Everyday Forms of State Formation

**Withdrawn from
Barnard College
Library**

D1498829

THE WOLLMAN LIBRARY

Barnard College

NEW YORK

EVERYDAY FORMS OF STATE FORMATION

Revolution and the Negotiation of Rule

in Modern Mexico

Edited by

Gilbert M. Joseph

and

Daniel Nugent

Duke University Press   Durham and London   1994

Sponsored by the Joint Committee on
Latin American Studies of the Social Science Research
Council and the American Council of Learned Societies,
with funds from the Andrew W. Mellon Foundation and
the National Endowment for the Humanities, and in
cooperation with the Center for U.S.-Mexican Studies,
University of California, San Diego.

© 1994 DUKE UNIVERSITY PRESS
All rights reserved
Printed in the United States of America
on acid-free paper ∞
Library of Congress Cataloging-in-Publication Data
appear on the last printed page of this book.
Fourth printing, 2003

Contents

III A THEORETICAL REPRISE

Foreword

Most conferences and the collections of essays they occasionally spawn achieve, at best, a paper-thin thematic unity. They resemble, in the telling phrase of Barrington Moore, "a dog's breakfast." The editors, in such cases, must labor mightily to fashion a tenuous conceptual thread in order to tie the essays together and convince a skeptical reader that they are all part of the same analytical enterprise.

This volume and the conference that generated it, by way of contrast, began with a sharply defined problem. The result is a collection of essays exhibiting a rare degree of empirical richness and thematic unity. Much of the credit for this belongs to Gil Joseph and Daniel Nugent for having thought through and stated the issues linking state formation, popular culture, and the Mexican revolution with such clarity. Credit is also due to those contributors, particularly Alan Knight, Bill Roseberry, and Derek Sayer, who took it upon themselves to clarify some of the major conceptual issues. Finally, *mirabile dictu*, the authors of each empirical study do, in fact, directly address the thorny relationship between hegemonic processes and resistance for that patch of the Mexican experience they examine. They are all, in other words, part of the same conversation—the same discursive community.

I am not, even remotely, a Mexicanist. And although I have thought about the issues of hegemony, domination, and resistance in the context of Southeast Asia, a foreword is hardly the place to raise complex conceptual problems, let alone presume to solve them. What I can do is suggest some lines of comparative inquiry that I suspect might be fruitful and, if it does not sound too irresponsible, throw out a few provocative questions about hegemony to which I cannot pretend to have definitive answers.

What was the local experience of the Mexican revolution? How was this experience embodied in local values and practice? What relation did these local values and practices bear to the postrevolutionary Mexican state and to the official "state cult" of the revolution? In one fashion or another, these questions are considered by virtually all the contributors to this book. The emphasis, in my reading of them, is on assessing the variable degree to which representatives of the state prevailed (i.e., in establishing and maintaining a large degree of hegemonic consent). Since, as most authors agree, such questions are processual and do not permit static or binary answers, attention is focused on the terms of the continually negotiated (and typically fragile) political equilibrium thereby created. A more rarely asked question—one both more dialectical and Gramscian—is also posed: to what extent has the state's hegemonic project itself been influenced by the force of popular experience and of mobilized popular expectations of the revolution?

The questions posed in the essays that follow bear a family resemblance to the enormous scholarly dialogue over the meaning and legacy of the French revolution. Maurice Agulhon, in his landmark work, *La République au village*, asked many of the same questions about the local variants of the French revolution (Agulhon 1970). He understood that the revolution bore, everywhere, the marks of its particular local development. Insofar as the actors, timing, social structure, and economic givens of any locality's revolutionary process were distinctive, it could be said that each municipality and each village had its own unique revolution. For one village the burning of lists of feudal dues might occupy center stage, for another the seizing of woodland and meadow, for another the burden of postrevolutionary conscription and threats against popular parish priests (as in the "counterrevolutionary" Vendée), and for another the end of an onerous tithe. Of course there were divisions within communities and, in principle, one could even say that each family (or each individual, for that matter) had its own particular French revolution. Agulhon also asked, as do many of the authors here, exactly what long-term institutional, symbolic, and ritual sediment the revolution left behind. If the French revolution is any guide here, and I suspect it is, Mexicans and Mexicanists will be quarreling about it and its legacy for more than a century to come.

As a non-Mexicanist interested in agrarian history and questions of domination, I find the sheer specificity and variety of revolutionary experiences described here of surpassing interest. Any carefully detailed empirical case is always far richer than the generalizations that can be extracted from it. Taking advantage of the richness of the case studies, I venture a few brief observations.

A revolution is also an interregnum. Between the moment when a previous regime disintegrates and the moment when a new regime is firmly in place lies a political terrain that has rarely been examined closely. State-centric descriptions of this period typically emphasize its anarchy, chaos, and insecurity. For many citizens and communities, however, it *may* represent a remarkable period without taxes and state surveillance, a period when perceived injustices can be reversed; in short, a respite of autonomy. In place of the "dual sovereignty" described so well by Charles Tilly, the term "vacuum of sovereignty" or "local sovereignty" might serve better. The end of the interregnum can often be conceptualized, then, as a reconquest, sometimes peaceful, sometimes violent, of the countryside by the agents of the successor state. One purpose of such reconquests is to replace the local "folk" variant of the revolution with the official version of revolutionary order. Taxes are a frequent bone of contention. Thus, for the Namiquipans described by Nugent and Ana Alonso the revolution did not include the state-sanctioned *ejido* or its tributary taxes; and for the peasantry of Tlaxcala examined by Elsie Rockwell, the revolution meant an end to school taxes.

Orlando Figes (1989) has examined local practices of schooling, taxes, land division, and governance in several provinces of European Russia during this brief postrevolutionary interregnum in order to understand something of the autonomous politics of the peasant community. A similar inquiry, begun so well in this volume, seems even more important in Mexico, for several reasons. First, the interregnum was much longer in Mexico than in Russia. Second, the Mexican revolution, to a far greater extent than the Russian, *was* a constellation of local revolutions that had taken root well before the new state was created. Finally, the revolutionary Mexican state was (had to be?) far more accommodating, and for far longer than the Russian, of the exotic local variants it encountered.

The various contributors seem to agree that if there is one basic social fact that conditions the postrevolutionary shape of state relations with localities, it is the local experience of political and military mobilization. It is all very well to examine the differences between the values and routines embedded in popular culture and those represented by the state and its agents. In this case, however, these popular values had often been the basis of mobilization that in turn produced the sacrifices, anger, memory, and patterns of collective action that transformed people and communities. People did not just "have" values they preferred; they had shown themselves and others that they could enact and impose those values, often against great odds. The essays by Joseph, Knight, and Nugent and Alonso emphasize the symbolic and political capital generated by this experience, while Florencia Mallon reminds us that this mobilization and the values fueling it had a prehistory, at least in Puebla, in the civil war of the late 1850s. In Russia there was also a "dress rehearsal" in 1905, but rural mobilization was not nearly so lengthy nor so institutionalized as in Mexico. This difference may go some way toward explaining the length of the interregnum in Mexico, the tenacity of its local heterodoxies, and the compromises the state was obliged to make. But not the whole way, perhaps. The postrevolutionary Mexican state, though surely a child of the Enlightenment and of nineteenth-century views of scientific progress, was far less determined, it seems, than was Lenin to force a high-modernist, centralized, utopian grid on society at no matter what cost.

How "rooted" is the revolution in popular culture and in the community? This is Agulhon's question, and also that of many contributors to this volume. Notice, however, that this question is not the same as asking how close—normatively and institutionally—the national and local expressions of the revolution are. A revolution can be firmly rooted despite substantial normative differences, provided these are differences the state is not committed to crushing. Rockwell's paper, for example, shows carefully how the school is a negotiated terrain in which minimum national/bureaucratic criteria are met and which, at the same time, serves as a host of quite different, if not contradictory, local interests. The two visions of school do not quite "map" on each other, but neither are they a source of great conflict. In the same fashion, one imagines that the prerevolutionary folk Catholicism of Michoacán described by Marjorie Becker might not have satisfied an archbishop's standards for orthodoxy. Nevertheless, the Mexican church had long made its peace with much, if not all, folk heterodoxy.

If the degree of normative misalignment is not necessarily a reliable indicator of conflict, then perhaps the degree of institutional misalignment might be. Shouldn't we expect institutional syncretism to make for a more seamless web between the national and the local revolution? The surprising answer, if I understand the import of the paper by Jan Rus, is no! In highland Chiapas, the traditional authorities (scribe-*principales*) and the cargo system they employ have come to represent the revolutionary establishment. In the process they have also become the agents of centralization and ladino influence, all in the name of the defense of tradition. Far from legitimizing the "institutionalized revolution," the resulting syncretism serves to delegitimize the state. The dynamic Rus portrays is strikingly similar to Romana Falcón's analysis of how the Porfiriato's assimilation of local bosses via the *jefaturas políticas* served to link Díaz's regime to the arbitrary exercise of personal power, thereby delegitimizing it among the populace. Institutional syncretism will apparently not legitimize a regime so long as it permits the local representatives of the state freely to violate the revolutionary values that their populace has, in fact, taken to heart.

The empirical studies as well as the synthetic essays by Joseph and Nugent, Knight, Roseberry, and Sayer all strongly suggest two further conclusions. The first is that we cannot simply take it for granted that state elites *have* a "hegemonic project" at all. This must be an empirical question, not a presupposition. Second, and more important, although one *may* occasionally be able to speak of *a* hegemonic project of state elites, one must always speak of popular culture and resistance to such projects in the *plural*. The strength and resilience of popular resistance to any hegemonic project lies precisely in its plurality. As Roseberry observes, it has no unitary counterhegemony of its own to impose; it seeks rather to evade. Since it does not speak with one voice, it cannot be silenced with a single blow of force or rhetoric. It may disguise itself in hegemonic dress and go on its merry—or not so merry—way, informally contravening official realities. It may, as do the determined villagers of Namaquipa, Chihuahua, described by Nugent and Alonso, refuse hegemonic dress and assert its own local claims to land and status. It may, finally, speak a language that is simply unintelligible within the prevailing discourse—much as some of the defendants during the Chicago conspiracy trial stood on the defense table and, rather than making a legal defense, chanted "Ooooom, Ooooom."

The analysis of hegemonic processes is a conceptual thicket in which more than one clever social scientist has been lost. In the interest of provocation and agnosticism, I will close with a few questions about hegemony that ought to be answered with some clarity before we can expect much conceptual advance. First, how cohesive, as a historical matter, are most elite hegemonic projects? Second, assuming that they can, at the level of ideas, be described as reasonably cohesive, how cohesive are they when they are translated into practice? What are the relative roles of ideas, routines, rituals, and "symbolic tribute" in this practice? Third, how confining are hegemonic projects? How easy is it to specify precisely what they require and what they exclude as a matter of principle? And finally, who are the audience(s) for hegemonic processes? How important is the normative alignment and consent of the popular classes as compared with, say, their practical compliance? How important are hegemonic processes for the cohesion, self-confidence, and moral purpose of the state elites themselves?

These are issues to debate for as long as one debates the meaning and legacy of the Mexican revolution. I believe, however, that there is no better place to begin confronting them than in this fine collection.

James C. Scott   *Yale University*

Preface

This book focuses on modern Mexico to examine a problem of extraordinary contemporary relevance: the manner in which local societies and cultures, revolutionary processes, and states are articulated historically. The idea grew out of a series of discussions between the editors and María Teresa Koreck at the Center for U.S.-Mexican Studies in La Jolla, California, where all were Visiting Research Fellows between 1986 and 1989. The three of us agreed that, despite impressive advances over the past two decades, historical writing on the Mexican revolution had fallen into something of a rut. Scholars continued to churn out impeccably researched local monographs, and the first important national syntheses in decades had just burst upon the scene. Still, debate continued in predictable channels: Had the revolution, warts and all, been a truly popular affair, so popular that it made a significant difference in the way power and resources were henceforth distributed and managed? Or had the revolution been betrayed by its own, Machiavellian, (not so) revolutionary leaders and the muscular central state they had resurrected?

Of course, there were arguments to be marshalled on both sides, and writers recycled them endlessly, plugging in a new locale or "region" with each successive iteration. Nevertheless, it struck us that from an interpretive standpoint, scholars seemed bent on transforming a complex revolutionary *process*—itself part of a broader, multistranded historical tapestry—into a single *event*. In the bargain they lined up in a historiographical rendition of the proverbial "Mexican standoff." On one side, the event was singled out as the culminating moment of heroic struggle in Mexican history; on the other, it was held to signal the ultimate triumph of the state over the people. Unfortunately, too rarely was the Mexican revolution studied as a culturally complex, historically generated process, in a manner that might illuminate the relationship between such abstract notions as "the state" and "the people."

As our discussion of these *inquietudes* came to include a broader range of Mexicanist and Latin Americanist colleagues, the three of us began to plan a research symposium that would also incorporate scholars working creatively across disciplines on similar empirical and theoretical issues in other parts of the world. Following a two-year planning process, an international conference on "Popular Culture, State Formation, and the Mexican Revolution" was held at the Center for U.S.-Mexican Studies early in 1991. The event brought a distinguished array of established and younger *mexicólogos* into dialogue with William Roseberry, Derek Sayer, and James C. Scott, scholars who had written on issues such as state formation, popular culture, resistance, and consciousness in Southeast Asia, Europe, and other parts of Latin America. Four days of intense discussion and debate among this diverse, interdisciplinary cast had the result of altering and enriching the frames of reference for considering state and popular participation before, during, and after "The Revolution."

International conferences do not come cheaply. The 1991 conference was funded by a variety of foundations and institutions. The lion's share of conference expenses was generously borne by the National Endowment for the Humanities (Conference Grant RX-21279-90). The Joint Committee on Latin American Studies of the Social Science Research Council (SSRC) and the American Council of Learned Societies covered the travel and lodging costs of the Mexican participants. The Center for U.S.-Mexican Studies and the Center for Iberian and Latin American Studies at the University of California, San Diego, and the University of California Consortium for Studies of Mexico and the United States (UC-MEXUS) each generously donated funds that were applied to both the planning and staging of the event. The Contracts and Grants Office at the University of North Carolina, Chapel Hill—particularly Contract Specialists Don Wood and Elizabeth Earle—provided dependable assistance at every stage of the conference's complicated funding history.

No less important for an international conference is a suitable locale. It should already be clear that we are deeply indebted to Wayne Cornelius, director of the Center for U.S.-Mexican Studies, and to his able staff. Wayne encouraged the project from its inception, and it took root in the lively exchanges of the center's Visiting Fellow Program. Graciela Platero, Patricia Rojas, and their assistants at the center deftly managed the nagging details of a four-day event whose participants came from several continents and spoke different languages; even more remarkably, they never lost their sense of humor.

We gratefully acknowledge the support of those colleagues who helped to shape the 1991 conference. Terri Koreck's ideas and energy were particularly instrumental in organizing the gathering and ensuring that it assumed the form it did. Besides the writers whose work appears in this volume, we also wish to thank the following people who contributed research findings and commentaries in La Jolla that have substantially improved the discussion found in these pages: Roger Bartra, William Beezley, Ann Craig, Adolfo Gilly, Peter Guardino, Alicia Hernández Chávez, Friedrich Katz, Martha Lampland, Jane-Dale Lloyd, Frans Schryer, Daniela Spenser, Paul Vanderwood, and Eric Van Young.

The present volume is the result of several years of collaboration among the editors, contributors, and individuals mentioned above. Following the conference, which generated a surprisingly coherent set of reflections for future research, participants spent the next year recasting their manuscripts. Scott, Roseberry, and Sayer were each invited to submit shorter pieces based on their engagement with the Mexican materials. The editors' introduction and Joseph's essay on Yucatán, while written more recently, owe a great deal to the deliberations in La Jolla.

Special thanks are due to the SSRC's Latin American and Carribbean Program. The program's Joint Committee found support for the conference in the council's darkest financial hours, then generously provided a publication grant to revise the manuscript for publication.

The editors are grateful to Joaquín Urquidi and Jennifer Gilbert, who provided draft translations of the essays by Falcón and Bartra, which were subsequently reworked into the versions that appear here. Thanks also go to Tim Henderson and Helen Robbins, who transcribed several of the commentaries from the La Jolla conference, to Eleanor Lahn and Bradley Levinson, who aided the editors in the revision process, and to Daniel Goldstein, who prepared the index. Finally, we express our gratitude to Ken Wissoker, our fine editor at Duke University Press, whose abiding commitment and good sense made this a better book.

Like the La Jolla conference, the present volume is structured in the form of a dialogue between theory and empirical research. The essays that frame the volume in parts 1 and 3 deal with the historiography of revolutionary Mexico, the pertinence of recent advances in social theory to Mexican research, the character of hegemony, the nature and power of the state, and future directions for the study of popular culture and state formation. The studies in the middle section of the book treat locales as distant and diverse as Chihuahua and Yucatán; indigenous peoples and peasant communities; "spontaneous," disorganized mobilizations and more formal political struggles; educators and the educated; culture industries and cultural consumers; academic history and popular history.

It strikes us that the events that have transpired in the six years since we first conceived this project on popular culture and state formation have only served to heighten the currency of the volume. In 1987, we began planning the project against the backdrop of zero percent growth in Mexico and the eruption of a popular political phenomenon—neo-Cardenismo—that most scholars, following the lead of the Revolutionary State, seemed bent on ignoring. Two years later, coincident in time with the collapse of states in the misnamed "Soviet" bloc of Eastern Europe, the Mexican state began to dismantle the institutions and legitimizing discourse of its own revolution. It did so with little opposition from the traditional left, which, as Barry Carr's essay in this volume demonstrates, has always been notoriously unprepared to look beyond its orthodox European models. Meanwhile, in the Western academy, revolution and social movements were ceasing to be fashionable intellectual commodities. "Revisionist" studies of revolutions betrayed held center stage. Left and right versions of "The End of History" crowded the scholarly journals and book-chat circuits. In 1991, we convened our conference in La Jolla at the very height of the first Gulf War, amid a gale of Bush administration hype that proved as clear an illustration of the state's ability to shape discursive frameworks as any in recent memory.

Today, as this book goes to press, the New World Order consolidates itself on both sides of the border. In Mexico City, intellectuals who three or four generations ago might have written for *Regeneración* now rewrite public school texts in order to refurbish the liberal, modernizing discourses of yesteryear for the North American Free Trade Agreement of today. But it is not enough to write a requiem for the Mexican revolution. That has already been done, several times and from diverse quarters. What is needed is a *truly* postrevisionist critique of Mexico's revolutionary past, one that is prepared to ride its long waves and is not deaf to its multiple voices and dialects—such as those that presently emanate from the highlands and jungles of Chiapas. It is this kind of critique, generated through experience and imaginative response to forms of oppression, control, and rule, that the present volume seeks to encourage.

Gilbert M. Joseph *New Haven, Connecticut*   Daniel Nugent *Tucson, Arizona*

PHILIP CORRIGAN

State Formation

Historians, anthropologists, and sociologists have now begun to recon-
stitute the appropriate paradigm for studying "the State." Although the
relevance of the latter concept is still disputed, many idealists (such as
Cassirer) and materialists (such as Engels or Lenin) have long defended
the relevance of this focus as an essence, objective facticity, second-order
phenomenon, spirit, cultural field, and so on; i.e., as *A Thing*. Marx attempts to disperse this essentialism-and-reification (Thingification), a
procedure furthered by Mao and Gramsci. This recent work centers forms
of social organization, particularly documentary organization, *as forms of
rule and ruling*. Key questions then become NOT *who* rules but *how* is rule
accomplished. This expanded conception of the political (opening to see
the political features of all economic, cultural, and "private" relations)
corresponds to a shift in dominant practices—within advanced capitalist
societies, dependent capitalist formations, and socialist countries—where
terms like "Governance" and "Entrepreneurialism" are now used extensively.

This refocusing of "How" questions as necessarily anterior to "Why"
and "Who" or "Whom" questions, has oriented relevant studies toward a
historical sociology of the type encouraged by Philip Abrams. It corresponds with quadruple challenges to, and crises of, legitimacy: socialist
forms, feminist critiques, antiracist analyses, *and* within the governance of

A version of this essay, with complete bibliographical references, was published
as "State Formation (entry for a dictionary) (1986)," in Philip Corrigan's *Social
Forms/Human Capacities: Essays in Authority and Difference* (London: Routledge, 1990),
264–68. It appears here in its present form with permission of the author and the
publishers.

capitalist formations—plus the rediscovery of much of Marx "lost" (i.e., unknown) to those Second and Third Internationalists who formed "Marxism" as it was experienced in the 1960s and 1970s. The stress here crosses disciplinary boundaries (including political theory; plus anthropology, sociology, and history, as has been indicated) and transcends the "boundary maintenance" practices that detach subjectivity from culture, culture from power, power from knowledge, "the state" from subjectivities.

The argument (for such it is and remains) for *state formation* runs as follows: no historical or contemporary form of ruling can be understood (1) as or in its own discursive regime or image repertoire terms; (2) without investigating the historical genealogy, archaeology, origination (and transmutation) of those terms *as forms*; (3) without an awareness of "Abroad," as in the "learning from 'Abroad,'" which is so evident, both as positivity or as the negativity of the impositions of cultural-political imperatives (for example with regard to Aid or U.S. AID); and (4) in ways that *silence* the generic and racist features of "politically organized subjection" (Abrams [1977] 1988).

What a "state-formation" approach promises is a way of overcoming (for the region of its focus) the antinomies (of both Marxist and bourgeois scholarship) between Constraint and Consensus; Force and Will; Body and Mind; Society and Self. In sum: the objective and the subjective (Mao 1966). These are, so it is argued, the disciplined, powerful, acknowledged archetypes of rationalism and the Enlightenment. In other words, patriarchy, racism, and class-ism become visible as constitutive features of rule (both precapitalist and capitalist; developed and colonized capitalist; vanguard and reformist socialism). Governance becomes unified with the "private" realm; indeed, seen as constitutive of that crucial "private"/"public" split; and sexualized subjectivities (as part of the media of modernity) enter "politics."

Centered here, finally, is the materiality of moral regulation and the moralization of material reality. What is natural, neutral, universal—that is, "The Obvious"—becomes problematic and questionable. Socializing Freud and Jung means psychologizing Marx (for example, Reich, among the most neglected political theorists of the twentieth century). Questions of "relevance" and "evidence" shift accordingly. Above all, these displaced and condensed realms of affectivity, bodily knowing, soulful aspirations, cultural symbologies, and personal associationism, come to be seen as sites/sights of maximally organized social forms (for the majority, that is, historical experiences of disempowerment, exploitation, oppression, domination, and subordination). Here there is a "happy isomorphism" ("elective affinity"?) with the work of distinctively *social* linguists, joining with them in the exposure and explication of ruling powers, hence State powers, as a social grammar. Rediscovered, but in a different place, is *the grammar of politics*.

I

Theoretical

Prolegomena

GILBERT M. JOSEPH AND DANIEL NUGENT

Popular Culture and State Formation
in Revolutionary Mexico

A central feature of the Mexican and Latin American past has been the continuing tension between emergent popular cultures and processes of state formation. Paradoxically, this relationship has for a long time been poorly understood, drawing the attention of scholars primarily when it has broken down, and particularly when it has erupted into sustained or apocalyptic episodes of mass insurrection or state-managed repression. Meanwhile, the dynamics of the state's day-to-day engagement with grassroots society have largely been ignored; indeed, Latin Americanists have rarely examined popular cultures and forms of the state simultaneously, let alone in relation to each other. The present volume brings together a series of studies and reflections that provide a new perspective on this complex issue.

Friedrich Katz engagingly set forth the terms of a paradox that we, as Mexicanist historians, anthropologists, cultural critics, and sociologists must address in our own work. Mexico is the only country in the Americas where "every major social transformation has been inextricably linked to popular rural upheavals" (Katz 1981b). In fact, three times within a century—in 1810, in the 1850s and 1860s, and again in the 1910s—social and political movements emerged that destroyed the existing state and most of the military establishment, then set up a new state

Critical readings by Ana Alonso and Hermann Rebel improved this text, to which the standard disclaimers apply.

and army. Nevertheless, in every case the changes in the countryside that these popular movements ultimately wrought were rather modest. Each of the upheavals resulted in the formation of states in which *campesinos* (and urban workers) played a subordinate role. Armies that began as preponderantly *campesino*-based forces soon became the guarantors of an increasingly oppressive social order, an order which, in time, was itself challenged and ultimately toppled. Why have Mexico's embattled power-holders repeatedly called upon *campesinos*, and why have the latter so often followed? Perhaps more important, what were the terms of engagement between the very different social groups involved, and how were those terms negotiated? These, Katz believes, remain the most tantalizing questions with which social historians of Mexico grapple. And while they are couched within a particular national-historical context, they simulta-neously raise the broader theoretical problem of the state's contested relationship with popular culture.

The original essays collected here all address this problem. They combine empirical analysis of developments in Mexico from the second half of the nineteenth century to the present with theoretical arguments that go beyond the specific case materials at hand. The volume's pur-posefully ironic title juxtaposes "everyday forms" from James Scott's pen-etrating analysis of peasant resistance in rural Southeast Asia (Scott 1985) and "state formation" from Philip Corrigan and Derek Sayer's study of the formation of the bourgeois state in England as a cultural revolution (Corrigan and Sayer 1985). While until now the important contributions of Scott, Corrigan, and Sayer to the study of power and resistance have largely been overlooked by Mexicanists, the contributors to this volume have all found that their work helps open up new routes toward under-standing longstanding, seemingly intractable problems in the history of revolutionary Mexico.

In this introductory essay, we first review—briefly and, we hope, contentiously—some centrally important themes and currents in the recent historiography of modern Mexico and its twentieth-century revo-lution. We then discuss theoretical controversies related to the contested meanings of popular culture, resistance, and consciousness on the one hand, and state formation on the other. Throughout, we draw on a diverse range of comparative social theorists—as well as Mexicanist and Latin Americanist scholars—in an effort to fashion an analytical framework for understanding *the relationship between* popular cultures and state formation in revolutionary and postrevolutionary Mexico.

INTERPRETATIONS OF THE MEXICAN REVOLUTION

Perhaps no other event has given rise to such an abundant and method-ologically sophisticated historiography among Latin Americanists as the Mexican revolution of 1910. Yet despite its strengths, this rich literature has suffered from a marked tendency to isolate and privilege the revolu-tion *as event*—as the supreme moment of popular resistance in Mexican history—rather than to study it as a culturally complex, historically generated process. Ironically, if most often unintentionally, many profes-sional scholars have joined the ruling political party in Mexico (the PRI or Revolutionary Institutional Party) in transforming the Mexican revolu-tion into "The Revolution." That "event" is variously described as having occurred between 1910 and 1917, 1910 and 1920, or 1910 and 1940,[1] and the debates about how to periodize the revolution not only highlight its complexity as a historical process during which popular resistance figured significantly, but also point to another process simultaneous in space and time: revolutionary and postrevolutionary state formation. How, then, might one characterize the relationship between popular mobilization and the culture(s) that inform it, and state formation in twentieth-century Mexico?

This pivotal issue was for many years ignored or elided in the early orthodox, "populist" vision of the revolution that appeared in the pioneer-ing works of participants and observers writing in the 1920s and 1930s. That orthodoxy depicted the upheaval in schematic and uncritical fash-ion as a unified event, a virtually spontaneous, agrarian revolution that swept up the entire nation in a clean break with an essentially "feudal" past. "The people" rose up indignantly, "anonymously," out of the Mexi-can earth and overthrew their old dictator, Porfirio Díaz, along with more visible local "bosses" (*los caciques*). And although the social struggle lost its way for years at a time while "The Revolution's" caudillos fought among themselves, it ultimately bestowed its expected fruit—land to the peas-antry and the nationalization of foreign-controlled extractive indus-tries—under President Lázaro Cárdenas in the late 1930s.

1. Despite the continuing claim represented in the official party's name, there is little dispute that "The Revolution" is over. In recent years, the PRI government has encouraged the sale of nationalized industries and enterprises (most recently, the Mexican national bank) to private investors, and "reformed" (read terminated) the agrarian reform enshrined in Article 27 of the 1917 Constitution.

In the hands of foreign commentators such as Frank Tannenbaum, Ernest Gruening, Eyler Simpson, and even John Steinbeck (who scripted the film *Viva Zapata!*), or those of José Valadés, Jesús Silva Herzog, and countless other *cronistas veteranos*, such populist renditions at times assumed epic—even mythic—proportions, and were in short order neatly codified by the new Revolutionary State (O'Malley 1986; T. Benjamin 1994). The empathetic and committed character of much of this early work, written when the social revolution was at high tide and the regime's revolutionary myth was just beginning to crystallize, certainly must frame (and mitigate) our criticism of it. Nevertheless, however much we might still enjoy late-night reruns of *Viva Zapata!*,[2] the old orthodoxy has long since become a historiographic artefact.

More recent interpretive currents represent significant advances over the earlier orthodoxy, above all because they question the seeming singleness of purpose that is built into the conceptualization of social revolution articulated in the first wave of studies of the Mexican revolution and codified by the rulers of the state since the 1920s. At least two conceptual approaches can be identified in the work of scholars who have investigated the Mexican revolution since the late 1960s. For purposes of exposition,[3] we will designate these approaches as "revisionist" and "neopopulist" (or "postrevisionist"), contrasting both with the older, orthodox view.

Revisionist studies (see, e.g., Bailey 1978; Carr 1980; Fowler-Salamini 1993; S. Miller 1988 for detailed discussions) have paid special attention to the relationship between the revolution and the state, portraying the revolution's significance in decidedly darker hues. The avalanche of mostly regional-level studies that appeared in the 1970s and 1980s indicated in compelling fashion that although the revolution may have begun with the active participation of truly popular groups in different regions of Mexico, it rapidly witnessed the ascendancy of aspiring bourgeois and petite bourgeois elements. These chiefs sometimes employed traditional

---

2. Or the much less commercial—and less visible—attempts of Sergei Eisenstein to portray the Mexican revolution at twenty-four frames per second. For an undeservedly neglected, highly irreverent (and decidedly *un-orthodox*) cinematic rendering of the epic revolution, see Sergio Leone's *A Fistful of Dynamite* (*Duck, You Sucker* in European release).

3. We are leery of abstract characterizations of the type that all too frequently—and rapidly—metamorphose into reifications. Cf. Sayer 1987 and below.

patterns of authority based on patron-client exchanges to co-opt and
manipulate the masses of peasants and workers. By the 1930s, the more
independent of these regional and local power holders were themselves
subordinated (if they had not already been eliminated) by the emerging
Revolutionary state. A modern Leviathan, the new state swallowed up
regional political configurations, eventually perfecting—in a manner
reminiscent of Tocqueville's revision of the French revolution—the for-
mula of political centralization and dependent capitalist development
that had begun under Porfirio Díaz's version of the *ancien régime* during the
three-and-a-half decades preceding 1910. (See, e.g., R. Hansen 1971;
Córdova 1973; J. Meyer 1976; Ruiz 1980; Brading 1980; Jacobs 1983;
Ankerson 1984; Falcón 1984; Pansters and Ouweneel 1989.)

An unfortunate consequence of revisionists' identification of the rise
of the Mexican Revolutionary state as the decisive accomplishment of the
decade of violence has been to relegate popular participation to a subordinated, almost inconsequential role. For example, in his essay on the
Mexican revolution in the *Cambridge History of Latin America* (1986), John
Womack advanced a revisionist thesis in particularly provocative, un-
equivocal terms. While admitting that peasant movements and labor
unions became significant forces and that Mexican society underwent
"extraordinary crises and serious changes" from 1910 to 1920, Womack
argues that continuity clearly took precedence over change: "The crises
did not go nearly deep enough to break capitalist domination of production. The great issues were issues of state." Drawn (kicking and screaming,
one assumes[4]) to the conclusion that "the subject is therefore no longer so
much social revolution as political management," Womack explains that
his essay is "short on social movements because however important their
emergence, their defeat and subordination mattered more" (Womack
1986:81–82).

Few would deny that most popular social movements in twentieth-
century Mexico were, in the final analysis, defeated or co-opted by the
state, or collapsed and imploded owing to contradictions internal to the
movements themselves. Nor is it difficult to recognize the value of an
approach such as Womack outlined in the 1980s for situating the Mexican revolution in relation to world-scale political and economic structures

---

4. We should recall that in 1968 Womack published the definitive study of
Emiliano Zapata and the popular movement he led until he was murdered by order of
Venustiano Carranza, the "First Chief" of the revolution and president of Mexico.

and forces. Finally, focusing the analysis on the political dimension of the revolutionary decade and the very material consequences the exercise of power had in reshaping—and destroying—the lives of millions of people, is a useful corrective to the romanticization of revolution and of putatively authentic popular and peasant insurgency that plagues much of the literature on Latin American social movements and rural protest.[5]

Revisionist interpretations of the Mexican revolution themselves appeared in large part as a response to the historical crisis of the Mexican state after 1968. That year (which Marshall Berman would probably call "a great *modernist* year"; see Berman 1992:55) started out with the hope and promise of the first Tet offensive in Vietnam, the Prague Spring, the days of May in Paris, and student mobilizations throughout Asia, Europe, and North America; it ended up with an intensification of bombing throughout Southeast Asia, police riots in Chicago, Russian tanks in Czechoslovakia and, in Mexico City, the massacre of hundreds of unarmed civilians in the plaza of Tlatelolco. Small wonder that in the 1970s and 1980s revisionists sought to stand the old revolutionary orthodoxy on its head. Nor is it coincidental that it was within this political climate that the new regional history of Mexico also came of age, with many revisionists among its charter members. Challenging the conventional wisdoms that reposed within a fraying *historiografía capitalina*, demystifying official interpretations of regional events while reclaiming local heroes, searching for historical roots and analogies that might inform the political activity of the present, the new regional and microhistorians issued a strong indictment of the stifling centralization of the postrevolutionary state (Martínez Assad 1990, 1991; Joseph 1991b; Van Young 1992b; Lomnitz-Adler 1992; Fowler-Salamini 1993).

Yet if revisionists have made important advances in reinterpreting the larger events and the political-economic context of the Mexican revolution from regional—rather than metropolitan—standpoints, they have been much less successful in extending the analysis down to the grass-

---

5. The naive romanticism that refuses to problematize notions of authenticity is evident in much of the writing on Che Guevara, or Lampião, or social bandits generally in Latin America (cf. Joseph 1990). We would argue further that romantic, sentimentalizing, or triumphalist accounts of revolution may result in a rhetorical softening and political defanging of the phenomena they treat. Ultimately, popular insurgency is reduced in the discourse of intellectuals to a quaint, even naturalized "trait" of Latin American culture.

roots.[6] Indeed, not only have they failed to understand the political consciousness of the revolutionary rank and file and the culture that informs that consciousness; in some revisionist accounts the popular dimension of revolutionary practice has been consigned to the dustbin of history.

But, as one of the premier critics of revisionist accounts has put it bluntly, surely the revolution was something more than "a series of chaotic, careerist episodes, in which popular forces were, at best, the instruments of manipulative *caciques*, of aspiring bourgeois or petty bourgeois leaders" (Knight 1986a:xi). Adolfo Gilly, in his seminal study, *La revolución interrumpida* (first published in 1971 and translated into English in 1983 with the somewhat unfortunate title *The Mexican Revolution*), demonstrated how popular armies from the south and the north came together (however fleetingly) in 1914–15 to directly confront the bourgeoisie. Where Womack underlines the "defeat and subordination" of popular social movements, Gilly draws attention to the vitality and efficacy of the popular presence during the period of armed rebellion in Mexico, 1910–1920. Adding fuel to this particular fire, Alan Knight emphatically argues that "there can be no high politics without a good deal of low politics. This is particularly true since, I believe, the Revolution was a genuinely *popular* movement and thus an example of those relatively rare episodes in history when *the mass of people* profoundly influenced events" (1986a:x–xi, emphasis added). Thus, he contends, the regionally diverse popular movements informing the "low politics" of the 1910–1920 period must be seen as "the precursor, the necessary precursor, of the *étatiste* 'revolution'"—the "high politics"—that followed in the 1920s and 1930s (1986a:xi).

Still, a challenge of this type to revisionist interpretations can be persuasive only if it specifies what is meant by *popular*, and who or what such phrases as *the mass of people* are intended to designate. Broad invocations of "the people" may naively play into the hands of Mexico's ruling party, a political party that, despite the definitive discrediting of its populist dream in the 1980s, still insisted into the 1990s that it was the party of an institutionalized *revolution* of the popular classes. Indeed, invocations of "the people," "the popular," and so on come dangerously

6. Of course, given the impoverished state of *capitalino* historiography and the underdeveloped nature of *archivos de provincia* in the 1970s and early 1980s, successful analysis at a "middle hermeneutical level" (see Freitag 1989) was no mean feat.

close to resuscitating the romanticism so characteristic of the early studies of the 1920s and 1930s. Nevertheless, the more recent work of the new populists and critics of the state does have the virtue, at least potentially, of taking seriously the grassroots social movements that have appeared intermittently throughout Mexico since 1910, as well as in preceding decades.[7]

In characterizing interpretations of the Mexican revolution advanced by revisionists and their successors, we have thus far underscored their salient differences as historiographical currents. Yet those differences mask the fact that at a fundamental level both lines of interpretation attempt to draw together the same set of issues; both seek to articulate popular culture, revolution, and state formation in the analysis of modern Mexico.

For example, revisionists and neopopulists alike have written volumes about local grievances and agendas and the capacity of local actors to give voice to them (e.g., Knight 1986a; Tutino 1986; Nugent 1988a; Joseph [1982] 1988; Katz 1988a).[8] The role of larger structural determinants, including ecological and economic crises that characterized Mexico's subordination within an unevenly expanding capitalist world system at the start of the twentieth century, has also been considered (Katz 1981a; Hart 1987; Ruiz 1988; Joseph [1982] 1988). Patterns of authority, recruitment and mobilization, and the gamut of relations between revolutionary leaders and followers that figured in the manifold process of mediation between the state, regional powers, and local society have all been explored to one degree or another (Brading 1980; Katz 1988a; Nugent 1988a; T. Benjamin and Wasserman 1990; Rodríguez 1990).

It is instructive, however, to differentiate between the ways each interpretive current conceptualizes the linkages between the state and

7. In addition to Knight, this new generation of populists might include John Tutino (1986) and John Hart (1987). The latter, for example, regards the Mexican revolution as primarily a great "war of national liberation," in which peasants and workers made common cause with the "pequeña burguesía" against the Yankees and their comprador bourgeoisie. See also Coatsworth (1988b:67): "In rebelling against the Porfirian regime, Mexico's peasants . . . called into question all that imperialism had accomplished in their country . . . [asserting] at gunpoint a different vision of what their country was about."

8. Other social historians have more generally (and tentatively) examined popular attitudes and ideologies, frequently dubbing them "mentalities." See, e.g., Van Young (1990, 1992a), Vanderwood (1987), and other contributors to the collections edited by Rodríguez (1990, 1992).

popular culture(s) in the Mexican revolution. Revisionists, mindful of the left-wing critique of the "new social history" as an apolitical and hence potentially romanticizing exercise in "history from below" (sardonically dubbed "proctological history" by Bernard Cohn [1980:214]; cf. Judt 1979; Stearns 1983), successfully establish the political dimension at the center of the *problematique*. They thereby demonstrate an awareness of the power relations that tie local society and culture into the larger contexts of region, nation, international economy, and a world-scale political arena (see Joseph 1986; and de la Peña 1989 on local and regional power). But as we have pointed out, their work frequently occludes the human subjects who made the Mexican revolution while, as Alan Knight has reminded us time and again, too often lapsing into "statolatry" (cf. Gramsci 1971:268). By centering their analyses on the relationship between the national state and regional leaders and movements (without extending the analysis down to the local level) they have, in gross fashion, "brought the state back in," but left the people out (cf. Nugent 1988b:15ff.).

On the other hand, critics of the revisionists make great claims for the popular classes' involvement in the Mexican revolution, claims based in large part on a sensitive reading of the revisionists' own well-documented, empirically rich local- and regional-level monographs (see, e.g., V. García 1992, which leans on the pioneering regional-level studies of revolutionary Veracruz by Falcón and S. García [1977, 1986] and Fowler-Salamini [1978]). In the process, more recent work has achieved a theoretical recognition of what was realized by those popular classes in historical practice, namely the articulation of distinctive forms of social consciousness and experience. Until now, however, those who have challenged revisionism have for the most part been reluctant to take that consciousness seriously and slow to examine its relationship to popular culture.[9] Yet as the work of James Scott, among others, and many of the essays in this volume reveal, such consciousness is predicated upon selective (and always contested) traditions of historical memory that reside and are nourished in popular "subcultures of resistance" (Scott 1985; see also Scott 1990; Adas 1982; Guha 1982a, 1982b, 1983b, 1984, 1985; Alonso 1992b; Hernández Chávez 1991; Nugent 1992; Koreck

9. Below we consider different notions of popular culture in some detail. Distinct from popular culture, *popular consciousness* refers to politicized forms of knowledge and identity that are consensually recognized by subaltern groups during particular historical conjunctures (cf. Lefebvre 1988, on the *quotidienne*).

1991; and the chapters by Becker, Carr, Joseph, Mallon, Nugent and Alonso, and Rus here; but cf. Rebel 1989).

The essays that follow go beyond previous interpretations of the revolution by fleshing out the variety of currents and modalities through which popular movements acted upon the revolution and the new state and played a role in the transformation of Mexican society. Moreover, beyond asserting that regionally diverse popular movements were necessary precursors of the "statist revolution" that followed in the 1920s and 1930s, these studies indicate something about the dynamics of state formation, and particularly the quotidian process whereby the new state engaged the popular classes and vice versa. The analyses are directed toward a clearer understanding of those aspects of social experience that actually changed, and toward identifying the agents and agencies of social transformation. Building upon insights into the continuities and discontinuities of power and the experience of popular resistance that have been gleaned from recent research on revolutionary Mexico and elsewhere, these essays demonstrate how popular involvement in the multiple arenas through which official projects were advanced invariably resulted in negotiation from below.

BRINGING THE STATE BACK IN WITHOUT LEAVING THE PEOPLE OUT

This volume goes beyond previous work on Mexico because our explicit concern is to fashion an analytical framework for simultaneously integrating views of the Mexican revolution "from below" with a more compelling and nuanced "view from above." This requires a concept of popular culture that can be analyzed in relation to a notion of state formation that equally recognizes the importance of the cultural dimension of historical process and social experience. Rather than begin with abstract definitions of these terms, though, we will start by underlining the immense value of research conducted outside Mexico for developing an appreciation of the relationship between popular culture and state formation.

For example, in uncovering the ordinary, everyday "weapons of the weak" deployed by peasants and in probing the informal "subcultures of resistance" that underwrite them, James Scott's studies of Southeast Asia represent the redirection of attention to subordinated groups and classes as historical protagonists (Scott 1977, 1985, 1987). Challenging the status scholars routinely grant to "organized" movements (class-based or other) as the only relevant framework for understanding "revolutionary" and other episodes of insurgency (Scott 1976, 1985, 1987, 1990), and drawing on notions of "moral economy" borrowed from E. P. Thompson, Scott's work and that of other Southeast Asianist scholars (e.g., Adas 1982; Kahn 1985; Scott and Kirkvliet 1986) has figured importantly in recent debates on the character of popular consciousness. Equally salient have been the studies that appeared in *Subaltern Studies* during the 1980s, Ranajit Guha's *Elementary Aspects of Peasant Insurgency in Colonial India* (1983), and the penetrating and engaging reviews and critiques of the work of the *Subaltern Studies* group (e.g., Bayly 1988; O'Hanlon 1988; Spivak 1985, 1988). Similarly, Steve Stern's programmatic essay introducing *Resistance, Rebellion, and Consciousness in the Andean Peasant World* (1987) and his critique of Wallersteinian world-systems theory (1988) have been instrumental in putting the issue of political consciousness back on the agenda for understanding rural revolt in Latin America.

What unifies these studies is their shared insistence that the character of popular experience and consciousness may only be specified in the historical contexts of unequal power in which popular culture is elaborated or manifested. The power of the state, especially the capitalist state, has been of signal importance in providing some of the idioms in terms of which subordinated groups have initiated their struggles for emancipation, particularly in the twentieth century. Drawing on a different Thompsonian metaphor—"field of force"—in his contribution to this volume, William Roseberry explores both the possibilities for, and limits to, the hegemony of the state. A line of inquiry taken up in most of the essays that follow involves the examination of what Roseberry calls hegemonic *processes*, which he and other contributors take pains to distinguish from the achievement of hegemony as *outcome* (see also Roseberry and O'Brien 1991; Roseberry 1989).

Our collective insistence on viewing hegemony, culture, consciousness, and experience *in historical motion* is motivated in large part by the closely linked conceptualization of state formation as above all a *cultural process* with manifest consequences in the material world. Here we draw on Philip Corrigan and Derek Sayer's study *The Great Arch: English State Formation as Cultural Revolution* (1985). In introducing their account of a specific example of cultural transformation that occurred over eight centuries in England, Corrigan and Sayer point to the shared recognition among sociologists, Marxists, and feminists that "the triumph of modern capitalist civilization involved a wholesale cultural revolution too—a revolution as much in the way the world was made sense of as in how goods were produced and exchanged" (Corrigan and Sayer 1985:1–2).

This revolution "in the way the world is made sense of" occurred (and continues to occur) both in the way subjects of the state elaborate their experience (a topic taken up below in our discussion of popular culture) and in the manner in which "state activities, forms, routines and rituals . . .for the constitution and regulation of social identities" (Corrigan and Sayer 1985:2) are also elaborated.

The analysis of English state formation presented in *The Great Arch* draws in no small part on Corrigan and Sayer's earlier collaborations with Harvie Ramsay, including their critique of Bolshevism in *Socialist Construction and Marxist Theory* (1978) and *For Mao* (1979) and their seminal article on "The State as a Relation of Production" (Corrigan, Ramsay, and Sayer 1980). In the latter essay, they point out how

> the real forms of State dominion are the apparently classless and eternal "rituals of ruling" and the categories of moral absolutism, not least the declarations concerning both "the national interest" and "rationality" or "reasonableness." What such rituals and categories make possible is a way of discussing political priorities which makes unsayable much of what are lived as political problems. (Corrigan, Ramsay, and Sayer 1980:17–19)

In subsequent writings, especially their 1982 essay, "Marxist Theory and Socialist Construction in Historical Perspective," and *The Great Arch*, Corrigan and Sayer draw on Marx, Weber, and Durkheim to elaborate their argument that "in a materially unequal society assertion of formal equality can be violently oppressive, [indeed] it is itself a form of rule" (1985:187). Systematically, they lay bare the capitalist state's repertoire of activities and cultural forms that have provided modes of organization, social practice, and identity, but that historians have too often ignored or dismissed as somehow natural. Again in *The Great Arch* they register

> the centrality within the social theories we have considered of state formation and its associated cultural revolution to ordering a society in which capitalist economy is possible: to invert the "standard" Marxist dogma. For Marx . . . these transformations . . . are integral to the making of a bourgeois social order, a civilization. Capitalism is not just an economy, it is a regulated set of social forms of life. (Corrigan and Sayer 1985:187–8)

Understanding how such a regulated set of social forms of life—i.e., capitalism—emerged in so strong a form in Mexico is not an easy task, particularly since that historical outcome is frequently masqueraded as the result of a popular, peasant war. But that is the paradox the following essays confront, and it provides a leitmotiv running through the volume's empirical studies. The basic assumption throughout is that popular culture and state formation can only be understood in relational terms (see Corrigan 1975; Mohanty 1992:2).

POPULAR CULTURE

Until very recently, there has been surprisingly little work done on popular culture in Latin America that attempts to understand it, above all, as an issue of power—a problem of politics. What has been done in this vein has largely been restricted to urban groups, and has focused overwhelmingly on the nature, reception, and consequences of mass culture under capitalism. Where Latin America's rural areas are concerned—and Mexico was preponderantly rural throughout the period under scrutiny in this volume—much work on popular culture is still framed within the terms of an older tradition of studies of folklore.

This venerable tradition, which over the years has been shrewdly appropriated and legitimated by Mexico's populist Revolutionary state (O'Malley 1986), largely ignores the broader sociopolitical dynamics in which rural communities are embedded. Instead, it perpetuates notions of a singular, authentic rural culture, routinely portrayed as the repository of Mexican national identity and virtue (cf. R. Bartra 1987, 1991; Monsiváis 1981; see also Carr's discussion below of how leftist artists and the Communist party in Mexico abetted such unitary constructions). Consonant with such a perspective, the term *popular culture* is used to refer to the "expressive culture"—the music, art, handicrafts, narratives, rituals, theater—of the *campesinado* (and of the urban underclass and working class, for that matter). Yet however much folklorists may lament how the purity of this peasant culture is being degraded by the inexorable onslaught of industrialization and modern "culture industries," their scholarship generally fails to relate issues of meaning to questions of power.

Recent work on popular culture in Latin America has taken a different turn. Influenced by the work of Gramsci and more recent Italian writers (e.g., Cirese 1979; Lombardi Satriani 1975, 1978), as well as the theoretical and empirical studies by the Argentine sociologist and art critic Néstor García Canclini (1982, 1987, 1988, 1990), scholars have come to recognize that popular culture cannot be defined in terms of "its" intrinsic properties. Rather, it can only be conceived in relation to the political forces and culture(s) that engage it. As García Canclini writes, "The 'popular' nature of any thing or phenomenon can only be established by the manner in which it is used or experienced, not by where it originates" (1982:53).

If the earlier notions of folklore mistakenly imbued popular culture with a primordial solidity, recent work on communications and mass media under capitalism has too often gone to the opposite extreme and emptied it of any content. Reliant on a notion of "mass culture"[10] as the culture produced by modern media of communication, education, and information technologies, studies from this perspective tend to view popular culture only as an expression—or symptom—of a global process of cultural domination and homogenization (e.g., Mattelart and Siegelaub 1979–83; Fernández Christlieb 1982; many of the essays in Aman and Parker 1991). This Manichean and apocalyptic view of mass culture often carries with it some of the romantic assumptions that plague the folkloristic approach; namely that the mass media are destroying all that is pristine and authentic in the cultural sphere and, moreover, that this manipulative strategy is being worked upon passive subjects.[11]

The empirical retort to this sort of argument has been persuasively issued by García Canclini (1982) and Rodrigo Montoya et al. (1979) for Mexico and Peru, respectively. First, capitalism in Latin America has so far not succeeded in ineluctably eradicating so-called traditional or pre-capitalist modes of production or forms of social life; more frequently those have been retained in a state of "partial integration." Furthermore, the more apocalyptic readings of mass culture take no notice of the variety of ways the media are "received" and their consequences negotiated on the ground.

Jesús Martín-Barbero (1987; n.d.) develops the critique further, arguing against one-sided, dehistoricizing views of the media's impact on society, and shifting the focus of inquiry from the media's own technological capacity to deliver an ideological message to the cultural resources of the receiving public. (For an earlier application of this kind of critique to film studies, see *Screen Reader 1* 1977; Burch 1969.) In Martín-Barbero's reading, the mass media act as vehicles or "mediations" of specific moments in the "massification" of society, not as its source. Thus

10. See Swingewood (1979) for a scathing critique of literary and sociological theories of "mass culture." Cf. Mukerji and Schudson 1991:1–61.

11. Cf. Alonso (1992a) and Nugent (1992) for elements of a critique of authenticity. For discussions of the analytical constructions to which popular cultural elements are put by practitioners, see Taylor and Rebel (1981); Rebel (1988).

"mass culture is not something completely external that subverts the popular from without, but is actually a development of certain potentialities already within the popular itself" (Martín-Barbero 1987:96; cf. de Certeau 1984; Mahan 1990; Yúdice et al. 1992). In other words—as Bartra, Rockwell, and Falcón indicate in their chapters below—the mass media, state-supported education, and even the agents and instruments of a repressive state bureaucracy not only can serve as points of resistance to state projects but *also* may provide opportunities for the shoring up and reconstitution of popular traditions.

In an effort to delve beyond the defects of both folkloristic and mass culture notions of popular culture, we use the term to designate the symbols and meanings embedded in the day-to-day practices of subordinated groups (see especially Nugent and Alonso below). Such a notion of popular culture does not *exclude* the analysis of expressive cultural forms; nor does it deny the possibility of a "mass culture" constituted predominantly via media of communication controlled by the "culture industries." But, it *includes* a host of meaningful practices that are overlooked by both other senses of the term, and, with Martín-Barbero, insists on challenging the proposition that "instruments" of mass culture may achieve homogenous effects throughout society.[12]

Designating popular culture as the symbols and meanings embedded in the quotidian practices of subaltern groups is not intended as a rigid formulation that might enable us to specify what the *contents* of those symbols and meanings are—a static, reifying exercise at best. Rather, our definition underlines their processual nature, and insists that such popular knowledge is constantly being refashioned and "read" (cf. Rebel 1989) within (and upon) the subordinate imagination. At once "socially constituted (it is a product of present and past activity) and socially constituting (it is part of the meaningful context in which activity takes place)" (Roseberry 1989:42), popular culture is neither an autonomous, authentic, and bounded domain nor a "little tradition" version of dominant culture. Instead, popular and dominant culture are produced in relation to each other through a "dialectic of cultural struggle" (S. Hall 1981:233) that "takes place in contexts of unequal power and entails reciprocal appropriations, expropriations, and transformations" (Nugent and Alonso, below).

12. Our argument about the three different notions of popular culture owes much to discussions with Ana Alonso and her consultations with Pablo Vila in Austin, Texas, in 1989.

As Nugent and Alonso go on to point out, the kind of "reciprocity" indicated here does not imply equality in the distribution of cultural power. What it does imply is a sequence of exchanges between—and changes within—the partners of exchange (cf. Mauss [1925] 1967).

> What is essential to the definition of popular culture is the relations which define "popular culture" in a continuing tension (relationship, influence, and antagonism) to the dominant culture. It is a conception of culture which is polarised around this cultural dialectic. . . . What matters is not the intrinsic or historically fixed objects of culture, but the state of play in cultural relations. . . . (S. Hall 1981:235).

This understanding of popular culture postulates a set of linkages between the production of meaning and relations of power that are radically different from those that figure in either folkloristic or mass culture conceptualizations. It is possible, for example, to view "the state of play in cultural relations" in spatial terms. Looking at matters from this angle, where folklorists might perceive dominant and popular cultures as autonomous and singular domains, mass culture theorists would regard the two as hierarchically integrated spheres, with the terms of their integration provided by the dominant culture itself. In contrast, we would argue for understanding popular culture as "a site—or more accurately, a series of dispersed sites . . . where popular subjects, as distinct from members of ruling groups, are formed" (Rowe and Schelling 1991:10). Given a plurality of decentralized sites or (better) spaces, diverse possibilities for resistance may emerge historically (cf. Corrigan and Sayer 1985). This perspective informs our critique of unitary readings of Mexican popular culture, and also our recognition of the multiple axes of difference in Mexican society that the official populism has worked to obscure. In the hands of the state, Carlos Monsiváis warns, "the term *popular culture* ends up capriciously unifying ethnic, regional . . . class [and, we would add, gender] differences and inscribes itself in a political language" (Monsiváis 1981:33).

STATE FORMATION

If the relations between popular and dominant cultures are constantly shifting and are part of the everyday struggle for power, then a study of popular culture can only be conducted alongside or in concert with a study of dominant culture and an examination of power itself, and particularly those organizations of power that provide the context for "everyday struggle." One organization of, or form for regulating, power that is critical in this regard is the state.

While the point has been made time and again, it bears repeating that the state is not a *thing*, an object one can point to (and thereby seize, smash, or destroy) (Corrigan 1990b; Sayer 1987; Oyarzún 1989). The difficulty of then specifying what exactly the state is has been answered in a variety of ways. For Engels, for example, the state was an active and transformative "institution" which "set the seal of general social recognition" on notions of property and the "right" of one class to exploit another; while for Weber "it" was a "human community" enjoying a legitimate monopoly on the use of force (Engels [1884] 1942:97; Weber [1918] 1958:78). A common feature of these characterizations of the state is that they indicate a relationship of power. An additional feature, perhaps more nuanced and complex in Weber—and later in Gramsci—than in Engels, is that they draw attention to how effects of power are achieved within society (Weber's "legitimacy"; Gramsci's [often misunderstood] "active consent"; cf. Weber [1918] 1958; Gramsci 1971:244). But whether the state is taken to be an institution or a human community, the problem remains with each of these formulations that they are still wedded to a notion of the state as a material object that can be studied. It is precisely this contention that needs to be challenged.

In a brilliant essay titled "Notes on the Difficulty of Studying the State," Philip Abrams wrote:

> We should abandon the state as a material object of study whether concrete or abstract while continuing to take the *idea* of the state extremely seriously. . . . The state is, then, in every sense of the term a triumph of concealment. It conceals the real history and relations of subjection behind an a-historical mask of legitimating illusion. . . . In sum: the state is not the reality which stands behind the mask of political practice. It is itself the mask . . . (Abrams [1977] 1988:75, 77, 82)

Abrams is not only arguing for an examination of the *effects* of power ("the real history and relations of subjection") but also indicating that in order to move away from instrumentalist or reified notions of the state we must highlight the practical and processual dimensions of "its" dynamic evolution or *formation*.

Reflecting their debt to Abrams in *The Great Arch*, Corrigan and Sayer, as we have seen, write about state formation as nothing less than a cultural "revolution . . . in the way the world is made sense of" (1985:1–2).

Influenced by Durkheim, for whom "the state is the very organ of social thought . . . [and] is above all, supremely, the organ of moral discipline" (Durkheim 1957:50, 72, cited in Corrigan and Sayer 1985:5), and also by Mao Zedong, their study draws attention to the *totalizing* dimension of state formation, linked to its constructions of "national character" and "national identity" (cf. Anderson 1983). But *The Great Arch* equally considers the *individualizing* dimension of state formation, which is organized through impositional claims embodied in distinctive categories (e.g., citizen, taxpayer, head of household, *ejidatario*, and so on) that are structured along the axes of class, occupation, gender, age, ethnicity, and locality. Rather than dwell on the traditional preoccupations of some social scientists, such as "nation building" (the project of certain modernizing elites) or the origins of some apparatus of power routinely called "the state" (cf. the "state*making*" literature represented in Skocpol 1979; Bright and Harding 1984), Corrigan and Sayer reconstruct for England a centuries-long cultural process which was embodied in the forms, routines, rituals, and discourses of rule.

Unfortunately, they point out, forms of the state have in the past "been understood within state formation's own universalizing vocabularies" (1985:7) without considering the determinate consequences of this misapprehension for subjects of the state. Subjects are repeatedly reminded of their subjected identities via rituals and media of moral regulation, and not only through their manifest, concrete oppression. In short, "states *state*"; and as both Sayer and Roseberry argue in their contributions below, in stating may appear to successfully establish a common discursive framework that sets out central terms around which and in terms of which contestation and struggle can occur. The common discursive framework provides a language articulated as much through driver's licenses, formulaic slogans, or red flags, as through words. Furthermore, as Roseberry suggests—again drawing on *The Great Arch*—this discursive framework operates not only in terms of words and signs but also necessarily involves a *material* social process; that is, concrete social relations and the establishment of routines, rituals, and institutions that "work in us." Raymond Williams makes the same point about any "effective and dominant system of meanings and values, which are not merely abstract but which are organized and lived" (Williams 1980:38).

These remarks serve to highlight not only the formidably material character of the state's power, but also its relational constitution vis-à-vis "its" subjects. An overweening emphasis on looking only at "the state" obscures an understanding of alternative forms of power and identity, of movement and action which create oppositional or popular cultures. Corrigan and Sayer write:

> Too often these have been sundered. State forms have been understood . . . without reference to what they are formed *against*. . . . Oppositional cultures are conversely comprehended through the grid of the various selective traditions imposed as if they were all there is to say and know about "culture." (Corrigan and Sayer 1985:7)

The last sentence calls our attention to one of the problems that has plagued writing on popular mobilization and peasant insurgency. In much of this scholarship, there has been a tendency to insist on the autonomy and distinctiveness of forms of "popular" resistance, as though they were self-generating phenomena sprouting in a sociocultural terrarium. Ranajit Guha, for example, identifies subaltern politics as "an *autonomous* domain," and "the ideology operative in this domain" as constituting a distinct "stream" of consciousness or discourse (Guha 1982b:4, 5). "There were," he writes, "vast areas in the life and consciousness of the people which were never integrated into [the] hegemony [of the bourgeoisie]" (Guha 1982b:5–6; cf. Scott 1985, 1990). Even as these stimulating and provocative formulations have inspired some Latin Americanist research (e.g., Joseph 1990, 1991a, and below; Nugent 1988b, 1993; Mallon below; Seed 1991; Escobar 1992), the work of the *Subaltern Studies* group has been criticized for making extraordinary claims about the autonomy of "the popular" or the subaltern (e.g., O'Hanlon 1988; Spivak 1985, 1988; Prakash 1992a)—not least by the subalternists themselves (Chakrabarty 1985, 1991; Guha 1989).[13]

But if popular culture is not a thoroughly autonomous domain, neither are "the meanings and symbols produced and disseminated by the state . . . simply reproduced by subordinated groups [and consumed in an uncritical, unmediated manner]. Popular culture is contradictory since it embodies and elaborates dominant symbols and meanings but also con-

---

13. The point to be made in their defense is that these arguments—advanced during the "first moment" of subaltern studies—were themselves a critical response to even more essentialist formulations such as Eric Hobsbawm's notion of "primitive rebels" (1959) and his continued reliance on categories such as "pre-political" to characterize peasant politics (1973; cf. Corrigan 1975). Other essentialist variants include the "heroic" histories of peasant/popular resistance, which are predicated on some notion of "authenticity" (e.g., Hart 1987. See Rus's chapter below for a sobering antidote to such sentimentalizations; also see Abu-Lughod 1990).

tests, challenges, rejects, revalues, . . . and presents alternatives to them" (Nugent and Alonso, below; cf. Gramsci 1971:333; Williams 1977:113–14). Our conceptualization of the relationship between state formation and popular culture does not regard the latter as a category semantically nested in the culture of the state, the way popular classes are subordinated by the state, the proletariat by the bourgeoisie, and so on. Rather, it postulates the articulation of state formation and popular culture, with each connected to, as well as expressed in, the other (see Foster-Carter 1978; Post 1978 on "articulation"). Yet if popular and dominant cultures are imbricated in one another, "the 'same' unifying representations from the perspective of 'the State' [are] differentially understood from 'below' " (Corrigan and Sayer 1985:6). This point is amply illustrated in the essays that follow.[14]

Mallon, Joseph, Rus, and Rockwell, for example, explore how the state's subjects in Puebla, Yucatán, Chiapas, and Tlaxcala consistently sought to refashion liberal and "revolutionary" discourses of citizenship when these proved threatening to local forms of identity. Similarly, Nugent and Alonso and Becker probe the differential understandings regarding land and forms of landholding that have long kept Chihuahuan and Michoacan villagers at odds with the postrevolutionary regime—albeit for very different reasons. Collectively, the essays point to the durability and flexibility of the "revolutionary" traditions through which both the state and its opponents have sought to legitimate their struggles, a point that would seem to differentiate the Mexican revolution from other twentieth-century social movements.

It should be clear that any attempt to understand Mexico at the start of the twentieth century involves more than an interest in an event—"The Revolution"—that is routinely singled out as the empirical point of reference and privileged object of analysis. The changes Mexico underwent during the first decades of the twentieth century may be regarded in our analysis as a theoretical object, drawing together the simultaneous processes of state formation and the emergence of forms of local consciousness. The essays in this volume deemphasize "The Revolution" as a circumscribed event; rather, they promote a multifaceted, processual view

14. See also Levinson (1993) and the collection edited by Beezley, Martin, and French (1994), which examines the interplay of public and popular rituals in Mexico from colonial times; see particularly the essays by Vaughan (1994) and Loyo (1994).

of the relationships between revolution and popular culture, and between popular culture and the state.

One way of rephrasing the questions that Katz posed, in asking what were the terms of engagement between Mexico's *campesinos* and power-holders and how those terms were negotiated, is to suggest that the problem has to do with the complex issue of the relationship between autonomy and subordination. To formulate a processual analysis of this problem, several of the volume's contributors integrate multiple time scales into their analytical frameworks, as students of resistance in the Andean world have done with notable success (Stern 1987). This enables them better to understand how popular cultures and forms of domination are reciprocally engaged during particular conjunctures, as well as over medium-range and longer periods; in other words, before, during, and after "The Revolution." It also helps them sort out the multiple forms that resistance takes, and gives the reader insight into how historical protagonists *as well as scholars* attempt to make sense of the transition from one form to another in the context of changing modalities of domination. In this regard, attention is paid to the particular values, visions, and memories embedded in local society. Each is constructed and reconstructed—or, better, "imagined" (see Anderson 1983; Roseberry 1991 and his essay below)—in specific political contexts inflected by distinctions of class, ethnicity, and gender (cf. Comaroff 1987). Such values, visions, and memories, the contributors argue, define awareness of the power of the state, and shape resistance to it.

These studies of local Mexican society during times of crisis, popular revolt, and state repression provide the beginning of a more adequate *political* history of Mexico's *campesinos* and their ongoing negotiations with both elite factions and the emergent Revolutionary State. At the same time, these essays illuminate the character and form of a process of state formation that is cultural as well as political. And while this hegemonic process never gave rise in Mexico to anything resembling England's "Great Arch," time and again it prepared the ground for a translation between popular and state ideologies, and for the construction of Mexico's *histories*. Thus, these essays not only enable us to recover more fully the agendas and consciousness of participants at different points on the social-class spectrum; they also deepen our appreciation of the state's unremitting efforts to contain and depict them.

ALAN KNIGHT

Weapons and Arches in the Mexican
Revolutionary Landscape

In this chapter I seek to link, on the one hand, empirical data and debates concerning Mexican history with, on the other, more general theoretical questions relating to revolution, popular protest, state formation, and "popular culture." I do so encouraged by the advice that I should roam the field in relatively uninhibited fashion, but also alarmed by the sheer size of the field, the complexity of its topography, and the redoubtable reputation of many of its inhabitants. The result is an exploratory essay which, by virtue of its generality, is necessarily superficial—but I hope not fundamentally misleading—in its treatment of both the empirical history and the comparative social theory. The essay is divided into three sections. The first offers some personal views concerning the analysis of the revolution; the second and third relate to two major theoretical paradigms that may help our understanding of the historical phenomena: namely, those associated with James Scott on the one hand, and with Philip Corrigan and Derek Sayer on the other (Scott 1976, 1985, 1990; Corrigan and Sayer 1985).

I

"A long, long time ago," Barrington Moore tells us, "there was a school of philosophers in China whose tenets called for a 'rectification of names.' They apparently believed that the beginning of political wisdom was to call things by their right names" (Moore 1969:162). Taking a leaf from these linguistic philosophers *avant la lettre*, it might be worth trying to clarify a few concepts (and perhaps prejudices). I admit to a certain impatience with analyses that begin with a lengthy "naming of parts" peroration. Such an exercise—favored by sociologists who have "gotten history," like Michael Mann and Anthony Giddens—sometimes seems to involve the mass baptism of old ideas with abstract neologisms. Labels and vocabulary are renovated, but the phenomena behind the names remain murky, and often no clearer than they were under their old nomenclature. (I am making the assumption that there *are* phenomena "behind the names" and that we are engaged in more than the arbitrary swapping of labels and unscrambling of free-floating texts.)

Many of the concepts encountered in the course of this inquiry are big, grand, and amorphous: revolution, popular culture, the people, mentality, hegemony. My own workaday belief is that the utility of such concepts becomes apparent only as—and to the extent that—they provide the machinery for making sense of concrete examples, in this case the history of modern Mexico. They are applied concepts, or "organizing" concepts. In some cases (consider hegemony, consensus, mystification, false consciousness, dominant ideology) there is a considerable overlap between concepts that may derive from quite different social science authorities and paradigms. To some extent, the historian can pick and choose between them (this I have elsewhere dignified as the principle of controlled eclecticism: Knight 1986a:2:83–84). The choice and refinement of concepts therefore depend upon a sustained and critical dialogue with the empirical data, that "arduous . . . engagement between thought and its objective materials: the dialogue . . . out of which all knowledge is won" (Thompson 1978a:229). Once that dialogue has been established, of course, it is then possible to back up and reintroduce the ("useful," "fruitful") concepts by way of preamble. So here is my own brief set of conceptual preferences.

First there is the very definition of what constitutes the *explanandum:* the Mexican revolution or, to put it another but still question-begging way, the history of revolutionary Mexico. We may choose to focus on the *armed* revolution, roughly 1910–20; but we should not overlook certain armed "precursor" movements prior to 1910, the major post-1920 rebellions (none nationally successful), the Cristero War of the 1920s, and the endemic rural violence that afflicted much of the country throughout the period. So the dates are somewhat arbitrary.

Even more arbitrary is the criterion of violence. The notion of revolution—as used here—implies violence, of course, but it implies a lot more besides, as I shall go on to mention (cf. Hobsbawm 1986:7).

Furthermore, a stress on violence—especially the "bottom-up" violence that is diagnostic of popular or social revolution—will lead us away from some important themes on the agenda. James Scott's own work can be roughly divided into his earlier studies of *revolutionary* episodes and characteristics and his more recent work on peasant strategies of resistance in distinctly *non*revolutionary situations. These are—to paraphrase Harry Truman—two halves of the same walnut, both theoretically and historically: any understanding of "why men rebel" must be paralleled by an understanding of why they do not; of why subordination, inequality, abuses (all the factors that supposedly lie behind rebellion) may also coexist with quiescence (in terms of actions, not necessarily beliefs) (Knight 1986a:1:165–66). And in the case of Mexico, as I shall suggest, there are obvious reasons for comparing the phase of extensive revolt and upheaval—during which time, I would argue, popular violence was widespread—with the preceding and succeeding phases of greater peace and quiescence.

Such a chronological wide angle is important for a second reason, which is linked to my other main theoretical concern: the analysis of the revolution at the macrosocial level. Here again, violence is only a part of the story, and the armed revolution is only a phase (albeit a crucial one) in a longer process of social, political, economic, and cultural change. From both points of view, therefore, we should look to the long term, and we should try to locate the period of armed revolution within its broader historical context. How broad will depend to a considerable degree on the arguments we wish to make. Some explanations of the armed revolution, for example, stress immediate causes, such as the recession of 1907 (Ruiz 1980: chap. 8; Hart 1987: chap. 6). Others roam back through the nineteenth century, searching out the oppressive colonial legacy or, on the contrary, the corrosive consequences of Bourbon and liberal reformism (Tannenbaum [1933] 1966; Guerra 1985). My own preference—at least for many of the causal arguments I would deploy—is for the generation or so preceding 1910 (Knight 1986a:1:153–54). The point is that the chronological framework should be open-ended, the approach open-minded. So, too, with the question of "outcome" (a loaded term, with excessively final, even teleological, implications). I don't want to repeat those old debates about the degree of deadness of the Mexican revolution (Ross 1966). Defined with sufficient ingenuity (or casuistry), the revolution will never die; it enjoys the immortality of royal lineages— *la révolution est morte, vive la révolution!*—which is the position of the present Mexican administration.

Whether dead or immortal, the revolution, thus conceived and described, is evidently a reification: it is a definite entity, possessed of an immortal soul or a quasi-biological life cycle. Pretty well all recent students of the revolution stress, in contrast, the shifting, multifaceted character of "The Revolution," a phenomenon that appears in quite different guises depending on the chronological and—rather more—the spatial standpoint being taken by the observer. According to this relativist approach—which I think we should firmly adopt—the term *The Revolution* is at best a catchall, useful for general conversation but fatal to detailed analysis. At the very least, then, we need to attach to our (hopefully) detailed analysis some clear guidelines: that such-and-such an argument or generalization relates specifically to the armed revolution, to revolutionary anticlericalism, to the revolution in Chihuahua or the Papagochi Valley, to General Fulano de Tal and the Fulanistas. This does not mean, incidentally, that the notion of a national revolution must be discarded, that the only proper arena of analysis is the region, the valley, the *municipio*, or (as some oral history tends to suggest) the individual. Each of those arenas of analysis, though undoubtedly useful, is itself somewhat arbitrary: it captures something, it misses a lot.

Regions or states encompass wide differences within their borders. The national historian may generalize about Morelos (a pretty small state), but specialists in Morelos will stress regional variations within the state. Even within regions, such as the Ciénega de Chapala of northwestern Michoacán, there are marked differences between communities; and within communities there are class, factional, and *barrio* differences. (The relationship of *spatial* to *class* allegiances seems to me a live question, which recent literature, with its strong "regional" emphasis, frequently raises but rarely explains; e.g., T. Benjamin and Wasserman 1990.)

This leads me to a plea: while, on the one hand, we need to preface our arguments and generalizations with clear indicators (of the scope of the argument or generalization), we also need to bear in mind the appropriate criteria for evaluating arguments and generalizations at these different levels. We should not try to measure molecules in parsecs or planetary orbits in angstrom units. For example, a community or regional monograph will rightly delve into the details of, say, factional groups and alliances and their day-to-day struggle for political power and position. A broader study, national or thematic, cannot encompass such detail; will perforce generalize; and in doing so will violate some of the nuances of the micro-study (of course, the micro-study will already have violated "reality" on a grand scale). High in the stratosphere, meanwhile, world system theorists will look down, generalize, and, in so doing, further violate the nuances of the national or thematic study (consider the recent Stern-Wallerstein debate: Stern 1988; Wallerstein 1988). It does not follow, of course, that world systems theory is inherently inferior to national history, which in turn is inferior to regional and local history. Or vice versa. Rather, it is a question of deciding what are the appropriate levels of generalization, and what are the criteria for judging the value of generalizations.

To take a crude but important example: there is disagreement concerning peasant participation in the revolution (for the moment, let us not worry about what *peasant* and *revolution* mean). The argument may be put in terms of a head count: how many peasants participated in the revolution? Or (a more useful question) how many of the revolutionaries were peasants? Or we may ask how important were "peasant" grievances or "peasant" actions (seizing land, fleeing haciendas, macheteing *mayordomos*, and so on). Even if we come up with plenty of data, we may be unable to agree as to its significance. First, because we may interpret *intentions* differently: is macheteing a *mayordomo* an example of class retribution, the outcome of a personal feud, an act of individual criminality, or the result of too much aguardiente? (Scott 1985:295–96; Joseph and Wells 1990a:173, n. 26; Scott 1990:188). Second, we may disagree because, from our different standpoints, we may adopt different criteria or significance. From a local viewpoint, for example, a rebellion may appear narrowly clientelist in make-up; from above and beyond, it may appear to fit a pattern of broader socioeconomic protest. The local view may, by emphasizing a given rebellion, give an impression of powerful revolutionary commitment, whereas the broader regional or national perspective may play down its significance. Or vice versa. These may seem platitudes, but they are designed to forewarn against a possible source of confusion and polemic: namely, the different criteria of relevance and significance that tend to be adopted depending on the level of analysis being attempted.

Let me address two other sources of conceptual obfuscation: the very terms *revolution* and *popular culture*. Let me begin with the latter, about which I feel less qualified to talk. *Popular culture*, like revolution, is, in my view, a useful portmanteau term, which we can legitimately use to carry a number of concepts when we want to move fast; but it is one that should be promptly unpacked as soon as we want to get down to serious business. Or, changing the metaphor, it is a useful peg on which to hang an important discussion; but as the discussion proceeds, the peg is quite likely to vanish—without the discussion necessarily collapsing to the ground for want of support. I say this because I share with Chartier and others a certain skepticism about so broad and encompassing a term (Chartier 1987:3–4, 11; cf. Kaplan 1984:1–2; Geertz 1973:4–5).

Much of what we may term *popular culture* is shared by nonpopular (elite? superordinate?) groups; e.g., certain national and religious symbols and practices. Of course, different groups assimilate, appropriate, and rework symbols in different ways. Scott rightly stresses the importance of "discursive negation"—the tactically shrewd appropriation of elite discourse by subordinate groups (Scott 1990:104–6). But it does not follow that the popular/elite divide is always paramount, or (I shall argue) that popular appropriation is invariably instrumental. In the case of (Mexican) religion, for example, some aspects of "popular" Catholicism are not confined to the "popular" classes; conversely, anticlericalism has assumed both popular and elite forms. Catholicism and anticlericalism therefore have straddled class. They could afford bridges, ideological and institutional, thrown across the class divide. (Consider the National League for the Defense of Religion and the Popular Union in the 1920s, or the anticlerical clubs—liberal, patriotic, mutualist—that raised recruits across a broad social spectrum.)

More generally, the so-called popular classes have displayed huge cultural variations based on region, religion, ideology, ethnicity, and the often crucial rural/urban divide (Knight 1984a:52–56). Critics rightly point to the simplicity and abstraction of Robert Redfield's "Great" and "Little" Traditions; but to ditch the "Little Tradition" in favor of "popular culture" may be another semantic rebaptism rather than a major analytical advance.

As regards *revolution*, I would like to be bolder and less negative. Definitions and theories abound. Many of them are pretty useless. As commonly used and defined, *revolution* implies both substantial mobilization and conflict *and* substantial sociopolitical transformation. Most analyses seem to embody these two associated—but analytically distinct—aspects (Huntington 1971:264; Skocpol 1979:4–5). Elsewhere I have discussed both the Mexican revolution and, to a lesser extent, other revolutions in terms of these two aspects, which I would distinguish as the descriptive and the functional (Knight 1990d). The first implies a definition or description of what revolution looks like: it involves violence, sustained mobilization (not of a purely coercive kind), and the clash of rival ideologies, groups, classes, this clash premised on the belief that the outcome matters in some profound way; and it leads, in turn, to significant upheaval, perhaps involving the situation of "multiple sovereignty" discussed by Charles Tilly (Skocpol 1979:11). This descriptive definition can encompass not only the so-called great social revolutions, which entail civil war, but also—if so desired—anticolonial revolutions or national liberation movements (such as the Algerian), as well as "failed" revolutions (such as Taiping). Peasant rebellions—of the kind analyzed by Scott—form part, often a crucial part, of such major historical episodes (Scott 1976:3; Wolf 1969, 1973). We may argue about the membership criteria for this fairly select club (how profound is profound, for example), and we may even wish to tighten the entry rules. But from a historical point of view, I think it is both possible and useful to distinguish such a broad category of rare historical episodes and to differentiate them, at least along some continuum, from individual revolts and coups.

The authors of comparative studies of "great" or "social" revolutions were not, in my view, inventing chimeras. This is not to say, however, that they came up with meaningful causal explanations, for I do not take the view that this category, select though it may be, conforms to clear etiological patterns. Nor is this surprising; what I have offered is a purely descriptive definition—a revolution looks something like this—and no common causal kinship is implied. From this descriptive point of view, revolutions are like wars (or better, "total wars"): they belong to a recognizable category, but there is no assumption that the members of that category derive from common causes.

Nor do I believe that revolutions display a common morphology. They do not—to take a favorite version—proceed through moderate, radical, and Thermidorean phases (cf. Brinton 1965: chaps. 3, 5–8). Of course, it is usually possible to identify such phases if one looks closely and imaginatively enough. But such identification often involves a priori presumptions and a certain amount of Procrustean hacking and stretching. I do not believe the Mexican revolution follows such a pattern; not least because the "patterns" of the revolution (and it did embody patterns, it was not just a series of random events) were too varied, spatially and temporally, to admit of such a neat and simple configuration. There were many miniradicalizations and mini-Thermidors affecting national administrations, state governments, or even local politics. Of course, there were some rough congruences, especially after the "institutional" revolution of the 1920s (another loose label and loose chronology) got under way: a broadly radical trend during the mid-1930s and a conservative trend— perhaps a protracted, low-key Thermidor—thereafter. But these trends do not really match the classic revolutionary timetable, derived from the

French revolution. Indeed, just as we no longer take the British Industrial Revolution as the yardstick against which to judge later processes of industrialization, so we probably ought to abandon the French revolutionary archetype. "It is time," Corrigan and Sayer advise, "the search for an 'English 1789' was buried once and for all" (1985:202). Indeed, abandonment is all the more necessary because that archetype probably caricatures the French revolution in the first place.

If, with respect to etiology and morphology, I find revolutions to be quite varied and disparate—"just so stories," in Wolf's phrase (1971:12)—I would argue differently for outcomes. Certain revolutions share a kinship in respect of what they achieve; and, I would further tentatively argue, this comparable outcome derives from certain shared socioeconomic features. Outcomes, in other words, are less randomly distributed than causes, and it is for this reason that "macro" studies of revolution, such as Corrigan and Sayer's, reveal interesting and often quite close parallels between discreet cases (e.g., Knight 1986a:2:517–27; Doyle 1990: chap. 17).

Here we switch from description to function; that is, outcome, result, "contribution to history." A "descriptive" revolution, such as Taiping, may fail, in that it proves unable substantially to transform society. Again, we can argue about what "transformation" implies. (My feeling is that some analysts expect "revolutionary" transformations to be so rapid and extreme that they readily disqualify virtually all revolutions from being truly "revolutionary." Perhaps "revolutionary" change is habitually less abrupt and extreme than generally supposed; revolutions—while still warranting the term—may be more conservative than we think.) Just as there are "failed" revolutions, however, so there are "successful" revolutions, cases in which "descriptive" revolutions—the revolutionary sound and fury—have brought "functionally" revolutionary transformations; that is, they were more than "sound and fury signifying nothing." The Mexican revolution is one of them. I would go further and suggest that the outcome in Mexico conformed to several of the notional requirements of a "bourgeois" revolution, and thus perhaps warrants membership in that subset of the "social revolution" category.

This distinction between description and function, or between process and outcome, has its problematic aspects, some of which have been mentioned. There is the familiar problem of interpretation: how profound is profound? What is "transformation?" (These questions still arise, of course, even if considerations of "revolutionary" status are ignored. Debating such status is just one among many means of trying to calibrate historical change.) There is also the problem of distinguishing the one from the other, process from outcome. Since it is moot when a given "outcome" has been reached, we may adopt different chronological stand-points from which to evaluate the transforming effect of the revolution. What had changed by, say, 1917? or 1934? 1940? 1992? We return here to the old question of the mortality of the revolution. As I have said, it is an anthropomorphic fallacy to assume a life cycle for revolutions: old revolutionaries die, revolutionary generations die, but the historical legacy of (especially successful) revolutions is never entirely spent; it lives on in socioeconomic structures, political institutions, rhetoric, myths, memories, songs, stories, statues, individual and collective commitments, family vendettas, and intellectual polemics. The 1988 presidential campaign showed that the historical legacy of the (Cardenista) revolution had by no means been entirely spent. So it is never possible to close the book and evaluate the "definitive" outcome of a revolution (recall Mao's famous quote: see Knight 1985b:28). Nevertheless, with the passage of time and the benefit of hindsight, it is surely possible to argue about the consequences—the outcome, the function—of major revolutions, making clear as we do the vantage point we are adopting. An evaluation of the Mexican revolution in 1920 will look substantially different from an evaluation of the revolution in 1930 or 1940.

This distinction between process and outcome is, I think, useful, and it may be particularly useful in the present context, since many of the debates—empirical and theoretical—that arise in the course of this intellectual inquiry can be subsumed under one of these two headings. Indeed, the distinction between process and outcome corresponds in some measure to the two fields of analysis associated with Scott on the one hand and Corrigan and Sayer on the other. I will therefore organize the rest of this paper accordingly. The second part will consider the process of the revolution, in light of Scott's work. As regards period, I focus on the armed revolution (conventionally termed, 1910–20), its causes (which I see as primarily rooted in the Porfiriato), and its aftermath (chiefly the period of "institutional" revolution, 1920–40). So it is the period ca. 1880–1940 that claims attention.

In seeking to understand what went into the revolution we need to bear in mind not only the familiar "causes" (I mean the conditions that supposedly generated protest and rebellion: commercialization, foreign investment and exports, land concentration, increased stratification, proletarianization, state building, the centralization of power, caciquismo, military repression, the monopolization of political power, economic recession) but also the more subjective lenses through which these conditions were perceived (e.g., *mentalités*, ideologies, individual and collective beliefs). The first set of considerations—the stuff of the national histories of the past (e.g., Ochoa Campos 1967, 1968)—involves grand generalization, macroanalysis, an "etic" approach that gives priority to the supposedly detached observer (Harris 1979:32–41). The second, closely associated with the regional, local, and oral history that now predominates, involves lower-level generalization (sometimes, alas, little generalization at all), microanalysis (as befits "microhistoria"), and an "emic" approach, which gives priority to the views, concerns, and motives of historical participants. This second ("emic") approach deserves close attention when we consider the *process* of the revolution: first, because it is powerfully represented in recent historiography; second, because it undoubtedly sheds light on "popular" motivation and participation; and third because it ties in with one of the two main theoretical paradigms we propose to consider—that of James Scott.

II

Scott's work is highly pertinent to our understanding of the process of the revolution—armed and institutional—in two broad ways. As I understand it, his work falls into two main halves: the first, represented by *The Moral Economy* (1976), seeks to explain popular, specifically peasant, protest and mobilization, within rebellious and even revolutionary circumstances (certainly circumstances that could be categorized as *descriptively* revolutionary; i.e., in which, outcome notwithstanding, there is substantial noncoercive mobilization in pursuit of goals that excite opposition, countermobilization, repression, and conflict). Scott's second major contribution, represented by *Weapons of the Weak* (1985) and *Domination and the Arts of Resistance* (1990), deals largely with peasants constrained by powerful systems of domination (a more common occurrence, of course). Here, although conflict is endemic, it is limited, low-key, and nonrebellious— and, *a fortiori*, nonrevolutionary (Scott 1990:102, 136, 199). Frequently, when social scientists present dichotomies (left-right, stable-unstable, popular-elitist), it is at once necessary to stress that these are points on a continuum rather than separate pigeonholes. In this case, the caveat is somewhat in order. But only somewhat. It is a feature of revolutions (certainly, I would argue, of the Mexican revolution; also, I think, of the French, Russian, German, Bolivian, Iranian, and perhaps the Cuban) that they happen suddenly, that they take observers and even participants by surprise. As Lenin said to Trotsky: "You know, from persecution and a life underground to come so suddenly into power . . . *Es schwindelt!* [It's mind-boggling!]" (Huntington 1971:272).

Thus, as I shall mention later, revolutions reveal some of the characteristics of the "world turned upside-down." That being true, the switch from a nonrevolutionary to a revolutionary situation—with all that implies in terms of subjective hopes, fears, and calculations—may be quite sudden and dramatic: more amenable to catastrophe theory than to the organicist, febrile metaphor (mounting malaise leading to a predictable fever) that has often been preferred in revolutionary analysis (e.g., Brinton 1965:69, 72, 250–53). It also means that the dominated, dissimulating peasantry may suddenly find themselves "empowered," briefly capable of enunciating the "hidden transcript" of the poor; while conversely their erstwhile dominators suddenly have to look to their class defenses (Scott 1990:102, 224). The *modus operandi* changes: the "weapons of the weak"—dissimulation, tactical deference, appeals to landlord paternalism—are discarded in favor of machetes, clubs, shotguns, and (since we are talking about metaphorical as much as material weaponry), guerrilla *focos*, peasant leagues, more radical "structural" demands.

According to Scott, the new circumstances also allow the expression of popular sentiments that, like subterranean streams coursing through invisible caverns, were previously latent, stifled by the system of domination. Thus, he convincingly argues, the radical discourse of the popular revolution is not some new invention, but is rather the outward manifestation of hitherto silent ruminations, as the streams break the surface and cascade down the cliffs. Now the "true," latent sentiments become apparent; popular "moral outrage" (to use Moore's phrase) or "righteous anger" (Scott's) is laid bare; the stolid, forelock-tugging peasant discards his mask and becomes the protagonist of mayhem and jacquerie (Scott 1976:167; Moore 1978; Knight 1986a:1:162, 167–68). (Given the importance, the catharsis, the "political electricity" of this shift in social relations, it seems inappropriate to mix up the armory: Scott, for example, cites Pedro Martínez as an exponent of the "weapons of the weak" amid the tumult of the Zapatista revolution; but was this a case of Schweikian "resistance" or individual self-preservation, even "freeloading"? Scott 1985:294; 1990:206.)

If the switch from quiescence to rebellion, from the "weapons of the weak" to the arsenal of moral outrage, is sudden—and made possible by the existence, under the mask of deference, of subversive sentiments—

what of the later return to quiescence, or at least of the termination of revolution and the creation, on the basis of repression and conciliation, of a new relationship between rulers and ruled? In the case of "failed" rebellions and revolutions, repression is the norm; though it may be assisted by peasant divisions, weariness, the need to plant or harvest—whether in eighteenth-century France, nineteenth-century Yucatán, or twentieth-century Mexico (Cobb 1972:xv; N. Reed 1964:99; Knight 1986a:1:277, 315, 318, 378; García de León 1985:2:29).

Peasant mobilization thus becomes a brief episode, inspiring, horrifying, but ultimately futile (i.e., lacking in practical consequences, certainly of the kind the peasant rebels envisaged). So it was with the French jacquerie, the English Peasants' Revolt, the German Peasants' War, the Taiping Rebellion, the Caste War of Yucatán. These were not inconsequential, of course; they served, at least, as cautionary tales, restraining elite or state demands; but they terminated in clear victories for the elites, and they certainly did not revolutionize society. But in the case of the Mexican revolution as of other "great" revolutions (certainly the French and the Bolivian), the peasantry were not just repressed but also conciliated. They were partly successful in achieving their goals; conversely, the landed class suffered real losses in terms of both political and economic power. The peasantry, however, remained the peasantry—diagnostically a subordinate rural class. In many respects (as revisionists, in particular, stress) the "victorious" peasantry changed one set of masters for another. Over time, therefore, the peasantry had to put aside their revolutionary weapons, literal and metaphorical, and take up once again the "weapons of the weak." But this shift was *not* sudden, nor, in the Mexican case, was it, or is it, complete. As Cobb observes, perhaps too cautiously, "It is likely always to take some time to push or ease the people out of a revolutionary situation once they are no longer needed" (Cobb 1972:85). If the genesis of successful social revolution is often sudden and dramatic, its termination—with the caveat just expressed, that termination is a slippery notion—is likely to be protracted and mundane; hence, perhaps, less studied (for which reason Hobsbawm [1986:7] refers to "the neglected problem of how and when revolutions finish").

In the Mexican case, outright resistance, violence, vigorous lobbying, and political mobilization continued throughout the 1920s and 1930s; and, even though the 1940s brought a different sociopolitical scenario, characterized by a more quiescent peasantry, it is a travesty of contemporary history to see that decade—or, indeed, the last fifty years as a whole—as a period of popular quiescence, docility, and inertia (cf. Voss

1990:301; Knight 1990a). True, we are now far from the popular insurgence of 1910–20. The conditions, grievances, and tactics of the Mexican peasantry have changed markedly and, to some extent, that change has involved the forging and deployment of new "weapons of the weak," appropriate for the battles of post-1920 and especially post-1940.

By the same token, elites have had to respond to these new circumstances: they have changed in terms of make-up, political representation, and *modus operandi*. The "weapons of the strong" are no longer what they were in 1910. But the point is that during the long postrevolutionary odyssey, Mexico's peasants, once proponents of social revolution, were once again constrained by a new system of domination, which in turn required them to develop new "weapons of the weak," albeit weapons much uglier and sharper than those wielded by the peasants of Sedaka. (A similar argument could be made for postrevolutionary Bolivia. See Kohl 1982; Albó 1987.)

Scott's dual paradigm therefore offers a useful and appropriate lens through which to view the process of the revolution. But *how* useful is it? At the risk of seeming churlish (etymologically a good peasant characteristic), let me deal rapidly with the many points at which Scott's analysis rings true, in order to focus on areas of greater contention. I am of the opinion—shared by others, like John Tutino—that the notion of moral economy is invaluable in helping to explain the causes and course of the Mexican revolution (Knight 1986a:1:158–60; Tutino 1986:16–17, 24; Joseph and Wells 1990a:182). If one looks at where, when, and why peasants rebelled, one fails to find a neat correlation either with standards of living (whether individual, collective, or regional) or with the fluctuations of the business cycle. As E. P. Thompson commented, it is an error to believe that "popular radicalism can be encompassed in cost-of-living series" (Thompson 1963:222). Nor can Guerra's idealist argument, which places great emphasis on the dissemination of freethinking ideas and new forms of sociability, explain peasant, as opposed to middle-class, protest (Guerra 1985).

Protest and revolt seem to derive in particular from the experience of communities that were facing a severe, even mortal, challenge to their existence—economic, political, social, and cultural (Warman 1976:89). The challenge emanated from an expansionist landlord class (including some petty rancheros and caciques as well as big latifundistas), a class that enjoyed ample political and other benefits during the Porfiriato; and from a state that both connived at landlord expansion and sought to implement its own project of centralization and social control (Helguera R. 1974:70,

72; Knight 1986a:1:92–95, 115–17). These are broad-brush statements. They do not, of course, apply to all peasant movements; still less to all revolutionary movements. (I am not explaining the civilian Maderismo of 1909–10 in terms of "moral economy"—although "moral sensibilities" might be a valid concept.) The proof of this contention is to be found in reviewing the numerous peasant movements that populated the revolution, often under very diverse national labels. (I shall pass on the separate question of whether these peasant movements were sufficiently powerful and numerous to qualify the Mexican revolution as a "peasant revolution" or "peasant war." In my view they were, but that is not the immediate question.)

A "peasant movement" does not, of course, have to consist entirely of peasants. It does not have to be led, in all cases, by peasants. Rather, across a range of indicators, it must be shown to elicit the spontaneous (not coerced) support of peasants in pursuit of objectives that the peasants voluntarily—indeed, eagerly—endorse. As regards leadership, I have little time for the quibble that makes, say, Zapata a ranchero and therefore an unrepresentative leader of the peasantry. In fact, Zapata was probably as much a peasant as most of his followers. The "ranchero" argument is, in this case, something of a red herring. In other cases—for example, Carrillo Puerto's attempt to rally the *campesinos* of Yucatán—the distance between middle-class (or petite bourgeois?) leadership may be more significant; and that distance yawns if we consider archetypal fixers like Portes Gil of Tamaulipas. Leadership must be judged in light of support, program, and achievements. Portes Gil pretty clearly sought *campesino* support in an instrumental way, in pursuit of his own political goals (Fowler-Salamini 1990). That did not make his *campesino* mobilization irrelevant, but it prevents us from seeing Portes Gil's PSF as a "peasant movement," unless that term is unwarrantably stretched. But other "mobilizers" (or mediators, linkmen, brokers—no doubt we will continue to add to the vocabulary) led peasant movements without themselves being peasants, and did so honestly and representatively (Craig 1983: chaps. 4, 5). What is at stake is the degree of rapport and solidarity linking leaders and led: what we might call the *organicitá* of the leadership (Knight 1989:42; Sassoon 1980:138).

If program and accomplishments are important, so too are style and culture. The leaders of peasant movements, whatever their social origin, had to conform to certain norms: if they were not of the peasantry by birth and occupation (as a good many in reality were), they had to show that they were of the peasantry in terms of culture and mores. This they signaled—some cynically, some genuinely—by their "dress, deportment, and speech" (Schryer 1980:15; Joseph and Wells 1990a:183).

Peasant movements, then, were numerous and powerful: in Morelos, Guerrero, Tlaxcala, the Laguna; in parts of Mexico state, Michoacán, Puebla, Veracruz, San Luis, Zacatecas, Durango, Sinaloa, and Chihuahua; and pockets of Sonora, Jalisco, Oaxaca, Tabasco, and Yucatán. Revolt correlated closely with the "free" villages (to use Tannenbaum's terminology. His statistics may be wrong, but that does not invalidate his essential insight concerning the centrality of the free village: Tannenbaum [1933] 1966: chap. 16; J. Meyer 1986). Conversely, although some hacienda peons joined the revolution, they were much less numerous and conspicuous. The moral economy explanation is therefore suggestive—although, partly for want of historical data, I do not think it can be definitively proven or, of course, disproven. There is good evidence of the "moral outrage" propelling peasants to rebel; conversely, there is, as I have said, scant correlation between rebellion and objective living standards; and the armchair abstraction of relative deprivation offers little by way of meaningful explanation (cf. Nickel 1988:379–82; Scott 1976:32, 187). Womack's description of the Zapatistas, "country people who did not want to move and therefore got into a revolution," could be extended to cover a legion of peasant revolutionaries (Womack 1968:ix).

Scott's thesis is also borne out by the generally moderate and retrospective character of peasant revolt. The Zapatistas embraced a moderate program of land reform that only radicalized over time, in response to events. (This process of radicalization is important and deserves attention. Backward-looking moderates can become forward-looking radicals under pressure of circumstances; revolutions, like wars, have their own inherent momentum. Or, in Scott's own terminology, revolutions can not only reveal hidden transcripts but help write new ones.) This at least initial moderation of purpose and focus on the past are, of course, traits shared by many peasant movements that aimed at the restoration of a past situation—somewhat gilded, perhaps—of security, subsistence, partial autonomy, and elite reciprocity (Scott 1976:187; Cobb 1972:80).

Some authorities—Arnaldo Córdova in particular—have therefore sought to deny the revolutionary status of such rebels: since the latter lack a suitably radical, national, and comprehensive blueprint, they cannot be revolutionaries; and the very term *peasant revolution* becomes an oxymoron (Córdova 1973: chap. 3). Those, such as Womack or I, who have argued for the effective revolutionary role of peasant rebels—formal ideology (*proyecto o propósito de carácter político*) notwithstanding—are labeled romantic *campesinistas* (Córdova 1989:14). Scott's strictures, which echo those of Lawrence Stone, are pertinent: "A historical examination of the rank-and-file of nearly any manifestly revolutionary mass movement will show that the objectives sought are usually limited, even reformist, in tone, although the means adopted to achieve them may be revolutionary" (Scott 1985:317–18; see also Scott 1990:77, 106; Knight 1986a:1:161, 314). Failure to recognize this bespeaks not only an indifferent grasp of history but also, as Scott suggests, a quaint adherence to the clapped-out certitudes of Leninism (Scott 1985:297; 1990:151, which further argues for the superior tactical value of "primitive" popular protest).

Finally, Scott's argument for the latency of subversive sentiments—and his critique of the notion of hegemony—is substantially borne out by the experience of 1910–11. Of course, we lack suitable studies of the late Porfirian peasantry: no proto-James Scott sounded out the *campesinos* of the time concerning their day-to-day struggle with landlords and caciques, or the subversive attitudes they entertained beneath a mask of docility. The anthropologists of the day were often too busy measuring skulls; and they tended to do so in the Indian south, which was the least rebellious region of the country (e.g., Gadow 1908; Starr 1908). Even a later generation of anthropologists, working in the postrevolutionary period, who might have tried to probe prerevolutionary states of mind, tended to confine themselves to synchronic snapshots, many of them taken through the lens of Durkheimian functionalism. They turned a blind eye to history and conflict alike. More recently, a few historians have resorted to oral evidence or have begun to plumb court records in the hope of reconstituting popular *mentalités* on the eve of the revolution; but we do not yet have studies of the scope and caliber of the French school.

For my own part, I was impressed by the scale of popular insurgence in and after 1910 (*sic*: it did not await the fall of Madero in 1913. Cf. Tutino 1990:41). Apart from the forms of protest recognized in conventional history—peasant insurrections, land seizures, and military campaigns—there was also plenty of "expressive" protest, suggestive of a popular "transcript" infused with class and ethnic antipathies; humiliation of the rich; lynching of *catrines* (city slickers); invasion of public space; for example, when the rebel horde swaggered through the muddy streets of Torreón, rode the trams without paying, lunched in Sanborn's, rode into cantinas on horseback, or subverted the traditional decorum of the Sunday *paseo* in Guadalajara, forcing the daughters of the *gente decente* to dance with scruffy *campesinos* (Knight 1986a:1:210, 2:40, 177, 577). Discourse sounded subversive, too. The word went about that taxes need no longer be paid; "The Revolution" justified the seizure of land (Knight 1986a: 1:220, 244–45, 280–81). Meanwhile, unpopular groups—landlords, *may-ordomos*, officials, army officers, pawnbrokers, moneylenders, Spaniards, Chinese—were the object of frequent attack, in both city and countryside (Knight 1986a:1:206–8, 212–13, 279, 286, 343–44, 382–83, 2:38, 44, 119–20). Women were seen filing into cities, carrying baskets with which to carry off the expected plunder. In Chiapas, the Indians of the sierra took up their old weaponry, banners, and icons, and, under alleged clerical auspices, rose in rebellion, terrifying the ladino population with "the bloody image of a caste war" (T. Benjamin 1989:108–10; García de León 1985:2:37–31). Examples could be multiplied; their incidence and signifi-cance could be debated at length. But it is hard to avoid the conclusion that Mexico, during and after 1910, experienced something of the "world turned upside down," that dramatic reversal of rank and class that has historically characterized popular revolt and revolution (Hill 1975; Scott 1990:166–72).

In terms of behavior, the change was startling. A mystified Luis Terrazas lamented that once-faithful peons were now up in arms, threat-ening their masters (Knight 1986a:1:182). Given the suddenness of this upheaval, it seems hard to believe that these radical and popular notions were born *de novo* in 1910, or that they were the product of Madero's highly moderate and respectable political program. Popular attitudes (or ideology, or culture) are probably quite deeply ingrained and resistant to sudden swings. Behavior, in other words, is more elastic than culture. I admit this was a problem that I considered, but never tried to resolve, in my study of the revolution (Knight 1986a:1:528, n. 577). To my mind, the important thing was not the prerevolutionary substratum of popular culture—which, in its sociopolitical guise, was very hard to get at—but rather the dramatic and decisive events of 1910–11 and after. These events, in my view, stemmed from a generation or so of mounting tensions and abuses, though not a generation of mounting popular protest. In fact, the latter half of the Porfiriato—that is, post-1893—was in this respect quieter than the first half; and the Porfiriato as a whole was quieter than either the 1840s or the years of the Restored Republic. (See F. Katz 1986a:11, 1988b:11; Coatsworth 1988a:39.)

My argument implies, and certainly welcomes, the notion of a sub-stratum of latent peasant radicalism that, as I briefly suggested, was vested in certain regions, communities, and families and manifested in certain "traditional" political attachments, many of "liberal-patriotic" hue (Knight

1985a:83, 1986a:1:162–64). This meant that peasant protest was far from the kind of mute, inarticulate, brutish violence that some studies have suggested. Peasants resembled Aristotelian political animals more than Pavlov's dogs or Skinner's pigeons (Knight 1986a:1:527, n. 558), even though peasant protest derived from basic socioeconomic trends and grievances of the kind stressed by "traditional" histories of the revolution (Tannenbaum and others), albeit in somewhat simplistic and statistically loose fashion. Socioeconomic grievances found expression in ideological and normative forms, many of which conformed to Scott's analysis by virtue of being retrospective, nostalgic, and quite moderate, especially at the outset.

So far I have, as promised, registered close agreement with many of Scott's arguments. For the Mexican revolution (as I see it), they work very well. But there are also some problems. The arguments work for many "revolutionary" zones and actors: regions, communities, *barrios*, clienteles, clans, families, and individuals. But not all Mexico was "revolutionary." Without resorting to the crude dichotomy of "revolutionary and non-revolutionary peasants," we have to recognize that, in Mexico as in France, or Russia, or China, or Bolivia, or Cuba, there was a distinct geography of revolution. Why, then, were some parts of Mexico notice-ably quieter after 1910: for example, much of the northeast (Nuevo León, Tamaulipas), parts of the center and Bajío (Aguascalientes, Guanajuato, Querétaro), much of the south and southeast (Yucatán, Campeche, and Quintana Roo)? We could debate at length the incidence and significance of peasant protest in these and other states (I am using states as rough geographical shorthand, without presuming uniformity within states). Assuming, however, that no one believes that peasant protest spread uniformly across the country, or that it was entirely nonexistent outside Morelos, as some revisionists come close to suggesting (Ruiz 1980:7–8), then some pattern of *relative* protest must have existed. In my view, the contrast between revolutionary Morelos or Tlaxcala on the one hand and, say, nonrevolutionary Yucatán or Jalisco on the other is obvious and demanding of explanation. But what lay behind it? Here Scott's arguments, as I understand them, encounter some problems.

According to the "moral economy" thesis, protest derives from the breakdown, under the impact of the market or the state, of a preexisting equilibrium, which, though exploitative, was tolerable in that it did not involve the denial of basic subsistence rights or the elimination of all reciprocity in the peasantry's relationship with landlords and the state. Just as this thesis serves to explain popular revolt in revolutionary regions, such as Morelos or Chihuahua, so it can help explain quiescence—by which I mean simply the relative absence of popular revolt—in certain others. In a community like San José de Gracia, where extremes of wealth were limited and where access to resources, though inegalitarian, was not undergoing some marked upheaval, the absence of a revolutionary thrust is not surprising; it is the exception that proves the moral economy rule. (So the *josefinos* spent the early months of the revolution observing Halley's Comet or watching Elías Martínez try unsuccessfully to fly on wings of straw matting from the top of an ash tree [González [1968] 1972:114, 118].)

In some other quiescent areas—perhaps rather more—it was less the absence of abuses and grievances than the prevalence and efficacy of social control that ensured tranquility, at least for a time. To a significant degree, coercion maintained the plantocracy in Yucatán, as well as in other parts of the south: Campeche, the Valle Nacional, the *monterías* of Chiapas. Here we enter a "weapons of the weak" landscape. It was not that the peons of Yucatán lacked grievances—these can be inferred not only from the muckraking revelations of John Kenneth Turner, but also from the record of sporadic popular protest in the last years of the Porfiriato (Joseph and Wells 1990a:169–74; C. Gill, 1991). Rather, they lacked the freedom to express their grievances or to confront the dominant plantocracy, which controlled a system of social control exceptional even by Porfirian standards, involving quasi-slavery, slave hunters, deported labor, and corporal punishment (Joseph [1982] 1988b:71–80; Knight 1986a: 1:87–89). So Yucatán's popular revolution remained sporadic, confined mostly to the interior, until Alvarado's dramatic irruption in 1915.

I do not think, however, that these cases of quiescence—whether the Arcadian quiescence of San José or the *Animal Farm* quiescence of Yucatán—can be wholly explained in terms of Scott's two principal arguments. In other words, quiescent peasants were not necessarily happy with their lot (since it was a tolerable lot, involving adequate subsistence); nor were they necessarily cowed into inaction, ground under by an effective system of coercion. A third consideration, applicable to some degree in both these cases, as well as in many more, was that of "hegemony," which Scott appears to discard. In my view, the notion of hegemony (or its various alternatives: mystification, ideological domination, false consciousness) should be used cautiously and sparingly, certainly not as some kind of blanket explanation analogous to those other mindless *passe-partouts*, "national character" or "human nature." But in certain circumstances hegemony, or something like it, seems to fit the historical pattern, just as the "moral economy" or the "weapons of the weak" seem to fit elsewhere.

By discarding notions of hegemony, Scott (especially in *Weapons of the Weak* and *Domination and the Arts of Resistance*) seems to posit a standard condition of peasant discontent and potential subversion in agrarian societies (Scott 1976:4, 1985:317, 1990:70, 72). In this he appears to approximate Skocpol's implied argument: that peasant oppression and discontent are *givens*, and therefore major rebellions and revolutions are determined by events and pressures acting upon the state, especially through the international state system—an argument which is at a loss to explain the outbreak of the Mexican revolution (Knight 1990d:2–3). In other words, in terms of the familiar pressure-cooker metaphor,[1] Scott and Skocpol envisage a boiling stew, screwed down by a stout lid. (Scott also stresses that the lid is so well screwed down that the stew boils silently and anonymously.) Explosions occur only when the lid is tampered with.

In contrast, it could be argued that different cookers display different levels of activity. Some are highly unstable, ready to blow at any moment (e.g., Morelos in 1910). In such cases, the lid cannot withstand the internal pressures; external tampering may or may not be important; and if tampering occurs, it is more trigger than cause of the explosion. And when the explosion comes, the stew hits the ceiling. Other cookers are bubbling, but the lid is so strong it can contain the pressure, at least until

---

1. The pressure cooker is yet another of the (loosely) hydraulic metaphors that litter the field (Scott 1990:9, 177–78, 181, 185, 216, 220). It is interesting to note that this is an image entertained not only by ivory-tower academics but also by those engaged in the practical assessment of stability and protest. Under the presidency of P. W. Botha, the British ambassador to South Africa observed, "what we were seeing . . . was an attempt to respond to the steam building up inside the cauldron by trying to nail the lid down harder and tighter" ("After Four Years, British Envoy Is Leaving a New South Africa," *New York Times*, 15 July 1991, A6). It should be added that Scott's discussion—and repudiation—of the notion of hegemony is subtle and nuanced. In particular, he makes a useful distinction between "thick" and "thin" versions of the concept, the first involving a positive popular endorsement of the status quo, the second implying no more than resigned acceptance. In arguing for the retention of the concept, I would emphasize the second—that is, a "minimal notion of ideological domination [that] has become almost an orthodoxy"—much more than the first. Scott, while agreeing that the second is "eminently plausible," still considers both concepts to be "fundamentally wrong," and vulnerable to "fatal" objections (Scott 1990:72–77).

serious tampering starts (e.g., Yucatán before 1915). A third category of cookers, I would suggest, are barely simmering—and may be no more than lukewarm. Stout lids are unnecessary, because there is little fire under the pot. Even if the lid is removed, the stew stays put.

It is this third category that deserves some attention. For one thing, can such a category be presumed to exist? Or does it, perhaps, exist only in developed industrial societies? The evidence for some kind of "hegemony" conditioning attitudes and behavior in, say, the United States seems to me to be strong; and (*pace* Giddens and perhaps Scott) I am not wholly convinced by the argument that modern states are endowed with hegemony-manufacturing capacities out of all proportion to traditional states (Giddens 1987:71–78, 209–12; Scott 1985:320–21, 1990:21, n. 3). Of course, Scott's arguments derive largely from purely peasant societies; hence comparisons with nonpeasant societies may be invalid. As peasants lose their peasant status and relinquish subsistence cultivation for wage labor, Scott argues, so they become "a hybrid species with its own unique characteristics" (1976:214–15).

Perhaps those unique characteristics include a vulnerability to "mystification" that their peasant forebears lacked. Even as regards those forebears, however, Scott recognizes, in *The Moral Economy*, that discontent is not a given; that there are degrees of discontent, which in turn would help explain the incidence of revolt as against quiescence (1976:239, n. 103). In contrast, the whole thrust of *Weapons of the Weak* is that compliance is coerced, not just physically but also by Marx's "dull compulsion of economic relations" (1985:246, 1990:66). Compliance does not indicate any peasant acceptance or legitimacy of the status quo; and given some relaxation of the system of domination, some tempting *apertura*, the mask of compliance will come off, and grudging compliance will give way to protest and rebellion. That happened in many parts of revolutionary Mexico as hidden transcripts became public. We may presume that Terrazas' subjects, tenants, and peons experienced such a transformation in Chihuahua in 1910.

But it failed to happen in many other parts of the country. And the failure, the absence of protest, cannot be wholly attributed to either material well-being or outright coercion. There are sufficient examples, both during and after the armed revolution, of *campesinos* spurning the tempting *apertura*. They did not rise up; they remained loyal to cacique and landlord; they opposed revolutionary reforms that promised them land, schools, or the dissolution of landlord authority (e.g., Amerlinck de Bontempo 1982; González [1968] 1972:174; Gledhill 1991; Margolies

1975:39). Even in revolutionary Morelos there were *campesinos*—like those of Tenango—who allegedly were "tied by solidarity (*ligados solidariamente*) to the hacienda in such a way that they could not perceive the magnitude of the exploitative relationship" they suffered (Helguera R. 1974:68). Conversely, it was not the poorest, those closest to subsistence crisis and destitution, who rose up; indeed, we may question whether Porfirian Mexico ever suffered a Malthusian crisis remotely comparable to the North Vietnamese famine of 1944–45. The closest Mexico came to Malthusian crisis was *during* the revolution, especially in 1917, the "year of hunger" (Coatsworth 1976; Knight 1986a:2:412–18).

How should these cases of quiescence be explained? I do not deny that in many cases, rational calculation induced caution. Peasants were leery of antagonizing powerful landlords or bosses, whose lapse of authority was perhaps only temporary. Reprisals might follow. The postrevolutionary agrarian reform was frequently stymied by the indifference or downright opposition of peons who feared that an ejidal petition would bring down upon them the wrath of the local landlord and his hired thugs (Craig 1983:74–75; Friedrich 1977:90–92). Peons, tenants, and sharecroppers were reluctant to risk old accommodations with landlords in pursuit of a notional future benefit (Knight 1991:93–95). To draw a significant parallel, which corroborates both *The Moral Economy* and *Weapons of the Weak*, I have repeatedly argued that foreign enterprises were *not* major victims of popular hostility and attack during the revolution, since the foreign enterprises in question, such as the big Anglo-American mining and oil companies, appeared on the scene neither as usurpers of the peasants' landed patrimony nor as gravediggers of peasant security (Knight 1987:21–25, 53–69). Quite the contrary; they provided jobs and higher wages. In the Mayo Valley, the United Sugar Company enjoyed fairly good relations with the local Indian peasantry; it was the mestizo and ladino landed elite who incurred peasant dislike (M. Gill 1955). A similar relationship emerged to unite highland Chiapas Indians and lowland German cafetaleros (Knight 1986b:56–60). No one would argue for a powerful affective bond linking foreign bosses and Mexican peasants and workers; yet the relationship, which survived the collapse of authority during the revolution, cannot be explained in terms of coercion either. Rather, the relationship was tactical, calculating, and utilitarian, amenable to a modified "weapons of the weak" analysis, one that stresses the "dull compulsion" of economics over outright coercion.

By the same token, some Mexican landlords retained the "loyalty"— i.e., the continued compliance—of their peasant workers during and after the revolution. Economic calculation, not coercion—or affection—was paramount. But economic calculation, while it explains a lot, cannot explain the whole picture. Why was compliance evident when, in the next state, the next valley, the next *municipio*, peasants were mobilizing, marching, and macheteing the *mayordomos?* And when, according to the evidence we have, the economic predicament of "compliant" as against "insurgent" communities was not always distinct, and indeed was sometimes similar?

Of course, some fault lines followed an economic rationale, either between states (a compliant Aguascalientes compared to an insurgent Morelos) or within them (a compliant northern Tlaxcala, an insurgent south) (Buve 1990:239–40). Within states like Puebla or Michoacán and regions like the Ciénega de Chapala or the Once Pueblos, however, there were also marked discrepancies, which apparently are not reducible to clear-cut economic differences. Cherán had "very inequitably divided fields," yet it was a bastion of clerical conservatism and the bugbear of its agrarista neighbor, Naranja (Friedrich 1986:162). The geography of revolution cannot, it seems, be reduced to economic patterns. "Red," "revolutionary," "agrarista" communities confronted conservative, clerical, anti-agrarista communities, and some communities were internally divided along these lines. The evidence does not prove that rebelliousness neatly correlated with absolute poverty or even with recent dispossession and landed conflict. Hence the revolutionaries often faced an uphill struggle when it came to mobilizing the peasantry, especially in those areas where peasant mobilization was "secondary"—i.e., where it did not build upon a prior autonomous peasant insurgence (Knight 1991:86, 89).

My argument, then, is that the incidence of peasant quiescence cannot be explained solely in terms either of coercion (which could not prevent successful rebellions in many places) or of careful peasant calculation, premised on economic—specifically, subsistence—considerations. After all, many peasant revolts, especially during 1910–15, flew in the face of rational calculation. As Scott has argued, peasant rebellion does not obey a Benthamite, felicific calculus. Individual calculation and self-interest are not likely to start revolts; rebels may have to "risk everything"; they may rise up "despite seemingly hopeless odds" (Scott 1976:3, 191; but cf. Scott 1990:220, n. 33, which sees "acts of madness" as "exceptionally rare"). And although revolts, once under way, attract their time servers, it is a travesty of the revolution to attribute popular mobilization primarily to self-interested calculation and careerism. Mortality rates alone would tell against that, unless we are to assume that peasants were too stupid to appreciate the risk of revolt. Saturnino Cedillo finally did well for himself, but his siblings suffered a fearful mortality.

In other words, just as protest and revolt had a normative and ideological dimension, so too did compliance and quiescence; and neither can be reduced to material calculation, even though that was often important, and sometimes paramount, as at Sedaka. The best example of this concerns peasant support for the church and opposition to revolutionary *agrarismo*, a stance neatly summed up in the words of peons of the hacienda Guaracha, addressed to Cárdenas: "No queremos tierra, queremos culto" ("We want not land, but our faith") (Gledhill 1991:36, 97). This is a topic central to our understanding of revolutionary history. In his rebuttal of the notion of hegemony, Scott largely bypasses questions of religion and magic (1985:320, 334; but cf. 1976:220–21, 236–37; and 1990:24, 115). In the Mexican—as compared to the Malaysian—case, this is not a bypass that we ought to follow. In Mexico, religion and revolution were inseparable. Both during the armed revolution and after, the church generally set its face against the revolution, and did so with the benefit of considerable popular support, especially in the center-west states of Jalisco, Michoacán, and in the Bajío; and pockets of the north, chiefly Zacatecas, Durango, and Nayarit. This phenomenon, which reached its apogee in the Cristero War of 1926–29, is a complex one and, although we have some good studies and one outstanding *magnum opus*, we are still far from understanding it.

The conventional revolutionary explanation tied the church to "reaction." The church aligned itself with landlords in opposition to the revolution's promises of reform, especially agrarian reform. The Cristeros were therefore economic actors: on the one hand landlords and rancheros, eager to preserve their estates; and on the other their pliant retainers, peons in both senses of the word. Some recent studies also interpret the Cristiada in terms of simple economic factors (Tutino 1986:343–45; Larín 1968). On the other hand, Ramón Jrade offers a subtler picture, stressing political and class divisions and arguing that "the Cristero uprisings were primarily a response . . . to the efforts of the revolutionary coalition to consolidate and centralize its power over the states" (Jrade 1985, 1989:13). (This, while true, begs the question: why did these efforts, which covered the face of the country, elicit such strenuous Catholic resistance in some areas but not others?)

In contrast, Jean Meyer, arguing the fundamental religiosity of the movement, maintains that the Cristiada was a highly heterogeneous movement, comprising representatives from all strata of society (1974c).

For Meyer, the Cristero was no *homo economicus*. Rather, the Cristiada knitted together a cross-section of Catholic society and included a massive popular contingent, which was in no sense the pliant instrument of controlling elites. Indeed, Meyer argues—perhaps overmuch, but the point is well taken—that *caciques* were scarcely represented in the ranks of the Cristeros and that the latter represented a genuine, autonomous, popular force, analogous in many respects to the Zapatistas of the preceding decade. The proof of this, in my view, can be seen in the dogged and protracted resistance the Cristeros put up during 1926–29 (and to a lesser degree during the "Second Cristiada" of the 1930s). Whether *caciques* and landlords were present or not, this resistance, taking the form of classic guerrilla warfare, would not have been possible without widespread, deep-rooted (as their enemies said, "fanatical") popular support and participation. Proof is also evident, during the 1930s, when the anticlerical, agrarista thrust of the Cárdenas regime was blunted by both popular indifference and outright popular hostility, especially in regions and communities of Cristero tradition. Indeed, there were even cases of agraristas—recipients of ejidal grants—who remained fervently ("fanatically") Catholic (Secretaría de Educación Pública [SEP] 1935).

To what should this popular peasant conservatism—reminiscent of the Vendée—be attributed? As I have said, elite coercion won't wash. Many of the elite quit the region during the rebellion (J. Meyer 1974c:43). Those who stayed were hardly in a position to sustain and lead a widespread rebellion on the basis of coercion. We have to accept a genuinely popular basis for the Cristiada and, to a lesser extent, for the "neo-Cristero" anti-Cardenismo of the 1930s, notably the Sinarquistas ("to a lesser extent" because, by the 1930s, outright civil war had ended and elites were, notwithstanding the newfound radicalism of the central government, better placed to exercise their authority and defend their position).

The strength of this popular base—Catholic, anti-agrarista, anti-revolutionary, and therefore, in some sense, conservative—can be interpreted in different ways. (And these interpretations, I should stress, are my own distillations of what are often complex and sometimes convoluted arguments.) One interpretation—roughly Meyer's—stresses the distinctive religiosity of the peasantry of west-central Mexico. While the historical roots of this religiosity can be dug up (J. Meyer 1974b:43–53; Sullivan-González 1989), the argument tends to take Catholicism as a datum, and to deny that it served as a front for ulterior motives. If this premise is accepted, the question whether Catholicism served as a form of "mystification" depends very largely on what one thinks about Catholicism, or Christianity, or religion in general—a question which, for want of time and temerity, I shall duck. However, the Mexican evidence certainly suggests a genuine (voluntaristic) attachment to Catholicism—including not just heterodox "folk" Catholicism but also the institutional church—that clashes with Scott's depiction of Catholicism, whether in medieval Europe or 1930s Spain, as *either* a source of "discursive negation" and popular dissidence *or* a hollow facade, imposed by elites upon a skeptical populace (Scott 1990:68–9, 215).

This clash is all the more striking if we see the Mexican church as more than a mere spiritual mentor and attribute to it a significant sociopolitical role (not necessarily that of tribune of the people). Several historians deny the transparency of religion and seek to relate both Catholicism and popular clericalism to sociopolitical factors. This may involve somewhat crude "opium of the people" reductionism or more subtle formulations. According to the traditional "revolutionary" explanation already mentioned, peasant conservatism and Catholicism obeyed the interests of the landed elite and attested to the power of the clergy. To the extent that this is true—that clerical authority bolstered a conservative, landed elite—this would seem to be a classic case of "mystification" (or "false consciousness," or whatever). Evidence for this is certainly not wanting. Priests preached against land reform, denounced the revolution, inveighed against "socialist education," and excommunicated those who succumbed to these heresies (Craig 1983:70–71; González [1968] 1972: 173–74; Friedrich 1977:48, 120). Allegedly, they even denied the last rites to dying agraristas and revealed the secrets of the confessional to the landlord's posse of thugs (Gruening 1928:218; Gledhill 1991:84). Most important, peasant flocks often allowed themselves to be shepherded by their *curas*. They declined to petition for land, fearing excommunication and hellfire; they attacked Protestants, believing that "the Government of Mexico is Protestant and . . . is trying to change the religion of our people into Protestantism"; they boycotted federal schools and ostracized the pioneer agraristas; they took up arms, either in brave defense of their faith or in brutal aggression against vulnerable schoolteachers (Gruening 1928:282; Raby 1974: chap. 5; SEP, 1935).

The fact—though neither the geographical extent, nor the historical origins—of this clerical hegemony seems certain. The traditional revolutionary explanation, stressing clerical connivance with exploitative landlords, snugly fits a "false consciousness" hypothesis. Indeed, the radicals of the 1930s talked in virtually these terms: socialist education was designed to break the ideological hegemony of clerics, landowners, and capitalists (SEP 1935). To the extent that they were right, a large chunk of the Mexican peasantry, their revolutionary experience notwithstanding, were languishing in the trammels of false consciousness. Not only did they not take up the weapons of the weak; they even shouldered arms in support of their clerical and landed exploiters. Clearly, this sits uneasily with Scott's general analysis. For while Scott concedes that "the major historical forms of domination have presented themselves in the form of a metaphysics, a religion, a world view," he doubts that these presentations have carried weight. The opiate ("general anesthesia," in Scott's words) doesn't work; the common people espouse religion to the extent that it is subversive, dissident, supportive of the "hidden transcript" (Scott 1990:68, 115, 215).[2]

A more subtle explanation, espoused by Jrade and even to some degree by Meyer, expands the rationale of Catholicism and sees it as weapon, symbol, and prize in the old battle between center and periphery, a battle aggravated by the experience of the revolution. Accordingly, the Cristeros fought not simply in defense of *caciques* and landlords but rather in defense of the *patria chica*, to keep the offensive revolution at arm's length, to maintain their local autonomy. While this argument does not posit a crude "false consciousness"—Catholic mobilization does not serve the interests of the landed elite *tout court*—it does imply some notion of hegemony. The conflict between the revolution and the church, fought out on the battlefields of Jalisco and Michoacán, is a struggle for

2. Scott's argument for the subversive potential of popular religion is well taken; Mexican history is replete with examples. On the other hand, it seems unrealistic to claim that religion achieves purchase and political significance among the popular classes only to the extent that it inspires protest (rather than, say, submission). Scott concedes that a "generalized respect for priests and for the faith they represent" can and does exist; he also recognizes—but excludes from discussion—the "voluntary and revocable subordination typified by entering a religious order" (Scott, 1990:24, 82, n. 33). If for "religious order" we substitute "religious community," we admit to a social and ideological formation—the Catholic church, the parish—membership in which is, at least in the case we are considering, to some degree voluntary, yet capable of exerting a strong influence on its members, sometimes even governing their political behavior. The religious arena may certainly offer spaces for popular appropriation and resistance, as Scott stresses, but it may also contain traps and culs-de-sac capable of imprisoning its popular adherents. And religion is only the best example of this phenomenon; secular political movements and philosophies (nationalism, for example) may turn a similar trick.

ideological and institutional supremacy (J. Meyer 1974c:63—64). More of this in conclusion.

A yet more forthright version of this interpretation is evident in some recent revisionist scholarship, notably that of Marjorie Becker (1987, 1988a, b). Becker's analysis is particularly relevant because she works explicitly within a "weapons of the weak" paradigm (i.e., the paradigm that rejects notions of hegemony and interprets peasant politics in terms of a quotidian resistance to domination, indicative of a latent subversive mentality). According to Becker, the Catholic peasantry of Michoacán— in particular, the Catholic peasantry of Janácuaro—contested the Cardenistas' imposition of a revolutionary program that was anticlerical, agrarista, and "socialist." In doing so they drew upon their own world view and traditions, and sought to defend the integrity and autonomy of their community. According to this scenario, the peasants of Michoacán deployed the weapons of the weak against a new and threatening engine of domination: the revolutionary state. The Cardenistas performed the same role as the UMNO fat cats of Sedaka. Note that this means a complete reversal of the traditional (i.e., revolutionary) interpretation of events, which saw these same peasants as suffering under the "reactionary" domination of landlords, priests, and *caciques*, a domination the revolution sought to break in the name of progress, emancipation, and egalitarianism.

While I do not so much question Becker's discussion of Janácuaro, I have doubts about her discussion of Cardenismo in general (whether as a Michoacán or national movement). There are two main problems, and they impinge directly upon the utility of the Scott paradigm for the analysis of this phenomenon. First, it is doubtful how far Cardenismo should be considered an effective engine of domination. The imperfections, limitations, and lacunae in its radius of effective action were striking (Knight 1990b). This is apparent from Becker's own evidence, as well as plenty of other sources. The Cardenista project was *not* imposed upon a cowed peasantry, nor was it the work of an undisputed elite; in both respects, therefore, the Cardenistas in general did not correspond to the unquestionably powerful village elite of Sedaka. In particular, the Cardenistas' power was political, and dependent on a distant and sometimes unreliable central government; whereas Sedaka's elite enjoyed secure economic power in the locality. In some villages the Cardenistas were the cocks of the walk, it is true; but in many they were not—they were isolated, vulnerable, and, in several cases, ultimately dead (Raby 1974: 128—37, 147—60; Vaughan 1987, 1991). As this comparison suggests, the political map remained highly variegated: red pueblos warred (sometimes literally) with clerical communities. No statewide political monopoly could be established; even municipal political monopolies were vulnerable. In such a fragmented and conflictual situation, the "weapons of the weak" argument appears somewhat inappropriate, certainly strained.

This leads to the second main problem: in the absence of any such monopoly, the peasantry retained some genuine political leverage, much more than the peasants of Sedaka seem to have enjoyed. Whether Catholic or agrarista, the peasants of 1930s Mexico all lived in a postrevolutionary society; the neap tide of popular insurgency had ebbed, but the waters remained agitated. Society witnessed sustained popular mobilization, rival propaganda, competitive (albeit dirty) politics, and endemic local violence. In such a Hobbesian world there was (*pace* some historians) still no Leviathan, no securely dominant elite, and no thoroughly dominated peasantry. The days of mass guerrilla war were gone, but, inverting Clausewitz, we may say that the (agrarian) politics of the 1930s were in many ways the continuation of the guerrilla war by other means.

The sheer heterogeneity of the political landscape—in Mexico at large, in Michoacán in particular—calls for an explanation that goes beyond either coercion or grudging economic compliance as the twin determinants of peasant politics. Basically, it requires a partial and cautious resort to the idea of hegemony. In my view, the polarized politics of the postrevolutionary period involved a battle for hegemony between rival elites (and here I am defining elites pretty broadly). As will be clear from what I have already said, I do not regard the peasants as inert subjects of this battle: they participated, they strove for a measure of autonomy, and they contributed to the manufacture of new ideologies and political practices (Knight 1990c:249–50). They could not be taken for granted. That was one of the great lessons of 1910. The destruction of the old system of Porfirian political domination left a vacuum that, in simple terms, the revolutionaries sought to fill and their enemies sought to contest.

Foremost among their enemies in the 1920s and 1930s were the Catholic church and the militant Catholic laity. Irrespective of whether we consider revolutionary anticlericalism to have been a progressive and emancipating force, as it claimed to be, or as an authoritarian imposition, or even as a smoke screen to hide more deeply rooted "socioeconomic" questions, in actuality it excited fierce feelings both for and against. The revolutionaries actively sought converts, and their Catholic opponents—

precise social counterparts, in some cases, of the revolutionary militants—resisted (J. Meyer 1974a:53). Furthermore, there is good evidence
that the peasantry was polarized along these lines. Becker stresses the
resistance of a brave, God-fearing peasantry to Cardenista domination,
but it is not difficult to find counterexamples of brave agrarista resistance
to landlord and clerical domination (Friedrich 1977; Craig 1983; Gledhill
1991). In other words, the revolutionary view was not all self-serving
myth.

If, as seems to be the case, Michoacán—or Mexico—thus resembled
a complex mosaic of political tesserae, what conclusions does this suggest? Since domination is, in this situation, fragmentary, vulnerable, and
contested, it is wrong to see the peasantry as locked in a windowless
prison, capable only of very limited quotidian resistance. The Sedaka
picture does not fit; nor is this surprising, given, as I have said, the still-
recent experience of social revolution, which strongly colored Mexican
perceptions and calculations. As Scott himself puts it: "Sedaka is not
Morelos" (1985:244). Furthermore, the absence of any political monopoly (or even oligopoly) does not imply either ideological indifference or a
bland pluralism; on the contrary, people were busily shooting each other
for their religious and political beliefs. The situation resembles the French
Wars of Religion rather than British Butskellism. Over and above material
grievances, and the subsistence ethic that accompanied them and under-
wrote peasant protest; over and above the quotidian calculation of res-
pites and benefits; over and above, therefore, the two main explanatory
devices Scott offers, and which together explain a great deal, we have also
to consider an additional plane of behavior or explanation (forgive the
spatial metaphor) that involved ideology, normative allegiances, and
hegemony. I do not say that this was the most important consideration,
and I share Scott's distaste for the "ideological determinism"—or "rabid
idealism"—now in vogue in many circles (Scott 1985: 317; Corrigan and
Sayer 1985:2). But I remain to be persuaded that "the notion of hegemony
and its related concepts . . . not only fail to make sense of class relations in
Sedaka, *but also are just as likely to mislead us seriously in understanding class conflict
in most situations*"—including, presumably, revolutionary Mexico (Scott
1985:317, my emphasis; see also Scott 1990:72).

Certainly there were a good many Mexican Schweiks, skeptical
plebeians who spurned church and state, clerical and revolutionary authority alike; or Mexican Candides who cultivated their *milpa* and preferred the cantina to either the chapel or the *escuela socialista*. But there

were also many Mexicans who took sides in the great social struggles of 1910 to 1940, exercising choices and contributing to outcomes. No doubt that was a special—*qua* postrevolutionary—situation; but it was not historically unique. Nor, we might add, has the passage of time entirely undone the work of the revolutionary era. The revolution—itself the result of a failed (Porfirian) hegemony—gave birth to a state that struggled to assert its authority in the face of powerful enemies possessed of their own counterclaims to authority. The common people of Mexico were both victims and participants in this secular struggle. And the outcome was, at least in part, a new hegemony, more durable than that of the past: a Mexican Great Arch, the work not only of elite architects but also of the calloused hands of common peons.

III

This leads us to Corrigan and Sayer's analysis, which also has an interesting bearing on the study of modern Mexican history. By stressing the need "to grasp state forms culturally and cultural forms as state-regulated," they broach not only the central question of state formation, which is a live issue in Mexican studies, but also the question of cultural change and its political significance (Corrigan and Sayer 1985:3). In this latter respect, they part company, at least to some degree, with Scott (especially the Scott of *Weapons of the Weak* and *Domination and the Arts of Resistance*). Of course, Corrigan and Sayer emphasize the importance of coercion; like Scott, they argue that "acquiescence . . . should not be confused with assent"; and they contend that their book "is not an argument for 'consensus' versus 'coercion'" (1985:197, 199). They appear also to discard the notion of false consciousness (1985:9).

Such undesirables having been evicted by the front door, however, a few fellow-traveling opinions are allowed to sneak in 'round the back. Invoking Durkheim, Corrigan and Sayer stress the "moral dimension of state activity," which is manifested in "moral regulation" and which forms a key part of the epochal "cultural revolution"; moral regulation involves "a project of normalizing, rendering natural, taken for granted, in a word, 'obvious,' what are in fact . . . premises of a particular and historical form of social order" (1985:3, 4). Durkheim gets a pat on the back for having revealed that "extensive moral regulation, [and] the organization of consent" are necessary prerequisites for civil order. The "moral dimension" of state activity is something Marxists, unlike Durkheimians, have failed to address (despite Marx's famous comment, "every bourgeoisie must be able to present itself as the representative of society as a whole"). Thus it is to be welcomed that scholars now project "a timely focus on the exercise of power as residing, at root, in forms of human relationship and the construction of different subjectivities" (1985:186, 191, 193, 205). "Capitalist order," Corrigan and Sayer go on, "has never been sustained [merely] by the 'dull compulsion of economic relations.'" The role of the state extends far beyond coercion to include "cultural forms," which penetrate deep into civil society: "the enormous power of 'the State' is not only external and objective; it is in equal part internal and subjective, it works through us. It works above all through the myriad ways it collectively and individually (mis)represents us and variously 'encourages,' cajoles, and in the final analysis forces us to (mis)represent ourselves" (1985:180, 199).

Thus, to take a concrete example, the unemployed feel a "loss of self-respect" (1985:198–99). (Interestingly, "as the need for their labor has plummeted," the peasants of Sedaka "have experienced a corresponding loss in the respect and recognition accorded them" by their peers as well as their superiors. If the "humiliation of idleness" is thus "internalized," does that not suggest a form of collective "misrepresentation" or even "mystification" [Scott 1985:239]?) More generally, Corrigan and Sayer argue, the state inculcates appropriate sentiments, national as well as economic (and it does so successfully—these are not vain "encouragements"). The imperialist British state managed "for long periods, with a fair degree of success, to bedazzle the domestically subordinated with the spectacle of empire"; the "boundaries of the possible . . . are massively, powerfully sanctioned in the magnificent rituals of state, catching us up with an emotional force difficult to resist" (1985:195, 199). (Compare, by way of contrast, Scott's dismissal of the hollow showmanship of the Laotian state. 1990:58–61.)

It is not my purpose to set Scott and Corrigan and Sayer at each others' throats like combatants in one of Geertz's Balinese cockfights. Their respective views could be reconciled (at some theoretical cost) by arguing that Sedaka is not only not Morelos, but is also not England; that Malaysian peasants are by and large immune to the blandishments of the state and the ruling class in a way that the English by and large have not been; and that this discrepancy points, perhaps, to a fundamental difference between "traditional," illiterate, agrarian societies on the one hand

and their "modern," literate, industrial counterparts on the other (a difference Scott recognizes but at times seems to blur).[3] In other words,
different spatial and temporal locations generate quite different theoretical conclusions. The latter serve at best as middle-range (?) hypotheses,
relevant only to their place of birth, or perhaps places substantially
similar to their place of birth. I am not sure whether either side wants its
hypotheses to be thus constricted, thus barred from roaming the world. I
have already quoted Scott to the effect that his thesis is meant to apply to
"class conflict in most situations," which position is reinforced by his
positive citation of Abercrombie, Hill, and Turner (Scott 1985:317; Abercrombie, Hill, and Turner 1980; Scott 1990:77, for a reasoned but sweep-
ing repudiation of hegemony). One goal of the present debate, therefore,
may be to try to test these hypotheses in a location—modern Mexico—
that offers both parallels and contrasts with Malaysia and England. We
may thereby not only shed light on Mexico but also find out how
global—as against parochial—these hypotheses are.

Applied to Mexico, Corrigan and Sayer's argument would concede
(stress?) the moral dimension of both prerevolutionary founts of authority and the Revolutionary state itself. In particular, it would recognize the
importance of the attempted "cultural revolution"—the battle for legitimacy, perhaps—that the Revolutionary state undertook from its inception, and that was characterized by nationalism, anticlericalism, agrarian
reform, labor mobilization, educational programs, artistic projects, and

3. Scott's analysis of Sedaka is very convincing; it is the broader application of
that analysis across time and space that is at issue. In *Domination and the Arts of Resistance*
the author roams a wide landscape: frequently, he stresses the specificity of "traditional," agrarian societies, in which peasants are constrained by powerful but illegitimate systems of "personal" subordination; his analysis, he says, is "less relevant to
forms of *impersonal* domination by, say, 'scientific techniques,' bureaucratic rules, or by
market forces of supply and demand" and, indeed, the "possibility of hegemonic
incorporation"—denied in the case of traditional agrarian societies—is apparently
countenanced in the case of modern industrial societies, possessed of job mobility
and civil rights (Scott 1990:21, n. 3, 22). Yet this distinction gets blurred in practice.
Scott invokes several "modern," industrial examples, both historical and psychologi-
cal, to support his general argument (112, 134). Conversely, his refutation of, for
example, medieval religiosity—and thus clerical ideological hegemony—is among
the less convincing parts of the book (68). In short, I remain doubtful whether the
traditional/modern watershed is crucial for our use (or rejection) of the concept of
"hegemony"; and, in the present case, I am not at all sure whether revolutionary and
postrevolutionary Mexico should be considered "traditional" or "modern."

party formation. Mexico's attempted cultural revolution can be seen as roughly paralleling England's achieved cultural revolution, which is the basic theme of *The Great Arch*. Such an approach stresses the long haul, and sees the armed revolution as one episode in a much longer process of nation building, state formation, and capitalist development, a process arguably begun with the Bourbon era, renewed with Independence and the Reforma, and further accelerated by the 1910 revolution. (This is a view some historians would share: see Semo 1978:299; Knight 1985b:3.)

The 1910 revolution accordingly did not instantaneously subvert one mode of production in favor of another. To believe that the 1910 revolution "should" have done this, that it was not a proper revolution because it didn't, and that other proper revolutions, such as the French, *have* done this is, as I have already mentioned, ahistorical, misleading, and stultifying (cf. Ruiz 1980). One thing recent debates about both the English and French revolutions have unmistakably shown is that the demise of feudalism and installation of capitalism was a protracted process, not the sudden accomplishment of revolutionary fiat (Hill 1981:118–19, 124). There is also substantial agreement, in these comparable cases, that the neat equation of revolutionary factions with social classes does not work; that revolutionary collective actors should not be depicted as "cardboard cutouts mechanically representing 'economic interests'"; and that the image of a bourgeoisie purposefully grasping for power, and therefore of a revolution as "a defined and dated event, in which political power visibly changes hands," is a gross oversimplification that should be seriously qualified (Corrigan and Sayer 1985:75, 85). But this does not mean that the armed revolution, the brief episode of political upheaval and popular mobilization, was of scant importance to the longer process, that it was a mere blip on the screen of history, or that revolution cannot be evaluated in terms of class conflict or of the epocal shift from one mode of production to another (Vanderwood 1987:232; 1989:312).

Thus I am sympathetic to the notion of locating "The Revolution" within a broader sweep of history without thereby negating the pivotal importance of "The Revolution" in the overall process. I am also alive to the dangers of this approach, to which Corrigan and Sayer allude, noting that its stress on continuity and linearity may bring it "dangerously close to Whiggery" (1985:201). The caveat is important, since there is probably already too much teleology and linearity—in short, too much Whiggery—straightjacketing Mexican historiography, whose subject I would see as a good deal more jagged, messy, and circuitous than many. (Maybe Corrigan and Sayer would say the same about England.) At any rate, it is feasible and, I think, illuminating to apply Corrigan and Sayer's model to Mexico, to relocate the Great Arch amid the cactuses of Anáhuac.

Many of the components of England's cultural transformation can be discerned, *mutatis mutandis*, in the broad process of change that characterized Mexico in the period since roughly 1760 (especially since 1880 and, *a fortiori*, 1920): the creation of a nation, a national market, even a fictive "national character"; the deepening of capitalism—i.e., commercial production, capital accumulation, and proletarianization—within that market, facilitated by improvements in the infrastructure (railways under Díaz, roads under Calles and Cárdenas); the resort to state intervention to develop the economy, "bourgeois laissez-faire" notwithstanding; this in turn linked to a "Baconian vision . . . that state control and direction could stimulate material progress" (Corrigan and Sayer 1985:83; cf. Córdova 1973:236–47, 268–76); the establishment of a more homogeneous society, notionally constituted of free citizens as against castes, slaves, or servile peons, all of whom were emancipated by liberal reforms, such as Juárez's nationally or Alvarado's locally (Corrigan and Sayer 1985:183); the encouragement of literacy, hard work, hygiene, and sobriety, all of which were deemed necessary, by both Porfirians and revolutionaries, for the nation's development (French 1990; Vaughan 1982); the breakdown of local particularisms and the inculcation of sentiments of loyalty to the nation and the state (*forjando patria*: a task that Porfirian ideologues like Sierra stressed and revolutionary activists like Gamio carried through); the erosion, in particular, of the power of the church, the most egregious antinational institution (recall Calles' promotion of a schismatic church, a distant echo of the Henrician Reformation); the demonization of enemies of the state project (Catholics in particular: Jacobites in England, Cristeros in Mexico) (Corrigan and Sayer 1985:196); even the establishment, in a postrevolutionary situation, of a political oligarchy—a *de facto* one-party state—based on patronage and graft, ultimately resistant to reform, and "conducive to capitalism, if in complex and contradictory ways"; namely "Old Corruption," alias the PRI (Corrigan and Sayer 1985:88–89; Porter 1990:112).

Lest some readers—historians in particular—blanch at these far-flung, perhaps farfetched comparisons (Calles as Henry VIII, Enrique Gorostieta as Bonnie Prince Charlie, Portes Gil as the Duke of Newcastle), let me also suggest a more synchronic and therefore, perhaps, more acceptable parallel: Fabianism, which, with its concern for social abuses, its Social Darwinist assumptions, its commitment to ameliorative state intervention, even its eager collection of statistics, all had powerful resonances in postrevolutionary Mexico. "Fabianism, gradualism, elitism, hierarchy, patriarchy, and a semiworship of 'the State' are key features that form laborism and the Labor party," Corrigan and Sayer generalize, offering a checklist of political attributes that are to be found aplenty in revolutionary Mexico (1985:172; cf. Córdova, 1973). Recall, for example, that the first genuinely mass party created out of the revolution was Morones' Partido Laborista, which name was not arbitrarily chosen (Garrido 1986:49). So parallels emerge in two dimensions. Over the long term, Mexican development seems to display some structural features that are strongly reminiscent of England's "cultural revolution" (to use the portmanteau term). In the short term, the Mexican Revolutionary state appears to adopt some of the specific characteristics of English Fabianism (to use another one)—perhaps as a result of direct emulation. (Of course, many similar, or even better, parallels are to be found elsewhere: for example, if we compare Mexican and French processes of postrevolutionary change. I focus on the English case not because it is necessarily the best or the closest, but because it is the case discussed in the *Great Arch*. In fact, the English, French, Mexican, and Bolivian revolutions all display certain common characteristics in respect of outcome that might repay comparative analysis, perhaps under the broad rubric of "bourgeois" revolutions.)

Pressing the English parallel further, and returning to the key question of cultural transformation and legitimation—which I take to be a potential point of issue between Corrigan and Sayer on the one hand and Scott on the other—it is worth recalling the strenuous efforts at cultural engineering undertaken by Mexico's revolutionary regime. These were not wholly unprecedented; there were Porfirian as well as earlier liberal and Bourbon attempts. And of course these efforts postdated and perhaps were dwarfed by centuries of Catholic proselytizing. But the Mexican revolutionary regime, like its counterparts in France, Russia, China, and Cuba, embarked on an ambitious program of "nationalizing and rationalizing" the Mexican people (Hunt 1984). This involved, for example, changing "the rituals of rule . . . [the] extensive theatricality of state repertoire" by commissioning didactic murals; building monuments; renaming streets; rewriting history; instituting new celebrations ("secular fiestas") designed to commemorate revolutionary anniversaries and heroes; extending education, especially rural education; ideologically rehabilitating the Indian; and blending indigenismo with nationalism (Corrigan and Sayer 1985:107; Friedlander 1981; O'Malley 1986; Knight 1990c).

That there was a state project of cultural transformation seems undoubtable. The revolutionaries, as I have said, firmly believed in notions of hegemony, even false consciousness (if not in those terms). But how successful were they? First, did they transform popular consciousness, legitimizing the revolutionary regime? (And if so, we may ask again, did they thereby foster a new "mystification" or "false consciousness"? Or, rather, did they successfully combat a rival legitimation—for example, Catholic conservatism—and thereby *demystify*, breaking the fetters of false consciousness?) Or was the revolutionary project a failure, a gimcrack façade behind which the common people, the peasants especially, grumbled and prayed to old gods, untouched by the new legitimation? Was it a case not just of "idols behind altars" but idols behind altars behind murals?

Answers are not easy to come by, in part because the questions are so intractable, in part because the research has scarcely been done. Scott is clearly right to stress that apparent compliance by no means indicates heartfelt allegiance; the parades of the PRI may be as contrived as those of the Pathet Lao (Scott 1990:58–61). And throughout, we must be cautious of the reification of "The Revolution" that these questions tend to encourage. There were different revolutions, hence different ideological shades, even after the process of institutionalization—and attempted legitimation—got under way. Allowing for these major qualifications, however, I think it can be argued that the revolution *did* succeed in establishing a partial legitimacy: partial in terms of the regions and groups that responded positively to its message, that "internalized" it and became carriers and agents of revolutionary ideology; and that, in doing so often molded and refashioned that ideology, since, as I have said, this was no one-way, top-down imposition.

On the other hand, some important groups were indifferent or downright hostile. In other words, the period 1910–1940 saw not a process of linear legitimation but a sequence of ideological battles, some violent and some peaceful; some fought locally and silently, some nationally and noisily. There was also a rough correlation of issues, in the sense that when, for example, the revolutionaries espoused agrarian reform and anticlericalism, their conservative enemies opposed the reform and supported the church. By the 1930s, international issues also bulked large and solidified these rival ideological alignments. Polarization involved the usual mythopoeic appeals to authorities and heroes. The revolutionaries harked back to Cuauhtémoc, Hidalgo, and Juárez; the conservatives to Cortés, Iturbide, and Alamán. The former (in some cases) flaunted the red flag; the latter favored the tricolor or the banner of the Virgin of Guadalupe. (To the Cristeros the red flag was suitable only for butcher shops. See J. Meyer 1974c:284–85, 287.) The former invoked the *leyenda negra* of Spanish colonialism; the latter denounced Protestants, freemasons, and gringos. While Cristero campaigns were suffused with Catholic religiosity (we are told), and the Catholic militants of the Unión Popular strove "to penetrate and thereby transform from within the fabric of social life," their revolutionary and anticlerical enemies sought to create an entire counterculture, a "surrogate religion," emulating while mocking Catholic practices with Red Mondays, socialist weddings, and secular fiestas—the last dedicated not, in high-minded Gallic style, to virtue, but rather to homely provender, such as the coconut or the banana (Friedrich 1986:156; J. Meyer 1974c:272–81; Jrade 1989:7; Martínez Assad 1979:45–48, 125).

This conflict over signs and symbols (has no one yet coined the neologism *semiomachy?*) has begun to attract some attention in Mexican historiography. (It is to be hoped that, as the attention grows, it will not encourage that kind of cerebral and rarefied "decoding" that has become so fashionable in other quarters.) Historians have to ask how and why such symbols were taken up by particular groups and with what degree of success and sincerity they were wielded—again, difficult questions. Here, I would make three main points. First, the ideological appropriation of symbols was historically conditioned; hence it was far from uniform. Revolutionary Tabasco contrasted with Catholic Jalisco and, as I have already said, there were many complex variations within states. The factors determining "revolutionary" allegiance were also varied. Among the most important was a record of agrarian struggle that, in Morelos, Tlaxcala, the Laguna, and parts of Michoacán, helped create support for the revolution in both its armed and institutional phases (even during phases when the national government soft-pedaled agrarian reform). With agrarismo came—generally, not uniformly—support for federal education, anticlericalism, and, in the later 1930s, Republican Spain and the petroleum nationalization. While this espousal of revolutionary causes was often instrumental—there are cases of agraristas who feigned anticlericalism, or of groups whose very agrarismo was superficial and tactical (J. Meyer 1974c:62; Buve 1990:255, 262)—it would be wrong to assume that revolutionary allegiances in general were skin-deep, expedient, or coerced (as many today tend to infer). Against the timeservers and opportunists we must set the honest, dedicated, and often vulnerable agraristas who sought to mobilize peasants in hostile circumstances; those of Lagos de Moreno, for example (Craig 1983). Success, in terms of revolutionary mobilization, therefore depended a good deal on local material circumstances. It is not surprising that the community of San José de Gracia—prosperous, mestizo, and populated by landowners—largely spurned agrarismo, while its nearby rival, Mazamitla, possessed of an Indian and insurgent past, was more receptive (González [1968] 1972:174–75).

If the material factor was crucial, historical predispositions were also important. By *historical predispositions* I mean the cultural and political attitudes that colored particular communities or regions. By invoking these as significant factors, I am conceding some autonomous role to "ideology" or "culture," although I accept that such factors blend with (I would not baldly state *mask*) other considerations. Revolutionary messages were eagerly taken up—whether in 1910, when the revolution began, or later, as it proceeded to institutionalize itself—by certain communities, families, and individuals who stood historically on the "left" (another shorthand term) or who, borrowing French political terminology, espoused the party of "movement" as against the party of "order." By that I mean those who adhered to the liberal, radical, and patriot tradition: those who in the nineteenth century had fought for independence, backed the liberals, and resisted the French, and who in the twentieth would rally to Madero and Cárdenas.

Of course, there were many discontinuities and inconsistencies in this long story. But I believe it can be shown that, in Mexico as in France, certain communities and regions acquired, through their historical experiences, political and cultural attitudes of considerable tenacity (Bois 1971). Though reinforced by the material factors already mentioned, such allegiances were in some measure autonomous and self-sustaining. They were often sustained by rivalry with neighboring communities of opposite affiliation, as well as by songs, societies, fiestas, and oral memory (Loera 1987:35–39). The armed revolution of 1910 helped cement old allegiances and create new ones. Meanwhile, it should not be overlooked that the Catholic constituency also proselytized, recruited, and changed its make-up. The Porfiriato witnessed a successful, though little studied, campaign of Catholic proselytizing, especially in center-west Mexico: a kind of Porfirian spiritual conquest (González [1968] 1972:70–71; García de León, 1985:2:21–24; Sullivan-González 1989). This, as well as—and,

I would guess, more than—the new wave of "social" Catholicism, gave the church and the Catholic constituency a bigger and stronger foothold, as would become apparent during the bloody Cristiada of the 1920s. And that episode, of course, created new martyrs and heroes, memories and songs. Not surprisingly, this constituency strenuously resisted the anti-clerical policies and socialist education of the 1930s.

It also did so with considerable success. Although the revolutionary regime defeated the Cristeros on the battlefield, its campaign to win hearts and minds had mixed results. Over the long term, it seems likely, education in Mexico has served to inculcate notions of nationalism. But the revolutionary program of the 1920s and 1930s was much more ambitious and radical than that. It sought, for example, to break the hold of Catholicism over the Mexican mind (especially the Mexican female mind), and it largely failed. It sought, at least in the 1930s, to foster a cooperative, class-conscious, "solidary" peasantry, in which it also failed more than it succeeded. That is not to say that revolutionary ideology failed to put down popular roots, or that it remained purely an elite ideology—serving, for example, to unite the revolutionary elite in the face of its enemies, as "dominant ideologies" are said to do, even if they do not achieve hegemony in society at large (Abercrombie, Hill, and Turner 1980; Knight 1992). Revolutionary proselytizing went deeper than that. But its successes were patchy, and they depended on prior material and cultural circumstances. We may go further and note that a kind of popular revolutionary ideology has survived, albeit chastened and increasingly at odds with the official "revolutionary" ideology of the PRI. This became evident in 1988, when Cuauhtémoc Cárdenas's campaign clearly tapped reservoirs of support in regions, like the Laguna, where Cardenismo had flourished fifty years before.

These radical and popular traditions are neither elite impositions nor wholly popular constructs. They are something of both. Just as Catholicism, a creation of the Spanish "Great Tradition," was appropriated and refashioned by the Mexican "Little Tradition" (more shorthand), so secular ideologies such as liberalism, anarchism, and socialism were transmuted and particularized as they were espoused by peasant communities (Knight 1990c:234, 250). New secular myths and heroes entered the traditional Pantheon: Marx and Madero rubbed shoulders with Jesus and the Virgin of Guadalupe; in martyrdom, Carrillo Puerto assumed a distinctly Christlike appearance. A foolish consistency was not the hobgoblin of popular minds. This new syncretism, building on older syncretisms, offered a bridge between elite and popular cultures, between high politics and low, between the Great and Little Traditions. Though it would be a considerable exaggeration to talk of a "dominant ideology," it would, I think, be true that the ideology of the revolution offered a set of ideas and symbols that many—not all—social actors could appropriate, espouse, and utilize in their dealings—and struggles—with one another.

In doing so, that ideology probably enhanced national political unity—which is not to say that it anesthetized civil society or "mystified" the populace into shortsighted obedience. At times it served to justify repression, to reinforce the cohesion of a narrow governing elite: "*la révolution en danger*," invoked against the church in the 1920s and the foreign oil companies in the 1930s, could also be invoked against the student movement in the 1960s. But at other times the ideology of the revolution—egalitarian, nationalist, populist—has given some purchase to popular groups and demands. For to the extent that the ruling party claims to govern in the name of the revolution, it cannot wholly, blatantly, and consistently flout the popular precepts that the revolution bequeathed. Nineteen ten was to Mexico what 1688 was to England. "Ruling groups," Scott observes, "can be called upon to live up to their own idealized presentation of themselves to their subordinates"; public transcripts embody elements around which popular groups can mobilize, pressing elites to conform to their high-flown principles (Scott 1990:54). Hence the periodic revivals of "revolutionary" policies and popular dialogue (the Echeverría presidency; even the Solidaridad program of the Salinas administration). Hence, perhaps, the less-flagrant repression of popular movements in Mexico compared to Central America or the Southern Cone.

What is fascinating about the present conjuncture in Mexican politics is not only the gap between revolutionary precepts and actual practice (which is hardly new) but also—perhaps more so—the overt abandonment of many of the precepts themselves. Where previous administrations have stuck to the symbols while shifting their practice, the administrations of the 1980s have scrapped the very symbols: by putting Cananea on the auction block, and more generally repudiating economic nationalism; by welcoming the Pope and reneging on revolutionary anticlericalism; by openly planning for the "flexibilization"—i.e., the official euthanasia?—of the *ejido*. Not surprisingly, and by way of evidence for at least a lingering revolutionary popular allegiance, the old slogans, memories, and epithets resurfaced in 1988 when Cuauhtémoc Cárdenas, son of Lázaro, campaigned for the presidency as an opposition candidate. "We don't want to continue as puppets of the PRI," wrote a deputation from Oaxaca to Cuauhtémoc. "As far as we're concerned you are the winner, and we are cleaning and oiling the weapons that were used in 1910 to overthrow a dictatorship" (Gilly 1989:73).

IV

In conclusion: Scott and Corrigan and Sayer provide illuminating but contrasting perspectives on Mexican revolutionary history. *The Moral Economy* offers a powerful phenomenological explanation of peasant discontent, rooting it in material circumstances and structural change while recognizing the importance of the moral and ideological dimensions of protest. Thus, the (etic) analysis of material and structural factors is married to the (emic) apprehension of peasant demands, symbols, and discourse. It "fits" the case—which, of course, was a case of widespread popular mobilization, in the context of a (descriptive) social revolution. With *Weapons of the Weak* and *Domination and the Arts of Resistance* Scott offers an alternative perspective, derived from a contrasting sociopolitical context (characterized by elite domination and peasant compliance), which can retrospectively aid our understanding of the Porfiriato and of the sudden *bouleversement*, the brusque change of transcripts, that marked its downfall. In short, these analyses afford explanations for the Porfiriato, its fall, and the brief but crucial ensuing period when the world was turned upside down. Their utility diminishes, however, as we enter the postrevolutionary period of reconstruction, state building, and ideological/institutional confrontation, especially between church and state (roughly 1920–40). Here, Corrigan and Sayer's analysis of "cultural transformation" is suggestive.

Corrigan and Sayer emphasize the need to see revolutionary phases —the "descriptive" revolutions—as episodes, albeit pivotal episodes, within longer and broader processes of change. Accordingly they direct our attention to the secular transformation of society, economy, politics, and culture that is subsumed under the metaphor of the Great Arch. In Mexico, the armed revolution catalyzed longer-term processes of change, an important part of which involved a sustained clash of rival symbols and ideologies. Peasants were active protagonists—not hapless victims—of these processes (hence Sedaka, a community unacquainted with revolution, is not a close parallel). Though still clearly subordinate—had they not been, they would no longer have been peasants—Mexico's *campesinos* enjoyed some limited but real political autonomy and leverage. They also displayed marked regional and cultural differences, which cannot be interpreted in terms of some prior material rationale without grave risk of reductionism. Material circumstances—the battle for land, water, and subsistence—were crucial, and probably the chief determinant of trends and allegiances. But, especially in the broad realm of religion, ideology and culture enjoyed at least a relative autonomy, nurtured and conditioned by historical traditions and experiences: the Reforma and French Intervention; the Porfirian "spiritual conquest"; the armed revolution and Cristiada. To the extent that these experiences were historically particular, so, on closer inspection, peasant politics seem to reveal "shifting loyalties, internal contradictions, personal squabbles, the role of personalities and of militant minorities . . . passion, confusion, credulity, myth, anarchy, noise" (Cobb 1972:121).

These experiences, in all their infinite variety, shaped the allegiances of individuals, families, *barrios*, *pueblos*, and regions—allegiances which, while they were strongly conditioned, were not necessarily determined (even "in the last analysis") by material conditions, by coercion, or by the "dull compulsion of economic relations." Did such variegated allegiances, whether revolutionary or conservative, reflect "false consciousness"; that is, a betrayal of "objective" peasant interests (bearing in mind that opposing sides of the debate attribute the manufacture of false consciousness to both revolutionary *and* Catholic elites, according to preference or prejudice)? That, perhaps, is a question better left to moral philosophers than to historians.

II

Empirical

Studies

FLORENCIA E. MALLON

Reflections on the Ruins:
Everyday Forms of State Formation
in Nineteenth-Century Mexico

"The owl of Minerva which brings wisdom, said Hegel, flies out at dusk."
Eric Hobsbawm uses these words in the concluding paragraph of his
recent book on nations and nationalism, suggesting that historians only
pay attention to a phenomenon once it is past its peak (Hobsbawm
1990:183). It is perhaps only fitting, then, that my discussion of state
formation in nineteenth-century Mexico should be titled "Reflections on
the Ruins." Starting in the mid-1980s, the Mexican state faced a major
challenge to its stability. Cuauhtémoc Cárdenas's 1988 presidential campaign called into question a half-century of PRI rule. Under Carlos Salinas
de Gortari, the response of the PRI to the Cardenista challenge has been
to jettison a good part of the revolutionary legacy as represented in the
Constitution of 1917. So how would an understanding of what has been
destroyed be helpful in any but the most antiquarian sense?

I begin with the assumption that the archaeology of political institutions has more than antiquarian value. As the products of previous conflicts and confrontations, institutions have embedded in them the sedi-
ments of earlier struggles.[1] Uncovering these helps us understand not
only the history of how they were formed, but also their present character
and future potential. From this perspective, digging deep can also help

---

1. My concept of institutions and structures as embedded struggle and agency
was helped by a reading of Poulantzas (1978) and Giddens (1981, 1987).

discern contemporary directions of transformation, paths of destruction, or even hidden continuities.

I have found the concept of hegemony to be particularly useful in this attempt at political archaeology. I do not, however, equate hegemony with a belief in, or an incorporation of, the dominant ideology. Instead, I define hegemony in two distinct, though sometimes related, ways. First, hegemony is a set of nested processes, constant and ongoing, through which power relations are contested, legitimated, and redefined at all levels of society. According to this definition, hegemony is hegemonic process: it can and does exist everywhere, at all times. Secondly, hegemony is an actual end point, the result of hegemonic processes. An always dynamic or precarious balance, a contract or agreement, is reached among contesting forces. Those in power then rule through a combination of coercion and consent. In the words of Philip Corrigan and Derek Sayer, this is a "cultural revolution": the generation of a common social and moral project that includes popular as well as elite notions of political culture.[2]

If we think of hegemony as process, politics at all levels become nested arenas of contestation, where power is being contested, legitimated, and redefined. Some political projects are always winning out over others, some factions are defeating others. The interactions among different political arenas—say, between communities and regions, or between regions and a central state—not only redefines each one internally, but also helps redefine the balance of forces among them. In this constant, complex interaction among terrains of conflict and alliance, there are moments of greater change or transformation: revolutionary or radical movements, moments when, in the words of James Scott, the "curtain is . . . parted" (Scott 1985:329). These can be explained by analyzing the historical articulation of different hegemonic processes into a broader coalition or political movement.

Here the definition of hegemony as end point enters in. The leaders of a particular movement or coalition achieve hegemony as an end point only when they effectively garner for themselves ongoing legitimacy and support. They are successful in doing so if they partially incorporate the political aspirations or discourses of the movement's supporters, articulating elements of earlier hegemonic processes to their emerging hegemonic

2. For the original definition of hegemony as the combination of coercion and consent, see Gramsci (1971). For the consolidation of the state as a process of cultural revolution, see Corrigan and Sayer (1985).

project. Only then can they rule through a combination of coercion and consent, control the terms of political discourse through incorporation as well as repression, and effectively bring about a cultural revolution.

Such a framework allows us to see political power as interactive, and more easily to understand its accumulation as a series of nested and interdependent processes. If the concepts of hegemony and counterhegemony are always interlaced, each hegemonic impulse involves a counterhegemonic impulse. Hegemony cannot exist or be reproduced without the constant, though partial, incorporation of counterhegemony.[3] Shifting alliances at one level affect relationships or coalitions in other political arenas. Discourses and political movements continue to exert influence and importance even after they have been repressed or submerged.

In this essay, I contribute to the broader process of political archaeology by uncovering the subterranean effects that nineteenth-century popular movements and discourses had in the early decades of the twentieth century, when statemakers in Mexico faced difficult decisions between hegemony and domination. I excavate in detail some of the nineteenth-century hegemonic processes in the *sierra de Puebla*, the Puebla highlands, that have direct relevance for our understanding of the 1910 Mexican revolution. By focusing on one especially rich case study, I am able to combine communal, regional, and national levels of analysis. In the communities, disagreements among factions were constantly negotiated along lines of gender, ethnicity, age, wealth, and ecological/spatial differences. In the region, conflicts over power continuously reconstructed and redefined the content of political culture. And at the national level, political and economic elites fought for hegemony among themselves through the construction of supraregional coalitions that could conquer and rebuild state power. Only through the combination of all three levels is it possible truly to comprehend the complexity of a hegemonic outcome.

The last part of my essay places the *sierra de Puebla* on a broader Mexican canvas—where hegemonic processes had a hegemonic outcome by 1940—and draws a comparison with Peru, where hegemonic processes have resulted in political refragmentation until the present day. In comparing Mexico to Peru I do not wish to develop the Peruvian case

3. Among the works that have inspired my analysis are Chatterjee (1983, 1986, 1987, and 1990); Guha (1982a, b, 1983a, and 1986); Spivak (1985); Williams (1977: esp. 108–14); Laclau and Mouffe ([1985] 1989); Davidson (1984); Arnold (1984); and Laclau ([1977] 1979).

systematically, which anyway is beyond the confines of this essay and this volume. Instead I wish to highlight the specific achievements of the Mexican political system between 1920 and 1940. It is certainly important to emphasize the repression, violence, and exclusion that formed an ongoing part of institutionalized revolutionary politics in Mexico over these years. But placing Mexico next to Peru—where hegemonic outcomes have been elusive throughout that country's postcolonial history—serves to emphasize as well the successful construction of civil and political society in twentieth-century Mexico. This will also allow us to trace some political continuities even through the crisis of the 1980s.

HEGEMONIC PROCESSES IN THE *SIERRA DE PUEBLA*: THE 1910 REVOLUTION IN NINETEENTH-CENTURY PERSPECTIVE

One of the explanations for the stability of the Mexican postrevolutionary state was its ability to reach down to the local level. After 1920, revolutionary statemakers began a process of articulation that would bring villages and municipalities into direct relations with the central government. This process reached its culmination during the presidency of Lázaro Cárdenas, who institutionalized the revolution through agrarian reform, socialist education, support for labor, and economic nationalism. Until Carlos Salinas de Gortari reversed most of the revolutionary policies of the Mexican state in the early 1990s, this would be the status quo.[4]

We can agree on this much, at least at an abstract level. We know less about how these policies were constructed, and why they found resonance, however conflictual, at the local level. Through the examination of specific hegemonic processes in the *sierra de Puebla* during the nineteenth century, I hope to show that the elements for many of these policies were already being generated, in villages and towns, during "the Liberal Revolution" and Restored Republic. The genius of revolutionary statemakers in the twentieth century was that they reached deeply into the reservoir of

---

4. The literature on the Mexican revolution is much too complex to cite thoroughly. For some useful introductions to the 1920s and 1930s, see Córdova (1974); Brading (1980); Hamilton (1982); Leal (1975a, 1975b); J. Meyer (1974a, b, and c); Medin (1982); Friedrich (1977); Falcón (1977 and 1984); J. Meyer, Krauze, and Reyes (1977); L. Meyer (1978); L. Meyer, Segovia, and Lajous (1978); L. Hall (1990); Knight (1990c); Joseph ([1982] 1988b).

these popular traditions. The "great arch" they built thus had a solid foundation in local popular culture.

THE DISCOURSE ON LAND: REVOLUTIONARY *EJIDOS* IN NINETEENTH-CENTURY PERSPECTIVE

To begin with a major centerpiece of Mexican revolutionary discourse: the *ejido*, and agrarian reform. As several authors in this volume show, and has also been suggested before by Jean Meyer and Marjorie Becker, state *ejido* grants were often problematic at the local level. The *dotaciones* were hardly ever the same lands that peasants had made their own through local and intimate processes of labor, naming, and struggle. Indeed, the Revolutionary state, through a sanitized official discourse of generosity, rendered itself as the magnanimous patron that recreated peasant communities in its own image.[5] And yet despite these problems, agrarian reform emerged as one of the spectacular successes, especially of the Cardenista regime. What made it so?

One possible explanation is that state policy on *ejidos* connected to earlier state-village discourses on *ejidos* and village lands, dating back at least to the 1855 "Liberal Revolution." As is well known, the original liberal laws on the privatization of corporate properties applied equally well to church and communal lands, calling for the privatization of both in the interests of developing a market society of individuals who could all be equal before the law. In practice, however, such principles proved to be illusory (J. Meyer 1971, 1984). After the original passage of the disamortization law in June of 1856, therefore, Miguel Lerdo de Tejada issued a series of clarifying decrees concerning the disamortization of small municipal or communal properties, which can be seen as an alternative interpretation of how liberal law could be applied to the communal and smallholding peasantry.

As Miguel Lerdo de Tejada explained in his original and most important circular, October 9, 1856, attempts to apply the June land laws had generated a number of confusions and abuses. The poorer peasants were being left out of the adjudication process because they did not have the money to pay the necessary fees, or because speculators beat them out in presenting petitions to adjudicate specific plots. It was necessary to

5. In addition to the essay by Nugent and Alonso in this volume, see Koreck (1991); J. Meyer (1974a, b, and c); and Becker (1987, 1989).

remedy these abuses, and to convince the poor smallholding peasantry that the law was meant to benefit them; otherwise, "[t]he law would be nullified in one of its principal goals, which was the subdivision of agricultural property." Thus Lerdo ordered that all plots with a value under two hundred pesos would be adjudicated for free, and, of necessity, to their de facto possessors, unless they clearly and specifically renounced their right to such plots.[6]

A month later, in a case brought before him by the village of Tepeji del Río, the president chose to declare the tradition of communal property, which he interpreted as the Spanish crown extending ownership of land to indigenous communities while prohibiting its sale or transfer, to be entirely relevant and legitimate in a liberal context. The villagers of Tepeji had requested, only a week after Lerdo's original circular, that their common lands (*de repartimiento*) not be included in those affected by the adjudication procedures. The president responded:

> the relevant lands should be held and enjoyed by the referred Indians in absolute property, receiving thus the right to pawn, rent, and sell them, and to dispose of them as any owner does of his things, and without the mentioned Indians needing to pay any cost, since they are not receiving the lands in adjudication, since they already owned them, but simply are being freed of inappropriate and anomalous impediments attached to that ownership.

In this interpretation, liberal legislation modified communal property rights only by allowing the free circulation of the plots; the identity of the proprietors, and the tradition of proprietorship, should remain otherwise unchanged.[7]

In the *sierra de Puebla*, the alternative interpretation of liberal land law already present in debates within the liberal state was articulated to an emerging regional discourse on the meaning of property. In three specific contexts—the liberal-conservative civil war (1858–1861), the French Intervention (1861–1867), and the early conflicts of the Restored Republic (1867–1868)—highland villagers and their allies molded their

6. Mexico, Secretaría de Hacienda y Crédito Público, *Documentos relativos a la espedición de títulos de propiedad de los terrenos llamados de común repartimiento, a los indíjenas que los poseen* (Puebla: Imprenta del Gobierno del Hospicio, 1869), 3–4: documento no. 43, "Circular de Miguel Lerdo de Tejada, Secretario de Hacienda y Crédito Público, a los gobernadores de los estados," Mexico City, Oct. 9, 1856. Both quotations from p. 3.

7. Ibid., 5–7. Quote, p. 7.

interpretation of property through political alliance, conflict, and discursive practice. In the discourse that emerged, the ownership of land was not foremost or most legitimately a question of individual or private rights, but instead was interconnected with histories of common right and usage dating back to the Spanish conquest. The humble and indigenous had greater legitimacy in conflicts over land, simply by their status: they were owners unless they expressly and publicly said otherwise.

The first conflict that helped form this discourse was a fight among liberal factions in highland Puebla between 1859 and 1860, where the main issue was local interpretations of the liberal land laws. The more radical faction, led by mestizo national guard commanders Juan N. Méndez and Ramón Márquez Galindo, was committed to protecting the rights of Totonac Indians in the lowland communities of Tenampulco and Tuzamapan over those of white *vecinos* in the adjudication of municipal land in the Teziutlán-Tenampulco area. By contrast, the more moderate liberal faction, led by Puebla ex-governor Miguel Cástulo de Alatriste, supported the claims of white residents in Teziutlán.

The contested terrain between districts or municipalities was especially difficult to define during processes of adjudication. Commercial agriculturalists from Teziutlán had rented or possessed lands in these regions—prime tropical lands for livestock or other commercial uses— and wished to privatize them. Municipalities were also not clear on where the dividing lines stood between them. Under such circumstances, the allies of Alatriste in Teziutlán began a process of liberal disentailment which they hoped would benefit them, using the most literal interpretation of the June 1856 law as their guide: land to whoever possesses it at the time. Márquez and Méndez, on the other hand, articulated the claims of villagers to the spirit of the 1856 law as represented in the clarifying circulars and decrees of October to November, and supported indigenous self-defense actions against white landowners adjudicating themselves municipal properties.[8]

8. AHDN, XI/481.3/883, "Parte del Comandante General del Estado de Puebla," June 29, 1832; XI/481.3/8166, "Acta levantada en la villa de Zacapoaxtla," Mar. 29, 1856; XI/481.3/5307, "Expediente sobre operaciones militares en Puebla y Veracruz," esp. Dec. 18, 1856–Jan. 6, 1857; *Diario Oficial* (Mexico City), June 13, 1858, pp. 1–2, in which the conservative government separates Zacapoaxtla from Teziutlán to form an independent prefectura; and ACEP, Book I, Sesión pública y ordinaria, Dec. 21, 1867, "Definición de distritos," ff. 37–37v. Much of this conflict, which continued through the 1860s, can also be seen in the documents on disentailment from the 1867–68 period, treated in more detail below.

When Rafael Avila, *vecino* of Teziutlán and a local political official appointed by Alatriste, protested Márquez's actions in his town, he couched the protest in terms of the first interpretation of liberal land law. He accused Márquez of offering weapons to the peasants from Tenampulco and El Chacal in order to expel Teziutlán *vecinos* from municipal lands, and predicted there would be a "caste war" if Alatriste did not take stern countermeasures. Three days later, Avila's predictions began to come true, from his point of view, when indigenous soldiers sent by Márquez invaded the town and sought to arrest the local officials in charge of the disentailment process.[9]

Yet it is instructive to view the conflicts from the perspective of the other interpretation of liberal law. If the original and legitimate right of proprietorship was the grant given indigenous communities by the Spanish crown, and if indeed one of the main purposes of liberal land legislation was the redistribution of land, then the indigenous peasants of Tenampulco, Tuzamapan, El Chacal, Jonotla, and associated villages had a better right to disputed municipal lands than did the wealthier white inhabitants of Teziutlán. Moreover, since these peasants had not renounced their right to the land in any legal or explicit way, any process of adjudication being carried out in Teziutlán was not only illegitimate but illegal. Indeed, in light of the circular of October 9, 1856, Avila and his ilk might well be considered "speculators." In this context the actions of indigenous peasants, when they attempted to recover the lands and when they tried to arrest the political authorities in charge of adjudications, were legally justified.

During the French Intervention, this more popular and populist interpretation of liberal land policy was articulated to the defense of the nation and loyalty to the nation-state. In March of 1864, while the Puebla highlands were under attack by interventionist forces, the military commander of Zacapoaxtla, José Mariá Maldonado, issued a circular to the commanders of the indigenous villages of Xochitlán, Nauzontla, and Cuetzalan. Maldonado's main purpose was to explain the reform laws, whose first beneficiaries, he said, were the humble classes. The liberal land laws were meant to save them from the abuses of a priestly elite and give them access to land. In the context of foreign invasion, Maldonado was, of course, interested in expanding the popular base for the resistance

9. ACDN, expediente de Ramón Márquez Galindo, ff. 60–60v, "Carta de Rafael Avila a Alatriste," Teziutlán, Mar. 12, 1860, quotes on f. 60, ff. 61–63, "Carta de Rafael Avila a Alatriste," Teziutlán, Mar. 15, 1860.

(Mallon forthcoming: chaps. 2, 4). But what is most interesting for our purposes here is that the discourse on land contained in his circular connected both to the national circulars and resolutions of October–November 1856, and to the articulations occurring in the 1859–60 conflict between Méndez and Alatriste.

According to Maldonado, the purpose of the disamortization laws was "to turn national property into private property, enriching multitudes of families"; and "communal lands in the villages should be distributed among the Indians in equal parts in order to meet their needs and without their having to pay anything." Yet despite his attempts at carrying out these dispositions in the fairest possible way, he continued, some people believed their interests had been hurt, in particular those who, "abusing the authority they had held, had grabbed for themselves the communal lands existing in the highlands, to the detriment of the villagers." Therefore, he ordered the village commanders, it was their duty to enforce the law and make sure that all white landowners (*de razón*) and those owning more than one *fanega* (approximately 1.6 acres) of land paid the necessary taxes to make their adjudications legal. Those unwilling to do so would lose access to the land, which would then be redistributed among the poor.[10]

To this point, Maldonado built on existing alternative discourses, selecting out community members, poor Indians, as especially entitled to justice under the reforms. In his discussion, as in the previous examples, property was tempered with justice, and put in the context of redistribution and a commitment to equality. But Maldonado went even further: he connected the right to property with the defense of the nation. "Since traitors have proven themselves undeserving of consideration by the government," he concluded, "all those who possess communal land in the villages and do not immediately seek a pardon, will have the lands taken away and distributed [to the poor]."[11]

In making the connection between defense of the nation and entitlement to property, Maldonado opened up a new line of argument about village lands. The ownership of property was not simply an individual issue but became reembedded in questions of collective behavior, collective good, and community responsibility. The community and its repre-

10. AHMZ, paquete 1863-65-64, expediente (exp.) 204, "Circular a los comandantes militares de Xochitlán, Nauzontla, y Cuetzalán sobre las leyes de Reforma," Zacapoaxtla, Mar. 18, 1864, ff. 10–11v, quotes on ff. 10v and 11, respectively.
11. Ibid.; quotation on f. 11v.

sentatives had the right to judge who was deserving and who was not, according to politico-moral principles. Those who defended the nation—soldiers of whatever rank—were entitled, by implication, to own land.

An analogous articulation occurred in December of the same year, when the liberal governor of Puebla, Fernando María Ortega, signed a decree giving the highland village of Xochiapulco formal ownership rights over the lands of haciendas Xochiapulco and La Manzanilla, as well as the lands of the then-extinct village of Xilotepec. Ortega also granted Xochiapulco independent municipal status, making it a *villa* instead of a simple *pueblo* and calling it Villa del Cinco de Mayo. As the new name for the community attests, the decree was justified in a discourse about entitlement, about the rewards that "good" citizens received, and about how the state could grant land in such a context. The three justifications appearing at the beginning of the decree were that the state had the right to reward the services of citizens and populations; that the inhabitants of Xochiapulco had "given eminent service in the noble cause of Mexico's Independence, and their soldiers, among other brilliant actions of war, distinguished themselves in the glorious battle of the Fifth of May"; and that, for the public good, it is sometimes necessary to take over property, after having estimated and paid its just price. The state was designated in the decree as the mediator between Xochiapulco and the *hacendados*. Access to land was legitimated, through a series of nested justifications, to all members of the community because of the village's role in the resistance to the French; but also, according to rank, to the soldiers who had fought on May 5.[12] In the end, therefore, the contextualization of private property, and of access to it, involved issues of service to the nation and to the community.

A third moment in the development of local and regional discourses on land occurred in the immediate postwar period, during the consolidation of the Restored Republic. While he was provisional governor of Puebla state in August 1867, Juan N. Méndez encouraged more populist interpretations of property rights by naming a commission, headed by Nahua general Juan Francisco Lucas, to oversee the adjudication of communal lands in the area. Building on the regional discourses constructed during the civil war and the Intervention, communities in the

12. "Decreto de Fernando María Ortega, General de Brigada, Gobernador y Comandante Militar del Estado de Puebla, a sus habitantes," Zacapoaxtla, Dec. 5, 1864; reproduced in Huerta Jaramillo (1985:122–23).

sierra de Puebla responded by connecting popular access to communal land with bravery and contributions made to the cause of the republic. The connections among these various discursive and political moments were especially clear in cases with an already established debate on property rights, such as Tenampulco, Tuzamapan, and Cuetzalan.

In March 1867, while the fighting was still going on, the villages of Jonotla, Tuzamapan and Tenampulco—the same that had joined with Méndez in 1860 to articulate a liberal counterdiscourse on land—met in communal assembly to consider the liberal government's circular on *desamortización*. All three communities were in agreement with the privatization, as long as the following conditions were met: that all adjudications would go to inhabitants (*vecinos*) of the village or the district; that the disentailment of the plots held by *vecinos* be done without charge; and that all preexisting problems of boundaries and land usurpations be resolved ahead of time and with justice. Perhaps most interesting, however, was the justification given for exemption from fees in the adjudication. Since the villages had collaborated assiduously and paid all their taxes during the 1860s—that is, during the wars—now they were entitled to their properties without charge. Jonotla and Tuzamapan mentioned especially the thirteen hundred pesos they had contributed to the resistance in 1863, while Tenampulco recalled always being on time with its contributions, plus having provided labor to build a field hospital in Espinal.[13]

In Cuetzalan, 1867 also saw the intensification of debate over the disamortization of communal lands. Back in 1862, the communal authorities in Cuetzalan's indigenous *barrio* of Tzicuilan had already petitioned José María Maldonado while he was military commander in Zacapoaxtla. They complained that several recent *vecinos* in Cuetzalan had been allowing their cattle to damage the crops of the *barrio*; and that, given Maldonado's reputation for "ideas . . . highly liberal," he would undoubtedly "incline . . . to be a decided supporter of the weak and especially the Indian race that always suffers [at the hands of] its dominators. . . ."

---

13. AHMTO, Gobierno, caja s/n 1866, exp. 71, "Sesión municipal de Jonotla," Apr. 13, 1868. For the 1864 discussion of who would get access to communal lands, see AHMZ, paquete 1863-65-64, exp. 204, Borrador de Oficios del Jefe Político de Zacapoaxtla, Zacapoaxtla, 1864, "Oficio al Comandante Militar de Cuetzalán," Zacapoaxtla, Feb. 9, 1864, quotation on f. 9. For the communal assemblies in Jonotla, Tuzamapan, and Tenampulco, see AHMTO, caja s/n 1866, exp. 71, "Actas de varios pueblos en las municipalidades de Jonotla, Tuzamapan, y Tenampulco," Mar. 9–16, 1867.

Maldonado indeed lived up to his liberal reputation, working out an agreement between the villagers of Tziculan and the three white *vecinos* in which all cattle needed to be removed from the area, ultimately renting some communal land to two of these three for a period of five years (Thomson 1991).

As of January 1868, however, the white *vecino* renters were ready to disentail their plots, and the indigenous villagers of Tziculan rebelled against what they saw as the continued abuse of their communal land rights. Echoing many of the notes of entitlement present in the earlier consideration of the liberal land laws by the communities of Tuzamapan and Jonotla, Cuetzalan's national guard captain Francisco Agustín made very clear in his letter to Ignacio Arrieta, the district's *jefe político,* that the people of Tziculan *barrio* considered their rights in communal land to be buttressed by their loyalty and connection to the populist Méndez faction in state politics (Thomson 1991:221–26; Agustín's letter is quoted extensively on p. 222). And that association was itself based on the complex construction of a popular liberal discourse on land, ongoing since the 1850s.

By the late 1860s and early 1870s, then, communities throughout the central and eastern *sierra de Puebla* were pushing for a collective, state-oriented interpretation of liberal land law. During the previous twenty years of struggle, they had learned to expect two things: first, that peasants had original and irrevocable rights to their communal lands first granted to them by the colonial state; and second, that the state could legitimately intervene to assure those rights against predatory land-owners, especially if the peasants were loyal supporters of the nation. As formulated by the liberal state and the peasant communities during the 1850s and 1860s, this alternative liberal discourse on property rights flew in the face of more purely market-oriented approaches. Yet at the same time, it had a firm basis in Lerdo's clarifying circulars of October–November 1856, and in local policy as formulated in the *sierra* through the late 1860s.

During the Restored Republic and in the second half of the Porfiriato, liberal statemakers would once again give priority to more purely market-oriented definitions of landed property. In both cases, the result would be rural rebellion. Only in the postrevolutionary decades did the principles of popular liberalism reemerge at the national level. In the 1920s, it was the exchange of land grants for loyalty to the nation; in the 1930s, legitimate state intervention to ensure the original communal rights to *ejido* property. The genius of land reform during these years was to resuscitate popular discourses and aspirations in place since the 1860s.

HEGEMONIC PROCESSES IN THE *SIERRA DE PUEBLA*:
THE CASE OF EDUCATION

Similar reverberations between nineteenth-century liberal discourse and postrevolutionary policy occurred in the area of education. Contributions to this volume, and other local work on postrevolutionary education, have begun to show the contradictory effects of state programs. In the 1920s and 1930s, state efforts to expand education combined attempts to enable rural populations and integrate them into the national society and economy, with less laudatory goals of social control. The response of local populations in both decades was also mixed. While some welcomed attempts to improve and transform local life, others resisted through absenteeism, the assassination of teachers, or, in the 1920s, the Cristero Rebellion.[14] As Elsie Rockwell makes clear in her essay, each local post-revolutionary school was constructed through daily processes of conflict and contestation. But here again are strong parallels with what occurred earlier in the Puebla highlands.

In the central Puebla highlands between 1867 and 1872, local offi-cials attempted to open public primary schools in municipalities through-out the Tetela district. In part, this effort was a response to popular aspirations that saw education as a way of opening doors to achievement, participation, and citizenship. Even before the end of the Second Empire, people in the *barrio* of San Nicolás had written to the Tetela municipal council about their desire to open a primary school. After explaining that they had saved one hundred pesos from a communal agricultural project, they tied the coming of "a stable and lasting peace" to the "prosperity and enlightened progress" they expected a primary school to provide for them. Judging from the number of schools that opened in Tetela munici-pality between 1867 and 1870, these aspirations were shared fairly widely. That such a large number of schools found the funds to open their doors when poverty and scarcity were widespread in the aftermath of a

14. On education during the 1920s and 1930s, see Raby (1974); Britton (1979); Lerner (1979); Vaughan (1982, 1990b, and 1992). On the Cristero Rebellion, see J. Meyer (1974a, b, and c).

decade-and-a-half of civil war and foreign intervention, lends further proof to the depth of the hopes pinned on education.[15]

But as it came to be practiced in this region over these years, the expansion of schooling also became a way of teaching people how to march to the state's tune. Children needed to be schooled in the ways of "civilization": getting to school on time, learning respect, making school a higher priority than the agricultural calendar or the family economy. Almost immediately, questions of enforcement and surveillance surfaced, as teachers experienced the frustrations of poor attendance and seeming nonchalance toward learning. In this context, education was no longer a popular aspiration to progress, in forms and with calendars that the people controlled. It became instead a potentially authoritarian and racist discourse about the need to force ignorant or religious villagers, almost without exception Indian, against their own judgment and for their own good, into the enlightened sphere of "science." And in the various municipalities of Tetela de Ocampo, it was local intellectuals—schoolteachers, justices of the peace, municipal officers, and officials of the local commissions on public instruction—who stood at the forefront of this battle and helped define the direction it would take.

There was a missionary quality to the attitude many teachers adopted. They were bringing understanding, knowledge, and civilization to the ignorant. In many cases they were sacrificing themselves as well, living in poor rural conditions to teach. It certainly must have been hard, in such a situation, not to take absences and other obstacles personally. And this was true in the 1860s and 1870s just as clearly as it would be in the 1920s and 1930s.

A particularly telling case was Valentín Sánchez, teacher of the *barrio* school in San José, who sent a letter to Tetela's municipal council in October 1871. He had been teaching in San José since April 1870, he explained. Parents and political authorities had shown nothing but indifference, with the result that "the advances of the youths have been few and insignificant." Sánchez admitted to feeling ashamed during the visits

15. The letter from the *barrio* of San Nicolás is in AHMTO, Gobierno, caja 9, exp. 3, "Oficio de los vecinos del barrio de San Nicolás al Ayuntamiento de Tetela de Ocampo," Feb. 16, 1867. Other examples of the early desire for education, as well as the difficulties involved, are "Oficio del preceptor de la escuela de la Cañada, Tiburcio García, al Ayuntamiento de Tetela," Jan. 16, 1867; and exp. 6, no. 52: "Oficio del Ayuntamiento de Aquixtla al Jefe Político de Tetela, sobre educación," Aquixtla, July 22, 1867.

of the local commission on public instruction because he was unable to show more advancement. "But what can a teacher do," he asked, "when the boys come only four, six, or eight days during a whole month?" As quickly as they learned, they also forgot. Of the forty-two boys registered in the school, twenty simply did not show up. The rest showed up only occasionally. Although he had written to the local authorities, they had done nothing. If something could not be done, Sánchez concluded, he would be forced to resign. On October 21, nine days after his original petition, the municipal council asked the local commission on public instruction to "bring the case before the relevant court, so that the children begin attending school or their parents receive the appropriate punishment."[16]

Sometimes the situation could escalate into personal confrontation. Donaciano Arriaga, teacher in La Cañada since 1867, brought a complaint before Tetela municipality in February of 1871. His problem was a familiar one: the boys were absent from school, when they came they were late, and the parents were not cooperating. What was different in this case was that Arriaga accused one father, Antonio Tapia, of organizing opposition to him among the parents, trying to remove Arriaga from his post. The only reason for this opposition, according to the teacher, was that "I constantly reprehend the insubordination to which the children are accustomed, the thefts that are not lacking among them, the pranks and various other things they do incessantly."

Arriaga felt a deep responsibility for all the boys, and seemed to focus on Tapia and Tapia's son as the root of all his difficulties. He could not discipline Tapia's son, he said, because Tapia would then "state publicly that the children are being mistreated unjustly, and that is why they do not advance with the current teacher." He also used Tapia's son as the example of his deepest frustration, when even if the boys were advancing their parents would not send them to school regularly.

> Several of the boys who are writing and principally this one [Tapia's son] because of the work his father is making him do, gets to school at eleven in the morning, and at four in the afternoon. . . .

Another difference in this case was that the justice of the peace in La Cañada was called in to investigate, and wrote a formal report. In it he

16. AHMTO, Gobierno, caja s/n 1871, exp. 5: "Oficio de Valentín Sánchez, preceptor de la escuela del barrio de San José, al Ayuntamiento de Tetela," Oct. 12, 1871.

confirmed the absences, tardiness, and insubordination of the children, and said that it occurred with the consent of some of the parents. He also reported on a personal meeting with Arriaga and Tapia. At that meeting Tapia admitted that, with two other parents, he had been attempting to establish a private school. But he apologized, saying that whatever he had done that could be causing problems had been "hot-headed and without reflection," and that he would not do it again. The justice of the peace concluded his report by confirming that several fathers had come to his office demanding a *barrio* meeting to establish a private school, but that he had refused to grant the demand. On March 25, more than a month after Arriaga's original complaint, the local commission on public instruction asked the local judge to arrange a meeting with the individuals involved in order to determine culpability and relevant punishment.[17]

The case of Donaciano Arriaga and the La Cañada school provides a particularly good window on issues that were common to most confrontations among local parents, schoolteachers, and municipal officials. A crucial component in most of these cases, but which emerges with particular clarity in the La Cañada case, was the struggle between parents and teachers over the labor time of the children. In the local agricultural economy, parental control over children's labor was a key component of the organization and division of labor more generally, and of the system of patriarchal authority (Mallon forthcoming: chap. 3). Interference by outsiders, whether teachers or municipal officials, was both unwelcome and potentially dangerous. Thus it was not a question of whether education was desirable or not in the abstract, but rather of who would control the educational process and who would bear the highest cost.

The debates around private schools are particularly telling in this context. They are a clear indictment of the way public schools were being run at the local level. As formulated by schoolteachers, municipalities, and commissions of public instruction, education was not serving the needs of the population, yet it was forcing the family economy to bear the highest part of the cost. If that was the case anyway, why not establish private schools? From the standpoint of the parents in La Cañada, a private school would allow those who bore the highest cost to also control the process.

For the local teachers and political authorities who found themselves

17. On the case of Arriaga, see AHMTO, Gobierno, caja s/n 1871, "Expediente promovido por el preceptor de la escuela del barrio de La Cañada," Tetela de Ocampo, Feb. 11–Mar. 25, 1871. All the quotations are included.

in the middle of the fray, however, it was difficult to see things in this light. Instead, they tended to take the conflicts over control very personally. They explained the situation through self-images in which they were struggling to bring civilization to the ignorant. In Xochiapulco, these images opposed a superior "science" to the superstitions associated with "religion," as can be seen in an 1870 conflict between the *barrio* of Cuauximaloyan and Xochiapulco's *cabecera*.

In early December of that year, ten *vecinos* from Cuauximaloyan complained to the *jefe político* of Tetela district that their municipal capital had promised to provide funds from the municipal treasury if the *barrio* wished to establish a school. What it had done instead, however, was to demand the monthly payment of a one-*real* tax from each individual in order to support the school in the *cabecera*. Meanwhile, the people in Cuauximaloyan were very poor, "without seeds, without corn, and without anything else because everything was lost in the past revolution." They asked the *jefe* to allow them to keep their money so that they could pay their own teacher.[18]

A week later the *juez municipal* in Xochiapulco responded angrily. In his view, the *barrio* of Cuauximaloyan had already agreed that primary education was important enough to warrant a contribution of one *real* per person. Then, after having agreed in a public assembly, they had presented a petition to the *jefe político*. People who had suffered more than those from Cuauximaloyan, the *juez* insisted, were not refusing to pay the tax. What was really going on, he concluded, was that

> they are more interested in building a church that they do not need, rather than building the most august of all temples, the one to science. For the first, there has been and is a peso [eight *reales*] per person to build the church; but for the second, there isn't even a *real* per month for the education of their own children; and furthermore: that for education, there are multitudes of elderly, there are many who are ill, poor, or [otherwise] employed; but not so for the church. . . .[19]

The issue of religion was important and contentious in Xochiapulco, a village owing its very existence to the "Liberal Revolution" of 1855.

18. Ibid., caja s/n 1870/73–74/78, exp. 113, "Ocurso de 10 vecinos del barrio de Cuauximaloyan al jefe político de Tetela de Ocampo," Cuauximaloyan, Dec. 6, 1870.
19. Ibid., "Informe del Juez Municipal de Xochiapulco, Juan Francisco Dinorin, al jefe político de Tetela de Ocampo, sobre el caso de Cuauximaloyan," Xochiapulco, Dec. 14, 1870.

When Dinorin accused the inhabitants of Cuauximaloyan of preferring religion to education, moreover, he did so in the context of a previously existing public discussion that had granted both church and school equivalent public legitimacy, in the sense of requesting communal labor for both. Indeed, only a month before the confrontation with Cuauximaloyan, the acting mayor of Xochiapulco had written to Tetela's *jefe político* requesting permission to organize a communal work party to build a small house or sanctuary for the village saints. Once the primary school had been completed, he explained, the municipal council had decided that they should invite the same *vecinos* who had built the school

> to cooperate with their voluntary labor . . . , so that in the same way they can help build a small house in which to keep the saints, that because of the war the then-enemies of the interests of the *pueblo* took them [the saints] to the *barrio* of Las Lomas, where they are abandoned, without the veneration of their owners.[20]

Earlier communal discussions had thus not privileged education over religion, except in granting first place to the construction of the school; both were considered legitimate. In fact, by denigrating Cuauximaloyan for its commitment to religion, Dinorin was tying into the anticlerical strands present in liberalism, using them to deflect attention from some important underlying issues. The struggle with Cuauximaloyan was not over education versus religion, at least not in any abstract sense, but about local *barrio* control over the schools and about the equitable use of revenue across all the *barrios* of the municipality.

The *jefe político* understood these important underlying issues, and his resolution of the conflict made this clear. Starting on January 1, 1871, he decided, Cuauximaloyan would have its own school. The Xochiapulco municipal council would name a teacher for the school and set the salary, paying it from the municipal treasury. The inhabitants of Cuauximaloyan and Atzalan *barrios* would continue to contribute to education through the Chicontepec tax, the same way as the inhabitants of the *cabecera* should continue to pay. If this tax did not cover the expenses of all the schools, the municipal council would find a way to make up the difference from other funds, distributing them equitably across the whole municipality.[21]

20. Ibid., "Oficio del alcalde municipal interino de Xochiapulco, Juan Martín, al jefe político de Tetela," Xochiapulco, Nov. 15, 1870.
21. Ibid., "Resolución del jefe político de Tetela de Ocampo sobre el problema de la escuela en Cuauximaloyan, Xochiapulco," Tetela, Dec. 15, 1870.

The *jefe político* in Tetela certainly had his hands full with disputes of this nature. Earlier in 1870 Juan José Galicia, a Totonac Indian from Tuzamapan, had protested to the *jefe* about the punishment he had received at the hands of the village mayor. The mayor, José Galván, then complained to the *jefe* for not requesting a report from him first. Apparently, Galicia had taken his son out of primary school when the boy had reached an advanced level, "reading quite well, writing at a second-grade level; in religion he had gotten as far as reciting the Our Father." Galván had punished Galicia, who then went to Tetela to protest, where he managed to get the *jefe político* to write Galván a private letter telling him to leave Galicia alone. Returning to Tuzamapan, according to Galván, Galicia

> began to tell [everyone] that only here were people molested, that in Tetela no one said anything, and allowed children to leave school; and such disorder has been introduced that [the children] have started getting too many colds, as is proven by the attendance lists and daily absences that I have included, so that you may answer by telling me what I should do, if I should leave them in this state, or if I should obey the law concerning [public] schools.

Throughout the document, Galván seems more interested in asserting his authority than in advancing education, and consistently justifies his actions and his superior knowledge by denigrating the Totonac families. He explains that the authorities were forced to punish families for not sending their children to school, and that they had succeeded despite grave difficulties, the proof for which lay in the fact that the children, "despite being dissembling and dull [*cerrados*] Totonacs, are [actually] too advanced." He later justified his authoritarian practices by asserting that, in his view, he had the obligation to bring education to the population despite their own worse judgment, "since as Totonac Indians, what is good [for them] appears bad."[22]

In Xochiapulco and Tuzamapan, existing conflicts or tensions were used by local intellectuals to explain why, as they saw it, the local population was resistant to education. Whether the previous conflict was about religion, as in Xochiapulco, or about ethnic negotiations over local power, as in Tuzamapan, the underlying issue was not education per se but the way it was being implemented and controlled.[23] The protests of local

22. Ibid., exp. 112: "Oficio del alcalde municipal de Tuzamapan, José Galván, al jefe político de Tetela," Tuzamapan, Apr. 4, 1870, which includes all the quotations.
23. On the problem of ethnic power sharing in Tuzamapan, see also AHMTO,

villagers about their lack of control over the process, their desire to find ways to make access to and organization of education equitable across *barrio* and ethnic lines, were transformed discursively into proof of their ignorance, their lack of understanding. This ignorance was then constructed as superstition in Xochiapulco, racial inferiority in Tuzamapan.

In both cases, we can perhaps understand the frustration and impatience of local teachers and municipal officials, when after much sacrifice and struggle a school was provided, only to have parents and children resist attendance. And yet from the perspective of the parents themselves, the discourses of superior civilization and enlightenment, the "for their own good" justifications that emerge from the authorities' frustration were anything but liberating. Indeed, these discourses and justifications could easily tie the local intellectuals who espoused them to wider webs of complicity and social control emerging in Mexico after 1867.

The struggles surrounding the 1855 "Liberal Revolution" helped hone a variety of racist discourses on social control that were used broadly, by conservatives and liberals, to justify the repression of agrarian social movements. They did so through the "othering" of the rural indigenous population—the identification of Indian peasants with ignorance, superstition, lack of political judgment, and tendencies toward violence and plunder. Conservatives served up these discourses as justifications for corporate and authoritarian politics: because of the large agrarian Indian population, democracy became equated with bloodshed and carnage; Mexico was not ready for broad participatory politics. Liberals articulated similar discourses in their efforts to control political power: peasants did not know how to act publicly; they needed strong leadership; when left to their own devices, only anarchy could ensue.[24]

Local discourses on education connected especially well to the liberal variants. Indian peasants, in this context, were not ready to participate in

Gobierno, caja s/n 1868, exp. 66: "Oficio de Antonio Sánchez, juez de Tuzamapan, al jefe político de Tetela, sobre las elecciones municipales en Tenampulco," Sept. 24, 1866, and "Oficio del nuevo juez de Tuzamapan, Nicolás Galicia, al jefe político de Tetela, sobre el arreglo en Tenampulco," Oct. 20, 1868.

24. I analyze the articulation of racist discourses by liberals and conservatives in Mexico in Mallon (forthcoming: esp. chaps. 2, 4, 6, 7, and 8). See also Mallon (1988). For a subtle and particularly interesting use of racism to "prove" that people cannot govern themselves and need a centralized state and effective leadership to be part of political society, see S. Nieto, "Legitimidad de la Administración Actual del Estado," parts 1–3, *Periódico Oficial del Estado Libre y Soberano de Puebla,* 1:64, 65, 67 (Mar. 27, 30 and Apr. 4, 1868), 1–2, in all three numbers.

the public sphere; they put their family interests and their religious beliefs before their civic duty to educate their children. Racism became, in this context, a nested discourse of control: local, regional, and national intellectuals of liberal persuasion had the obligation to educate the masses in spite of themselves. The liberals were to create the citizen, through a process of education and surveillance.

The education campaigns of the 1920s and 1930s seem an eerie reprise of many of these issues. The combination of education and surveillance, of enabling mixed with social control, is also present in the missionary teachers' campaign of the 1920s and the socialist education movement of the 1930s. So is the combination of local enthusiasm and resistance. In a sense, these later campaigns were successful at tying local populations to the state precisely because they connected to previous debates in village society, to questions and issues raised in an ongoing way for six or more decades. But the key to the postrevolutionary state's success in rural communities would be the alliance with local intellectuals—with the schoolteachers and political officials who had seen themselves, over the years, as fighting the lonely fight against ignorance and superstition. These people would be crucial, not only in the education campaigns, but also in the reconstruction of local politics.

MUNICIPAL AUTONOMY AND COMMUNAL HEGEMONY: DEMOCRATIC PATRIARCHY IN THE *SIERRA DE PUEBLA*

Along with land for those who work it, political autonomy has long been recognized as the second key ingredient of the 1910 revolution's popular program. Voiced alternatively as municipal autonomy, an end to the *jefes políticos*, or, in Womack's translation, "a real vote and no boss rule" (Womack 1968:55), this aspiration for political voice inspired many to support revolutionary transformation. Yet precisely for this reason, it is especially puzzling to find that, with the institutionalization of revolutionary rule in the 1930s, local governments became the proxies of an invasive central state. The *municipio libre*, won through blood and struggle, became the local feeding trough or proving ground for PRI members.

How did this happen, and what made the process of postrevolutionary centralization so successful? Once again through the analysis of parallel processes in the nineteenth century, I will show that statemakers in the twentieth century succeeded because they tied into the preexisting debates over power, legitimacy, and justice that had made up village politics since the colonial period. By allying with particular sectors of the community, most notably the younger male intellectuals, postrevolutionary leaders formed enduring links between the institutionalized party and rural constituencies.

In the Puebla highlands, village politics and communal institutions were arenas in which power was negotiated and accumulated throughout the colonial period and into the nineteenth century. Conflicts over power helped transform and rebuild local institutions again and again over four centuries. These transitions were not smooth or functional, and we know too little about them yet to do more than speculate. But what had emerged by the mid-nineteenth century—combining the disruptions and changes set into motion by colonialism with the new experiments in municipal government brought about by independence—was a new form of communal hegemonic process. Organized around a civil-religious hierarchy of officeholding that unified municipal and *cofradía* posts into a single cargo system, this new form of politics was a negotiated solution among communal factions, especially between younger and older men or spatially organized lineages and neighborhoods, over how to redefine and control power at the local level (Mallon forthcoming: chap. 3).

In one sense, this new cargo system helped negotiate age-old generational tensions that had existed among men in Nahua culture. While men of different generations collaborated in their control of women's labor power, sexuality, and reproductive potential, older women and men collaborated in the reproduction of generational authority and privilege. These crosscutting ties and conflicts, sometimes represented and worked out within families and households, were also at the root of communal politics. Even before the Spanish conquest, the military had provided an alternative route for younger men to circumvent the power of elders. In the early colonial period, younger Indians had once again sought power through alliances with Spanish officials, attempting to bypass the generational and patriarchal authority of the older men. And with independence, the emergence of the *municipalidad* also provided younger, more educated men with a different source of local power and of mediation with the emerging postcolonial state (Mallon forthcoming: chap. 3).

By providing a sequential, age-defined path along which men could pass in their progressive attainment of communal authority and prestige, the cargo system helped reorganize and manage those enduring conflicts over power. The cargo system combined political and religious offices and made all positions subject to surveillance by a council of elders, or *pasados*—older men who had finished their service to the community, having occupied all the offices in the civil-religious hierarchy. Thus it also provided for communal supervision over the new institution of the *municipalidad*. Yet given the power still held by *pasados*, the cargo system combined legitimacy with conflict even as it sought to deflect the latter.

The civil-religious hierarchy, with a clearly defined ladder of cargos through which all could theoretically rise, was in reality divided into an upper level (*cargos principales*) and a lower level (*cargos comunes*). Ideally, the two levels were separated only by the ages of the men occupying them; but in reality, not all individuals serving in the *cargos comunes* made it up into the *principales*. The *pasados* oversaw the proceedings, nominating and approving candidates for the different positions, further buttressing the differentiation. Often the division also reproduced regional, ethnic, economic, and *sujeto-cabecera* distinctions. Politically dependent villages (*sujetos*) that were poorer or predominantly Totonac would have less representation in the upper reaches of the cargo system than their Nahua or more prosperous *cabeceras*. At the same time, however, these divisions were not set in stone; there was room for individual or group mobility into the status of elder or *principal*, depending on such factors as wealth, outstanding service or talent, war or rebellion (when younger men might evidence special qualities), and especially the separation of a *sujeto* population and the establishment of a new, autonomous cargo system.[25]

Some of these potential conflicts and divisions could be worked out in the communal assemblies. Carefully constructed arenas of communal discourse where different interest groups, factions, or individuals sought collective approval for their projects or status, assemblies had a well-established, almost ritualized practice with concentric circles of power represented within them. The choice of language—whether Spanish, one or more indigenous languages, or some combination of them all—constantly helped rebuild relations of authority. Spanish, for example, represented a speaker's ability to mediate with the larger society and political system; but *pasados* who did not speak Spanish could call on their proven communal authority to bypass the symbolic power of the dominant language. In addition, women and younger men could, in the largest and most important communal assemblies, serve as a chorus of approval and disapproval, even if they possessed neither the generational or gender

25. The analysis in this paragraph was inspired by Carmagnani (1982) and by conversations with Steve J. Stern. Dow (1974:147–56) also suggests that the cargo system becomes increasingly selective at the top; only about half of the men, he calculates, manage to earn the status of elder. See also Arizpe (1973:121–24).

status nor the linguistic ability to speak up. Thus local indigenous leaders, through the cargo system and council of elders, could counteract the accumulation of power by younger or more acculturated mediators— whether in the position of municipal officials or municipal *secretarios*—by calling on the support of the community as a whole, reinforced within the discursive space of the assembly. Yet new leaders could emerge in the same space, bypassing some of the rigidities of *pasado* authority, by calling on collective approval from the communal chorus (Sierra Camacho 1987).

As practiced and reproduced in the *sierra de Puebla*, then, the community was constantly reconstructed through a complex network of conflict and cooperation that tied women, men, and generations to each other in families, *barrios*, villages, and *cabeceras*. Crosscutting ties of generation, gender, and ethnicity defined the community as a combination of families, internally organized according to patriarchal age structure. Local leaders, without exception male, gained authority and prestige by holding office in a parallel structure of religious and political posts in an ascending order of importance. The older a leader was, the more offices he had held, the greater his authority; ultimately, the council of elders oversaw all other forms of political activity. And it was this combination of families and elder patriarchs that gave the community its identity and legitimacy: "Our community, composed of its families and *pasados*" was a customary way of opening a political petition or other document.[26]

The relationship between family and community was a reciprocal one. The authority of elder males, as well as their responsibility to look after the common welfare, was clearly understood in both institutions; and the maintenance of this authority in one institution reinforced its maintenance in the other. In the community, *pasados* had the obligation continuously to earn their authority and prestige by advising, represent-

---

26. For the use of familial language when referring to the community, see especially AHMZ, paquete 1863-65-64, exp. 222, "Oficio del Juez de Paz de Taitic al Comandante Militar y Jefe Político de Zacapoaxtla," Aug. 2, 1863; ibid., legajo 37, "Carta de Francisco Cortés al Capitán D. Juan Francisco Lucas," Cuetzalan, Mar. 23, 1863; and AHMTO, Gobierno, caja s/n 1866, exp. 71, "Acta de la Guardia Nacional de Tetela de Ocampo rechazando las condiciones impuestas por Ignacio R. Alatorre." For the political role of *los pasados*, see ibid., exp. 7, "Acta del pueblo de San Francisco Zoquiapan sobre adjudicaciones de terrenos," Mar. 11, 1867, and "Acta del pueblo de Tenampulco sobre adjudicaciones de terrenos," Mar. 16, 1867; AHMZ, paquete 1869, exp. 111, "Relativo a la ley de desamortización en el pueblo de Yancuitlalpan: Copia del acta de los vecinos de Santiago Yancuitlalpan sobre escoger un terreno para ejido," Jan. 17, 1869.

ing, and risking themselves for the common good. Patriarchs within families had parallel responsibilities. Just as *los pasados* had to protect the community as a whole, male elders in families had the obligation to look after and protect their dependents. Given the interdependence of the two institutions, moreover, community authorities could legitimately intervene in families to preserve the mutuality of family reciprocal relations. An abusive patriarch threatened not only his own dependents but also the collective fabric of the community. Thus he had to be subject to community authority in the last instance.[27]

It is in the mutually reinforcing relationship between family and community, and in the reciprocal obligations that tied different community and family members to each other, that we find the basis for communal hegemony. Justice for all was identified not with complete equality, but with the reciprocal relations maintained by the "good" patriarch. *Pasados* were just if they protected their community and sacrificed themselves in the common interest. Municipal officials were just if they mediated equally between citizens and assured everyone's access to subsistence, as a good father would. State officials were just if they were responsive to the needs of all their "children."

In this context, it is especially interesting that Juan Francisco Lucas, the most outstanding and prestigious leader of the guerrilla resistance against the French, became known in his later years as "el patriarca de la sierra" ("the patriarch of the highlands"). He took seriously his obligation to watch over the common good, even as he grew older, wealthier, and more powerful. At one point, for example, he petitioned local municipal officials to carry out a *deslinde* (legal fixing of boundaries) between his estate and the neighboring village. As he explained in the document, it was not a question of settling conflicts but of preventing them; he wanted to make sure that everyone was happy with the boundary and that good relations were maintained. The role of the good patriarch was to guard the peace by acting justly.[28]

In a situation where the justice of the good patriarch functioned,

27. In a personal communication, Steve J. Stern has confirmed a similar role for community authorities as checks against abusive patriarchs in Oaxaca in the late colonial and early national periods.

28. AHMTO, Gobierno, caja 11, "Solicitud de Juan Francisco Lucas al P. Ayuntamiento de Tetela de Ocampo," Dec. 1, 1868. For Lucas's general importance in the *sierra* during the last decades of the nineteenth century, see LaFrance and Thomson (1987: esp. 4–9).

then, everyone would benefit. Beyond the individual family or household, it was the *pasados* who most embodied this principle. Their status reflected resources and commitment, authority and service; they earned it by personifying the ideal characteristics of the good father. The same characteristics also earned them the right to oversee and mediate political relations in general, keeping the peace between individuals as well as in the community as a whole. And as long as the elders did their job correctly and justly, everyone had the obligation to continue struggling for the common principles of communal hegemony; for the best way to achieve justice was to assure the survival and viability of "las familias y los pasados."

If communal hegemony was organized internally around a gendered and generational concept of justice, equally important to its overall reproduction was the form taken by relations with the broader society and economy. People who had the skills for such mediation—namely, the education, language proficiency, and contacts to handle political or economic interactions outside the community—were still subject to the supervision and control of the collectivity, especially as embodied in the elders. They, too, had to earn the privilege of representing the community. Negotiations over who held the offices of mediation, including municipal *secretario* and *juez municipal*, usually balanced community prestige acquired through the *cargo* system against the skills learned in school, regional trade, or other sectors of the broader society. Compromises might entail a trade-off, with a locally prestigious but often non–Spanish-speaking or illiterate *juez* or *alcalde* serving alongside a ladino, mestizo, or acculturated Indian *secretario*.[29] But whatever the outcome in a particular

29. Arizpe (1973:123); Sierra Camacho (1987). In some documents from the nineteenth century, moreover, it becomes clear that the various offices of local government were negotiated ethnically, often with the more indigenous leader occupying the *alcalde* or *juez* position and the mestizo or ladino occupying the *suplente* or *secretario* role. See, for example, AHMTO, Gobierno, caja s/n 1866, exp. 71, "Acta del pueblo de S. Martín Tuzamapan desconociendo al gobierno imperial," Aug. 25, 1866, "Acta del pueblo de Jonotla desconociendo al gobierno imperial," Aug. 24, 1866, and "Acta del pueblo de Zapotitlan desconociendo al gobierno imperial," Sept. 3, 1866; caja s/n 1868, exp. 66, "Oficio de Antonio Sánchez al jefe político de Tetela," Tenampulco, Sept. 24, 1868, and "Oficio del nuevo juez de Tuzamapan al jefe político de Tetela," Oct. 20, 1868; and AGNEP, Huauchinango, caja 2 (1861–70), libro 1863, "Arrendamiento de algunos solares comunales por Manuel Antonio, alcalde de Michiuca, suplente José Francisco Telles, y algunos pasados," Nov. 23, 1863.

case, the maintenance of communal consensus rested on the twin pillars of internal justice and successful external mediation.

Just as independence helped articulate emerging civil-religious hierarchies to postcolonial municipal institutions, the "Liberal Revolution" of 1855 introduced yet another wave of new dynamics into the reconstruction of communal consensus. In the *sierra de Puebla*, from the 1840s on, economic and commercial growth generated new opportunities in trade and agricultural production, especially in areas like long-distance trade or commercial agriculture, which, according to existing divisions of labor, were the province of men. Additional opportunities for education and migration, moreover, potentially opened up alternative routes to economic and political influence for younger men, who might not need to wait around for their inheritance and might use new skills to build new alliances at the community level.[30]

Thus the two decades of guerrilla resistance that followed the 1855 revolution occurred in communities already embroiled in new processes of internal tension and change. The "Liberal Revolution" itself, by providing the terrain on which to hammer out radically new concepts of citizenship and political participation, set the scene for yet another reconstruction of communal hegemonic processes. While not abolishing internal gender, ethnic, and generational hierarchies, the presence of liberal guerrilla forces along the center-east fringe of the Puebla highlands called into question the forms of hegemonic communal politics that had emerged between the late colonial and early postindependence periods.

Liberal guerrilla warfare in the Puebla highlands increased the potential power of young men, especially Indian men, by making possible their participation in the national guard battalions that spearheaded the resistance. Officers were elected to head the battalions, often according to criteria of dedication and bravery that had little to do with age or ethnicity. Nahua Indians without last names fought shoulder to shoulder with mestizos. The national guard also played a new role in mediation with the larger society; through its officers and the actions of its men in

30. For a more extensive discussion of the commercial trends in the 1840s and beyond, and how this might lead to intensified conflict between villages or municipalities, see Mallon forthcoming: chap. 2. My speculations about how such changes might open up new spaces for younger men are based on what did happen in the twentieth century with additional commercial, wage labor, and migration opportunities. In addition to Arizpe (1973) and Dow (1974), see Taggart (1975) and Nutini and Isaac (1974).

combat, villages were integrated into the liberal movement, receiving recognition or rewards for their bravery and dedication.[31]

Potentially at least, this new access to power and influence by the national guard was a challenge to the *pasados'* monopoly on power, and might have created tensions with older communal officials or practices. Yet national guard soldiers and their leaders occupied their intermediate space between the liberal state and communal politics with a great deal of creativity and dynamism. Locally, they combined local indigenous concepts of community and collective responsibility with radical definitions of liberal citizenship, nurturing a democratic vision of how society should be organized. According to this perspective, elected municipal officials should be responsible to all of the community's citizens, distributing tax and labor obligations, as well as revenues, in an equal manner. Regionally and nationally, the national guard units used their position in local society, and the ideology of reciprocity that stood at the center of communal consensus, to conceptualize a more egalitarian relationship to the central state. The people should have the right to choose their own representatives, and to demand responsiveness and access to political and economic participation for all. As defined by the national guard of highland Puebla, then, the nation was made up of all its citizens, and the state had an equal obligation to underwrite the prosperity of all (Mallon forthcoming: chaps. 2–4).

What emerged from this interaction of communal hegemony and liberal struggle was what one could call, following Judith Stacey, "democratic patriarchy" (Stacey 1983:116–17, 155–57). At its core were the ongoing negotiations among male villagers over the sources for and legitimation of local power and prestige. In these negotiations, national guard troops held new access to state power and control over the local means of violence and self-defense. Yet any reference to or use of communal solidarity by the national guard had to gain the approval of the *pasados*, those custodians of "legitimate" communalism who were themselves the very embodiment of communal notions of justice—of the concepts of reciprocity and responsibility contained in the idea of the good patriarch. This mutual recognition of power and influence, then, underlay the construction of "democratic patriarchy."

---

31. For descriptions of the role of the national guard, see Mallon (forthcoming: chaps. 2, 3, 4, 5, and 7). See also Thomson (1990).

Equally important to the concept, however, was the oxymoronic tension between democracy and patriarchy. Democracy, in this case, meant the extension of influence and prestige to men who had previously stood on the fringes of the communal power structure. Patriarchy signified the ongoing exclusion of women from the expanded definition of citizenship. And the oxymoronic tension was also present in the social and cultural struggles through which democratic patriarchy, as an emerging form of popular political culture, was built.

Democratic patriarchy was not only a negotiation among men, but also an attempt by village peasants, both women and men, to confront the new political possibilities emerging with the "Liberal Revolution." Literally in the heat of battle, the men and women of these villages struggled to bridge the gap between their own dynamic and contested concepts of mutuality and justice, and the ideas of individual freedom and equality contained in nineteenth-century liberalism. Situating these ideas in the context of indigenous communalism and reciprocity, highland peasants tempered the individualism and strengthened the promises of equality those ideas contained. In so doing, they fashioned a liberal vision quite distinct, in class and ethnic terms, from that held by many citified intellectuals (Mallon forthcoming: chaps. 2, 4). At the same time, their vision was a gendered one, in which the possibility of equality was necessarily mediated by existing patriarchal traditions and relationships.

In the myriad struggles that occurred in the *sierra de Puebla* during the "Liberal Revolution" and the French Intervention, the year 1868 proved to be a watershed. With the defeat of the Empire and the reestablishment of the Republic (1867), the power and autonomy of popular liberalism began to decline. As the disentailment of community lands began in earnest, the importance of a unified communal response also loomed large. Under such conditions the independent power of the national guard began to decrease, and communal hegemony once again was reorganized around a revitalized generational axis. This reorganization provides the best explanation for the events that occurred in 1869, when the Nahua villages near Cuetzalan, unhappy with the abusive privatization of communal lands going on in their region, participated in a regional rebellion in alliance with the national guard units from Xochiapulco and Tetela de Ocampo. Officials at the Mexican Defense Ministry were confused about what to do with the captured guerrilla leaders. All the military sources insisted that these leaders were dangerous and should be sent into internal exile. Yet in Mexico City, those in charge had a hard time believing this judgment; the average age of the prisoners was ninety-two![32]

But perhaps the best evidence for this new revitalization of generational politics is to be found in the transformation of Juan Francisco Lucas. Born in 1834, his baptism certificate records no last names for either of his parents or him. At the young age of twenty-one, he joined and soon led the national guard battalion from Xochiapulco, rising in a single decade to the rank of general, carrying on a personal correspondence with the president of the republic, becoming *compadres* with influential figures, including Porfirio Díaz himself.

His youth and lack of connection to a regular *cargo* system might have given ethnic leaders pause. Their ambivalence is certainly reflected in two petitions from the *pasados* and authorities of Cuetzalan in 1863, when they refer to Lucas alternatively as "Señor Capitán Don Juan Francisco Lucas," then as "Señor Don Juan de Político," almost as if they thought he was masquerading as a political authority. Yet at the same time, throughout the years of the "Liberal Revolution," even as he respected communal leaders and authorities, Lucas had the ultimate say in the region under his command. Perhaps things changed after 1867, when some of his former allies turned against him and he found among his new allies many of the older *pasados* whom he could earlier have challenged or circumvented.

In 1868, Lucas married Acención Pérez, daughter of one of Tetela's wealthiest and most prominent mestizo citizens, thereby ultimately inheriting one of the few larger *fundos* in the region and using it as base for the ongoing rebellions in the *sierra*. In the end, as we have seen, he would be known as "el patriarca de la sierra"; but at his wedding, three months short of his thirty-fourth birthday, General Juan Francisco Lucas lied about his age. In declaring himself thirty-five, he symbolically recognized the changes already in the wind. For the rest of the nineteenth century, the popular liberalism of the national guard would have to sacrifice potential democracy for communal survival. Twenty-year-old national guard captains would once again surrender communal space to *pasados* and their allies.[33]

32. AHDN, exp. XI/481.4/9893: "Correspondencia entre el Comandante Militar de Veracruz y el Ministerio de Guerra y Marina, sobre los prisioneros de guerra de Zacapoaxtla," Sept. 19–Oct. 1, 1868, ff. 211–14v; "Oficio de Rafael J. García al Ministerio de Guerra y Marina, adjuntando copia de la lista de presos de Zacapoaxtla," Oct. 12, 1868, ff. 218–19.

33. For the process of inheritance related to the will of Francisco Pérez and the

By the late nineteenth century, the tendency of younger men to rise and challenge generational authority in village politics had come to characterize most periods of war or political flux. Indeed, since the conquest, compromises among generations, ethnic groups, and villages had helped fashion at least three institutional and discursive transitions in local society: the ladder of civil posts was associated with colonial *gobiernos de república;* the civil-religious hierarchies were articulated, after independence, with the new municipalities; and the seemingly ephemeral democratic patriarchy allied *pasados* with the national guard in the 1855–67 period. With the 1910 revolution, village-based militias would once again attempt generational and ethnic negotiations with communal leaders; once again they would involve gendered relations of power.

During the 1910 revolution, the call for municipal autonomy that fired the popular imagination contained the twin promises of a return to communal democracy and to familial solidarity (which often meant that all men would have authority over "their" women). Yet as is well known, promises of popular democracy were stillborn in the period of postrevolutionary consolidation.[34] Ilene O'Malley has explained this by examining the process through which images of male revolutionaries emerged in official revolutionary culture. Bourgeois class domination, she suggests, was articulated through the construction of distinct masculinities for different revolutionary heroes. State control was made effective through the discourse of patriarchy, which was used against all women but perhaps even more importantly against male lower-class rebels, who emerge, in

---

fundo Taxcantla, see AGNEP, Tetela de Ocampo, caja 1 (1869–1880), libro 1869, ff. 7v–9v, "Hijuelas de la testamentería de Francisco Pérez," Oct. 18, 1869. For the use of Taxcantla as the base for the Xochiapulquenses in the period 1869–72 (even Porfirio Díaz retired there to recover from a wound during the rebellion of La Noria), see *El Siglo XIX* (Mexico City), Dec. 22, 1869, p. 3; Jan. 9, 1870, p. 3; Dec. 14, 1871, p. 3; *Diario Oficial,* Jan. 9, 1870, p. 1; Jan. 10, 1870, p. 3; Jan. 16, 1870, p. 3; Mar. 5, 1872, p. 3 [reference to Díaz]; and *Publicación Oficial de Puebla,* Jan. 11, 1870, p. 4. For the two references to Lucas from Cuetzalan, see AHMZ, paquete 1863-64-65, leg. 37: "Dos oficios de las autoridades de Cuetzalan a Juan Francisco Lucas," Mar. 23, 1863. For Lucas's baptismal and marriage records, see (Lic.) Francisco Landero Alamo, *Zacapoaxtla,* available in the municipal library, Zacapoaxtla, pp. 8–9.

34. Reed (1969) makes the patriarchal underpinnings of the popular Villista movement especially clear. Some of the underlying gender implications of communal democracy for the Zapatista movement are clear in Womack (1968). Additional analyses of women in the revolution of 1910 can be found in Macías (1982) and Salas (1990).

this new system, as the perpetual adolescents confronting the benevolent yet firm authority of the bourgeois father (O'Malley 1986).

It is useful to remember here that the metaphor of adolescent rebellion is not simply a trope used by the postrevolutionary state. In the Puebla highlands, we have seen that generational conflicts stood at the very center of the negotiations that constructed communal political cultures and helped define the contours of democratic patriarchy. The brilliance of the postrevolutionary state, therefore, lay not only in the discursive manipulation of masculinity, but also in the ability to connect to the generational conflict as metaphor and practice in popular culture.

It is tempting to suggest, in this context, that the institutionalized revolution of the 1930s and beyond represented the institutionalization of democratic patriarchy. In the *sierra de Puebla,* the spread of the coffee economy, increasing opportunities for labor migration, and the erosion of access to land in *sierra* villages all helped loosen the ties of gerontocracy, generating new options for women and for younger men in the labor force and the market economy (Arizpe 1973; Dow 1974; Nutini and Isaac 1974; Taggart 1975). The essay by Jan Rus in this volume provides tantalizing hints that similar trends developed in Chiapas during the Cardenista years; and we can speculate, based on indirect evidence, for the country as a whole. A massive, state-sponsored agrarian reform; the spread of commercial agriculture and increasing opportunities for labor migration; the erosion of communally based forms of access to land—all these trends helped loosen the ties of gerontocracy across the board. The importance of mediators and local intellectuals, most often younger men with more years of education, everywhere increased under the hegemony of the Partido Revolucionario Institucional. In a sense, if the *pasados* won the battle with the national guard after 1867, they lost the war after 1920.

Seen from the side of communal hegemonic processes, then, the emergence of the postrevolutionary *municipio libre*—with its combination of effective populism and authoritarianism—becomes easier to explain. As was the case during the "Liberal Revolution," the populism involved effective ties with younger intellectuals at the local level. For these ambitious villagers, predominantly though not exclusively male, the PRI became the ticket to local power and influence. At the same time, using the metaphors and practices of democratic patriarchy for the purpose of social control reconstructed authoritarianism because it ensured that the patriarchal side of the dyad continued to dominate the democratic side in Mexican politics.

THE 1910 REVOLUTION IN NINETEENTH-CENTURY AND
REGIONAL PERSPECTIVE

From the perspective of local or regional hegemonic processes, it becomes much easier to explain the successes of the postrevolutionary state in achieving a hegemonic outcome. Though I have limited my analysis here to three specific areas of policy—agrarian reform, education, and local government—similar forms of discussion could probably take place for other areas. If we consider William Roseberry's point (developed in his essay in this volume) that hegemony is not complete agreement or ideological acceptance but the establishment of a common discursive framework, then the twentieth-century Mexican state was hegemonic precisely because it tied into existing debates and discourses in local society.

On the question of agrarian reform, popular liberalism had already defined, in the second half of the nineteenth century, the state's right to intervene in favor of some people's access to the land, and had tied the right to land to defense of the nation. Obregón and Cárdenas would rely on these traditions. On the issue of education, nineteenth-century schoolteachers and municipal officials had already been fighting to overcome local resistance around school attendance and discipline. The oppositions between education and religion, education and ignorance; the equation of resistance with superstition and of schoolteachers with the missionaries of science and enlightenment—all these discourses would find deep resonance among village intellectuals. Finally, articulating local municipal governments to existing debates and discussions around democratic patriarchy, as well as privileging younger males as mediators, also tied the postrevolutionary *municipio libre* to communal hegemonic processes that had been ongoing since independence.

My analysis of democratic patriarchy thus suggests that the sometimes puzzling combination of populism and authoritarianism that underlay PRI rule is a legacy of the ongoing articulation of communal hegemonic processes to the construction of national politics. In Mexican political culture, enduring authoritarianisms coexist uneasily with recurring and stubborn democratic counterhegemonies. Both have their roots in the dynamic and contradictory constructions of communal and national hegemonic politics.

HEGEMONIC PROCESSES AND HEGEMONIC OUTCOMES: REGIONAL
POLITICAL CULTURES AND STATE FORMATION IN MEXICO AND PERU

As Peru and Mexico entered the twentieth century, their states had much
in common on the surface. In Peru, Nicolás de Piérola and his successor,
Eduardo López de Romaña, headed governments interested in order,
progress, and economic development. They wished to bring their country into the modern era, and they presided over the beginning of substantial U.S. investment in production and in construction of new roads and
railroads. In Mexico, Porfirio Díaz oversaw similar, if much more dramatic, trends. In both countries as well, states rested on coalitions whose
centers were composed of entrepreneurial, landowning classes, in combination with foreign capital. The reproduction of these states and of the
coalitions that supported them necessitated, at various points and in
various forms, the violent repression of social movements and popular
resistance. But overall, the veneer was one of prosperity and order,
modernization and progress (Mallon 1983; Cosío Villegas 1956).

What was not so obvious on the surface was that each of these states
had been formed and consolidated in a historically different manner. In
Mexico, Porfirio Díaz came to power as a hero of the popular resistance
against the French Intervention and Second Empire, riding the crest of a
coalition composed of multiple regional counterhegemonic movements.
Each regional movement had a distinct internal dynamic, based on the
particular historical process through which its own political culture had
been constructed and on its particular experience during the French
Intervention, Second Empire, and Restored Republic. But the coalition as
a whole gave Díaz a mandate to build national politics on the basis of
negotiation and incorporation rather than repression and domination
(Mallon forthcoming: chaps. 4, 5, 8).

What remained to be seen, in 1876 and beyond, was what Díaz
would do with this mandate. To some extent, he fulfilled his promises
during the earlier Porfiriato, at least in central Mexico. Governors and
other political officials in the state governments were initially veterans of
previous liberal struggles who had earned their constituencies' trust. They
served as mediators between local populist politics and the national
government. Even as power was consolidated, then, regional movements
and coalitions continued being heard—if not always listened to. Such
was the case during the administrations of Juan Nepomuceno Méndez
and Juan Crisóstomo Bonilla in Puebla; such was the case, somewhat more

belatedly, with the governorship of Manuel Alarcón in Morelos. But somewhere along the line, the balance of the coalition keeping Díaz in power began to change. Its center came to rest less and less with the popular movements or alliances that had brought Díaz to power, and shifted increasingly toward a Mexico City-based entrepreneurial class and its associates among foreign investors (Guerra 1985, 1988:1:78, 79, 98, 101, 2:22; Womack 1968:13–15; Goldfrank 1979:151–53).

For the popular movements that spearheaded the 1910 revolution, this shift in the Porfirian balance of forces was an important precipitating factor. In Puebla, when octogenarian Juan Francisco Lucas refused to answer the call of his *compadre* Díaz and joined the revolution instead, it was with a sense of broken promises. In Morelos, when the ex-Porfirian villages of Anenecuilco and Ayala declared for the revolution, it was after a nakedly fraudulent election stole the state governorship from Francisco Leyva's son Patricio and installed the first direct representative of the planter class. When landowner Pablo Escandón campaigned in Cuautla in 1909, the first words out of the mouths of the crowd that met him at the train station were the same counterhegemonic slogan from 1810 and 1855–61: "¡Mueran los gachupines!" ("Death to the Spaniards!").[35]

In Peru, by contrast, Nicolás de Piérola took power from a tarnished Cacerismo unable to stabilize a ruling coalition. After the War of the Pacific (1879–1884), President Andrés Cáceres had been unwilling to identify wholly with either his earlier enemies, the landowners who had collaborated with the Chilean occupation, or his ex-allies, the peasant guerrillas who had spearheaded the resistance to the Chilean army (Mallon 1983, 1987; Manrique 1981, 1988). By 1894, the death of Cacerista president Remigio Morales Bermúdez initiated an armed conflict for control of the state between the Caceristas and the Democratic party led by Piérola. By March 1895, Piérola had taken Lima and had begun the reorganization of the state.

The Pierolistas aimed to construct a state that was "relatively autonomous," free from the particular interests of classes or political factions. They reasoned that such a state, constituted above the political fray, could bring true progress to all the country's citizens and establish ef-

---

35. On Juan Francisco Lucas joining the revolution, see LaFrance and Thomson (1987); LaFrance (1984:88); and "Breves datos biográficos del señor General don Juan Francisco Lucas, proporcionados por el ex-Teniente Coronel Martín Rivera Torres," Personal Archive, Donna Rivera Moreno, Xochiapulco. On the process in Morelos, see Womack (1968:10–36; quote on p. 33).

fective and legitimate authority across the entire national territory. Establishing effective authority, however, directly contradicted the maintenance of state autonomy; and this contradiction was at the center of the process through which the Pierolista state established domination.

Beneath a positivist discourse of progress and modernization lay the age-old practices of political favoritism and violent repression. The "modern" Peruvian state, in its initial Pierolista form, was constructed by negotiating a zig-zag course between these contradictory markers of progress and cronyism, modernization and repression.[36] Piérola thus built the state on the corpse of the nineteenth-century popular movement, through an open alliance with sectors of the *hacendado* class in different Peruvian regions.

The impact of these alliances and contradictions was especially clear in emerging definitions of citizenship and the nation. In 1895, the first Pierolista congress ratified an earlier constitutional reform by the last Cacerista legislature that limited the right to vote to those who could read and write. For the first time since independence, Indians and other community members were not included in the suffrage. The justification for this change was made clear by the 1895 Senate commission: "The man who does not know how to read or write is not, nor can he be, a citizen in modern society."[37]

36. On Morales Bermúdez's death and the subsequent civil war, see Basadre (1970:93–128). The desire for a "disinterested" state emerges most clearly in the letters of Domingo F. Parra to Piérola. As special envoy, general troubleshooter, and personal friend to Piérola, Parra often wrote directly and sincerely of the overall concept and ambitions of the regime. See esp. BNP, Archivo Piérola, caja (antigua) 53, 1895–97, Correspondencia Oficial y Particular, "Carta de Domingo F. Parra a Nicolás de Piérola," Huancayo, May 14, 1896, and "Carta de Domingo F. Parra a Nicolás de Piérola," Huancayo, May 18, 1896. Also Archivo Piérola (1895–1897), Correspondencia Oficial y Particular, "Carta Reservada de Domingo F. Parra a Nicolás de Piérola," Ayacucho, Apr. 29, 1897. For the appearance of similar discourse in the writings of others, see BNP, D4505, "Memoria del Prefecto de Huancavelica," 1895; Archivo Piérola, caja (antigua) 53, 1895–97, Correspondencia Oficial y Particular, "Carta de F. Urbieta a Nicolás de Piérola, sobre la carretera al Pichis y el enganche de peones," Jauja, Apr. 5, 1897, "Carta de E. Zapata a Nicolás de Piérola," Tarma, Feb. 19, 1897, and "Carta de E. Zapata a Nicolás de Piérola," Tarma, Mar. 19, 1897. Some sources on the "relative autonomy" of the state are Poulantzas (1969, 1973, and 1976); Miliband (1970, 1973); Laclau (1975); Carnoy (1984); Hamilton (1982); and Evans, Rueschemeyer, and Skocpol (1985).

37. Peru, Congreso Ordinario de 1895, *Diario de los Debates de la H. Cámara de Senadores* (Lima: Imprenta de "El País," 1895), 443.

Rather than through serious consideration of the concerns and demands of peasant movements, domination was thus reestablished through the fragmentation and isolation of political constituencies and of their ability to fight back. Divide-and-rule rather than incorporation; neocolonial reunification rather than national consolidation. The discourses about savagery and primitiveness that accompanied and legitimated hierarchy were in fact generated by an alliance between ambitious local notables and a supposedly "national" state unable effectively to incorporate the demands and visions of indigenous peasant guerrillas. This same state, in its Pierolista form, climbed into the twentieth century on the backs of a peasantry repressed through blood and fire. As it came, it elaborated the myth of its own benevolent indigenismo, a myth parallel to that of an isolated and passive peasantry with no interest in the outside world.

Peru's subsequent political history suggests that fragmentation and clientelism also impeded the further consolidation of a truly national state. In the 1920s and again in the 1960s, when new waves of popular movements renewed the possibility of a national revolution, the legacy of repression through fragmentation was lengthened and strengthened instead. It would not be until the end of the 1970s that illiterates were once again granted the vote in Peru.[38]

Returning to the imagery of Corrigan and Sayer, we can consider state formation in Mexico and Peru as cultural revolutions extending over a long period of time, during which people constructed each "great arch" with historically and culturally distinct materials. I have not examined the whole duration of the process here, but I hope to have made clear how very different was each "great arch" when it was done. In Mexico, whatever the chinks and missing bricks, the second half of the arch was completed, and the foundation has held pretty well. This endurance is due to the strength of popular political culture, submerged and repressed during the nineteenth century but reconstituted and reconstructed in the first half of the twentieth. Its partial incorporation into the postrevolutionary state helped build hegemony in Mexico, precisely through the establishment of a common moral and social project. Arguably at least, the survival of such a project into the 1980s, frayed and worn as it has become since 1968, helps explain why the political crisis of the last few years has still been fought out within existing state structures.

38. It was only with the Constitution of 1979 that illiterates once again had the right to vote.

In Peru, solid construction of the "great arch" stopped somewhere around halfway, and the rest of the structure was composed only of veneer. The greater fragmentation of popular political cultures, their more successful repression through neocolonial "divide-and-rule," impeded the mounting of a successful challenge to state authority in the 1920s. The subsequent story in Peru, therefore, has been a series of successive marginalizations of counterhegemonic movements, and the failure to build a common social and moral project—though not for lack of trying. The crisis of the 1980s emerges, in this context, as a collapse of state authority. It has been fought out not within state structures but in the armed conflicts that increasingly eat away at their margins.

A similar distinction emerges if we view the comparison from the perspective of hegemonic processes. In Mexico, the nature of nineteenth-century hegemonic processes allowed for the reemergence of a broad and powerful popular movement that transformed the succession crisis of 1910 into a major social revolution. By 1940, this had resulted in an effective and hegemonic state. In Peru, on the other hand, a more fragmented popular legacy was unable to transform the crises of the 1920s and 1960s into social revolutions. Though fairly broad agrarian and urban popular movements did take place, especially in the 1960s, the ultimate result was further repression and crisis rather than hegemony. This difference in hegemonic processes lies at the root of the distinction between a functioning though frayed Mexican state in the 1990s, and a Peruvian state in the advanced stages of decomposition.

A final image clinches these differences. Contrast Cuauhtémoc Cárdenas, counterhegemonic hero at least in part because his father built the hegemonic state, and Sendero Luminoso, active precisely in those areas of central Peru where nineteenth-century guerrillas also fought. For Cárdenas, the conflict is over what the hegemonic legacy really means. For Sendero, it is about the total bankruptcy of the Peruvian state. In Puebla and Morelos in 1988, villagers fought about the legitimacy of the process through which their votes were counted; in the early 1990s, they struggle over the true meaning of the agrarian legacy of 1910. In Junín and Ayacucho, the struggles between Senderistas and the anti-Senderista village militias called *rondas* continue to reproduce the figure of the ever-vigilant guerrilla, eternally on the margins of a nonexistent nation.

ROMANA FALCÓN

Force and the Search for Consent:
The Role of the Jefaturas Políticas of Coahuila
in National State Formation

The making of the set of activities, institutions, and social forms accepted as "legitimate" that go into shaping a national state, capable of imposing its domination and something of its world view on society's different strata, involves long historical processes fraught with accidents and contradictions. The case of Mexico is no exception.

According to Corrigan and Sayer's very broad perspective in *The Great Arch* (1985:2–4, 141–42), modern state formation should properly be understood as a profound cultural revolution, one that tends to impose a "moral regulation" on the most disparate spheres of a society. The formation of a state is not an event that can be considered concluded at some point; rather, it is a process that is always being constructed, sustained, and reconstructed by particular agents and agencies. The formation of a state is, in essence, a continuous and difficult interweaving, in part violent and in part consensual, between individuals and social groups on the one hand and those who govern and dominate on the other.

In this making of a modern state, those who govern always strive to make less obvious or less visible the systematic inequalities that characterize any society. Such inequalities in modern societies are always structured along lines of profound differences of class, gender, ethnicity, religion, and occupation. Corrigan and Sayer have applied the notion of

This work is part of a broader study of the *jefaturas políticas* in the states of Coahuila and Mexico during the Porfiriato.

"moral regulation" to those attempts to render as normal, natural, and legitimate what are in fact particular premises of historically constructed social orders. Hence the vital importance that this "moral regulation" acquires for any relations of domination, and the reason the attempt to achieve it plays such a central role in the construction of modern states. From this point of view, force and consent are the two inseparable elements that explain the intricate relationship that, over time, unifies and opposes institutions and agencies of government against the other various components of the social fabric.

The purpose of this essay is to take Corrigan and Sayer's perspective as an inspiration, albeit not in the sense of adopting it as a general model that might "explain" the historical construction of the Mexican state, but rather as a series of concepts and metaphors that can facilitate the interpretation of these processes. Within this larger problematic, this study will concentrate on examining the variety of mechanisms, formal and informal, through which the agencies of government entered into an intense and multifaceted relationship with society's different strata. Their objective was to construct a relatively centralized command structure, but one capable of imposing its policies on people in the far corners of Mexico, as well as up and down the social hierarchy. Sometimes these relations of domination were sustained by openly coercive forms; sometimes they were based on attempted forms of "legitimacy" and consensus or, more often, on attitudes that the dominated perceived, or liked to perceive, as consensus.

The focus of this study is an institution created during the first century of Mexico's independence. It was designed to perform an essential role in the complex social, political, economic, and cultural integration associated with the gradual construction of the state and the nation. The *jefaturas políticas* flourished toward the close of the colonial period along with the liberal Constitution of Cádiz of 1812; and, with ups and downs, they held sway throughout Mexico until they were definitively abolished by the revolutionary Constitution of 1917. This powerful institution—which, curiously, has not received the scholarly attention it deserves—was created precisely for the purpose of supporting efforts to shape Mexican society within an integrated nation, a centralized political structure, and a relatively modern state, though one that was always authoritarian. In reality, however, many of these efforts fell short of success.

Before taking up the substance of this study, it is worth briefly introducing these personages. The reader should bear in mind that in the course of this first, turbulent century, no single, general evolution produced the *jefaturas políticas*, but rather several, at times contradictory, evolutionary processes, given the great diversity of local forms that the institution adopted. To begin with, the institution itself assumed various names: *gefes de departamento* (department chiefs), *gefes de partido* (district chiefs), *gefes de policía de departamento* (department police chiefs), *jefes políticos* (political chiefs), and *prefectos* and *subprefectos políticos* (political prefects and subprefects), among others. What's more, although some of the powers delegated to the *jefaturas* were very similar in many of the country's federal states—for example, their duty to maintain the "public peace"—others merely bore a vague resemblance or varied considerably.

The complexity and diversity of this institution stand out in an analysis of its role in relation to one of the central problems of the early period of independence, which is also paramount in state formation: the dispersion or concentration of political and military authority. On occasion, the *jefes políticos* acted in the spirit in which they had been conceived: as centralizing forces, anxious to extend the links of domination forged in the state or national capital. But at many other times they assumed the opposite position: they became the spokesmen and agents of powerful regional interests—landowners, merchants, or local elites—and they sought to further local autonomy. Thus, a closely related question is the problem of whom the *jefes políticos* represented. Although they usually answered directly to the state governor—at least this was true during the long regime of Porfirio Díaz (1876–1911)—they were often appointed or their functions defined from Mexico City. At other times, when they directly represented powerful local factions, the *jefes políticos* helped to preserve the delicate regional balance of power.

Another important variable, one that gave rise to many social tensions, was the formal method for selecting the *jefes políticos*. In some places, such as Puebla, the governor chose among three candidates presented to him. In others, such as Chihuahua early in the Porfiriato, these public officials were elected by popular vote. In still others, such as Coahuila between 1874 and 1882, they were elected by the municipal authorities of the district. But by and large—as eventually in Chihuahua, Coahuila, the State of Mexico, and San Luis Potosí—they were simply appointed to and removed from office at the governor's pleasure (Falcón 1988:429).

The central idea underlying this study is that Mexico's *jefaturas políticas* as an institution were designed to organize power and society. Indeed, within their particular limits, the *jefaturas políticas* played a decisive role in state formation, as much in those projects that involved force and coercion as in those that aimed at consensus and legitimacy.

In the formal workings of the government, the *jefes políticos* headed complex and relatively useful political machines that allowed them to bridge different social spheres. They did this in at least three senses: by linking the dominant class with the dominated, national and state power with municipal and village authority, and the propertied classes with the dispossessed. Thanks to their wide repertoire of legal, political, military, financial, judicial, and clientelistic resources, the *jefaturas políticas* could extend their reach to the inhabitants of the smallest settlements, *rancherías* (hamlets), haciendas, mining camps, and towns. Their contribution to modern state formation was their strategic function as intermediaries—formal or informal, but virtually inevitable—between those who exercised power and those excluded from it.

The *jefaturas'* domination was not anchored solely in their extensive legal functions, which, at least in theory, helped to consolidate the system. In practice, their delegated powers were easily parleyed into an even greater authority, which fostered extended networks of patronage and clientele. Beyond that, the *jefes políticos* imposed their dominance through traditional, personalist, petty, corrupt, and inefficient means, often to the detriment of the formal image and capacity of the state. Nevertheless, it was precisely this combination of legal functions and personal dominance that enabled these functionaries to run relatively efficient political machines, and to utilize them for integrating, channeling, or repressing those who made demands or refused to accept the rules of the game imposed by the oligarchy. That meant peasants, Indians, artisans, and laborers; members of the middle class; large landowners, merchants, manufacturers, *caciques*, and *caudillos*; trade unions, political parties, and factions; village and municipal authorities.

On the other hand, this institution orchestrated many of the functions, rituals, and laws aimed at governing the conduct of individuals. It attempted to make such practices of power routine, customary, and seemingly normal; to give them the appearance of legitimacy and acceptability. In this way the *jefaturas* combined coercion with practices aimed at achieving the internalization of the individual's subjection. They interwove force with consent.

This essay will focus on the principal forms—whether coercive or aimed at securing acceptance, or at least the image of acceptance, among the dominated—through which the *jefaturas políticas* tried to instill in the common people of Mexico the world view, laws, policies, routines, and rituals of state and of its ruling elites.[1] Special attention will be paid to the relationship between this institution and the groups and individuals that formed the lowest strata of society, given that these people were the ones most subjugated and least able to defend themselves.

The *jefaturas políticas* attempted to shape the customs, thinking, behavior, and identity of the common person, as well as the way that person conceived of his or her place in the world. The institution's major role in administering the laws and rituals of government served to define people as citizens, voters, taxpayers, militiamen, soldiers, property owners, workers, tenants, the unemployed, "vagrants," and other categorizations useful to the general structure of domination. All of these were eventually translated into individual and collective forms of organization, representation, and identification, forms that the Mexican state and its particular agents could consider and treat—or not—as legal, or else as "legitimate."

Within this overall project of regulation, the *jefaturas* also helped further one of the Porfirian regime's central legitimating goals: economic growth and integration. In this sphere, the *jefaturas* helped to regulate private property and, what constitutes the other side of the coin, to police and regulate those who did not have property. Beyond that, some of the principal powers delegated to the *jefaturas* were those relating to political dominance and the use of armed force. Because of their coercive and openly violent features, these powers usually entailed dramatic costs— sometimes death—for people in the small communities.

This essay deals with the state of Coahuila, located in Mexico's northern desert. Its time frame is the last thirty years of the nineteenth century and the first decade of the twentieth; that is, the period spanning the long administration dominated by General Porfirio Díaz.

In principle, this account seeks to record the interaction of state agencies with individuals and social groups, giving equal weight to both forces. For historians, however, this objective is often impossible to achieve. This essay is based on local, state, national, and foreign archives,

1. Elsewhere I have examined in depth the way this institution contributed, in northern Mexico, to imposing the concept of nation and the world view held by settlers of Mexican and Spanish origin on the world view held by the native inhabitants—the pejoratively labeled "savage Indians" (Falcón forthcoming). I have also detailed the diverse types of legal powers that the *jefaturas* enjoyed, as well as the fundamental changes they underwent during the first century of independence (Falcón 1991).

which, although they contain numerous letters, complaints, petitions, and other communications from particular persons—often, indeed, from the lower classes—basically provide a "history from above." If it is not the only possible perspective, it is at least, and fortunately, an essential one.

Finally, it should not be forgotten that reality and history are plagued with paradoxes and contradictions. Up to this point, it might seem that this essay aims to buttress the idea that the *jefaturas políticas* played a decisive role in imposing the state's domination on society. That would be far from the purpose or findings of this study. The *jefes'* very excesses, their corruption, ineptitude, and inflexibility, translated into structural weaknesses for the old regime. Ultimately, an analysis of this institution is as indispensable for understanding the gains of the Mexican state as it is for explaining the Porfirian regime's eventual decline and fall. Once put into action, the grandiose ideas that constituted the project of the Mexican state, its laws, and its forms of government typically lost the spirit that supposedly had animated them. In mundane, quotidian affairs, they were reduced to petty and distorted expressions.

THE REALM OF THE PRIVATE

Taking the case of England as an example, Corrigan and Sayer insist that the "moral regulation" from which the dominant class needs to derive part of its "legitimacy" is painfully constructed through constant, mutually formative struggles between those who have the necessary power to further their own project and those whom they dominate. Particularly significant among such formative struggles are those through which government regulates a series of matters impinging on private life, property, and the domestic world of the family.

In Mexico, the *jefaturas políticas* were one of the important government agencies for introducing the rules, activities, and rituals through which the state attempted to extend its reach into the private life of the individual. The *jefaturas* enjoyed this privileged position because the institution was conceived precisely as a link between federal and state authorities and local entities—the villages and municipalities. Equally important, the law also made the *jefaturas* the reverse channel through which "all manner of complaints, questions, and claims of villages and individuals" should flow to the highest level of government.[2]

2. *Ley orgánica del artículo 78 bis de la constitución, dado por el gobernador interino constitucional, 25 de agosto de 1874*, arts. 2, 3, 12, 29; *Constitución del Estado de Coahuila dada el*

The law gave this institution a major role in the task of implanting the rules and rituals related to "social morals." Such matters ranged from regulating public amusements to dealing with policies of enormous philosophical and political significance in forging a national identity. A particularly notable issue was the secularization of society and the separation of church and state, an issue that remained at the heart of the principal transformations and major conflicts of nineteenth-century Mexico.

Virtually from the outset, the young nation was engulfed in a struggle to delimit the ecclesiastical and civil spheres of power. In 1867, after the defeat of the French invasion (which the church and the "conservative" faction had supported), the so-called liberals managed, weapons in hand, to restore the republic. They obtained the political and military power, as well as part of the needed legitimacy, to impose their national project.

The new ruling elite seemed confident that it could map out in detail the political and social structure of the emerging state, as well as its primacy over the church, by creating a powerful government legal structure. The *jefaturas políticas* constituted one part of the administrative apparatus designed to carry out the reform laws that, beginning in midcentury, proclaimed that primacy. The *jefaturas* were also to help construct a "liberal" Mexico, one the laws themselves defined as entrepreneurial, secular, and free—free from both the old ties of the colonial past and the disaster and turbulence of early independence. In a climate still feverish from the bloody civil war, the process was not without violence.

Thus it was during this period that in many parts of Mexico, laws were promulgated establishing and reshaping the *jefaturas políticas* as powerful organizing mechanisms. The law enacted in Coahuila in August 1874 reiterated or updated many of the original powers that, since 1827, had been delegated to what were then called *gefes de departamento* (Falcón 1991). The Coahuila law specified that the *jefaturas políticas* should concern themselves particularly with official state tasks and activities and should see to it "that the relevant laws are fully complied with." The *jefaturas políticas* thereby became one cog in the complex machinery through which state agencies attempted to appropriate, in this case, the rites and ceremonies marking the chief events of a person's life: birth, death, marriage, and even divorce.[3] In keeping with the tone of the

---

21 *de febrero de 1882*, art. 89, para. 4. According to article 87, paragraph 22, the *jefes políticos* were charged with seeing to it that all public offices were furnished with collections of the requisite laws for "settling business."

3. *Ley orgánica . . . 1874*, arts. 15, 16.

reform laws, and superseding the ecclesiastical authority that heretofore had kept the official registry and, even more important, had legitimated such events, the Mexican state now imposed its own legitimating authority. Clearly, to surmount the ideological and political force of religion and the clergy in nineteenth-century Mexico was overwhelmingly one of the ruling elite's aspirations. For the great majority of Mexicans, however, the true rituals and sacraments continued to be those administered by the church. Still, the civil authorities formulated their own rituals and ceremonies, seeking to put their own stamp on those moments that are of prime importance in every society.

Because education is also a fundamental element in state formation and in regulating social classes, the civil authorities also concentrated their efforts on the schools. In the Mexico of the last third of the nineteenth century, with the conservative faction recently defeated on the battlefield, education was a highly controversial issue and the source of a good deal of violence. In Coahuila, the *jefes políticos* were charged with enforcing some of the new rules aimed at secularizing schools, thereby remanding to the state this task so vital to the creation of a national identity. Establishing such primacy was a process fraught with tensions, given the opposition of the church and many social sectors, which saw the move as an intrusion into areas considered to be outside the state's jurisdiction.

In Coahuila, as in many other parts of Mexico, severe constraints were placed on religious schools. Consequently, the *jefes políticos* of the Restored Republic and the Porfiriato regularly had to decide cases such as that of the *Hermanas de la Caridad* (Sisters of Charity) of Saltillo, who in 1875 asked the *jefatura política* of the Central District for permission to continue their traditional work in education.[4] The constitution promulgated in 1882 by Governor Evaristo Madero—grandfather of the future revolutionary leader—emphasized that the *jefes políticos* should exercise control over educational matters and required them to preside over all meetings of "public instruction whenever they deemed it necessary in order to minister . . . to the well-being and needs of the people." The *jefes políticos* consequently were obliged to devote much of their energy to looking after the primary schools in villages, settlements, *rancherías,* and haciendas, and to making sure that students were supplied with essential school furniture and learning materials.[5]

4. AMS, PM, c.118, exp. 3, 2f, "Solicitud a la Jefatura Política del Centro," 1875.
5. *Ley orgánica* . . . 1874, art 4; *Constitución* . . . 1882, art. 108, 87, paras. 22, 28; AMS,

Another central influence in state formation is the government's capacity for producing statistics, censuses, and other basic information. This reveals the very weight and form of rule that the central government is able to impose on society. The preservation and systematization of facts not only constitutes a powerful tool for defining reality in accordance with particular interests and for establishing routines to benefit the structure of domination, it also shapes how people identify themselves and define their place in the world (Corrigan and Sayer 1985:21). Under the Coahuila law, the *jefes políticos* could require all offices and employees to provide any information the *jefes* thought necessary for the administration of good government. This allowed them to keep detailed lists on the most diverse topics, from agricultural production in the municipalities to monthly population changes.[6]

As it did all over the world in the nineteenth century, growing state involvement in Mexican private life led to the introduction of new practices in the field of public health. Once again, the *jefaturas políticas* participated in no small way. They guarded their districts against the spread of contagious or endemic diseases—terrible scourges that decimated the population; they saw to it that municipal public health boards were established; they carried out vaccination campaigns.[7] They also enforced standards of public health and cleanliness in barracks, jails, and certain town and village establishments, such as butcher shops.[8]

Historically, in other processes of state formation, such as that of medieval England, it was common for authorities to devote much of their energy to regulating dramatic performances, publications, and other types of private and social entertainment—the act of "making public" in all its forms. In Coahuila, the *jefaturas* regulated a portion of these activities, thereby accustoming people to accepting the government's authority extended into yet another part of their private lives. Townsfolk and villagers had to apply to the *jefaturas* for permission to take part in

---

6. JP, c.7, e.13, Report to the Jefatura Política, Central District, on outlays for children's school and meeting room in the municipality of Patos, 1885.

6. *Constitución . . . 1882*, art. 108, 87, para. 28; AMS, JP, c.9, exp. 1, no. 5259, Report to the Jefatura Política, Central District, Jan. 7, 1891, on changes in population occurring in Saltillo in December 1890.

7. *Ley orgánica . . . 1874*, arts. 23, 24.

8. AMS, PM, c.128, e.14, 5f, no. 1056, Petition from the Office of the Commander's General Headquarters to the Jefatura Política, 1885; ibid., c.223, e.101, 4f, no. 11972, Jefatura Política, Central District, to the Ayuntamiento of Saltillo, 1876.

games during fairs and to organize private gatherings. As late as the 1880s, the Coahuila government drafted detailed regulations for dances. *Tertulias* (small informal gatherings), which generally took place in private homes, were exempt from paying taxes as long as they advised the *jefatura política* first. On the other hand, masked balls, song fests, and other highly popular activities had to pay a tax so they could count on permission to take place.[9]

Equally or more important than private and special occasions was the regular observance of civic celebrations, festivities that helped create a unifying identity throughout the country. To regulate and impose these observances as custom was to foster an identity that might at least appear to rival, or even overshadow, the one emanating from the *terruño*, the locality associated with long-held customs, traditions, and religion. The *jefaturas* saw to it that key state celebrations were observed with all due magnificence: for example, the commemoration of independence from Spain or the recent victories of the "liberals," such as the battle of the Fifth of May, when the Mexicans defeated the invading French army.[10] The *jefaturas* also supervised all protocol connected with government activities, notably the governor's annual address and the various municipal, state, and national elections.[11] Obviously, the man or woman on the street must have perceived many of these state celebrations merely as external rites and rituals, difficult to internalize or accept. It is impossible to determine how deep or how rapidly such efforts penetrated to create individual conceptions of a national identity.

In matters pertaining to private life, certain of the *jefes políticos'* actions were entirely removed from the strategy of creating routines and seeking consensus. Indeed, some of their actions tellingly marked the government's coercive character. Nowhere is this clearer than in the judicial sphere, where these functionaries enjoyed powers that enabled them to exercise great dominance over the common people. The Coahuila law charged the *jefes* with overseeing the establishment and functioning of jails, church and charity hospices, and hospitals.[12] In addition, the law

9. *Periódico Oficial* (Saltillo), June 10, 1880; AMS, PM, c.123, e.52, 1f, no. 582, Jefatura Política, Central District, to the Ayuntamiento of Saltillo, 1880.

10. AMS, PM, c.121, e.41, 54 fjs, no. 407, Jefe Político, Central District, to the Ayuntamiento of Saltillo, 1878.

11. AMS, PM, c.4, e.102, Secretaría General de Gobierno to the Jefe Político, Central District, Jan. 30, 1886.

12. *Ley orgánica . . .* 1874, art. 4; *Constitución . . .* 1882, art. 108 and 87, subparagraph 22.

endowed the *jefes* with such broad and diffuse judicial authority that when, in their opinion, "public security" required it, and by written order, they were empowered to break into and search houses, arrest people, and turn them over to the appropriate judge. It is interesting to note the importance that the law granted to the *jefes'* particular judgment; also the moralistic tone with which it authorized them to fine "individuals who disobeyed them or were disrespectful, punishing, in a correctional facility for such offenses, with up to fifteen days of arrest according to the circumstances, those unable to pay the fine."[13] This task the *jefes* carried out with apparent consistency and precision, judging from the detailed registries of those imprisoned by their orders.[14]

So broad and vague were the *jefes'* judicial powers that they could order offenders to serve out their sentences by laboring, under the *jefes'* supervision, on public works for the "benefit of the district."[15] This frequently led to corruption and abuse. Many *jefes políticos* ordered certain detainees to be placed "at their disposal," so that when certain "formalities" were completed, they could harness the prisoners' labor for their own benefit and that of other private individuals, family members, or favorites. The wide margin of interpretation that the laws left to these functionaries—to define, for instance, what precisely constituted an "act of disrespect for authority"—fostered the personal, clientelistic empires they accrued. It was not at all unusual for them to deprive individuals of their liberty at whim or convenience, to imprison all sorts of opponents, and to appropriate the labor not only of prisoners but also of drunkards, vagrants, even villagers and rancheros. If ever an image was impressed in the popular memory, it was that of the *jefe político* as hatchet man, the source of all manner of excesses and outrages. That is precisely what the regime that arose from the Mexican revolution sought to abolish once and for all.

Furthermore, in a political structure such as the Díaz regime, humble citizens had virtually no way of redressing the acts of functionaries other than to file formal complaints or engage in the kind of "everyday" forms of resistance and "infrapolitics" that James Scott presents so evocatively in his recent work (see, e.g., 1985, 1990). Typical of the former was the

13. Ibid., arts. 17, 19.

14. AMS, PM, c.128, e.20, 18f, no. 1062, Registry of prisoners sentenced by the Jefatura Política, Central District, 1885.

15. AMS, JP, c.10, exp. 31, Constancio de la Garza to the Jefe Político, Central District, May 9, 1890, referring to two persons under arrest.

accusation made against the *jefe político* of Sierra Mojada, which appeared in an opposition newspaper in 1893. It asserted that the official had used the labor of several prisoners not for public works "but for a water tank that was being constructed in his house," a practice so normal in his case that "for that he incarcerates even for insignificant offenses."[16]

Another example of this arbitrary behavior that took place in 1888 is worthy of particular note because it highlights one of the few formal defenses that wronged parties could bring against the *jefaturas* and how, in a political system as hierarchical as the Díaz regime, the case had to be pleaded all the way to the president himself. On this occasion, Díaz saw fit to reprimand the governor for the

> unjustly energetic conduct of the *jefe político* of Sierra Mojada who . . . commits many abuses, for example ordering the police to haul in as many persons as they may find in an inebriated state and sending them the following day to work in the mines he owns, particularly if among these same persons there are good miners[,] . . . and other similar things that have agitated those people to such a state of violence . . . [that] I have considered it my duty to draw your attention [to the matter].[17]

PROPERTY OWNERS AND THE DISPOSSESSED

A profound and highly complex relationship exists between the formation of modern states and the establishment of propitious conditions for capitalist development. In Porfirian Mexico, economic growth and modernization—which in certain sectors, such as communications, was quite impressive—became, almost explicitly, the regime's principal source of legitimacy. Throughout Mexico, the *jefaturas políticas* did their part to advance the economy and private enterprise. In Coahuila, the *jefaturas* tried to shape society in aspects ranging from the creation of new patterns of economic interaction to the regulation of private property and the containment and discipline of those who had none.

One such project was the institution of a uniform system of weights, measures, and coinage throughout the country, supplanting the particular practices and traditions of each locality. Here, the *jefes* had to confront the rejection, by small commercial enterprises in Coahuila's towns and vil-

16. *Diario del Hogar* (Mexico City), June 15, 1893.

17. CPD, leg. 13, c.14, doc. 6785, Porfirio Díaz to José María Garza Galán, July 11, 1888.

lages, of the decimal system imposed in 1884. Similarly, one year later, they strove to overcome the public's resistance to the decimal silver coins the federal government sought to introduce.[18]

In terms of directly affecting the economic situation of individuals and businesses, the *jefaturas* had the authority, under certain conditions, to modify property assessments for tax purposes. Given the enormous power they derived from this function, the *jefaturas* were swamped with petitions for "capital reductions" from large landholders, merchants, manufacturers, and ordinary citizens. Typical was the memorial for tax relief submitted to the *jefe político* of the Central District by Camila Ramos in 1890. Ramos pointed out that, inasmuch as for some time the municipality of Ramos Arizpe had been "undergoing a notable decline due to crop failures," with the ensuing loss of revenues, she no longer had enough "even to cover my expenses."[19]

Other powers related to the use of land and water allowed the *jefaturas* to foment capitalist development. Ever since the formation of the state of Coahuila and Texas in the third decade of the nineteenth century, the *jefaturas* had played a role, albeit a rather modest one, in gradually eradicating what many considered one of the chief obstacles to Mexico's overall development: corporate social organizations, such as guilds, community groups, and above all, communal landholdings. The government's intense battle against them was colored by elements of moral and racial superiority. As the century wore on, the *jefaturas* in Coahuila extended the scope of their power over property by issuing decrees related to specific cases. Thus, on the same day that the Restored Republic reinstated the *jefaturas*—August 19, 1874—the local executive decreed the compulsory and immediate privatization of land and water in the old community of San Esteban.[20] During the Porfiriato, this type of order was by no means unusual. The *jefes* regulated the amount of water the local *ayuntamientos* (town councils) could sell, and *hacendados* and rancheros routinely applied

18. AMS, JP, c.1, e.23, 1f, Comandante de Infantería to Jefatura Política, Central District, Nov. 9, 1885, requesting it to obligate merchants to accept without discount the coins already being used to pay Mexican soldiers. The provisions for the adoption of the decimal system appeared in the *Periódico Oficial*, Feb. 23, 1883, indicating that the decimal system would be obligatory as of Jan. 1, 1884.

19. AMS, JP, c.10, exp. 71, Camila Ramos to Jefatura Política, Central District, Aug. 22, 1890.

20. Decree 205, Aug. 19, 1874, issued by Antonio García Carrillo, jefe político, San Esteban.

to the *jefes* to obtain the rights to watercourses, the scarcest and most valuable resource in those desert lands.[21]

The times when the *jefes'* intervention really stood out, however, were those critical occasions when tensions between classes and social groups came to a boil. This occurred whenever serious conflicts arose over property, or between laborers and owners of plantations, mines, or factories. Inasmuch as the *jefes'* primary responsibility was to maintain public security and ensure the social peace, their presence at those moments served to remind the opposing parties that the state could always resolve matters by force, if necessary. Yet, being able to *prevent* violence was a matter of great pride to the *jefes políticos*. It also showed their mettle to their formal superiors like the governor, or informal superiors like General Bernardo Reyes. Chief of military operations in Coahuila and factotum of northeastern Mexico in the 1890s, Reyes was Díaz's personal agent for controlling the region. Thus in March 1894, the *jefe político* of Sierra Mojada boasted to Reyes of having been "summoned to maintain order, and there was no turmoil" when, without making use of the police, he was able to prevent the destruction of a line of boundary stones marking the hacienda La Explotadora.[22]

In several ways, not limited to their strictly legal functions, the *jefaturas* acted to spur the economic boom under way in Coahuila during the Porfiriato. Indeed, few other Mexican regional cases illustrate more transparently the close link between this institution and the growth of dependent capitalist production. Particularly important was the *jefes'* ability to build personal contacts with men "of great drive and weight" in the region. Thus, in 1892, when it was decided to extend the commercial functions of the U.S. consulate at Piedras Negras, the consul's first act was to call on the local *jefe político*, an uncle of Governor José María Garza Galán. The *jefe*, according to the consular representative, showed great courtesy and interest in creating a climate conducive to improving commercial and diplomatic relations between the two countries. An hour after the interview ended, the consul, much to his surprise, was in turn called on by the *jefe político*, accompanied by an entourage of the "principal local

21. AMS, JP, c.9, exp. 6, Case records on the sale of water in Villa de Patos, Mar. 11, 1890; AMS, PM, c.133, exp. 68, 5 fjs., Jesús María Siller to Jefe Político, Central District, 1890, application for a watercourse.

22. CEHMC, FDLI, carpeta 20, leg. 3926, Bernardo Reyes to Fernández Leal, forwarding the report of the Jefe Político of Sierra Mojada, Mar. 15, 1894; ibid., leg. 3833, doc. 1, Reyes to Romero Rubio, Mar. 20, 1894.

residents" and officials. The procession was led by a marching band and followed by a servant who offered goblets of wine. The *jefe* toasted the President of the United States, and the consul responded by drinking to the health of President Díaz. Undoubtedly, one might say, this ritual was intended to contribute to the molding of local society. The consul actually noted as much, reporting that he highly valued "this courtesy for the good effect it cannot fail to have upon the attitude of the residents of Sierra Mojada."[23]

The *jefaturas* played a pivotal role in the development of the mining sector. Indeed, their task as mining promoters was sometimes so crucial that Díaz himself made a special effort to see that they were doing their job. Of the relatively scarce correspondence about the *jefaturas políticas* that passed between the *Palacio Nacional* and the *palacio de gobierno* at Saltillo, an important part consisted of reprimands from Díaz to the governors when he believed that certain *jefes* were hindering or inadequately fostering the progress of these businesses. A notable case in point was the abuses committed by the *jefe político* of Sierra Mojada described earlier. This prefect illegally imprisoned miners and compelled them to work without pay in his own mines.[24]

Besides showing the *jefes'* self-aggrandizement and ineptitude, such tensions mirror the typical clashes between public officials at all levels, as well as between officials and the very industrialists and capitalists whose interests these government agents were supposed to favor. Taken together, such frictions reveal the complexity and the weakness of the Porfirian machine. They also demonstrate that the projects of the Mexican state frequently fell far short of defining what would actually happen.

Nevertheless, the *jefaturas'* vital function for the advancement of mining appears frequently in the political elite's internal discourse, and figures prominently among the stated reasons for establishing the *jefaturas* as an institution. As Governor Garza Galán wrote to Díaz, it was precisely because of the economic boom flourishing in Sierra del Carmen that, in early 1889, he had decided to establish a *jefatura política* there "for the greater organization of those affairs and in order to guarantee the interests that should develop."[25]

The foresight of this move rapidly proved itself in favor of the mine

23. NA, RG 84, Consulate at Piedras Negras, Despatch Book, c.8, f.221, Consul to the Assistant Secretary of State, June 1, 1892.

24. See the quotation cited at note 17.

25. CPD, l.13, c.4, doc. 1947, Garza Galán to Díaz, Feb. 16, 1888.

owners. In August of that year, three hundred miners declared one of the relatively few strikes of the Coahuilan Porfiriato. Immediately, Garza Galán arranged with General Reyes to send in a detachment of federal forces, which, according to the press, would serve "to reestablish order." Privately, Garza Galán's reason was more specific: "for the purpose of backing" the *jefatura's* authority "in its acts of trying to subdue the strikers who have disturbed the peace." Against those the governor called the "ringleaders," the authorities decided to exercise full severity, underscoring their abiding interest in strengthening ties between the capitalist elite and the government. They dragooned the leaders into the federal army and sent them far away from Coahuila, where they could be properly "cared for."[26] Thus the *jefaturas'* nominal role in promoting mining translated back to their fundamental function of imposing order and discipline on the common people.

It is important to emphasize the clear sense of class implicit in the acts of Coahuila's authorities throughout the Porfiriato, the *jefes políticos* included. As the 1889 strike shows, severe punishment was almost inevitable whenever those opposing the regime belonged to the broader base of the social pyramid. Conversely, whenever the opponents belonged to factions of the same economic and political elite, the regime responded with amnesty, negotiation, courtesy, and partial acceptance of their demands (Falcón 1988). Such was the case in the armed rebellion of mid-1893, in which the protagonists were "notables" from business and the local government; they represented, among other prominent families, that of Venustiano Carranza, the future revolutionary leader and president. Thus, like other officials throughout the structure of domination, the *jefaturas* utilized the state's armed forces selectively, according to their opponents' place in the social hierarchy.

Recourse to arms was not the sole coercive tool with which the *jefaturas* and other state agencies disciplined and controlled the laboring poor. Few legislative acts reveal so dramatic a sense of class underlying the definition and coercive treatment of society's lowest strata as the laws on vagrancy. With deep roots reaching back to the colonial period, the Coahuila law during both the Restored Republic and the Porfiriato required the *jefaturas políticas* to punish "those who had no trade," or who did not habitually work at one, with penalties ranging from six months' to two

26. CEHMC, FDLI, Copiadores (cop.) 1, doc. 113, f. 129, Reyes to Garza Galán, Aug. 8, 1889; *El Tiempo* (Mexico City), Aug. 15, 1889, quoted in Leticia Reina, *Las luchas populares en México en el siglo XIX* (México, CIESAS, 1983), p. 354.

years' labor on public works or the equivalent in penal servitude. Thus the Mexican state, practically speaking, made it a crime for a laborer to abandon his job and his employer; it thereby intended to guarantee a labor force always at the disposal of those who had the resources to employ it. In 1882, Coahuilan law emphasized that it was the *jefes políticos'* "paramount obligation . . . to persecute vagrancy . . . and to impose on vagrants the corrective penalties prescribed by the law."[27]

Needless to say, such legislation became yet another source of the personal dominance and clientelism so characteristic of Porfirian magistrates, *ayuntamiento* members, and *jefes políticos*. It permitted them, for example, to incarcerate whomever they wished on the charge of being a "vagrant," and thereby create yet another source of free labor for supposedly public works.

FORCE AND PACIFICATION

Max Weber's classic conception of the state stresses the state's claim to a monopoly on the legitimate use of force. According to this paradigm, one of the main elements in state formation relates precisely to the regulation of this power: defining who has legitimate access to arms, under what conditions, and for what ends. The growing success of this particular claim to legitimacy positions the state as an impersonal power over and above society.

Consequently, a major contribution of the *jefaturas políticas* to the formation of a national, central authority structure derived from their wide-ranging, though vaguely defined, powers to help decide who should participate in the various armed brigades, how these forces were organized and regulated, and when and against whom this last recourse of domination was to be used. Such prerogatives allowed the *jefaturas* to impose themselves directly and dramatically on the common people, particularly the inhabitants of small communities. Hence also came the hatred they brought on themselves throughout the country.

To begin with, the *jefes políticos* of Coahuila could deploy armed units whenever they deemed it necessary to maintain "the public peace, good order, the security of individuals, and the security of inhabitants' prop-

27. *Ley orgánica* . . . 1874, art. 8, which makes reference to Decree 186 of July 16, 1874; *Colección de leyes y circulares expedidas en el Estado de Coahuila de Zaragoza* (Saltillo), Decree 473, Feb. 27, 1882.

erty." In the early, extraordinarily difficult years of the state of Coahuila and Texas, keeping the peace was the *jefes'* central preoccupation, though success did not always crown their efforts. The *jefes* could ask the military commanders for "the assistance of armed troops needed to establish public peace and the security of the roads." They could also exercise certain prerogatives of "inspection and command" over the civil militia forces in their districts. All of this endowed the *jefaturas* with the power of life or death over the people of Coahuila. That power peaked at the beginning and at the end of the institution's life cycle: during the first decades of independence and during the first years of the Mexican revolution.

In the 1820s and 1830s, the *jefaturas* kept the militia forces under tight control. They supervised the drawing of lots by which militia members were selected, and made sure that those selected who did not enter active service paid the corresponding fee. They attempted to improve what were hardship conditions for the militiamen by helping to coordinate and finance their military campaigns, furnishing them with arms and medical officers.[28] In the last third of the nineteenth century, when permanent militias had already ceased to exist, the *jefaturas* held similar powers over the national guard. But Coahuila's Porfirian constitution, dating from 1882, introduced an element of centralization and control: the *jefes políticos* could still deploy the state's police and public security forces, but their commands were "immediately subject to the orders of the executive."[29]

During the long years of Porfirian rule, these functionaries derived from their military powers a direct and incisive influence over the general population. They served as a channel of communication between the civil and military authorities. They also were responsible for part of the maintenance of certain security forces. Notwithstanding that the need to take up arms was deeply ingrained in the Coahuilan character—given the people's extensive struggles against "savage Indians," bandits, and invaders—the obligation to pay for the maintenance of military forces usually proved extremely burdensome for villagers and the poor. As late as the 1880s, "the citizens of all towns and villages" were obliged to contribute to the support of the public security force in districts like Río Grande. When the people refused to keep paying, the *jefe político* had to

28. Falcón (forthcoming); *Reglamento para el gobierno económico y político del Estado Libre de Coahuila y Tejas* (dado el 15 de junio de 1827, art. 7).

29. *Ley orgánica . . . 1874*, arts. 18, 25; *Constitución . . . 1882*, arts. 108, 87.

look for a new way of defraying such expenses.[30] In another case, from 1876, fighting against the "savages" brought the *jefe político* of Monclova enormous power over the inhabitants. He was able to concentrate in his office political, fiscal, and military functions. As he declared to the Coahuila state government,

> By virtue of the authorization that the Gov[ernor] has given me in the Treasury and War departments, the residents of this district have disbursed two thousand pesos . . . out of their own pocketbooks in order to be ready to repulse [Indian] aggressions.

So onerous was the financial burden on the villages and smaller towns for fighting the "savages" in Monclova, Cuatro Ciénegas, Sacramento, San Buenaventura, and Múzquiz that the *jefatura* itself requested that these communities be exempted from making contributions. The *jefe político's* argument stressed the sacrifices the settlers had already made.

> Every moment, [citizens] are pressed into military service to pursue the Indians, without their consent and without any kind of compensation. In view of these sacrifices, which these people have made and will continue to make, not just at the present time but from time immemorial, might not the exemption I request be granted to them? I think so, for the President of the Republic who embraces the cause of this country's progress and better- ment . . . surely understands the war of extermination and devastation that the savages are waging.[31]

Another example of the drama and urgency surrounding the war contributions took place in the last decade of the century. In February 1890, the village of Villa de Fuente obtained from the governor a reduc- tion in the taxes that the *jefe político* had decreed, seeing how "sad and pitiful" it was to listen to

> the complaints presented . . . by poor residents here, all because of having a quota of two reales imposed for the support of the Public Security Forces of this district. They tell me I take the bread out of their mouths, that day's sole sustenance for their families. For they are all *jornaleros* [day laborers], and on a day they do not work they do not eat.[32]

30. *Periódico Oficial*, Oct. 15, 1880.
31. AGN, FG, leg. 1262, exp. 3, Jefe Político of Monclova to Secretaría General de Gobierno, Feb. 28, 1876.
32. AGHECZ, leg. 111, doc. 4577, Municipal President of Villa de Fuentes, Monclova, to Secretaría General de Gobierno, Feb. 21, 1890.

An even more serious burden for the settlers was that in moments of emergency the Porfirian *jefaturas* could arrange to have certain citizens impressed into armed units to fight the Indians (or other opponents of the Porfirian regime). Thus, these government offices were the first link in the chain of command through which the executive dictated orders to the municipal presidents. This "blood quota" was an abusive practice that people could do little to stop. A case in point involved a former U.S. soldier who was arrested in 1880, supposedly by order of the judge and the *jefe político* of Piedras Negras. The U.S. consul filed a formal complaint, charging that this act was "unjust and contrary to [the Mexican] laws," and warned the *jefe político* that he "would inform my government of the facts." The consul's protest notwithstanding, the *jefe* simply refused to free the U.S. citizen. The consul put his finger on the heart of the matter when he reported,

> Only the poor and friendless are treated in such a way. . . . No Mexican official who perpetrates such arbitrary acts on poor citizens is afraid of incurring any responsibility.[33]

Thus the local *jefaturas* often had the power to decide such vital questions for villagers and citizens as the obligation to go to war, sometimes without any remuneration. In terms of the construction of a modern state, it is striking that as late as the last decade of the nineteenth century, Mexico still had not clearly designated the agencies responsible for monopolizing and attempting to legitimate the state's power to use force. In this context the *jefaturas políticas* were local centers of power that concentrated any number and variety of functions. The office thereby betrayed its primitive character, and its position as an obstacle to the processes of modernization and administrative and political rationality. Once again, the great projects of the state cast only a pale reflection in everyday life.

DISCRETIONARY POLITICAL AUTHORITY

Among the main ways the groups and forces in a society are channeled for the purpose of shaping a modern structure of domination is the organization of formal political life, the relations between citizens and

33. NA, RG 59, "Despatches sent by the U.S. Consul in Piedras Negras," Consul to Assistant Secretary of State, Aug. 15, 1880.

their government institutions. In this sphere the laws of the time once again favored the *jefaturas políticas*.

As prescribed in the regulation of 1827 as well as the law of 1874, the primary obligation of the *jefaturas políticas* was to be the link between the state and national government and the authorities and inhabitants of the basic cells of society. The least of their duties was to inform the public of orders and decrees; what was truly important was to enforce compliance. From this function they derived vast dominion over individuals and lower-level authorities, capped by the obligation to exercise surveillance over both the population and public officials. They were expected

> to inform the government . . . of the infractions . . . of the constitutions, the general one of the Republic and the particular one of the state; and of the laws laid down by the civil state. . . . And they will do the same with regard to any abuses they may note in the administration of justice, and in the administration of public revenues.[34]

The *jefaturas* were a hinge that articulated, or at least mediated, two frequently clashing powers. On the one hand, local authorities, such as communities, villages, factions, *caciques*, caudillos, and the wealthy, were accustomed to lording it over the Coahuilan deserts and prairies. On the other hand, state and national authorities, especially during the extended reign of the Porfiriato, were achieving a certain degree of stability, strength, and centralized power.

By law, and often in real life, the *jefaturas* were the essential instrument of the governor and the president for imposing the state's presence and control on its regions, towns, and villages. But at other times they did just the opposite: as zealous champions of regional elites or community interests, they acted as bulwarks of local autonomy against state or national efforts to concentrate authority.

The *jefaturas* were endowed with many tools for maintaining the strictest control over political life in the diverse corners of Coahuila. But perhaps their most powerful weapon—one that revealed the fragility of the groups that struggled to preserve regional autonomy—was their authority to "suspend with justified cause any or several of the members of the *ayuntamientos* . . . and village officials . . . when they failed to fulfill their duties."[35] This prime source of formal and informal power was used and abused frequently; on occasion the *ayuntamientos* would completely

34. *Reglamento . . . 1827*, art. 76; *Ley orgánica . . . 1874*, art. 22.
35. *Reglamento . . . 1827*, art. 63; *Ley orgánica . . . 1874*, art. 10.

change composition, their entire membership replaced with individuals proposed by the *jefatura*.

The *jefes políticos* had to make at least one annual visit to all the towns and villages in their jurisdiction and report to the government on where it would be appropriate to establish new *ayuntamientos*. This was one of the issues of greatest contention in the nineteenth century. Local communities, as well as powerful regional factions, ardently desired the political and economic clout that accompanied municipal status. The debate not only bespoke the profound legalism that dominated political life and discourse at the time; it also constituted one of the most sensitive barometers of the tension between dispersive and concentrating forces of power. On this specific point, the *jefes políticos* played a role of paramount importance. On the basis of their recommendation, municipalities could be founded or abolished.[36]

The *jefaturas* also had power over the management of municipal funds. They could "supervise the good investment of villages' municipal funds, examining the accounts of their revenues and expenditures," which the villages were obliged to submit annually. Moreover, the *jefaturas* could take initiatives, proposing to the government "such excise taxes as they considered advisable for [municipal] works of common utility, conservation, or repair." If such projects were approved, the *ayuntamientos* would appropriate the funds, and the *jefe político* would be responsible for investing them. Equally important was the *jefaturas'* strategic position whenever the municipalities or villages wished to undertake "extraordinary expenses." In such cases, the *jefes políticos* were not only the obligatory channel of application, but also the authority empowered to express a formal "opinion" on the matter.[37]

Given all of these powers over the life of the municipality, it is easy to explain why communities emphatically rejected the *jefaturas*. That rejection was made particularly clear in August 1874, when the institution was reinstated in Coahuila's formal political structure after almost a quarter-century. In the interim the municipalities had functioned freely and, more important, had assumed most of the *jefaturas'* powers. From a "zero-sum" political perspective, the *jefaturas'* reinstatement was a net loss for the

36. *Ley orgánica . . . 1874*, arts. 9, 14; *Reglamento . . . 1827*, art. 62. In those years, it was frequently decided in Saltillo which municipalities should be set up and which ones abolished.

37. *Ley orgánica . . . 1874*, arts. 5, 6, 13; *Reglamento . . . 1827*, arts. 36, 37, 58, 59, 60.

municipalities. Thus the *ayuntamientos* of Saltillo, Patos, San Buenaventura, Sacramento, Múzquiz, Abasolo, Salinas, Matamoros, Candela, and Valladoras—which collectively accounted for 44,548 inhabitants, approximately half of Coahuila's population—formally, if fruitlessly, opposed the reestablishment of the *jefaturas*.[38]

The *jefaturas* effectively controlled electoral politics: they were empowered to intervene at every step of the supposedly democratic elections that governed Mexico and Coahuila. They supervised all the rituals of rule, seeing to it that elections were held on the designated dates and in the prescribed fashion; that funds were appropriated to that end, and that new elections were convened whenever *ayuntamiento* positions became vacant.[39] All this contributed to shaping an image of domination over society, an appearance of an organized, efficient political structure—one with a clear organic unity integrating municipalities, states, and the republic.

The Porfirian regime carefully observed the details and appearances of a formal democracy while emptying it of all content. In Coahuila, Díaz and his representatives, including the *jefes políticos*, attempted to impose their control on society. They routinely used any of a number of "expedients": the composition of a slate of candidates "who could serve the center should the necessity arise"; negotiation between government agents and candidates seeking to win by "popular vote"; oversight of the polls "in order to influence the results of the election in question" by exerting pressure at the moment of voting and the moment of ballot counting. At times they also acted as government informants (Falcón 1989:119–29).

The iron hand with which the *jefaturas* excluded any opposition leadership is easy to document (Falcón 1989). A typical example occurred in the 1886 state gubernatorial elections, in which Díaz upheld the reelection of General Garza Galán, notwithstanding the considerable internal opposition this generated. A few hours after the polls closed, the *jefe político* of Múzquiz proudly informed the president that in his jurisdiction the elections had taken place "amid the greatest order," with the

---

38. The twenty *ayuntamientos* that accepted their reinstatement encompassed a population of virtually the same size: 48,601. *Periódico Oficial,* Aug. 3, 1874.

39. *Ley orgánica . . . 1874,* arts. 11, 20; *Reglamento . . . 1827,* arts. 24, 64; *Constitución . . . 1882,* art. 89, para. 6. An example of compliance with these obligations is found in AGHECZ, 1888, Primer, leg. 107, exp. 4131, election of senators, deputies, and president of the republic in the various districts of Coahuila.

result that absolutely every single one of those voting had cast the vote for the official candidate. As if that were not enough, this *jefe* told Díaz what he wanted to hear:

> With respect to the election of deputies, magistrates, and judges, the candidates from Mr. Garza Galán's circle, like his own candidacy, won with no opposition. I am informed that the same was true throughout the entire state.[40]

This informal style of domination reigned supreme throughout the Porfiriato. Two years later, after the 1888 state supreme court elections, Governor Garza Galán described to Díaz how the justices supposedly were elected. His letter is remarkable for its legitimating discourse aimed at strengthening the political elite's cohesion.

> [E]lectoral activities were brought to a successful conclusion . . . resulting in the election of the persons you yourself agreed to. . . . We have done a little better than expected, since, without exerting the least pressure or violence, these elections have been exceptional . . . above all for the uniform show of adherence they presented. . . . Throughout this entire state and in each village, no other will is possible or admissible save your own. . . .
>
> I should mention to you that my *compadre*, General Zermeño [the *jefe político* of Parras de la Fuente], acting in this case with characteristic energy, turned up at this Colegio with one hundred voters as uniform and as loyally devoted as the hundred produced by this Central District. . . .[41]

Just as in other spheres, the *jefaturas'* political activity overlapped other functions. It was not unusual for the *jefes* to resort to military force to achieve electoral control. Also fairly common was the other side of the coin: interference in the political struggles waged by military commandants. Those who suffered the most from such pressures and abuses were the common people of villages and rural communities. For example, a few months after the state constitution of 1882 was issued, the general-in-chief of the military zone complained to the Ministry of Government (Secretaría de Gobernación) in the nation's capital about the attitude of the *jefes políticos* of Matamoros and San Pedro. Both were calling to arms the residents of their municipalities before the upcoming elections, thereby giving rise to a climate of violence. The general asked the Ministry of Government what attitude he should take,

40. CPD, l.11, c.2, doc. 0671, Jefe Político of Múzquiz to Díaz, Jan. 18, 1886.
41. CPD, l.13, c.14, doc. 6787, Garza Galán to Díaz, July 1, 1888.

assuring [you] with no fear of being mistaken that I can put a stop to anybody in this vicinity, including the authorities themselves if ordered to do so; but otherwise I will have to continue to witness [these *jefes'*] violent proceedings, . . . without being able to put a stop to them, seeing as how they are so well masked under the guise of legality.[42]

Needless to say, such interference in the electoral process only extended the *jefes'* personal domains. At the same time, and from the early moments of the Porfiriato, the rules governing access to power were narrowed, the participation of the bulk of the inhabitants was blocked, and the essentially authoritarian and centralized character of the Díaz regime was reaffirmed.

A final political privilege accentuated the violent nature of the *jefaturas'* rule. They had the authority to break into and search a house or to send any person to prison whenever they deemed that "public security" required it. Such privilege not only allowed them to crush any brewing opposition; it also led to serious abuses of the poorer inhabitants of Coahuila, especially those who questioned the established system.

The history of Coahuila and of Mexico is crammed with examples of such suppression. In 1876, the *jefe político* of Parras de la Fuente informed the governor, in a tone redolent of pride and moral superiority, that he had detained a Mr. Chapman, who, in his opinion, had been "engaged in stirring up all individuals who are restless and revolutionary in spirit in order to promote an uprising." He had also held one Mariano Domínguez,

who, after being among those involved in riotously disturbing the peace . . . is also known to be among those who inform the disaffected living outside the District about the situation of this municipality. . . . This dangerous man is capable of bringing us into a conflict, which I have endeavored to avoid in this way, obviating any occasion for [his] causing harm to the village.[43]

CONCLUSIONS

The purpose of this essay has been to shed light on the workings of one of the most complex and important government agencies of the Porfiriato,

42. AGN, FG, leg. 1240, exp. 2, 1878, Official letter, General-in-Chief of the second and third military zones to Secretaría de Gobernación, Jan. 6, 1883, quoted in Falcón (1991).

43. AGN, FG, leg. 1262, exp. 3, Jefe Político of Parras de la Fuente to Governor of Coahuila, Mar. 6, 1876.

in order to gain an understanding of how the Mexican state attempted to mold and dominate society, especially the groups and individuals in its lower ranks. In the process, this study has also sought to contribute something of the Mexican experience to the discussion of the formation of modern states. The *jefaturas políticas* functioned as powerful outposts of government, whose purpose was to extend the dominion of Mexico's national and state authorities across the full spectrum of society. The *jefaturas* concentrated forms of social regulation and discipline through which individuals and groups might gradually be organized. They also sought to impose a language or rhetoric of domination, one that would attribute an apparent unity, structure, and independence to government practices.

In all the means by which this institution established its complex links to society's diverse groups, in what it did or failed to do, its activities turned on a single axis—coercion and violence at one extreme, and consensus and legitimacy, or its appearance, at the other. On the one hand, the *jefaturas* sought to inculcate "correct" ways for people to identify, organize, and conduct themselves, in order to establish the routines and the apparatus of government as something relatively "natural" and reasonable. On the other hand, the *jefaturas* regulated particular groups, especially the powerless, with an iron fist, exercising what theorists generally regard as the essence of the state: its claim to the "legitimate" use of force.

The *jefaturas* touched the lives of the inhabitants of far-flung, small communities in a wide variety of matters. Furthermore, as representatives of the triumphant "liberal" faction, the *jefaturas* sought to usher in the national project the "liberals" had fought for: one in which the power of the state would prevail over both the church and the factions that proposed alternative projects. This form of state the liberals conceived as modern, dynamic, and secularized.

The *jefaturas* tried to persuade the population to remember and celebrate those experiences in the country's past that were most relevant to the construction of a national identity. They also collaborated in the task of identifying people in terms of discrete categories—citizens, taxpayers, militiamen, soldiers, the unemployed, "vagrants," and so forth—through which these people could be governed, thereby creating socially acceptable individual identities and self-images. In sum, the *jefaturas* attempted to prescribe ways of seeing the world and each person's place in it.

In helping to consolidate Mexico's economic development, the *jefaturas'* role concentrated on government's control and regulation of private property and, much more decisively, the often violent control and subjugation of the unpropertied. Moreover, their broad and vaguely defined powers to decide who could have access to arms implied life-and-death power over many individuals and communities.

Finally, in the strictly political sphere, the *jefaturas* assembled complex machines with which to dominate local politics. They were in a position to use force to quell the desire of communities, villages, *caciques,* and the wealthy to exercise greater autonomy from the government, although this was not always the *jefaturas'* intention. Based on the law and on their own powerful clientelistic networks, the *jefaturas* frequently could control elections and individual candidates, as well as restrict the political and financial liberty of villages and municipalities.

In sum, from the very beginning of the Porfiriato, these public officials had tools to minimize the strength of opponents, social groups, political parties, communities, and any person unwilling to accept the conditions imposed by the structure of domination. They could grapple with powerful *caciques, hacendados,* and capitalist entrepreneurs; or, with greater violence, with trade unions, strikers, peons, peasants, and the common people of villages and *rancherías.* The political and military machinery at the *jefaturas'* disposal led them almost naturally to shape an extremely authoritarian and closed structure of power.

In theory, and sometimes also in practice, the *jefaturas políticas* served as a point of articulation between diverse spheres: between individuals who lacked power and influence and those who dominated them; between those who defined and ruled the formal political world and those who had no access to it; between those who controlled weapons and those who had to suffer violent actions or serve in armed forces against their own will; between the power of the federal government and that of regions, municipalities, villages, and individuals; between the propertied and the dispossessed.

Yet if any one characteristic of the *jefaturas políticas* remained stamped on the public imagination, it was their constant abuses, the *jefes'* harsh rule for their personal benefit and that of their followers, their half-veiled forms of authority that weighed most heavily on the humblest inhabitants. Their outrages, so grievous to society and the individual, far from helping to buttress the authority of the Mexican state, had the opposite effect, fomenting an enormous hatred toward the *jefaturas* and the domination the institution represented. All of this undermined the legitimacy of the system, accentuated its deeply entrenched exclusionary and authoritarian features, and contributed significantly to the downfall of the old regime and the advent of the Mexican revolution.

It is important to note that, even if seen only from a legal point of view, the very wide range of powers conferred on the *jefaturas* made them "primitive" agencies; to a great extent they compressed and combined functions that in a modern state tend to be differentiated. In this sense, the *jefaturas* can also be seen as obstacles to the formation of a structure of domination with an outward appearance of efficiency and modernity.

Nor is it possible to conclude this study of the *jefaturas políticas* without raising a fundamental question: how successful were they? To what degree did they manage to mold society and "legitimize" state policies and practices? How much and in what ways did they contribute to changing the behavior and the perspective through which the inhabitants of this young nation saw themselves and saw Mexico? It is impossible to give a conclusive answer. Few documents reveal what was thought and felt by the bulk of Porfirian society—the humble and perhaps dispirited laborers of the land, the mines, and the factories.

We might speculate that the *jefaturas'* impact was quite modest; that in many domains, especially in those not dependent on the state's coercive actions, the old traditions and ways of seeing the world persisted with enormous strength. The great legislative and political ideals remained far removed from the localized, everyday world and the hearts and minds of the common people. We can document the repression and the authoritarianism of the *jefes políticos* and the Porfirian regime they served; but the opposition they engendered, carried on within the passive daily routine of the people of Coahuila, we historians can only surmise.

GILBERT M. JOSEPH

Rethinking Mexican Revolutionary Mobilization:

Yucatán's Seasons of Upheaval, 1909–1915

A compelling analysis of the period of transition joining the decline of the Porfirian Old Regime and the emergence of the new Revolutionary state remains a high priority for historians of modern Mexico. Especially intriguing are the 1909–1913 years marking the rise and fall of the national liberal reform movement of Francisco Madero. Clearly, many of the restraints that the Porfirian state had imposed on popular movements were lifted during the Maderista interlude, and extremely divergent local movements began to emerge in Mexico's different regions. Surprisingly, except for important work on Morelos, Puebla, and Tlaxcala in Mexico's central core, or more recently on the northern state of San Luis Potosí, little has been done to explain the mobilization of these movements or to examine their eventual fates (Womack 1968; Buve 1975; LaFrance 1984, 1989, 1990; Ankerson 1984; Falcón 1984). Yet they are of great importance in understanding the character of the "epic revolution" (1910–1917) and the kind of state that emerged from it.

The Yucatecan variant of this *apertura maderista* holds particular interest. Like other regions of Mexico during the period, Yucatán witnessed

The author gratefully acknowledges support by the National Endowment for the Humanities; the Center for U.S.-Mexican Studies, University of California, San Diego; the National Humanities Center; and the Institute of Latin American Studies of the University of North Carolina, Chapel Hill, in the research and writing of this essay. He also wishes to thank Allen Wells, who has shared ideas and data over the course of a long and enriching collaboration; and Marie Lapointe and Lucy Defresne, who generously made available one of their oral history interviews.

the opening of new political space; the movement of new actors and political alliances into this space; and, in short order, a series of local revolts, some orchestrated, others more spontaneous and uncoordinated. However, whereas in much of the rest of Mexico these homegrown swells led inexorably to civil war and the destruction of the traditional oligarchical order, in Yucatán the Old Regime survived. Consequently, the Mexican revolution had to fight its way in from without, in March 1915.

This salient difference frames the basic questions of my larger study with Allen Wells of late Porfirian and early revolutionary politics and society (Joseph and Wells forthcoming). First, how did the traditional oligarchical order manage to ride out the first challenges to its power by mid-1913, despite frequent and widespread protest and revolt throughout the Yucatecan countryside during the preceding four years? Second, what was the nature of this rural protest; what characteristic forms did resistance take among peasant villagers and hacienda peons? Equally important, how was such resistance woven into long-term patterns of resistant adaptation? And finally, how was resistance repeatedly mobilized and then dissolved during the Maderista period, and what role did regional elites and the state play in controlling the insurgency?[1]

The puzzle of Yucatán's failed rural rebellions is also fertile ground for examining one of the central concerns now engaging historians of revolutionary movements in Mexico and elsewhere: namely, the degree of continuity between revolutionary-era forms of authority and consciousness and those of the old order. For example, who were the new men who led these Yucatecan revolts and filled the vacuum created by the weakening of the central state in 1910? How did they recruit and maintain their followers? To what extent did these revolts led by local chiefs (contemporaries referred to them as *cabecillas* or *caciques*) tap into local subcultures of

---

1. Our study of how an entrenched oligarchical regime maintains itself in the face of popular insurgency may generate insights of some relevance to students of other areas, particularly modern Central America, which resembles Yucatán in certain structural respects. Like El Salvador's coffee growers, Yucatán's henequen planters demonstrated the capacity to "hang on," to resist seemingly inevitable structural change, even in the face of escalating social challenges, the outbreak of local rebellions, and ultimately the mobilization of multiclass coalitions. Indeed, it is striking that so little attention has been given in the Latin Americanist historiography to *integrating* the study of popular movements and rebellions with examinations of the efforts of elite establishments to foment, prevent, contain, and crush such rebellions. Most often these problems are treated separately. Of course, the present volume seeks to redress this imbalance.

resistance and represent truly "popular," autonomous rebellions against the interests and values of the Old Regime? This is what Alan Knight, giving new voice to a venerable populist current of revolutionary interpretation, contends. Or were they more significant in permitting new, upwardly mobile elements (with ties to existing elites) their first access to a clientele among the masses, on whose backs they would one day consolidate a more efficient version of the Old Regime? This is what numerous self-proclaimed "revisionist" writers have recently argued (see, e.g., Carr 1980; Brading 1980; S. Miller 1988; Fowler-Salamini 1993, for in-depth discussions).[2]

Clearly, the revisionists have succeeded in situating the Mexican revolution in relation to world-scale forces of change and in focusing attention on important continuities between the Porfirian regime and the new Revolutionary state. Yet, with Alan Knight, I would contend that they often reduce the revolution to "a series of chaotic, careerist episodes, in which popular forces were, at best, the instruments of manipulative *caciques*" (Knight 1986a:1:xi). In Tocquevillian fashion, they posit the rise of a Machiavellian central state as the key element—some even argue the only important element—of the epic revolution. But such "statolatry," as Knight terms it, provides a false homogeneity to the complex history of the Mexican revolution. Moreover, it ignores the pressures from below on the state; it mistakenly stresses the inertia of peasants and workers and the unbroken political hegemony of elites and middle strata. Such a view is problematic for any decade after 1910, and is particularly misguided for the period prior to 1920, or for the Cardenista *sexenio* (1934–1940) (Knight 1984b). Finally, until now, in spite of their reification of "a Leviathan state," revisionists have not been particularly clear just what this state is or how "it" so successfully managed to swallow up Mexico's popular cultures like so many minnows. Indeed, the Revolutionary state has remained something of a black box conceptually; most often it has

2. In his provocative, two-volume study, Alan Knight makes a forceful case for the existence of truly popular movements during the first decade of violence. Also see Hart (1987), whose work, apart from its grand thesis, contains a treasure trove of information on the external environment that conditioned revolutionary Mexico; and the final chapter of Tutino (1986). Knight and Hart build on the classic populist thesis set forth sixty years ago by Frank Tannenbaum (1933) and a variety of Mexican writers (e.g., Jesús Silva Herzog and José Valadés). For a critical discussion of both currents of interpretation with representative citations, see Nugent's and my introductory essay to this volume.

been cast as an ominous presence hovering above (but eerily removed from) the mundane workings of Mexican society.

In our introductory chapter to the present volume, Daniel Nugent and I advance the argument that what is needed is a synthesis of populist and revisionist interpretations—one that integrates their contributions but in the process transcends them. This will entail a broader application of the type of analysis that many of this book's contributors provide: for starters, a more sophisticated reconstruction of peasant and worker mobilizations (and demobilizations); and a greater appreciation of the impact these popular movements registered—locally, regionally, nationally, occasionally even internationally—on Porfirian and Revolutionary state projects of social transformation. Here, analysis of revolutionary-era mobilizations must go beyond the kind of broad assertions of resistance and empowerment that populist scholars have provided in their national histories (e.g., Tannenbaum 1933; Hart 1987; Silva Herzog 1963; Valadés 1963–67).[3] Rather, through close examination of popular political cultures, scholars must endeavor to *deconstruct "the popular"*; that is, to show how apparently "primordial" sociocultural forms—notions of community, the peasant economy, ethnic and gender identities—are, in fact, historically constructed (O'Brien and Roseberry 1991). In the process, such an approach would begin to generate empirical elaborations of both the character and the limitations of subaltern consciousness, situating the production of this consciousness in dynamic relation to ongoing, often quotidian, processes of domination and state formation. It would thereby avoid the excesses of much recent scholarship on resistance in Latin America and elsewhere, which overemphasizes the "authenticity," the "irreducible integrity" of subaltern cultures, and consequently ascribes an unwarranted autonomy to the politics and ideology of popular struggles.[4]

3. Knight's masterful synoptic history is less vulnerable to this critique. While it forcefully argues the case for a popular agrarian revolution, it is far more sensitive to regional and local nuance, and it consistently seeks to historicize the broad issues it narrates (not for nothing does it number well over a thousand pages!). Still, as Nugent and I emphasize in our introductory chapter, while Knight "has achieved a theoretical recognition of what was realized by [the] popular classes in historical practice, namely the articulation of distinctive forms of social consciousness and experience," he has not grounded that popular presence and consciousness in a sustained analysis of popular culture. To be sure, he was constrained by his sources and the considerable demands of writing a narrative that embraces all of Mexico.

4. See Nugent and my introductory chapter for a critique of essentialist readings of popular culture, and references to the lively, ongoing debate in Asian studies about

Only then, with these conceptual elements in place, will we have any prospect of reconstructing more precisely how popular agency in the multiple arenas through which state projects were promoted typically led to some measure of negotiation from below. (For some of the results that have already been achieved, see particularly the companion essays in this volume by Mallon, Nugent and Alonso, Becker, Rus, and Rockwell.)

In the spirit of similarly practicing something of what I preach, let me now turn to the seasons of upheaval that gripped Yucatán intermittently during the Maderista period. My research, which is based in large part on an extraordinarily rich set of personal testimonies from criminal court records in the Archivo General del Estado de Yucatán[5]—as well as on oral traditions and more standard sources—enables me to focus on the villagers and peons who participated in the revolts led by Yucatán's incipient revolutionary chiefs and statebuilders.

This is precisely what the "elite historiographies" of both the left and the right have failed to do. Most historians of Yucatán have passed over the Maderista period to focus on the more celebrated, radical regimes of Salvador Alvarado (1915–1918) and Felipe Carrillo Puerto (1922–1924), when Yucatán was hailed as the social laboratory of the Mexican revolution (Joseph 1986: chap. 5). When historians have addressed the Maderista seasons of upheaval, they have typically portrayed them in the manner of contemporary "official" discourse—as the voiceless, brutish, and ultimately inconsequential outbursts of vengeful peons. Local writers of both conservative and Marxist stripe have "explained" the unleashing of these violent riots and revolts as little more than the work of unscrupulous (choose: leftist or *hacendado*) "outside agitators" preying on the credulous minds of ignorant *campesinos*.[6] Of course, "it is no longer possible to

how subaltern politics and consciousness should be conceptualized. For a provocative recent exchange, see Prakash (1990, 1992a); and O'Hanlon and Washbrook (1992).

5. While social historians of the colonial period have used criminal court records to great effect, these sources have been sadly underutilized by students of modern Mexico. To some extent this reflects the destruction of judicial archives during the revolution of 1910.

6. For a representative conservative view, see Gamboa Ricalde (1943–55: esp. vol. 1); cf. the orthodox Marxist treatment by Betancourt Pérez (1983). For their part, professional (largely foreign) scholars have chosen—in the best revisionist fashion— to inflect the pivotal role of nonideological, self-serving "warlords"; e.g., see Franz (1973: chaps. 1–3).

deny peasantries intellectual or ideological attributes, to equate peasantry with the 'idiocy of rural life,' or even to assume that the intellectual/ ideological content of peasant revolutionary consciousness must necessarily be imported from 'outside,' through the medium of urban contacts, the vanguard party or whatever external agency" (Knight 1981).

SUMMER OF DISCONTENT[7]

The most significant clues for understanding both the outbreak and the limitations of the Maderista revolts lie in the history of the two preceding decades. Like so much of regional Mexico, Yucatán was thoroughly transformed by the requirements of North American industrial capitalism and governed by its fluctuating rhythms during the last quarter of the nineteenth century. The production of henequen increased furiously during the Porfiriato, as annual exports rose from forty thousand bales of raw fiber to more than six hundred thousand bales. A small, landed elite of three to four hundred families cultivated henequen on estates throughout the northwestern quadrant of the peninsula. But these *hacendados* were not independent actors. A much smaller, more cohesive group of about twenty to thirty families constituted a hegemonic, oligarchical *camarilla* (or *casta divina*, as they were called, and came to call themselves early in the century). This ruling faction, based on the Olegario Molina-Avelino Montes *parentesco* (extended family), had homogeneous interests, a relatively closed membership, and, owing in part to its collaboration with the principal buyer of raw fiber, the International Harvester Company, such control over the economic and political levers of power that it was able to thwart the opportunities of rival elite groups in late Porfirian society.

The economic leverage afforded by the partnership between Harvester and the Molina-Montes *parentesco* had a complementary ripple effect in the political arena. Not only was Olegario Molina governor of the state of Yucatán during the first decade of the century, but his relatives and associates filled the upper echelons of the state bureaucracy. As was typical throughout Porfirian Mexico, the ruling oligarchical clique was subsequently incorporated into the national superstructure. In 1907, following his first term as governor, Molina himself joined Díaz's cabinet as minister of development (*fomento*).

7. This section summarizes findings developed at length in two of my earlier essays with Allen Wells (1986, 1990b).

The henequen boom earned millions for the Molina-Montes *camarilla*. Yet for the great majority of Yucatecan henequen *hacendados* (or *henequeneros*), who collectively constituted one of the wealthiest classes in Porfirian Mexico, economic conditions were among the least secure. In most cases these *henequeneros* were not only big spenders but speculators, constantly seeking new ways to maximize profits amid the problematical fluctuations of the export economy, and often overextending themselves in the process. For every genuine success story, many more *henequeneros* existed in a perpetual state of indebtedness and fiscal instability that periodically led to bankruptcy. With increasing frequency throughout the period 1902–1915, such members of the *henequenero*-merchant bourgeoisie became indebted to Molina's *casta divina* and were forced to advance their future product at slightly less than the current market price to cover present obligations. Moreover, it was access to foreign capital, and Harvester's capacity to funnel large amounts of it at critical junctures, that helped Molina and his oligarchical faction acquire mortgages, purchase estates outright, and consolidate their hold on regional communications, infrastructure, and banking—all of which guaranteed control of local fiber production and generally worked to depress the price.

Declining fiber prices during the last years of the Porfiriato served to heighten tensions within the regional elite and crystallized the belief among most *hacendados* that the Molinista *camarilla* was unwilling to countenance any loss of economic control. By 1909, accommodation no longer seemed possible. Political activity and, if necessary, rebellion increasingly were perceived as the only means to restore a more equitable reapportionment of the spoils of the henequen economy.

The national liberal reform movement of Francisco Madero, with its democratic rhetoric, emboldened subordinate factions of the *henequenero* class and their middle-sector allies to challenge Yucatán's ruling oligarchy. Two rival parties, led by disgruntled factions of the landed elite, moved to center stage as soon as political space opened up during the Maderista period. These two parties were known popularly as "Morenistas" and "Pinistas" after their respective standard-bearers, Delio Moreno Cantón and José María Pino Suárez, who were journalists. Financed by its *henequenero* supporters, each party rapidly attempted to construct alliances reaching into the middle class intelligentsia, the small urban working and artisan class, and—most important, but until now not really explained—into the Maya peasantry (*campesinado*).

For the purpose of this essay, I will focus particularly on this variegated peasantry. The rise of henequen monoculture dramatically transformed the lives of the tens of thousands of *campesinos* who comprised the labor force. (For a more detailed discussion of social conditions on henequen estates, see Joseph and Wells 1988.) The plantations devoured almost all the independent peasant villages in the henequen zone, located roughly within a radius of seventy to eighty kilometers of the state capital, Mérida (see map 1). By the turn of the century, the great majority of the free Maya *pueblos* in the zone had lost their land base.[8]

These *pueblos* had already been stripped by the whites of the wealth of their *cofradías* (religious brotherhoods) at the end of the colonial period. Now, the erosion of village lands rendered obsolete the extended patrilateral kin networks that had sustained reciprocal labor exchanges and had underwritten a hereditary political-religious elite. By presiding over the yearly round of fiestas central to the community's religious experience, this Maya elite had orchestrated a syncretic Catholicism that culturally resisted white domination—promoting what Nancy Farriss has termed a "collective enterprise of survival" (1984).

Now, increasingly unable to hold off the expanding henequen plantations, Yucatán's *campesinos* were first pulled onto the estates and then relatively isolated on them. *Henequeneros* made sure their work force was a heterogeneous group, combining large concentrations of Maya workers with smaller numbers of ethnic and linguistic strangers—Yaqui deportees, indentured Asian immigrants, and central Mexican *enganchados* (contract workers; literally "hooked ones"). Not only did Maya peons have little contact with their fellow workers on other estates; they were also isolated from potential allies in the urban areas. Yucatecan proprietors hoped that these precautions, coupled with an intensified labor regime and a multitiered system of surveillance and repression—which included the state's national guard, federal and state battalions, private bounty hunters, and the state bureau of investigation (ominously called *la policía secreta*)—would preclude another Caste War.

This preemptive strategy extended into the discursive realm as well, where the *henequenero* elite attempted to *reinvent* the prevailing terms of regional ethnicity. During the darkest days of the Caste War, when the whites were besieged in Mérida by rebel Maya insurgents, those Maya peons and villagers who had fought with the whites or performed essential tasks for their troops had been accorded the title *hidalgo* for their efforts (e.g., see Bojórquez Urzáiz 1977, 1979). Then, once the whites

8. This process of agrarian dispossession in northwestern Yucatán was already well advanced before the onset of the *auge henequenero*. See Patch (1976).

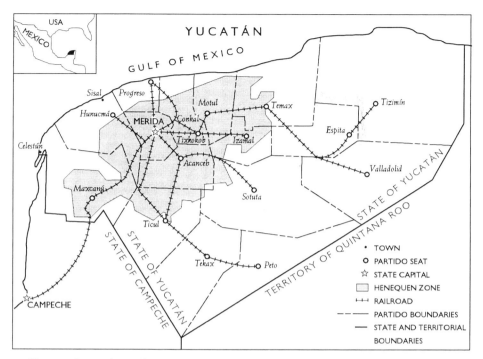

Yucatán during the revolutionary era.

had gained the upper hand and the so-called *indios bravos* had retreated into the bush across the Quintana Roo frontier, the Maya who remained in the northwestern henequen zone came to be known euphemistically as mestizos. Thus, at least as a matter of official policy, the ethnic classification of *Indian* ceased to exist in Yucatán.[9]

Indeed, contemporary *campesino* testimonies and the oral histories I have gathered underscore the fact that in Yucatán the term *mestizo* has come to differ from the standard Mexican usage. It connotes a person or attribute—that is, a style of dress or abode—that is at root Maya but has been influenced over time by Hispanic culture (e.g., see Joseph and Wells

9. E.g., see CGPD, Memorandum, Manuel Sierra Méndez to Porfirio Díaz, "Apuntes breves sobre la situación de Yucatán, las providencias que sería conveniente tomar al iniciarse la Campaña de Indios y sobre algunos otros puntos que relacionan con la misma," June 9, 1897, 22:14:006780-95; and cf., AGEY, RJ, "Toca a la causa seguida a Juan Jiménez y socios por el delito de provocación al delito de rebelión," 1913. Yucatán's unique ethnic categories are discussed in Thompson (1974); Bricker (1981:92, 253); and A. Hansen (1980:122–41).

1987:27–40, esp. 29). Certainly well before the turn of the century, Yucatán's Maya-speaking peons and villagers had come to distinguish themselves from the *indios bravos* who had never capitulated to the state or federal governments.[10] In fact, they consistently referred to themselves as mestizos or *campesinos* or simply as *pobres* (poor people), and never as *indios* or Maya.[11] At the same time, these peons and villagers held few illusions that the *dzules*—the *señores*, the white masters who dominated regional society—regarded them as anything other than *indios ignorantes y borrachos*. These were certainly the terms the planters often used in their "off-stage" descriptions of their workers; the same terms repeatedly found their way into contemporary criminal court records.[12] The classic planter aphorism with regard to the Maya work force was "El indio no oye, sino por las nalgas." This sardonic justification of the lash is best translated in polite company as: "The Indian only hears with his backside."[13]

Despite the various precautions they took—and, no doubt, because of the draconian nature of some of them—Yucatán's white masters lived in constant fear of Maya uprisings. The *hacendados'* fears were justified. Interestingly, unlike the Porfirian elites themselves, modern writers have dismissed the peons' capacity to protest the demands of their masters, except, perhaps, in cases when the workers reached their boiling point and then lashed out senselessly.[14] To be sure, the planters effectively utilized both carrot and stick, blending paternalist incentives and a measure of security with restrictive mechanisms of coercion and isolation.

10. For archivally based discussions of this perception of cultural difference, see Joseph and Wells (1988:224–33); Wells (1985: chaps. 4 and 6, passim); also N. Reed (1964: part 3); and Joseph (1986: chaps. 2 and 3).

11. E.g., interviews with Marcos Ku Peraza and Alicia Trejo Hernández, Peto, June 14, 1982 (courtesy Drs. Marie Lapointe and Lucy Defresne); Jesús Campos Esquivel, Dzilám González, Dec. 26, 1986, Jan. 2, 1987; Melchor Zozaya Raz, Temax, Dec. 31, 1986; and Saluz Tut de Euán, Opichén, Aug. 12, 1991.

12. E.g., AGEY, RJ, "Toca a la causa seguida a Hermenegildo Nah y socio por los delitos de robo y destrucción en propiedad ajena por incendio," 1912; "Toca a la causa seguida a Visitación González y Magdalena Alcocer de González, por injurias a funcionario público y resistencia a la autoridad," 1914.

13. This aphorism appears in contemporary travelers' accounts, such as Frost and Arnold (1909:324), and is cited in numerous secondary treatments of Yucatán's "época de esclavitud" ("age of slavery").

14. A recent portrayal of the Yucatecan *peón acasillado* as quiescent is found in Knight (1986a:1:89). For a discussion of the literature on henequen workers during the Porfiriato, see Wells (1985: chap. 6, and 1984:213–41, esp. 214–16).

It is hardly surprising, therefore, that their peons lacked the revolutionary potential—or, as Eric Wolf has put it, the "tactical mobility"—manifested by the villagers, cowboys, miners, and *serranos* who made up the revolutionary armies of central and northern Mexico.[15]

Nevertheless, Wells's and my research in criminal court records recasts prevailing notions about peons' inability to resist their masters. While henequen monoculture's characteristic structure of domination restricted the potential for self-generated insurrection on the estates, as we shall see it frequently could not prevent peons from joining the revolts that originated on the periphery of the henequen zone during the early years of the revolutionary era. Moreover, although Yucatecan peons were not as overtly rebellious as villagers outside or on the fringes of the zone, this does not mean they did not resist the monocultural regime. Their personal testimonies—as well as a careful reading of estate records, correspondence between bishops and planters, and travelers' accounts— suggest that peons partook of "quieter" and "everyday forms of resistance," which were safer and more successful over the long run in contesting, materially as well as symbolically, the stepped-up work rhythms and other exploitative aspects of henequen monoculture.[16] On the whole, peons rejected the weak, paternalistic ethos of their masters, demonstrating their dissatisfaction in a variety of ways, most commonly by running away, shirking, and alcoholism. To a lesser extent, they clandestinely burned henequen fields; engaged in brief, ultimately futile localized acts of violence; and in a frighteningly high number of cases, committed suicide.[17]

Meanwhile, on the fringes of the henequen zone, along the southern range of stunted hills known as the Puuc, and south and east of the prime henequen haciendas of Temax, independent smallholders stubbornly guarded their lands and autonomy against the incursions of local *hacen-*

---

15. Wolf (1969: Introduction). Tutino writes more explicitly: "In places where the most radical economic changes of the Porfiriato occurred, where established peasant communities were suddenly incorporated into the export economy as export producers, there was little revolutionary insurrection after 1910" (1986:296).

16. Wells and I discuss the promise and potential pitfalls of researching "everyday forms of resistance" in "official records"—court cases; estate records, such as *cuentas de administración*; and church archives (1988:244–54). See also Joseph (1990:7– 53, esp. 18–25).

17. For an in-depth discussion of each of these "routine" forms of resistance, with numerous references from AGEY, RJ, see Joseph and Wells (1988:244–54).

dados and Molinista *jefes políticos*. White proprietors and labor contractors already exercised control over a significant number of these village-based *campesinos*, and intra-*pueblo* factionalism was rife.[18] Nevertheless, when a village's traditional ejidal lands hung in the balance, bonds of solidarity among villagers were accentuated. In a variety of cases, significant group-ings of villagers opted to fight local authorities rather than submit to the surveying and parceling of their traditional lands.[19]

With increasing frequency after 1907, state authorities failed to contain social unrest in these peripheral areas, since insurgents and a proliferating number of "bandits"—often the same people, despite the state's delegitimizing labels—could easily slip off into the bush.[20] It was here, on the fringes of monoculture, that the concept of *un hombre libre*—a free and independent man—became part of the daily lexicon of the smallholders, petty merchants, and artisans who populated the rural towns and *pueblos*.[21] It is hardly surprising, then, that these transitional areas proved to be fertile recruiting grounds for both the *cabecillas* and the clienteles of the first rebellions of Maderismo.

SEASONS OF UPHEAVAL: MOBILIZATIONS

How, then, did Yucatán's bickering "summer of discontent" fester into several violent seasons of upheaval that shook the oligarchical order? And once such insurgency had been unleashed, in 1909–10, how did the old order successfully forestall a general conflagration until the revolution

18. E.g., see C. Gill (1991: chap. 3) for an incisive account—based largely on oral history—of how planters came to exercise a personalistic control over villagers in the Puuc.

19. A perfect case in point was the southern pueblo of Santa Elena in the *partido* of Ticul. This town in the Puuc had fought the incursion of local surveyors at the turn of the century and would become a prime staging area for revolutionary violence during the Madero period. See Wells (1985:103–4). Hunucmá and Opichén pro-vided similar agrarian pockets of resistance. Microhistories of the agrarian struggles of these and other localities from ca. 1880 to 1915 will appear in Joseph and Wells (forthcoming).

20. E.g., see ACEY, RJ, "Testimonio de la causa seguida a Herminio Balam y socios por los delitos de homicidio y robo por asalto," 1911; "Diligencias practicadas con motivo del asalto y robo hecho a Absalón Vázquez, administrador de la finca Uayalceh," 1911; and cf. Joseph (1990:20–23).

21. Interviews with Jesús Campos Esquivel and Melchor Zozaya Raz.

was imported by General Salvador Alvarado's formidable Constitutionalist army in 1915? Although I can only work in broad strokes here, let me focus on the mechanisms and consequences of both the mobilizations and demobilizations that were carried out in Yucatán between 1909 and 1915. In the process, I will attempt to mark out the agendas and political consciousness that elites and *campesinos* brought to the insurgencies of the period.

However outraged they may be, *campesinos* generally wait for evidence that powerholders are weak or divided before they will take the risks attending insurrection.[22] News of such opportunities was often brought to *campesinos* by dissident elites—in some cases their own *patrones*—or by individuals of more modest station whom Wells and I call "hingemen." These were local, rural *cabecillas* who typically spoke Spanish well enough and had some cultural experience in the dominant society which complemented, indeed often enhanced, their standing in the subordinate rural society. Although such brokers did not *cause* rural revolts, they often precipitated them and played a role in organizing rural insurgents and establishing their links with other groups.[23]

Typically, Morenista and Pinista elites and middle-class intellectuals, based in Mérida, would plan a revolt, frequently timing their regional uprising to coincide with a national-level event or conspiracy. Then, through an extended network of middlemen, including local *cabecillas*, and spies and couriers known colorfully as *orejas* and *madrinas* (literally, "ears" and "godmothers"), these dissident elites would mobilize sympathetic elements (and often "press" or coerce reluctant ones) in rural towns, villages, and haciendas.[24]

The linchpins of these networks remained the *cabecillas* of the free villages on the periphery of the henequen zone. These local chiefs not only had access to Mérida and rural towns but also to the estates, typically through commercial and labor arrangements involving themselves or

22. Thus, to paraphrase one recent commentator (Tutino 1986:22), from the perspective of poor *campesinos*, rural rebellions result from critical meetings of grievances and opportunities.

23. For the case of one particularly well documented "hingeman," see Joseph and Wells (1987). The term *hingeman* originally appeared in Brown (1982).

24. For two cases that graphically document these networks of recruitment, complete with hingemen, "orejas," and "madrinas," see AGEY, RJ, "Causa seguida a José Policarpo Mendoza y socios por el delito de rebelión," 1912, and "Toca a la causa seguida a Juan Jiménez y socios."

their kin. In most cases, the *cabecillas*, their kin, or their trusted clients sold goods to the estates or worked on them as supervisory personnel. They came to know who were the "good" and "bad" overseers, what constituted the peons' principal grievances, and how (and through whom) to exploit them.[25]

Making sense of the consciousness of participants in rather fleeting moments of rural collective action—episodes that rarely leave a cultural trace—is no easy task. As rich as they are, contemporary judicial testimonies and recently gathered oral traditions permit us to speak more confidently about the character of Yucatán's mobilizations than about the motivations of the villagers and peons who joined or refused to join them. Indeed, many students of social movements wonder whether we can ever determine individual motivations with any degree of accuracy. The task is made even more daunting when we must work retrospectively, with incomplete data. Particularly in the tumultuous context of riots and rebellions, the insurgents themselves may not even be conscious, at the moment they join a band, of what motivates them. One Yucatecan peon, Marcos Chan, tersely remarked at his trial: "They asked me if I wanted to join them and I said yes."[26] How can we begin to know what went through his mind? How can we know if he would have acted differently a day or a week later if presented with the same choice? Some structuralists find the exercise of assessing motivation so subjective (and some would add, so "trivial") that they completely discourage asking why people acted, and seek only to understand how they acted and with what outcomes (e.g., see Foweraker 1989; Skocpol 1979: esp. 16–18).

These critics raise a valid point. A careful reading of the court records suggests that individual *campesinos* may have joined or refused to join insurgent bands for a plethora of conscious (often interlinked) motivations: economic calculations, family and fictive kin ties and responsibilities, and an urge for revenge among them. Moreover, beyond these surface motivations there were, no doubt, other unconscious, psychologically based factors that entered into individual behavior choices. For example, psychologists (beginning with Le Bon's aristocratic and racialist

25. E.g., see AGEY, RJ, "Toca a la causa seguida a Juan Jiménez y socios," and "Copia certificada de constancias en la causa seguida a Bernabé Escalante por suponérsele presunto cómplice del delito de homicidio, para la continuación respecto de José Osorio, Juan Campos y socios," 1912.
26. AGEY, RJ, "Toca a la causa seguida a Juan Jiménez y socios."

treatment at the turn of the century) have documented the collective lowering of thresholds of inhibition in mobs and other crowd phenomena (Le Bon [1909] 1952; Rudé 1964: esp. 3–16; Van Young 1992a:337–53). In fact, some episodes of Yucatecan insurgency resembled public fiestas in which large concentrations of people, accompanied by the community band, defected en masse.[27]

And what role did gender relations play in motivation? In certain cases I found mothers, wives, and sisters egging on their male relations, in effect challenging the machismo of their men. In one notable example—which produced a jacquerie—Martina Ek graphically exhorted her husband and son to take action against a plantation overseer: "C'mon, why don't you kill that bastard (*cabrón*) now that you have the chance; you can bet he wouldn't go soft on you!"[28] On numerous other occasions, village-based *campesinas* protected and frequently "took the heat" for male relatives being pursued by state security forces for "banditry" and "sedition." Frequently they were also at the forefront of initiatives in the *pueblos* to resist the *leva* (forced conscription into the army or national guard). These actions often provoked verbal and physical attacks on the women by state agents, which infuriated their menfolk and gave rise to celebrated local riots and revolts in which men and women both played active roles.[29]

Here Temma Kaplan's conceptualization of "female consciousness" in working-class struggles in Spain and Mexico, as well as other parts of Latin America and the developing world, is particularly helpful for understanding the motivation of these *campesinas yucatecas* (and, by extension, that of their male relations). The lives of these *campesinas* revolved around

27. E.g., RDY, May 16, 1911. Of course, European social historians, such as E. P. Thompson and George Rudé, have at the same time inflected the "moral content"— the appeal to customary rights or "natural justice"—that informed (eighteenth- and nineteenth-century English and French) crowd phenomena, and enhanced its "capacity for swift, direct action." See Thompson (1974:401 and 1971); cf. Rudé (1964: esp. chaps. 14 and 15).

28. AGEY, RJ, "Toca a la causa seguida a Luis Uc y socios por los delitos de amenaza de injurias," 1913.

29. E.g., see AGEY, RJ, "Toca a la apelación interpuesta por María Isabel Reyes y Agustina Poot contra el auto de fecha 20 de mayo de 1914 en que se les declara formalmente presas, en la causa que se les sigue por el delito de ultrajes a funcionarios públicos," 1914 (wife and mother-in-law shield insurgent *cabecilla*, are verbally abused and fondled by police, and fight back, provoking a *tumulto*). For female-led insurgency against the *leva*, see Domínguez (1981:178–205); Civeira Taboada (1974:108–9); and Bolio Ontiveros (1967:57–62).

their perceived role as nurturers and preservers of life in the family and community. When their obligation (and perceived *right*) to feed and protect their loved ones was threatened by police, military recruiters, and other agents of the state, they not only challenged their men to perform their own customary roles, they engaged in disruptive behavior in the public arena. Thus, in mounting an effort to obtain their customary rights as family caretakers, these *campesinas* politicized the networks of everyday life. In the process, they often became outlaws and were generally judged by their betters to have "made spectacles of themselves."[30]

Certainly a variety of conscious and unconscious motivations and variables, as well as numerous other contingencies, come into play when we are called to ponder why individuals participate in riots and rebellions. We might say that the political behavior of insurgent groupings is typically *overdetermined*, the product of multiple and complex social and cultural wellsprings.[31] But ultimately, in grappling with these episodes of resistance and rebellion, I feel compelled to attempt a general explanation of why they took place and why villagers and peons decided to join

30. T. Kaplan (1982:566; 1987:444–46; 1992). Logan (1990:150–59) discusses female consciousness in present-day urban contexts, particularly Mérida, where many housewives are recent arrivals from the countryside.

Consider, for example, the circumstances affecting women's choices in the remote southeastern pueblo of Yaxcabá (Sotuta district) in the spring of 1911. The village was working under a tight deadline to prepare its *milpa* when military recruiters arrived. While their menfolk worked in the fields (only men make *milpa*), the women petitioned the recruiters and local political authorities to rescind the *leva* order. They pointed out that if the men were forced into the national guard, the village's livelihood would be jeopardized; moreover, in these times of violence, the men were their only protection—not only from the gathering Maderista rebellion, but from the *indios bravos* directly to the east. When the authorities would not budge, the women exhorted their men to resist. After several hours of "deliberation" in the local cantina, the men—joined by the women—attacked the *comisaría municipal*. Interviews with Clotilde Cob, Yaxcabá, Oct. 2, 1977, Dec. 15, 1977; Domínguez (1981:188–93).

31. Joseph (1990, 1991: esp. 166); cf. Van Young (1992). Scott (1990:217) trenchantly observes: "Once all the structural factors that might shed some light on [outbreaks of protest and insurgency] have been considered, there will be a large and irreducible element of voluntarism left." He cautions, therefore, to leave some analytical space for historical breaks, for moments when things change dramatically, almost in Jekyl-Hyde fashion; for possibilities that are inherent in practices that on the surface would seem to indicate otherwise. Cf. the similar caveats by Knight and Sayer in their contributions to this volume.

them—to offer at least a proximate cause, to pass through the eye of the needle, as it were.

In order to do this, we are obliged to look beyond individual insurgents' own beliefs about their actions and read those beliefs against the structural conditions that affected the individual as a member of a group(s) and as a part of a larger social formation. In effect, this means that the full range of "external" power relations must be considered, in addition to people's own "internal" perceptions of their conditions and behavior (see Taylor 1979:128–42; Stern 1987a:3–25).

I have sketched out the dynamic relations of domination within the henequen zone during the final years of the Porfiriato. Similarly, I have examined the severe threat that the expansion of the fiber estates posed to the existence of the poor but free villagers on the zone's less-controllable fringes. This threat was often compounded by the abuses of collusive political authorities at a juncture when the economy was deteriorating but political space was widening. Often such egregious acts by *jefes políticos* or other identifiable superiors—which in the case of one notorious political boss routinely included the expectation of *jus prima noctis*[32]—had the effect of transforming routine suffering into an unbearable sense of outrage so propitious to rebellion (Moore 1978: esp. 468–71; Tutino 1986: chap. 1).

Edward Thompson provides a salutary guidepost for the challenging task of understanding the consciousness of villagers and peons during episodes of insurgency:

> The consciousness of a worker is not a curve that rises and falls with wages and prices; it is an accumulation of a lifetime of experience and socialization, inherited traditions, struggles successful and defeated. It is this weighty baggage that goes into the making of a worker's consciousness and provides the basis for his behavior when conditions ripen and the moment comes. (Quoted in Winn 1986:v)

Thompson's insight may be profitably read against the evidence of the period. Hingemen often received an ambivalent reception when they

---

32. Interview with Marcos Ku Peraza; AGEY, RJ, "Acusación formulada por don Arturo Cirerol contra don Máximo Sabido, Jefe Político de Peto, por los delitos de abuso de autoridad y allanamiento de morada," 1913. The perpetrator in question was Arturo Cirerol. Ku Peraza recalls: "Back then, they didn't charge you anything to get married. But first the señor took your woman, first *he* had her, and *then* you got married." (To punctuate the point, Ku first referred to the act in Maya.)

arrived on henequen estates seeking adherents between 1909 and 1913.[33] Bad as conditions had become, many peons still eschewed a strategy of direct confrontation. It is likely they believed that, as in the past, such actions were doomed to failure, and that the spoils that might temporarily be won were not worth the loss of the modicum of security that the estate still provided—not to mention the potential loss of life and limb.

Some required more information before standing up to the *patrón*, and assertively sought it out. Contemporary testimonies and more recently gathered oral traditions reveal that in a variety of instances peons (individually and in groups) essentially *negotiated* with *cabecillas:* one *sirviente* pointedly asked a Morenista chief, "*Bueno, jefe,* exactly what *jornal* [wage] does your revolution provide?"[34] In another instance, after a hurried discussion upon the arrival of a Morenista band, several peons served notice to their *amo* (master) on the spot: "*Patrón,* we're leaving your service because of the violence and uncertain state of things [*la intranquilidad*]."[35] The recollections of one of them suggest that familial responsibilities and longstanding grievances played an important part in the mental calculus that was done.[36]

Yet not all *henequeneros* were perceived by peons to be losing their grip, nor had all abandoned paternal incentives; while conditions were generally deplorable,[37] they varied from estate to estate. No doubt, many *sirvientes* favored a strategy of continuing to extract what security they could and resisting the demands of monoculture in more "routine," less risky ways. Some peons, such as Alonso Patrón Espadas' *acasillados* at Sacapuc, remained genuinely loyal (and even affectionate) to a patron widely renowned for his generosity and kindness.[38]

33. Episodes that reveal much of this ambiguity and complexity are ACEY, RJ, "Toca a la causa seguida a Pedro Chi por el delito de destrucción de propiedad ajena por el incendio," 1912, and "Toca a la causa seguida a Juan Jiménez y socios."

34. Interview with Melchor Zozaya Raz; cf. ACEY, RJ, "Toca a la causa seguida a Juan Jiménez y socios."

35. ACEY, RJ, "Causa seguida a José Policarpo Mendoza y socios"; interview with Encarnación Parra, Libre Unión, Oct. 24, 1984.

36. Interview with Encarnación Parra.

37. As fiber prices continued to decline during the final years of the Porfiriato, the straitened planters passed the burden downward, reducing wages, restricting initial advances to peons as well as credit in the *tienda de raya,* and slashing other customary paternalist incentives, such as access to *milpa* plots and medical care. For a fuller discussion, see Joseph and Wells (1988).

38. Interviews with Hernán Menéndez, Mérida, Apr. 13, 1987; Alejandra García Quintanilla, Mérida, June 9, 1985; and Lina Cruz, Sacapuc, June 10, 1985.

Like the leaders of other peasant or slave revolts, Yucatán's *cabecillas* were not above "pressing" in order to secure recruits. Nor could they afford to be, in challenging such a formidable monocultural regime. As a rule, every effort was made first to appeal—in Maya—to the ties of family and communal origin that frequently bound villagers and peons, as well as to invoke shared grievances of class and ethnicity. When they had the luxury of time, the insurgents would also throw open the doors to the *tienda de raya,* slaughter the *patrón's* cattle, and fete the peons with an impromptu banquet—thereby demonstrating largesse and solidarity while pointing up the master's impotence. Moreover, *cabecillas* always made a point of first attempting to woo, manipulate or coerce those personnel on the estate who had a high degree of influence with the peons: the schoolteacher (*maestro*), the drivers and overseers (*mayocoles*), and occasionally even the *hacendado's* administrator (*encargado*). This task was made easier when the *cabecillas'* intelligence suggested that such individuals inhabiting rural society's middle ranks might be disgruntled with their current arrangements and chafing for advancement. Typically, it was only when these various inducements and recruiting strategies failed that *cabecillas* began to intimidate the peons directly, first making threats and then making violent examples of the *patrón's* favorite *sirvientes.* Frequently, they assembled the peons and threatened to raze their huts, burn their *milpa,* and confiscate their possessions if they did not join the revolt—and worse if they betrayed them to the authorities.[39]

Of course, a debate has always swirled around the uses of what Eugene Genovese, writing in the similar context of Afro-American slave revolts, calls "revolutionary terror." Genovese uses the term descriptively, even approvingly. In other words, leaders of slave revolts or peasant insurgencies appreciate that their mobilizations do not proceed in the abstract. Yucatán's *cabecillas* knew that whatever sympathies the peons might have harbored for the cause, they had long been conditioned to submission and would fear any resort to violence. That being the case, such peons had to be made "to confront a new reality." Genovese writes:

> [Rebels] who have not lost their senses must conclude that they will have no prospects until the cost of collaboration rises to the level of the cost of rebellion. For only then will people be free to choose sides on grounds of duty. And it serves no purpose to pretend that "innocent"—personally

39. Two court cases that document pressing in particularly rich detail are AGEY, RJ, "Causa seguida contra José Policarpo Mendoza y socios," and "Toca a la causa seguida a Juan Jiménez y socios."

inoffensive and politically neutral—people should be spared. The oppressor needs nothing so much as political neutrality to do business as usual: It is his *sine qua non.* He who wills liberation in a context that does not permit peaceful change wills revolutionary terror. No slave revolt that hesitated to invoke terror had a chance.[40]

Of course, this need to employ force to generate solidarity—a seeming contradiction in terms—has universally led insurgents' opponents to ignore pressing's *unifying function.* The "official mind" of the state has regarded pressing solely as proof of the coercive nature of rebellion, or at least portrayed it as such. Indeed, Yucatecan planters and state authorities did not stop talking about *sirvientes* who had been "seized," "forced" by "outsiders" to become part of a growing "contagion"; and many latter-day historians have drawn much the same conclusion.[41] But such one-sided depictions of pressing, as Indian historian Ranajit Guha points out, fail to grasp the essential ambiguity of the phenomenon, which is symptomatic of a lack of uniformity in peasant consciousness itself. "For no class or community is ever so monolithic as completely to rule out lags or disparities in its members' response to a rebellion." In this context, Guha contends, pressing "is primarily an instrument of . . . unification and not of punishment." Insurgents use "their mass and militancy . . . to resolve a contradiction among the [subaltern] themselves, not between [them] and their enemies" (Guha 1985:197–98).

Willingly or with some persuasion, significant numbers of peons took the risk and joined rebellious villagers in the popular insurgencies. Throughout 1910 and early 1911, the tenuous alliance between dissident elites in the cities and influential rural brokers in the interior continued to grow as the elites secured arms and cash, and the new, local *cabecillas* recruited in their *pueblos* and on neighboring estates.

In short order, however, the Morenista and Pinista elites came to reconsider the wisdom of their mobilization of villagers and peons. By the

40. Genovese (1979:11). For equally pertinent accounts of the dynamics of pressing in actions by eighteenth- and nineteenth-century Indian *ryots,* nineteenth-century English peasants, and former slaves in the postbellum "rice kingdom" of South Carolina and Georgia, see Guha (1985); Hobsbawm and Rudé (1968); and Foner (1983: chap. 3), respectively.

41. AGEY, RJ, 1910–1913, passim.; Gamboa Ricalde (1943–55:1); Betancourt Pérez (1983); Franz (1973: chaps. 1–3). Also see the periodic reports of U.S. consuls, which reflect the perspectives of state officials and the planter elite, in NA, RG 84, SD-CPR, 1910–1913, passim.

spring of 1911, the latest round of local riots and revolts had begun to spin out of control.

What the elites did not fully consider as they constructed these rudimentary insurgent networks was that the incipient rural rebels also had their own agendas, which were rarely congruent with the elites' rather limited political projects. Gradually, from the aborted Candelaria *conjura* (plot) in October 1909, through the failed rebellion in Valladolid during the late spring of 1910,[42] to the more freewheeling revolts that periodically rocked the state during 1911, 1912, and the first months of 1913, locally based popular mobilization had begun to evolve a life of its own, one that took little heed of elite political posturings. Yucatán's competing elites had opened a Pandora's box and, try as they might, they could never successfully harness the rage that exploded in peripheral areas like Hunucmá, the Puuc, and the eastern district of Temax.

Here, on the fringes of monoculture, throughout 1911 and 1912, estates were overrun by marauding bands who "liberated" peons and property alike—occasionally from the very Morenista or Pinista planters who had initially fomented the mobilization. On some estates, jacqueries erupted from within. In a variety of *cabeceras* (municipal seats), rebels dynamited the houses and stores of local notables, attacked the armories of national guard detachments, and summarily "brought to justice" abusive prefects, municipal authorities, and estate personnel.[43] They held Halachó, a good-sized *cabecera* in the Puuc, for two days and began naming their own municipal authorities.[44] Occasionally, popular *cabecilla*-led bands, joined by local peons, raided the *hacendados'* living quarters, then smashed henequen processing plants and tore up stretches of Decauville tram tracks in the best Luddite fashion.

Yet while the damage was extensive, the violence was rarely arbitrary or gratuitous. Targets were purposefully chosen, and none of the three

42. Although much of the literature on the outbreak of the Mexican revolution in Yucatán has focused on the failed rebellion of Valladolid in 1910, I contend that the uprising in the eastern portion of the state was just one example of the kind of revolts that surfaced during the last years of the Porfiriato. Cf. Menéndez (1919) and Betancourt Pérez (1983).

43. For *ajusticiamientos populares*, e.g., see AGEY, RJ, "Causa seguida contra Pedro Crespo y socios por el delito de homicidio, rebelión y robo," 1911, and "Causa seguida a Bernabé Escalante."

44. Ibid., "Toca a la causa a José Dolores Cauich y socios por los delitos de rebelión, robo y destrucción de propiedad ajena," 1912.

elite factions—Morenistas, Pinistas, or Molinistas—remained exempt. An elaborate effort was often made to symbolically negate the power of the *patrón* and manifest the inversion in power relations that was being played out. For example, in Hunucmá district, on the western fringes of the henequen zone, where agrarian discontents had simmered since the penetration of fiber cultivation in the 1880s and 1890s, the rebels dispatched their victims in a brutal, ritualistic manner. Thus, at hacienda San Pedro, Bonifacio Yam, a despised retainer of the planter, Pedro Telmo Puerto, was decapitated with a machete in the presence of the peons.[45] At hacienda Hoboyna, Herminio Balam slit the throat of Miguel Negrón, the estate's overseer, from ear to ear, then drank from the rivulet of spurting blood out of the palm of his hand. "How *agridulce* (sweet and tangy) the blood tasted," he would later observe to family members and *amigos de confianza.*[46]

In such popular *ajusticiamentos,* carried out under cover of Maderismo, personal vendettas were often bound up with longstanding communal grievances. Consider the celebrated action of Pedro Crespo, a Morenista *cabecilla* in Temax district. On March 4, 1911, Crespo rode into the *cabecera* just before dawn; rousted the corrupt *jefe político,* Colonel Antonio Herrera, and treasury agent Nazario Aguilar Brito from their beds; and hauled them, clad only in their skivvies, to the central plaza. All the while, as members of his band shouted "Down with bad government!" and "Viva Madero!", Crespo vented his rage on the stunned Herrera: "You bastard, you killed my father! For nine years you were on top and screwed me and the *pueblo,* but now it's my turn!"[47]

45. Ibid., "Toca a la causa seguida a Herminio Balam y socios por los delitos acumulados de encubridor de homicidio, destrucción de propiedad ajena y robo," 1913. The events described in this case took place in August 1911. One old-timer would later recall that this *ajusticiamiento* was quite a contrast from the floggings of lazy or disorderly *sirvientes* that he and his fellow peons had been obliged to watch during "the age of slavery." Interview with Marcos Ek, Hunucmá, June 7, 1982.

46. AGEY, RJ, "Testimonio de la causa seguida a Herminio Balam y socios por los delitos de homicidio y robo por asalto," 1911.

47. My reconstruction of the Crespo episode rests largely on the following sources: AGEY, RJ, "Causa seguida contra Pedro Crespo y socios"; and interviews with Melchor Zozaya Raz and Jesús Campos Esquivel. Temaxeños remember Crespo as a man with a foot in two worlds, "un mestizo de buen hablar"—a Maya *campesino* who spoke Spanish well and could handle himself in town. For a fuller account of Pedro Crespo's long and interesting political career as a *cacique revolucionario,* see Joseph and Wells (1987).

The tables were indeed turned. Handpicked as district prefect around the turn of the century by Temax's powerful Molinista planters, Herrera had been the dominant figure in the district's political life, and his physical presence made him even more menacing to local *campesinos*. Hulking in stature, with his shaved head and long, gray beard, Herrera often took on the dimensions of a mad monk or an avenging prophet. Only days before, during the carnival revels of Shrove Tuesday, although too cowed to make a statement about the *jefe político*, Temaxeños had mocked his subordinate, Aguilar Brito, as "Juan Carnaval," shooting an effigy of the tax collector in front of the municipal palace. Now, in the same central plaza in the wee hours of the morning, Pedro Crespo was cutting the despised prefect down to size. In a final act of humiliation, Crespo strapped Herrera and Aguilar to chairs and riddled them with bullets in the same spot in front of the town hall where Aguilar had been "executed" during carnival. The bodies were piled into a meat wagon and then dumped at the gates of the town cemetery. (In a ghastly irony, the treasury agent would later be interred in the same coffin "Juan Carnaval" had occupied the preceding Shrove Tuesday.[48])

After years of exploitation and racial degradation, Maya *campesinos* suddenly found themselves enthusiastically discussing their actions in the country stores and at Saturday night fiestas (*jaranas*). The following is a reconstruction of a typical exchange, drawn from contemporary testimonies: "I lit the dynamite that blew up the boiler," offered Fulano. "I knocked down the stone markers around the new field," commented Mengano. "Imagine," interjected Zutano, "All these fine clothes were paid for with the loot that the *dzules* extracted from the ribs of our *pueblo*."[49] At various junctures in 1911 and 1912, such popular insurgency threatened to ignite the henequen zone itself.

Clearly, Madero's liberal movement was a bundle of contradictions; but the single greatest cleavage was the marked difference in world views between contending urban elites on the one hand, and the rural insurgents they had unleashed on the other. Despite their bickering, Morenista and Pinista elites both espoused a return to something approaching

48. For a persuasive symbolic analysis that explores how patterns of ethnic conflict can be "read" from historical accounts of Yucatecan carnival as well as from observing present-day rituals, see Bricker (1981:150–54).

49. E.g., see AGEY, RJ, "Causa seguida a Guillermo Canul y socios por los delitos de daño y destrucción de propiedad ajena," 1912; and "Toca a la causa seguida a Pedro Chi."

the political liberalism of Benito Juárez. Beneath their ideological state-ments and rhetorical embellishments was a gnawing desire to return to the traditional, nineteenth-century model of political power that would permit them to garner their proper share of the henequen spoils. Such elite liberalism, of course, had all the while sanctioned the breakup of village lands in the name of progress.

Meanwhile, personal testimonies and an extraordinary, rambling "epic poem" titled "The Fifteenth of September," written by a twenty-year-old, village-based insurgent from the Puuc named Rigoberto Xiu, reveal that Yucatán's popular rebels were *also* imbued with liberalism, but of a very different stripe.[50] *Their* liberalism invoked liberal heroes and traditions like Padre Hidalgo and Independence, Juárez and the War against the French. Yet consonant with the personal testimonies of so many other insurgents, the liberal tradition to which Xiu appealed was not the inevitable march of progress the elites celebrated. Rather it was a bloody, often bleak, but utterly "moral" struggle over centuries to preserve one's freedom and dignity against external forces of oppression.

SEASONS OF UPHEAVAL: DEMOBILIZATIONS

Ultimately, a variety of planter and state strategies, as well as certain structural factors, explains why in Yucatán political conflict and popular insurgency stopped short of the generalized rebellion that occurred in many other parts of the republic. To begin with, in Yucatán the old order had certain "built-in" advantages that permitted it to contain festering discontent and pull itself back from the brink. The peninsula's remote location—there were no roads connecting Yucatán with central Mexico until well after World War II—impeded communications with revolu-tionary chiefs in Mexico's core and in the north, and made coordination of joint campaigns virtually impossible.

Second, the coercive and highly regulated system of social control that landowners and the state had fashioned during the henequen boom worked to impede collaboration between villagers and peons and to keep local outbreaks isolated. As we have seen, the *henequeneros* never succeeded in keeping the plantations hermetically sealed; indeed, rural *cabecillas* and their intimates frequently penetrated the estates, chiefly as peddlers and

---

50. Ibid., "Causa seguida a Rigoberto Xiu y socios por rebelión," 1909; interviews with Jesús Campos Esquivel and Melchor Zozaya Raz.

part-time workers. Yet despite the ties of kinship and communal origin that frequently linked members of insurgent bands to groupings of peons on neighboring estates, over the long haul it was extraordinarily difficult to mobilize a diverse peasantry balkanized by different social and productive relations.[51] Contemporary testimonies are redolent with references to long-running animosities and vendettas between villagers and peons. If the freewheeling Maderista riots and revolts could bring these *comuneros* and *acasillados* together around shared grievances, not infrequently they also served to drive them further apart, bringing simmering antagonisms to a boil and providing a convenient cover for the settling of old scores. "Look, Juan, there is one of those chicken thieves from [hacienda] Suytunchen," an insurgent screamed to a fellow villager from Sierra Papacal; "let's break the bastard of his bad habit once and for all."[52] In Yucatán and elsewhere during the epic revolution—notwithstanding the rosy claims of some populist historians—villagers and peons were rarely amalgamated in durable alliances, let alone constituted a *"campesino* class" that struggled against landowners.[53]

The "social memory" of the Yucatecan planter class might itself be viewed as something of a "structural" factor. The *hacendados'* obsession with the specter of the Caste War gave them second thoughts about unleashing a full-scale mobilization of Maya villagers and peons. Although Morenista and Pinista planters itched to defeat the Molinista oligarchy, the majority of them feared that arming the rural masses would undermine the elaborate mechanisms of social control that had so successfully underwritten the henequen boom. That certain elites did take such a chance and did arm *campesinos* throughout the state demonstrates the divisions in the dominant class and the sense of desperation of some *henequeneros.* More often than not, however, rebellious *campesinos* had little fire power, typically only their field machetes or the antique, muzzle-loaded shotguns they used for hunting.[54]

51. This is precisely the argument Scott (1985) makes with regard to Malaysian peasants. He goes on to argue that in such highly controlled agrarian societies, peasants historically have had greater recourse to "quieter," more routine forms of resistance. The significance of such "everyday forms of resistance" on Porfirian estates has already been noted.

52. AGEY, RJ, "Toca a la causa seguida a Juan Jiménez y socios."

53. Hart (1987) advances in most extreme fashion the populist notion of a peasantry unified in struggle.

54. AGEY, RJ, 1909–1913, passim.

Nevertheless, even with the structural obstacles arrayed against it, popular insurgency was reaching dangerous new levels and threatening to engulf the henequen zone late in 1912. This obliged the planters and their new ally, the national military state of General Victoriano Huerta, to fashion new strategies to defuse the insurgency early in 1913.[55]

Probably nowhere in the republic was the new military dictator so enthusiastically received as in Yucatán. His assassination of Madero was applauded by Yucatán's rival elites, who, by and large, approved of Huertismo's subsequent Porfirista solution to the problems of "banditry" and "anarchy" (read popular insurgency). Huerta's imposition of authoritarian military rule institutionalized a political stalemate among Yucatán's three contending elite factions, the Molinistas, Morenistas, and Pinistas; but it also allowed them an opportunity to reach an accommodation—*un acomodamiento de desleales*, as it were—that would preserve the social peace.

With the issue of state power resolved, at least temporarily, justice was meted out alternately with Porfirian shrewdness and verve. The Huertista government declared a general amnesty, then made it clear in a run of edicts and local court decisions that "banditry"—i.e., new crimes against property, resistance to authority—would be punished with the greatest severity. To be sure, Yucatán (like any society, even a highly controlled one) did not lack "professional" criminals; thieves and rustlers had plied their trade before the seasons of upheaval, and found even greater possibilities during them. Yet here the use of the term *banditry* by the Huertista state and Yucatán's three elite *camarillas* was an attempt to seize the discursive high ground to meet a specific *political* challenge. Much like the more recent concept of "terrorism," "banditry" became more a part of the "metalanguage of crime" than a specific crime itself. It allowed the state and the planter class to mark violent or potentially violent behavior by "dangerous classes" in society.[56] It is interesting, that only months before, two of the elite *camarillas* had been in the habit of referring to at least some of these "bandits" (i.e., "their" bandits) as

55. The following discussion of demobilization draws heavily on Joseph and Wells (1990b).

56. Indeed, even banditry's etymological origins (the Latin *bannire*, meaning to banish) suggest this process of exclusion, in which a boundary was created between the bandit and society. (The process is cast in even bolder relief in the case of the analogous term *outlaw*.) For a fuller discussion of the state's use of labeling to criminalize popular protest and resistance, one that draws on a venerable Anglo-Saxon literature on the sociology of deviance as well as the recent linguistic turn in critical inquiry associated primarily with French scholarship, see Joseph (1990:18–25).

"revolutionaries" and "insurgents." From the "bandits'" standpoint, their activities remained essentially the same. In Hunucmá district, for example, they operated as individuals, in small informal groups, or in larger insurgent bands, depending on the options that circumstances provided; but always with a view to defending the remnants of a shrinking agrarian patrimony and settling accounts with despised power figures.

As for the military state, while it made examples of several villagers, sending them before a firing squad for rustling and robbery, it solicitously courted and ultimately cut deals with the most strategically placed popular *cabecillas*. In exchange at least for their quiescence, these local chiefs in the fringe areas, who had demonstrated their ability to turn out hundreds of fighters, were granted a measure of political autonomy—which had always been their principal goal. Some received commissions in the state militia, and for several the deal seems to have been sweetened with a choice *terrenito* (piece of land).

Meanwhile, the planters made some adjustments of their own. As we have seen, even during the height of the fiber boom, Yucatán's monocultural regime had depended on more than mere coercion; its "idiom of power" included paternalistic incentives and did not preclude at least the opportunity for henequen workers to address the state's courts with their grievances (Joseph and Wells 1988). Now, early in 1913, faced with an escalating popular revolt, the planters were forced, at least in the short run, to make greater concessions.[57]

Like earlier slave rebellions in the Caribbean and the U.S. South, Yucatán's popular seasons of upheaval elicited the drafting of a reform agenda by progressive planters and actual material concessions on some estates, even as the revolts provoked more severe measures of control on others.[58] In general, after 1913, the local courts, which were still planter-controlled, were more disposed to addressing (and occasionally even redressing) the most egregious abuses against peons.[59] This also suggests parallels with the plantation regime of the antebellum U.S. South, where,

57. Or, as Knight (1986a:1:221) has put it for Mexico as a whole: "to wheedle and promise, as well as repress."

58. E.g., see Genovese (1979:110–13). Progressive planters coalesced in the Liga de Acción Social in 1909. See Chacón (1981:118–31).

59. E.g., see the court system's judicious handling of the notorious San Nicolás case, involving *henequenero* abuse of peons (consistent use of leg irons, floggings with wire, etc.). AGEY, RJ, "Toca a la causa seguida a Pedro Pinto y socios por los delitos de lesiones y atentados contra la libertad individual," 1914.

as Genovese and others have shown, the law fulfilled something of a hegemonic function, providing at least the appearance of a disinterested standard of justice in the minds of the subordinate class (Genovese 1974:25–49).

Finally, in a culminating gesture in 1914, Yucatecan rural workers secured a decree that abolished debt peonage. Although it was never implemented, and seems to have been issued only as an expedient to buy the plantocracy time, the decree provided an important precedent that later revolutionary governments would enforce after 1915 (see, e.g., Paoli and Montalvo 1977; Joseph [1982] 1988: parts 2 and 3).

By mid-1913, the countryside had essentially been demobilized, but the passage of the peonage decree a year later attests to how tenuous the social peace really was in Yucatán. The dominant class's honeymoon with Huertismo would be brief. To meet the mounting Constitutionalist revolutionary challenge against him in the rest of Mexico, Huerta repeatedly raised taxes on the Yucatecan monocrop as well as military levees on the *henequeneros'* already scarce labor force. Thus, elites and working people alike found Huertismo increasingly odious. In mid-1914, just before Huerta fell, popular insurgency was again under way in the Puuc, and several riots flared in the henequen zone itself.

Only with some difficulty thereafter did Yucatán's uneasy alliance of elite *camarillas* maintain the old order following the arrival of Constitutionalist rule in 1914. Not only did bargains have to be renegotiated with some popular *cabecillas*, but an understanding also had to be reached with the new governor from Mexico City. It was at this crucial juncture that the toothless peonage decree was issued. Then, in January 1915, when bribes and blandishments no longer served to forestall the reforms of the next Constitutionalist governor, the old plantocracy buried its factional differences and mounted a last, futile rebellion to preserve the *ancien régime*. The leaders and paymasters of this revolt, staged ostensibly to uphold "state sovereignty," were Olegario Molina, Avelino Montes, and other heavyweights in the old Molinista *casta divina*. Yucatán, it appeared, had come full circle.

REVOLUTIONARY LEGACIES

Or had it? I would argue that Yucatán's *campesinos* had been changed by their participation in the Madero-era seasons of upheaval from late 1909 through early 1913. Indeed, the fact that the so-called sovereignty movement of 1915 was able to muster so little popular support would seem to offer testimony of something of a shift in *campesino* attitudes and tactics. Alvarado's seven-thousand-strong army made short work of the Yucatecan force of fifteen hundred, a good many of whom were students and merchants, sons of the Meridano and Progreseño middle and upper classes. A few *cabecillas* turned out their men, but the majority sat out the debacle of the Yucatecan oligarchy and then came to terms with Alvarado, a Mexican revolutionary populist whose program had more to offer the Yucatecan popular classes.[60] Among the myriad social reforms he implemented, Alvarado quickly put teeth back into the decree outlawing debt peonage.

In fact, much documentation exists to support the judgment that in remote, oligarchical Yucatán, as in other parts of Mexico, old, deferential habits were giving way to a new assertiveness and empowerment—to what Knight has called "a new plebeian insolence" (1986a:1:169). The judicial records and press reports between 1910 and 1915 reveal a variety of complaints from plantation overseers and the owners themselves that their peons no longer doffed their hats or kissed their masters' hands.[61] In 1915, Alvarado's newly installed military tribunals received waves of petitions from peons demanding that their masters raise their salaries and improve their working conditions. In one colorful instance, the rendering of a positive decision by a revolutionary tribunal was not enough to satisfy the leader of a delegation of peons. He continued to rail about the haughtiness and cruelty of his overseer until he was found in contempt and forcibly removed from the chamber.[62]

The sudden launching during the 1909–1913 period of the political careers of popular *cabecillas* like Pedro Crespo, Juan Campos, and José Loreto Baak provides another indication of change in both the political and mental realms. Contemporary testimonies and the interviews I conducted with old-timers in selected fringe municipalities suggest that the precipitous rise of these local chiefs was as satisfying to their *campesino* followers as it was disconcerting to the plantocracy. Such *cabecillas*, who have received far too little attention in the Mexican revolutionary historiography (but see Joseph 1980:193–221; Joseph and Wells 1987; Buve

---

60. The collapse of this "last stand of the oligarchs" is treated in the final chapter of my forthcoming book with Wells.

61. E.g., see AGEY, RJ, "Incendio en la finca Texán," 1914; and RdY, Mar. 31, 1914.

62. AGEY, RJ, "Diligencias contra Juan Córdova," 1915.

1985; and Falcón 1984), under Alvarado and Carrillo Puerto would consolidate their clienteles into intermediate power domains, midway between larger regional political machines and purely local *cacicazgos*. Typically smallholders, artisans, petty merchants, or some combination of these, they emerged from the middle rungs of rural society to mobilize and represent the rural masses throughout the republic, bridging the cultural and ideological gap between *campesinos* and townspeople— between "insiders" and "outsiders."

No doubt a series of culturally informed, longitudinal studies of such *jefes menores* or intermediate *caciques*—the "flesh of the Revolution," in the words of Carleton Beals (1931: chap. 13)—would go a long way toward creating the synthesis of the Mexican revolution that appears to lie in the offing. Such studies would focus on the relations these *caciques* forged with the emerging Revolutionary state on the one hand, and their local clienteles on the other. My investigation of several of Yucatán's *cabecillas* has enabled me to trace them from their beginnings as notable political actors in 1909–1910 through the consolidation of their power domains in the 1910s and early 1920s, until their demise or transformation into official party functionaries in the 1930s (and even the 1940s, in at least one case). It has also cautioned me to reject neat, overwrought interpretations of the Mexican revolution and encouraged me to fit together elements from both populist and revisionist approaches.

With Alan Knight, I would agree that *cabecillas* such as Crespo, Campos, and Baak provided a brand of leadership to villagers on the periphery of the henequen zone that was eminently popular: home-grown, locally focused, and organically legitimate (in the sense of the Weberian model of "traditional authority"). Such authority both reflected and helped to shape the character of village-based insurgency during the seasons of upheaval. These leaders had no encompassing national or even regional vision. They responded to, and by their actions reinforced, their followers' determination to preserve autonomy and subsistence and at the same time to undermine, actually and symbolically, the authority of the dominant class and the state. Their "ideology" was written in their revolts, and often emerges in their testimonies. Crespo candidly told the press: "Our goal is to overthrow the authorities and then see what happens."[63] Or as Juan Campos summed it up: "to fight tyranny and slavery and remain a free man."[64]

63. DY, Mar. 6, 1911.
64. Interview with Campos's son, Jesús Campos Esquivel, Dec. 26, 1986.

Where such organic leadership and organization was weak or virtually absent, among the ethnically diverse settlements—I hesitate even
to call them true communities—of estate peons in the heart of the more
systematically controlled henequen zone, the forms of protest were
different. Resistance normally took on a more "routine," day-to-day quality, escalating into short-lived eruptions of violence that were often
provoked by the incursions of *cabecilla*-led bands between 1910 and early
1913 (Joseph and Wells 1988:244–64).

Because of the rather parochial, defensive nature of popular authority
and ideology, Yucatán's popular movement was destined to be rather
fragmented and brittle. The village-based *cabecillas* might successfully
mobilize and represent their local clienteles, but they often just as actively feuded with and repressed factional rivals and only with great
difficulty made common cause (and never lasting alliances) with neighboring entities or with the peons.[65]

I should emphasize that I am not affirming any larger theoretical
judgment about peasant consciousness—that it is narrowly obsessed with
local struggles over land, subsistence, and a desire simply to be left alone.
Nor am I validating essentialist notions that the little world of the village
or hacienda bounded the ideological horizon of peasants. My earlier
emphasis on the appropriation and reformulation of liberal ideology by
Yucatecan peasants should make this clear. Moreover, scholars working
on the Andes have persuasively argued that peasants often had a keen
awareness of political worlds beyond the immediate locale, and possessed
a flexibility of consciousness far more complex than the predictable
parochial obsessions with land, autonomy, or subsistence security (see,
e.g., the essays in Stern 1987b: esp. chaps. 1, 2, and 9). Nevertheless,
given the formidable constraints imposed by Yucatán's monocultural
regime, particularly an "idiom of power" that effectively combined reinforcing elements of isolation, coercion, and paternalistic security, it seems
legitimate to conclude that a parochial orientation and a defensive obsession with local rights did indeed prevail among the Yucatecan peasantry
during the seasons of upheaval.

For a variety of reasons, then, it is not really surprising that the
popular movement led in Yucatán by the new men of the 1910s was
welded without great difficulty (and often with their assistance) into the
ever-more-powerful national state of the 1920s and 1930s. In a sense,
Yucatán, despite its marked regionalism, provides a vivid illustration of

65. E.g., see AGEY, RJ, "Toca a la causa seguida a Juan Jiménez y socios."

what is increasingly regarded as a commonplace of Mexican political culture and revolutionary history: the propensity of local popular elements and movements—invariably undemocratic themselves—at first to suspect, then to work cautiously with, and finally to legitimate authoritarian regional and national caudillos and the institutionalized regime they ultimately established.

Pedro Crespo, *cacique* of the village of Temax and of central Yucatán from about 1911 until he died in 1944, whose early career we have already glimpsed, serves to illustrate this principle (Joseph and Wells 1987). Representing the grievances of most Temaxeños (as well as harboring his own personal vendetta), Crespo rebelled in 1911, then reached a series of separate understandings with Maderismo, Huertismo, revolutionary Yucatán's homegrown variant of "socialismo," and ultimately with what evolved into current-day PRIismo. But it is too easy to argue, like the revisionists, that Pedro Crespo "sold out." Up to the 1930s, political life in Temax and its environs proceeded with a high degree of local autonomy from the state, in large part due to Crespo's shrewdness. Under his *cacicazgo*, moreover, Temaxeños regained most of their traditional village lands. Later, during the Great Depression, with henequen irreversibly in decline, Crespo skillfully negotiated an arrangement with the most powerful planters and the state to keep the fields in production and minimize layoffs.

It is significant that to the day he died, Crespo lived in much the same manner as his rustic followers: he spoke Maya among friends, wore the collarless white *filipina* shirt, and lived in the *kaxna*, the traditional wattle-and-daub-cottage with thatched roof. What interested him most was political power, not wealth. The Mexican revolution had offered him a chance, and he had seized it. He viewed himself, and is still regarded in Temax, as a *líder nato*—a born local leader, a chief. As such, he did what was necessary to preserve, even extend, his *poderío* (power domain). This entailed constant political vigilance and negotiation: deals might be made with powerful planters and *had* to be made with an ever more muscular, bureaucratic state, but they never called on Crespo to sell out his clientele, accumulate great wealth, and leave Temax for Mérida. Indeed, precisely because he was a *líder nato*, he was incapable of transcending his locality and breaking with the political culture that had produced him.

In the process, Pedro Crespo played an important role in promoting those routines and rituals of rule that, when all is said and done, allow "The Mexican Revolution" to stake its claim as part of a *cultural* revolution in state formation (Corrigan and Sayer 1985). Organizing local *ligas de resistencia* and, later, official party clubs and youth groups; scheduling weekly *veladas culturales* (cultural soirées); officiating at patriotic acts of commemoration (such as the anniversary of the death of Revolutionary Martyr Carrillo Puerto); and energetically promoting "socialist education" and *béisbol* teams in some of the remotest *pueblos* and hacienda communities of central Yucatán,[66] Crespo effectively bridged the cultural and ideological gap between Temaxeños and the Revolutionary state for several decades. Today, forty years after his death, Crespo remains at the service of the state's cultural project. Duly incorporated into the Revolutionary Pantheon alongside more famous regional icons like Alvarado and Carrillo Puerto, he is commemorated when the Revolution's litany of triumphs is read in Temax every November 20.

Some of Yucatán's other *cabecillas* were more ruthless and economically acquisitive than Pedro Crespo; nevertheless, they still approximate him far more than they do Carlos Fuentes' fictional composite, Artemio Cruz. All were leaders who ruled over factionalized, stratified local worlds, who sought to balance between the centralizing new state with its project of capitalist transformation on the one hand and their own local clienteles on the other, all the while clinging to political power (be it control of local agrarian commissions, municipal presidencies, or other vehicles). Those like Crespo (or Peto's Elías Rivero) who managed this balancing act, who were particularly able to translate between popular and state ideologies, endured. Those not as politically or culturally adroit (such as José Loreto Baak) were replaced by factional contenders, who then took their turn at applying the new rules of the game to the old political culture.

To date neither the revisionists nor the populists have provided a particularly satisfying treatment of how the postrevolutionary state was formed. It is one thing to affirm, with the revisionists, an essential continuity in the Porfirian and revolutionary elites' desire to create a national, capitalist society. It is quite another to deny agency to popular political cultures and reduce their leaders to mere instruments of an emerging Leviathan state. I would contend that in Yucatán and elsewhere, the

66. For an examination of how the official party used baseball in Yucatán during the 1920s and 1930s to mobilize popular support and *forjar patria* (construct the nation) in both sociocultural and infrastructural terms, see Joseph (1988:29–61). The state was so successful in its campaign that *béisbol* has become the regional pastime, an anomaly in a nation where elsewhere *fútbol* is the people's game.

revolutionary process forever changed the terms by which the Mexican state would be formed. Indeed, it is the state's partial incorporation of popular demands since 1920 that helps to distinguish Mexico from countries like Peru and El Salvador today. As Florencia Mallon points out in her chapter in this volume, one has only to juxtapose the contrasting images of Cuauhtémoc Cárdenas and Peru's Sendero Luminoso to appreciate this point. For Mexico's latter-day Cardenistas, the struggle is clearly circumscribed within the framework of the revolution, the nation, and the state; for the Senderistas, it is about the total bankruptcy of the Peruvian state and the absence of a nation.

At the same time, my Yucatecan data also present a compelling argument for subjecting romantic, populist approaches to much closer scrutiny. The data challenge us to specify just what is so popular about "the popular," and caution against applying facile, essentialist notions of class, communal, and ethnic solidarity to real social worlds. As we have seen, Yucatán's diverse *campesinado* had for many decades been divided by different social and productive relations; strong peasant communities had ceased to exist in the northwestern henequen zone long before the Caste War and the subsequent onslaught of monoculture. Even on the fringes of monoculture, peasant villages were stratified and contentious, communal bonds were fragile, and could only be mobilized to confront a serious external threat.[67] Similarly, ethnic identity was anything but "primordial" or solidary; Maya ethnicity had undergone several important reconstruc-

---

67. In a recent, richly suggestive essay, Gavin Smith argues that peasant participants in the relatively successful present-day Peruvian land invasions he has studied "are committed both to the importance of the differences among them *and simultaneously* to the ongoing production of an image of themselves as internally homogeneous and externally distinctive" (Smith 1991:181, emphasis added). In other words, with communal heterogeneity a given, points of difference must constantly be negotiated, and *contentiousness* becomes an integral part of the process whereby community and a culture of resistance are forged. In the case of the Peruvian land invaders, such "acting in unity . . . required a *continuous process* of the intense negotiation of meanings—a process, moreover, in which the attainment of cultural unity was never complete but was always unfinished business throughout the intense periods of resistance" (p. 204). Smith's thesis deserves to be tested in the Mexican revolutionary context, although written and oral sources rarely support such fine-grained historical ethnography. In the case of Yucatán, embattled *campesinos* rarely had the autonomy or mobility that Smith's *comuneros* possessed. Thus, although negotiated strategies of resistance were essential in the face of monoculture's onslaught, they were difficult to achieve, and tenuous at best.

tions since the days of the Yucatec Maya's "collective enterprise of survival" during the colonial period.

Yes, Yucatán generated a popular rural movement during Maderismo, but it was a far cry from the telluric national groundswells conjured up, for example, by writers such as Frank Tannenbaum and José Valadés or, more recently, John Hart. The broad-ranging histories of such populists, past and present, provide heroic images and stirring accounts, to be sure; but Yucatán's revolutionary experience—as well as others detailed in this volume[68]—alerts us to other perspectives and histories that such universalizing renditions tend to elide or pass over entirely.[69]

68. See particularly Rus's essay on highland Chiapas, Nugent and Alonso's on western Chihuahua, and Becker's on northwestern Michoacán.

69. Again, Knight's magnum opus (1986a) is less deserving of such criticism (see n. 3, above). Unlike other populists, Knight is consistently alive to regional variation and refuses mechanically to deduce the behavior and consciousness of historical actors from structural relations of production or, worse, to assume that they are the product of some preexisting consciousness.

ELSIE ROCKWELL

Schools of the Revolution: Enacting and Contesting State Forms in Tlaxcala, 1910–1930

In the history of Mexico, public schools almost invariably have come to be associated with the state. Nineteenth-century liberal discourse, which defined a public, political role for education, certainly contributed to this conception, while the educational policies of the 1920s and 1930s further reinforced it. Yet such a view presupposes a state powerful enough to develop and control a public school system, and through it mold a national consciousness.[1] During the first decade of the Mexican revolution (1910–1920), this condition did not exist. Although a nominal federal administration continued during these years, the prerevolutionary state was effectively dissolved (Womack 1986:107; Knight 1985:15–17). The relative weakness of the successive governing groups gave way to diverse regional conflicts and realignments. Indeed, the formation of a new central power, founded on a different network of relations and alliances, would proceed gradually over the course of the following decades.

I am grateful for the careful reading and comments on previous versions of this essay by Gilbert Joseph, Bradley Levinson, William Beezley, Raymond Buve, Mary Kay Vaughan, Susana Quintanilla, and Oresta López.

1. President Plutarco E. Calles's *Grito de Guadalajara* in the 1920s is often cited to indicate the state's intention of using the school to shape "the consciences of children and of young people . . . in order to banish prejudices and create a new national soul." See Josefina Z. Vázquez (1970:153). Alan Knight (1986a) has been particularly insistent on the dangers of attributing social changes, such as those wrought through the Mexican revolution, to an all-powerful state.

The rural schools that developed in the postrevolutionary era were not simple expressions of a preexisting state; on the contrary, they contributed in a crucial way to the formation of a more centralized state. As schools were established, new channels—mediated by teachers—were created between rural constituencies and local and federal authorities. Yet the story has another side. Schools were only minimally funded and controlled by the postrevolutionary governments. Villagers contributed in a number of ways: by making specific social and pedagogical demands (typically rooted in traditional liberal views of public education), by donating their resources and time to school construction, and by participating in schools' day-to-day operation. In turn, rural schools came to constitute new spaces where relations with the state were negotiated and where the fabric of local civil society[2] was reinforced.

AN ETHNOGRAPHIC APPROACH TO THE HISTORY OF RURAL SCHOOLING

My interest in postrevolutionary schooling stems from an earlier ethnographic study of rural schools in Tlaxcala, which called into question—as fieldwork tends to do—existing theoretical frameworks.[3] That field research revealed a series of local conflicts over several issues, among them the social obligations of teachers, plans for celebrating civic holidays, ways of teaching and disciplining children, styles of building schools, the uses of school grounds, and the payment of fees (see C. Aguilar 1991; Mercado 1986; Rockwell and Mercado 1986). Those conflicts could not be interpreted simply as a univocal "popular opposition to schooling." Teachers as well as villagers were often divided on the

2. The term *civil society* is not used here as a synonym for *society,* or to indicate a uniform "subject" that rises against the state. Rather, it is formed by the historically constituted relationships that make public, collective action possible. The networks that constitute civil society may predate or follow the process of secularization. See Pereyra (1984:205–19) for a convincing interpretation of Gramsci's 1971 conception.

3. The research project, "Teaching and Its Institutional and Social Context (1980–1986)," was coordinated by Justa Ezpeleta and the author with the collaboration of Ruth Mercado, Citlali Aguilar, and Etelvina Sandoval. Some of the ideas and field examples used in this essay are the product of collective work during the project, and are also reported in other publications, including Ezpeleta and Rockwell (1983), Rockwell (1986), Rockwell and Mercado (1986), and Mercado (1986).

issues, and the conflicts often led to open negotiation at school meetings—or to a more implicit kind of negotiation, in which various strategies of control and resistance were used to influence the outcomes.

In studying these negotiations, we found that the bases of present-day resistance could often be traced to the way schools had been constructed in the decades immediately following the Mexican revolution. Indeed, two quite different conceptions were at play: rural schools were originally geared toward social action and local participation, while the subsequent model of schooling privileged technical and professional imperatives and curtailed local control. Although the more bureaucratic model had largely displaced former practices by the 1980s, many parents and older teachers continued to press for compliance with traditional school norms and to resist "modernizing" policies. These findings served to direct my attention to the history of rural schooling.

During the nineteenth century, different models of elementary schooling coexisted in Mexico. In a sense, there was no strict separation between public and private education: government regulations and subsidies were often bound up with local, parochial, and corporate initiatives to provide a limited access to free schooling. In rural areas, villagers and hacienda proprietors would hire "private" or "domestic" teachers to comply with the public obligation to educate children. Despite the liberal regimes' emphatic support of the idea of universal, compulsory, lay education—codified in the 1857 Constitution and subsequent liberal laws—and Justo Sierra's far-reaching proposal for federal education in 1905, one cannot equate the official provisions for schooling with the actual existence of a public school system by the end of the Porfirian regime.[4] After 1915, Venustiano Carranza promoted municipal control of elementary schooling, and different parts of the country entertained alternative schemes for financing education. A federal system was reestablished only after the Obregón regime redefined educational policy in 1921, yet the incursion of this federal system into the various regions encountered an assortment of preexisting arrangements.

Because of the persistence of some deep-seated prerevolutionary patterns of education in the second and third decades of this century, the revisionist critique of the official history of education has tended to

4. I use Michael B. Katz's conception of a "public school system" (1987), which emphasizes the appearance of a professional administrative body as the defining element.

downplay the effects of the Mexican revolution on schooling.[5] The recent trend has been to discover and emphasize the continuity of practices established in the colonial or Porfirian periods with those found in the postrevolutionary years (Vázquez 1970; Vaughan 1982; Meneses 1986; Gonzalbo 1991). Some studies argue that after the revolution, educators simply implemented the nineteenth-century liberal program, rather than creating a new project. I will argue in this essay that the revolutionary movement did generate changes—at times unforeseen— both in the structure of public education and in the everyday life of schools in rural areas.

A variety of theoretical and methodological problems complicate research on schooling. The emphasis on the individual militancy of teachers (Cockroft 1967; Raby 1974; Knight 1989) has overshadowed the social history of schooling itself, as Mary Kay Vaughan correctly reminds us (1990a:47). The notion of schools as "state apparatuses" or instruments that forge national consensus, inculcate ideologies, train labor forces, and transform identities pervades much of the literature. Yet this "reproductionist" vision is increasingly being questioned by authors who prefer to historicize schooling—that is, to conceive of it as variable, subject to diverse social and political forces and uses.[6]

Historical analyses of schooling that draw exclusively on the documentation of official public discourse (laws, reports, programs, and textbooks) sometimes assume that school systems actually accomplish what governments claim—such as constituting free citizens or disseminating a rational world view—and that they change uniformly when central policies are modified. In reality, school practices are extraordinarily diverse and often at odds with official policy. Furthermore, the state's educational proposals at any given moment are not necessarily coherent, and they are redefined as they filter down through the respective govern-

5. Mary Kay Vaughan (1990) has recently reviewed research on nineteenth-century Mexican education centering on the current debates, some of which I take up in this essay.

6. Reproductionist theory has several versions, to which scholars such as Althusser, Bourdieu and Passeron, Foucault, and Corrigan have contributed. Among those who have questioned this model of schooling, stressing the idea that relationships between the social classes and schools are historically constructed, are Willis (1977), Wexler et al. (1981), Reed-Danahay (1987), Ezpeleta and Rockwell (1983), and Vaughan (1994).

ing agencies. Indeed, the obvious complexity of the process has often encouraged a contrary interpretation. It has been argued, for example, that Mexican rural schools succeeded in disseminating neither the liberal nor the socialist ideologies proclaimed by authorities at different moments. This argument nourishes the revisionist view that state policies scarcely affect the continuity of basic schooling patterns established sometime in the past. It also—as Alan Knight warns in his essay in this volume—underestimates the cultural transformations that the revolution brought about. Significantly, neither interpretation views schools as the products of social history.

From an ethnographic perspective, it is clear that schools, like other institutions, are socially constructed. In my view, ethnography should attempt to uncover the "undocumented history" of this process of social construction (Rockwell 1986). A school's "undocumented history" consists of those sociocultural contexts and resources—both constraining and enabling—that structure social action. At any given moment in school history, persistent local practices and beliefs interact with government initiatives to mold school life. "Everyday forms of resistance," such as those documented for other contexts by James Scott (1990:108–35), contribute "hidden transcripts" that also constitute classroom realities. The dynamics of discourse and practice, of change and continuity, are as complex in schooling as in any other sphere of culture. Only as the ethnographic dimension is incorporated into the history of rural schools can such constitutive practices lose their exclusive identification with the state.

An ethnographic approach can thus recover the diversity and complexity among rural schools in the decades that followed the revolution. It should not be surprising to find differences even within the same region, as a consequence of the variety of local histories that produces schools.[7] This study focuses on the densely populated central region of Tlaxcala, where multiple social threads interweave to fashion an intricate cultural formation. At the beginning of the twentieth century, the peasants of the region were "solidly anchored in the political-religious systems of the Indian community" (Buve 1989:195). Most held small, individual land

7. For example, the impact and meaning of socialist education during the Cárdenas period differed greatly from region to region. See the comparative work done by Vaughan (1991, 1994); Valdés Silva (1990), Camacho (1992), and Civera (1988).

parcels in the Malintzi foothills or worked as hired laborers on nearby haciendas. Yet many villagers also worked for wages in the local textile mills, where contact with labor movements in Puebla and Orizaba spurred participation in the strikes of 1906–1907. The local population drew, as well, on its own popular liberal tradition and its history of protest as it entered the revolutionary movement in 1910.

The revolution in Tlaxcala followed a characteristic course, albeit with distinct subregional variations (Buve 1988, 1989; Ramírez Rancaño 1991). The local *agrarista* movement, affiliated with Zapatismo and headed by caudillo Domingo Arenas, was able to maintain control of the southwestern region between 1916 and 1917 and initiate the distribution of haciendas among peasants and military leaders. Rival Constitutionalist forces took over the governorship in August 1914 and controlled the northeastern part of the state, leaving a "transition zone" (Buve 1989:223) in the center, where struggles continued until Arenas was defeated in 1917. During the following decade, the local *cacique* Ignacio Mendoza controlled the governorship and, with the strong backing of presidents Alvaro Obregón and Plutarco E. Calles, reoriented agrarian policy through the more conservative, bureaucratic channels of the *comisiones agrarias* (agrarian reform commissions). Three successive governors in the 1920s used political and labor organizations, coupled with force, to secure relative stability (Ramírez Rancaño 1991; Buve and Falcón 1989).[8] Local educational reforms were constantly initiated during this period, and were an important factor in the reorganization of the state in Tlaxcala.

My analysis in this essay draws on field notes[9] as well as documentary evidence from Tlaxcala for the 1910–1930 period. The next two sections trace the fundamental changes that occurred in the organization and funding of public education after the revolution. The fourth and fifth sections explore the ways local culture pervaded school life, even as local culture—and the civil society it mediated—was in turn modified by the presence of schools. Though certain perennial concerns—many of them deposited in earlier forms of schooling—can still be found in rural

8. The three were Rafael Apango (1921–1924), Ignacio Mendoza (1925–1928), and Adrián Vázquez Sánchez (1929–1933).

9. Information was gathered through interviews and observation during the ethnographic study (see n. 3) conducted in the municipalities of Juan Cuamatzi (Contla) and Santa Ana Chiautempan in central Tlaxcala.

Mexico, I will argue that at certain points in time, and particularly during the 1910–1930 period, the relationship between the state and schooling in Mexico had been fundamentally redefined.

RENEWING THE LIBERAL COMMITMENT TO PUBLIC SCHOOLING: 1910–1914

The existence of public schools depends on the structures established by states to finance and regulate education. In Tlaxcala, the provision of schooling before 1910 differed from what the postrevolutionary regimes constructed, because it operated through a system of appointed councils rather than through an educational bureaucracy. During the Maderista period, the educational precepts of the 1857 Constitution were the acknowledged banner; a "revolutionary" conception of education was slow to emerge. Nevertheless, the existing mechanisms for providing funds and for controlling schools gave way under the revolution's impact. A look at the way the prerevolutionary structures were dissolved will serve to clarify the subsequent processes of state formation in Tlaxcala.

Tlaxcala was noted for its significant advances in education during the nineteenth century. Compulsory elementary schooling had been decreed in 1868 by the liberal governor Miguel Lira y Ortega, who outraged conservatives by stating that Indians had "as much right to education as the children of those who are unaware of their origins and still believe they rule this country" (cited in Angulo 1956:11). Thereafter, the Tlaxcala government assumed a stronger role in supporting schools than did many other state governments, and raised the state to second in the nation in schools per capita, though efforts declined between 1900 and 1910 under the Porfirian governor, Próspero Cahuantzi.[10]

The 1882 Law of Primary Instruction and the 1897 bylaw defined the structure for regulating and financing schools which was still functioning in 1911.[11] The laws set up a "public instruction fund" to be financed

10. See AGET, FRRO, 301-75, 1910, the comparative table of statistics signed by Miguel E. Schulz, Sección de Archivo, Estadística, e Información, Secretaría de Instrucción Pública y Bellas Artes, Dec. 1909.

11. *Ley de instrucción primaria del Estado de Tlaxcala*, Tlaxcala, decreed Jan. 20, 1882, under Governor Mariano Grajales (Tlaxcala: Gobierno del Estado, 1882); and *Reglamento de instrucción primaria en el Estado Libre y Soberano de Tlaxcala*, decreed Oct. 1897, under Governor Cahuantzi (Tlaxcala: Imprenta del Gobierno, 1898).

through a monthly head tax and fixed portions of the state and municipal budgets.[12] The fund also tapped other sources to support schools, such as fines, sales taxes, and, notably, the proceeds from communal land (*terrenos de adjudicación*) assigned to public education.[13] The local congress redistributed the total amount collected each year, allocating it to specific schools. This system achieved a relatively equitable fiscal distribution among Tlaxcala's municipalities, a situation not always found in other parts of Mexico. In 1910, for example, several of the wealthier municipalities, such as Huamantla, received a smaller portion of the educational budget than the taxes they actually collected (with the exception of the capital, Tlaxcala, where nothing had been collected since 1901), while some of the more indigenous municipalities received a larger share.[14] Nevertheless, funding for public schools was concentrated in the municipal seats (*cabeceras*) and larger towns, where village children were expected to attend school.[15] Actually, only about one-fourth of all children were in school, and very few reached the third grade.

At the time, a professional administrative body did not yet exist for education in Tlaxcala. The governor personally attended to such matters as hiring and firing teachers, scheduling dates of examinations, and rewarding or punishing individual students. The *jefes políticos* (prefects; see Falcón's essay in this volume) reproduced this personal authority at the district level, controlling finances and intervening directly in the operation of both public and private schools. A series of honorary councils (*consejos de vigilancia*) were appointed at the state, district, municipal, and local levels to aid each locality's highest-ranking political authority in overseeing the schools.

Though the state government was responsible for the provision of schools as a public service, the structure rested to a great extent on the

12. AGET, FRRO, 302-26, 1911, the "Corte de Caja de la Tesorería del Estado de Tlaxcala" for Dec. 1910, which specifies income and expenditures for each municipality.

13. Contracts for the use of these plots refer to regulations contained in the "Circular General," Oct. 9, 1856, and the "Circular del Gobierno del Estado," Jan. 10, 1868. See example in AGET, FRRO, 310-33, 1912.

14. On Tlaxcala's lack of collections, see AGET, FRRO, 304-14, Ramón A. Flores to the Secretario de Gobierno, Nov. 22, 1911.

15. By law, all communities of more than one hundred residents were to have a school, yet in practice few village schools existed. Haciendas were obligated to employ teachers for the workers' children.

local elites, who served on councils and examining juries and as private tax collectors who received a percentage of revenues. Inspectors were sometimes appointed, but their only function was occasionally to visit and report on schools. Certain of the more literate townspeople exerted considerable influence in school matters by sending frequent petitions and complaints, which the governor would personally resolve. Teachers, proposed yearly by the local authorities, did not form a cohesive group, and were forbidden to take part in politics.

In spite of regulations to the contrary, during the years preceding the Maderista uprisings many Tlaxcalan teachers were active in local anti-reelection clubs, and had close ties with radical groups in Puebla, where many had studied. Several later became military chiefs, political activists, and secretaries to agrarian leaders, and held offices in the local government.[16] As a result, Tlaxcalan authorities were particularly responsive to educational demands in the years following the outbreak of the 1910 revolution.

When the Tlaxcalan Anti-Reelection party candidate, the former labor leader Antonio Hidalgo, was elected in 1911, some towns, particularly those which had participated in the movement, believed the Maderista governor would heed grievances that had long gone unattended. For example, the *vecinos* (residents) of San Bernardino Contla wrote:

> During the whole period of his government, Cahuantzi never wanted to protect our unfortunate town. . . . Several times we requested a raise in the budget for instruction in our town, but it was never granted. We understand that the *cacique* Cahuantzi never wanted to favor us because this town has always been opposed to his regime, because he dishonestly usurped its interests, as everyone knows. . . . Since we sacrificed ourselves to overthrow our tyrant, now we wish to be rewarded for our sacrifices, by being granted an increase in the budget, to sixty pesos, in order to be able to have an intelligent person as teacher of the boys' schools, for the children's happiness. . . .[17]

The residents of Contla had not paid the school tax since 1910, alleging that the revolution had abolished all taxes; but Hidalgo ordered them to

16. Methodist pastors and teachers, such as José Rumbia, and teachers trained in Methodist schools in Tlaxcala and Puebla were among the most active in these groups. See Bastian (1986).

17. AGET, FRRO, 305-70, Vecinos of Contla to the C. Gobernador, Jan. 3, 1912.

meet their obligations and then increased their budget. Many local accounts trace the origins of their rural schools to Madero's regime, yet there is nothing to indicate a radical change in the structure of schooling during this period. As in other spheres of public life, the intention was basically to implement the 1857 liberal constitution.

After Hidalgo was ousted in January 1913, the schools continued to operate much as they had before. The *jefes políticos* still disciplined students and controlled the public instruction fund. They added to their functions the control of schoolteachers' ideological expressions; for example, one removed the principal in Barrón-Escandón for defacing the effigies of Díaz and Cahuantzi in his school.[18] Ingeniero (engineer) Justiniano Aguillón de los Ríos, a noted prerevolutionary educator, represented Tlaxcala, as he had the three previous years, at the annual national convention on primary education. At these gatherings such issues as federalization of primary education, the curriculum, and coeducation were debated, apparently without any formal discussion of the ongoing events of the revolution.[19] As in other spheres of elite culture, in education the uprisings were viewed as but a passing disruption of institutional life (see Monsiváis 1985).

The education files of 1912–1915 contain few direct references to the regional upheaval that was then taking place. Yet some of the documents written in the obligatory bureaucratic style take on new meaning when contemplated in the larger context of the revolution. For example, authorities received a steady flow of village complaints regarding teacher desertions and school closures owing to frequent, debilitating episodes of "banditry." The most important signs emerged in the financial sphere: it became increasingly difficult to collect the public instruction tax, even with the help of soldiers; and this responsibility was finally transferred from the prefects to the municipal presidents. In 1913, a decree ordered all land belonging to the public instruction fund to be "redeemed" by those who could prove legal possession, undermining yet another source of funding for the schools.[20] It became clear that the prefects, though still formally in charge, had lost much of their power, even before their final

18. AGET, FRRO, 322–23, Presidente Municipal of Barrón Escandón to the Prefecto Político, June 5, 1913.

19. The National Convention for Primary Education met yearly from 1910 to 1914, in spite of the drastic changes of government during these years (Meneses 1986:92–115, 134–50).

20. For example, reports in AGET, FRRO, 321-40, 1913, and 329-57, 1914.

demise in 1914. The educational system reached a crisis point during these years: fifty-five schools were closed, including those of Contla.[21]

Teachers were among the first to denounce the situation. In January 1914, the respected principal Isabel H. Gracia sent Governor Manuel Cuéllar a written exposition on the problems and possible reforms of public education.[22] Gracia expressed his motive as "a desire to fight against that great enemy 'ignorance,' which causes [so many] upheavals." In his view, schooling was to be regarded as a remedy for, rather than a consequence of, the revolution.[23] He nevertheless insisted that teaching methods should "not exclude any social category or occupation from public schools," thereby echoing the popular demand for universal free schooling.

What Gracia proposed was actually the creation of a professionally administered school system, in which an acting director of education would replace the existing *consejos de vigilancia*. Of the latter, Gracia wrote: "They are constituted mainly by artisans, industrialists, or scientists who have a higher education but lack even the rudiments of pedagogy, who intervene in these delicate matters with no professional knowledge. . . . Thus, they become . . . a cancer within the organism of the school."[24] He appended a long series of proposals for establishing and sustaining a qualitatively different system of education. Though ignored at the time, the substance of Gracia's plan was consistent with the opinion of national educators and was taken up by subsequent governors (see Meneses 1986:168–70).

In the particular state formation that marked the late Porfiriato, the regime succeeded in exercising fairly strict control over public schools without the existence of a bureaucracy; but this condition would eventually be modified. One immediate effect of the revolution of 1910 was a

21. For example, reports in AGET, FRRO, 327-38 and 325-43, 1913, and 333-47, 1914.

22. AGET, FRRO, 329-15, 1914, "Exposición pedagógica que rinde el C. Profesor Isabel H. Gracia al C. Gobernador del Estado Señor Coronel Don Manuel Cuéllar, concreta a los incovenientes que ha podido observar en su prolongada labor pedagógica, y los proyectos que propone para la reforma del actual Reglamento de Instrucción Primaria," Jan. 14, 1914. In 1918 it was presented to the local congress by Gracia's son, Ezequiel Gracia, then serving as state deputy.

23. The *vecinos* of Analco expressed a similar argument; they requested a teacher to "illuminate our children . . . so that they would no longer serve as cannon fodder (*carne de cañón*)." AGET, FRRO, 317-6, Feb. 8, 1913.

24. AGET, FRRO, 329-15, 1914.

renewal of the liberal commitment to public, secular, elementary education rather than the creation of a "new" school. Initially, equal access to schooling was considered more important than changes in educational content or discourse. The basic structure through which the Porfirian state had provided and regulated public schools continued to operate, though it was already being undermined by the violence and the demands of the revolutionary movement.

RESTRUCTURING PUBLIC SCHOOLING: MUNICIPAL, STATE, AND FEDERAL PROJECTS

An abrupt break in schooling occurred when the Constitutionalist forces took over the Tlaxcalan government in August 1914. In areas that had experienced armed conflict, some schools had been used as barracks or had been abandoned; others remained beyond government control. The state military commander, Governor Máximo Rojas, immediately sent a dispatch ordering all schools closed "pending reorganization of public instruction."[25] This state of affairs lasted more than eight years. As different laws and measures were enacted—and different political alliances were established—the central issue became whether the municipal, the state, or the federal government would fund and operate the schools.

The first impulse followed Carranza's December 1914 decree establishing the free municipality (Fabela 1963:118–19). Porfirio del Castillo, Tlaxcala's acting civil authority, attempted, according to his own report, to "make the free municipality a reality" by transferring schools to the local authorities (del Castillo 1953:212).[26] Yet crucial measures, such as the renewal of taxation, were necessary to reopen the schools. Del Castillo ordered "personal contributions" to be collected for education, and asked local authorities to propose "apt persons" as state teachers.[27] Most munici-

25. AGET, FRRO, 333-26, "Acuerdo del Gobernador Provisional y Comandante Militar del Estado con el Secretario General del Gobierno," Sept. 15, 1914.

26. Porfirio del Castillo, a former teacher and colonel, became the acting civil authority as secretario de gobierno under provisional governor Máximo Rojas from August 1914 to May 1915. He was appointed provisional governor for the term from May 1915 to July 1916.

27. "Informe presentado al Ministro de Gobernación por el C. Gobernador del Estado Libre y Soberano de Tlaxcala, Coronel Porfirio del Castillo," Imprenta del Gobierno, Jan. 1916; AGET, EP, 21-4, 1915, Receipts of Circular no. 2, Feb. 1915; AGET, EP, 21-17, 1915, Acuerdo no. 4, Mar. 1915.

pal presidents had difficulty collecting funds, and some even requested the governor's intervention. Though committed in principle to municipal control, del Castillo then strengthened the state educational system, setting a tax on pulque, proposing a fourfold increase in the education budget, renewing the staff of the teacher-training institutes, and ordering work on a new education law. His 1915 decree, which reinterpreted in radical *laicista* terms the anticlerical educational clauses of the *Leyes de Reforma*, foreshadowed the 1916–1917 federal constitutional debate and became the first ideological redefinition of education during the revolution in Tlaxcala (del Castillo 1953:210–15).

The state's Constitutionalist governors in the years that followed, Daniel Ríos Zertuche and Luis M. Hernández, confronted the limitations of the plan to turn schools over to the municipal governments. The successive decrees and drafts of the pending education and municipal laws decreased the responsibility of municipal authorities by limiting the municipality's obligation to *cabecera* schools, thus leaving rural schools to the state system.[28] The laws that were finally ratified allowed but did not obligate municipalities to run schools, though they required municipal authorities to contribute.[29] Other measures reduced the proportion of municipal funding to one-third, and later to one-fifth, of the budget. This portion was to be paid directly to teachers, who often complained that they did not receive it, and therefore worked fewer hours. Some effects of the municipalization proposal had actually verged on privatization. Villagers of Aztatla requested state schools, arguing that they were too poor to pay a "private" teacher in order to fulfill their legal obligation; those of Cuautenco paid their "contributions" directly to the teacher, bypassing the municipal treasury.[30] By the end of the decade it was clear, in Tlaxcala as in other parts of the country, that most rural municipalities lacked the

28. AGET, FRRO, 344-36, Comisión de Legislación Escolar, Aug. 18, 1917; AGET, FRRO, 391-1, 1918, Proposal for the law regulating municipal government. Various drafts and references to these proposed laws are found in AGET, FRRO, 346-29, 1917, 350-26, 1920, and 353-15, 1919; and AGET, EP, 59-36, 1920.

29. See *Ley de educación primaria para las escuelas del Estado de Tlaxcala*, Sept. 27, 1917 (Tlaxcala: Imprenta del Gobierno, 1917); *Constitución del Estado Libre y Soberano de Tlaxcala* (Tlaxcala: Gobierno de Tlaxcala, 1918); and *Ley orgánica del municipio en el Estado L. y S. de Tlaxcala*, Feb. 9, 1919 (Tlaxcala: Talleres Gráficos, 1938).

30. AGET, FRRO, 335-43, *Vecinos* of Aztatla to the Gobernador, Feb. 19, 1916; and AGET, FRRO, 369-6, Agente Municipal of Cuauhtenco to the Gobernador, Jan. 4, 1922.

means to sustain schools.[31] Furthermore, the control of public schooling was one means used by governors to strengthen their hold on those regions that were still under the sway of the revolutionary movement.

The state government continued to finance many of the schools that had existed before the Maderista rebellion. Nevertheless, it no longer had specific revenues for public instruction, and education had to compete for scarce funds that were often diverted to cover the cost of military actions. The resulting financial crisis led to such measures as closing the normal school and assigning only one teacher to work shifts at both the boys' and girls' schools in many towns. In addition, famine and epidemics led to school closures. The state system would not recover from this disruption for years to come.

At the same time that it was attempting to municipalize public schools, the state government laid the foundation for a professional administrative body, creating the office of director of education in 1917. Together with a group of "honorary technical inspectors"—actually principals of the larger schools—the first directors, Pedro Suárez and José María Bonilla, took a more active role in promoting and regulating existing schools.[32] For a time, they insisted on local control of education, though in practice they initiated central supervision. The inspectors propagated the new educational doctrine of the 1917 Constitution, interpreting for teachers the meaning of nationalism, laicism, and integral education.[33] It was during this period that the term *Revolution* began to be used, not only as an explanation of school closure but also as justification for reopening schools. One finds numerous statements such as, "Schools are one of the principal orientations of the Revolution . . . and through them must come the exaltation of the Fatherland [*Patria*]."

Three successive laws were passed, in 1921, 1926, and 1929, that

31. Apango reported in 1921 that most municipal governments refused to pay their share of the budget. "Informe de la gestión administrativa del 1° de abril 1920 al 31 de marzo 1921, que rinde el Gobernador C. Rafael Apango." This outcome was similar in other parts of the country, despite the 1917 Constitution (Vaughan 1982: 2:206–22; Meneses 1986:184–89).

32. Both had a revolutionary background. José María Bonilla had apparently acted as secretary to Zapatista leaders in northern Puebla. Pedro Suárez was Carrancista, yet he rescued his friend Bonilla when Bonilla was taken by the Constitutionalist forces (Nava 1978).

33. AGET, FRRO, 351-17, "Atribuciones del inspector técnico honorario," Aug. 17, 1918; AGET, FRRO, 346-29, Inspector's report, Oct. 13, 1917.

codified some of the changes that had occurred in public education during the previous decade.[34] Though the texts of the three laws are very similar, the variations in those sections relating to school administration reveal an important tension that had developed between the two predominant tendencies of the postrevolutionary system: a strengthening of local control and the development of a professional bureaucracy.

Besides restating the doctrine of compulsory and free public education, the 1921 law formalized the administrative structure, giving ample functions to the director of education. At the same time, it set up *juntas de educación* to aid (*secundar*) the director by overseeing final oral exams and exacting fines from parents who would not send their children to classes, just as the previous *consejos* had done. The state system also charged these *juntas* with obtaining the local funds that were indispensable for constructing and operating a school. Rather than levying a general education tax, the government expected the elected *juntas* to determine the contributions parents should make to finance all local expenses except teacher salaries. The 1926 bylaw specified a new procedure for electing *junta* representatives: students were to deposit their parents' ballots, in order "to prepare children for the functions of citizenship." This attempt evidently clashed with the growing role of the bureaucracy, and the 1929 law modified this measure, subordinating the *juntas'* actions, and particularly their management of funds, to the inspectors' authority.

Though legally established in 1921, the professional administration of the state system developed slowly. When Ingeniero Aguillón de los Ríos became director of education in 1923, he had one inspector and one secretary, and personally answered all correspondence, which mostly amounted to authorizing teacher appointments and salaries. Most requests for schools were still channeled through the municipal presidents directly to the governor. Teachers were hired for certain schools, negotiated salaries individually, often resigned (alleging health problems or lack of pay), and were later rehired in other towns. They could be proposed, retained, or removed by municipal presidents or local *juntas*. They were also under continual surveillance from villagers, who could pressure to change those who were not to their liking.

34. *Estado L. y S. de Tlaxcala. Ley de educación primaria del estado. Edición oficial* (Tlaxcala: Imprenta del Gobierno del Estado, 1921); *Estado L. y S. de Tlaxcala. Ley de educación pública y reformas* (Tlaxcala: Imprenta del Gobierno del Estado, 1926); *Ley de educación pública del Estado de Tlaxcala* (Tlaxcala: Imprenta del Gobierno del Estado, 1929).

Aguillón was a charismatic leader, known to many of the teachers; he used his personal authority to create a sense of *magisterio* among them and interceded on their behalf with the state authorities. He organized two-week "winter courses" on the revolutionary goals of the rural schools, set up teacher "cooperatives," and headed the mutualist society founded to aid teachers in case of illness.[35] These actions both responded to and promoted a growing professional identity among the disparate group of teachers—an identity that would result in the organization of unions and pressure groups in later years.[36]

Gradually the bureaucratic authority of an incipient school system replaced the personal authority of the governor. In the later twenties, several full-time inspectors were appointed and became a "consultative council" to the director. They reported on available buildings and on private schools; they systematized statistics, kept service records, assigned teachers to schools. As the school system grew, the authority of the municipal presidents in educational matters was slowly undermined. Increasingly, controversies over the right to determine the date for public examinations, or to keep the school keys, revealed the deepening confrontation between teachers and local authorities.

During the twenties, prerevolutionary educational concepts and practices were rearticulated and combined with a new ideological adherence to the revolution. The 1926 law, issued under Governor Ignacio Mendoza, was phrased in a radical new language, emphasizing the scientific, practical, agricultural, and civic training of the students over book learning. The bylaw prescribed a local version of the "school of action" program, a proposal associated with Moisés Sáenz and other educators who at the time were setting up the federal school system at the Secretaría de Educación Pública (SEP). The program caused considerable debate, and some teachers argued that results were worse in 1927 than in previous years. The governor defended it, arguing that with the new programs, "intellectual culture had been reduced . . . but teaching was

35. AGET, EP, 82-52, "Breve informe acerca del estado de la instrucción pública durante el año de 1923," signed by Aguillón de los Ríos, Mar. 8, 1924; and AGET, EP, 115-12, "Plan general para los cursos de invierno," Dec. 23, 1925.

36. About 15 percent of the teachers were certified; by 1926 slightly over half were women. See Aguillón de los Ríos, "Breve informe . . . ," Mar. 8, 1924. Though not yet unionized, some teachers collectively petitioned for higher salaries. AGET, FRRO, 374-25, Aguillón to the Secretario de Gobierno, July 13, 1923.

more practical, and was therefore more effective."[37] During the 1929 pedagogical conference, teachers interpreted the proposal in different ways. Some claimed that it contained old ideas in a new guise; others welcomed those aspects that reflected the fundamental shift that was occurring in attitudes toward children. All approved the elimination of public oral exams, together with the local supervision they implied.[38] It was this sort of structural change that was to have the most lasting effect on the balance between the state and local forces.

FEDERALIZATION: NEW FORCES ENTER EDUCATION

The federal government began to enter the realm of education throughout the republic in 1922, after President Obregón reversed Carranza's policy and endorsed José Vansconcelos's proposal to establish the Secretaría de Educación Pública. The impact of federalization, however, would depend on the political patterns of each state. In Tlaxcala, Obregón and Calles succeeded in disarming and subordinating the regional power group led by Mendoza. The federal government gained the loyalty of peasants by offering security and land as well as education, and at times by temporarily fostering local autonomy (Buve and Falcón 1989:112–14). Mexico City's strategy rested on the belief that an incipient network of federal schools would give the central government a crucial presence in the southwestern region of the state, where peasant mobilization was still strong.

Tlaxcala was the first state selected to test the proposed federalization policy. The school system was to be headed by an "educational council" formed by representatives of the federal, state, and municipal governments. Vasconcelos had envisioned the creation of educational councils in each locality, with members elected to represent parents, teachers, and municipal authorities; these councils in turn were to elect, from among their own members, representatives to the state council.[39]

37. "Informe de la gestión administrativa comprendida del 1° de abril de 1926 al 31 de marzo 1927, que rinde el C. I. Mendoza, Gobernador Constitutional del Estado de L. y S. de Tlaxcala, ante la H. XXIX Legislatura," 1927.

38. See AGET, EP, 245-4, 1929, discussion in the minutes of the Congreso del Educación del Estado, Temas de Estudio y Dictámenes, Tema: "Escuela de la acción."

39. *Proyecto de ley para la creación de la Secretaría de Educación Pública*, signed by José Vasconcelos (Mexico City: Universidad Nacional, 1920), 41–42.

But as time for implementation of the plan was very short, Vasconcelos ultimately took a different tack in Tlaxcala. The corresponding file in the state archive contains identical minutes signed by every municipal president, stating that, "after long deliberation," Fausto González (at the time state director of education) had been proposed as "municipal representative" and approved by the local governing body (*cuerpo moral*).[40] The federal government thus legitimized its intervention in a domain that had been reserved for municipal government, and then named its own representative to head the council.

Federal funding was vital to renewing public schooling in the state, and it constituted 50 percent of the state budget in 1922. Nevertheless, at this point the central government had established only tenuous authority over the claims of both the state and the municipal powers.[41] The council's own report at the end of 1922 candidly stated that "no fundamental innovation was imprinted on the legislation and functioning of the schools." The following year the council was dissolved, the state system retained its original schools, and the federal system initiated in earnest its expansion into rural areas.[42]

Because the federal system offered better salaries and school provisions, it was attractive to both teachers and villagers. It revitalized state schools that had been abandoned or had requested transfer to the federal system; and it deployed younger teachers, some from out of state, who put into practice the innovative ideas propagated by the SEP. These federal teachers would promote the creation of new schools and begin classes in rooms provided by residents. Some encountered opposition from local *juntas*, as villagers objected to coeducation and to the absence of public exams, and preferred the state teachers whom they knew and felt they could control.[43] Federal teachers were not under the jurisdiction

40. AGET, FRRO, 368-12, 1922, "Consejo de Educación. Informe a los Ciudadanos Diputados Secretarios del H. Congreso del Estado" and related documents.

41. For example, the Contla president cited the 1921 law: "Municipal governments being directly responsible for making effective the legal obligation of providing education. . . ." AGET, FRRO, 369-6, Presidente Municipal de Contla al Secretario de Gobierno, Mar. 21, 1922.

42. Within ten years, the federal system had taken over or established one hundred schools in Tlaxcala, primarily in rural areas. See AGET, EP, 82-52, 1924; and AHSEP, Tlaxcala, 252-7, 1935.

43. For example, the petitions from several communities in AGET, EP, 246-4, 1929.

of state authorities; they soon found they could denounce municipal presidents for not collaborating, and count on the support of national political leaders.

Initiatives for establishing a federal school often came from the villages, and implied a certain degree of independence from the municipal *cabecera*. The creation of a local school meant that villagers would no longer be obliged to send their children to the town school or to contribute to its maintenance. Over the years, each small village or *barrio* began a struggle to establish its own school. Disagreements occurred between neighboring villages when only one was chosen as the site for a school that children from both localities would attend. The conflicts involved "both self-esteem and a certain amount of village politics," in the words of one inspector.[44] Social differences within villages also fueled controversies: school projects typically mobilized local groups that had particular political or financial interests—such as those arising out of the restructuring of local society during these years—and received less support from those who saw little profit in schooling.

As school projects got under way in the smaller communities that had been under the jurisdiction of the municipal authorities, the *vecinos* would often seek to upgrade their administrative status (to, for example, an *agencia municipal* or *pueblo*). The *barrio* of Aztatla, for instance, asked for official recognition of their representative as *agente municipal* in the very act of soliciting a school.[45] The newly formed agrarista colonies also sought to bypass municipal authorities by soliciting a federal school through agrarian organizations. The process could involve changes in the denomination of localities, or their annexation to neighboring municipalities.[46] One teacher in Tlachco was accused by Contla authorities of taking his students to the *fiestas patrias* of neighboring Santa Cruz in support of secessionist schemes. Thus the age-old movement toward becoming a *pueblo* (Guerra 1985, 1988:279–301; Chevalier 1989), revitalized during the revolutionary movement, aided the expansion of the rural school system. In the process, the federal government "created relationships that linked peasant communities with the state" (Taboada

44. AGET, FRRO, 351-22, 1919, Inspector's report, Apr. 13, 1919. See also numerous petitions in AGET, FRRO, 369-2, 1922.

45. AGET, FRRO, 335–43, 1916, Presidente Municipal of Aztatla to the Goberador, Feb. 19, 1916.

46. Changes of municipal delimitations are reported in AGET, EP, 145-70, 1926; and in AHSEP, Tlaxcala, exp. IV-161 (IV-14/21175).

1985:55) and strengthened its control over local power centers; state governing networks correspondingly weakened.

Similarly, the SEP files of the late twenties reflect a different orientation to education. The most novel sign was a new educational discourse, that of the *misiones culturales*, which stressed the social role of schools and promoted community projects.[47] The ideas of educators in the SEP, such as Manuel Gamio, Moisés Sáenz, and Rafael Ramírez, slowly filtered down through courses given by the *misiones* to both federal and state teachers. In the late twenties, younger teachers, often from a more rural background, had a sense of being involved in a new sort of schooling, one that responded to the rights of peasants and workers. It was not without its controversy: one distinguished state teacher requested reassignment to an urban school because, although she wanted to experience the "new Mexican school," she preferred working where she could apply the "general laws of human understanding" and was not limited to basic literacy (*desanalfabetización*).[48]

A less visible aspect of the federal project was a conscious attempt to "proceed in a rational manner."[49] This implied a new sort of regulation, contained in the categories used for precise classification of students and schools, the questionnaires on all aspects of village life, the formal procedures for presenting documentation and displaying quantitative evaluations through graphs, and a constant communication between a number of federal agencies and the teachers. The federal school redirected peasant demands through the newly formed channels, and at times redefined the content of these demands in line with services offered by the central government for such projects as agricultural credit, reforestation, and public health.

The strengthened links between the government and the governed in rural villages were constructed as much through patronage relations as rational design. During the twenties and thirties, teachers began to forge alternative connections between authorities and peasants, while still drawing on the patriarchal traditions of the prerevolutionary period. Many teachers had backing beyond the educational sphere, among local

47. The *misiones culturales* were federal teams of experts who gave practical courses for in-service teachers. The courses were held in rural villages, and teachers undertook community projects as part of the course work.

48. AGET, EP, Contla, ref. 209–10, 1929, leg. 2.

49. AHSEP, Dirección de Educación Federal, Tlaxcala, 794–14, 1925, Report of Inspector Rafael Villeda.

campesino leaders, party members, and former students or relatives (who were often also former teachers) employed in the state or federal government.[50] Sometimes patronage networks corresponding to different parties and factions—at both the local and the federal levels—clashed because of their common interests in obtaining popular support and in forging clientelistic relationships with local elites. Through these connections, and often owing to these conflicts, teachers were able to procure resources and services for the villages.

The construction of the postrevolutionary school system did not have to follow precisely this course. It was locally produced by a convergence of diverse forces. The attempt to turn schools over to the municipalities had nourished, and in some cases created, grassroots demand for schools. Through schooling, the struggle for local autonomy joined hands with the federal government's incursion into rural areas, as villagers found in federal schools a means to enhance their own position. At the same time, teachers pressed for a system that would extend their own professional interests and ideals. The constitutional delegates in 1917 had defended universal lay education in the liberal tradition, and Vasconcelos had essentially conceived of the federal program as a "civilizing mission" (Vaughan 1982:1:206–22). None of these actors had envisioned that a federal school system would be materially instrumental in the construction of a strong state.[51]

This possibility became manifest as the central government, led by Calles, faced escalating peasant demands and attempted to control local forces. In the later twenties, when postrevolutionary agrarian policy became increasingly conservative, the expansion of rural schooling may have been politically motivated by an attempt to offset the demand for land. Thus Governor Adrián Vázquez Sánchez (1929–1933), noted for his antiagrarian stance, nevertheless advanced schooling in the rural areas of Tlaxcala. Yet public schooling was also very much a popular demand, in many cases closely connected to local agrarian movements. Besides renewing the liberal tradition, the revolution had brought a new sense of empowerment, of the right to gain access to a basic public service that could break down social barriers to the literate world.

50. Although from a later period, the autobiography of Claudio Hernández (1987) gives an excellent account of this process.

51. Vasconcelos actually had argued that the state would eventually withdraw from education when this mission was accomplished. See his *Proyecto de ley para la creación de una Secretaría de Educación Pública Federal* (Mexico City: Universidad Nacional, 1920), 24.

THE SOCIAL CONSTRUCTION OF SCHOOLING

One of my key arguments is thus that the development of rural schools in the postrevolutionary years owed as much to popular claims and resources as to any "rational" designs of the newly forming state. Both before and after the revolution, public schooling was locally subsidized in a number of ways; villagers paid numerous fees and donated materials, animals, land, tools, and books.[52] Everyday school life was socially constructed at the local level, with labor that was not necessarily controlled or financed by central authorities. In fact, many of the school's constitutive elements were much more the product of local knowledge than of official disposition. In the next several pages, I sketch the manner in which local knowledge and culture came to constitute a significant portion of school practices.

Signs of popular culture surface in the documents of the local school committees. The successive legislative reforms of the twenties were in large measure aimed at regulating the actions of the *juntas de educación;* nevertheless, these councils often functioned in traditional ways. Though the *juntas* were responsible for managing resources to build or maintain the school, it was possible to bypass official control of funds by entrusting specific projects to other committees, such as *comités pro-construcción* or *pro-mejoras materiales,* or ad hoc committees, in charge of such tasks as building chicken coops or cleaning out the well.

The practices of some of these committees reflect those of the traditional cargo or *cofradía* system, sustained by *barrio* and *compadrazgo* networks (Nutini and Bell 1980). Under this system, religious festivities are financed on a rotating basis by the *mayordomos* and their collaborators; each contributes substantial amounts to cover expenses and collects voluntary contributions from kin. The arrangement was used following the revolution for funding a variety of local projects, such as the restoration of churches or the celebration of patriotic fiestas (Buve 1982:277). One informant from Contla who explained the local *barrio* organization insisted, "This is how all public offices, including the presidency, should be organized."[53] The ritual kinship networks, the fixed sequence of rotating cargos, the mechanisms for selecting *mayordomos*—all of these tradi-

52. Eklof (1990) describes a similar position of Russian peasants during the late nineteenth century.

53. Interview with the juez local, San Bernardino Contla, Oct. 8, 1981, by Ruth Mercado.

tional bases of politicoreligious organization contrasted starkly with the more "egalitarian" categories of "citizen" or "parent," and with the rules for universal suffrage and taxation proposed by federal school authorities.

Documentary evidence of the use of the *cofradía* system for school projects is scarce, since minutes were drawn up according to official regulations; nevertheless, some traces can be found. In 1929, for example, the Yancuiclalpan and Tlalcuapan *juntas* included members representing each *barrio* rather than each grade, as specified in the official regulations.[54] Minutes of some school meetings mention the *principales*, who offered to undertake projects. To resume work on the school building in Ixcotla, the *junta patriótica* made available the funds that had been collected for fireworks for the local fiesta. Other reports account for donations in kind by committee members or note large contributions made by members of the *junta*, in addition to the fee collected of all parents.[55]

In many of the villages of Contla and Chiautempan, residents continued to use these traditional mechanisms to defray the high costs involved in building or enlarging a school. Apparently it had for some time been a viable alternative to the official measure, by which costs were divided equally among all adult males of the village. Committee heads were named at public meetings by a show of hands; they in turn would invite collaborators to help sponsor and raise funds for specific projects. For example, during a contested election in San Miguel, collaborators threatened to withdraw their offer, arguing that rival committee members should find their own sponsors.[56] Committees vied for public recognition of the additions they "had left the school," and were remembered by the older inhabitants (Mercado 1992). Thus, while drawing on private resources and time rather than enacting state forms, this local strategy made possible the construction of free public schools in these rural villages.

The process by which traditional social structure became the basis for the organization of rural schools can probably be traced back to the time when communal lands were allocated for the public instruction fund. Proceeds from these plots were at times unofficially used to promote local fiestas in addition to providing funds for the school, and were thereby linked to the *mayordomía* system. The use of communal lands for the

54. AGET, EP, c. 248, 1929, Actas de Juntas de Educación for Ixcotla, Tlaltelulco, Tlalcuapan, and Yancuiclalpan.

55. Ibid., and the "Libro de actas" of the agencia municipal, Xaltipan, Contla.

56. AGET, EP, 1929, leg. 15, Actas de Instalación de Juntas de Educación, San Miguel Contla.

school fund implied a commitment to collective projects; yet internal differences often cropped up. In 1913, for example, Totolac villagers complained of certain individuals who claimed the land, and threatened to "renounce their membership in the community that had existed, as it was no longer their will to continue ceding the product of those plots."[57]

After these lands were privatized, the structures for communal funding were redefined.[58] Head taxes were abolished, but the contributions requested by local authorities were not completely voluntary. One elderly woman recalled: "We were always mortified by the fees. . . . If a fee wasn't paid, one faced confiscation. Quickly, the pig must be sold, or the agents would come and take the burro" (cited in Mercado 1986:42). She added that there was always work to do, sometimes for the church, sometimes for the school, and "the government did not help at all." The Ixcotla *agente* in 1922 asked the governor for documents with which he could justify collecting fees from "debtors" who did not want to cooperate in building the school—yet no law was available.[59] The traditional mechanism of rotating sponsorship provided an alternative structure, yet not all agreed to participate. In Ixcotla, it was said that the wealthier had often opposed school projects, while men involved in the local cargo system were more apt to take responsibility for, and receive the corresponding prestige from, community social projects. Thus participation in traditional structures did not impede, and in some cases even strengthened, support of the local school. In villages such as Ixcotla and Xaltipan, the same groups contributed, in alternating periods, to the construction of the school and of the local church. Through each project villagers gained political distance from municipal authorities, both civil and religious.

The line between so-called traditional and modern involvement in schooling thereby blurred. Since the nineteenth century, a pronounced popular liberalism, one very much rooted in local society, had endured in the area (Knight 1985a:63). This could be seen, for example, in the appropriation of the *fiestas patrias*, the celebration of Independence Day. Civic ritual, including altars to Hidalgo and Morelos, had been intro-

57. AGET, FRRO, 320-1, Vecinos of Totolac to the Gobernador, and related documents, Mar. 15, 1913.

58. In the 1920s, rural schools, particularly those on *ejidos*, had *parcelas escolares*. Parents generally cultivated the land, and the proceeds were used to cover some school expenses.

59. AGET, FRRO, 369-2, Agente Municipal of Guadalupe Ixcotla to the Gobernador, Feb. 27, 1922.

duced in the nineteenth century in explicit competition with religious ritual, and the practice continued in the 1920s. State-promoted patriotism became part of popular culture, as well as being a civic obligation. Although *juntas patrióticas* were named each year to sponsor the festivities, teachers were often required to organize the ceremonies.[60] This was only one of the specific social obligations that villagers demanded of teachers. Teachers were also expected to place their literacy skills at the service of the village, and to take an active role in soliciting other governmental services.

In response to the expectations of villagers, many rural teachers also subsidized the existence of schools, in effect dedicating time far beyond the regular school day. Many were able to continue teaching through the lean years only because they had other means of subsistence, for instance, as carpenters or cultivators of small plots. Teaching was a family trade; siblings and spouses supported (and often substituted for) each other, enabling teachers to survive in rural villages.[61] Teachers also frequently contributed teaching materials, buying books and making or improvising classroom furniture and other necessities. Very few had studied pedagogy, so most obtained their training through a network of relatives and former teachers who supported their first years of learning on the job.

Within the ambit of daily life, teachers appropriated different practices and concepts for their work. These everyday appropriations often ended up accounting for more of the actual content and method of teaching than those proposed by the official manuals and regulations. The worldview of teachers owed as much to the homespun tradition of liberalism that they imbibed at home or in various literate circles as to the government's normal schools (Vaughan 1990a:48–51). In fact, most teachers never attended normal school, and it was often the more liberal families that allowed daughters to become teachers.

Certain documents and testimonies permit us to catch glimpses of how children participated in the social construction of schooling—since their presence was indispensable to the existence of schools. Though school attendance was legally mandatory, the law was contested throughout these years; the very frequency of injunctions to exact fines or police the streets suggests that such measures at best had only a temporary

60. On the role of *juntas patrióticas*, see Thomson (1989) and Vaughan (1994).

61. Many autobiographies in the collection *Los maestros y la cultura nacional* (SEP 1987) tell how teachers learned to teach and managed to survive with help from relatives, especially wives.

effect. Many children resisted schooling, fleeing the dismal conditions of most schoolrooms, the discipline of harsher teachers, or the ridicule from students of a higher social status to seek other activities they deemed more profitable or bearable.[62] One wonders why many (at least one out of four) actually stayed in school, in the absence of effective coercion and despite the frequent privations of these unsettled years.[63] Besides parental pressure, certainly their own interest in what was taught in class must have been a factor, as were the affective ties formed between teachers and individual children. Thus some teachers tell of children who warned them of—or even defended them against—local opposition.[64] Still, it is difficult to document with any precision the everyday emotional and intellectual experiences that alienated children from or bound them to schooling.

Ethnography helps in reconstructing the ways children played their part in the social construction of everyday school life. The prevailing theoretical emphasis on the "disciplining of bodies" (Foucault 1979) and the "production of selves" (Corrigan, Curtis, and Lansing n.d.) through schooling has often hidden children's collective power to impose relations, rhythms, and forms of learning. Nowhere is it clearer how "selves"—that is, social actors—produce schools than in the complex network of interactions among children, in their own appropriation of the space and time of schooling. They must, of course, negotiate their preferred activities with teachers, and although the teacher's will often prevails, the process of negotiation often forces teachers to modify their ways.

This was particularly true in indigenous villages (see, for example, Paradise 1991), such as those of Contla and Chiautempan at the beginning of the century.[65] Even today, the Nahuatl language, which only the elderly are said to speak, is used by some of the students of the rural villages when they joke among themselves or do not want a teacher to

62. Though it was prohibited by law, children found many opportunities for work. See ACET, FRRO, 341-33, Aviso, Jan. 22, 1917.

63. Inspectors reported low attendance in some schools because of revolutionary skirmishes, epidemics, and other dangers, such as the ravines or rivers children had to cross to get there.

64. Interview with Claudio Hernández, Amaxac de Guerrero, July 1992, by Elsie Rockwell and Oresta López. See also, ACET, EP, 1935, leg. 1, Acta de Junta Tepeyanco, July 6, 1935.

65. The federal director of education in Tlaxcala, Alfonso Alanís, reported in 1925 that 54 percent of the population was *indígena*. AHSEP, Tlaxcala, 794-14, 1925, "Informe general," Mar. 30, 1925.

know what they are saying. Elders recall that as children they generally spoke Nahuatl during class, except when called on by the teacher to repeat something in Spanish. Many of the rural teachers spoke Nahuatl and, though this practice was not officially promoted at the time, bilingual teachers were often obliged to use their native language to make themselves understood by their pupils.

Children, especially in large groups, are potentially subversive. As schools were opened to more children, and as young teachers had to persuade them to attend, the need to negotiate the very conditions of classroom teaching became more apparent. Older residents maintain that discipline was stricter in former days, though they seem to have preferred it that way. Yet even the oldest teacher we observed in Contla, Fidel Morales—trained before the revolution and noted for instilling both fear and learning in his students—negotiated with the children, responding to their claims and accepting their corrections.

Thus, besides the state, villagers, teachers, and children all had a stake in schooling. It is not surprising, therefore, that the rural schools of the postrevolutionary years were not merely "hegemonic instruments."[66] If hegemony was in play, it operated within a "field of force around which people define[d] fundamental social relationships," as William Roseberry argues in this volume. The few traces of ongoing confrontations that reached the official record provide a clue to the various motives and forces involved. The letters that scribes wrote for villagers and directed to the governors were often couched in venerable, formulaic phrases: the children were not learning, they were wasting their time; teachers did not open the schools, they had other occupations, or their behavior was unacceptable.[67] Teachers responded that these complaints were "slanderous," reminded authorities that "villagers, as is their routine custom, allege that teachers don't attend to their duties," and complained in turn that villagers did not support the school.[68] The rhetoric on both sides often hid other motives, particularly those engendered by issues of religion and politics, domains in which teachers were forbidden by law to intervene.

As would be expected, the renewal of liberalism and laicism became a

66. For discussions of the state's hegemonic role, see Raby (1989) and Taboada (1985).

67. Some of these offenses were specified in the 1898 bylaw. Complaints against teachers abound in the files.

68. AGET, EP, 23-9, 1918, Director of Ixtacuixtla to the Gobernador.

source of conflicts, which were not always resolved in the same manner. Teachers often appealed to the liberal views of authorities to contradict the villagers' accusations, and argued that the real issue was their refusal to teach religion. Sometimes, liberal slogans helped teachers retain their jobs; in other cases, such slogans were useless against parents' complaints about a teacher's age, deafness, or drunkenness. Furthermore, the religious issue could cut both ways. In Tlaxco, the teacher complained that her assistant was instigating parents against her, accusing her of being a Protestant. In Tlacotepec, by contrast, villagers denounced a teacher for "serving as a priest" and dividing the village.[69] In spite of frequent protests, central Tlaxcala was relatively free of the violence that surrounded schools in other states, where the Cristero Rebellion was being waged during the late twenties (Ramírez Rancaño 1991).

As different revolutionary factions took over various parts of the state, teachers were also caught up in partisan politics. One teacher, married to the daughter of a follower of Máximo Rojas, reported that he was being attacked by local ranchers of the conservative *Liga de Agricultores*, who denounced him to the Arenista band. This group of parents had withdrawn their children from school, arguing that they were not going to be healers (*curanderos*) and therefore did not need to learn anatomy.[70] Teachers were found on opposite sides of conflicts, yet they also formed common occupational ties that resisted political division.

In this field of contending political forces, many sources of opposition to schools appeared. Still, it would be inaccurate to polarize an account of schooling by assuming, as it were, that a uniform traditional "society" always opposed the "state" schools, represented by the teachers.[71] Information interpreted as evidence of a strong, univocal opposition to schooling can actually indicate a variety of motives at play. For example, it has been argued that in some communities, schools were accepted for their political and social role, even as low attendance figures revealed an everyday form of resistance (Lira 1983; Vaughan 1990a:47). It is logical to assume that other variables accounted for the irregular patterns of school attendance, which averaged about two-thirds of enrollment figures. Ob-

69. The cases are reported in AGET, FRRO, 335-26, 1917, Directora de Tlaxco al Gobernador; AGET, EP, 111-22, 1924, Vecinos de Tlacotepec al Director General de Educación, Apr. 8, 1923.

70. AGET, EP, 23-9, 1918, Vecinos of Ixtacuixtla to the Gobernador.

71. See, for example, the dichotomous view proposed by François-Xavier Guerra (1988:394–426).

viously, economic factors—the material impossibility of sending children to school—were involved in many cases. Furthermore, rural communities used the school in a way that did not presuppose, as we do today, the value of universal literacy. Parents would often select some of their children, those thought to do best at learning Spanish and writing, and keep them in school as long as this objective was being achieved. In Indian communities, especially, the ability to write was considered to be the specialized skill of scribes, who could be hired if the need should arise. In the long run, the concentration of knowledge of the written word in the hands of a few led to a concentration of power. Scribes in fact often became the gatekeepers to village governing authorities. Resistance against this sort of exclusive power may have given added impulse to universal schooling in the late 1930s, when attendance began to increase.

Beneath the reported incidents lie signs of a different sort of resistance, less spectacular and perhaps more effective. Instead of opposition to schools as such this region manifested a popular resistance to poor teaching and an implicit demand for higher-quality schooling. References were sometimes made to the children: "Even they say they are not being taught well."[72] Xocoyucan parents complained that they preferred to give their children other occupations, "so they would not waste their time . . . as the worksheets they had presented were done by their teacher, not by them."[73] Other parents objected to the teachers' use of antiquated methods, or to their haughty attitudes toward peasants, which were reminiscent of the Porfiriato.[74] Some struggled to retain teachers, convincing authorities to reject their midyear resignations, which the parents felt would retard their children's progress.[75] A degree of local control over the school tempered the state's authority in this respect.

Through these various channels, local culture influenced the everyday experience of schooling. In order to work in rural schools, teachers had to comply with village requests. They used a wide range of resources,

72. AGET, FRRO, 306-40, 1912, Vecinos of Contla to the Gobernador, Jan. 4, 1912.

73. AGET, FRRO, 330-26, 1914, Vecinos of San Diego to the Gobernador, Jan. 30, 1914.

74. AGET, EP, 369-14, 1933, Vecinos of Tlacochcalco to the Gobernador, Apr. 20, 1933.

75. AGET, FRRO, 312-51, 1915, Agente Municipal of Xochiteotla to the Gobernador, Aug. 3, 1915.

some gathered from the new "school of action" program, others the product of collective experience. Teachers reinterpreted state educational policies in terms that appealed to local knowledge.[76] Indeed, the acceptance of schooling hinged greatly on teachers' ability to turn the school into a social space amenable to local values and interests, as well as conducive to new cultural practices.

RURAL SCHOOLS AND THE CONSTRUCTION OF CIVIL SOCIETY

Besides drawing on local knowledge and resources, the social construction of schooling reinforced the network of social relations that constitutes civil society. In the course of my research, I have asked whether rural schools broadened horizons by giving "a sense of belonging to a form of social integration other than that mediated by the priest" (Ezpeleta and Rockwell 1983:75). In the transition from pre- to postrevolutionary rural Mexico, the local structure of domination shifted from the prefect, the hacienda administrator, and the parish priest to the military *jefe* and, later, the government official. Schools may have been instrumental in building the new system, but they also broke up some of the ties that bound the old one. In the process, new and unforeseen civil spaces and relations were created in peasant society.

In attempting to see schools as social and cultural spaces and not just as political instruments, we must keep in mind their particular characteristics. Unlike in the factory and the marketplace, where material appropriation occurs unilaterally, benefiting only dominant groups, in schools a popular appropriation of social domains and cultural contents is always a possibility. One place to look for signs of this process is in the use of space and time. The rural school established new gathering places, where state hegemony might be forged but a collective will could also be expressed. In Mexico's rural schools, the "authoritative organization of spaces, of times, of identities" (Sayer, in this volume) enacted by the state encountered alternative orders.

Because of the way local groups subsidized public education, they came to have a sense of possessing rural schools. Villagers would often decide the style of building they would finance, even after the 1929 law

---

76. Many autobiographies in *Los maestros y la cultura nacional* document the various ways this was achieved.

attempted to set a uniform plan.[77] Committee members were responsible for the school; they would turn the school over to incoming teachers and receive it at the end of the school year. They regularly kept watch over school grounds; safeguarded official papers, supplies, and key; and were even entrusted with the students' drawings and texts pending grading, if a teacher resigned before the end of the school year.[78] Committee members held meetings without the teachers' presence, and decided whether they would accept proposed educational changes.[79]

Rural schools represented a new public space, generally located in the center of the villages, facing the chapel. During the later twenties particularly, many schools also included other spaces: gardens, workshops, open-air theaters. Village schools served, for a time at least, as town meeting halls. When classes were over, schools might be used alternately as offices, market places, playgrounds, and dance halls. All of these public uses bothered the modernizing school principals of later years, who sought to redefine school space and fence it in.

Time was another dimension that schooling disturbed. Subtly, it wrought a series of changes in the organization of daily life. Time that children had spent elsewhere, learning other things, was soon devoted to their schooling. Among the everpresent items in the school inventories of the 1920s were bells and clocks, and the inspectors stressed punctuality. Sometimes it was the villagers who insisted that time not be wasted.[80] Yet the use of time was not immediately controlled: rather, it was continuously redefined, with local *juntas* in charge of establishing the preferred schedule and suspending classes on religious holidays.[81]

The inspectors' insistence on punctuality seems to have reflected the growth of industry in the region, as E. P. Thompson has suggested for England (1967). For example, in the course of our fieldwork, one of the

77. For example, AGET, EP, c. 248, 1929, leg. 2, Tenenyecac, Juntas de Educación.

78. AGET, FRRO, 325-43, 1913, Director of Tetlanohcan to the Gobernador, Oct. 29, 1913.

79. For example, AGET, EP, 1935, leg. 11, Director of Santa Cruz to the Gobernador, Apr. 19, 1935.

80. Terrenate parents requested that classes begin early in January, reminding authorities that children lost 114 days a year due to Saturdays, Sundays, and the *fiestas patrias*. AGET, EP, 71-33, 1922, Jan. 11, 1922.

81. See for example, AGET, FRRO, 1913, 320-69, Jefe Político of Hidalgo to the Gobernador, Apr. 30, 1913; and AGET, EP, 1929, leg. 15, Actas de Instalación de Juntas de Educación.

older principals of the area was heard to reprimand a mother, saying, "How is your son to learn to arrive at the factory on time if he does not come to school at eight?" Yet in postrevolutionary days, as in more recent times, the everyday use of school time was actually negotiated between teachers and pupils. The former often lived in distant towns and would arrive and leave earlier or later than scheduled, "in accordance with the local customs"; the latter did errands before classes and went home for lunch at recess. School time was not, in these schools at least, anything like ideal factory time.

The construction of the school generated new forms of association and decision making in addition to renewing traditional ones. The 1929 law recommended forming "societies for the practice of modern social habits," including antialcohol groups, cooperatives, mutual societies, and sports clubs. The principle of election was a significant change; inclusion of elected, rather than appointed, representatives in the *juntas* distinguished those bodies from their Porfirian predecessors. As the formal procedures of democracy were introduced, they blended with local customs. Thus the secret ballot recommended by law probably did not substitute for a show of hands, while the official assemblies allowed local forms of organization to enter school life. Other proposals were appropriated and transformed: the public accounting of school funds became a permanent practice; the *cooperativa* (cooperative), on the other hand, was often taken to mean *cooperaciones* (contributions).[82] One particularly important effect of the reforms of the twenties was the legitimate space opened for women in organizing local affairs. One mother was included in the *juntas* as "representative of the children," and a series of "societies," such as *sociedades de madres, comités pro-infancia,* and *ligas femeninas,* were promoted. Children were also exposed to these new practices of civic life, and thereby carried their imprint into the following decades.

After the revolution, schools established practices that extended well beyond the classroom. Though teachers had fulfilled important civic functions before the revolution, after 1917 their social role was enhanced. Teachers brought to rural schools some urban traditions, such as theater presentations and *veladas literarias,* which became, in the words of one inspector, "brilliant social commentaries" for these towns. Teachers were also asked to speak on civic duties in the marketplace for the "popular

82. See ACET, EP, 1929, leg. 15, Actas de Instalación de Juntas de Educación; and ibid., 245-3, 245-4, 1929, the discussion that took place during the Congreso de Educación, Tema: "Cooperativismo."

masses," as well as to offer evening classes for adults.[83] Through the intensification of civic ceremony that followed the revolution, the state disseminated an official revolutionary discourse (Vaughan 1994, Taboada 1985).

Nevertheless, popular appropriations of the revolution were also evident. In 1918, the *vecinos* of Contla named their school after their local hero, Juan Cuamatzi, though authorities did not register the name for years.[84] One federal inspector was surprised to find in 1926 that the Zacatelco girls' school only celebrated the local agrarian leader Domingo Arenas; every student had heard of his deeds, whereas only four could identify the nation's president.[85]

As teachers made their presence felt outside the schoolroom, they became part of a civil network, not only a state network. Though they generally had more pronounced urban mores, their social class differences were rarely marked. A 1917 circular required teachers to wear pants and shoes, no doubt reflecting the fact that their everyday dress was often similar to that of villagers.[86] Many rural teachers gained villagers' confidence by intentionally sharing their meals and customs. Others counted on their knowledge of Nahuatl to win over communities that had previously been hostile to teachers. Most state teachers were locally born; the better ones were sought by villagers who knew of the quality of their work in other schools.

Teachers in Tlaxcala were likely more integrated into the local society than was true in other areas of Mexico. Central Tlaxcalan villages, though deeply involved in popular Catholicism, generally did not have resident priests; teachers were often accorded moral authority in civil matters.[87] Teachers who remained in one school for years became part of the community through *compadrazgo* and participation in local affairs. Moreover, the teachers' role as brokers with government authorities had another side to it: advocacy. Many teachers recognized an obligation to denounce local injustices, either out of a sense of moral indignation or because of their adherence to liberal ideas. Younger federal teachers,

83. AGET, FRRO, 341-33, 1917, Circular 15, Apr. 21, 1917.

84. AGET, EP, 29-13, 1918, Report of the Director of Contla.

85. AHSEP, Tlaxcala, 1928–1937, exp. IV-161 (IV-16/6262), Inspector's report.

86. AGET, FRRO, 341-33, 1917, Circular 30, May 24, 1917.

87. By contrast, in places such as Los Altos de Jalisco, where the clergy had strong family ties with local inhabitants, opposition to the advance of federal schooling was effective (Brading 1988:169).

recognizing their modicum of independence from the local authorities, were particularly outspoken. Their activities served to recast the image of rural teachers, signaling the political conflicts that were to develop during the 1930s.

The rural social order was also altered, in ways that are sometimes difficult to capture, by the intensity of association among school children. Indeed, one educator in 1914 criticized schools as "meeting places where children only learn to play, and find excuses for obtaining from their parents more money than is needed for supplies, which they use to buy toys and, shamefully, obscene objects."[88] In school, children encountered new forms of social control but also found respite from the discipline of the field or factory, where they worked as apprentices to their fathers or relatives. In the classroom they encountered a different sort of discipline, which, though rigorous, was often collectively negotiable.

Just as local cultural forms persisted in everyday school life, new forms of relation were also constructed within the schools' characteristic environment. No other social space gathered together such a large number of children, with only one adult, for such a lengthy period of time. Also new was the ostensible purpose of the gathering, the acquisition of knowledge through a particularly discursive mode. Listening and speaking took on novel forms—for example, public oratory—which were, to some extent, transferable to other settings. Since the postrevolutionary social context in Tlaxcala favored the use of writing, literacy skills acquired in school were often lasting. Before the revolution, many peasants had learned to read in the workplace or in military service rather than in school. Yet, during the twenties, most initial engagement with the written word in rural areas occurred in the classroom. The appropriation of literacy—as incipient as it was—helped transform the hierarchical relationships that had shaped prerevolutionary society.[89]

Coeducation also changed existing patterns of social relations. After the revolution, school enrollment of girls approached that of boys.[90] The

88. ACET, FRRO, 329-15, 1914, Director of the Instituto Científico y Literario to the Gobernador.

89. Gains in literacy rates (over 60 percent in Tlaxcala in 1920) were slow in postrevolutionary years, but qualitative changes may have occurred. See Rockwell (1992).

90. In 1923, Aguillón reported that about four thousand girls and fifty-five hundred boys were enrolled in state schools, and regretted the gender difference. ACET, EP, 82-52, 1924. By the late twenties, the proportions were almost even.

larger urban and *cabecera* schools remained separate for boys and girls well into this century, because these locales had the resources and population to maintain a dual system. Thus, coeducation developed first, "for economic reasons," in rural areas, where it was allowed by law when enrollment was low.[91] During the twenties, village teachers increasingly worked with boys and girls together, though seated in separate rows, rather than maintaining the previous scheme of separating them by shifts. As enrollment grew, some villages, such as Ixcotla, requested two teachers, one for girls and one for boys, to keep up with the urban model. Eventually, however, additional teachers were assigned to the lower grades; for practical reasons, children were separated by age and achievement rather than by gender, even in the face of parental opposition. Over several generations, the daily encounter between boys and girls in schoolrooms must have redefined gender relations in ways that are still undocumented, but which certainly went far beyond the official discourse aimed at dignifying women.

The new sense of space and time that emerged in rural schools began to penetrate other spheres of village life. The resulting transformation of cultural and social practices was not necessarily a function of state domination, or even of modernization. The alternative networks and representations that emerged through schooling were constitutive of civil society, and probably had a greater effect on local social relations than the ideological content of official texts that historians have been so quick to analyze.[92]

REDEFINING RURAL SCHOOLING AND THE STATE

Drawing a contrast between the rural schools of this period and those of later years highlights the specificity of the dynamics found in Tlaxcala. As is generally recognized, the relationship between the postrevolutionary state and rural schooling gradually changed. The Cárdenas administration financed an important increase in the number of rural schools in the country and attempted to articulate a coherent national policy—named

91. See ACET, EP, 245-4, 1929, discussion in the minutes of the Congreso de Educación, Tema: "Coeducación."

92. Meneses for example, summarizes studies on the texts used in the twenties and concludes that they continued to represent Porfirian values rather than revolutionary ideals (1986:492–94).

"socialist education"—that drew on the experiences of the previous decade and mobilized new political forces. This policy met with considerable opposition and was drastically redefined in later years. However, a more significant and lasting structural transformation was occurring— even in the late thirties—at the everyday level. Two critical processes that marked this transformation were the redefinition of teachers' work and the delimitation of the social space of rural schooling.

Teachers in the thirties continued to dedicate many an evening and weekend to social activities; at times this activity was driven by civic obligation, at times by political militancy. Gradually, teachers' groups began to demand for themselves some of the rights they proclaimed for peons and factory workers. The 1929 education law was the first piece of legislation to regulate teacher promotions and labor rights in Tlaxcala. Nevertheless, the additional services that teachers performed in their communities persisted for years, and eventually came into conflict with the unions' efforts to regulate working hours. Even now, school authorities attempt to strike a balance between community obligations, such as the nighttime celebration of Independence Day, and the rights of teachers (C. Aguilar 1991).

Over the years, the social space of rural schools has also changed. Power has increasingly shifted to the principal, though villagers still attempt to defend their traditional prerogatives. For example, they still seek to exercise a customary right to oversee teachers' work and to defend classrooms, built decades ago, that are scheduled to be replaced with more modern buildings. Principals have points of leverage: when a school is much in demand, they can condition a child's entry on payment of individual construction fees, displacing the older committee system of sponsoring collective projects. Even so, some parents continue to resist, armed with a growing awareness of the government's constitutional obligation to provide free schooling.[93]

As rural schools in the region became "modern," they were invariably fenced in—though some fences had telling holes in them, with paths that led through the fields. With a closed gate, students whose parents had not yet paid dues could be left out, time schedules could be imposed, town meetings had to be held in other places, and greater distance could be established between parents and teachers. An increasing number of gov-

93. The negotiations surrounding the construction of school buildings, and the forms of control and resistance manifest in the process, were studied by Ruth Mercado (1986, 1992).

erning agencies entered rural areas, taking over functions once assigned to the teachers, though the latter are still called on to secure villagers' cooperation.

The model of schooling that replaced the one constructed in the decades immediately following the revolution operated with a different rationale, one that had fewer explicit ties with the social sphere in the rural communities. Yet this model probably had more profound effects. Through more subtle processes, schools began to contribute to the individuation of subjects in the society (Holloway 1980; Corrigan and Sayer 1985). The sort of coercion that operates through the definition of distinct social categories was increasingly present in everyday school life in the late thirties. The state's new presence in schooling was manifested in the differential classification of teachers and students, the selective channeling of knowledge, and a host of seemingly innocuous bureaucratic procedures. In the long run, such "routine" state forms served to counteract, at the everyday level, the potential for collective organization that had also been generated by postrevolutionary rural schools.

In the context of this more recent rationalization (and bureaucratization), resistance has taken forms that were originally introduced by the state-promoted rural school of the twenties.[94] Schools are therefore sites where state forms are both enacted and contested; yet it is not easy to assess accurately (or even distinguish between) the presence of the state and the strength of popular resistance. It is only locally that a history of mutual appropriations can be traced. The state has clearly incorporated or taken advantage of local resources and traditions; by the same token, *vecinos* have adopted and reinterpreted practices originally advanced by the schools.

States exert power in multiple combinations of public and private means, as Gramsci warned (1971). Domination, the concentration of power, may be expressed in different forms: at times it is attached to governing authorities; at times it is channeled through other spheres, such as the church or the market. State hegemony is challenged especially in those spheres where a basic service is claimed, and offered, as a condition of legitimate rule. In the case of public education, more is involved than sheer domination; more, even, than the regulation of everyday life.

94. Ana María Alonso (1988a) analyzes a similar process for Namiquipa, Chihuahua, where villagers originally backed by the state to fight Apaches resisted the state's subsequent modernization policies.

In Mexico, the protean changes of the state have taken it through several phases in this century (and another phase is currently in the making). In spite of revisionist claims of a basic continuity of the liberal project, a fundamental shift occurred after the revolution, and this shift is clearly visible in schooling. The Porfirian state in Tlaxcala was character-ized by a concentration of personal power and an increasing disregard for local voices. The regulation of schooling, as of other spheres of life, remained in the hands of political prefects and local, nongoverning elites.

When this form of state was undone, and while most of the revolu-tionaries were still busy on the battlefield, schooling was taken up as an issue by various contending forces. Several interests converged at this point—the villages' struggle for autonomy, the teachers' civilizing mis-sion, the children's need for knowledge—that together made the expan-sion of rural schools possible. Through schooling, state forms—such as the electoral process that ignited the revolution—were used and abused; government resources were reallocated, and central authorities increased their power in the rural areas. But at the everyday level, local culture tinged school life, teachers' networks sustained it, and peasant children made something of it.

During a later phase—which in some villages has occurred only recently—this sort of school was enclosed: teachers defended their work-ing hours, villagers found other spaces of contestation, and children, other forms of diversion. In the process, schooling accomplished some of its implicit missions, regulating the time and delimiting the space where children learned and producing workers and citizens. But schooling also empowered. As we know, selective access to knowledge can buttress the unequal distribution of power, but popular access can destabilize it. The power "to define the boundaries of the possible" (Sayer, in this volume) through schooling finally opened boundaries where more was possible than had previously been the case.

Most recently, another form of the state has been emerging. Through a neoliberal plan for "educational modernization," it seeks to "return schools to civil society" by exacting greater local contributions and privatizing public services. As the logic of the market system channels resources toward the more prosperous areas of the country, the compen-satory funding of state-financed public schools may be curtailed. Rural schools are being abandoned, and are apparently no longer needed to construct the political networks that support those in power. Signifi-cantly, the continuity of high-quality, state-funded public education has become a legitimate popular demand.

As central government is undone from within, the state is being reconstituted in a different guise. As in other Latin American countries (and elsewhere for that matter), the new form of rule tends to dismantle systems of public education and proposes to return the educating function to other agencies. At the same time, the new state increases its effective domination of popular classes. Perhaps, as James Scott has suggested, ultimately "the system may have most to fear from those subordinates among whom the institutions of hegemony have been most successful" (Scott 1990:107).

DANIEL NUGENT AND ANA MARÍA ALONSO

Multiple Selective Traditions in Agrarian Reform and Agrarian Struggle: Popular Culture and State Formation in the Ejido of Namiquipa, Chihuahua

The point of departure for this paper is the notion that there is a relationship between popular culture and state formation, that neither is an autonomous process or sphere of action or representation. Our aim here is to understand this relationship by analyzing peasant reactions to the formation of the *ejido* in Namiquipa, Chihuahua, and examining *some* of the ways in which *some* peasants envision the state and construct their own identities in relation to, and against, it.[1] The argument relies on

We thank all the participants at the 1991 conference in San Diego, especially Adolfo Gilly and William Roseberry, who commented specifically on this paper. Parts of it have been presented to American Anthropological Association meetings in Washington, DC, in 1989 and New Orleans in 1990; to a University of North Carolina History Department seminar; and to the Anthropology Department at the University of Arizona. The argument is greatly improved thanks to the commentary and critiques in those contexts from Philip Corrigan, Nick Dirks, Jane Hill, and Daniela Spenser. Thanks also to Ellen Basso, Gil Joseph, Paul Liffman, Carlos Vélez-Ibáñez, and Drexel Woodson, who commented on earlier drafts.

1. The *ejido* is a system of land tenure based on indigenous Mesoamerican systems but equally derived from fifteenth-century southern European systems (Mendieta y Núñez 1981:72–73). We use the term to designate a territorial unit (which may range in size from less than one hundred to more than one hundred thousand hectares) created in accordance with laws formulated during the Mexican revolution

materials derived from ethnographic and historical study of Namiquipans' involvement in political struggle before, during, and after the revolution of 1910 as well as of the postrevolutionary Mexican state's agrarian reform.

We understand popular culture to be the symbols and meanings embedded in the day-to-day practices of subordinated groups. At once "socially constituted (it is a product of present and past activity) and socially constituting (it is part of the meaningful context in which activity takes place)" (Roseberry 1989:42), popular culture is neither an autonomous, authentic, and bounded domain nor a "little tradition" version of dominant culture. Instead, popular and dominant culture are produced *in relation* to each other through a "dialectic of cultural struggle" (Hall 1981:233) that takes place in contexts of unequal power and entails reciprocal appropriations, expropriations, and transformations. Reciprocity does not imply equality in the distribution of power; but, while domination "has real effects . . . these are neither all-powerful nor all-inclusive" (S. Hall 1981:233).

The forms, routines, rituals, and discourses of rule of the state play a key role in the dialectic of cultural struggle. State formation is a "revolution . . . in the way the world is made sense of"; that is, a "cultural revolution" (Corrigan and Sayer 1985:1–2). While the latter expression indicates a nod in the direction of Mao Zedong thought, its inspiration derives no less from Durkheim, for whom "the state is the very organ of social thought . . . [and] is above all, supremely, the organ of moral discipline" (Durkheim 1957:50, 72, cited in Corrigan and Sayer 1985:5). State formation thus refers neither to "nation building" as a project of certain elites, nor to the *origins* of some apparatus of power called "the state." Rather, it encompasses processes through which the identities of subjects of the state are constructed via media of moral regulation, quotidian administration, and ritual, as well as through manifest, concrete

---

and agrarian policies implemented since 1920. Ideally composed primarily of lands susceptible to cultivation, the *ejido* can be characterized by a variety of types of relations of production. In Namiquipa, for example, fields of agricultural land designated and recognized as "ejidal plots" (primarily *temporal*, or rain-irrigated fields) are assigned to individual *ejidatarios* and devoted to the cultivation of beans and corn. The common grazing lands of the Namiquipan *ejido* are open for use by any member of the community with cattle and so are the common forests, where people forage for firewood, cut fenceposts, log pine trees, and from time to time establish stills for the manufacture of *sotol*.

oppression. Yet the meanings and symbols produced and disseminated by the state are not simply reproduced by subordinated groups. Popular culture is contradictory since it embodies and elaborates dominant symbols and meanings but also contests, challenges, rejects, revalues, reaccents,[2] and presents alternatives to them (cf. Gramsci 1971:333; Williams 1977:113–14). Examining a concrete example of the relationship between state formation and popular culture should advance our understanding of this dialectic of cultural struggle.

THE MEXICAN REVOLUTION, AGRARIAN ACTIVISM, AND AGRARIAN REFORM

The Mexican revolution (1910–1920) has captured the interest of countless scholars. The result has been a proliferation of arguments about the revolution and how to characterize it, periodize it, decry it for its shortcomings and challenge it, or authenticate and celebrate it. But any serious effort to analyze the Mexican revolution involves recognizing the importance of popular demands for land and liberty that were expressed, however unevenly, in the decades after 1910 (Warman 1978, 1988).

After the revolution, Mexico became the first nation in the Americas in which an agrarian reform was systematically implemented by the state. Between the 1920s and the 1970s, millions of hectares of land were taken from Mexican and foreign-owned estates and redistributed to peasants; by 1980, more than twenty thousand *ejidos* had been established in the countryside (Sanderson 1984).

Postrevolutionary agrarian reform in Mexico has spawned a literature almost as vast and varied as that concerning the revolution. Contentious issues addressed in this literature include whether the success—or failure—of the agrarian reform should be attributed primarily to forces internal to particular communities, to the organization of agricultural labor itself, or to the internationalization of capital and labor. The optimistic view is that the agrarian reform functioned as a socially just set of brakes on the more invidious aspects of capitalist development in the countryside (e.g., Silva Herzog 1969; Simpson 1937; Tannenbaum 1929). The more critical (or perhaps pessimistic) view is that by co-opting popular demands and erecting an institutional structure through which the production process in agriculture was organized, the postrevolutionary state

---

2. See Volosinov (1986) on the multiaccentual character of the ideological sign.

strengthened its own position at the service of capital and against peasants (e.g., Hamilton 1982; Stavenhagen 1970; A. Bartra 1985).

The key institution through which the Mexican state implemented agrarian reform was the postrevolutionary *ejido*. In most *ejidos*, household heads (usually males)[3] hold usufruct rights to specified plots of land within the *ejido* which they work individually, i.e., relying principally on their own and household labor (Whetten 1948; Mendieta y Núñez 1981; Reyes et al. 1970). The state reserves for itself the authority to issue credentials to *ejidatarios* (members of the *ejido*) and to be the final arbiter of who enjoys rights to land. According to agrarian legislation, ejidal lands belong to the state (A. Bartra 1985:16–21) and are administered by community-based organizations whose functionaries are elected by the *ejidatarios*. The law of December 19, 1925 mandated that *ejidatarios* could not sell their usufruct rights (Mendieta y Núñez 1981:236); moreover, those rights might be revoked. The latter point provides one of the terms of struggle with the state in Namiquipa: from a Namiquipan point of view, when the state is the landlord, land tenure is insecure.

Our intent is not to deny the genuine accomplishments of the agrarian reform in Mexico: millions of hectares of land were expropriated from large estates and redistributed to peasants. However, we are persuaded that the *ejido* has functioned semantically within what Marx might have called "the ideal historiography" of the Mexican state, its "so-called cultural history" ([1857] 1973:109), to promote a populist revolutionary nationalism that establishes a privileged role for the state as paterfamilias and arbiter of social conflicts while eliding relations of domination. The *ejido* is a crucial element of the "selective tradition"[4] through which the postrevolutionary state has constructed its legitimacy and secured hegemony—however tentatively. The stress within official rhetoric on the "traditional" indigenous roots of the *ejido* (versus the extent to which it is a creation of the postrevolutionary state) has served to emphasize the putatively "genuinely popular" character of this system of land tenure while effacing the state control over the peasantry and over agricultural

3. In the official discourse of agrarian rights the *ejidatario* is a male subject (see, for example, *Ley federal de reforma agraria*, 1982). Angelina Casillas Moreno notes that in Julimes and El Ejido, Chihuahua, no women secured land via formal requests from the *ejido* organization; women with rights to *ejido* land had obtained these through inheritance from fathers or husbands (Casillas Moreno 1985:61).

4. Raymond Williams defines *selective tradition* as "an intentionally selective version of a shaping past and a preshaped present, which is then powerfully operative in the process of social and cultural definition and identification" (1977:115).

production it has secured. The popular has been appropriated by the populist in order to construct an image of the state as the true representative of the nation and of its "authentic" children, *el pueblo.*

Armando Bartra's characterization of state-co-opted agrarismo (agrarian activism) explains the outcomes of a wide range of popular struggles for land in terms of the relationship of popular movements to a (culturally constituted) capitalist state, which, in stating the "rules of the game," unalterably transformed and muted, even negated, the thrust of those popular movements. Agrarismo was, in this account, "the route through which the new State [was] able to create for itself a solid base among the masses." The agraristas of the 1920s, Bartra writes,

> constituted a peasant movement of a new type, one which in principle recognized or acceded to *the rules of the game of the postrevolutionary State.* This was a peasant movement which, from the moment it admitted that its rights to land came from the State, recognized the legitimacy of the new social order, and accepted its own subordinated role (Bartra 1985:23, our translation and emphasis).

But not all rural Mexicans became agraristas in the 1920s; and in contrast to the general trajectory of agrarismo described by Bartra, the participants in the Namiquipan popular struggle for *tierra y libertad,* for example, did not simply endorse the rules of the game mandated by the national state. Instead, they challenged these rules. And what we want to explore here are the terms in which they did so.

That abstraction we call "the state" (see Abrams [1977] 1988) is not the only author of a selective tradition. This paper argues that Namiquipans' selective tradition construes the *ejido* and the relationship between peasants and the state in ways that contrast with the populist heroics of Mexico's official history and challenge the power of the state. This active *envisioning* of the state by Namiquipan peasants is a potent representational and practical form, through which

> possibilities of the future are inflected by the past. But this relationship between present and past is neither direct nor univocal. The pre-figuring of the present by the past is always mediated by social memory and by the historical circumstances of social groups. Thus, the present also shapes the past because social groups reconstruct their histories as the history they live changes (Alonso 1986:5).

A critical point is that this alternative selective tradition has been produced by Namiquipans through an engagement with the state, and not in isolation from it. The crucial task for analysis, then, is to uncover the complex relationships, the terms of a "dialectic of articulation," between the community—constituted, as John Comaroff suggests, by an "internal dialectic"—and the state as those relationships shift over time (Comaroff 1982:146).[5]

During our fieldwork (June 1983 to October 1985) we learned about agrarian struggles and political conflicts in the present and the past, both in the *ejidos* of Namiquipa and Cruces and in neighboring *colonias agricolas.* One of the central insights we obtained through archival research and through conversations with Namiquipans and Chihuahuans was that in agrarian struggle in this region, the control of land and the organization of production on it are intimately linked to *the meaning* of the land, and whether such an ascription of meaning is perceived to be generated from within the community or from without. Of course, popular perceptions may be no less partial than official or "state-ed" ones, and cannot be taken at face value. The problem, then, becomes one of analyzing modalities of resistance focused on competing claims about how land is held and worked, in which the outcomes, while they do not definitively overthrow the state's rules of the game, do not endorse them either. Such an analysis requires not just an anthropological but also a historical perspective.

A CONCISE AGRARIAN HISTORY OF NAMIQUIPA

Namiquipa is today the center of a rural municipality of some forty thousand inhabitants located approximately two hundred miles south of

---

5. Comaroff's "two dialectics" provide, in our view, a useful and, above all, *concise* restatement of a number of insights that emerged from the literature on peasants and the state, theories of dependency, and the articulation of modes of production written in the 1960s and 1970s. In this connection see Long (1984) and Roseberry (1989: 88ff., 145–74). Nugent (1991:93–94) discusses how rural Mexico during the Porfiriato (see Katz 1986b) may be understood in terms of the way the dialectic(s) of articulation and the internal dialectic(s) shaped one another. A critical feature of that process was the way "the so-called primitive accumulation of capital" (Marx [1867] 1906:784–805) affected laboring masses in the Mexican countryside during the period. From the standpoint of the peasantry, primitive accumulation had consequences both structural (separation of producers from means of production) and cultural. Peasants had to reorient their practice in light of the transformation of land from a *subject of labor* in their communities to a commodity—one they could not afford to purchase—that circulated in spheres of exchange having little to do with community life. (See also Chaterjee 1982; Cardoso 1980; Marx [1857–58] 1973:471–72;

the U.S. border on the eastern slope of the Sierra Madre Occidental. Namiquipans consider themselves to have mostly "Spanish blood"; indeed, many of them are the descendants of Indian-fighters, of the "gente de razón" (people possessing reason) who "defended civilization" from "indios bárbaros" (barbaric indians)—that is, the Apache—for more than a century. From 1778 until 1821 the community was the headquarters of a *compañía volante*, a "flying company" of presidial soldiers serving the Spanish crown in the conquest and defense of New Spain's northern frontier. Civilian colonists cooperated with presidial forces.

A *bando* (decree) issued by Teodoro de Croix, governor of the Internal Provinces of New Spain, on November 15, 1778, awarded each of the communities known today as Namiquipa, Cruces, Galeana, Casas Grandes, and Janos corporate land grants of more than 112,000 hectares in exchange for the settlers' commitment to fight the Apache and establish viable agricultural communities (see Nugent 1993:43–50). These land grants were more than sixty times the size routinely stipulated for communities (whether of indigenous or nonindigenous peoples) in the region. To the end of developing a "warrior spirit" among non-Indian peasant men, the colonial state promoted a construction of gender and ethnic honor that predicated masculine reputation, access to land, and membership in a corporate community on valor and performance in warfare against "barbarians" (Alonso 1988a).

The peasants' defense of the land from Apache bands contesting control of the region was a protracted and bloody struggle that was not concluded until 1886. After independence and through the 1860s, anti-Apache campaigns were largely initiated and coordinated by the *gente de razón* and Tarahumara inhabitants of the communities of western Chihuahua, with little financial or military assistance from the state or from *hacendados* (owners of large estates), many of whom abandoned their properties in the nineteenth century (AMCG, passim). By the 1870s and 1880s, important Chihuahuan landowning families—notably the Terrazas—partly financed and coordinated Apache campaigns, and many peasants from towns such as Namiquipa, San Andrés, and Ariseachi fought under the leadership of Col. Joaquín Terrazas (Jordán 1956; F. Katz 1988c:537; Lister and Lister 1966; Terrazas 1905; AMCG, passim.).

After 1885, however, the residents of northwestern Chihuahua found themselves face-to-face with the barbarism of surveying companies, state

Nugent 1988b:16. Cf. Rosaldo 1989:196–217; Scott 1985; and Corrigan and Sayer 1985, on the state and "its" subjects.)

officials, and landlords. Between 1880 and 1910, most of the lands earlier assigned to these communities—with the exception of Namiquipa's grant—were successfully invaded by Mexican and North American landlords and incorporated into cattle estates. The processes of agrarian dispossession, social differentiation, and loss of popular control over local politics precipitated by those invasions go some way toward explaining why the inhabitants of these towns participated as substantially as they did in movements of nonviolent protest and armed rebellion against the state in the decades before 1910, and in almost every stage of revolutionary struggle in Chihuahua in the decade following 1910 (Almada 1964; Wasserman 1980; F. Katz 1981; Alonso 1986, 1988a; Lloyd 1988; González Herrera 1988; Olea 1961; Duarte Morales 1968; Rubén Osorio, personal communication).

In contrast to their neighbors, Namiquipans never lost control of their land to surveying companies or haciendas during the decades following the conclusion of the Apache Wars, just as they had never surrendered to the Apache and abandoned their lands during the previous century of warfare. In 1885 Namiquipans persuaded a surveying company's representatives to respect their rights to the sixty-four *sitios de ganado mayor* of land (over 112,000 hectares) that constituted the community's colonial land grant.[6] The president of the republic affirmed the legality of Namiquipa's colonial concession in 1889[7] and in 1893 the federal government once again provided de jure confirmation of the Namiquipans' corporate rights to land.[8] Since the mid-1860s, Enrique Müller, a *hacendado* with close ties to powerful Chihuahuan families, had been advancing claims to about forty thousand hectares of Namiquipa's land as part of his Santa Clara estate, but Namiquipans prevented Müller from effectively seizing them.[9] Attempts by petit bourgeois outsiders (small ranchers and merchants who immigrated to Namiquipa after the end of the Apache Wars) to wrest control of the land from local peasants were also largely unsuccessful until after 1904, when Enrique Creel began his term as governor of Chihuahua.

In 1904, Creel revised the Chihuahuan constitution to eliminate the last vestiges of peasant control over local politics and passed a municipal tax law that substantially increased the state's share of peasant surpluses

6. ATN, 1.71 [06] E 75669; 1.24 [06] E 17.
7. Ibid., 1.22 [06] E 182, Aug. 21, 1889.
8. Ibid., 1.24 [06] E 178.
9. AMCG, box 10, exp. 122.

(Almada 1964:21–26, 81–83). Most important, Creel's Municipal Land Law of 1905 put on the market whatever land was still controlled by rural communities in Chihuahua, intensifying and generalizing peasant discontent and delegitimizing the state and federal governments in the peasants' eyes (see Lloyd 1988; Alonso 1988a; Nugent 1993). Wealthy ranchers, *hacendados*, municipal and regional officials of the state, and—certainly in the case of Namiquipa—petit bourgeois immigrants purchased vacant lots, grazing land, fields, and even house lots out from under existing residents who, though descendants of colonial-period settlers, could not produce "legitimate" titles to their properties.

Within Namiquipa, petit bourgeois immigrants, with the support of higher-level government officials, had by 1904 assumed control of the municipal administration. That provided these *foráneos* (outsiders) the power required to undermine the land rights of peasant *originarios* (those who considered themselves descendants of Namiquipa's original colonists). The first step was to charge the peasants rent for the small plots they cultivated without "legitimate" titles; by 1906, approximately half of Namiquipa's peasant families were paying rent for their plots.[10] What was at issue for *originario* peasants was not so much the money as the circumstance that the exaction of rent denied the legitimacy of their claims to land.[11] The second step increased the size of the *ejido* (heretofore an extension of land reserved for common use within the land grant) by a factor of six, from the standard 1,755 hectares to 10,530 hectares, so as to free more land for the market.[12] The third step was the effort to alienate these 10,530 hectares under the umbrella of the 1905 Municipal Land Law. (More than 5,000 hectares were actually sold between 1905 and 1910. See Lloyd 1988:90–97; Nugent 1993:68–72.)

Sales of municipal land meant that Namiquipan peasants who in the past had enjoyed rights to work land within what was now defined as the "municipal *ejido*" found their fields sold from under them. The local political boss, who by law had to approve all land sales, favored petit

10. AMN, box 2, 1906.

11. AMCG, box 73, exp. 625, Jefe Municipal y Comandante Militar Cenobio Varela, Namiquipa, to Jefe Político Distrito Guerrero, May 17, 1911; AMN, box 3, unsigned letter, Oct. 8, 1907; ibid., letter signed Victoriano Torres, Jefe Municipal, Apr. 28, 1906.

12. ATN, complaint from the peasants of Namiquipa to Porfirio Díaz, July 28, 1908; AMN, box 2-bis, exp. 1900–1905, complaint from the peasants of Namiquipa, transcribed to the Jefe Municipal by the Jefe Político, Urbano Zea, Dec. 27, 1904.

bourgeois immigrants and excluded *originario* peasants from purchasing land. The 1905 law provided the legal pretext for an invasion of 8,775 hectares of the peasants' colonial land grant (the *terrenos de común repartimiento*).[13] Moreover, common usufruct rights to water and timber were violated as these were transformed into commodities and sold or rented by the local political boss to petit bourgeois outsiders.[14]

Responding to the Municipal Land Law, Namiquipans formed a "private civil society" (La Sociedad Civil Particular, or SCP) to defend the rights of *originario* peasants to their colonial land grant. The founding document of the SCP, from May 1906, outlines a regime of land tenure.[15] It bases its terms on those in the 1778 *bando* and the century of struggle it had taken to fulfill them. The document pointedly affirms that only Namiquipan families who are descendants of the original colonists should enjoy rights to work the land and have access to the commons. While the SCP was ineffective until 1911 (its leadership jailed, its petitions ignored), after that date and through the 1920s, it provided a local, popularly based organization through which *pueblo* lands were administered.

From 1905 on, then, Namiquipans were drawn into direct conflict with local officials of the state. Nonviolent forms of resistance to processes of agrarian dispossession and political domination were increasingly ineffective. In October 1905, a representative of the Namiquipan peasants wrote to Ricardo Flores Magón—then attempting to organize the revolution in Mexico—expressing readiness to fight against "the authorities governed by the Dictatorship" of Porfirio Díaz.[16] This attempt to seek outside sources of support failed. However, five years later, Namiquipan peasants—who, as former Apache fighters, possessed military skills and some weapons—threw their support behind the emergent movement[17] that directly challenged Terrazas-Creel power in Chihuahua

13. AMCG, box 73, exp. 625, May 17, 1911.

14. For example, see AMN, box 3-bis, Jefe Político Urbano Zea to Jefe Municipal, Namiquipa, Jan. 25, 1907, notifying him of the Chihuahuan government's approval of a contract between the municipal council and José Casavantes for the cutting of timber in *común repartimiento* lands. For protest against this by Namiquipan peasants, see AMCG, box 56, exp. 508, Jefe Municipal to Jefe Político, Nov. 22, 1906.

15. AGNCh, Protocolos, Namiquipa, libro 1, May 26, 1906.

16. BL, MB-18, box 26, fol. 8-C, from Concepción Cervantes, Namiquipa, to Ricardo Flores Magón, St. Louis, MO, Oct. 13, 1905.

17. The movement, largely middle class and even *haut bourgeois* in origin, was led by Francisco I. Madero, a landlord from Coahuila. See S. Terrazas (1985).

and appeared to provide an overarching organization through which to channel and direct peasant discontent into a national revolution.

On the morning of November 20, 1910, SCP Vice President José Rascón y Tena rode in with his brothers and cousins from their rancho, joining more armed men in the *barrio* of La Hacienda. The insurgents soon took the plaza of Namiquipa in a battle during which Félix Merino, the police commander, was killed. Victoriano Torres and Pablo Porras, the political bosses who had presided over sales of municipal lands after 1905, were quickly run out of town.[18] During the winter of 1910–11, contingents of Namiquipans joined the Maderista uprising throughout western Chihuahua, many later participating in the battle of Ciudad Juárez, which brought about the downfall of the Díaz regime (BN.AFM; Olea Arias 1961; Duarte Morales 1968; Calzadíaz Barrera 1979).

In May 1911, as the Díaz government collapsed, Namiquipans petitioned revolutionary authorities to expropriate the lands alienated by the 1905 Municipal Land Law and return them to local peasants.[19] When their petitions received no action, they took matters into their own hands. In July 1911, the municipal president of Namiquipa (recently elected by the revolutionary peasants) prohibited all those who had purchased land under the 1905 law from working it.[20] Peasants ripped down the new fences enclosing more than five thousand hectares of land.[21] The revolutionary authorities at the district level responded to this locally initiated agrarian reform by ordering that the expropriated lands be returned to their petit bourgeois "owners" and that the peasants settle their grievances in court. This superior order was ignored.[22]

The Maderista regime's failure immediately to redress popular agrarian grievances contributed to mobilizing some support among Chihuahuan peasants in 1912 for the Orozquista movement, which was backed by the Terrazas-Creel grand family as well as other prerevolutionary Chihuahuan oligarchs. Though José Rascón y Tena, one of Namiquipa's

18. Interview with José Rascón Iguado, Ciudad Chihuahua, June 1984.

19. AMCG, box 73, exp. 625, May 17, 1911.

20. Ibid., July 1, 1911.

21. AMN, box 5-C, exp. 1918, letter from Mariano and Dolores Carrasco referring to the destruction during the revolution of the fences on lands bought under the 1905 law.

22. AMCG, box 74, exp. 627, from the Jefe Político Interino of Guerrero to the Jefe Municipal of Namiquipa.

agrarian activists and revolutionary leaders, briefly supported Pascual Orozco, Jr., the majority of Namiquipan revolutionaries continued to fight on the side of the Madero government. Most Namiquipan revolutionaries thought that an Orozquista government would not confer on them the same *garantías* (guarantees) as had the Madero administration.[23] Adherence to the Maderista movement had resulted in the recovery of control over the municipal administration, for example, which allowed Namiquipan peasants effectively to marginalize the local petite bourgeoisie. What's more, Orozco's connections with the landed oligarchy were known; and he also was a distant relative by marriage of Victoriano Torres, the hated prerevolutionary Namiquipan *cacique.*

Instead, from March 1913 through much of 1916, the municipality became an important center of Villismo, the armed, popular movement from the north that destroyed the prerevolutionary state but in the end failed to establish an alternative, popular regime throughout the country. Starting in 1913 (and possibly earlier), the SCP started giving *originario* peasants usufruct rights to plots within the *común repartimiento* lands.[24] In April 1913, local revolutionaries, following the orders of General Francisco ("Pancho") Villa, confiscated the neighboring Müller estate, Santa Clara, in the name of the revolution (Calzadíaz Barrera 1979:102–3). In line with Villa's pragmatic policy of not confiscating U.S.-owned property in Chihuahua, the William Randolph Hearst hacienda of San José de Babicora, located to the west and south of the town, was left intact. Until early 1916, Santa Clara was administered by two local Villista officers, Telesforo Terrazas and Candelario Cervantes.[25]

The confiscation of the hacienda Santa Clara was a significant step in the redressal of local agrarian grievances. Enrique Müller had been trying to invade Namiquipan lands since 1871. Moreover, once the agrarian struggle had been won, the main beneficiaries of Villa's confiscation without compensation of the estates of the landed oligarchy—formally decreed in December 1913—were to be dispossessed peasants, revolutionaries, widows, and orphans (F. Katz 1981a:139–40).

23. See, for example, ASC, box 7, Sectional President, Cruces, Namiquipa, to General-in-Chief Victoriano Huerta, Chihuahua, July 19, 1912.

24. Though most of the SCP records were destroyed (interview with José Rascón Iguado, Chihuahua City, 1984), "certificates of possession" given out by the SCP beginning in 1913 are found in AMN and AJMN.

25. The latter was a nephew of Concepción Cervantes, who had been corresponding with the PLM in 1905. AMN, AJMN, passim.

By the middle of 1916, "The Revolution" in Mexico, and Villismo in particular, had no center. Villa had disbanded his army, the División del Norte, in December 1915, and had initiated his guerrilla period the following March with his celebrated attack on Columbus, New Mexico. While about 100 Namiquipans (20 percent of the five-hundred-member force) participated in the Columbus raid, the immediate consequences for the town were devastating, at least from the standpoint of sustaining a viable, and Villista, resistance to outsiders of whatever provenance. Five thousand U.S. soldiers occupied Namiquipa from April to June 1916 (Alonso 1988c). Even before their withdrawal, some Namiquipans (a few of whom had collaborated with U.S. occupation forces) formed the Defensa Social, a local militia that eventually (at least ostensibly) owed fealty to Ignacio C. Enríquez, the Carrancista general commissioned with the task of ridding Chihuahua of Villistas and establishing Constitutionalist order in the region. While the Defensa Social of Namiquipa was among the first to be established in Chihuahua (Alonso 1988c), by 1917 such militia were organized throughout the state, their actions coordinated by Carrancista officers or intermediaries (Rocha Islas 1979). Though some of Villa's Namiquipan followers joined the Defensas Sociales, others continued fighting by Villa's side until his surrender in 1920 (Osorio 1990:186ff.).

Between 1910 and 1920, then, Namiquipans appealed to a range of external forces (Constitucionalista, Villista, even *yanqui*) to validate their claims to land. But while the Villista guerrilla forces scored some notable victories in Chihuahua (including battles against Defensas Sociales from Namiquipa), from the late summer and early autumn of 1916 until Villa's surrender and retirement to Canutillo in 1920 (he was assassinated three years later), many Namiquipans no longer perceived Villismo as a viable avenue through which to press agrarian demands. Not only did Villismo lack a supralocal institutional framework through which to validate agrarian claims after 1915, but Villa was no longer able to guarantee protection to his adherents or the towns from which they came (F. Katz 1988d, González Herrera 1988).

During the 1920s, the struggle to validate the community's rights to lands continued. Namiquipans appealed to the Revolutionary state to defend their rights against the claims of *hacendados*. However, they also opposed attempts by the state to consolidate its power over the peasantry through the *ejido*, and they resisted efforts to reduce the SCP's role in administering local agrarian affairs.

In 1921, Reyes Ortíz took office as municipal president of Namiquipa. Along with Cornelio Espinosa (president of the SCP from 1906 to 1922) and José Rascón y Tena (vice president of the SCP from 1906 on), Ortíz had been active in the struggle to validate Namiquipa's rights to land before the revolution.[26] Despite their shared history of agrarian activism, however, Espinosa as SCP president and Ortíz as municipal president came into conflict. In 1921, each claimed exclusive rights to administer the lands of Namiquipa and to represent the community in agrarian questions.[27] While their conflicts reflected a personal struggle for leadership of the community rather than major social or ideological differences, they did have consequences for the *pueblo* as a whole. Both the SCP and the municipal council were giving peasants permits to cultivate lands and, at times, the different authorities gave several individuals rights to the same plots.[28] Ortíz charged rent to peasants cultivating plots within the "municipal *ejido*" and, in general, challenged the legitimacy of the SCP with his actions, insisting that the local apparatus of the state should administer the lands of the community.

Conflicts between the Ortíz administration and the SCP were mediated by Mariano Yrigoyen, a deputy of the Chihuahuan congress, and on July 30, 1921, the municipal council agreed to accept the SCP's authority to administer the land grant. In practice, however, Ortíz continued his earlier policy. Espinosa died in 1922, and Ortíz resigned his post as municipal president on June 24 of the same year (probably because of popular feeling against him). Conflicts between the SCP and the municipal council continued, however, as Ortíz's replacement, Anastacio Tena, continued renting "municipal land" and issuing permits for cultivation in the *terrenos de común repartimiento*. Meanwhile, Tena's municipal council named Ortíz as Namiquipa's agrarian representative in the ongoing con-

26. Though Ortíz, born in 1866, was a *foráneo*, his family had immigrated to Namiquipa in the late 1870s or early 1880s; that is, before the end of the Apache Wars. Ostensibly, the SCP was wholly composed of *originarios*; however, Ortíz and two of his brothers were among the *foráneos* admitted into the organization when it was founded in 1906. This was probably because birth in the community was not the only criterion defining an *originario*; fighting the Apache was another. Ortíz acted as the community's agrarian representative in 1901. Ironically, he drafted a petition to the national government complaining that Namiquipa's *común repartimiento* lands were being invaded by *foráneos*. ATN 1.24(06), exp. 23, Mar. 20, 1901.

27. AMN, box 6-D, passim.

28. For example, AMN, Justicia, box 1, case of Gabino Carrasco vs. Eulalio Vásquez, Mar. 1925.

flict between the community and the owners of the hacienda de Santa Clara.

In 1919, the heirs of Enrique Müller had renewed Müller's original efforts to claim forty-thousand hectares of Namiquipan land as part of hacienda Santa Clara. The ensuing dispute with the town was presented to the governor of Chihuahua for arbitration.[29] He ruled in March 1922 that the rights of the *pueblo* of Namiquipa to the disputed land were unquestionable, the Santa Clara claim without merit. The governor was Ignacio C. Enríquez who, while not a strong advocate of agrarian reform since his preferences ran toward the development of large-scale capitalist enterprises, irrigation works, and so on,[30] probably supported the Namiquipans out of political expediency.

Namiquipa was (and is still) considered to be one of the most "revolutionary" *pueblos* in Chihuahua, and the community's men had (and continue to have) a reputation throughout the state for bravery, rebelliousness, and fighting skills. Hence, Chihuahuan government functionaries often made concessions to the community to curtail political discontent. This point is aptly illustrated by the state government's attitude toward the SCP between 1921 and 1925. In addition to the rulings favoring the SCP over the Ortíz administration in 1921 and Namiquipa over Santa Clara in 1922, the municipal president and council were expressly forbidden from playing an active role in the administration of Namiquipa's lands after 1923. Jesús Mucharraz, *procurador general de justicia interino* of Chihuahua, clearly expressed the reasons behind the government's position. Writing in 1925, Mucharraz commented that he had seen "testimonies of General Enríquez and the Secretaría de Fomento (Development) in which they give importance to the agreements and resolutions" of the SCP, adding that since the SCP "is a Society integrated by many Members, all agriculturalists of the region, a resolution dictated against their interests could give rise to serious conflicts and upheavals between the Government and the Society."[31]

29. ASC, Secretaría del Gobierno del Estado, Chihuahua to the President of Cruces, Namiquipa, Sept. 23, 1921; President of Galeana to the President of Cruces, Oct. 4, 1921, informing him that the municipal council of Galeana, like those of Cruces and Namiquipa, had agreed to accept the governor of Chihuahua as mediator in the conflict with heirs of Enrique Müller.

30. AGN, CNA. Actas 8:13ff.

31. AMN, Justicia, Procurador General de Justicia, Jesús Mucharraz, Chihuahua, to Agente Subalterno del Ministerio Público, Reyes Ortíz, Namiquipa, Feb. 18, 1925.

The Chihuahuan government's attitude toward the SCP contrasts with that of the Comisión Nacional Agraria (hereafter CNA), the agrarian reform apparatus of the national state, and its regional branch, the Comisión Local Agraria (hereafter CLA). In 1922 the CLA authorized the municipal council headed by Ortíz to give out land permits until a Comité Particular Administrativo (CPA), the local ejidal organization, could be established in Namiquipa.[32] Beginning in 1925, the CNA did everything possible to replace the SCP, the autonomous peasant organization, with the CPA, the local branch of its own administrative structure.

Anxious to obtain legal guarantees for the community's land rights and to block any efforts by the owners of Santa Clara to usurp their land, 133 Namiquipan men (including the SCP vice president, Rascón y Tena) submitted a petition to Governor Enríquez and the CLA on November 18, 1922, requesting restitution of all lands from the colonial-period grant that had been invaded by neighboring landowners.[33] Four years later, the state affirmed the *pueblo's* collective rights to the land, ruling that an *ejido* be granted as a *restitución*, not a *dotación*.

Restitución involves a restoration of lands that have been taken away from peasants illegally; *dotación* is simply a grant of land to peasants from the state. According to Nathan Whetten, since prior possession of lands by peasant communities was difficult to document systematically, and illegal dispossession difficult to prove to the satisfaction of the state (and the capitalist regime of property), the architects of the agrarian reform invented the method of *dotación* in order to have the legal means to distribute more land (Whetten 1948:129–30). Insofar as this was merely a procedural distinction—and the desired end of delivering land to the peasantry was the same in both events—Whetten may be correct. But from the standpoint of Mexican peasants, restitution involved the post-revolutionary state's recognition of their prior rights to land, whereas

---

Ortíz was once again trying to discredit the SCP so as to persuade the Chihuahuan government to curtail its activities; but he got no support from higher-level functionaries.

32. AJMN, July 16, 1923. According to a 1919 CNA circular, municipal councils could not administer *pueblo* lands. AMN, box 5-D, Secretario General Poder Ejecutivo, Ramo de Fomento, Chihuahua, Circular no. 1260, Aug. 15, 1919, transcription of CNA circular, July 11, 1919. For protest against Ortíz's issuing of land permits as municipal president during 1921–22, see AMN, box 7, José Rascón y Tena, Vice President, SCP, Namiquipa, to the President and Municipal Council, Aug. 13, 1924.

33. AGCCA, exp. 24:432(721.1), Nov. 18, 1922.

dotación involved a gift of land from the state and therefore, underlined peasants' subordinated position (see Nugent 1993: 90–92).

The Namiquipan postrevolutionary *ejido* was enormous, almost one hundred thousand hectares.[34] Furthermore, land-tenure arrangements in Namiquipa, formalized by the SCP and practiced since the time of the *presidio*, appear substantively similar to the terms of revolutionary agrarian legislation and of the *ejido* system. Arguably the peasant movement in Namiquipa *succeeded*, and did so in a way (*pace* Bartra) that challenged its subordinated role in the new social order. With a *restitución*, the peasants secured recognition from the state of what they fought for, and not the other way around; that is, the state did not secure from the Namiquipans a recognition of the legitimacy of the state's stating—as Corrigan and Sayer (1985:3) remind us states do—what their rights to or in land were.

At first glance it seems the Namiquipans were relatively privileged beneficiaries of the agrarian reform. But at the same time, the granting of *ejidos* by the state in Chihuahua appears paradoxical and leaves some questions unanswered (González Herrera 1988; Nugent 1990). Why, for example, did a majority of Namiquipa's *originario* peasants, many of them ex-revolutionaries, reject the postrevolutionary state's "solution" to their agrarian problem? What were the implications of an *ejido* for state control over peasants and over agricultural production? What, in other words, was the meaning for Namiquipans of the land that the state "restored" to the community, and how did that differ from the meaning of the *ejido* in the selective tradition of the state?

THE *EJIDO* IN THE SELECTIVE TRADITION OF THE STATE

Article 27 of the Mexican Constitution of 1917 offered a solution to the problem of the inequitable distribution of agricultural land in society. The central principle of article 27 was, "the property of the lands and waters comprehended within national territory corresponds originally to the Nation," and thus to the state as its legitimate representative (Mendieta y

---

34. AGN, CNA.RP. Of this territory, in 1926 some 302 hectares along the Río Santa María were *riego* (irrigated fields), and another 5,900 hectares were *temporal* (seasonal, rain-irrigated) fields. In addition there were 22,257 hectares of *monte* (mountainous terrain) and more than 65,000 hectares of *pastal* (grazing land). See AGRA. Almost half the land classified in the 1920s as grazing land proved suitable for cultivation in subsequent decades, provided certain preparatory work was performed.

Núñez 1981:193). The vision of the state articulated there and in post-revolutionary agrarian legislation is a paternalistic one, according to which the state becomes the privileged arbiter of society.

> Paternalistic theories view the state as an independent and supernatant entity, one that ideally calms the transient tensions of the social organism and intervenes to promote justice. . . . This paternalistic conception under-pins most theories of the state as an independent variable and is preferred by elites the world over because it gives them a choice role. . . . [T]his view rationalizes and reinforces obvious inequalities. . . . *They* [urban elites] are to represent the interests of the people, defined, by them, according to the universal principles of Justice and Reason. (Trouillot 1990:20)

Though in practice the Mexican state was far from being "an independent and supernatant entity," postrevolutionary officials actively promulgated this paternalistic vision in order to re-present their partiality as neutrality. The legitimacy of the state's role as neutral arbiter and representative of "the public interest" rested on its reification, on its transcendence of particular social interests. But if the power of the state could be used to expropriate large estates and regulate private property in the name of the "public interest," it could also be used to secure control over revolutionary peasants and agricultural production.

Early land distributions were *political* solutions to *political* problems. *Ejidos* were established in Zapatista communities in the state of Morelos in the 1920s, for example, not because the postrevolutionary state was particularly enamored of the idea of destroying sugar plantations and reinstituting cultivation of corn, beans, and vegetables, but because the Zapatistas had participated in a decade-long armed struggle for the land and had *already* reclaimed it for their villages. When the CNA decided on individual petitions, political considerations frequently outweighed prag-matic, technical, or economic considerations regarding the ultimate dis-position of the land or the (legally defined) "legitimacy" of the claim. For that matter, the issue of how specific *ejidos* in particular regions would or would not address the agrarian question in a socially just manner figures only indirectly in many of the CNA's deliberations.[35]

For example, during a CNA meeting held June 23, 1926, Ing. Luis León, the Commission's president, emphatically opposed restituting lands to Namiquipa, Cruces, Galeana, Casas Grandes, and Janos, declaim-ing that he knew

---

35. CNA. Actas, passim.

the ideology of the inhabitants of those places. . . . What those peasants do is set themselves up in distinct places, forming their ranches and underutilizing the rest of the land (AGN, CNA.Actas 14:292–94 23-vi-1926).

Manuel Fitzmaurice, who had prepared the files for the five towns, argued strongly against León and in favor of restitution, suggesting finally

that in the event that the President is opposed it would be a good idea to send some Agricultural Engineers to inform the *pueblos* in person that the restitutions are not going through, something which might cause many difficulties, of which the President of the Republic is doubtless aware (Ibid.).

President Calles signed a resolution endorsing the Namiquipa and Cruces restitutions on August 5, 1926. Favorable resolutions for the remaining three *pueblos* were issued over the next few months.

In western Chihuahua, the list of towns in which *ejidos* were established in the 1920s reads like a roll call of the most famous *pueblos*, whose inhabitants had initiated the armed struggle in Mexico in 1910 and, earlier still, had fought in the Apache campaigns (Nugent 1993:95, 182). The early Chihuahuan *ejidos* can be regarded as trophies intended to transform revolutionary peasants into supporters of the new state; hence their establishment bore echoes of the colonial period when the Spanish crown granted land to colonists. But if Chihuahuan *ejidos* of the 1920s were in a certain sense throwbacks to the colonial period, they were also an anticipation of the future, a future which in the eyes of CNA functionaries was to be characterized by a more rigorously regulated relationship—of domination/dependence—to the new state order.

These relations of domination and dependence are particularly evident in the way the "beneficiaries" of the agrarian reform—Namiquipans in particular—are characterized in the minutes of the CNA meetings in Mexico City.[36] The official discourse of agrarian reform is permeated by a characterization of peasants as ignorant, illiterate, traditional, of largely Indian origins, and economically backward because they lack entrepreneurial spirit. Such politically irrational, wayward children, so the story goes, must be protected from their own worst selves for their own best interests and those of society as a whole by the state as paterfamilias.

As "the centre of a reverberating set of power relations and political processes" in which different but interlinked forms of identity and domi-

36. See, for example, the León-Fitzmaurice exchange discussed in text of this chapter.

nation are both constructed and contested, the state plays a major role in the production of the sociocultural categories of class, ethnicity, and gender (Connell 1987:130; cf. Mohanty 1992:21–23). Nowhere was this more in evidence than in the agrarian reform of the 1920s, when the subjectivity of peasants was constituted in such a way as to render their subjection to the state both rational and just. Furthermore, the *campesino* and the *ejidatario* are implicitly represented in the discourse of the state as male subjects, but subjects of a particular type.[37]

> The tradition-centered patriarchal authority that was criticized at the level of public politics by liberal rationalists . . . represented the hegemony of a particular kind of masculinity in domestic life. . . . [T]he hegemony of this [prior] form of masculinity was challenged and displaced [under the modern, bourgeois state] by masculinities organized much more around technical rationality and calculation. . . . This did not eliminate other masculinities. What it did was marginalize them . . . (Connell 1987:130–31).

In other words, the discourse of agrarian reform, constructs peasant subjectivity along lines of gender as well as class and ethnicity. Peasant women are denied the agrarian rights allocated to men. But peasant men are also subjected as "sons" of the state. Significantly, this construction of peasants' subjectivity is substantively similar to that advanced by the Porfirian state in the decades before 1910. But after 1920, the "solution" was no longer to achieve "Order and Progress" by proletarianizing peasants (thereby freeing lands for development by capitalists who *did* have the entrepreneurial spirit) but by "reforming" them through the *ejido.*

A key point about the agrarian reform process—also well illustrated in the minutes of the CNA meetings—is that it was profoundly *distant* from the communities and people whose lives it was designed to reorder. The distance was physical, social, and rhetorical. CNA meetings took place in Mexico City, far from the affected communities. They were not attended by peasants but by members of the CNA—lawyers, bureaucrats, schoolteachers, and politicians, few of whom had risen through the ranks of the popular movements. They articulated the norms of the agrarian reform in edicts, proclamations, fact-finding rulings issued in state-controlled publications, and a host of internal memoranda circulated

---

37. See C. Gill (1991) for an analysis of how a dominant discourse—in the example he discusses, that of the planter class in nineteenth-century Yucatán—may appropriate and reinforce a particular, existing set of notions of masculinity, but for its *own* ends.

within the CNA and the CLAS. The language of the agrarian reform was laden with legal niceties and technicalities, and invocations of a national *patria* few peasants could relate to (F. Katz 1988d; Anderson 1983). The language was stripped of local references recognizable to the beneficiaries of the land redistributions; their respective communities, their *patrias chicas*—landscapes impregnated with generations of work, struggle, and meaning—were reduced to or recast as so-and-so many hectares of such-and-such a category of land for this-and-that type of use. As Corrigan and Sayer remind us, "The power involved in recording, preserving, and retrieving 'facts'—defining realities—is one that grows rapidly by being used; behind the individual records is a formal authority which establishes routines and rituals, each buttressing the other" (1985:21).

However rapidly this power of the state grew from the 1920s onward, actually securing possession of agricultural land was a slow and tiresome process for many peasant communities (but again, Namiquipa excepted). Even in cases where popular demands were rapidly met, the CNA would try to impose *particular* solutions on communities rather than implement or accommodate popular demands precisely. Petitions for *restitución* of lands were routinely negated; but sometimes the very same territory was granted to the community as a *dotación*.[38] When finally an *ejido* was granted, in other words, it was to figure as a gift from the state; a gift for which peasants were expected to express their gratitude, demonstrating their indebtedness by becoming the loyal subjects of the state. But if this new strategy of indebtedness "worked" with some peasants, it did not succeed as well with others, as the example of Namiquipa demonstrates.

ANOTHER SELECTIVE TRADITION

Much of the evidence for an alternative, Namiquipan selective tradition is in the form of "hechos, no palabras" ("deeds, not words").[39] This can be illustrated by some examples of Namiquipans' disruption of state rituals. Ironically, our description is based largely on CNA engineers' narratives.

38. Between 1916 and 1980, only 17 percent of requests for restitution were granted, in contrast to 79 percent of the requests for *dotación*. During the same period only 214 restitutions were made, compared to 21,289 *dotaciones* (Sanderson 1984). In other words, only about 1 percent of the *ejidos* in Mexico were formed through the state's recognition of peasants' prior rights to land.

39. PRI slogan from the 1980s.

On August 29, 1925, the municipal president of Namiquipa called on the *pueblo's* men to attend a meeting during which they would elect representatives to the CPA and receive provisional possession of Namiquipa's *ejido.*[40] Despite the municipal president's threat that those who did not attend the meeting would be penalized "according to the law," fewer than forty peasants showed up.[41]

Almost exactly a year later, on August 22, 1926, the municipal president called two hundred Namiquipan men to participate in another state ritual during which agricultural engineers from the CNA would give the *pueblo* definitive possession of the *ejido.* According to one of the engineers present, during the course of this ritual, "a disagreeable incident occurred, provoked by a certain number of the members of the so-called Civil Society [the SCP] . . . who refused to receive the lands in accordance with the Agrarian Law."[42] Another engineer noted that the group of Namiquipans, led by the directors of the SCP, said they were unwilling to accept the Agrarian Law because "they believed that the Presidential Resolution was not necessary for the lands to continue to be theirs, since previous Governments also had declared that the lands belonged to them."[43] Arcadio Maldonado, a local revolutionary leader and SCP member, told the CNA representatives that "the *pueblo* feared the linking of the [presidential] resolution to the Agrarian Law," adding that the Namiquipans were "happier with their own pieces of paper [*escrituras*]."[44] Though the engineers insisted that 118 of the 200 Namiquipans in attendance were willing to accept the *ejido,* that figure is belied by the fact that only 22 were willing to sign their names to this effect (and several of these signed twice), especially after the 81 "inconformes" sarcastically claimed they had "forgotten" how to sign.[45]

40. AMN, box 8, Aug. 29, 1925.
41. The Acta de Deslinde (AMN, box 8-B, Sept. 1, 1925) ratifying the boundaries of the *ejido* and the Acta de Posesión Provisional (AMN, box 8-B, Sept. 1, 1925) ratifying acceptance of the *ejido* were signed by only 35 and 39 *vecinos,* or community members, respectively, not counting the municipal president, the CPA representatives, and the engineer. Only 32 persons voted in the election for CPA representatives. AGCCA, exp. 24:432(721.1), May 27, 1927. See also note 45.
42. AGCCA, Bienes Comunales, exp. 24:432(721.1).
43. Ibid.
44. Ibid.
45. Ibid. Most Namiquipan men were able to sign their names; those who could not would find someone else to sign for them. Significantly, of the twenty-two who did sign, only seven had signed the Certificate of Provisional Possession a year earlier;

But some did sign, just as four years earlier some had initiated the petition for restitution of Namiquipa's land. The first signature on the 1926 document belongs to Francisco V. Antillón, leader of the Defensas Sociales in 1920 and a longtime local protégé of Ignacio C. Enríquez. Antillón's endorsement of the idea of the *ejido*—like his mentor's earlier support of Namiquipan land rights—may well have had more to do with an interest in climbing the ladder of state politics than to any strong commitment to agrarian reform in Chihuahua.

In the months that followed, Namiquipans complained to the Chihuahuan government about "irregularities" in the CPA's administration of the *ejido*, and in May 1927 they called for the removal of the CPA president, who was none other than Reyes Ortíz.[46] Elections for new CPA officers were held on February 6, 1928, and Ortíz was replaced by Adolfo Delgado, a founding member of the SCP and its interim president in 1924.[47] According to the CNA representative present for the election, more than 60 percent of the *ejidatarios* attended the meeting, and all of them stated

that they did not want the Agrarian Law, that they were better off before, that recently the extension of the land was less than what they possessed earlier, that they did not need cooperatives, that they were happy to work only with their plows. . . . Likewise they showed themselves unwilling to contribute the 15 percent [of their harvests to the CPA], saying that they were willing to pay [property] taxes, if possible one hundred pesos each, but not to pay the 15 percent [quota to the ejido].[48]

eight of the twenty-two went on to sign a 1928 document affirming that they were willing to pay taxes on their lands so long as these were "respected as private property" (i.e., *not* included in the *ejido*). AMN, box 9, Sept. 23, 1928.

46. Besides alleging irregularities in Ortíz's administration of the CPA, Namiquipans complained that Ortíz held another public post (*Subagente del Ministerio Público*) and that "the distribution of lands he has made is not based on the law and . . . all the *ejidatarios* know nothing of his administration, only he knows what he has done." AGCCA, Bienes Comunales, exp. 24:432(721.1), Ing. Ignacio Solís to the Oficial Mayor of the CNA, May 27, 1927. Solís commented that "antiagrarista concepts are expressed" by Namiquipans. The Official Mayor responded that Namiquipans' opinion as to the status of the lands should be ignored. AGCCA, exp. 24:432(721.1), June 2, 1927.

47. AMN, box 9, (month unknown) 21, 1924. The complaints against Ortíz include his charging the community of Namiquipa 1,086 pesos when he served as their agrarian representative in 1921. See AGCCA, exp. 24:432(721.1), petition from SCP officers to the President of Mexico, Namiquipa, May 17, 1925.

48. AGCCA, exp. 24:432(721.1), Certificate of Election, Feb. 6, 1928.

A few days later, the CNA official wrote that during the election meeting the Namiquipans, led by Arcadio Maldonado and Antonio Duarte, another founding member of the SCP, had uttered "pure barbarisms to which I paid no attention," adding that by refusing to sign anything to do with the Agrarian Law, they demonstrated "a total lack of consciousness and an absolute ignorance, refusing to understand the explanations [that were] made to them; some of them said that they had forgotten their names."[49]

In disrupting these state rituals, Namiquipan men deployed an insolent humor that refused to take seriously the state's rules of the game and contested the power of inscription that codified those rules (much as earlier rebels and revolutionaries had derided the power of the official word by urinating on government documents). Their humor played with the stereotype of the illiterate, ignorant, irrational, backward, reactionary, recalcitrant peasant that was upheld by the bureaucrats of the agrarian reform. The presumed rationality and expertise of the latter were put into question by the Namiquipans' sarcasm. Paradoxically, it was through their feigned ignorance of their own names or their ability to sign them that Namiquipans refused to play the role of docile and grateful *ejidatarios*. In doing so, they made a mockery of these populist state rituals in which the state's authority was contingent on the *pueblo's* submissive authorization of its acts. Peasants' sarcastic challenges to the state's power of codification, their claim that they were "happier with their own pieces of paper" and "better off before," and their refusal to sign or give their names, were all interpreted by CNA representatives as signs of "absolute ignorance." The different ways of understanding the implications of the Agrarian Law— that of Namiquipans on the one hand and CNA representatives on the other—indicate an almost total disjuncture between the selective tradition of the Namiquipans and that of the state.

Recalling Armando Bartra's characterization of agrarismo as "the route through which the new state is able to create for itself a solid base among the masses" (1985:23), we argue that this insight can also provide the basis for a critique of the penetration of the power of the state into community affairs. Namiquipans were antiagrarista because they were *aware* that agrarismo consolidated forms of state control that they opposed. But why? Why did some of the earliest and most privileged beneficiaries of the agrarian reform reject its provisions? Why did they

49. Ibid., Alejandro Muñoz, Ayudante Dibujante, Chihuahua, to Ing. Ignacio Solís, CNA delegate, Feb. 15, 1928.

prefer to pay taxes if they could work their lands as *propiedades particulares* (private properties) rather than as ejidal plots?[50] Why did they "fear" the Agrarian Law? What distinguished the meanings Namiquipans ascribed to their land and the ways they had been holding and working it from the terms mandated by the postrevolutionary agrarian reform?

According to Teodoro de Croix's *bando* of November 15, 1778 (copy furnished by José Muñoz Franco of Namiquipa), *jefes de familia*, male nuclear family and household heads vested with traditional patriarchal authority, would have corporate rights to the land grant as a whole and to common pasture and woodlands, as well as rights to individual agricultural and house lots. Local authorities were responsible for the distribution of lots as well as water rights, and for the regulation of collective uses of common lands. Descent was another key criterion for access to land since rights were to be transmissible by inheritance. Locality also defined access to the means of production since *originarios* were to be preferred over *foráneos* in the internal distribution and sale of land. Finally, rights to land were contingent on fighting the Apache. According to the *bando*, peasants were to be given title to their individual holdings, but in practice this was not done. Instead, male family heads had *derechos de posesión* (rights of possession) to specific lots, usufruct rights to common pastures and woodlands, and property rights only as members of a corporate community. This agrarian regime continued to operate in the *pueblo* until 1904, when petit bourgeois *foráneos* wrested control of municipal administration away from the *originario* peasants.

Thus for Namiquipans, rights to land did not emanate from legal titles but from membership in a community, from the uninterrupted possession and continuous working of the land and the fulfillment of military obligations. For the community as a whole, land rights were an emblem of "civilization," of the Namiquipans' identity as *gente de razón* and difference from the landless, nomadic, "barbaric Indians" who "lived like animals," eating wild plants and animals and "stealing" livestock (Alonso 1988a). Furthermore, land rights were a sign of masculine honor and a

50. On September 23, 1928, about five hundred Namiquipans attended a meeting organized by José Rascón y Tena, José Cervantes, and Arcadio Maldonado, at which they named representatives who would determine how much tax each of them owed. They were all willing to pay taxes so long as their lands were respected as private properties "in accordance with the grant made by the Caballero de Croix and recognized by the Government of the Union"; that is, Porfirio Díaz's regime. AMN, box 9, Sept. 23, 1928.

crucial key to the consolidation of men's patriarchal power (Alonso 1988a, 1988b, 1992b).

By working on their lands, Namiquipan men not only ensured the material reproduction of their household and community but also realized themselves as honorable patriarchs. The trope of "fecundating" the land recurs in Namiquipan agrarian petitions both before 1910 and during the 1920s. Going to the *labor* (field) was key to the production of masculine identity since the socialization of the "natural" self is accomplished through the domestication of nature. A man who is "hardworking" (*muy trabajador*) is a "man of respect" (*hombre de respeto*) who fulfills the obligation to "maintain his family" (*mantener su familia*) entailed by a fully socialized masculinity. Such a man is considered to be a good *jefe de familia* and a *buen vecino*, a good community member. *Derechos de posesión* to land are key to this self-realization through productive activity; the self-mastery and autonomy integral to masculine honor and identity are actualized through work on one's own fields. As aspects of masculine identity, power and autonomy can only be achieved if a man is his own master; that is, if he controls both his work and the subject of his labor, the land.[51]

In practice, *derechos de posesión* differed from property rights only in that they were not legitimated by individual legal titles but by permission granted by the municipal council, which administered the *pueblo's* corporate property, or, after 1906, by the SCP. But whereas property was acquired through market transactions, *posesión* was obtained by virtue of membership in the community, inheritance, labor on the land, and fulfillment of obligations to the *pueblo*, including military duties. Both the SCP charter of 1906 and the agrarian reform implemented by the SCP in Namiquipa during the revolution echoed the conditions set out in the *bando*. *Derechos de posesión* were to go to *originarios* who defended the land and who fulfilled their duties to the community.

The Namiquipan regime of land tenure actually anticipated the postrevolutionary *ejido* system, but with one major difference. If the subject of land rights within Namiquipan practice was a *buen vecino* and a *buen jefe de familia*, the subject of land rights within the *ejido* system was a loyal and

51. See Alonso (1988b:23–24, revised as Alonso 1992b), where the remarks made here on masculinity, rights to land, and control over productive activity are further developed. On the distinction between work and labor, see Calagione and Nugent (1992). On land as the subject of labor, see Marx [1857–58] (1973:471–72), [1867] (1906: 198–99); Chaterjee (1982).

docile "son" of the state. If the former system of land tenure was the result of a dialectic of articulation that had played itself out for the prior century and was apprehended in local consciousness—in a manner consonant with the internal dialectic of community formation—as the community's own vision, the new regime of land tenure was experienced as an imposition from without, as a form of state domination. Namiquipans detected ways the Agrarian Law would undermine their control over the land and the production process, which was key to the personal autonomy and self-mastery integral to local ideals of masculinity. In addition, their historical experience had taught Namiquipans that they had good reason to fear the state.

Namiquipans' vision of the state in the past as well as the present has been, like the state's own, a paternalistic one. Positively, the state is the *padre* (father) of the *patria* (motherland), the people, and the *patria chica* (little motherland or local community). The state as *padre* is the government as the good, wise, and beneficent father who protects and respects the sovereignty of the *patria chica* and the honor of his "sons" and "daughters." But negatively, the state as *padrastro* (stepfather) is the government as the bad father who encroaches upon local sovereignty, penetrating and redrawing the boundaries that should ideally subsist between state and community.

In the decades prior to the revolution, Namiquipans came to see the Porfirian state as a *padrastro*. During that period, historical memory was deployed to contrast an idealized vision of "the Primordial Society" (a term taken from Rosaldo 1987)—of a frontier past when "brave" patriarchs protected the *pueblo* and "civilization" from the onslaughts of "barbaric" Apaches, and when the state was a beneficent *padre*—with a corrupt present in which rights to land, community sovereignty, and masculine autonomy were abrogated (Alonso 1988a, b, 1992b).

The same historical memory was invoked in texts dated from after 1910. In 1918 members of the SCP refer to de Croix's *bando* and the compact between the colonial state and the colonists of Namiquipa as a "grand and beneficent project."[52] And in 1922 Namiquipans wrote,

> The traditional History of our pueblo as that of the State [of Chihuahua] marks a period of continuous War against the Apache tribes, and the settlers of these isolated regions had to withstand this struggle with true stoicism

52. AMN, box 5-C, "Acuerdo referente al terreno de *común repartimiento*," Namiquipa, Feb. 3, 1918.

and abnegation for more than seventy years, and even though they frequently fell beneath the knife of the Savage, they never abandoned their *posesiones* because this signified losing them, a condition imposed by the Decree of Colonization.[53]

In 1929 the Namiquipan CPA agreed to set aside one *sitio de ganado mayor* as municipal land on the condition

> that the house lots, lands, and water rights that were distributed in conformity with the *bando* . . . cannot be acquired as property by the Municipality. Likewise, the *posesiones* that the descendants of the first acquirers occupy today shall be respected . . . since it should not be forgotten that until the Year of 1885, the *vecinos* of this *pueblo* did not cease to suffer the aggressions and threats of the barbaric enemies, almost on a daily basis. . . .[54]

That Namiquipan agrarian petitions in the 1920s deployed the same historical memory as that which figured in prerevolutionary protests against loss of agrarian rights,[55] indicates that the struggle against the postrevolutionary state was not so different from the struggle against the Porfirian state.

Ironically, the terms of a still earlier—colonial—state project, as reinterpreted by members of the community, were deployed to contest a later state project. The *pueblo's* colonial charter was invoked as the blueprint for the continued reproduction of the community, rather than the postrevolutionary state's Agrarian Law. By stressing the colonial origins of their land rights and locating an agrarian ideal in the colonial past, Namiquipans put into question the postrevolutionary state's rhetoric of progress. Namiquipans argued that prior governments (notably including that of Porfirio Díaz) had already approved their agrarian arrangements. The selectivity of this version of history is particularly ironic, given that Namiquipans had earlier fought against the Díaz regime when they saw it as undermining their agrarian rights, the sovereignty of their community, and the prerogatives of its patriarchs. But by invoking Díaz in the 1920s, they further undermined the socially progressive pretensions of the post-

53. AGCCA, Bienes Comunales, exp. 24:432(721.1), Namiquipa, Nov. 18, 1922.

54. AMN, box 6, Namiquipa, July 15, 1929.

55. Indeed, two of the 1920s petitions were simply updated rewrites of an earlier 1908 petition: AMN, box 7, José Rascón y Tena to Municipal President, Namiquipa, Aug. 13, 1924; and AGCCA, Namiquipa, Nov. 18, 1922, are rewrites of ATN, July 28, 1908. A more extended discussion of the historical memory articulated in these petitions can be found in Alonso (1988a and b, or 1992b).

revolutionary state, implying that its vision of agrarian justice was even more unjust than Díaz's.

While perhaps reinforcing the official stereotype of the backward and irrational peasant, this strategy and the alternative selective tradition that informed it also challenged the postrevolutionary state's vision of national progress. For Namiquipan men in the 1920s, the *ejido*, far from offering a blueprint for progress, was instead recognized as yet another state-sponsored *despojo* (dispossession) of the community patrimony as a whole and of *jefes de familia* in particular, a *despojo* that would pave the way for other forms of state intervention in the production process and in *pueblo* life that they considered illegitimate. That is one reason they feared the Agrarian Law.

The law itself had been formulated by Carrancistas, against whom Namiquipan Villistas had fought during the revolution. Indeed, Carrancistas had treated peasant communities with so little respect (appropriating their crops and livestock, arresting and executing people, and raping women) that during the revolution a new term had been coined: *carrancear*, to steal.[56] This association of theft with Carrancismo was hardly dispelled when a CLA engineer first measured the *ejidos* of Namiquipa and Cruces in 1925 and assigned only fifty-seven instead of sixty-four *sitios de ganado mayor* to Namiquipa. Because of an error in the measurement, the other seven *sitios* were awarded to Cruces and to the hacienda de San José de Babicora, in effect depriving Namiquipa of more land than it had actually lost to neighboring haciendas in the decades before 1910![57] Nor was the notion of Carrancismo as theft dispelled by the demand that Namiquipans turn over 15 percent of their harvests to the administrative committee of the *ejido*. For Namiquipans, this was tantamount to paying rent to the state for lands they considered their own. "According to the inhabitants they prefer to abandon the *pueblo* rather than recognize the 15

56. After 1916, many Namiquipans turned against Villa and formed local militias to fight him. They did not see themselves as Carrancistas, however, but as defenders of the *patria chica* (Alonso 1988c). Although during the guerrilla phase of his movement Villa commandeered food and supplies from peasants and ordered reprisals against communities and individuals (including Namiquipa and Namiquipans) who would not support him, his earlier relations with Chihuahuan peasants had been extremely positive (Alonso 1988c) and indeed, for many, remained positive until his murder in 1923 (see Osorio 1990).

57. AGCCA, exp. 24:432(721.1), petition from the SCP, Namiquipa, May 17, 1925.

percent of their products because they maintain that such a procedure constitutes a form of *despojo*."[58]

Efforts by the CPA, following orders of the CLA, to gather data on the number of hectares of corn Namiquipans planted and the livestock they owned also met resistance. The collection of information was perceived not as a neutral act but as a form of state regulation of the production process. One Namiquipan petition, signed by 288 men, comments: "These acts [of information gathering], Mr. President, come to demonstrate clearly that now there is an attempt to confederate[59] [make the property of the federal government] lands that we esteem in justice to be ours, because they have been transmitted from fathers to sons and fecundated with the constant work of much more than a century."[60]

In light of their conviction that the agrarian law represented a *despojo*, an attempt to "confederate" their lands and place them under the control of the national state, the majority of Namiquipan men asserted, in a general assembly held on February 19, 1928, that with the issuance of the community's colonial charter, "*Namiquipa left the dominion of the nation.*"[61] They would therefore administer their lands not according to the Agrarian Law but according to their colonial charter, in which, "with paternal care, are fixed all the measures necessary to the formation and conservation of these *pueblos*" and their system of land tenure.[62] In short, the response of the majority of Namiquipan men to the presidential resolution of 1926 was that the national state had no dominion over their lands, nor could it "restitute" lands over which Namiquipans had never lost de facto control.

The history of state formation in Mexico (and of popular resistance to different national projects) can be read in terms of state efforts to co-opt or undermine those particularisms that have challenged state power by serving as alternative bases for envisioning political community (An-

58. AEN, Adolfo Delgado, President of the CPA, Namiquipa, to the Procurador de los Pueblos, Chihuahua, May 6, 1928.

59. The phrase *attempt to confederate* in Spanish is *se pretendende confederarlos*. At the time, the federal government was often referred to as *la federación*.

60. AGCCA, exp. 24:432(721.1), petition from 288 Namiquipans to the President of Mexico, Namiquipa, Jan. 29, 1926, protesting the formation of the *ejido*.

61. AEN, Delgado to Procurador de Pueblos, Namiquipa, June 6, 1928, explaining why the Namiquipans opposed the Agrarian Law.

62. AMN, box 7, José Rascón y Tena, Vice President of the SCP, to the Municipal President and Council, Aug. 13, 1924.

derson 1983). Yet it would be misleading to characterize Chihuahuan peasants as antinationalist. Late nineteenth- and early twentieth-century peasant petitions provide evidence of a nascent nationalist consciousness. But among Chihuahuan peasants, nationalism and localism[63] coexist as modes of imagining community, facets of a "contradictory consciousness" (Gramsci 1971:332) that are selectively actualized in practice in response to concrete historical circumstances. The assertion in 1928 that Namiquipa "had left the dominion of the nation" a century-and-a-half earlier was motivated by localism, by fear that the Agrarian Law would undermine community sovereignty; but it was motivated also by the perception that the national project embedded in this law would increase peasant subordination to the state.

During the same general assembly of February 19, 1928, Namiquipans invoked the state's own laws as a basis for rejecting the *ejido* and the Agrarian Law. They cited a circular issued by the CNA on July 11, 1919, according to which "the owners of the *ejidos* are the *pueblos* themselves [and] . . . the law of 6 January 1915 . . . revives the juridical capacity of the *pueblos* to possess *ejidos*, though on condition of reducing them later to private property."[64] They added, "Constitutional Article 27 orders all respect for lands possessed *en nombre propio a título de dominio* for more than ten years when their areas do not exceed fifty hectares."[65]

Namiquipans' insistence on holding the land as *pequeña propiedad* (small property) in the 1920s was not a sign of a new (or an old) capitalist individualism (*pace* Díaz Soto y Gama[66]) or of a fundamental change in their own vision of land rights. The personal autonomy central to local ideals of masculinity rooted in the colonization of the frontier was an important value that inflected Namiquipans' notions of land tenure and of

63. On localism, see Alonso (1988c).

64. AMN, box 5-D, Ramo de Fomento, Circular no. 1260.

65. AEN, Delgado to Procurador de Pueblos, Namiquipa, June 6, 1928.

66. Antonio Díaz Soto y Gama wrote, "For the northerners . . . the solution [to the unequal distribution of land in the 1920s] resided in dividing the huge *latifundia* and creating a great number of small private properties." Quoted in Mendieta y Núñez (1983:184). Recent research on the agrarian question in the north, however, has uncovered examples in Chihuahua in which "classical" demands—for land and freedom, for return to villagers of stolen lands—were articulated by inhabitants of former military settlement colonies such as Namiquipa, as well as by hacienda workers, Amerindian communities, and migratory workers, the "semi-industrial, semi-agricultural" working class of Chihuahua (F. Katz 1974; Nugent 1990:299–302; see also F. Katz 1988d:243; González Herrera 1988).

the organization of work on the land; but it would be a mistake to confuse this with capitalist individualism. Namiquipans' valuation of the person was informed by a sense of a collective subject, by their vision of the *patria chica* as a community of equals that is a "form and product of struggle" with outside forces (Roseberry 1991:22). Namiquipans' argument for holding individual plots as *pequeñas propiedades* formed as a strategic response to historical circumstances, since the lack of "legitimate titles" had resulted in agrarian dispossession before the revolution (especially during the period 1905–1910). In the 1920s and 1930s, Namiquipans came to believe that working small properties rather than ejidal lands would guarantee greater security of land tenure, control of the production process, and autonomy from the state.

This is precisely why the state did not want to recognize Namiquipan lands as *pequeñas propiedades*. As Adolfo C. Besson, organizer of the Secretaría de Agricultura y Fomento (poder ejecutivo federal) wrote in 1928, Namiquipa was "one of the most rebellious and richest *ejidos*, where the Government could obtain great benefits" if the peasants could only be made "to understand that they should obey the Laws of the Government." This, he adds,

> will be the only way in which some benefit can be obtained from said *pueblo*, because, otherwise, time will pass and the inhabitants will get more enamored of the idea that they are small property owners, and as a consequence, will refuse to recognize in all its parts what the Agrarian Law establishes for them.[67]

As Namiquipans were aware, agrarian reform legislation did allow for the recognition of some *pequeñas propiedades* within *ejidos* (Mendieta y Núñez 1981:199–200, 214–15). However, the owners of small properties were not to be peasants who lacked the proper entrepreneurial spirit, but capitalist farmers. Significantly, neither of the two *pequeñas propiedades* legally recognized within the Namiquipan *ejido* in 1926 belonged to peasants; they were both owned by petit bourgeois *foráneos*. The existence within the *ejido* of hundreds of small properties worked by peasants was regarded by the state not as a beacon of progress but a sign of rebelliousness. For what concerned the state was fomenting dependence and doc-

---

67. AGCCA, exp. 24:432(721.1). Cf. the remarks of Luis León, cited above in this chapter, p. 227.

ility among *ejidatarios* from whom "benefits" could be extracted, whether in the form of the surplus product of their labor or political support.

Sometime during the 1930s, the SCP ceased to function,[68] and the *ejido* took over the administration of Namiquipa's lands. The hundreds of small private properties recognized by the SCP did not, however, devolve to the *ejido*. By the 1930s, Namiquipans "belonged" to an *ejido* that comprised an abundance of land, including the small properties—largely irrigated land—and virgin fields that could be assigned to future generations of cultivators. In most other *ejidos* throughout Mexico, by contrast, the *dotaciones* or *restituciones* generally were scarcely sufficient to provide a livelihood at the time the *ejido* was created. But by the 1970s in Namiquipa, the only way to invest more individual cultivators with control of land was by fractioning existing plots, or introducing alternative crops that could be cultivated more intensively on smaller plots. Namiquipans' solution was to put in apple orchards. But that only points to another peculiarity of the *ejido* of Namiquipa.

The possibility of cultivating cash crops provides one avenue through which Namiquipans can evade state control and appropriation of the products of their labor; an alternative to the production of basic grains for the state monopoly. But the issue of who profited, cultivators or merchants,[69] begs the question of why people would plant orchards—with the considerable technical input, capital investment, and time they require—on ejidal lands since, according to agrarian legislation, those belonged to the state. The solution is quite simple: Namiquipans only put orchards on "small properties." There were about three hundred such *pequeñas propiedades* within the borders of the *ejido*, most having originated in *posesiones* given out by municipal administrations until 1904 and by the SCP from 1913 to the 1930s. As we indicated earlier, the concept according to which Namiquipans designated these lands small private properties was emphatically not a recension of the notion of property in a capitalist system, but the transformation of an earlier notion of *posesión*. The latter

68. Available documentation sheds little light on how this came about. We were told by José Rascón y Tena's son that "agraristas" burned the SCP archive at his father's ranch sometime in the 1930s. Interview with José Rascón Iguado, Ciudad Chihuahua, June 1984.

69. See Alonso (1992a) and Nugent (1992) for discussions of many Namiquipans' seeming insensitivity to the character of their exploitation by merchants and a capitalist market for their "independently" produced goods.

concept was based on local arrangements and practices regarding possession and use of agricultural lands that Namiquipans had elaborated over the prior century-and-a-half.

CONCLUSIONS: PROPERTY, PRODUCTION, POPULAR CULTURE, AND THE STATE

In our effort to understand popular responses to the establishment of an *ejido* in Namiquipa, we found it necessary to analyze both the social relations and the meanings and forms of identity embedded in land-tenure arrangements, along with community-state relations (see Nugent 1989a). If the construction of forms of identity is key to hegemony, as Gramsci (1971), Williams (1977), and others have argued, it is also key to popular practices that contest relations of domination.

The different notions of agricultural land that were operative in Namiquipa have diverse implications both for the peasantry's relationship to the state and to capitalism, and for constructions of identity. The three categories of land are ejidal land, capitalist property, and the "small properties" of the Namiquipans, which really involve a recension of the earlier notion of *posesión*. Working ejidal land implies subordination to the state, an acquiescent peasantry. Owning capitalist property is strongly linked to notions of individualism and "freedom"—the freedom to exploit others. Working "small properties" that are a transformation of *posesiones* implies personal autonomy (or at least required a struggle *for* autonomy) from *patrones* and from the state—an autonomy that is central to ideals of masculinity and is predicated on a selective tradition of resistance to perceived illegitimate forms of domination. The subject of that resistance and protagonist of that struggle, however, is a collective subject: the community, the *pueblo* as simultaneously people and locale.

Autonomy differs from individualism in that the concept of personhood on which the former is predicated recognizes the social and material embeddedness of identity. Thus, the *buen jefe de familia* is also the *buen vecino* who fulfills obligations of both work and defense to the community and respects other *vecinos'* land rights. While the household was and remains a basic unit of production and consumption in Namiquipa, access to means of agricultural production has always been mediated by suprahousehold forms of organization, whether the political authority of presidial captains in the colonial period; community organizations after independence, such as the popular municipal councils; or, after 1906, the

SCP. Thus, though "production was not communal, the community constituted an important relation of production" (Roseberry 1991:22). No
less important in providing the conditions for production to take place
was collective struggle for the *pueblo's* land, whether against "barbaric"
Indians, *hacendados, foráneos,* or the state itself.

When the postrevolutionary state attempted to impose a new organizational form, the *ejido,* to mediate access to means of production in the
1920s, it met resistance. Namiquipans' vision of the *patria chica* and of the
role of the community in land tenure and production explains the high
level of unity and collective organization manifest in their opposition to
the *ejido.* One further consequence of this sense of a community of equals
that is a "form and product of struggle" against outside forces and the
identities thereby engendered—very much bound up with the form of
working the land Namiquipans elaborated—was that it provided a brake
on processes of internal social differentiation.[70] Additionally, it militated
against *acaparamientos de tierras* in both the pre- and postrevolutionary
periods, and this selective tradition continues to be an important force
limiting *acaparamientos* today.

Acaparamiento de tierras is common both in *colonias agrícolas* (where the
state has sold twenty-five-hectare parcels outright to cultivators, and
individuals have consolidated large estates by purchasing contiguous
parcels) and in *ejidos* (the example of Cruces springs to mind). In *ejidos,* a
handful of *ejidatarios* claim the best land, enclose common pastures, and
are locally regarded as *los ricos,* while poor people are systematically
excluded from the ejidal census, prohibited from enjoying access to
cultivable land, and reduced to sharecropping or working as wage-
laborers for the *ejidatarios.*

In your garden-variety "irregular" *ejido* one finds systematic violations
of provisions of the Agrarian Law relating to eligibility to cultivate, the
transfer of usufruct, and limits on the amount of cultivable land any
individual may control (see, e.g., Feder 1971; Cockcroft 1983; Hewitt de
Alcántara 1984; Stavenhagen 1970). Individuals assume control of multiple ejidal plots; individuals lie about the size of their plots, which may be
considerably larger than the twenty-hectare legal limit; plots of cultivable

---

70. Our seeming lack of attention in this essay to internal differentiation along
class lines in the community is due neither to a romantic or heroic notion of the
peasantry nor to a notion of peasant communities as homogeneous, but instead to the
knowledge that such differentiation was limited and did not play a significant role in
the opposition to the *ejido* by the majority of Namiquipan men.

ejidal land are purchased, rented, sharecropped, used as collateral for debts. The best irrigated land in the *ejido* of Galeana, Chihuahua, was "sold" by the ejidal commissioner to Mormons in the 1960s and 1970s. The *ejido* in Casas Grandes was blocked by influential property owners in the region, including many Mormons, but from an earlier wave of settlement.[71] As Jim Cockcroft put it: "'Rent parcels?' groaned one Sonora peasant in 1963. 'Why here entire *ejidos* are rented out'" (Cockcroft 1983:170).

While some of the violations of the Agrarian Law noted above occur in Namiquipa, what qualifies Namiquipa's as the "most irregular" *ejido* is that it has undergone very little consolidation of its extensive lands (either ejidal land or "private properties"). We think this is as much a function of the construction and reproduction of locally meaningful practices for administering land tenure as it is a function of the socially just provisions of the *ejido*-based agrarian reform. Furthermore, we would emphasize that the construction of such local practices is rooted in popular culture and historical memory, both of which, in turn, are constantly transformed (cf. Marx [1867] 1906:197–98).

The situation in Namiquipa may be explained by demonstrating how the relationships of popular movements to a culturally constituted state developed from the 1920s onward, but also in light of the prior century of development.[72] This long-term perspective integrates historical and anthropological modes of understanding and provides a clearer sense of process and transformation than a static approach that would seek to analyze sociocultural practices in terms of somewhat wooden, absolute, and over-generalizing "contradictions," such as that between state and peasantry (or capital and labor, or accommodation and resistance; on which see Calagione and Nugent 1992). Such a concern with process and history also entails a recognition of the importance of popular forms of historical memory and their strategic deployment in political struggle.

The regime of land tenure implemented in Namiquipa since the 1920s is a popular alternative to the state's rules of the game, but this does not mean that it developed in pristine isolation from state policies and

71. On the sale of ejidal lands in Galeana, see AGRA 23-399, Sept. 12, 1979. On the *ejido* of Casas Grandes, see AGN, CNA.RP, Jan. 1927. Information on its disposition from Jesús Vargas, personal communication.

72. Cf. Stern (1987), who underlines (among other valuable methodological points) the utility of employing multiple (and lengthier) time scales in the analysis of peasant mobilization and consciousness.

official discourses, or that it is the heroic expression of some authentic peasant essence. It is the product of a long history of struggle over not only the disposition of the land but the meanings attributed to it. Moreover, the collective creation of this alternative regime of land tenure involved the conjunction of an internal dialectic and a dialectic of articulation from the colonial period on. As Raymond Williams argues, nearly all alternative or oppositional sociocultural practices are "tied to the hegemonic: . . . [T]he dominant culture . . . at once produces and limits its own forms of counterculture" (1977:114). However, as this essay demonstrates, the character of this conjunction is partly the product of a dialectic of cultural struggle that is marked by complexities and contradictions not easily captured by the dichotomy of accommodation *or* resistance. Thus, even if the alternative is tied to and limited by the hegemonic, it is not reducible to it. The state's rules have been restated, refracted through the terms of another selective tradition. Hence the hegemonic is also tied to and limited by the alternative, even if cultural struggles take place in contexts of unequal power.

The apparent localism of the Chihuahuan peasantry was a product of concrete historical processes, of the specific forms that conquest and colonization had earlier assumed on the frontier, and the ways those in turn shaped community-state relations in subsequent decades (see Nugent 1989a).[73] Despite the postcolonial state's attempts to weld the imagining of a national community to the defense of frontier territory, the form of "patriotism" that emerged during the Apache Wars was eminently regional and parochial. Among militarized peasants, such as the Namiquipans, allegiance to and defense of the *patria chica* took precedence over loyalty to the nation. The link between frontier warfare and the imagining of political community is particularly evident in the Namiquipan notion that the *originarios*, or true members of the *patria chica*, were the descendants of settlers who had fought the Apache. In 1929 the CPA even suggested using the 1880 census, formulated five years before the end of the Apache Wars, to determine who was an *originario* and, as such, had *derechos de posesión*.[74]

Once we descend from the "macropolitical panorama" to examine regional and local modalities through which powers of the state succeed and fail to achieve certain effects of domination (de la Peña 1981:259–

73. Alonso (1988a) includes an extended discussion of warfare between colonists and indigenes.

74. AMN, box 6, text of a CPA *acuerdo*, Namiquipa, July 15, 1929.

60), we gain an appreciation of the degree to which what is at issue, even in struggles as seemingly straightforward as "the struggle for land [and freedom]," is not just a determinate territory but the very definition of land itself. In other words, the struggle is concerned as much with the production of meaning as it is with control over production and the labor process.

Our research provides a basis for critiquing some of the ways the postrevolutionary state has attempted to rule the peasantry through the implementation of agrarian reform. This paper was largely written before Carlos Salinas de Gortari's reforms to Article 27 of the Constitution of 1917 were announced. It should *not* be read as an argument *for* capitalist privatization of agricultural land, which the current regime hopes to rationalize and extend even into the ejidal sector. Meanings of the land and practices related to working it that Namiquipans developed in the century-and-a-half before 1926 appear to have anticipated features of the *ejido* as well as of privatization, but are not reducible to either. Instead, they point the way to an alternative, to community-based forms of land tenure in which the subject of the land is neither a ward of the state nor an individualist entrepreneur, but a member of a rural collectivity with significant autonomy in the administration of its lands who retains a large measure of independence in the organization of production and the disposition of the products of labor, despite the constraints of the arrangements generated by a democratically controlled community organization.

MARJORIE BECKER

Torching La Purísima, Dancing at the Altar:
The Construction of Revolutionary Hegemony
in Michoacán, 1934–1940

The *campesinos* of Michoacán did not make their state a major theater in the Mexican revolution of 1910. Yet Michoacán's Catholic hierarchy found the revolution deeply disturbing. Throughout the period of armed conflict, Michoacán priests attempted to refurbish Catholic ideological influence among *campesinos*, and by the 1920s the clerical campaign to

This essay draws partly on research conducted for the author's doctoral dissertation (Becker 1988a), for which the generous support of the Inter-American Foundation and the Yale University History Department are gratefully acknowledged. Most of the research for the present essay was conducted more recently in Michoacán during the summer of 1988 and between June and November 1989. This research was supported by a Faculty Fulbright Research Fellowship, a National Endowment for the Humanities Summer Stipend, an American Council of Learned Societies Grant-in-Aid, and a University of Southern California Faculty Research and Innovation Fund Grant. It is not always easy for progressive scholars to empathize with the resistance of counterrevolutionary peasants nor to appreciate scholarly efforts to reconstruct their historical trajectory. For this reason, I am particularly grateful to Gil Joseph, Friedrich Katz, Jean Meyer, James C. Scott, and Emília Viotti da Costa for their warm support of my work. Finally, one of the central goals of my work has been to develop a more deeply nuanced and human understanding of the historical actors populating my prose. To the extent that I am beginning to accomplish this, it is much due to the warm friendship of Carolyn Dewald, Carolyn Gurman, Steve J. Stern, and Dale Wall. I particularly acknowledge Florencia E. Mallon, whose comments over the years have been unusually generous, incisive, and alert to my form of perception.

promote popular conformity was well under way. Central to this effort was La Purísima, the Virgin Mary depicted in her most chaste aspect. Images of the Virgin with ivory-hued skin, features irrevocably downcast, graced the walls of many churches. Priests frequently sang her praises. It is probably not going too far to say that La Purísima dominated the plazas.

In July of 1935, President Lázaro Cárdenas's cadre of revolutionaries in the northwestern Michoacán village of Ario Santa Mónica contested that domination. Entering the church secretly, they seized the images of La Purísima and hid them in their homes. The next afternoon the Cardenistas torched the Virgin. With the image of spiritual overseer in ashes, young girls entered the church to dance before the altar.[1]

For Michoacán, an area steeped in Catholic tradition, this was a serious challenge to the established culture. In fact, as I hope to demonstrate in this essay, that event, along with similar events throughout the state, eventually led to a transformation of the postrevolutionary state. Yet until today, both the Cardenista effort to reconstruct the women of Ario and the women's responses have remained buried. Instead, postrevolutionary governments have offered us a myth of secular redemption (Becker 1988a:1–25). In this myth, Cárdenas is styled as something of a latter-day Jesus, a redeemer who traveled from village to village performing wonders. Always ready to hear *campesinos* out, he was the first Mexican head of state since the hapless Maximilian to listen to *campesinos* as they detailed their troubles. Most spectacularly, while Cárdenas multiplied no loaves or fishes, he divided large estates into peasant plots. In response, *campesinos* crowded around to pay homage to him and his government.

This is a luminous image and a generous one. As one of my informants put it, "Cárdenas opened the nation's pocketbook and threw the money to the people."[2] Perhaps because of this achievement and the ways it coincided—on paper, at least—with the radical hope at the heart of Emiliano Zapata's agrarian revolution, the scholarly literature tends to

1. AMZ, Gobernación, exp. 17, Ignacio Verduzgo and others to municipal president of Zamora, July 8, 1935; series of interviews with Mari Elena Verduzco, Apr.–July and Nov. 1990; Esperanza Rocha, May 13 and June 2, 1990; Concepción Méndez, June 9 and Nov. 3, 1990; and Soledad Barragán, June 6, 1990; conversations with Carmen Valadez, Apr.–July and Nov. 1990, all in Ario de Rayón, Michoacán.

2. Interview with Cardenista teacher and ideologue José Corona Núñez, July 12, 1985, Morelia, Michoacán.

reproduce this official story.[3] While debate surrounds Cárdenas and the state he constructed, the controversy tends to focus on motivation. Populists such as Tannenbaum (1950) and the Weyls (1939) contend that Cárdenas's land program was a pure-hearted response to the agrarian grievances that fueled the revolution, while revisionists like Angiano (1975) and Córdova (1974) emphasize that the land redistribution was a demagogic concession to the peasantry.

In other words, whether they have viewed Cárdenas as redeemer or as tarnished messiah, scholars have shared an insufficiently political image of the peasantry. They have reduced peasant needs to bread.[4] They have limited peasant political activity to occasional, if boisterous, risings triggered by sustenance crises. Once their nutritional requirements are met, the suggestion goes, peasants no longer participate in the construction of the state. State making, in turn, is portrayed as normally fairly aloof from peasant concerns (Brading 1980). Even in the best of this work, state responsiveness to peasant demands is viewed as a one-time concession (Hamilton 1983; Aguilar Camín 1980). In short, there is a strange, exponential Pavlovianism here—the state responding to peasants responding to their bellies.

Clerical imagery seems appropriate for a place as deeply and variously Catholic as Michoacán. Yet an examination of the relationship between Cardenistas and the women of Ario reveals that Cardenismo should not be likened to lightning-bolt messianic activity. Rather, a comparison to the work of the early Spanish missionaries seems more apt.[5] For like the sixteenth-century friars, the Cardenistas in Michoacán determined to undermine the previous ideological order and to create institutions reflecting their state-making project. And like the early friars, the Cardenistas sought popular identification with their program. Expressed in more contemporary terms, the Cardenista effort to bring the revolution to Michoacán and win acceptance of their program might be called a hegemonic project in the making.[6]

3. The implementation was a different matter. See Becker (1988a).

4. This emphasis on *campesino* "creaturely" characteristics is strongly reminiscent of Sarmiento (1952).

5. The Cardenistas compared themselves with Catholic priests. For an analysis of this tendency, see Becker (1987).

6. Without exploring the historical process through which it came into being, Herbert Marcuse persuasively describes the results of one such project (1966). The

This meant that Cardenistas sought to persuade peasants to abandon the old clerical order and embrace the new state as their own. Yet when Cardenistas made this proposal to the Ario women, the women hardly responded as economic ciphers. Instead, they behaved like people no longer trapped on the dance floor with a single partner. For before the emergence of Cardenismo, the church was the women's only institutional partner. Dependable yet ambiguous as partners, priests flattered women with pretty words and insisted that women adopt a submissive public stance.

By torching La Purísima and orchestrating the dance before the altar, the Cardenistas hoped to replace the church's role as lead partner. Some women were willing to dance with the Cardenistas, while others refused point-blank. But most—at last possessing a choice of partners—chose a more adventurous course, moving in time first with the church, then with the state. In the process, the women not only choreographed a new dance but persuaded the state to include it in its repertoire.

WOMEN AND THE MARRIAGE OF PIETY AND PROPERTY

It is common to refer to sociological variations among population groups as mosaic tiles, but in thinking of Michoacán's rural population, the image of puzzle pieces seems more useful. For in Michoacán the divisions were so extensive that elites—whether priests or Cardenistas—would again and again ponder how *campesinos* could fit together. Geography flung them into dozens of small villages. Ethnic variation was a factor, for while most *campesinos* were mestizos, one-fifth of the 1920 population was classified as Tarascan Indians (Foglio Miramontes 1936:2:138). Poverty was certainly a common rural condition, but the population was marked by hundreds of minute economic distinctions. Similarly, while most men worked on large estates, their jobs ranged from water carrier to cowboy. Not least, male and female *campesinos* were assigned different lots in life.

work of Walter Benjamin (1968), Gramsci (1971), Genovese (1976), Marcuse (1966), and Laclau and Mouffe (1989) has been central to my thinking about hegemony. Laclau and Mouffe particularly appreciate subordinate classes' capacities to forge alliances that can, at times, affect the terms of domination. Moreover, their work serves as a timely corrective to the often reflexive tendency to grant priority to economic causality. In addition, Mallon uses the concept of hegemony in a particularly thought-provoking way (Mallon, forthcoming).

What did these people have in common? Catholic priests had long attempted to provide an answer. For many years, the church hierarchy had played a dominant ideological role in northwestern Michoacán. Through an impressive array of schools, lay organizations, and churches (Verduzco, in Staples 1989:57–62), it disseminated three principles that both produced considerable behavioral conformity and effectively reproduced the ties between large property owners and the church. First, the hierarchy proclaimed private property both just and sacrosanct. Second, the church promoted relationships based on inequality. While it did recognize fairly egalitarian human ties, hierarchical, male-dominated relationships were Catholicism's stock in trade. The model was the Holy Family, constituted of an all-knowing father, a mother whose family status derived from her connection to males, and a son subservient to the father but dominant over all others. The third principle, women's submission to men, derived from the second.

In rural Michoacán, these principles came alive. The small group who owned the vast fertile valleys testified to the continuing dominance of private land ownership. These landowners, frequently connected by kinship, monopolized property in northwestern Michoacán (Verduzco, in Staples 1989:61). In a state virtually devoid of industry, this meant that *campesinos* were completely dependent on *hacendados* for employment. And population growth during the nineteenth-century heightened this dependency (J. Meyer 1984:32). Within such a context, the hierarchical social relationships mandated by the church materialized. Peons learned as children that on sighting a landlord (or his bad-guy stand-in, the *mayordomo*), they were to doff their caps and murmur, "Ave María."[7] At the same time, relationships of equality among *campesinos* seem to have been particularly fragile. Rafael Ochoa, an Ario *campesino* born on a hacienda, remembered his father's efforts to organize his fellow peons against the landlord's unfair treatment. The issue was the boss's failure to pay the peons as their contracts stipulated. But while peons turned out for Ochoa's midnight meetings and pledged their support, when the encounter with the landlord occurred, Ochoa's companions melted away.[8]

7. Series of interviews with Rafael Ochoa, Ario de Rayón, May–July and Nov. 1990. In interviews conducted in Zamora, Ignatio Espitia, a *campesino* born on a Zamora-area hacienda, and Vicente Pérez, a *campesino* who became a Cardenista agrarian leader, reported similar uses of deference couched in Catholic terms. Interviews with Espitia, 1985; interview with Pérez, 1985, Zamora, Michoacán.

8. Interview with Ochoa. Ranajit Guha offers a theoretical acknowledgment of

In other words, the peons were caught in a net of frustration. As men they were taught to view violence, aggression, and competition as instinctive and distinctive signs of manliness.[9] Yet how could they display these traits in everyday life? In the workaday hacienda world, private property was forever tantalizing and forever beyond their means. Even their thankless jobs were not safe, for population growth forced them to compete with fellow peons (who, in this face-to-face world, were frequently neighbors or relatives). And violent expression of their frustration could lead to the chain gang.[10]

If there was a ruffian quality to this life, I believe that it was mitigated for men by the subordination of women. Women enacted the fiction that they were inferior to men in a number of ways, but let us consider three. First, women fed men, and no matter how poor they were, they made this into something of an everyday ritual. This could take on a number of forms. The poorest women followed wheat harvesters, gleaning. Bending down, gathering remnants for their men and family, they might have stepped out of the Old Testament. Other *campesino* women filed out to the fields at mid-morning, with lunch for their men. Most frequently, men returned from work to a meal prepared by a woman. Whether or not we want to drag up the associations with comfort and nurturance, it is clear that women's work rhythms were not marked in this way.[11] Second,

---

the existence of popular betrayal in a different historical context in Guha and Spivak (1985:15).

9. Mexicanists have hardly begun to pursue issues of mestizo culture. Indeed, Alan Knight denies the existence of "mestizo society" or "mestizo social personality" (1986a:1:6). Still, without making much theoretical ado over the issue, Luis González shows mestizos living out culturally reproduced traits of manliness, such as breaking horses, branding cows, and climbing trees ([1968] 1972:89). For a reconstruction of mestizo culture, see Becker (forthcoming: chap. 2).

10. Interview with Ochoa. For use of the chain gang at the Guaracha hacienda in northwestern Michoacán, see Gledhill (1991:74).

11. The information on women hauling lunch out to the fields came from Ochoa, while Verduzco provided the verbal portrait of women gleaning. That women were in charge of food preparation is what historians used to refer to as "common knowledge." I checked this idea, however, through a series of interviews focusing on men's and women's work, with *campesinos* Verduzco and Rocha and with middle-class Cardenistas such as Tomás Rico Cano and Jesús Múgica Martínez. Interviews with Verduzco and Rocha; interviews with Rico Cano, 1990, Morelia, Michoacán; interviews with Múgica Martínez, 1989, 1990, Morelia, Michoacán.

women played a similar role in the realm of work and leisure. Men's work was grueling and long, but it ended at sunset. Women's work was grueling and almost endless, allowing men a semblance of free time and rest, luxuries that women almost never enjoyed.[12] Finally, unlike the men's fellow workers, women did not compete with them. The contention here is that this behavior not only subsidized capitalism, it also afforded men respite from the daily abuses they experienced.[13]

THE ROMANCE OF PURITY

In the rural Michoacán of the 1920s and 1930s, this marriage between large landed property and the Catholic hierarchy persisted (Verduzco, in Staples 1989:61). And at the grassroots level, social relationships that the hierarchy mandated remained intact. Yet while Jean Meyer (1974c:18) and González (1978:107–28) suggest that the hierarchy maintained ideological influence over the vast majority of Michoacán's population, many priests and Catholic ideologues sounded a note of panic in their official proclamations. Most dramatically, the church feared socialism, and priests reproduced the Pope's antisocialist stance in sermons. Re-

12. Interviews with Rocha, Méndez, Ochoa, and Verduzco regarding men's and women's work. This was also true of ranchero society in San José, as depicted by González ([1968] 1972:49).

13. For analyses of this kind of subsidy, see Hartmann in Sargent (1981:1–42). For an early attempt to move beyond efforts to prioritize either gender-based or class-based oppressions, and to understand the ways both patriarchal and capitalist social relations characterize work and home life, see Kelley (1979:216–27). Analyses pointing to the specific ways women's work has made family subsistence possible in dependent capitalist economies have been prominent among Latin Americanists to a much greater extent than among scholars focusing on gender in the United States and Europe. This is probably because widespread and enduring immiseration of vast sectors of Latin American populations, a condition that has affected women with singular severity, simply has not cut into such vast sectors of the Western European or North American populations. But for Latin Americanists, this has at times led to an overly economistic approach, which has been played out to the exclusion of approaches pondering other kinds of exploitation and other possible forms of resistance. See, for example, the essays in Nash and Safa (1976, 1986). For a sophisticated example of this approach, see Deere (1990). And for important exceptions, see Mallon (1987b) and Behar (1990).

iterating the doctrinaire view regarding private property, the Pope contended, "as men are naturally unequal in strength and intelligence, so they must be unequal in terms of what they own; the church commands that property rights, rooted in nature, are inviolable."[14] That sounds unyielding enough, and it is right to view this as a justification of an inequitable social order. Yet if the hierarchical attitude was stiff-necked, it was also anxious. A journalist writing for a Catholic periodical expressed the fear that socialism would erode society, "heating the blood of the workers with flashy words, promising to redistribute land, oxen, carts, money, and even the wives and daughters of the rich." The socialists "foster hatred against the rich. And they remove Christian resignation."[15]

In addition, a host of everyday delinquencies raised hierarchical hackles. Priests were particularly concerned about deception, and false pretenses seemed to abound. Foreigners, sporting credentials from the Eastern—not the Roman Catholic—church, begged for alms.[16] Women, though specifically prohibited from singing in church, "tried to pass themselves off as members of the community by positioning themselves with the faithful and singing their hearts out."[17] And *campesinos* played sacred music on a host of instruments "that can never be permitted in church, such as kettledrums and tambourines."[18]

It appears that these fears led the church to romance. Dipping into its storehouse of cultural wares, it began to reestablish what might be called an institutional flirtation with La Purísima. La Purísima was a hierarchical representation of the Virgin Mary, emphasizing her chastity and humility. This relationship between the Purest One and the hierarchy stretched back at least to 1851, when the church proclaimed her patron saint of Zamora, the most important town in northwestern Michoacán. To celebrate her inauguration, priests organized processions and fiestas. A committee met to develop blueprints for a church to be built in her honor (Tapia 1985:1–4).

14. APC, caja 11, "Carta pastoral de los prelados de la provincia de Michoacán," Junta provisional celebrada en Celaya, Feb. 1920.

15. "Mueran los ricos . . . mueran los ricos," *La Hoja Social: Quincenal de Propaganda Católica* 36 (Nov. 22, 1922), 1.

16. APC, caja 13, Sacramental y Disciplinar.

17. APC, caja 11, "Reglamento de la música sagrada que deberán observarse en la provincia eclesiástica de Michoacán."

18. Ibid.

Drawing on that legacy, in sermon after sermon priests recreated a portrait of a deeply self-sacrificing woman.[19] In sermons, pastoral letters, and iconography, priests attempted to disseminate that model.[20] As "the immaculate daughter of God, the virgin mother of God, the purest wife of God the Holy Spirit," she was chaste. As a woman who had allowed the male God to have his way with her, she was portrayed as a model for women who were to be "submissive to their husbands, who must love their wives with fidelity and constancy."[21] Then, too, La Purísima was generous beyond generosity. As she reputedly told the faithful, "I am a loving and tender mother for whomever asks my help in their pain and suffering. There is nothing to fear in my help and protection."[22]

In this attempt at what might be called clean seduction, priests whispered a double message in women's ears. Mary was crowned in purest gold, housed in the best places, and protected from work (unless an occasional procession through Zamora's dusty streets counts as work). And none of this finery came her way because of her wealth or power, for she had been but a poor Jewish woman from Nazareth. Furthermore, Mary was not praised for the great public exertions entailed by fighting wars, creating legislation, or building fortunes out of Zamora's fertile valleys. Instead, priests commended her selflessness and loyalty to others' needs.

Without any intention of trivializing the clerical project, it seems clear that the priests were no lovers agog at the beauty or the natural charm of their beloved. Rather, the church viewed their partners as Pygmalions-in-the rough. After all, to invoke Mary as model for women was to summon forth a woman historically rewarded for her connection

19. For a perceptive exploration of the ambivalence surrounding the Virgin as a female model, see Warner (1976). The counterpoint is Douglas (1966), who attempts to reconstruct the original context for certain purity customs, including those of traditional Jews and "new" Christians. But in a misguided effort to obscure the continuities between traditional Jewish and Christian ambivalence regarding women and virginity, Douglas falls into Catholic apologetics. Indeed, she champions Paul's approach to women and women's virginity as "setting a standard of freedom and equality which was against the traditional Jewish custom" (1966:157).

20. My iconographic evidence comes from participant observation of the churches in Zamora, Ario, Pátzcuaro, Jiquilpan, Morelia, and Jarácuaro, Michoacán. I have benefited from my art historical training at the University of Madrid.

21. APC, "Carta pastoral."

22. APC, Sacramental y Disciplinar.

to two male aspects of God. Mary was rewarded because she did God's will, obeyed when he commanded. Her crown, her power to intercede were borrowed—sanctity on loan. And the postrevolutionary message was similar. The church rewarded women—and by inference, the population as a whole—for keeping their rambunctious behavior under wraps. In a word, women were to be rewarded for conformity.

Double message or no, from all the available evidence, La Purísima was enormously popular among women. This is not to imply that the varied female population of Michoacán meant identical things by their individual reverence for the Virgin. Rather, women might turn to Mary to intercede in problems like children's illnesses, as Mari Elena Verduzco recalled; or, like Esperanza Rocha, they might hope for "protection against the revolutionaries" pushing her to abandon Catholicism.[23] Whatever the purpose, many women burned candles before the Virgin. Others organized processions to visit her. They turned to her in prayer for special intervention.[24]

But why? Why were women so taken with a model of female abnegation? In part, people seize on existing cultural patterns as raw material for cultural reproduction. That is, although popular cultural inventions certainly occur, they must be as rare as elite cultural inventions. Most people probably turn over in their consciousness whatever elements have been presented to them. In a context in which women were relegated to unpaid and unnoticed work, it seems reasonable that an image celebrating that role might have offered them some compensation, however slight.

More than that, women may have derived great satisfaction from the cult of the Virgin at a relatively small price. There was, for one thing, the matter of miracles. In an area where ordinary material ability to solve problems was limited by poverty, Michoacán women routinely turned to miracles as antidotes.[25] And the Virgin, as the immaculate mother of Jesus, was certainly the quintessential miracle worker.

Finally, though this point is admittedly quite speculative, the price—symbolic identity with chastity and modesty—may have seemed relatively small to women. Unchastity, after all, commonly meant the yearly birth of a child, which multiplied women's work. Similarly, to forgo modesty would have meant acting out openly assertive roles, but women

23. Interviews with Verduzco and Rocha.
24. Ibid.
25. Interviews with Méndez and Rocha.

had not rehearsed such roles. In short, for at least some women, the church's advances may have seemed both comfortable and gratifying.

TORCHING LA PURÍSIMA

In the best of circumstances, the Michoacán Cardenistas' program would have been ambitious. Their plan was to reconstruct the countryside through a combination of land redistribution and cultural transformation. By breaking up the haciendas, Cardenistas hoped to develop a prosperous peasantry able to feed both its own families and the urban population. In addition, the revolutionaries planned to recast peasant culture, the peasants' ways of seeing the world, through a "socialist" education program. In this program, rural teachers and agricultural agents who identified with Cardenismo would sport varying faces of liberalism.[26] Depending on who they were and what situation they found themselves in, the Cardenistas stressed agrarianism, national unification, or anticlericalism.

Circumstances, however, were hardly optimal. The Cardenistas themselves were a heterogeneous group. Almost all of them were from Michoacán, but they came from different towns and villages, from poverty and from the middle class; they were mestizos and occasionally Indians, men and women (Becker 1989:236). In addition, the landlords clung tenaciously to their property, and the Catholic establishment posed a formidable—and very immediate—threat. In 1926 the church hierarchy incited peasants to rise against the government, unleashing the Cristero Rebellion. For three years, Cristeros fought a bloody civil war against the government, and in Michoacán that war was particularly virulent. In addition, priests used their pulpits to denounce the governmental program. They insisted that hellfire awaited peasants accepting land from the government, and they threatened parents who sent their children to the Cardenista schools with excommunication.[27]

26. For an exploration of various understandings of Mexican liberalism, see Knight (1985a).

27. This threat appears in APC, caja 13, Sacramental y Disciplinar, "Normas del Comité Ejecutivo Episcopal a los Sacerdotes y a los Católicos." In addition, these threats were freely acknowledged by a number of ardent Catholics, including Francisco Elizalde, Father Joaquín Paz, and *sinarquista* Santiago del Río. Interviews with Elizalde, July 19, 26, 1985; Paz, Aug. 12, 1985; del Río, Aug. 22, 1985, all in Zamora, Michoacán.

That threat did not strip all Cardenistas of their idealistic approach to transforming the *campesinos*. Parodying the church, Cardenista José Corona Núñez designed a credo alive with belief in the common man. He claimed that it was not Jesus—"that man who sits up there on the velvet throne, crowned in gold"—who deserved reverence. Rather, he said, it was "you people, whom they call the wretched, [who] are the roots that nourish the soul of the country."[28]

Yet redemption was only possible, many Cardenistas believed, if women were transformed. For Cardenistas tended to view women as a sort of clerical fifth column. As school inspector Policarpo Sánchez put it, "The men play only secondary roles. It is the huge phalanx of devout women who pull the invisible strings behind all the propaganda against the educational work."[29]

This sense of threat lent the Cardenista engagement with women a decidedly uneven cast. On the one hand, the revolutionaries could be attractive suitors, and not because their platform emphasized women's rights. Except as widows, women did not receive rights to governmental land. The revolutionaries, however, established women's leagues, in which women learned that Cárdenas championed their husbands' (and by implication their families') rights to governmental land. In the leagues revolutionaries also discussed the evils of alcoholism, a real women's issue as long as women were in charge of stretching the limited family budget to feed their families. Claiming that alcohol "causes so much damage to our humble homes," women in the Liga Femenil de Lucha Social "Ricardo Flores Magón" of Zamora went so far as to petition that "all the cantinas be banished."[30]

On the other hand, because women were viewed as potentially unreliable, the Cardenistas began to play the roles of jealous suitors, trying to smoke out traces of their clerical rivals. Cardenista leaders closed the churches, outlawed public Catholic worship, and charged the women's leagues with the task of monitoring religious observances. At times the leagues concentrated on the enemy without, the nonagraristas. A woman from one of Ario's wealthiest families, Concepción Méndez,

28. Interview with José Corona Núñez.

29. AHSEP, caja 412, Policarpo L. Sánchez, professor, inspector federal, Michoacán; interview with Elizalde, July 25, 1985.

30. AMZ, Gobernación, exp. 17, loose documents, María Gallegos, secretary general of the Liga Femenil de Lucha Social "Ricardo Flores Magón," to municipal president of Zamora, July 18, 1938.

possesses vivid memories of league members' vigilance. "I used to spend time with my friends in the plaza talking. The women from the leagues would casually approach us, just waiting to hear what we had to say, if we mentioned baptisms or the church."[31]

Sometimes Cardenistas found potential treachery closer to home, in the agrarian community itself. Initially, they tried to stop it by issuing anticlerical orders. Esperanza Rocha, a devout Catholic married to an agrarista, remembers, "in the *liga* they wouldn't baptize our children. They prohibited it. We had to baptize them with honey," a pseudo-spiritual concoction that Rocha claims the Cardenistas whipped up.[32] When suggestion was not enough, the Cardenistas threatened women who practiced Catholicism with the loss of their ejidal lands.[33]

Social transformation proceeds slowly, and the countryside was full of nooks, crannies, and opportunities for subversion. Perhaps these considerations led the Cardenistas to dramatize their plight in Michoacán. We cannot know.

All we know is that a group of Cardenistas entered the church by night. There they found themselves face to face with the delicate Virgin. What did they think? Did her pale, delicate skin put them off, when they knew their women were browned and wrinkled in the sun, with no hope of refinement? Or did she stir up the embers of betrayal? Did they think of their mothers allying with the church? Whatever their thoughts, they kept them to themselves as they clutched the Virgin and other icons under their arms and hid them in their homes. The next morning, Catholic women peering out their windows witnessed the Cardenistas building a bonfire in the plaza. They unwrapped La Purísima, laid her on the fire, and watched her go up in flames.

DANCING AT THE ALTAR

With the icon in ashes, Cardenistas appropriated the church. They hired a band and issued invitations to their wives, daughters, and girlfriends.

31. Interview with Méndez.
32. The origins of this concoction are disputed in Ario and in Zamora, with anti-Cardenistas sustaining Rocha's contention. They attribute the concoction to Salvador Sotelo, a Cardenista teacher who spent many years in Ario. According to Jesús Tapia, however, Sotelo denied involvement with this sticky issue, throwing it back onto the women's leagues. See Tapia (1986:215–16).
33. Interview with Rocha. Also, documents cited in Becker (1988a:205–7) suggest this outcome. See, for example, AMZ, loose documents, 1937.

When the women entered the church it would have looked very different. The priest was gone. The image of the Virgin was missing. The band was playing contemporary popular music. And suddenly the women, too, were not quite the same. Their Catholic training, their lessons in humility began to recede, and the women, suddenly transformed, began to dance before the altar.

What, though, was the nature of the transformation? Three Ario women have tried to explain it: Méndez and Rocha, whom we have seen, and Soledad Barragán, allegedly one of the dancers. In interviews, these women developed distinct verbal images of the dancers, but in each case they drew on the language of purity, damnation, and loss.

These women's renditions are particularly valuable, because they help unearth a buried story. Yet before approaching them, it must be emphasized that these women do not recreate the dancers as they were. After all, they create the images through oral history or verbal memoirs. Such oral documents share with written records a failure fully to enter the hearts and minds of others. Neither form of documentation is transparent.

Although illusions of transparency may be the hobgoblins of positivist (or exceedingly hopeful) minds, these memoirs do present a real problem. They were created in a different historical context from the one they attempt to reconstruct. In this case, in advance of the evidence, it can be stated that these women's renditions of the dancers are reasonable but exaggerated approximations. The Cardenistas' anticlericalism both threatened the order of purity and ultimately resulted in its partial comeback. Thus the women's recollections are probably distorted in two directions. On the one hand, wealthy women had a scare: poor women they had barely considered threatened their world. Their partial recovery of that world in the years since the event has sharpened their tongues. Poor women, meanwhile, have reentered a pact with Catholics of all classes. This has tended to undermine their original bravado, and they now speak cautiously.

Méndez, then, had most to fear from the dancers. Her wealth meant that she possessed the most tangible stake in the habits and practices that the regime of purity had promoted. She lived largely among the wealthy. She shared her work routine, her Sundays, and her holidays with her wealthy relatives. When she went to church, she sat in front with her elite *compadres*. She and her wealthy friends developed Catholic rituals in which "we divided up and each of us sang a stanza of a hymn from a different street corner." It was a habit she remembers as "such a pleasure."[34]

34. Interview with Méndez.

The experiences of poor women were, and have remained, largely obscure to her. While Méndez and the poor women who walked by her house "always greeted each other," until the torching that was probably the extent of their communication. But then Méndez saw the flames out her window. She heard the dance from the back of her house. One of the agraristas' wives even dropped by to insult her.

These women's emergence from what Méndez had probably viewed as a shadowy crowd may have led her, in her latter-day interview, to reconstruct women who had experienced complete transformations. From women who generally conformed to the order of things, they became godless hussies. "They were shameless. They wanted to destroy everything, everything that had to do with believing in God." And for Méndez, their loss of purity was absolute. "Those who have already died have been paid with a painful death."[35]

Rocha, on the other hand, recreates women who remained much the same. To be sure, she views the dance as a misstep: "What they did was wrong." Then again, experience has made her alert to the context. Priests and men routinely demanded obedience from women. Women were to honor both their biological and their spiritual fathers. In Rocha's own experience, this demand was crisscrossed with conflict. She recalls, "the Cardenistas wanted me to keep from baptizing my children, so I told them that this was my house and that I am in charge here. But my husband and his family all went the other way and wanted me to, as well." Without spelling out the contradiction—that priests both wished to dictate moral absolutes and expected women to take responsibility for autonomous moral decisions—Rocha refuses to leave the women holding the bag. "After all, they were young, and they were just doing what their fathers put them up to."[36]

Barragán even further downplays the women's transformation. Indeed, though Méndez, Verduzco, and Rocha claim that she was one of the dancers, Barragán certainly does not deck out her past in flamboyant colors. On the contrary, if the story were left to her, we would not know that the church had once been a dance floor. Nor would we see the women as flirting with the damnation said to await the impure, for Barragán refuses such an interpretation. Rather, though she does not say this either, she implicitly refutes the gossip of the day, that revolutionary women were prostitutes.[37] To her it seems important to view the dancers

35. Ibid
36. Interview with Rocha.
37. Interviews with Méndez, Verduzco, and Rocha. For the information regard-

as ordinary poor women. "Look, I don't want people to think that this was a fancy dance, that these were fancy dancers like they have today. No, the women wore plain clothes, just whatever they had on."[38]

THE NEW CHOREOGRAPHY

Why do these women use Catholic clay to mold life into the dancers, when it has been stressed that the dance shook up the *pueblo?* Here it is instructive to return to the village in the 1930s, when La Purísima lay on the ground in ashes. Identification with her cult had lent women their first taste of prominence, yet that identification had also been used to reinforce women's submission. Perhaps it is not surprising that the Cardenista bonfire electrified the *pueblo.* Though schooled in deference, many women realized that something had changed. In response, some of them seized the opportunity to act in the public sphere.

Ario women acted in at least four distinct ways. The village's prominent women abandoned the *pueblo.* As Mari Elena Verduzco describes it, the revolutionaries destroyed what she romantically sees as an unruffled past. "Before the Cardenistas came, there was no hatred here. They sowed dissension."[39] With the revolutionary presence established in Ario, elite women and their families fled to nearby Zamora. There they used the well-funded Catholic institutions to serve as a sort of fortress, protecting them from the necessity of sending their children to government schools.

At least a handful of poor women adopted an equally definitive stance. Yet where the wealthy found Cardenismo repugnant, poor women discovered new opportunities in Cardenismo. For the dancers, the Cardenista tune allowed them to shake off old taboos. In a vicarious sense this may have been true for the crowds of women who hurried to the church to witness the spectacle. Consider for instance, Carmen Barragán. Barragán was the wife of an agrarista, and according to her daughter Soledad, "Though she was very Catholic, she saw things clearly for what they were. Things like justice." It would seem that part of the injustice she felt centered on ways wealthy women dominated the poor. In all events, for

---

ing alleged prostitution, I am grateful to lifelong Zamora resident Francisco Elizalde. Because of his close ties to both devout Catholics and revolutionaries, Elizalde's testimony was particularly useful. Interview with Elizalde, Nov. 1990, Zamora, Michoacán.

38. Interview with Barragán.
39. Interview with Verduzco.

her Concepción Méndez was a sacred cow, and she took her on. As Méndez herself put it, "That shameless girl, she's not even worth a peanut, came by. She knocked on my door and she spat in my face. That little no account."[40]

Then there were the poor women like Rocha, who chose a more complex alternative. They recognized that their families needed government land to survive. Yet they found government assaults on Catholic worship disturbing. In response, they reproduced and intensified a spiritual division of labor. Rocha's husband joined with other men in accepting land and attending agrarian meetings denouncing Catholicism. This led Rocha to "wear the image [of the Virgin] hidden for protection against what they were doing against God."[41]

For still other villagers this personal insurance policy was inadequate. And, to again press our metaphor into service, they responded to the state's invitation to dance. In a letter to the government Dolores Manjarez, Concepción Pérez, and Guadalupe Méndez joined with a number of men in mouthing a few words of the governmental tune. As they reminded the municipal president, they were "Mexicans exercising their rights," rights "consecrated in the Central Constitution of the Republic." But if the government had expected to lead, swinging their partners to its tune, these women had other ideas. They would dance with the Cardenistas, they implied, only if the government would reopen the churches and "recognize that everyone is free to practice whatever religious belief suits them."[42]

THE CONSTRUCTION OF REVOLUTIONARY HEGEMONY

Hegemony, as Gramsci reminds us, does not mean that subordinate classes completely abandon their ideological perspectives (1971:52, 55, 161). Rather, as Mexican *campesinos* have long demonstrated, in the context of elite ideological domination, *campesinos* might well forge alliances with elites. They might use elite language for their own purposes. They might negotiate.[43]

40. Interview with Méndez.

41. Interview with Rocha.

42. AMZ, Gobernación, exp. 17, Ignacio Verduzgo and others to municipal president of Zamora, July 8, 1935.

43. On the surface, such behavior resembles what James C. Scott (1985) has

Or, like the handful of Ario women who wrote to the government, they might gamble. When Cardenistas approached them on the dance floor with promises of government land, they agreed to step in time to the Cardenista rhythm. In effect, they were saying that hellfire or no, they could not stand in the way of their husbands' ability to feed their families. But when the band struck up an anticlerical number, the women chose to sit it out. More than that, they turned to the government requesting access to churches, physical spaces the Cardenistas viewed as hotbeds of subversion. The women apparently believed that considering the uncertainties of revolution in their village, access to miraculous intervention could not be forsworn.

It is important to remember that these women had received little formal education. They had been trained to maintain a shadowy presence in public. If they disagreed, they did so in their kitchens, at the streams where they washed clothes, or in the closets in the back of their minds. In that context, the women's engagement with Cardenismo was no small accomplishment. They took advantage of the presence of rival suitors to reveal a decided strategic intelligence. They behaved as though they recognized their value, both to the Catholic hierarchy and to the government.

Cárdenas also gambled. He reopened the churches, even though he knew the Ario women were not alone in calling for a different clerical policy. *Campesinos* throughout the state were disgruntled (Becker 1988a: 232–95). The Cristeros may have returned to their villages, but the countryside was smoldering. After the Cristero Rebellion, Cárdenas knew very well that such religious fervor could lead to violent antigovernment resistance.

Nonetheless, to establish his hegemony Cárdenas gambled. He gambled that his state, a state that monopolized violence and the means of production and that had now persuaded a recalcitrant peasantry to negotiate with him, would prevail. Sixty years later, the hegemonic state Cárdenas established remains intact. Who is to say that his gamble did not pay off?

---

baptized "everyday resistance." While I have critiqued certain aspects of Scott's analysis, it is perfectly plain that I consider Scott's notion that subordinate classes are not *ideologically* dominated both insightful and humane. Still, I now question the assumption that scholars can distinguish between "authentic" or disguised meaning; or, indeed, that behavior cannot mean many things at once. For an analysis of the limitations of everyday resistance in Michoacán, see Becker (1989).

JAN RUS

The "Comunidad Revolucionaria Institucional": The Subversion of Native Government in Highland Chiapas, 1936–1968

"The Revolution" has two meanings among the Maya peasants of high-land Chiapas. On the one hand, there was the revolution of the 1910s, which in the highlands was little more than a civil war between an occupying federal army, the Carrancistas, and bands of local, counter-revolutionary landowners who fought them for control of the region between 1914 and 1920. Indians were excluded from this revolution. More than excluded, they were mistreated by both sides, which fought battles across their land, requisitioned their food and labor, and punished entire villages thought to have collaborated with "the enemy." In spite of isolated gains by communities that managed to make fortunate alliances with the combatants or temporarily escape the demands of landowners who had fled the war zone, this revolution, the "time of Carranza" in the Maya languages of the highlands, is generally remembered with distaste.

The second revolution, which for Maya peasants was the real revolution, was the "time of Cárdenas" in the late 1930s. This was the period when the benefits of "the new Mexico"—among them agrarian reform, labor unions, and an end to debt contracting and peonage—finally reached out to include them as well. With some justification, the years

I would like to thank Andrés Aubry, Jan de Vos, Angélica Inda, Gil Joseph, Nancy Modiano, Daniel Nugent, Diane Rus, and Vern Sterk for their generous comments on an earlier version of this paper.

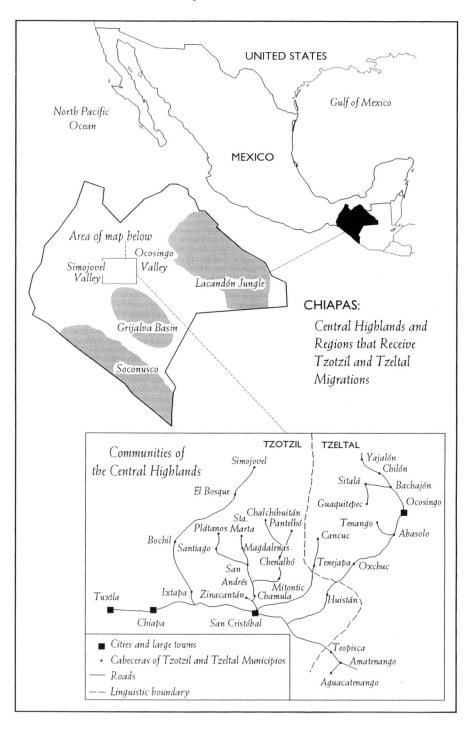

CHIAPAS:

Central Highlands and
Regions that Receive
Tzotzil and Tzeltal
Migrations

from 1936 to the beginning of the 1940s are sometimes referred to in Chiapas as "la revolución de los indios."

As revolutions go, however, this was a peculiar one. Although the myth of the "time of Cárdenas" is that it empowered the Indians and brought them new rights, a closer look reveals that in the long run it actually led to a more intimate form of domination. To make their reforms work, the Cardenistas and their successors reached inside the native communities, not only changing leaders but rearranging the governments, creating new offices to deal with labor and agrarian matters at the same time that they were granting vast new powers to the officials charged with maintaining relations with the party and state. To some extent, the result of this process—the centralization of political and economic power within communities and the tying of that power to the state—resembles the caciquismo, or "bossism," that characterizes Mexican rural society in general. In Indian communities like those of highland Chiapas, however, with their own corporate traditions of social and political organization, both in turn inextricably linked to local religious beliefs, the changes introduced by the Cardenistas required ideological and political adjustments beyond those mandated—or perhaps even conceived—by the reformers. With the passage of time, it turned out that they had managed to co-opt not only the native leaders who were their direct collaborators but also, ironically, the very community structures previously identified with resistance to outside intervention and exploitation—independent self-government, strictly enforced community solidarity, and religious legitimation of political power. As a result, by the mid-1950s, what anthropologists were just beginning to describe as "closed corporate communities" had in fact become "institutionalized revolutionary communities" harnessed to the state.

The purpose of this essay is to try to describe how this happened. To do so, it will look in some detail at the ways native communities' defenses were breached in the late 1930s to bring them the "fruits of the revolution"; and then at the ways the changes of that period worked themselves through community structures during the ensuing decades. For the most part, the discussion will focus on the Tzotzil-speaking community of Chamula, the most populous and important *municipio* in the Chiapas highlands. Since the process of subordinating and binding native governments to the state was regionwide, however, examples for comparison will also be drawn from the other Tzotzil and Tzeltal *municipios* immediately surrounding Chamula.

In the final section, this essay will try to show how the co-optation of native community structures that began in the late 1930s continues to affect economic and political development in the highlands communities today. As it will argue, the close relationship between the state and "traditional community structures" that dates from this earlier period has led in recent years to the anomaly of the state enforcing "native traditions" *against the natives themselves* to maintain order, and has forced many Maya peasants to search outside their communities for alternative ways of organizing themselves.

INDIANS OF HIGHLAND CHIAPAS ON THE EVE OF CHANGE, 1930–1936

In the mid-1930s, the Tzotzil and Tzeltal Indians of highland Chiapas lived under conditions that had changed little in almost fifty years. As before the revolution of the 1910s, their basic problem was a lack of cultivable land. While peasants in other parts of Mexico, even other parts of Chiapas, had benefited from at least cosmetic agrarian reform following the revolution, these Maya peasants continued to live in the same densely populated, relatively infertile niches in the mountains that they had occupied since their best lands were stripped from them in the mid-nineteenth century. Agrarian reform agents and surveyors, agraristas scared off by the local landowners' *guardias blancas* when they could not be bribed, had made virtually no impact on the cattle and corn ranches that monopolized the region's best plateaus, nor on the cane and coffee *fincas* that filled the surrounding deep valleys (Rus and Guzmán 1990:1–17; García de León 1985:2,197ff.).[1]

This chronic land poverty, in turn, continued to force the Tzotzils and Tzeltals to seek work as seasonal migrant laborers in Chiapas' lowlands, just as it had before 1910. Such work was badly paid, performed under miserable conditions, and the Indians often returned after several months with debts as large as the wage advances with which they had left home (Baumann 1983; Rus et al. 1986). In the mid-1930s, for example, as many as twenty thousand Indians from the region around San Cristóbal, the highlands' principal city, were making the yearly trek to the coffee plantations of Chiapas's southwestern mountains and coast. This entailed an eight-day walk each way for which not only were they not paid, but

1. For the Tzotzils' own view of this situation, see, for example, SRA.Tuxtla, Expedientes/Chamula.

during which they were forced to buy their own food, pay for the privilege of sleeping as a group on a veranda at night, and satisfy transit taxes as they passed through towns along the way (Pozas Arciniega 1952; Rus forthcoming). Moreover, in spite of a minimum wage of 1.30 pesos a day during this period, the prevailing rate for highland migrants on Chiapas' coffee plantations was only 30 to 50 centavos—and that only if they could finish their *tareas*, or daily work quotas. Harsh as these conditions may seem, however, they were better than those experienced by the men of the northern highlands who cut mahogany and other fine woods in the *monterías* of the Lacandón jungle, or those of the extreme western and eastern highlands who worked in the cane and corn fields of neighboring lowland *fincas*. As one old man from El Bosque summed up the lives of all the Tzotzils and Tzeltals in these years, "Even our bodies were not our own."[2]

To complete this picture of a region in which the revolution had little impact, it should be noted that although the Constitution of 1917 outlawed the administrative apparatus through which the state itself had guaranteed Indian laborers to the lowland plantations before 1910, in Chiapas the government continued to bear a major share of the burden of contracting workers right through the mid-1930s. Officially, it could no longer charge the taxes and fees that had formerly compelled Indians to accept unfavorable contracts, nor could it pursue and return to their "creditors" those laborers who fled before their wage advances were repaid. Extra-officially, however, the state government managed to achieve many of the same ends through the institution of the *secretarios municipales*. These were ladino (that is, non-Indian) officials, appointed from the nearest Spanish-speaking town, who acted as tutors to the native governments of Indian *municipios*, maintaining their civil registries, collecting taxes on labor contracts, and advising them on Mexican law. Informally, but more important, they also sold alcohol and acted as agents for the *enganchadores*, or contractors, who organized gangs of Indian workers for the plantations. Not only did they make wage advances in the contractors' name—often in the form of liquor and other goods sold on credit—but they used their position to keep track of community members who returned home before working off their debts. Although the *secretarios* of the 1920s and 1930s may not have had the same legal authority to pursue and arrest such runaways as the prerevolutionary *jefes políticos*, they could discipline them

---

2. Jan Rus, "Kipaltik interviews," unpublished notes, on deposit in INAREMAC.BD.

almost as effectively by seeing to it that in the future they were denied the labor contracts and other credit they needed to survive (Rus forthcoming).

Cut off, then, from the possibility of agrarian reform, forced by their poverty to accept unfavorable contracts for distant labor, and watched over by ladino authorities who kept their records and controlled their access to outside work, most of Chiapas's native communities of the immediate postrevolutionary period drew inward, shunning all unnecessary contact with the outside world. In Chamula, for instance, it became a rule even before the revolution ended that the community's *presidente municipal* could not be bilingual (as he usually had been before 1914) but had to be a monolingual, Tzotzil-speaking elder (*principal*) who had completed a career in the community's hierarchy of traditional civil and religious offices. Only in this way, it was argued, could he be trusted not to betray his neighbors to outsiders, whether by "selling" them to ladino labor contractors or acting precipitously in matters that might bring reprisals from ladino officials.[3]

Perhaps in part this rule was simply an attempt to make a virtue of necessity. Given the harsh economic conditions of the 1920s and 1930s, young, working-age men could rarely afford to serve for a year without pay in any case. As a result, when chosen even for lower-ranking offices they often fled, leaving, one might argue, no one but old men to conduct community government. The extent of cultural revitalization during this period, however, suggests that deeper forces were at work. At the same time that the community was entrusting its affairs to older, more traditional authorities, it was reviving and embellishing fiestas that had not been celebrated since the late nineteenth century. For the first time, native curers were not only allowed but encouraged to conduct ceremonies in the community church. Even the dress of officeholders became more specialized (Rus forthcoming). The overall impression gained from oral histories is of a people retrenching—strengthening and elaborating their community's internal government and culture to help them through a period when they had little control over their lives beyond that community.[4]

3. Interviews with Salvador Gómez Osob, July 9, 1975, and Salvador López Tuxum, Oct. 29, 1975, both of Chamula; and Manuel Castellanos Cancino, San Cristóbal, Nov. 8, 1975, and Dec. 30, 1976.
4. Interviews with Salvador Guzmán López, Aug. 11, 1990; and Mateo Méndez Aguilar, May 21, 1976, Aug. 14, 1990, and Aug. 27, 1991, both of Chamula.

Nevertheless, there was more to the resistance organized by the "traditionalist" leaders of the 1920s and 1930s than just symbolism or passive noncooperation. Beneath their deceptively calm surface, Tzotzil and Tzeltal communities of this period were also engaged in a tenacious, often violent struggle to keep ladinos from interfering further in their lives. By its very nature, the role of community leaders in this struggle is somewhat shadowy, but perhaps some cases from Chamula in the early 1930s can illustrate its effect. Case 1: In 1931 or 1932, an *enganchador* rode into Chamula's backcountry with two *pistoleros* to collect a debt from a particularly stubborn coffee worker. According to a witness who was a boy at the time, the men of several hamlets, convoked by the *principales*, overwhelmed the interlopers, dismembered their bodies with machetes, and threw them down a sinkhole. "*Laj k'op,* end of problem."[5] Such cases occurred often enough during the 1930s to keep alive the ladino saying, "If nightfall catches you in Chamula, you can go to sleep . . . but you won't wake up again." (The same refrain also exists for Oxchuc, Cancuc, and Chalchihuitán, among others.)

Case 2: From the early nineteenth century on, Chamulas permitted no ladinos to live anywhere in their *municipio* except the small *cabecera,* or town center. In 1933, however, by command of the state government, a school was built in a hamlet away from the *cabecera,* in a "residential area." Within months a group of men burned it, and it was never rebuilt. No outsider, even a teacher, could be permitted to gain a toehold in that part of their territory the Chamulas considered their refuge from ladino exploitation.[6]

Case 3: In 1934 it was rumored that anti-Catholic "Quemasantos" from the state capital were coming to burn the saints' images in Chamula and other communities. Organized by their *principales* and *ayuntamiento,* the Chamulas hid their saints in houses scattered throughout the *municipio* and, in spite of the expense, maintained a small army that for months guarded the roads leading to the *cabecera.* Had the Quemasantos appeared, there is no doubt that the community would have fought them.[7]

All of these, again, were acts of resistance undertaken to defend the

5. Interview with Pascual López Calixto of Chamula, in Rus et al. (1986:5).

6. Interviews with Salvador Sánchez Diezmo, Dec. 31, 1976; López Calixto, July 2, 1975; and Gómez Osob, Sept. 7, 1975, all of Chamula.

7. Interviews with Sánchez Diezmo, Dec. 31, 1976; Castellanos Cancino, May 16, 1976; and Teodosio Martínez Ramos, parish priest of Chamula in 1934, Feb. 23, 1977. See also Aubry (1991:76).

community's "interior," to protect—not increase—its members' "traditional" prerogatives and resources in their home space. Given the violently repressive atmosphere of the highlands during the 1920s and early 1930s—the private armies that defended major *fincas*, the gunmen who worked as bodyguards for labor contractors, and the state police and army units that took their orders from local politicians—Indian leaders in Chamula and elsewhere were convinced they could not afford to confront ladinos beyond their communities, or struggle openly against the established order represented by the *secretarios municipales* and other authorities.

Even so, there were exceptions. In Zinacantán, for instance, community leaders from 1920 on included young men who had worked in the ladino world as sharecroppers and peddlers, and who thus knew of the new agrarian laws and were bold enough to try to use them. At their instigation, the Zinacanteco *ayuntamiento* began filing petitions for the expropriation of nearby ladino ranches as early as 1925, almost eight years before any of its neighbors (Wasserstrom 1983:172–74). Aggressive young leaders also were active in Chenalhó and Oxchuc, communities with substantial ladino populations, where the Indians' struggle for autonomy in the 1920s took the form of movements in favor of separate, native-language schools (Arias 1985:99–100; Gómez Nich 1976:179–81). Indeed, despite the prevailing conservatism, even in Chamula there were young, bilingual men during the 1920s and early 1930s who knew about the agrarian reform and tried—albeit unsuccessfully—to persuade the traditional leadership to try to use it to acquire more land (Rus forthcoming.) While none of these young reformers had much success during this period, and while ladino authorities often harassed and jailed those who persisted, their very existence demonstrates that behind the public caution of the native *ayuntamientos*, many Tzotzils and Tzeltals were ready for change.

THE "INDIANS' REVOLUTION," 1936–1944

Given the unbending conservatism of the highlands' ladino elite in the 1930s and the generally defensive character of native resistance, it was almost inevitable that when change finally did come to the region it would need a strong push from outside to get started. As it happened, that push was provided by the election of Lázaro Cárdenas as Mexico's president in 1934. Both before and immediately after his election, there was a struggle within the ruling Partido Nacional Revolucionario (PNR) between those who argued that Mexico had to make urgent economic and social reforms to keep from slipping back into social warfare, and others—revolutionary caudillos, and the propertied classes who had by now made peace with them—who were comfortable with the postrevolutionary status quo and resisted any attempt to change it. Cárdenas represented the reformist side of this debate. His project, briefly stated, was to mobilize peasants and workers around the country, incorporate them into a new ruling coalition, and then use the power derived from their organization to neutralize the conservatives and push through the necessary reforms.

In the case of Chiapas, where radical labor and peasant organizations had existed in the 1920s, only to be repressed or co-opted by the early 1930s by the conservative state branch of the PNR, the first part of this task involved reviving those organizations and binding them to the national, Cardenista wing of the party. Indeed, even before Cárdenas himself took office his supporters in the state announced that this would be their strategy. In a widely publicized federal labor commission report exposing the "virtual enslavement" of Chiapas's Indian workers, they argued that since the conservative state government had proven incapable of enforcing labor codes in Chiapas, the federal government should organize the native work force and take over that function itself (Urbina 1944:20ff.; Pozas Arciniega 1952:31–48).

Although stung by the criticism (see Guillén 1934), Chiapas's conservative governor and state PNR were not so easily eclipsed. In the fall of 1934, before the Cardenistas could act, the governor and his supporters attempted to forestall them by strengthening their own tame worker and peasant organizations, holding out to grassroots leaders the promise of state government patronage in return for political loyalty.[8] Eventually the contest for control came down to the 1936 gubernatorial election. On one side was the candidate of the state party, backed by Chiapas's landowning politicians and the labor and peasant organizations they had spawned; on the other the candidate of the national party, backed by Chiapas's federal employees, incipient Cardenista labor and peasant movements, and ultimately Cárdenas himself (T. Benjamin 1989:186ff.)

This was the context in which the Cardenistas first brought the

8. Interviews with Castellanos Cancino, 1975–76. Castellanos Cancino worked for the state PNR's labor-peasant organization before 1937, and for the Cardenistas after.

revolution to the highland Indians. Together, the Tzotzils and Tzeltals represented one-third of Chiapas's population in the 1930s. They also represented the bulk of the migratory work force that made possible the state's export agriculture. Despite their numbers and economic importance, however, no one had bothered to organize them politically. Clearly, if they could be mobilized and bound to the national PNR, they would become an important component of the peasant and labor coalition with which the party hoped to take over control of the state.

The man chosen to direct this mobilization, Erasto Urbina, had first come to prominence through his participation in the 1934 labor commission. An immigration officer, he had acted as the commission's guide and chief informant on its fact-finding trip through the coffee-producing region along the southern border with Guatemala (Urbina 1944:20ff.). His qualifications, however, went beyond that. For one thing, he spoke fluent Tzotzil and Tzeltal: "Not like a ladino, but like us," according to the Chamulas. Some accounts have it that he had learned the language as a child growing up in San Cristóbal, where he had accompanied his grandfather on commercial trips to the Indian communities of the surrounding mountains. According to others, his mother was herself a Chamula who had gone to the city to work as a maid. In any case, in addition to being an effective emissary to the Indians, Urbina was also extraordinarily sensitive to their exploitation. As a result, he was detached from the Immigration Service early in 1936 and put in charge of the Cardenistas' campaign in the Indian highlands.[9]

Before the 1936 election, the Indians' votes had always been cast in community blocs by their *secretarios municipales,* who in turn took their orders from the chief of whatever political faction was most powerful in the surrounding region; typically, again, the *secretarios* owed their jobs to such chiefs. What Urbina did during the spring of 1936 was to recruit bilingual backwoods ladinos he had known in his youth—many of them described today as *pistoleros*—to join him on an "election committee" to visit all the highlands communities, "announcing" the candidacy of the national PNR's candidate for governor, Efraín Gutiérrez. Given, on the one hand, Urbina's federal credentials and the public's general uncertainty of just how much power he actually had, and on the other the rough nature of his companions, it is not surprising that none of the local officials with whom he dealt seem to have disputed his orders on how to

9. Interviews with Carlota Zepeda, widow of Erasto Urbina, Sept. 10 and 26, 1975, Dec. 6, 1976.

vote. During the primary election in April and again in the final election in July, the members of Urbina's "committee," now commissioned as "federal election inspectors," returned to the various native *municipios* in pairs, heavily armed, to oversee the *secretarios'* collection of the vote. When the results were tallied, Gutiérrez, on the basis of this highland vote, had won a resounding triumph. He took office as governor on December 1, 1936. Erasto Urbina was named director of the state Departamento de Protección Indígena (DPI) and became Gutiérrez's proconsul in the highlands.[10]

Urbina moved quickly that December and January to replace all the *secretarios municipales* with members of his "election committee." At the same time, in mid-December, he also started the legal procedures to organize a union, the Sindicato de Trabajadores Indígenas (STI), which would enroll all the region's migrant coffee workers (Urbina 1944:20ff.). The national PNR had only won an election in 1936; now it had to win the Indians' loyalty and cement the new alliance.[11]

Even before he officially took office, Urbina had realized that he would not be able to work effectively through the traditional old men who controlled the native *ayuntamientos*. Nor did he choose to work with the bilingual go-betweens, the *escribanos*, or "scribes," who had translated for the previous *secretarios municipales*. In Chamula as elsewhere, these were mature men who had made a career of working for ladinos, and Urbina undoubtedly considered them both compromised and unlikely to accept his direction. During the ten months from August 1936 through June 1937, therefore, he sought out bilingual and, when possible, literate young men in all the *municipios* under his jurisdiction and had them appointed as *escribanos* to their communities' *ayuntamientos*. Groups of these young men traveled with him when he visited their communities, acted as translators in the offices of the DPI in San Cristóbal, and worked closely

10. Interviews with Francisco Porras, Oct. 24, 1975; Francisco Liévano, Oct. 28, Nov. 13, 1975, Jan. 14, 1976; Celso Villafuerte, Nov. 6, 1975; and Clemente Pérez, Feb. 3, 1976, all members of Urbina's 1936 "election committee" and later *agentes montados de protección indígena*. The DPI's complete name was the Departamento de Acción Social, Cultura y Protección Indígena. See also T. Benjamin (1989:193–94).

11. Interviews with Porras, Liévano, Villafuerte, and Pérez. Pozas (1944:175–76) argues that the STI was actually formed and the process of hiring workers was taken under government control because the *enganchadores*, by simultaneously cheating the *finqueros* and embittering the workers, were ruining the coffee business in Chiapas. While this might be true, it seems by itself an insufficient explanation for the reformist policies of the late 1930s.

with the new *secretarios* to bring to heel those ladinos who had businesses in the Indian hinterland by organizing boycotts of stores, threatening labor contractors considered to be exploitative, and driving out ladino alcohol merchants.[12]

Meanwhile, Urbina and his assistants were also at work on other fronts to prove to the Indians that the new government not only had their best interests at heart but would act quickly and decisively to further them. Within weeks of taking office, for instance, on February 13, 1937, Urbina and some of the more intimidating members of his election committee, now engaged as *agentes montados* of the DPI, invaded and turned over to an accompanying group of Chamulas the first of many highland *fincas* they would expropriate during the next two-and-a-half years.[13] Apparently judging the procedures of the agrarian reform to be too slow—they had, after all, never worked in the highlands—and there being in any case some doubt about whether many of the region's *fincas* were even liable to expropriation, Urbina and company simply seized the properties in question and left it for someone else to sort out the niceties of legal procedure and indemnification (Urbina 1944:56–58).

At the same time that he was gaining stature with the Indians by acquiring land for them, Urbina was also moving rapidly to organize them as laborers and attach them firmly to the government. During the summer of 1937, the various Indian *ayuntamientos* "elected" STI delegates, all of them chosen from among the young scribes Urbina had attached to the *ayuntamientos* just a few months earlier. When these delegates in turn elected the union's first officers, five proved to be Chamulas, the eldest, the *secretario general*, only 22 years of age.[14] Finally, on August 9, 1937— just before hiring began for the fall coffee harvest—the STI began its first

12. Interviews with López Tuxum, Oct. 5, 1975; and Gómez Osob, July 9, 1975. According to Gómez Osob, during the most critical months of 1937 Urbina had the most important young scribes sleep in his house because their lives were in danger. See also interviews with Porras and Liévano.

13. As one of the expropriated landowners wrote: "El 13 de febrero de 1937, el Sr. Erasto Urbina . . . llegó a mi rancho San Antonio Las Rosas . . . con un grupo de individuos armados, y sin tramitación legal, ni pedimento alguno de tierras, estando mi mencionado rancho ocupado totalmente con ganado vacuno y caballar, lo entregó en unos cuantos minutos a un grupo de Chamulas, so pretexto de ser terrenos ociosos. . . ." Alberto Rojas to President Cárdenas, transcribed in expediente of the *ejido* Las Ollas, Municipio de Chamula, SRA.Tuxtla.

14. Sindicato de Trabajadores Indígenas, *Libro de Actas*, 1937–1946, photocopy in the author's possession; see also interviews with Zepeda.

massive inscription of workers in San Cristóbal. By the end of the year almost twenty-five thousand Indian workers were enrolled, and it was illegal to hire coffee pickers who did not have a union card (Urbina 1944:37–43).

While the Indians' labor conditions saw immediate improvements as a result of the STI—no more confinement while awaiting departure to the *fincas*, no more abuses of debt; no more *tiendas de raya*; uniform, documented wage advances—perhaps the union's main impact was to place the government between the coffee planters and their labor supply (Pozas 1944:177–78; Urbina 1944:43–46). Although the *enganchadores* resisted for a time—some of them apparently even joined an attempt to have Urbina assassinated in June 1938—this mediation was eventually accepted, and the government settled down to the task of assuring the coffee zone a steady flow of workers.

Under the new system, the plantations and their contracting agents were relieved of the tasks of recruiting laborers and disciplining those who ran away. Instead, these became the responsibility of the STI's own young officers. Acting through their municipal *ayuntamientos*, they now used the native police to round up more workers when they were needed to fill monthly hiring quotas, and applied traditional sanctions—including time in community jails—to those who left their *fincas* before fulfilling their contracts.[15] Meanwhile, the STI never called a single strike, nor do any of the surviving Indian officers recall ever having participated in the bargaining sessions between *finqueros* and state government officials. In the words of one, "Don Erasto called us [the young STI officers] his soldiers, and we did as we were told." In return for a substantial improvement in working conditions, then, the state—that is, Urbina—not only penetrated the Indians' internal community governments, but enlisted them in the task of subordinating the state's landowners and planters to the national government and party.[16]

The final element of the new regime's assertion of control in the Indian *municipios* came at the end of 1938, when the DPI announced that beginning with the new *ayuntamientos* taking office on January 1, 1939, it would deal only with municipal presidents who were bilingual. While some communities—Zinacantán, for one—apparently accepted this decision without protest, in others—particularly Chamula—it provoked a crisis. There, as elsewhere, the traditional elders had until this point been

15. Interviews with Porras; and with Liévano, Oct. 28, 1975.
16. Interview with López Tuxum, Oct. 5, 1975.

willing to compromise their power as the price of Urbina's reforms. But now, with no proof the reforms would continue, he was asking them to surrender power. Aroused by one of the old scribes deposed by Urbina in 1937, Chamula's leaders for a number of weeks seemed prepared to defy the edict, and several other communities looked ready to follow their example. In December 1938, however, the former scribe leading the protest was mysteriously murdered, and soon thereafter the DPI and Chamula's *ayuntamiento* reached a compromise that became a model for the rest of the highlands. For the time being, Chamula would have two municipal presidents: one a monolingual old man who had come up through the traditional cargo system, the other a young *escribano del presidente*, who would be considered only an aide to the president in Chamula but would represent the community as its *presidente municipal* in dealings with the government.[17]

Thus, after decades of organizing their communities in such a way that they would serve as a defense against exploitation by outsiders, between 1936 and 1940 the Tzotzils and Tzeltals suddenly found the very structures of those communities being commandeered by the state and party—outsiders—as part of what was proclaimed their common struggle against exploitation. Moreover, the scribes who had facilitated this transformation had begun to acquire powers far beyond those of traditional native leaders. By 1940, they were no longer simply *escribanos* subordinated to the traditional *ayuntamientos* but had also become labor union officers, heads of their municipal agrarian committees, leaders of local branches of the official party (known after 1937 as the Partido Revolucionario Mexicano, PRM), and representatives to the regional committee of the Confederación Nacional Campesina (CNC).

Some communities assimilated these changes with relative ease. In Zinacantán, for instance, the scribes who had worked with Urbina since 1937 were not as young as those in other *municipios*. Rather, they were experienced leaders who had participated in the community's struggle to obtain land from the agrarian reform since the 1920s. As a result, their new powers were viewed as simply an extension of functions they had already served for many years, and resentment was apparently minimal

17. Interviews with Gómez Osob, July 9, 1975; López Tuxum, Oct. 5, 29, 30, 1975; and Castellanos Cancino, Aug. 8, 1975, June 5, 1976. In his contemporaneous description of these events, Pozas (1944:319ff.), while supportive of Urbina's efforts to improve the treatment of Indian workers, expresses reservations about his political intervention. See also Pozas Arciniega (1977:2:10ff.).

(Edel 1966; Wasserstrom 1983:173ff.). In Chenalhó, by comparison, the principal scribe who worked with Urbina was also an older man, but unlike the leaders of Zinacantán, he had been suspicious of the government's sudden eagerness to help his community and had at first resisted Urbina's request to become a collaborator. For his caution Urbina had him jailed until he agreed to cooperate (Arias 1985:91–106). Eventually, however, this man's insistence on working through his community's traditional leadership structure, and his own withdrawal from "Erasto's service" as soon as he was able in 1940, meant that the DPI-PRM penetration of Chenalhó was never as complete as it was in other places.[18]

Despite these counterexamples, however, in most of the highlands the new leaders represented by "los muchachos de Erasto" were still perceived in 1940 as somehow not quite legitimate, as having been grafted onto the community's "real" leadership by government fiat. This was certainly the case in Chamula, where the bilingual presidents insisted on by the DPI continued to share office with the "traditional" presidents from 1940 through 1942. Similar arrangements were also worked out in, among other places, Tenejapa (Medina 1991:173–74, 186–87), Cancuc (Guiteras Holmes 1992:77ff.; Siverts 1965:339–60), Oxchuc (Siverts 1969:174ff.), and perhaps Mitontic, in all of which experienced elders were grateful for the reforms introduced by Cardenismo but jealous of their control of their own communities.[19]

At this point, with the Cardenista reorganization of highlands threatening to stall, a simultaneous change occurred in the internal governments of most of the highlands communities that suggests a guiding hand, although there is no direct evidence of its existence. In late 1942, the *escribano-presidente* chosen to serve Chamula for 1943 volunteered to serve an important—and costly—religious *cargo*, or office, in 1944, as soon as he finished his presidency. One of the complaints of the traditional elders had been that the "new" Indian politicians had not served an apprenticeship in lower-ranking civil and religious positions—positions that, because of the time and expense involved, could usually be filled only by jailing the men chosen until they agreed to accept. By volunteering, this young man, Salvador López Tuxum (incidentally, the first *secretario general* of the STI), signaled both his acceptance of the traditional route to

18. Interviews with Vicente Vázquez, June 4, 1987, and Eulogio Ruíz, June 2, 1987, both of the *municipio* of Chenalhó.

19. For Mitontic, interview with Mariano Gómez López and Marcelina Rodríguez López, Aug. 12, 1975.

becoming an elder and his desire to legitimate the unusually high political rank he had already achieved. But there was more. The sale of liquor had been illegal in Indian *municipios* since June 1937. During the same week that López Tuxum volunteered for religious office, the DPI quietly announced that it would permit liquor to be sold by current and *prospective* religious officials in Indian communities, both out of respect for its ritual meaning and to help defray the costs of office.[20]

Within a matter of months, so many new volunteers had applied for religious service that waiting lists were instituted in communities throughout the highlands. Prominent on all of them were the young men who had first come to power through their ties to Erasto Urbina. In Chamula, both López Tuxum's gesture in asking for a cargo and his association with the newly authorized sale of alcohol, which promised to become a lucrative business, reconciled the traditional elders to him and his cohort. On January 1, 1943, he assumed office as Chamula's sole *presidente municipal* (Rus and Wasserstrom 1980:472–75). The process of penetrating the Indian communities' defenses and binding them—willingly—to the reformist state and its party was complete.[21]

REACTION, 1944–1951

Although Erasto Urbina remained in Chiapas until 1944, after 1940 he was no longer involved in the day-to-day business of the DPI. From 1940 to 1942 he was the *diputado local* of the central highlands in the state legislature, and during 1943 and 1944 he was San Cristóbal's municipal president. Meanwhile, with the end of Cárdenas's term in 1940, the pace of change in Mexico and Chiapas slowed drastically. After 1940, agrarian reform essentially stopped. In the immediate vicinity of San Cristóbal it

20. Interview with López Tuxum, Nov. 7, 1976. This, incidentally, resumed an older tradition in which religious *mayordomos* were the only ones permitted to sell alcohol in Chamula; this was reported by the parish priest as long ago as 1855. See Inda (1986:59).

21. In the case of the *colonia* of Los Chorros in the *municipio* of Chenalhó, the surviving scribe-*principal* from the late 1930s said that when Urbina was preparing to leave office in the early 1940s, he explicitly instructed the people of the *colonia* to buy a saint and start a *mayordomía* as a way of legitimizing their local officials and strengthening the community. This is one of the clearest cases of Erasto's—and the state's—attempts to use native religion for political ends. Interview with Vázquez, June 4, 1987.

was not until the 1970s that new lands were added to those expropriated and returned to the Indians by Urbina before 1940. Similarly, whatever pretensions the STI had ever had of preparing the Indians to run their own autonomous labor movement evaporated after 1940 as the union settled into the more mundane task of assuring the flow of native workers to the lowlands.[22] Nevertheless, it did continue to inspect plantations and provide at least a minimal level of protection against abuse. Following Mexico's declaration of war on the Axis powers in mid-1942, however, even that level of defense of Indian interests disappeared as German coffee holdings—more than two-thirds of Chiapas's major plantations—were seized and placed in the hands of a state trust (T. Benjamin 1989:209, 214). Since the government itself now managed the *fincas*, it was decided that an "adversarial" syndicate was no longer needed, and the STI was reduced to nothing more than recruiting workers.[23]

Despite government policies that tended more and more to run counter to their interests after 1940, the Tzotzils and Tzeltals remained solidly in the official party's camp during every election, state and federal, from 1936 on. On election days, the appropriate number of ballots was delivered to their *ayuntamientos*, and their scribes handed them back, all appropriately marked, when the election officials returned in the evening. By the time the PRM became the PRI (Partido Revolucionario Institucional) in the mid-forties, the former self-defensive, closed communities of the Chiapas highlands had become integral parts of the party's local machine.

What makes this faithfulness particularly remarkable is that after 1944 the ruling party's politics became even more conservative; in Chiapas, becoming frankly hostile to Indians after 1946. In that year a new governor took office, and Alberto Rojas became his director of the Departamento de Protección Indígena. Rojas was an *enganchador* who was an enemy of Erasto Urbina, not only on that account but also because the first highland property Urbina had invaded in 1937 had been his. Within months of assuming power, he disbanded the STI, bringing its functions of registering migrants' wage advances and monitoring working condi-

22. Interviews with Castellanos Cancino, Sept. 6, 1975; and Zepeda, Sept. 26, 1976.

23. According to the STI's *Libro de Actas*, the union's board of directors met every month from 1937 through 1941 and certified every contract for workers on the coastal plantations during that period; from 1943 through 1946 it met only once a year and certified no contracts.

tions directly into his own office at the DPI. No Indian any longer had a role in this process, even as an employee; it was now a paper formality handled by the *enganchadores* themselves. Rojas also tried to undo the land expropriations of the late 1930s, albeit without success. Finally, in late 1946, he withdrew funding from the native schools that were Erasto Urbina's last official accomplishment, even refusing to pay the Indian teachers their last three months' salary.[24]

Nor was Rojas's DPI the only institution to attempt to put the Indians "back in their place" during this period. In 1946, San Cristóbal's first conservative municipal government in almost ten years tried, with the governor's blessing, to levy transit duties and market taxes on Indians bringing goods to the city's market or just traveling through. And then, in 1949, the state government once again changed its laws regarding the production and sale of alcohol to Indians. Permission for native religious officials to sell liquor was withdrawn, and instead a state monopoly was established. Henceforth, any alcohol not purchased from an official *expendio* (identified by a tax stamp on the bottle) was to be seized and its possessor jailed. This touched off a virtual war, "La Guerra del Posh" (*posh* is Tzotzil for liquor), with the two holders of the monopoly, Gustavo Morales and Hernán Pedrero, on one side and the state's numerous small-scale producers and their mostly Indian customers on the other. Between 1949 and 1954, bands of *fiscales*, commissioned by the state government (Pedrero, conveniently enough, was also secretary of finance) but paid by Morales and Pedrero, roamed the Indian *municipios* ransacking religious officials' homes, seizing alcohol at fiestas, and stopping people on isolated trails to unpack and inspect their cargo.[25]

24. About the STI: the last date in its *Libro de Actas* is Dec. 30, 1946. Rojas did not permit its charter to be renewed for the next two-year period (interview with Castellanos Cancino, Feb. 21, 1976). About land reform: Beginning in 1946 and continuing through 1947, there are numerous letters in the Chamula files of SRA, Tuxtla in which Rojas, as "Jefe del Dpto.," certifies that on closer questioning, the people of this or that *ejido* have decided they no longer need more land. For example, regarding the Chamula *ejido* of Romerillo, Apr. 10, 1947: ". . . los colonos . . . categóricamente declaran que . . . no se están interesando por adquirir nuevas tierras." It is interesting that all the literate scribes have disappeared by this point, and the documents filed by Rojas bear only thumbprints whose authenticity he testifies to himself. About the schools (*centros de castellanización*): interview with Castellanos Cancino, Nov. 16, 1975.

25. Interviews with Castellanos Cancino, Aug. 8, Sept. 6, 1975, Jan. 17, 1976; Ricardo Pozas, Dec. 4, 1975; Manuel Ballinas, Jan. 20, 1976; Pablo Ramírez Suárez,

What is ultimately most interesting about this period of renewed oppression, however, is not the oppression itself but the Indians' reaction to it. Despite everything, year after year they continued to furnish their votes to the candidates designated by the PRI, to send delegations when national PRI campaigns came to Chiapas, and to participate in the CNC and other official organizations. They also continued to elect Urbina's former scribes to their municipal presidencies and to cooperate at least formally with the DPI. They did not, in other words, withdraw into themselves as they had during and after the revolution of the 1910s; nor did they break their ties to the state and official party.

What they did do, however, was resist the offending policies when and how they could. Their leaders in this resistance were the same former scribes who simultaneously served as their link to the government that was promulgating those policies. In the case of the market and transit taxes of 1946, for instance, the Chamula scribes, with the cooperation of their colleagues from Zinacantán, San Andrés, Mitontic, and Chenalhó, organized a blockade of the roads leading to San Cristóbal and enforced a boycott of the city's market. After a week in which no food entered the city from the Indian communities and at least one tense confrontation with San Cristóbal's municipal police at the blockade point (the border between San Cristóbal and Chamula), the Indians won, and the new taxes were lifted. For the first time since perhaps the 1860s, the Tzotzils themselves had organized an act of collective resistance across community boundaries, and the young bilingual "elders" gained immensely in stature when it succeeded.[26]

More important for the future course of politics within native communities, however, was the reaction to the "Posh War." Once again the former scribes took the lead in organizing their communities' opposition. Unlike the tax fight, however, this time a great deal of money was involved on both sides of the dispute, and the adversary—the *policía fiscal*—was armed and unlikely to give up easily. (Ironically, the core of the fiscal police were former members of Urbina's *agentes montados*, some of

Oct. 14, 1976; and López Tuxum, Nov. 7, 1976. See also published interviews with Maruch Gómez Monte, in Rus et al. (1986:14–15); and with Salvador Pérez Díaz, in Rus and Guzmán (1990:10–11).

26. Interview with Castellanos Cancino, Jan. 30, 1976. There is no evidence that former indigenistas—many of whom were still in the region from 1947 to 1951, although all were out of government service—helped organize this resistance. As for Urbina, he was away from Chiapas between 1944 and 1950, serving a series of PRI appointments in Guanajuato and Baja California.

whom had been around since the "election committee" of 1936. Presumably, their intimate knowledge of the Indian leaders and territory was one of the factors that recommended them to Morales and Pedrero.) To make the resistance work, then, the scribes not only had to regulate the production and distribution of clandestine liquor in the face of armed ladino patrols, but also had to maintain discipline over a widely dispersed peasant population such that no one would inform the *fiscales* of where the alcohol was hidden (the state government offered rewards for such information).

In Chamula, as elsewhere, this discipline was accomplished by defining the defense of *posh* as a religious matter to be dealt with through religious sanctions. As a result, numerous accounts tell of informers being executed as witches and traitors by their neighbors, with the knowledge of the native *ayuntamientos*, between 1949 and the mid-1950s. It was a bloody strategy, but it worked: while the *fiscales* could raid Chamula and other communities, they rarely caught more than an unfortunate drunk with an unstamped bottle.[27] Meanwhile, the former scribes had for the first time appropriated traditional religious categories and sanctions to further a project that benefited primarily themselves and a small group of powerful allies. By the war's end, they had both won new esteem from the older, traditional *principales* and strengthened their own grip on the levers of power in their communities.

Ironically, then, the result of the conservatives' attempts during the late 1940s to pare back the gains Indians had made in the preceding decade was to produce an Indian leadership ever less dependent on the government for its position. No longer able to count on agrarian reform or the prosecution of labor abuses to justify their authority, the former scribes instead began shoring up their status as traditional community leaders, including, increasingly, spearheading resistance to the government and the state. Although formally and publicly the scribe-*principales* may have continued to defer to the state government, by the end of the 1940s they actually derived more power from their covert opposition to it.

THE "COMUNIDAD REVOLUCIONARIA INSTITUCIONAL," 1951–1968

This estrangement between Chiapas's state government and the native communities of the highlands continued well into the 1950s. At least at

27. Interviews with Castellanos Cancino, Jan. 17, 1976; and Ballinas, May 24,

first, however, until perhaps 1952, it appears to have been of little concern to the conservatives who dominated Chiapas's politics. In the wake of World War II, commodity prices were low, with the result that the state's agricultural production also declined to its lowest levels since the 1920s (T. Benjamin 1989:209, 214–29; Vivó 1959:37). Accordingly, the demand for highland laborers during the second half of the 1940s was also low. From the perspective of the ladino elite, there was thus little incentive to maintain good relations with the native communities, much less worry about their welfare. This panorama of economic decline and ethnic alienation began to change only with the introduction of new factors from outside the state at the beginning of the 1950s.

The first and perhaps most important of these was a sharp rise in world commodity prices at the very end of the 1940s. In Chiapas, as in the rest of Mexico, this produced a boom in commercial agriculture that lasted for the next two-and-a-half decades. Locally, the first effects were felt in the coffee industry of Soconusco, where production finally returned to its prewar levels in 1950–51 and continued to rise every year thereafter. Almost simultaneously, rising prices also led to increases in the amount of land under cultivation in the interior lowlands, particularly the Grijalva basin but also the Ocosingo and Simojovel valleys and eventually the Lacandón jungle. As a result, by 1960 Chiapas was not only Mexico's largest producer of coffee, but had also become the leading source of corn and beans for the national market and one of the top three suppliers of sugar, rice, cacao, tropical fruits, and cotton. In addition, as more and more of the land cleared for crops was left fallow in the form of pastures, the state also doubled its production of beef (T. Benjamin 1989:223–24; Castillo Burguete 1988:70–74).

If in the first instance this agricultural boom was a result of the rapid growth of world markets, it also owed much to government policies that, right from the beginning of the 1950s, encouraged large landowners to increase production to take advantage of those markets. Thus the expansion of Chiapas's road network, begun in the early 1940s but vastly accelerated during the 1950s, opened formerly isolated lowland *fincas* to new forms of exploitation. Meanwhile, the government also issued "certificates of inaffectability" to reassure the owners of those *fincas* that they would be safe from agrarian reform, and provided them with easy credit, crop insurance, and eventually guaranteed prices to ensure the financial

1975, Jan. 20, 1976. See also Guerrero Tapia (1979: chap. 5, "La negra leyenda del alcoholismo").

resources that would make their enterprises profitable (T. Benjamin 1989:223–24; Wasserstrom 1976; 1983:178ff.). The only element lacking to assure their success was a steady supply of cheap, willing labor. And so, in the early 1950s, the government also took a hand in redirecting part of the stream of Tzotzil and Tzeltal migrant laborers away from the coffee plantations of Soconusco and the small-scale ladino farms of the central highlands toward the new commercial agriculture of the interior lowlands.

It did this in two ways. First, in 1951, the state and federal governments began constructing roads that connected the newly opened regions of the lowlands directly to the native *municipios* of the central highlands. By itself this measure was almost sufficient: the Indians' own need to work guaranteed that they would find their way to the opportunities at the roads' other end (Wasserstrom 1983:178ff.; Vogt 1969:29–30). To encourage the highlanders further to change their destination, however, in 1954 the Immigration Service, at the behest of state politicians, began quietly permitting undocumented Guatemalans to cross the border to work on the coffee plantations of the Soconusco. Ostensibly, this was done only to replace Tzotzils and Tzeltals who had already begun to shift to the interior lowlands. In reality, it had the effect of pressuring even more of Chiapas's own Maya to abandon the coast for the interior because they could not compete with Guatemalans for the low wages the latter would accept.[28]

Under these circumstances, the trickle of Indians from the central highlands who had always worked in the nearby lowlands soon became a torrent. From the beginning of the 1950s, men from the southern end of the region—particularly Zinancantecos (Wasserstrom 1983:180ff.; Cancian 1972:110ff.) but also Chamulas—followed the new roads into the Grijalva basin, where they cleared brush and then sharecropped corn for

28. Interview with Castellanos Cancino, Aug. 8, 1975; Rus, "Chamula work history interviews," unpublished interview notes, 1975–76; Robert Wasserstrom, interview with the director of the Asociación de Cafetaleros, Tapachula, Feb. 15, 1976 (personal communication). According to the director, the first agreement (*convenio*) between the Asociación de Cafetaleros and the Departamento de Migración actually dates from 1952. However, it was not until 1954 that significant numbers of Guatemalans began replacing Tzotzils and Tzeltals in the Soconusco. Not coincidentally, this chronology corresponds to the rebirth of the Sindicato de Trabajadores Indígenas (1952) and its first impact on hiring in the central highlands (for the harvest of 1953–54), discussed in the text. See also Reveles (1974).

three or four years before returning the now improved lands to their ladino owners and moving on.[29] By the mid-1950s, workers from more northerly communities—among them Oxchuc, Altamirano, Yajalón, and Bachajón—were repeating this pattern in the region of Ocosingo, while others from the west—San Andrés and Plátanos—were copying it, with variations, in the region between Bochil and Simojovel. Meanwhile, highland Indians were also beginning to clear lands and prepare the way for ladino ranchers and commodity merchants along the roads just then penetrating the Lacandón jungle: people from Oxchuc, Bachajón, and Yajalón in the western jungle neighboring their homelands beginning in the mid-1950s (Esponda 1986:255ff.); and from Chamula, Huistán, Tenejapa, and San Andrés in the more distant eastern jungle by the early 1960s (Calvo et al. 1989).[30]

Not all those who joined this new migration to the interior lowlands, it should be noted, were sharecroppers or jungle colonists. Although precise percentages are necessarily hard to come by, the large majority from most of the highland communities were more likely to be wage laborers, *jornaleros*, working either for ladino landowners or for their own more enterprising compatriots who were renting on shares or colonizing. Still others continued to work as contract plantation laborers, although by the 1960s these, too, tended to find positions on the coffee, cane, and corn plantations adjacent to the central highlands rather than on the coffee *fincas* of the coast. In any case, with the development of the interior lowlands, the focus of highland labor had definitively changed.[31]

The final "outside" factor that changed the relationship of Chiapas's highland Maya to the state was the choice, in 1951, of San Cristóbal as the site of the Instituto Nacional Indigenista's first regional development program, the Centro Coordinador Tzeltal-Tzotzil. Founded as an experiment in gradualist, nonradical development—the only kind acceptable to the national administrations that followed Cárdenas—the Centro Coordinador offered the Indians not a continuation of the radical economic reforms of the Cárdenas period but schools, health care, and, through its legal department, some protection against the more outrageous forms of local exploitation. (These included being forced to clean the city streets as

29. Rus, "Chamula work history interviews."

30. Idem., "Kipaltik interviews"; interview with Castellanos Cancino, Aug. 8, 1975.

31. Idem., "Chamula work history interviews." A testimony illustrating the shift to the *fincas* of the interior is found in Rus et al. (1986:24–26).

a punishment for being out after dark, or being compelled to use ladino-controlled markets in *municipios* with ladino populations, because ladino police broke up the Indian ones.) (See Aguirre Beltrán et al. [1976].) These were moderate benefits, to be sure; but in 1951, after almost six years with no Indian policy at all—six years in which the government had actually been decidedly anti-Indian—they were not inconsiderable ones.

From the first, INI worked with Erasto Urbina's former scribes. From its perspective—that of reform-minded social scientists from Mexico City—the scribes were popular, progressive leaders, and by entering the highland communities through them, INI hoped its programs would find immediate acceptance. In the nine *municipios* closest to San Cristóbal, INI hired and trained forty-six former scribes as bilingual teachers during the winter of 1951–52, and by the fall of 1952 had installed each in a new primary school in his home community.[32] In most *municipios*, INI also opened health clinics, each staffed by one or two former scribes as *oficiales sanitarios*, and started cooperative stores, also manned by former scribes, as an alternative to the overpriced rural stores owned by ladinos (Aguirre Beltrán et al. 1976:113–46, 185–263).

Not surprisingly, the Centro Coordinador was not well received, at least at first, by Chiapas's local politicians.[33] Not only did it threaten their capacity to control the Indians themselves without federal interference— a capacity they were perhaps overestimating—but its personnel con-sisted largely of former Cardenistas who were once again expected to "stir the Indians up" against *finqueros*, labor contractors, and ladino politicians. Their worst fears seemed to be confirmed in 1952 when INI revived the Sindicato de Trabajadores Indígenas—a measure the state government tried mightily to stop. On the other hand, the state government con-tinued to prosecute the "Posh War," over INI objections, until the summer of 1954; and the governor and his supporters were able to prevent INI from taking a role in the legal administration of the Indian *municipios* until the end of 1953. (This meant that during INI's first two years the *secretarios municipales* acted as a virtual opposition in many *municipios*.)

Finally, however, by the fall of 1953, it must have become clear to

32. Kenneth Weathers (1952), "Informe: Promotores del Centro Coordinador," unpublished report to the director of the Centro Coordinador.

33. Indeed, according to Aguirre Beltrán (1988:17–18), in 1951 the governor of Chiapas actually threatened to close the Centro Coordinador and expel Beltrán, Erasto Urbina, and Manuel Castellanos Cancino from the state for obstructing enforcement of the *aguardiente* monopoly.

Chiapas's ladino leaders that there was no longer anything to be gained by continuing to resist INI. On the one hand, they once again needed a direct connection to the Indian labor on which the state depended for its prosperity—a connection they had lost when they dismantled the institutions of the Cárdenas reforms. On the other hand, INI's swift acceptance in the native communities and the federal government's evident commitment to a long-term policy of improving the Indians' conditions must have convinced the politicians that if they did not move quickly to reassert their authority over Indian affairs, they might soon lose it altogether.

Thus a compromise was reached between the state and federal governments, the local conservatives, and INI's indigenistas. In return for a voice in the legal and political administration of the Indian *municipios*, INI reoriented its projects along capitalist lines more congenial to Chiapas's elite (and, it must be said, more in keeping with larger national policies of the time that favored the development of private enterprise in general). Cooperative stores that had been managed for INI by former scribes were now turned over to their managers and became private businesses; trucks that had at first been entrusted to community cooperatives were increasingly owned individually by former scribes and their families; and agricultural and other demonstration projects that had originally been conducted on community land were now relocated to private holdings, particularly those of the former scribes.[34] In the abstract, these changes were supposed to hasten the accumulation of capital in the Indian communities and the assimilation of these communities to the national economy and society. In concrete terms, what they favored was the partnership of wealthy ladinos and a privileged Indian elite.

Finally, to complete the circle, a liaison office was established between INI and the state office of Indian affairs, now renamed the Departamento General de Asuntos Indígenas (DGAI). When the "Posh War" officially ended, in mid-1954 (through face-saving measures negotiated by the first liaison officer, Manuel Castellanos Cancino), many of the erstwhile *fiscales* returned to work in "la causa indigenista," some as *secretarios municipales* under the DGAI, others as employees of INI itself. Since the liaison officer was also the PRI delegate to the native *municipios*, he and the DGAI's network of new *secretarios municipales* not only coordinated elections, but made it their business to guarantee that INI projects were

34. Interviews with Pozas; Castellanos Cancino; and Pérez. See also Pozas's published account of this shift (1976).

channeled to politically reliable supporters. Government policy in the highlands was again unified, as it had been under Erasto Urbina.[35]

Meanwhile, behind the scenes, there was another side to this reconciliation between Chiapas's elite and the federal bureaucracy, between the DGAI and INI. According to one of Chamula's scribe-*principales*, soon after the Centro Coordinador was founded, certainly by 1952, the alcohol monopolists Pedrero and Morales had discreetly arranged a truce with the leading former scribes in each of the *municipios* involved in the "Posh War." The monopolists would halt raids on the scribes' communities; in exchange, the communities would make regular payments—bribes—to the monopolists' agents in San Cristóbal.[36] (Of course, the scribe-*principales* on one side, and the *fiscales* on the other, all having worked for Erasto Urbina, were well known to each other.) In Chamula and other communities, then, these payments were collected—and a commission for collecting them received—by the same former scribes who, during the preceding five or six years, had been consolidating control over their communities' traditional sanctions and boundaries precisely in battles like that *against* the *posh* raids. By 1951–52, in other words, Chiapas's ladino elite—the same elite that had perpetrated the conservative reaction of the preceding six years—had already recognized the emergence of a cadre of native leaders with whom it could do business. Such leaders were capable of controlling their communities as *principales* through "tradition," on the one hand, and of negotiating "reasonably," from a position of familiarity, with ladino officials, landowners, and merchants on the other. Thus, when these ladino political and economic bosses finally arrived at their accord with INI in 1953, they had already been dealing secretly with the native leaders who were also INI's closest collaborators for a couple of years. In a sense, the rapprochement between INI and the DGAI simply aligned public institutions with the political and economic reality that already existed. The only innovation, and it was a significant one, was that INI, by turning over to the scribe-*principales* as private citizens projects they had originally managed as INI employees, in effect subordinated itself to the ladino elite's decision to control the native communities through a hand-

35. Interviews with Liévano, Oct. 28 and Nov. 13, 1975, Jan. 14, 1976.

36. Rus, interviews with scribe-*principales* and ladino merchants and indigenistas, 1975–76. Some ladino residents of Tzotzil and Tzeltal *pueblos* alleged that following his accord with the scribe-*principales*, Hernán Pedrero himself undertook to provide the Indians with the materials for their "clandestine" stills. Interview with M. E. of Bachajón, July 31, 1990.

ful of favored leaders. Participation in INI projects now became a way of reinforcing that political alliance, a kind of reward dispensed to the chosen native elite; a federally financed payoff.[37]

After 1953, the state—meaning both the apparatus of government and the economic and political elite whose interests it served—settled into a pattern of depending more and more openly on its handful of favored scribe-*principales* to make the Indian communities do as it wished. INI, the "public face" of Indian policy, having treated the former scribes as simply a convenient entrée to the native communities in 1951, now came to depend on them to impose projects that might otherwise have taken years to put across. In 1958–59, for example, INI compelled those scribe-*principales* who were also bilingual teachers to use their traditional offices and powers—at the risk of losing their jobs—to force parents to send girls to school. Perhaps because Indians themselves were judged to be the ultimate beneficiaries of this policy, it has been carefully recorded.[38] Meanwhile, however, out of public view, INI regularly exploited the scribe-*principales*' authority to advance projects whose benefits were not primarily for Indians. As early as 1951, for instance, it had called on the scribe-*principales* of Chamula to silence the owners of cornfields who objected to having roads to other *municipios* built across their land. Later, following the reconciliation of INI and the DGAI in 1953, one of their first joint acts was to use their ties to the scribe-*principales* to persuade communities to accept the construction of a series of communication towers atop their sacred mountains. And finally, in the early 1970s, the same institutions used the same means to force community members in Chamula and elsewhere to allow PEMEX, the national oil company, to drill on their

37. Interviews with Pérez; and with Pozas, Dec. 4, 1975. Pérez was INI's instructor in storekeeping, Pozas the director of the Centro Coordinador in 1953 when the stores were still cooperatives. In addition to controlling stores and agricultural projects, the scribe-*principales* in Chamula had also begun limiting access to *promotor* jobs by the late 1950s. They did this by driving away from the *escuela albergue* in Chamula's *cabecera* all sixth-grade students who were not from their own families. Diane Rus, "Education interviews," 1975–76 (personal communication). Ironically, INI's efforts over the years to upgrade the Indian teachers by requiring more preparation abetted this elitism by making it ever more difficult for poor families to afford the additional years of schooling.

38. For example, for Oxchuc, Morales Sánchez (1976:131–38) and Santis Gómez (1976:149); for Chamula, interview with López Calixto, Sept. 15, 1975. See also Köhler (1975:336–40).

land.[39] In all these cases, as in the government's relations with Indians in general, results were all that mattered, and the scribe-*principales* had the power to cut short debate in their communities and impose results.

Like the government, wealthy ladino "patrons" also strengthened their relationships with the scribe-*principales* as the 1950s progressed. In 1954, in one of the most notorious examples, Hernán Pedrero and Jacinto Robles, who, like Pedrero, owned a coffee *finca* in the valleys just north of the central highlands, helped Salvador López Tuxum, the most important of the Chamula scribe-*principales*, to buy his first truck. The timing is particularly telling: on the one hand, INI and the state had just begun encouraging private ownership of trucks and stores; on the other, after an eight-year hiatus, López Tuxum had just resumed his post as *secretario general* of the Sindicato de Trabajadores Indígenas. Years later, Indians who worked on Pedrero's and Robles's *fincas* after the mid-1950s would remember them as the two most exploitative in the entire region, and yet strangely immune to government and syndicate attention.[40] Nor was this case unique: throughout the 1950s and 1960s, other wealthy ladinos helped the leading scribe-*principales* of most of the communities of the highlands buy land, acquire trucks, and become soft-drink and beer distributors. In return, the recipients of these favors quietly blocked agrarian reform petitions, guaranteed wholesalers sole access to their community's stores, and looked the other way as *coyotes*—sharp-dealing commodity merchants—short-weighted the produce they bought from community members. By such means—carefully dissembled—the leading scribe-*principales* had become, by the 1960s, not just powerful, but often quite wealthy.[41]

39. Interviews with Castellanos Cancino, Jan. 30, 1976, Mar. 3, 1976; Gómez Osob, July 8, 1973; and Pablo Ramírez Suárez, Nov. 14, 1975. See also Köhler (1975:176–82). More recent instances of this kind of coercion are the use of native elites to pave the way for film and television crews at fiestas and to open churches and religious ceremonies to tourists.

40. Rus, "San Cristóbal ladino interviews," 1975–76; and "Los Chorros contract labor interviews," 1986–88, INAREMAC.BD. In 1971, Pedrero and Robles helped López Tuxum and a group of associates buy a nine-hundred-hectare *finca* of their own on land that a group of neighboring Indians had for decades been requesting as an *ejido*; they thereby conveniently placed the Chamulans as a buffer between the petitioning community and a second, even richer Pedrero *finca*.

41. Rus, "San Cristóbal ladino interviews"; "Los Chorros interviews," 1986–88. For abuses by the scribe-*principales*, see also Arias (1984). In 1976, for example, López Tuxum and his young sons owned two stores and five trucks, controlled the Pepsi,

Not that the former scribes were only or always villains, of course. They also provided their neighbors with useful connections to government agencies, acted as translators and advocates in legal matters, and served as a source of loans (although typically at interest rates of 5 to 10 percent a month during the 1950s and 1960s). In general, however, these services were little more than side effects of their success; for by the 1960s, they and their closest relatives held all the best government jobs, owned most of the stores and trucks, and possessed a disproportionate share of community land.

Farther-reaching than the scribe-*principales'* individual political and economic roles, however, was the way they changed the meaning of native leadership and tradition. Whereas before 1936 the structures of the "corporate community" had helped to preserve a safe haven from ladino control and exploitation, by the second half of the 1950s those structures, through the agency of the scribe-*principales,* had been co-opted by the state and incorporated into its system of control in such a way that much of the time they actually served its interests as against those of the Indians. The meaning of tradition had been stood on its head.

CULTURE AND POWER IN THE COMMUNITIES OF THE 1950s AND 1960s

The question that arises from this increasingly close association between the scribe-*principales* and the ladino state is, how did it play itself out within the native communities themselves? Given that as recently as the 1930s, the governing structures of those communities had served precisely to prevent ladinos from penetrating the Indians' home territories, how were the scribe-*principales* now able to play—or justify—their new role as the ladinos' partners?

The short answer appears to be that at least at first, through the 1950s and perhaps the early 1960s, most community members seem not to have realized how close the relationship had become. The same strong ideology of community, the same xenophobia with respect to the "outside" and protectiveness of the "inside" that had characterized the communities of

---

Coca-Cola, and beer distributorships for the fifty thousand Chamulans, and held controlling (sole?) interests in four *fincas* totaling more than two thousand hectares. All in addition to their loan business, in which capacity they functioned as Chamula's bank, financing scores of sharecroppers at interest rates of 5 to 10 percent a month.

the 1930s kept its momentum right through this period, and most high-landers seem simply to have assumed that as *principales* the former scribes continued to be the chief defenders of that ideology. They therefore accepted with little question the scribe-*principales'* decisions about community politics and development. This, in turn, was just the result ladino leaders had hoped for when they began exercising control of the high-land *municipios* through native elites instead of continuing to try to impose it through *secretarios municipales, fiscales,* and assorted ladino police. The coherence of the Indian communities, coupled with their unquestioning loyalty to their leaders, made for "indirect rule" at its most efficient.

As for the scribe-*principales* themselves, as they became ever more compromised by their relationship to the state from the early 1950s on, they seem to have made an ever greater show of their "Indianness," of their belief in and defense of native culture. According to testimonies about Chamula in the 1950s and 1960s, for example, from the time the scribe-*principales* assumed real control in the late 1940s, they took great care to justify their decisions, no matter how self-interested, in terms of "tradition" ("the way the ancestors did things") and the need for the community to be unified ("to be of one soul"). This they did whether they were urging resistance to the state (as in the case of the "Posh War"), cooperation with it (as in the fights over road construction), or actions that mostly benefited themselves (as when ordering sanctions against their political rivals).[42] Clearly, "tradition" was never an absolute injunction or body of laws but a set of values to be interpreted in specific cases. By the early 1950s, however, the scribe-*principales* were almost alone in their power to do the interpreting. Once they had chosen a course of action, their fellow community members were faced with an almost religious obligation to go along with it.

Meanwhile, as the 1950s and 1960s progressed, the same regionwide economic and political conditions that had facilitated the scribe-*principales'* unprecedented accumulation of power and wealth began to change the lives of their constituents as well. In particular, the opening of new lands to sharecroppers and colonists soon led to the rise of a class of young entrepreneurs in most highland communities. As time went on, not

---

42. The Tzotzil phrase for "being of one soul" is *jun ko'onton*. Traditional Chamulans believe that even permitting a dissident to exist in their territory can destroy this "oneness" and cause God and the saints to withdraw their protection from the entire community. Individual dissidence and nonconformity are therefore blamed for such collective calamities as drought, crop failure, and epidemics.

only did such men begin to make more money than most of their neighbors, but by the very nature of their work they also tended to become both more individualistic and more accustomed to dealing with ladinos directly, without intermediaries, than those who remained in plantation or communal settings.[43] As the scribe-*principales* soon realized, if such men were not resubordinated to the group, reintegrated into the community structures that were the basis of the scribes' control, they could easily become rivals, whether as cultural brokers, sources of loans, or even informal authorities themselves. And if this were allowed to happen, the unity on which the corporate community—and the scribes' own power—depended would disappear.

The solution, in communities around the highlands beginning in the mid-1950s, was that almost as soon as young entrepreneurs arose, they were incorporated into the religious cargo systems. The process was fairly straightforward, and again Chamula can serve as an example. Having used religious cargos to legitimate their own premature and unprecedented ascension as *principales* in the early 1940s, the former scribes now began obliging younger men to make the same gesture. The only difference was that in the 1950s, participation in the religious cargo system was made a prerequisite not just for selling alcohol but also for owning a store in one's hamlet, lending money to one's neighbors, eventually buying a truck—the same lucrative, nontraditional enterprises that were opening up to young lowland farmers and government employees as they accumulated capital of their own. Young men who dared to undertake such enterprises without first taking the precaution of enlisting in the cargo system were considered to have entered into competition with those who did "serve the community." These miscreants were subjected to sanctions that ranged from, at the most lenient, being summoned to the *cabildo* and given immediate, forced cargos to being beaten, having their property destroyed, or even being accused of witchcraft.[44] In some communities,

43. In the case of Chamula, approximately one-third of the working-age men earned their living from the Grijalva basin and Lacandón jungle in 1975, while half continued to depend on the coffee *fincas* (Wasserstrom 1980:11–12). Variation in these proportions from community to community might go a long way toward accounting for differences in levels of political combativity among *municipios*.

44. Rus, "Chamula work history interviews." An interesting question is why this same change happened at about the same time in many different communities. One possible explanation is that the scribe-*principales*, as *promotores*, were constantly in contact with each other through INI during the critical period, and thereby could

notably Chamula but apparently following the model of Zinacantán, the system required service in a series of increasingly costly religious offices to justify undertaking increasingly profitable enterprises. (This, of course, was unlike the conditions for Chamula's scribe-*principales* themselves, most of whom served only one cargo near the beginning of their careers in the 1940s and never served again.)[45]

This strategy seems to have had most success and to have led to the greatest expansion of ceremonial life in the densely populated communities of the central and southern parts of the region (Chamula, Zinacantán, Tenejapa, Huistán, perhaps Mitontic, and San Andrés). Young men in such communities, however economically successful they might become as sharecroppers or migrant workers, still had no place to live besides their home *municipios* and therefore, however reluctantly, submitted to the *principales'* demands. In the northern highlands, on the other hand (Oxchuc, Tenango, Bachajón, and Yajalón), where it was possible for young men to escape the scribe-*principales'* control by simply leaving home and moving permanently to the neighboring jungle, that was precisely what increasing numbers of them did as the 1950s progressed. In the process, many also became Protestants as a way of emphasizing their rejection of the *principales'* demands (Esponda 1986:255ff.; Rus and Wasserstrom 1981:163–72).[46]

---

share successful governing strategies with each other. Ladino indigenista officials, for their part, deny any role in suggesting or coordinating the shift. Interview with Castellanos Cancino, Jan. 24, 1976. In any case, with some variation from community to community, the meaning of religious cargos apparently was extended during the 1950s in Chamula, Zinacantán, Mitontic, San Andrés, Tenejapa, and Cancuc, but apparently not in Chenalhó nor, at least for long, in the communities of the north (Oxchuc, Bachajón, Yajalón, and Altamirano).

45. Interview with López Tuxum, Oct. 5, 1975. Parenthetically, this new role for the cargo systems, combined with the improved economic conditions of the 1950s and 1960s, produced one highly visible result: an increase in the size and lavishness of the communal religious ceremonies classically associated with the self-defensive, closed structures of communities under economic and political stress. This increase has been studied most in Zinacantán, where it has been attributed variously to a "nativistic, revivalistic" reaction to modernization (Vogt 1969:609–10); to native government's attempts to preserve its traditional "function" of reconciling individual wealth to community solidarity by expanding in the face of economic growth (Cancian 1965); and, most recently, to the elaborate political apprenticeship forced on younger men, since the generation of the early 1940s was suddenly and uniquely endowed with control of the new *ejidos* (Collier 1989:111–23).

46. By way of comparison, during the 1950s change took a different course in

As for the state's reaction to these internal changes in the workings of the native communities, the official position from the mid-1950s on, derived from that of the anthropologists at INI, advocated nonintervention in "traditional community affairs." Thus pressures applied to potential rivals of the scribe-*principales* through the cargo systems or through "religious" sanctions were, conveniently, "internal" matters for the Indians to work out themselves. "Conveniently" because at the same time, of course, INI and the state were continuing Urbina's old strategy of working exclusively through the scribe-*principales*, and that strategy was much more effective if the former scribes remained unchallenged within their communities.

Meanwhile, when the state itself conferred jobs and other government resources on the scribe-*principales* it was not considered "intervention"; nor was it when, as the 1950s progressed, interested ladino patrons also showered them with lands and other benefits. Essentially, only intervention that undermined the authority of the scribe-*principales*—by definition "traditional"—was forbidden. As a result, when young men began to stand up against the scribe-*principales* in the northern Tzeltal communities in the late 1950s, INI and the DGAI encouraged them to leave their homes and move to the jungle rather than "fight tradition" (Beekman and Hefley 1968; Siverts 1969:175–84; Esponda 1986:255ff.). Similarly, when innovators in Amatenango suffered an epidemic of "witchcraft" murders in the early 1960s, Indian affairs bureaucrats dismissed the crimes as unprosecutable, leaving the *principales'*—and thus the state's—control of the community intact.[47]

---

those Tzotzil and Tzeltal communities on the edges of the highlands. There, Urbina had not played a role, and the economic opportunities of the 1950s and 1960s benefited not the native communities but the ladino landowners who held much of the land in their *municipios*; for example, Simojovel, Bochil, and Carranza. In these cases, the political and economic interests of younger and older men were virtually no different, and therefore ceremonial service had no reason to be anything more than what it had always been: relatively inexpensive, often paid for cooperatively, with officeholders selected by former officers at the last moment before they were to serve.

47. According to Nash (1970:244–47), of thirty-seven murders in Amatenango between 1938 and 1965, thirty occurred in the five years after 1960; the principal victims were "innovators" who ignored the traditional government while pursuing new economic opportunities. The rationale was that their "sudden" wealth was evidence of witchcraft, or that their "deviant" behavior endangered the community's integrity. Amatenango's population in 1960 was 3,105.

As they became more widely known, in turn, conflicts like these, in which the state sided almost exclusively with the scribe-*principales*, only reinforced the former scribes' ability to control rivals without having to call on state support. Not that such ability was in serious doubt, at least for the time being. Most highland natives were not individualistic entrepreneurs. For them, community solidarity and the threat of collective action remained their best defenses against mistreatment on the *fincas*, for instance, or being cheated in the marketplace. It was thus an article of faith that what the scribe-*principales* were defending when they punished a rival was the "tradition" that kept everyone safe from a dangerous outside world. If the relatively few cases of dissidence that came to INI's and the DGAI's attention were decided in favor of the former scribes, most community members saw that not as evidence of the state's influencing native government, but as proof of the scribes' own power to stand up for native tradition and to influence the state.

EPILOGUE

Between the mid-1950s and the late 1960s, then, the state had not only recognized the scribe-*principales* as sole leaders of their communities, but by enriching them and supporting them politically had given them power over those communities greater than that of any of their predecessors. Contrary to expectations that this strategy would provide a permanent solution to the problem of managing the Indian communities, however, by the early 1970s, native governments all over the highlands were engulfed in conflict. While these battles took on particular characteristics in each community as a result of their different histories, economic niches, and even the personalities of their leaders, in important ways they were everywhere the same. Essentially, they were the product of the contradiction between the centralizing influence of the state's administrative policies from the late 1930s on, leading to the creation of the scribe-*principales;* and the leveling, democratizing tendencies of its development policies, giving rise to a generation of younger, better-educated men eager to pursue their own opportunities without interference from the former scribes.

Perhaps no event better signals the beginning of this period of turmoil than the Chamula mutiny of 1968. Shortly after taking office in January of that year, Chamula's municipal president—one of Urbina's original scribes—imposed a tax on all adult men of the community, ostensibly to pay for reconstruction of the town hall. Many community members, however, believed that he and his cronies were keeping a large share of the receipts for themselves. Instead of simply accepting this graft as they might have a few years earlier, three thousand community members— one quarter of Chamula's adult men—marched into San Cristóbal to demand that the state remove their president. Not surprisingly, the appearance of this angry "Indian mob" ("chamulada") caused a panic in the city; and within hours, INI and the state government had agreed to finance the town hall themselves and return the protesters' money.

While Chamula's former scribes and the ladino officials in charge of Indian affairs apparently believed that they had once again managed to co-opt dissent and restore order, in reality this fight over the town hall was just the first skirmish in a struggle that continues to this day. During the months following the march, the former scribes took reprisals against the young school graduates and entrepreneurs who had led the protest. Instead of disbanding, though, these men redoubled their efforts to organize their neighbors and redefined their goal as nothing less than overthrowing the political monopoly of the scribe-*principales*—whom they now for the first time referred to as *caciques*. Within a year and a half, they had progressed to the point of nominating the first-ever alternative candidates for municipal office; and when their candidates inevitably lost that and succeeding elections, they staged demonstrations in San Cristóbal and the state capital, Tuxtla Gutiérrez. In addition, in an attempt to give their movement some authority within Chamula and gain legitimacy beyond it, they successively sought the support of the Catholic church, opposition political parties, and ultimately, Protestant missionaries.

In response to these attacks on their control, the scribe-*principales*, in turn, applied ever more repression. They rallied "real Chamulas" to their side by pointing out the dissidents' disrespect for native religion, community solidarity, and the injunction against introducing ladinos into community affairs; then, from the early 1970s on, they expelled hundreds of dissenters from the community as "enemies of tradition." The state, for its part, hoping to retain control of Chamula through its alliance with the scribe-*principales* and their successors, made itself an accomplice in these actions by retreating to its pose of noninterference in "internal community affairs."[48]

48. Interviews with Castellanos Cancino, Aug. 8 and Nov. 13, 1975. See also Pablo Iribarren (1980), "Misión Chamula," a fifty-page, offset-printed history of the Chamula conflict compiled for the Diocese of San Cristóbal, in INAREMAC.BD.

From the suddenness with which it arose and the strength with which it grew and sustained itself in the face of fierce repression, Chamula's opposition movement clearly seems to have welled up from a deep dissatisfaction among many Chamulas about the prevailing direction of community life. Nor were the Chamulas alone. By the mid-1970s, more than half the *municipios* of the highlands had active opposition movements. And by the early 1980s, the expedient of expelling political opponents had spread from Chamula to those communities, generating thousands of exiles who, in turn, founded dozens of new colonies in San Cristóbal and the Lacandón jungle. In all of these, and, by this time less openly, even inside the traditional *municipios* themselves, the effort to define new, "posttraditional" forms of community that would be truer to the Indians' own developing sense of themselves continues to this day.

Given this context, the following scenes, both of which occurred during the 1988 presidential campaign, are not only understandable but seem poignantly reflective of the ongoing struggle. In one, the governor of Chiapas, arriving in the main square of Chamula in his helicopter, emerges resplendent in native official garb and exhorts the Indians assembled to "defend their traditions" against those who would destroy them by undermining community solidarity or introducing foreign religious practices. Carefully left out of his peroration is that the "enemies of tradition" are other Indians from the same community. In the other scene, the son of Lázaro Cárdenas, Cuauhtémoc, stands in the *zócalo* in San Cristóbal challenging the hundreds of Indians pressing to get close to him (many of them exiles from their home communities) to join with him in making a new, democratic revolution.

ARMANDO BARTRA

The Seduction of the Innocents:
The First Tumultuous Moments of Mass Literacy
in Postrevolutionary Mexico

The Mexican people were initiated into reading through the comics, or "historietas." During the late 1930s and throughout the 1940s, millions who previously had not experienced the pleasures of the written word lost their literary virginity submerged in the seductive pages of the "monitos." As with all initiations, this inaugural reading contained something of the sinful. For the educated minority and the lovers of belles lettres, the unforeseen popular passion for the "pepines" was a transgression, a type of wholesale spiritual prostitution of the innocents, which had to be restrained in the name of morality and proper literary custom. Better a society of pure illiterates than a nation of contaminated readers.[1]

But the urgency of these new readers—the result of widespread literacy campaigns—was uncontrollable, and millions of Mexicans sacrificed their literary purity to the demonized pages of the "chamacos" and

1. In this essay, the term *historieta* (comic strip or comic book), is used virtually interchangeably with several other colloquial terms: *monito, pepín, paquín,* and *chamaco.* The discerning reader will note, however, that in this essay the terms are used somewhat chronologically; the *historieta,* or short story, portrayed in comic-strip form, was the term first used. *Monito* (or "little monkey") refers to the comic books or magazines in which the historietas appeared. *Pepines, paquines, chamacos,* and similar terms affectionately refer to the comic books by the names of their popular main characters—Pepín, Paquín, Chamaco, and so on. Finally, *monero* refers to the artist-writer who drew the characters and wrote the text.—*Eds.*

"pepines." Unlike "serious" books and magazines, the monitos did not inhibit the beginner; nor did they demand promises or prolonged compromises. They were simple, accessible, and disposable. Depending on the client's tastes they could be romantic, passionate, or cruel. And they were cheap: not more than ten centavos for a half an hour of pleasure. Thus the pepines occupy the first place as an example of our popular culture in the printed word.

The material in part 1 of this essay is drawn from a pair of chapters in volume 2 of *Puros cuentos*, which comprises observations supported by a thorough survey of the history of the Mexican comic.[2] That study pays particular attention to the first decades after the Mexican revolution, but it does not attempt to explore extensively the role of the monito magazines in the formation of Mexico's contemporary popular culture, and it only marginally refers to the comic's role in the educational policies of the postrevolutionary state. Nevertheless, that analysis, however provisional and tentatively linked to periodizations of postrevolutionary Mexico, can provide the basis for somewhat more comprehensive propositions regarding the role of the mass media in the formation of this country's popular culture. These latter issues are addressed in part 2 of this essay.

I

In the 1920s, the founding of the modern Mexican historieta was enacted by a handful of illustrators and writers, who published their efforts in the Sunday supplements of the daily newspapers. This generation, which included Pruneda, Acosta, Tilghmann, Arthenack, Audiffred, Neve, and Zendejas, nationalized the language of the comic and introduced styles and original characters such as Don Catarino, Chupamirto, Mamerto, Adelaido, El Señor Pestaña, and Segundo I. But the founding moneros made their initial advance toward a meager public composed of newspaper readers, less than 5 percent of the population at the end of the 1920s. For a decade they challenged the imported comic strips for newspaper space; but by the beginning of the 1930s they had lost the battle, and the Mexican historieta was in open retreat before North American comics.

In a country of illiterates with a persistent but marginal press, the transformation of the historieta into a cultural phenomenon of the masses

2. A. Bartra and Aurrecochea (1988 and forthcoming).

had to wait until the 1940s. In that decade a new, multifaceted public created by official education and the literacy campaigns appeared. The historieta, finally freed from the daily newspapers and supplements, had its own and potentially more popular vehicle: the magazines of monitos. The expansion of the historieta's readership began symbolically in 1934 with the appearance of *Paquín*, the first commercially successful specialized publication. The historieta magazines began to proliferate during the second half of the thirties, and the passion for monitos soared and stabilized during the forties, when various publications were produced daily. As editions grew unchecked, the consumption of pepines by people of all ages became a national vice.

In Mexico the comics have always had a predominantly adult audience, but for a long time the publishers chose to place them in the children's section. In the early years of their appearance on the scene, too, the monito magazines reinforced this emphasis, as evidenced by the names of the first and most famous of the comic book heroes—Paquín, Paquito, Pepín, Chamaco. But in fact, as their popularity soared in the forties, the comics were primarily purchased by adolescents and adults, and publishers were quick to apprehend the true profile of the market. Some magazines—the minority—continued to be directed at children, but the majority focused on older readers. *Pepín*, which at the end of the thirties had been subtitled *El chico más famoso del mundo* (*The Most Famous Boy in the World*), was transformed halfway through the forties into a daily *Diario de novelas gráficas para adultos*.

While defining their public, the comic magazines also adjusted their form and content. The pepines were born large and grew smaller. At first they adopted the tabloid format of their North American counterparts, but soon they shrank to one-fourth the size, becoming pocket magazines, portable literature to read on the trolley or the bus. At first they were published weekly, later three times a week; but the readers were insatiable, and finally the most successful ones appeared daily. Initially they offered a modest and mimetic local product alongside the dominant imported comics. But with time, the nationally produced historietas took the place of the imports and imposed their individual styles and themes.

The combination of open-ended serials and single, conclusive pages appearing weekly characterized the earliest series, but after the publication interval was shortened the adventures were increasingly extended, and "to be continued" became the norm. At first, line drawing predominated, but soon the halftone and the photomontage invaded the magazine page. Some of the earliest publications were printed on flat press (*prensa plana*) with black ink, but soon rotogravure and sepia tone came into common use.

Thus, as the formats and periodicity were adjusted through trial and error, so the style and thematic lines were defined along the way. It was like colonizing a great, unexplored continent, and the first forays groped their way along. The publishers, writers, and illustrators experimented without restraint or mercy; they tested everything, they invented, they improvised. Reduced sales signaled swampy terrain and impassable paths; a serial's commercial success opened a road, and within weeks, dozens of imitators were traveling on it. At the end of the thirties and during the forties, the creators of the Mexican comics made incursions into all imaginable genres, inaugurated the most diverse themes, and explored a wide range of narrative and graphic styles. In little more than a decade they discovered the principal veins of popular sensibility and began the plunder. Thereafter, everything would be continuations, parodies, rehashes—good or routine, but redundant—until the times changed and a transformed public with new demands exacted, with renewed insistence, greater imagination from its comic book artists.

But in the historietas' conquest and colonization of the Mexican people, the fearless illustrators and writers were hardly soldiers of fortune. Capital was the true motor of the expansion of historietas, and the monero "boom" of the forties coincided with the process of the original accumulation of two or three great fortunes. The men who gave us the comics were not missionaries in a spiritual conquest but zealous merchants hungry for clientele. They had no cultural vocation—they were neither socially engaged or estranged—they merely sought profits. And look what they obtained: the largest journalistic enterprise in the country, and one of the most extensive in the world, the García Valseca network, was created on the strength of pepines, and two enormous publishing consortia, Novedades Editores and Publicaciones La Prensa, were consolidated thanks to the monito magazines.

Enter the Word, With the Pepines

Popularization of the historieta required an extensive, literate population. Until the 1940s, the Mexican people had been mostly illiterate. In the elitist educational system of the Porfirian regime, reading and a familiarity with books, magazines, and newspapers was the privilege of a few. At the end of the nineteenth century, less than a fifth of the population knew how to read and write; and when, in 1910, the old regime collapsed, it left behind a 75 percent illiteracy rate. Publication statistics reflect this reality. *El Imparcial*, an exceptional newspaper for its time, achieved a surprising circulation and revolutionized the concept of journalism. Yet by the end of the first decade of this century its circulation numbered only about one hundred thousand, and that in a country of fifteen million inhabitants.

A revolution with a popular base and a desire for justice could not ignore the problem of illiteracy. The Constitution of 1917 and the National Education Law established free, secular, and mandatory primary instruction, assigning fundamental responsibilities for education to the state (see chapter 6 in this volume). The education campaigns after the revolution may have been more showy than effective; but in the long run, the unquestioned expansion of public education and the modest but continued advances in adult literacy combined to modify the Mexican educational profile. By the end of the thirties, 42 percent of the population could read and write. By the middle of the forties, literate people outnumbered illiterates, with one peculiarity: the largest percentage of illiterates corresponded to people of advanced age, while the majority of those under twenty-five had learned or were learning to read and write.

While under the old regime reading was a privilege of the wealthy and the small middle class, by the fifth decade of the century, many workers and peasants were literate. For the first time, reading and writing were widespread, popular practices. But what would these millions of newly literate people read? During the forties, the answer emerged loud and clear: they would read pepines or nothing at all.

By the middle of the 1940s, the potential demand for the printed word comprised about ten million readers. The output of the traditional publishing industry, however, did not even remotely approach this figure. In 1935, when the spectacular historieta expansion was about to begin, nearly a thousand periodicals were being published in Mexico. Total magazine circulation numbered perhaps in the tens of thousands, while the daily papers, sixty in all, did not print even half a million copies per day. Thus, while public education and literacy campaigns were making significant inroads into the potential reading population, the publishing industry continued to serve a small sector of traditional readers. The discovery of the unexploited commercial demand for the printed word can be traced to three newspaper empires—García Valseca, Novedades Editores, and Publicaciones La Prensa, whose leaders would soon transform themselves into the czars of the monitos, saturating the market with paquines, pepines, and chamacos.

In less than ten years after 1934, historieta circulation figures took an impressive jump, and by the middle of the forties they had reached the same order of magnitude as the literate population. Some significant statistics appear in the December 13, 1945, issue of the magazine *Cartones:* "At present, four historietas are published daily in the capital that together turn out *half a million* copies, with a readership that reaches *two million* every day. There are also three specialized weekly historietas whose press runs total approximately *one million copies.*" Combining these figures, we arrive at four-and-a-half million copies per week. If we accept the realistic hypothesis that each issue averaged four readers, we find eighteen million weekly historieta readings in Mexico in 1945. This does not mean that eighteen million people read one issue every week; there simply were not that many literate people. It is more realistic to suppose that some two million fanatics devoured a monito magazine as quickly as possible every day while another four million, less impassioned, read one issue every seven days. The rough estimate of six million significantly approaches the number of Mexicans who knew how to read.

This does not take into consideration that *Cartones* was itself a comic, and its estimate of the competition's circulation was conservative. There are those who maintain, with good reason, that *Chamaco* published seven hundred thousand copies daily, and others who believe its publication runs reached one million. The writer and illustrator Ramón Valdiosera did not exaggerate when he maintained that *Chamaco's* moneros were "the masters of the literate public." And perhaps he was also accurate in suggesting that in many cases, the historietas were the true incentive behind literacy: "Many people learned to read in order to understand the pepines. They were motivated by the desire to know what the cartoons said. One who read said to another, 'Look, pal, this is the one who tames the bull so that he will kill Joselito,' and so they began to read."

Vasos Comunicantes: Vessels of Communication

The historietas were not the only popular taste. While the pepines were being transformed into reading for the masses, other industries of dissemination discovered a potential consumer in the humble *pueblo.* From the twenties on, but above all in the thirties and forties, Mexicans met at the cinema, around the radio, at sports events, and in the realms of nightlife—live theater revues, dance halls, and cabarets. What historietas and other popular publications shared with these modes of diffusion was the collective leisure of the masses. Far from competing among themselves, these different media coexisted harmoniously and nourished each other. Among those of a narrative, literary nature—cinema, radio serials, and historietas—the symbiosis was complete and the genres, themes, plots, and characters passed from one to the other with remarkable fluidity.

During this period popular literature was revitalized, and alongside reissued series of nineteenth-century classics appeared newspaper serials with modern genres such as police stories, science fiction, and chronicles of "the Revolution." Although in Mexico pulp fiction did not achieve the popularity of the historietas, those inexpensive literary magazines also experienced a modest rise in popularity. In the mid-thirties, when the first monitos appeared, some "pulps"—*Emoción, Detectives, Misterio, Novela de Aventuras*—were already on the market, and were joined at the end of the decade by *Detectives y Bandidos, Cuentos y Novelas,* and, a little later, *Vida y Cuentos.*

Halfway between the "pulp" and the comic book, the first historieta magazines published as many monitos as literary serials, and their hybrid content encouraged the movement of genres from one idiom to another. In this way, one of the strongest themes of the nineteenth-century serial, the cloak-and-dagger adventure, was rapidly adopted by the historieta. If in 1935 *Paquín* published episodes of *El Jorobado* or *Enrique de Legardere* or *Sheridan Le Fanu* in their literary versions, soon *Chamaco* launched an interminable adaptation of *Los Pardaillant* by Miguel de Zevaco, realized by the monero Melesio Esquivel.

In the twenties and thirties, the new genres of popular literature became acclimatized to Mexico. Detectives proliferated in the weekly magazines, bearing autochthonous names like El Tejón, by Méndez Armendariz, and Pancho Chávez, whose author paradoxically signed himself Nick Carter. So did futuristic heroes such as Juan Cuauhli Sinoki, a character in "Around the World in 24 Hours" by Carlos M. Samper.

One national form of the serial was the novelized chronicle of the Mexican revolution, particularly the saga of its more "literary" protagonists. This was a thematic line, begun by writers, that would later feed the cinema, radio, and comics. Among these narratives, Pancho Villa was far and away the best-seller. Initially the Villista narratives came from *corridos* (popular ballads), but in the postrevolutionary period the novels of Martín Luis Guzmán or Rafael F. Muñoz and, in a more popular vein, the interminable anecdotes of Elías Torres, transformed the Centaur of the North into a character of testimonial literature.

In 1935 the voice of Domingo Soler brought Villa to the radio in a series of "radioscenic episodes" broadcast by XEFO, which also promoted the film *Vámonos con Pancho Villa,* directed by Fernando de Fuentes and based on the novel by Muñoz. Here is a case in which radio and cinema simultaneously appropriated a historical character already plundered by literature. The monitos wasted no time in joining the Villista ranks. In 1936 Ignacio Sierra, taking his script from Elías Torres, began to publish a biography of the hero in historieta form in *Semanario sucesos para todos.* The Centaur of the North thereby became one of the first protagonists of the Mexican historieta drawn realistically, and the first national historical personage to be transformed into the regular hero of a comic book series.

During the thirties and forties, soccer, bullfights, boxing, and wrestling gained a wide and passionate audience. Sports competition and bullfights are tragedies, comedies, farces, or melodramas that move even the most respectable spectator to shout, and create unblemished heroes alongside odious villains. Sports has the added advantage that its Manichaean symbols are interchangeable according to the affinities of each fan. If literary serials, comics, movies, and radio dramas capture their readers, spectators, and listeners through conflict and dramatic tension, commercial sports also resort to suspense, except that the drama unfolding before our eyes is not a representation but an actual confrontation. Sporting events, therefore, resemble the narrative genres found in popular culture. And the sports spectacle—collective catharsis and the rite (or cry) of national identity—provides invaluable material for the other media.

In the thirties, specialized magazines proliferated: *Ases y Estrellas, Mujeres y Deportes, La Afición, Fútbol, Ring,* and so on. In 1941 the first daily rotogravure sports magazine appeared—*Esto,* from the García Valseca network—and the cinema flirted with sporting themes in films such as *Campeón sin corona* (*Champion Without a Crown*), by Alejandro Galindo. But it was the moneros who truly capitalized on the Mexican's proverbial affection for the vicarious enjoyment of sports. The pepines transformed their pages into fields, mats, and rings, populated by countless heroes.

Another deep vein of Mexican popular sensibility is the love of violence and cruelty. Terrible events and a profusion of blood have always been a persistent theme as well as the proprietary turf of the street press (*prensa callejera*), from the leaflets of the colonial era to the bloody crime reporting (*nota roja*) of modern journalism. If during the revolution all journalistic information made up one enormous "red line," with the reestablishment of peace, crime coverage modified the dose of (distanced) terror that readers demanded. In the thirties, at the same time the monitos were consolidating their position as reading for the masses, a type of specialized publication destined to make history in the Mexican press was gaining strength: the crime magazine. With its "alibi" of covering the police blotter, it provided a veritable gallery of daily horrors.

All the crime magazines published comics, but that was the least of the connections between the two media. More important was the surreptitious transfer of *nota roja* styles and themes to the historieta, infusing the Mexican monitos with a markedly truculent tone. This was not primarily the spectacular but external violence typical of the North American comic. Doubtless that, too, was present. But more importantly, the Mexican historietas—especially the series that were set in the slums—conveyed a social and individual violence that reflected the rough everyday life of their readers. It was a far cry from the aseptic treatment of violence found in the North American imports.

Sports and crime are typically masculine themes, and in general the magazines that exploited them also rewarded their readers with photographs of more or less naked women. The erotic press was not a postrevolutionary phenomenon: since the end of the nineteenth century the repressed monster of the libido had buried its hairy pornographic ears in gentlemen's magazines such as *México Galante* and *Frivolidades*. In the twenties, salacious journalism reappeared with more plebeian features, and by the thirties it was one of the permanent themes in the popular press, the sexuality of ink and paper enjoying its corollary in the flesh and bone of the people of the night.

An extension of this phenomenon were the magazines "for adults." Frequently these were consulted in barbershops, a "zone of tolerance" in which bearded voyeurs could succumb to their secret reading pleasure. This "press of the barbershop," combining spicy text with lascivious photographs and pornographic drawings, transformed the trivial act of getting a haircut into a ritual of erotic initiation, provoking perverse associations in several generations of Mexicans. In this manner, fairly explicit sexuality came to the historieta. It was not an easy transition from the supposedly infantile monito to the porn comic, but once it was clear that adults made up the greater part of the readership, the heroines began to become sexualized. Thus, in time, was the well-mannered Adela Negrete, created by José Guadelupe Cruz in the pages of *Paquito* in 1935, transformed into the luxuriant superwoman of "Adelita and the Guerrillas."

Amusement and leisure are common places and collective spaces where multitudes congregate and where all the communication media intermingle. In the thirties and forties, cinema, radio, the popular press, commercial sports, and nightlife nourished one another in a snug symbiosis. The historietas were one of the fundamental axes of this motley culture, mercantile but beloved. The publishers, illustrators, and writers contributed and stole, innovated and plagiarized. And within this universal give and take, deep lines of specialization were forming in the monitos, the popular narrative most frequented by Mexicans in the past half-century.

From Favorite Characters to Specialized Genres

The birth, splendor, and decline of the pepines embraced a bit more than two decades. Between 1934, the year Francisco Sayrols published *Paquín,* and the mid-1950s, when *Chamaco* and *Pepín* disappeared and *Paquito* and *Paquín* changed character, the historical cycle of the traditional comic book characters was completed. By the mid-1950s, the monitos of multiple series developed over successive adventures had been marginalized, and the reign of comic books and volumes of historietas in novel form had begun.

During this period, fundamental developments took place. The monito magazines consolidated their market; a powerful, specialized publishing industry arose; the consumption of historietas became a popular habit; a flourishing society of professionals took shape; and the styles, treatments, and themes characteristic of the modern Mexican comic were born. Any attempt to trace an inherent logic in this varied historieta landscape would be risky and necessarily simplistic, for during these years, extremely diverse tendencies coexisted and were juxtaposed. Nevertheless, a certain underlying order and more or less identifiable tendencies appear. First, the obvious: the birth of the pepines inverted the *malinchista* tendencies of previous years, and by the end of this period the majority of historietas published in Mexico were national products.[3] In the twenties, the first generation of local moneros had succeeded, for a

3. The pejorative adjective *malinchista* derives from the quasi-mythical figure of *La Malinche,* the young woman given by indigenous lords to the Spanish conquistador, Hernán Cortés, following contact along Mexico's Gulf Coast. For a time she served as Cortés's translator and concubine, thereby helping the foreign invaders impose their will and rule on Mexico's indigenous societies. In contemporary Mexico both noun

while, in getting space in the daily papers; but by the beginning of the thirties, the imported comics again had predominated. To explain that defeat, the low cost of materials from foreign syndicates must be mentioned, along with the indisputable quality of their series and the cosmopolitan tastes of the Mexican middle class, the newspapers' enlightened readership.

But although the first commercial historieta magazines began with imports, publishers soon discovered that the new, larger public was capable of consuming more or less mimetic national products. This was the era in which José G. Cruz signed himself "Rolf Stern" and named his characters Sally, Best, Dick, or Brenty. In time, it occurred to the artists that Mexican readers had, or could develop, a certain sensibility; and that if they embraced the imported series they might also love historietas with local flavor, identifiable characters, and native treatments. Examples of comics produced not only in Mexico but for Mexicans were the humorous series of Gabriel Vargas, Rafael Araiza, or Bismark Mier; the sports stories of Ramón Valdiosera, Cervantes Bassoco, or Francisco Flores; the slum melodramas of Cruz or Manuel del Valle; and the tender mawkishness of Yolanda Vargas and Antonio Gutiérrez, to mention only a few.

The first pepines adopted the half-tabloid format of North American comic books, but soon halved that format once more. In the forties, historieta magazines in quarter-tabloid format dominated the market. The paquines, paquitos, pepines, chamacos, and chicos had a more or less standard format of thirteen by sixteen centimeters, which at first might seem claustrophobic. Actually, one of their pages was equivalent to the area of a newspaper comic strip, but with an alternative distribution of frames. Initially the transition was impoverishing, but with time the small format became common and the Mexican moneros developed a language appropriate to the new dimensions. Initially, the general rule was that a page contained two vignettes—eventually this would grow to three or even four—although pages containing a single vignette were not uncommon.

Just as the reduced size and less well defined image of the television set, as compared to the movie screen, results in the prevalence of closeups over long shots, so the pepines, small and poorly printed, privileged the closeup over the panorama, the simple sketch over the finished detail, a

and adjective are popularly used to gloss a range of forms of external penetration of the nation.—*Eds.*

few characters over a multitude, and the intimate over the epic. During the pepines' heyday, Mexican moneros could not count on the roomy spaces that allowed Foster to unfold his airy saga of Prince Valiant, favored the vegetal and anatomic baroque of Hogarth's "Tarzan," and made possible the dynamic composition of Raymond's "space operas." Nevertheless, moneros like Arturo Casillas and Francisco Flores were able to insert open scenes of medieval battles or the wide, seagoing world of piracy into the narrow pages of their publications. The best of these small magazines demonstrated that there was room for anything in a pepín that knew how to accommodate it.

While the space of the historietas was conditioned by the page size, its (discontinuous) time was circumscribed by the extension and periodicity of the installments and chapters. Once again, during the thirties and forties these dimensions were drastically modified. With the general acceptance of the monitos, lengthy, open-ended stories in installments became the dominant narrative structure. Historietas that began and ended on one page were relegated to miscellaneous magazines, and some were published as daily strips. The narrative flow of series in installments depended on the length of the chapters. In the daily papers and supplements, the visual dimensions were the page, the half-page, and the strip; but in the monitos, the extension was flexible and, in principle, could be larger, because the books were bound in gathered sets of thirty-six or more pages. Nevertheless, the pepines were integrated by diverse series of about six pages each (they could have as few as four or as many as twelve pages). Thus our cartoon heroes of the thirties and forties led syncopated lives, interrupted every fifteen or twenty frames by the inevitable "to be continued."

The adventures of El Flechador del Cielo, Los Charros del Bajío, Adelita, Aguila Roja, or Don Jilemón Metralla y Bomba advanced by fits and starts, since each installment had to begin, develop, and reach a final crossroads that would be postponed until the following chapter. The best narrators of our historietas were expert in their use of "to be continued," true masters of suspense capable of generating expectations every six pages. They resorted to limitlessly baroque schemes and a licentiousness of plot that permitted them to extricate their heroes from the worst quagmires in a couple of frames and conduct them to a fresh situation in a few more.

While the extension of the installments conditioned the narrative structure, the rhythm of the story also depended on the frequency of its appearance. Paper heroes might come to life once a month, every fifteen days, weekly, or in even shorter intervals, and this cadence determined their greater or lesser intimacy with the reader. By 1938, the most successful monitos were beginning to appear every day; and in this way the series with the greatest impact appeared as often as the daily newspaper comic strips. But whereas the strips were brief—three or four frames—the pepín episodes were much longer: four, six, up to twelve pages in each installment. In this sense, the Mexican historietas of the late thirties and forties were the fastest in the world—not for the internal cadence of their dramatic development but for the length and frequency of their chapters. That translates into an average rhythm of more than forty pages a week, or up to eighty-four when there were twelve-page installments.

Once they began appearing daily and in fairly long episodes, the pepines slipped into the everyday life of their readers. Millions of monito fanatics would begin their daily journey by sampling two or three fictional worlds, and their chosen heroes would provide material for impassioned commentary throughout the day. The personalities of politics, sports, and the theater might be flesh and blood, but they were inaccessible to the average person, who could only approach their lives through the communications media. In this sense, the protagonists of the historietas were no less real to Mexican readers than the other inhabitants of the "wider world" brought to them by the media. All were paper heroes or villains, living passionate but inaccessible lives that called for vicarious enjoyment. In practical terms, María Felix had the same stature as the fictional Adelita; the villainous Monje Negro was as real as Adolf Hitler or Josef Goebbels; Don Jilemón Metralla y Bomba as true as Luis N. Morones.

Aware of this "parallel reality" that their characters were assuming, some moneros added to the confusion by incorporating actual historical figures. This was a game. The mixture of fiction and reality did not approach schizophrenia, but it was pleasurable and necessary sport, a practice of participatory evasion and complicity whose rules were respected by moneros and readers alike. It was also a potentially critical experience, because the authors as well as the public grew used to distancing themselves from the narrative and its protagonists.

The Mexican pepines constituted an intense, vital experience for their readers, again in part because of their periodicity. The paper heroes had a daily existence: vigils of six or more pages and the inevitable night of "to be continued" reduced to less than twenty-four hours. The adventures developed day after day, and some were prolonged for years. They were historietas as real "as life itself," but more entertaining.

The Serious Comic

The personalities, settings, and plots of the first realistically drawn comics were, in general, hardly realistic: cosmic heroes of the twenty-fifth century; white Herculeses who reigned over elephants, gorillas, pygmies, and other African fauna, to mention only a few. The moneros' first incursions into the "serious" historieta followed the same line. Some were simply copies, while others, like "El Flechador del Cielo," by Alfonso Tirado, incorporated local and historical color. But whether their exoticism was cosmopolitan or vernacular, the historietas concentrated on heroic adventures and exterior action. It was a rich vein, and some Mexican moneros who began in this era exploited it for several decades. Cervantes Bassoco created his version of Tarzan in 1943, and forty years later Wama, transformed into Tawa, was still swinging from the lianas.

In time, the Mexican action comic began to develop its own variants. Besides the classic and racist Western, typical of a colonized country where the indigenous minorities were nearly exterminated, there appeared in Mexico the tale of the *charro*, or cowboy. This comic was presented in a mestizo context in which everyone except the landowner was dark, and its preferred historical context was not the conquest of the West but the revolutionary heroism of 1910. The cloak-and-dagger genre was cultivated French-style in Esquivel's endless series "Los Pardaillant," but slowly the native variants gained strength, situating themselves in the colonial period and drawing loosely upon the texts of Artemio de Valle Arizpe and González Obregón.

The sports saga was not invented in our country. In 1928, the North American Ham Fisher created the boxer Joe Palooka, and a year later the splendid Elzie Chisler Segar was incorporating the fighter Popeye into her series "Thimble Theater." Yet although they did not begin in Mexico, the sports historietas expanded and overflowed here. The styles of Segar and Chester Gould and the satiric tone of "Thimble Theater" inspired Rafael Araiza in his series "A Batacazo Limpio" ("Clean Fighting"), and Cervantes Bassoco's first character was Flat Foot, hero of the boxing ring. If boxing and its stories came to us by way of the United States and were nationalized, soccer, the bullfights, and later, wrestling were translated into comic form by enthusiastic moneros like Valdiosera, Flores, Cervantes Bassoco, and Casillas.

The Mexican varieties of the "serious" comic adapted the genre to history, geography, and national preferences, but they respected the fundamental rules of the game: they had to be adventures of pursuit and evasion, the protagonists virile heroes or macho women, and the plots based on external action. Their public could be youthful, juvenile, or adult, but presumably was masculine. To the girls, young women, and ladies, proverbially genteel and sensitive, were destined the romantic tales and tearful melodramas.

This assessment of public tastes is as sexist as it is debatable, since the Mexican pepines always had a wide spectrum and were acquired in a fairly indiscriminate manner by all types of readers. What is certain is that the romantic comic or "rose" historieta—which substituted intimate, sentimental action for external, heroic adventure—began to dominate in the late 1940s. Love and its intricate terrain changed from an added, but incidental, feature of bizarre plots, to the fundamental thread leading through countless stories. The heart of the romantic began to prevail over the heart of the adventurer.

The amorous drama is not the exclusive property of any geographical, historical, or social sphere; and our rose historietas explored all spaces, times, and classes. But in the 1940s, the passions loosed in the tearful Mexican historieta tended to situate themselves in the slums. The readership which would determine commercial success was composed chiefly of people of the *barrio*. The historietas offered them a sentimental education whose points of reference were the street, the neighborhood, or the cabaret.

For a popular urban medium such as the historieta, the coarsely realistic melodrama was the genre par excellence, and the *arrabal* (slum) its perfect setting. The world was wide and alien, but the *barrio bajo* was origin and destiny. People could leave the *arrabal* by the force of their fists, but in the long run, defeated by life and repentant of their frivolity, the deserters returned to the "fifth patio," where there waited the child or soulmate they had abandoned, and inevitably, the heart of a self-sacrificing mother.

The predominance of characters in conflict and intimate melodramas over conventional heroes and exterior action, combined with the prevalence of the *barrio*, cantina, and cabaret over exotic or cosmopolitan settings, introduced a new violence to the Mexican historieta of the forties. Both the humorous comic and the escapist adventure had always been marked by extreme physical violence; the onomatopoetic "boom" of the balloon captions responded, at least in part, to the need for graphic show of power. This aggressiveness, as spectacular and showy as it was arbitrary and external, was present in our comics from the beginning; but in the forties it began to attach itself to a less conventional violence. The *"BRAOOOM!"* and *"POW!"* of the North American comic could do little to represent the viciousness of a stab in the back during a cantina brawl. Children abused by an alcoholic father in the sordidness of an outhouse were poorly served by *"SNIF! SNIF!"* Once they had penetrated the world of sensual misery, the pepines adopted the savagery of the *nota roja* and moved away from the sanitized violence of conventional comics.

If the pepines did not invent the sports story, neither did they originate the tale of poverty. The United States was not always a consumer's paradise; and following the stock market crash of 1929, poverty was visible. In 1932, Martha Orr created the series "Apple Mary" ("María Manzanas" in Mexico), about an elderly street vendor. By 1939, however, the Great Depression was history, and the pauper heroine had ascended socially and adopted the new name of Mary Worth. Of course, in the underdeveloped countries, such miracles do not occur: poverty is not a waystation but an ugly, permanent state. Not surprisingly, the "miserabilista" comic was here to stay.

The naturalist vocation in the historieta of the 1940s found its most appropriate technical expression in the use of a single ink and the halftone technique. The Mexican pepines claimed to be as real "as life itself," and the new technique was a further step toward that goal. "With the halftone drawing," Valdiosera remembers, "people felt that the historietas were more credible. They commented on how much they looked like photographs." But if the photographic image was the height of verisimilitude and the comics aspired to realism, why not make historietas directly with photographs? The moneros accepted the challenge and in the early 1940s invented the photomontage, anticipating by some years the Italian *fumetti*, which appeared in 1947.

Stories with photographic sequences were almost as old as the art of Louis Daguerre. They had been published in Mexico since the end of the nineteenth century in magazines such as *El Mundo Ilustrado*, with images by Arriaga and Lupercio, among others. In the twentieth century, photographic reportage frequently appeared in the national press, executed by such professionals as Casasola and Devars. Nevertheless, these short illustrated stories were not photohistorietas, since they lacked balloons, and dialogue or explanatory text appeared in captions. Photomontage was another matter. It involved substituting photographs for drawings while maintaining the language of the historieta. That meant superimposing balloons and explanatory text, tracing outlines, drawing onomatopoetic words, and, where necessary, cutting and reassembling different photographs, retouching them, and frequently painting in the missing elements.

The Mexican photohistorieta of the forties was not a foray into a new narrative genre; it was an amplification of the language of the comic, developed by professional moneros who found the photographic collage a useful extension of the pen and the brush. It was also, and above all else, an effort to introduce the greatest truth possible into the historietas by appropriating the photograph's proverbial fidelity to the real. The originator of the first Mexican photomontages was arguably either Valdiosera—who in 1943 made "Pokar de Ases" for the magazine *Pinocho*—or Cruz, who at about the same time published photographic series such as "Remolino y Tango" in the pages of *Pepín*. In any case, after that date the new technique was adopted by other historieta artists, such as Flores, who began inserting photographs among the vignettes of "Gitanillo," a bullfighting series also published in *Pepín*.

In the humorous comics of the 1920s, the accompanying texts were secondary to the illustrations. But when the historieta decided to treat "serious" themes and "human" drama, the moneros began to feel that their drawings fell short of the moral, social, and philosophical implications of the plot. Accordingly, they underscored their elevated intentions with increasingly pompous and grandiloquent prose. In series of great "human weight" and didactic and moralistic pretensions, such as "Don Proverbio" by Carlos del Paso and Antonio Gutiérrez or "Brumas" by Leonel Guillermo Prieto and Arturo Casillas, the prologues and introductions took up entire chapters, and the action frequently was interrupted by extensive commentary on the implications of an act or the complex emotions of the protagonists.

The ultimate exponent of the supporting text was José Guadelupe Cruz, who possessed an astonishing ability to convince readers that they faced the sublime in historieta form. From his first efforts, published in *Paquín*, the young José Guadelupe fell back on kitschy prose:

> That night the cadavers of the Monje Negro and María, over whose lives tragedy and drama had beaten their wings, were shrouded. . . . A halo of mystery seemed to envelop the black coffins, and to look at them recalled a history written with tears and blood. . . . *to be continued*.

The authors of the romantic and moral historietas were faithful to the two basic principles of kitsch: "Sentiment that is not gripped by emotion is not sublime, nor is it sentiment, nor anything at all"; and "A phrase without metaphor is like a life without love." They filled their stories with purple prose, stamping Mexican comics with the strong verbal cargo they have borne into our own day. In exchange, the moneros brought their readers an impressive arsenal of literary formulas that enabled the expression of intimate emotions and transcendent convictions. For better or worse, the bolero, the tango, radio theatre, Spanish-language films, and the comics taught us to speak. They put words to unspoken sentiments and forged memorable phrases for an urban Mexico in formation, whose experiences, but for these media, would have gone unnamed. And since that which is not named does not exist, the work of our popular writers also has been an enterprise in sentimental construction.

The protagonists of our first modern historietas were popular character types refined through caricature. Just as their image was stylized, their speech was satirized: in the monitos, all the fricative consonants of the Chinese were *l*'s; Yankees only conjugated in the infinitive; Syrian and Lebanese creditors changed the *ies* to *aes*; Spanish shopkeepers shouted "¡Ole!" and spoke with the zeta; and uncultured Indians underscored all of their statements with *ansina, mesmamente,* and *sí, señor.*

A certain nationalistic culture dating from the aftermath of the revolution favored popular character types who were imbued with a patriotic curiosity and an entomological bent. The variants of our national condition, including the local ethnic minorities, were classified, defined, and reduced to types; and the same occurred with modes of speech. The comics of the era manifested this compulsion with a gallery of physical and verbal stereotypes: peasants like Don Catarino, Mamerto, and Segundo I; wretches (*peladitos*) such as Chema and Chupamirto; gringos like Smith and Lind; and so on.

In the action comics, which unfolded in frenzied or cosmopolitan settings, a neutral or direct Spanish was generally used. Transnational heroes such as Drake, Alex, Wings, or Tawa inhabited series that rarely had recourse to local expressions, but in which colloquialisms abounded. The balloon captions of the weepy melodrama or the adventure, on the other hand, lent themselves to a more luxuriant language. In the romantic series, both the supporting text and the dialogue tended toward sentimental exaltation and its literary counterpart, baroque verbal expression. While authors underscored the transcendence of their stories in long accompanying passages, the protagonists, conscious of their role, developed interminable monologues. For example:

> Only I know the hell I went through at the side of that man! . . . I was his slave and did everything he ordered me to without rebellion. Why did I humble myself so? He took me throughout the country from brothel to brothel, living off of me and other women. He hit me as no one would hit even a poor beast. . . . One horrible day I will never forget . . . he left me! . . . He abandoned me because I was no longer what I was before: I was losing my figure. . . . I was going to be a mother!

The Dictatorship of the Reader

In less than fifteen years, the Mexican comic found new means of diffusion, changed its format and frequency, diversified its themes, and modified its graphic and argumentative treatments. This profound transformation may be explained in part by the commercial decisions of the great publishers and distributors, by the initiative of the editors or artistic directors, and by the creativity of the writers and artists. But ultimately the reason for the success of comics lies neither within the industry that produced them nor, exclusively, outside it. In Mexico the state did not dictate cultural policy; neither did readers clearly have the capacity to frame their needs systematically or the force to impose them. The key to understanding the course of the historietas therefore lies neither in who produced them nor in who consumed them; rather, it is buried somewhere in the complex relations between the two foci of cultural production and consumption. Basically, this is a commercial nexus: the culture industry, like any other, looks for profits, and in this respect the public simply represents potential consumers of its products. But this merchandise will be purchased only if it satisfies a need that publicity, with all its magic, cannot create from scratch. To sell the monito magazines it was necessary to produce historietas that the readers "desired," and the ability to discover those needs was what made certain publishers successful.

This is not to suggest that the mass communications industry is incapable of creating needs and conditioning tastes. But its point of departure is the satisfaction, albeit commercial and alienated, of actual requirements. Popular sentiment can be manipulated, but first it must be captured. In the products of the communications media, therefore, can be read as much the producers' mercantile miserliness and brittle ideology as the signs of its consumers' cultural identity. They are faces of a single coin, inseparable but looking in different directions.

The true ideologues of the culture industries are not so much their political agents as those responsible for marketing—the technicians who can detect the slightest fluctuations in demand. Today the greatest publishers of historietas possess sophisticated marketing systems. In the 1930s and 1940s they depended mainly on intuition—an intuition that was validated or rectified by sales reports. But it was also an intuition always fed by a direct relationship with readers.

For the first comic fanatics, the monito magazines were as familiar as the open-air tent theater (*teatro carpero*). Whereas the singers, dancers, or actors of the *farándula populachera* (troupes that played to the "rabble") were encouraged or condemned at the top of the spectator's voice, the historieta illustrators were supported or criticized by letter. Readers of comics in the thirties and forties passionately followed the vicissitudes of their favorite heroes, and they were exacting and critical. Those writers and artists who may have started out blindly or by imitating the styles of imported comics were soon besieged by complaints, demands, or threats. At times the readers virtually took the helm of the historietas themselves.

This intense and mutual nourishment between the historietas and their readers flowed through the writers and illustrators, who, as a result, acquired public personas. No longer anonymous, they themselves were transformed into protagonists of a collective cultural adventure. The successful moneros became as famous as their characters, and their images regularly appeared beside those of their paper heroes. Cervantes Bassoco would interrupt the narration of "El Pirata Negro" to wish his readers a Merry Christmas or Happy New Year. Araiza dedicated several frames of "A Batacazo Limpio" to announcing that the illustrator "Manny" Moran had arrived from the United States and would be collaborating on the series. Valdiosera drew himself and recounted his biography at the beginning of a chapter of "Alex" that took place in the port of Tuxpan, "where I learned my first letters."

With the authors as protagonists and the public as interlocutors, the historietas and their characters were demystified and revealed for what they really were: fictions of ink and paper, games of the imagination that were enjoyed or suffered by moneros and readers alike. The emotional letters to the authors ("How can you make your hero suffer so? We love him; he is an idol in our home") lend credence to the notion of a triangular relationship in which the reader placed himself on the same level as the author in terms of a character's destiny. Between the passionate identification and the critical distance, the reading of historietas became a participatory experience, the kind that can be found only in manifestations of popular culture such as the tent theater or theatrical revue.

II

The material presented above provides a basis for examining, among other things, the new pillars of popular culture in Mexico that emerged in the decades following 1920, and the privatization of cultural experience that occurred during the same period. Another set of issues turns on how to characterize the mutual enrichment of the culture industries and the popular classes, as well as what could be called, for lack of a better expression, the plagiarizing creator. These are among the critical topics I will address by way of conclusion.

The Solitary Reader

After the revolution, Mexico urbanized very rapidly. The capital ceased to be the symbolic territory of the *catrines* (well-to-do): its streets and *colonias populares* crowded with migrants from the countryside, Mexico City became the crucible of new signs of identity. At the same time, the communications media began to supplant artisan folklore as a material base of popular culture. Radio, cinema, comics, recorded music, sports events, and metropolitan nightlife were the new or renewed means of communication. Their wide dissemination found its major outlet first in the urban areas and then, gradually, throughout the entire country.

Widespread literacy campaigns caused the consumption of popular culture to shift from sites of collective, almost always gregarious enjoyment to intimate settings. The new and solitary vice of reading privatized cultural experience for the first time and multiplied the "readers"— strange people who cried, exulted, or laughed alone, their gaze fixed on the printed page. The existence of "read" experiences—that is, shared by many but acquired in private—substantially modified the modes of sentimental education and obliged the moneros to reconsider their narrative methods.

In their attempt to move from the social laugh to the bedside chuckle, the humorous comics of the twenties and thirties resorted to the long-established routines of the *teatro carpero*. But the formulas that could

awaken contagious laughter in a public already congregated and pre-
disposed to it failed in the historieta. To extract a smile from the solitary
reader, the moneros had to reinvent humor. It was as a result of this
reinvention that the form of printed speech most familiar to Mexicans in
this century evolved. The historieta was the vehicle for the first intimate
cultural pleasure, a role it shared only with radio and musical recordings
in the first half of the century. Then and since—indeed, up to the present
day—magazines and daily newspapers (and behind them, books) have
followed at a remote distance.

It is said that folklore is popular in a creative sense, while the products
of the culture industries are popular only in terms of their mass consumption. This simplification obscures the indirect but important participation
of the reader in the configuration of Mexico's first comics. The culture
industry, no doubt for commercial reasons, tried to discover the needs of
its public before attempting to induce tastes, and this encouraged an
intense, mutual enrichment between authors and readers. Reading, however, is not simply an act of consumption but also of appropriation.
Consumers thereby participated in the genesis of the comics of that era.
The creative pleasure of newly discovered reading, moreover, brought
the reader's cultural baggage to the fore. Therefore it is urgent to begin
the historical rescue and systematic study not only of the virtually unexplored products of culture industry, but also of the multiple, diverse
reading experiences that must have taken place and that can be intuited
only from a contextualized rereading.

It is also sometimes said that the mass media homogenize their
offerings, and thereby the experience and cultural profile of their audience. From this perspective, by acceding to the messages of the postrevolutionary culture industry we Mexicans have sacrificed our spiritual
diversity to become "the masses." The reality is not so simple or Manichaean. Given the broad range of access to the messages of the culture
industry, clearly some of the old particularities of geography, ethnicity,
and class have fractured, and the more universal premises of identity have
been created. The result is a cultural environment that is still differentiated, but whose diversity is more elective than determinist. Indeed, the
mass media may bring about a potentially freer cultural plurality, fostering
not only more elaborate and sophisticated means of dissemination but
also the recomposition of minority groups.

Seen in this light, the birth of the Mexican commercial historieta was
more laudable than ominous. Before the forties, there was no publishing
industry for the masses, which meant that the great majority of Mexicans

were excluded from reading. The monito magazines, with print runs of more than a half million copies and national distribution, created the first truly mass readership in the country's history. Initially the industry's orientation tended to homogenize that public through magazines "for everyone." But that "tabula rasa strategy" lasted only a short while. If only three or four comics dominated the market in the 1940s (*Pepín, Chamaco, Paquín, Paquito*), by the 1950s the industry's publishing strategy was oriented toward a diversity of offerings and a multiplicity of options.

The "Plagiarizing" Creator

The most creative years of the Mexican culture industry were also the time of an opening to the outside world and an unchecked plagiarism— since originality does not flourish in isolation but in happy contamination. To act with self-confidence and without guilt is more creative in the end than cloistering oneself in search of inspiration in one's own "roots." As was the case with the entire culture industry following the revolution, the comics had no "cactus curtain." But this opening to the world was seen by almost all the intelligentsia as simply a foreignizing parody, and it provided even more arguments for the group's satanization of the comics industry.

In "high culture" the universal gaze is cosmopolitan, while provincialism is reprehensible myopia. In the "low culture" of popular consumption, on the other hand, the assimilation of models and formulas coined in other countries is seen as selling out to the foreigner. The truth is that imitation can be either creative or commonplace; the final product depends on the cultural vigor of its authors or creators. Protectionist and defensive self-absorption weakens rather than fortifies, because it permits creators neither to value their own creation nor to utilize their comparative cultural advantages.

The forties were the golden years of the Mexican historieta, but the powerful imagination our moneros displayed was not a creation "in vitro," nor was it born in the greenhouse of cultural protectionism. Original genres and styles resulted from the creative assimilation of North American models. Import substitution took place in the cultural sphere and its benefits were increasingly exported—benefits, in the historieta's case, manifested in the growth of the great syndicates, the multiplication of their services, and the distribution of Mexican comics throughout Latin America. This was the result not of protectionism but of competition within the local industry and, above all, among its creators. It was a propitious competition, since Mexican *moneros* faced products of national distribution which, owing to simple economies of scale, were very cheap. If our comics, like our theater, our radio, and our commercial music, survived and even conquered markets in spite of their technological inferiority, it was because they exploited their comparative advantages: they were comics of a cosmopolitan nature, but made by and for Latin Americans.

At the very moment when new media were offered to the Mexican masses on a commercial scale, the material conditions needed to transcend the old particularisms were also created, giving rise to a national culture based on a more elective and less fatalistic new plurality. Popular culture became international as it developed a flow of insights and messages that did not recognize borders. Mexican film, radio, commercial music, and comics were on a par with what was manufactured elsewhere in the world, since they had to compete with imports for a well-informed and therefore demanding public. Under these conditions the creation of unique styles in these media was a work of authentic nationalism, and should be understood not as exteriority and isolation but as a specific difference—as the Mexican version of universal culture.

In these years of extensive consumption of popular culture and intense creation in the communications industry, the preoccupation with "Mexican character," with the so-called national identity, gained strength. This attempt at self-definition came from the intelligentsia, but was encouraged by the state; not surprisingly it rested on questionable premises. One recent critique regards it to be a deceptive and alienating intellectual current, one that packaged and stereotyped us while ignoring realities perhaps less "profound" but more real. As such, it lent itself to manipulation, premeditated or otherwise.[4]

There is much to this critique. But if, apart from dismantling the construction from the inside, we consider the old discourse on "Mexican character" and "identity" in the context of the extensive and multicolored popular cultural effervescence of its era, what is most obvious is its astonishing lack of documentary support. Those who fall prey to such reflexive exercises generally possess an adequate understanding of the various areas of elite culture and more or less extensive notions about folklore. But such resources are wholly insufficient when *lo mexicano* is

4. For a provocative analysis of this intellectual current of self-definition, see R. Bartra (1987).

bubbling up in the melting pot of the culture industry. With no basis other than a cultivated spirit and some intuitions gained from a life shared with one's elite companions, the search for *lo mexicano* quickly becomes superficial.

In the first half of the twentieth century, the basis of a national identity developed through the accumulation of experiences shared by the majority of Mexicans, thanks to the media of mass communication. During the same period, the "nature" of what is Mexican was explored as if searching for an ultimate common denominator; that is, through an examination of specific differences, the three or four shared traits that distinguish us—a kind of search for definition in the Aristotelian sense of the term. It was a hopeless enterprise. *Lo mexicano* is, if anything, an articulated diversity; an ongoing synthesis that is subject to multiple determinations. And it is in the construction of this concept—not in attempts to define it—that our premises remain modest but challenging: to recover, depict, and critically analyze the great watersheds of the popular culture industry of the twentieth century.

Thanks to the nationalism of the state since the revolution, a formidable culture of Mexican folklore has developed that unfortunately has no corollary in other spheres. Today, we know more of the weavings, clay bowls, and masks—in short, of an artisan industry in full withdrawal—than we do of the history of radio, recorded music, or the comics. Thus, we know little of the history of the dynamic culture industries that, for better or worse, have shaped our identity. Without question, these same culture industries merit criticism for this state of affairs, a judgment that, if severe, seems well founded. Be this as it may, disqualification as an alibi for ignorance can no longer be tolerated.

BARRY CARR

The Fate of the Vanguard under a Revolutionary State:

Marxism's Contribution to the Construction

of the Great Arch

Marxists and Communists in Mexico drew on a variety of traditions. In particular they had to look to Europe and to their own nation. They responded to the European roots of the revolutionary socialist ideas they espoused and the world-historical character of their cause, and to the international movements (the Comintern, the Soviet Union, the Fourth International) that served as guide and inspiration. They also responded to indigenous popular and radical traditions (or rather to their own constructions of these traditions), the heritage of Mexican anarchism, and the challenge of a revolution and a revolutionary state that, while it never burst through the boundaries of capitalist social and economic relations, did detonate and occasionally support actions that pushed these boundaries to the limit.[1]

It is important to bear this in mind in the light of that tradition of Communist historiography which has underplayed the extent to which

1. The Cardenista years, for example, were marked by the expropriation of foreign-owned petroleum companies, experiments with worker and peasant self-management, and a massive expansion of agrarian reform, which included attacks on important citadels of agrarian capitalism. At the same time, the state supported the unification of the country's fragmented peasant and labor organizations, albeit on terms that prevented the creation of a united worker-peasant bloc. Hamilton (1982:140–44); Knight (1985b:27).

Marxism was necessarily superimposed on pre-existing modes of thought which it incorporated rather than displaced, and which were regarded as being intrinsic to the new outlook (Samuel 1980:23).

This dominant historiographical tradition has also emphasized teleological and reductionist interpretations that overstate the importance of Communist parties' subordination to the dictates of Moscow and demonstrate more concern with structure than with agency. What follows from this multistranded character of Marxism and Communism is, first, that it is impossible to understand the history of Marxists and Communists without paying attention to the ways they dialogued with traditions, experiences, and actions *outside* the formal tradition they espoused. This explains the saliency of the left's appeal and many of its triumphs, as well as some of its failures. Second, because Marxists and Communists were inevitably caught up in contradictory practices, their actions often had unintended consequences. Aiming to subvert and transform the character of the capitalist state, the Mexican Communist party (PCM) in some ways acted to strengthen it, encouraging its "revolutionary" and "progressive" pretensions.[2] For example, tied to a radical popular vision of art (as expressed in the muralist tradition) and committed to building on previous waves of national-popular struggles, the PCM won great prestige among the intelligentsia and people.[3] But it probably also deepened artistic and cultural mystification of the past and political manipulation of Mexican history as carried out by the Revolutionary Family.

Similarly, while from the vantage point of 1993 the global defeat of the older left's project is clear, this outcome cannot be explained solely by

---

2. The most eloquent discussion of how the left assimilated elements of revolutionary nationalism, and how in turn the bourgeois ideology of the Mexican revolution stole the clothes of the revolutionary left, is still that of José Revueltas (1980).

3. The list of Marxists and Communists (or at least people who made contact with these traditions at some point in their lives) who shaped large areas of Mexican life *before* the great explosion of Marxism in the late 1960s is enormous. It includes writers like Juan de la Cabada, Carlos Pellicer, Efraín Huerta, José Mancisidor, Eraclio Zepeda, José Revueltas; musicians, singers, and composers like Silvestre Revueltas and Concha Michel; and painters and muralists like Diego Rivera, David Alfaro Siqueiros, Frida Kahlo, Xavier Guerrero, José Chávez Morado, and Leopoldo Méndez. The list of social scientists (especially economists, sociologists, and historians), educators, and state-sector bureaucrats who passed through the PCM or Lombardismo would be many times larger.

reference to the far-sighted, all-seeing genius of the Leviathan state or the repression launched by that state against the left, although both these factors played a crucial role. One of the arguments of this chapter will be that the productivist and statist strains within the culture of Mexican socialism weakened the left's critical stand and enhanced the "revolution-ary" state's capacity to assume the role of sole legitimate interpreter of what was "national" and "popular." The Marxist left, then, played its role in constructing the Great Arch in Mexico.

This article ranges widely throughout the period 1920–1950. It is not a study of any one particular conjuncture, although it draws on a number of particular moments in the history of the left (Carr 1992). It is informed throughout by concerns shaped by my reading of the history of Marxism and Communism in other areas, particularly Britain. After an introduction to the two dominant Marxist traditions in Mexico (represented by the PCM and the fusion of Legal Marxism and revolutionary nationalism that has been labeled Lombardismo), this study discusses some of the features of Marxist culture as it has developed since the mid-nineteenth century and notes the ways in which elements of this ideological and cultural matrix facilitated and obstructed the development of the left in Mexico. This is followed by brief discussions of the revolutionary muralist move-ment, the development of Lombardismo during the 1930s and 1940s, and certain aspects of the PCM's involvement in agrarian struggle in the Laguna region.

The Marxist left had pretensions of constituting a vanguard—of being the privileged interpreters and activists of the people. Its organiza-tional structure, practices, and concerns reflected this; hence the central-ity of themes like hierarchy, centralization, the necessity for disciplined militants, the influence of party organs, the policing of orthodoxy, identi-fication with global struggles by the working class and peasantry, and the defense of the Soviet Union. But its members and the oppositionists it influenced (and Marxists influenced a constituency much wider than the membership lists of Marxist parties alone would suggest) were motivated by a complex series of concerns. Some of them have already been mentioned, but there were others: moral and ethical preoccupations; a search for prior collective traditions; and, on occasion, opportunism and expectations of personal enhancement.[4] On the other hand—and this

---

4. We need to remind ourselves again and again that some of the strongest motivations activating the left are ethical rather than material. For an eloquent statement of this point, see Shanin (1990). Talking about Eastern Europe and the

point will be stressed several times in this chapter—the culture of the radical left also shaped aspects of the dominant "official" culture of revolutionary Mexico which sometimes appropriated elements of the left's cultural baggage and employed it in ways that sought to contain popular action.

COMMUNISM AND LOMBARDISMO: THE VANGUARD PARTY LEGACY

The Mexican Communist party, the oldest political party in Mexico (it was founded in 1919), was never a mass party.[5] Its membership peaked in the late 1930s (during the presidency of Lázaro Cárdenas) at between thirty-five and forty thousand; apart from that era, however, PCM membership rarely exceeded ten thousand. A corollary is that, except for brief periods of its existence, the PCM's links with the Mexican working class and peasantry were weak and not very durable. This is not to suggest that the party was outside the history of worker and peasant struggles in Mexico. Far from it. During the middle and late 1920s, the PCM maintained an extremely important presence in the newly emerging peasant movement, the National Peasant League (Liga Nacional Campesina). The party played a crucial role in the peasant struggles of the mid- to late 1930s, particularly in the Laguna region of Coahuila and Durango, northern Sinaloa, parts of Sonora, and the Soconusco area of Chiapas; and it had small but important areas of influence among miners and railroad workers in the 1920s.

The Cárdenas era (1934–1940) is widely believed to have been the golden age of the PCM. The party regained its legality, which it had lost in 1929. Then, after an initial period of confusion regarding its attitude toward the radical popular and anti-imperialist policies of the new government, it embraced Cárdenas and the newly formed official party, the Partido de la Revolución Mexicana (PRM), as the incarnation of the

---

Soviet Union, Shanin notes, "the people who supported socialism and became its most effective activists did so mostly out of moral compulsion—an applied ethic of right and wrong in political and daily behavior. . . . Some supported socialism also out of a particular aesthetic in the ways they viewed humans and human endeavor—a kind of beauty assumed and set as a goal" (1990:69–71).

5. The PCM was formally dissolved in 1981. Since that year, fragments of the former PCM have formed part of several united left parties: the PSUM, the PMS, and currently the PRD.

Popular Front. Free from official harassment, the PCM played a formative role in the creation of a number of important national industrial unions in the 1930s. Incorporating teachers, railroad workers, petroleum workers, and miners, these organizational efforts had a measurable impact on PCM membership. In certain states in the late 1930s, for example, up to one quarter of the party's members were teachers. The party was also, for a while, the dominant force in the most important state federations of the newly formed Mexican Workers' Confederation (CTM).

With one or two exceptions, however, the PCM was unable to maintain a consistent presence in these sectors. This resulted partly from growing anticommunism in the "official" trade union movement and partly from sharp repression by the state. The latter was especially harsh during the late 1940s and early 1950s, as well as during the epic labor struggles of 1957–1960, which mobilized hundreds of thousands of teachers, telegraph operators, and railroad workers. The PCM also lost thousands of dedicated members during the frequent purges it undertook in the 1940s. The party's decision to back Vicente Lombardo Toledano's effort to create a broad left party, the Popular party (Partido Popular), in 1947 also cost the PCM a number of its best cadres.

By the early 1960s the Mexican Communist party could count on the active support of three main groups: a very small number of teachers, mostly in the Federal District; small, isolated clusters of railroad workers who had escaped the repression of 1958–1960; and a numerically significant but in practice very weak group of peasant affiliates in the Laguna region. Not until the student-popular movement of 1968 and afterward (more particularly in the mid-1970s, with the formation of powerful unions of university teachers and administrative workers) did the party acquire a considerable base within the ranks of teachers and other college employees. At the regional and local level, however, the PCM was able to establish a significant presence in several small cities and *municipios*. This was the case, for example, in Juchitán, Oaxaca, a town with a long history of oppositional activity closely linked to issues of Zapotec cultural identity. There, the party established an uneasy alliance with the main protagonist of the *juchiteco* left, COCEI (Rubin 1987:136–37; Gutiérrez 1981). In the village of Alcozauca (population 2,200) in the Montaña region of Guerrero, a PCM schoolteacher was elected *presidente municipal*, and thereby won control of the heavily Mixtec municipality in 1981.[6]

6. The election of Abel Cabrera (a teacher with thirty-five years' experience in the region) was a reminder that not all teachers and *normalistas* were insensitive agents

The PCM, for much of its life, pursued a strategy that was increasingly out of kilter with the realities of Mexican society, particularly in the period 1940–1960. In statements analogous to those of most other Latin American Communist parties, the PCM argued that Mexico was an imperfectly formed capitalist society, a semifeudal formation characterized by the existence of substantial feudal or precapitalist sectors. This argument led the party, for example, to neglect the growing political importance of proletarianized peasant groups outside the reform sector of agriculture. Thus, until the early 1960s, the PCM centered its concerns in the agricultural sector exclusively on its traditional base among groups of *ejidatarios*.

It also accepted the argument that the task of the Mexican revolution of 1910 was to consolidate the construction of capitalism with a nationalist and anti-imperialist program and a mass base among workers and peasants, which would permit a transition to socialism. This position echoed almost exactly the arguments developed by labor leader, theorist, and Popular party founder Vicente Lombardo Toledano. Accepting the thesis of the essential continuity of the Mexican revolution led the PCM, on different occasions, to propose liquidation of the party organization and even affiliation or merger with the official party of the Mexican revolution, known since 1946 as the PRI.

LOMBARDISMO

The idea of creating a broad, united-front party embracing the independent left and sectors of the ruling party had long been a dream of Lombardo's (Millon 1960; Krauze 1976: chap. 11; Chassen de López 1977). He had first proposed such a party in the late 1930s, and the idea caused a major fracas in the Communist party. In 1947–48 the concept reemerged with greater energy during discussions between Lombardo, left-wing labor and peasant leaders, and members of the national intelligentsia.

---

of a modernizing, rational, redistributionist state. The Communist party's presence in the Montaña was closely linked with democratic struggles in Mexico's largest union, the SNTE. Furthermore, many teachers played a major role in the region; some had been involved in the Consejo de Pueblos de la Montaña (CPM) since adolescence. One of Alcozauca's most famous sons was an activist of national fame, Othón Salazar, a leader of the 1958 teachers' movement in Mexico City. The CPM was the main vehicle through which the party worked. See Lagarde and Cazés (1980:3); Mejía Pineros and Sarmiento Siva (1987:97–101).

Lombardo proposed a party that would support the national democratic, antifeudal, and anti-imperialist goals of the Mexican revolution. It would work for rapid industrialization as part of a broader commitment to promoting national economic independence, and for a deepening of land reform. It would struggle against the Mexican right, which Lombardo identified as the *sinarquista* movement and the National Action party (PAN) and, to a much lesser degree, conservative forces within the PRI.

None of these goals differed from those of the PCM. This was not surprising, since Lombardo's vision was grounded in the Popular Front and National Unity concepts developed by the Comintern since the mid-1930s. Lombardo's strategy and tactics were different, though. Like the PCM, he was prepared to support "positive" steps taken by the ruling party, but his interpretation of what constituted a progressive move was much more generous. Under Lombardo's guidance, the Popular party was reluctant to condemn the PRI by name and when this was not possible, a careful distinction was always made between the actions of "reactionary" forces within the PRI and the figure of the president himself. In the final instance, Lombardo during the late 1940s had no problems expressing loyalty to both President Miguel Alemán and Joseph Stalin.

In spite of Lombardo's cautious approach to criticizing the PRI, the official party and its sectoral affiliates, especially the CTM, did not look kindly on the new organization. The onset of the Cold War was partly to blame, but the PRI, understandably, also saw the new party as a threat to its mass base, as well as a personal vehicle for Lombardo that might challenge its patronage networks and those of its mass organizations. Lombardo's firm hold over the new body was indisputable; his authoritarian imprint was visible from the earliest days of the Popular party and even in the negotiations that preceded the party's formal establishment in June 1948. Between September 1947 and June 1948, for example, the party's national coordinating committee did not meet even once. During the 1950s the party's decision-making apparatus barely functioned (Villaseñor 1976:136–37). Intraparty quarrels were common throughout the 1950s, and peaked between 1956 and 1958 in a series of arguments between Lombardo's inner circle of relatives and friends and the allies of a leading party intellectual (and former Communist), Enrique Ramírez y Ramírez (Schmitt 1965:82–87).

The Popular party's program did not mention socialism or Marxism at all, but called for a series of measures that would promote a form of state capitalism and a people's democracy (Millon 1960:161). In ways that were never explained, this was to lead to the establishment of socialism. By the mid-1950s, however, the party had adopted socialism as its goal. It changed its name to the Popular Socialist party (PPS) in 1960.

The key element in Lombardo's vision of socialism was the creative action of the state. The state—which Lombardo maintained was dominated by a nationalist bourgeoisie locked in permanent battle with reactionary capitalists and landowners at home and imperialism abroad—was interested in pressing for state capitalism and the nationalization of key resources. But the only way this drive could be translated into socialism was by creating a national front in which workers, peasants, intellectuals, the petite and nationalist bourgeoisie, and progressive sectors of the PRI could join forces. Socialism in Lombardo's vision became "the prolongation and extension of state capitalism" (R. Bartra 1982:186).

The Popular party developed a small but strategically important base among sectors of the peasantry and working class. It also developed a substantial base within the Mexican intelligentsia. In the late 1950s and early 1960s, the newsmagazine *Política,* edited by party member Manuel Marcué Pardiñas, helped publicize the Popular party line. In addition to the nationally renowned intellectuals who passed through the party at different points in its first decade, many teachers and students, especially in the rural teacher-training colleges, joined the PP, influenced by the militant nationalism and materialist rationalism featured in the discourse of the Lombardistas. The links between the PP(s), teachers, and teacher trainees meant that at the local level the Lombardistas were closely in touch with popular struggles, particularly among peasants and rural workers where rural teachers enjoyed prestige. Therefore, the actual practices of PP supporters and members at the regional level often diverged quite strongly from the cautious line articulated by Lombardo and the national leadership. In Chihuahua, for example, the first Mexican attempt to organize a guerrilla movement (at Madera) in the aftermath of the Cuban revolution was led by teachers and students who had been members of the PP.

THE MULTISTRANDED HERITAGE OF MARXISM

Marxism and socialism, especially of the Second and Third International varieties, were traditions, ideologies, and practices that carried within them many features of the mid- and late nineteenth-century capitalist societies in which they emerged. In particular, they bore the imprint of positivism, modernism, and evolutionism.[7] They celebrated modernity and progress, paying particular attention to the victory of science over nature and the revolutionary and transformative power of technology on the productive forces—hence the glorification of industrialization common in much Soviet and Comintern discourse from the 1920s to the 1940s.[8] They welcomed the victory of science over superstition.[9] (In some cases this involved adopting ideas of birth control and eugenics, sex education, and certain limited notions about economic and legal emancipation of women.[10]) They also emphasized the power of optimistic rationalism[11] and the centralizing and "nationalizing" thrust of the state as it challenged parochialism and particularistic identity. Marxist and Communist currents articulated a left variant of the culture of modern politics, based on such practices as mass meetings, sale of newspapers, and pamphleteering—activities oriented toward a literate or semiliterate urban population. The left traditions also welcomed massification and proletarianization, partly because of the assumption that the proletariat was the agency of revolution, and partly because of the belief that capitalism spelled the end of peasantry in any case. The vitality of the

7. I acknowledge that these tendencies are more present in Marx's followers and vulgarizers than in Marx's own writings, which convey considerable tension between, say, "evolutionist" perspectives and a sternly antiteleological stance. See Corrigan and Sayer (1983).

8. For a marvelous evocation of the enthusiasm with which Communists embraced modernity, "newness," and mass society, see the work of Raphael Samuel (1985:40–43). Although the context there is Britain, much the same thing could be said about the moods and enthusiasms of Communists and Marxists everywhere before the 1950s and 1960s. Even the most superficial skimming of the pages of PCM organs, such as *El Machete, La Voz de México,* and *Nueva Epoca* (note the emphasis in the title) and of the writings of Communists (both rank-and-file and cadres) would reveal this to be the case.

9. "Science [provides] a bridge between the accumulation of capital and the broader social scene. Applied science underscores industrialization and thereby the extended reproduction of modern economy, while the accumulation of capital and industrialization determines the contemporary rise of science" (Shanin 1983:261).

10. In Mexico, these particular concerns were most clearly expressed in the work of Felipe Carrillo Puerto, governor of Yucatán (Joseph [1982] 1988b:216–19).

11. The peak of rationalist optimism in progress was reached with the publication in 1964 of the little book by Lombardo titled *Summa.* Therein the doyen of Mexican Marxism offered the country's youth a path that would "lead them out of the cave of ignorance and suffering into the splendid light of truth" (R. Bartra 1982:181).

debate still raging between *campesinistas* and *proletaristas* in Latin America attests to the continuing importance of these themes in Marxist discourse.

The insistence on privileging proletarian action partly explains the ambiguity among so many Marxists about the revolutionary potential of peasants. In Mexico, Marxists and Communists began with some awareness of the need to secure the support of peasant smallholders, although there was hostility to the *ejido* form in the early years of the PCM. But by the mid-1930s, and building on the rural mobilizations of agricultural workers that preceded the expropriations carried out by the Cárdenas government, the PCM had become fixated on the political significance of the agricultural proletariat and the large-scale land transformations implemented in the Laguna, Michoacán, northern Sinaloa, Baja California, and Chiapas. *Ejidatarios* in some of these regions became a key constituency of the party through the early 1960s. This led Mexican Communists, as already noted, to ignore (until the 1960s) the problems of smallholders and the rapidly increasing number of peasants who had neither land nor work.

Rationalism was closely linked to atheism and anticlericalism for many socialists; and hostility to the church, priests, and religious belief was greatly amplified by the anarchist strain in the Mexican radical tradition. Until the 1960s, Mexican Communists and Marxists, with only a few exceptions, were firmly atheistic and anticlerical.[12] The left shared the vision articulated by the ideologists of the Revolutionary state, which saw peasant religiosity as retrograde, a product of clerical and landowner manipulation. Clearly, many peasants saw the church in a different light—as a valuable cultural, educational, and moral resource. This difference could cause major problems in mobilizing sectors of the peasantry, as witness the horrific experiences of some of the more dramatically Jacobin *maestros rurales* in the 1930s. In Alcozauca ("the first Communist *municipio* in Mexico," as it was called in the early 1980s), one of the first responses to the election of a "red" mayor was the departure of the local Catholic priest. But by this time the PCM was sufficiently aware of the local population's religious sensibilities, and it made strenuous efforts to persuade the bishop to replace the *cura* (Myers 1981:16–19).

12. One interesting exception is the singer, collector of *corridos*, and early feminist Concha Michel. Michel (for a while the *compañera* of PCM general secretary Hernán Laborde), quarreled with the party in the 1930s over the naive economism of its treatment of male-female relations. Michel preached an early version of "feminist theology" and called for the establishment of a *república femenina* (B. Miller 1984:25).

The Marxist and Communist left celebrated sobriety, order, and self-discipline in a world where many of the subordinate classes were viewed as "dangerous," drunken, and "ignorant." In other words, along with a deep sense of commitment to social transformation, there was a certain moralizing tone to the discourse of the Mexican left. This emphasis was a leftist version of the notion of respectability, understood as "an internal discipline in personal behavior," which (to note Stuart Macintyre's comments about workers in the Vale of Leven in Scotland) "gave the worker the self-respect and confidence he needed to think for himself and to fashion his own procedures."[13] Favorable references to discipline are also sprinkled through the formal statements and more informal conversations of the Mexican left. In the "red" *ayuntamiento* of Alcozauca, for example, the PCM mayor, Abel Cabrera, gave great play to the assertion that the local folk were impressed that "llevábamos una lucha correctamente disciplinada." Of course, it is difficult to judge whether such statements reflect a degree of wishful self-deception on the part of "professional" party cadres. The people of Alcozauca may have had other ways of making sense of their decision to vote for the Communist party.

Praise for the local Communists' proven honesty and for their practice of acting *dentro de la ley* in a region where the PRI was implicated in the worst traditions of caciquismo, suggest that the PCM was benefiting not only from the familiar "legalism" of *campesinos* but also from the longstanding concern shown by Mexican reformers for reestablishing the democratic functioning of local communal institutions like the *municipio*. The agendas of participants in protest contain multiple (and often contradictory) ideological strands.

Anti-alcohol campaigns, viewed as a necessary element in the struggle against underdevelopment, were also part of this moralizing stance. A Laguna peasant once remarked in an interview that what he most remembered from talks about the Soviet Union given by returning PCM delegates was the news that alcohol was banned in the first workers' state. Soviet citizens, he fondly believed, drank only natural fruit drinks. When the broad-left First Congress of Socialist Students met in June 1934, it called, among other things, for "the suppression of worship and the

13. The quotation continues: ". . . this discipline was thus a precondition for the development of working-class organizations in the Vale. . . . Hence respectability could assume a variety of political forms; with very few exceptions, the leading Communists came from respectable families, and in their lives they exemplified a characteristic responsibility and moral concern" (Macintyre 1980:91–92).

transformation of all religious buildings into lay schools, libraries, and *anti-alcohol centers*" (Martínez Assad 1979:91–92. My emphasis).

The importance of the rural schoolteachers (*maestros rurales*) in the world of the PCM during the 1930s and 1940s takes on added meaning in the framework of this discussion of the culture of Marxist politics.[14] The *maestros* were often organizers of worker syndicates and peasant unions, political activists, and cultural "middlemen," and were deeply committed to social and economic transformation of the masses. They were what Raby has called the "organic intellectuals of Cardenismo" (1981:82). They could also be viewed as agents of the central government (echoes of patron-client relations here) and pioneers of rationalism and modernism.

Teachers could indeed be rather dogmatic in their interpretations of ideology—Jacobin rather than just anticlerical—and could interpret socialist education in a very formalistic and positivistic fashion.[15] Many teachers, it is now clear, were rejected by peasants for the unwelcome intrusion on the "Little Tradition" and *campesino* vision of what constituted a legitimate social and cultural order that their actions were seen to represent (Becker 1987). On the other hand, we should beware of creating a new (and essentialist) black legend that would construct *campesinos* as unproblematically opposed to scientistic and modernist projects. Listen to the peasants of Xochihuehuetlán, Guerrero, as they write to Lázaro Cárdenas in 1936 supporting their *maestro socialista*:

> Así es que la enseñanza socialista es el bien del adelanto, del mejoramiento y del desarrollo de los campesinos, y nada es cierto que sea la enseñanza del protestantismo y masonismo aún cuando eso sea así, hay que ver por el adelanto de la ciencia del porvenir y del progreso (Bustamante Alvarez 1987:409).

Large numbers of Mexican Marxists tended to privilege scientific detachment and "retraction from the subjective, and especially from ethics, for 'science's sake'" (Shanin 1983:264). A particularly spectacular incident that played up this theme concerned the fate of the novel *Los días terrenales*, written in the late 1940s by José Revueltas, the most brilliant

14. In the state of Guerrero, 90 percent of the *maestros rurales* were members of the PCM in 1939. Four of the six federal inspectors were also Communists. See (Bustamante Alvarez 1987:407).

15. A February 1938 PCM conference on education condemned "la tendencia a considerar el trabajo educativo como lucha anti-religiosa y reconoce que esta tendencia es una de las supervivencias de la ideología anarquista." In PCM [1938] 1980.

creative writer to emerge from the Marxist tradition. The dogmatism and blindness of the PCM leadership is a recurring theme of the book.

> En el Comité Central era impossible que comprendiesen, no por falta de honradez para ello, sino por que simplemente no podían ver las cosas a través del compacto tejido de fórmulas en que estaban envueltos; no podían razonar sino dentro de la aritmética atroz que aplicaban a la vida. . . . Era imposible, a menos de sustituirlos a todos con gente un poco menos cadáver que ellos. . . . (Revueltas 1979:92).[16]

In existentialist fashion, Revueltas dissects the religious-style orthodoxy of political leaders (*curas rojos*), whose reliance on mechanical phrases and formulas blocked any attempt to achieve personal authenticity. The book is one of the first and certainly the most effective statement of humanistic Marxism published in Mexico. At a time when the naive optimism of socialist realism still dominated most creative writing by socialist authors, *Los días terrenales* caused an immediate, subversive shock. Here was a leading socialist writer with impeccable revolutionary credentials portraying a world of revolutionary commitment in which the class struggle was accompanied by an exploration of individual dilemmas and frailties. "They wanted beautiful and perfect revolutionaries; I never knew any; I just spoke about the people who were there" was Revueltas's comment late in his career (Frankenhalter 1979:44).

Finally, the importance of statism needs underlining in the twentieth century, and especially in the post-1917 history of Marxism and Communism, where the state is preserved and even worshiped (no withering away here!) and where the "party" substitutes for the revolutionary, class-conscious working masses. In Mexico, where a relatively weak development of civil society and a burgeoning state with leviathan intentions (many of them unfulfilled, one should quickly add) emerged as one of the centerpieces of post-1920s development, this feature of the Marxist and Communist tradition was particularly fateful. All the more so because,

16. Revueltas had been expelled from the Communist party in 1943. His response to the criticisms that *Los días terrenales* provoked revealed how narrow the limits of tolerance for deviant behavior were on the left. After defending himself against charges that he had broken with his revolutionary past and rejected the prime role of a vanguard workers' party, the novelist published a long piece of self-criticism in July 1950. In his letter of July 26, Revueltas acknowledged most of the criticisms made by his opponents and reaffirmed his commitment to the principles of socialist realism. He then withdrew the book from circulation.

from the late 1930s to 1960, the PCM (and the Lombardistas even later) subordinated the socialist project and sacrificed its independence to the logic of merging, incorporating, capturing, or reforming the octopuslike official party (the goals differed from year to year). The authoritarian practices inherited from international Stalinism were therefore magnified by the statist left's tendency to assimilate the ultranationalism and anti-democratic features of Mexico's ruling party.

The similarities between the style and structure of "PRI politics" in Mexico and the political culture of Marxism and Communism made movement from the latter to the former quite easy. This partly explains why so many people found the transition quite painless. Well-known examples include Enrique Ramírez y Ramírez (via the Partido Popular), Angel Olivo, Germán Parra, and Octaviano Campos Salas. It was not entirely in jest that the PCM was described as the PRI's unofficial cadre training school.[17]

COUNTERVAILING TENDENCIES

The socialist and Marxist traditions welcomed modernity and saw it as the necessary condition for the transformation of humanity. Nevertheless, especially in the nineteenth century and certain moments of the twentieth century, their critique of capitalism bemoaned the eclipse of older traditions and structures in which use values (for example, communal land use) allegedly preserved a homogeneous society. This orientation had, of course, always been present in the anarchist tradition, which strongly molded the early development of Mexican Marxism and socialism. The libertarian movements had a more welcoming attitude towards preindustrial and especially peasant society and were more hostile to the notion of state-organized power. They were also more open to the central importance of the themes of collective regulation of life and production, and self-management (present in the idea of free associations of producers and units of self-government; encapsulated in the peasant village and the "autonomous" *municipio*). In other words, this "proto-socialist" and

17. A claim made by many, including the PRI's Guillermo Martínez Domínguez. See Monsiváis (1979:256). The writer and poet Efraín Huerta captured this tendency brilliantly in one of his *poemínimos*: "A mis viejos maestros de Marxismo no les puedo entender: / Unos están en la cárcel—otros están en el poder" (Huerta 1974).

libertarian tradition competed with the vanguardism of the PCM and the regulated, administered collectivist ideal (with the specialized administrator and cadre in control) that was at the heart of Lombardismo.[18]

Outside the libertarian tradition, this rather more ambivalent attitude of the left toward modernity, and some of its icons of revolutionary romanticism, can be glimpsed in the history of Marxist and Communist parties in many areas of the world. The importance of "medievalist" concerns in British radical traditions from William Cobbett through William Morris and Raymond Williams is a case in point (Samuel 1980: 28–29; Williams 1961; Schwartz 1982:56; E. P. Thompson 1976).[19] In Britain, the Communist Party of Great Britain (CPGB) attempted to rediscover and recreate the democratic traditions of the national-popular by incorporating the concept of the "Good Old Cause" and the rights of the "Free-born Englishman" into its 1930s and 1940s Popular Front–inspired effort to prove the natural "English" roots of Communism. As the CPGB historian James Klugman put it:

> We became the inheritors of the Peasants' Revolt, of the left of the English revolution, of the pre-Chartist movement, of the women's suffrage movement from the 1790s to today. It set us in the right framework, it linked us with the past and gave us a more correct course for the future (cited in Schwartz 1982:56).

In the same vein, the Communist Party of the United States, through its Kansas-born leader, Earl Browder, proclaimed in the mid-1930s that Communism was "twentieth-century Americanism."[20]

Are there Mexican equivalents of this tendency on the left? To some extent, the PCM's embrace of the muralist movement in the 1920s (in which party members figured prominently) represented an attempt to generate a distinctively "national" and "popular" reading of Mexican history and politics.

During the period of the Popular Front and National Unity (1936–1945), Communist party cells and units were frequently named after heroic figures from the liberal/nationalist reading of Mexican history:

18. This is not to say that anarchosyndicalism, to take one of the many strands of antistatist practice, was hostile to industry, science, and progress. For a provocative discussion of Spanish anarchosyndicalists' "fervent" belief in progress and production, see Seidman (1991:42–56).

19. The cruder, more political CPGB appropriation of Morris's life and works can be seen in the first edition of E. P. Thompson's book.

20. On the CPUSA in the 1930s, see Klehr (1984).

Comité Cura Hidalgo, Comité Benito Juárez, Comité Anáhuac, Comité
Morelos, Comité Zapata, Comité Belisario Domínguez, Comité Cuauhtémoc, to name some examples among PCM groups active in the Federal
District.[21] Significantly, when a group of independent Marxists, socialists,
and revolutionary nationalists (including some expelled PCM figures like
Hernán Laborde and Valentín Campa) joined together in a new organization in the mid-1940s, they called it the Círculo [de Estudios y Acción]
José María Morelos.[22] As discourse theorists are constantly reminding us,
the proper answer to the question "What's in a name?" is "Everything," and
the names under which Mexican Communists chose to organize themselves give a clear message about their collective intentions vis-à-vis
Mexican history.

Efforts by the left to appropriate nationalism, however, created many
problems. First, the unproblematic posing of the concept of "national-
popular" necessarily obliterated important discontinuities in the historical
process. Popular struggles have, after all, experienced periods both of
success and failure. Second, a historically naive assumption was at work,
that "the people" were natural repositories of progressive truth, or as it has
been recently put, that "the forward march of the people is necessarily
democratic" and that an "authentic radical popular culture exists, resilient
or impervious to dominant interventions, such that it can be called on as
unambiguously 'ours'" (Schwartz 1982:87). Note that on the first point
the Mexican left's unproblematic celebration of the "national popular"
echoes the historicist thrust of the official ideology of the Mexican
revolution, which is fond of blurring the contradictory experiences and
projects of different figures in the Revolutionary Pantheon. Thus this
ideology celebrates both Emiliano Zapata and Venustiano Carranza (vic-
tim and assassin—or at least the intellectual author of an assassination) in
one breath (O'Malley 1986:126–28). It should be added that this is also a
very masculinist reading of the national-popular tradition.

21. NA, RG 84, 800C, box 57, vol. 264, "Communism, General," report titled
"Organization of the PCM," W. K. Ailshie to Secretary of State, July 6, 1943. Other
cells took on the name of a work location or trade (*sastres, Hacienda*) or a figure in the
revolutionary socialist tradition (Tina Modotti, Julio Antonio Mella).

22. "Los ideales de Hidalgo sólo se realizarán plenamente con un partido del
proletariado" is the title of an article in the magazine *Unidad Socialista* on which a
number of the Marxist and socialist independents collaborated. Anonymous (1946).
Hernán Laborde around this time also invoked historical precedent. His article "La
virgen de Guadalupe ha sido la campeona de nuestras luchas" provoked an angry
response from his former *compañeros* in the PCM. Laborde (1946:3).

MEXICO: STATE AND NATION

In Mexico, Marxists and Communists also set out to articulate a project for revolutionary transformation that intersected national traditions and popular culture. In so doing they had to face up to a tough competitor: the Revolutionary state, whose expansion after 1920 (even if analysts have exaggerated it) greatly overshadowed civil society. They confronted an official party that anchored its legitimacy in programs of land reform, nationalization of selected foreign enterprises, and defense of national sovereignty, and that managed to control and integrate the agrarian and worker masses through a series of mass organizations. In the process the state gained a wide, if increasingly unstable, base of support and sustained the illusion that the ruling party represented the interests of all classes.

More important, the ruling party attempted to monopolize the rhetoric of revolution itself, demonstrating its awareness of how the concepts of nation and nationalism were tied to the revolutionary process. The official discourse of the Mexican revolution was engaged in what Corrigan and Sayer argue is a central concern of all states that "attempt to give unitary and unifying expression to what are in reality multifaceted and differential historical experiences of groups within society, denying their particularity" (1985:4).

The strengthening of the state apparatus in Mexico, its growing tutelary relationship over mass organizations, accelerating public ownership of resources, and other aggrandizements were widely viewed by the left as "strengthening the nation." This was a familiar theme in statements of statists at all points on the political spectrum. The argument was a central assumption of the state bureaucracy, for example, while a large portion of the Marxist left adhered to a radical nationalism defined as the nation's recovery of its resources (with the state acting "on the nation's behalf"). As one of the key ideologues of the statist left put it succinctly: "Crecemos y avanzamos en nuestra historia, nacionalizando."[23]

THREE MOMENTS IN THE HISTORY OF THE LEFT

Communism and the Muralist Movement

The experience of the muralist movements of the 1920s and early 1930s was as close as the Mexican Communists ever got to the CPGB's Free-born

23. The statement was coined by Rafael Galván. Cited in Córdova (1984:27–33).

Englishmen project of the 1930s and 1940s. The Mexican muralists were iconoclastic figures (regarded by their more austere colleagues as politically "unreliable").[24] In their artistic work they maintained a certain critical independence from the PCM. But Diego Rivera, David Alfaro Siqueiros, and Xavier Guerrero made a crucial contribution to the Communist party in its first decade and won it enormous prestige over the years.

The muralists' work reflected the diverse and sometimes contradictory currents within the heritage of Marxism. They celebrated modernity, "science as progress," the triumphs of the Soviet Union (the first workers' state), proletarian internationalism, the primacy of the party, and "the masses in action" (Tibol 1972:288; Azuela 1986:15–129). In their work they condemned the decadence of the bourgeoisie, the aggressiveness of imperialism, and the corruption of the church. At the same time, these artists, Rivera in particular, celebrated dimensions of Mexican life and history allegedly untouched by modernity, affectionately portraying a preindustrial society and emphasizing Indianness, the village, autonomous science and handicrafts. Modern science and technology promised an expansion of human potential but at the same time threatened to enhance exploitation and domination. Hence Rivera's portrayal of the conquistadors as automatons, and his fascination with the destructive power of war technology at the service of fascism. Similarly, while the muralists were intensely "Mexican" and anti-imperialist, certainly in Rivera's case there was also an enormous ambivalence toward the major site of imperialism, the United States. Admiration and fascination for the United States was partly a product of Rivera's interest in fusing orally transmitted indigenous, artesanal art with the new possibilities opened up by industrial culture, and especially the new forms of communication— cinema, radio, and television, in which Rivera showed an early interest.

More significant for our purposes, some of the muralists' work also tended to mimic, and be mimicked by, the official artistic view of the Mexican revolution. This tendency reinforced the statist conception that the "state gives expression to popular values, whether revolutionary or national, and arbitrates their interests" (García Canclini 1988:480). There

24. Rivera was expelled from the PCM in 1929. He flirted with dissident currents in the U.S. Communist movement (the Lovestoneites) and with Trotskyism before returning to the PCM fold in the 1950s. Siqueiros never abandoned the world of the orthodox PCM, but he was expelled or marginalized from the party on numerous occasions.

is a certain anti-*gachupín* sentiment visible in the muralists' work; the revolutionary army is often represented unproblematically as an "army of the people" (with scenes of soldiers educating peasants), as though army connivance with landowners and employers, military repression of agrarian and worker revolt, or the armed forces' self-enrichment never existed. The notion of a single, uninterrupted continuum of revolutionary heroes is also present; for example, in David Siqueiros's mural in the Museo Nacional de Historia in Mexico City, where Emiliano Zapata is presented marching beside Francisco Madero and Venustiano Carranza.

Most important, the representation of indigenous popular culture in the muralists' art was mediated by the concerns of adherents to the "Great Tradition," urban intellectuals in particular. Distortion and romanticization of historical processes inevitably resulted. For all its brilliance, mural art rarely incorporated the self-generated culture of the indigenous population or acknowledged the historical and social processes that produced it. Thus staunchly anti-imperialist muralists of the PCM, curiously, reproduced some of the dichotomies inherent in the discourse of imperialism according to which indigenous peoples were represented as more "real" or "authentic"—closer to nature—than the European invaders and their mestizo successors. In this sense the PCM muralists, especially Rivera, unwittingly contributed to the deepening of folkloric treatments of popular culture and to a Mexican version of what has been described in some English-speaking countries as the "heritage industry."[25]

25. Until the late 1970s, Mexican Communists did not assign high priority to work among indigenous people. At the local level, however, individual Communists were necessarily obliged to deal with the indigenous components of *campesino* life. The classic case here is Primo Tapia, a bilingual former Wobbly and then Communist who organized peasant leagues in Tarascan areas of Michoacán in the early 1920s. See Friedrich [1970] (1977); Embriz Osorio and León García (1982:17–90, 185–90). For a brief period during the *maximato* and early Cárdenas years (1929–1935), the PCM invested energy in organizing work in Chiapas and Tabasco, particularly in the coffee areas of Soconusco and in banana zones, where many workers were Zapotecs from the Tehuantepec isthmus. The PCM commissioned members who came from the Zapotec-influenced town of Juchitán in Oaxaca to organize unions on the United Fruit Company plantations "a que agiten en zapoteco." Nevertheless, even in this region the party's work was mostly among wage laborers working in capitalist agriculture, and it failed to address the peculiar needs of adjacent Chole, Tzotzil, and Tzeltal indigenous regions (such as the Los Altos area). The autonomy of indigenous culture and society was generally not recognized—and seen only as subordinate to universalist categories such as class. Marxism was thoroughly mestizized in Mexico! On the PCM in Chiapas, see García de León (1979; 1985:187–218).

The ambiguities in the Communist muralists' relations with the state are revealed with particular clarity in the 1920s. The revolutionary governments of that decade tried to create a popular culture that would attach the masses' loyalties to the defense of the state and deepen the equation "state equals nation." The state's efforts, particularly associated with the work of José Vasconcelos, President Obregón's education minister, involved an expansion of primary schooling, the creation of cultural missions, and the cultivation of artisan skills. The PCM muralists both challenged and confirmed these state goals. In their work they exalted *both* Zapatista armies and the international proletariat, but did so on walls donated by the government. They thereby facilitated what Carlos Monsiváis has called "la conversión de esa cultura del pueblo en alta cultura y santuario turístico" (Monsiváis 1981:35).[26]

The biography of David Alfaro Siqueiros, the *enfant terrible* of Mexican Communism, contains several episodes in which the revolutionary artist endorsed the "progressive" thrust of presidential policy during periods of major repression of worker and student movements. For example, just three years after the infamous October 2, 1968, massacre of several hundred people in the Plaza of the Three Cultures, Tlatelolco, Siqueiros praised the style and content of the government of President Luis Echeverría. Echeverría had been Interior Minister at the time of the massacre. Siqueiros declared that the new government was moving toward "un estado progresista y avanzado" (Siqueiros 1971:2).[27]

Lombardismo Redux

The laboratory in which the left did most to appropriate and contribute to generating the ideology of revolutionary nationalism was Cardenismo, and the most important architect of this endeavor was Vicente Lombardo

26. The conflation of a politically neutered muralism and growing state interest in "tourism" was seen very clearly in the production of Siqueiros's last great mural, *The March of Humanity on Earth and Toward the Cosmos*, in the second half of the 1960s. The mural was placed in a cultural center attached to a large skyscraper hotel, the Hotel de México. For a very interesting analysis of the meaning of this event, see Leonard Folgarait's recent study (1987).

27. Siqueiros had published his views in a letter, *llamada a los comunistas*, in two newspapers in January 1971. In spite of protests from the PCM, Siqueiros continued to make similar declarations. Finally, after the Corpus Christi Day massacre on June 10, Siqueiros was excluded from the party's central committee.

Toledano. The major socioeconomic advances achieved during the middle years of the Cardenista *sexenio* form the essential backdrop to the PCM and Lombardo's enthusiastic belief in the anticapitalist potential of the Mexican revolution. The politics of the Popular Front greatly facilitated this process. In the era of popular frontism, anything that smacked of "classist," sectional concerns was to be subordinated to the national-popular and antifascist project. All other options—such as struggles for greater honesty and democracy within the newly founded CTM and attempts to halt the subordination of socialist goals to the newly emerging corporativism of the state—were seen as divisive.

But the PCM and Lombardistas were only able to make this stance plausible because Cardenismo accentuated many tenets of the ideology of the Mexican revolution, tenets that most directly coincided with the dominant concerns of Second International and Soviet Marxism. Thus the Marxists' struggle to replace "fanaticism" with "reason" found echoes in the Cardenistas' socialist education program. Socialist enthusiasm for science and technology was confirmed by Cárdenas's decision to establish an institute of technical education, the National Polytechnic Institute (Instituto Politécnico Nacional, IPN) to compete with the National University, which was widely, and with some reason, viewed as a bastion of the right.[28]

Similarly, the push for industrialization initiated during the Cárdenas *sexenio* and accelerated in the 1940s corresponded closely with a key element in the culture of Marxism and Communism. The argument that national independence and sovereignty could be equated with the goals of industrialization and the development of a "national capitalism" was already well established in the PCM and among the Lombardistas. Intellectually, its roots lay in the assumption, common in all the Latin American parties of the Third International, that the region's "semicolonial" status and the survival of a significant sector dominated by the social relations of feudalism imposed the need for an alliance between revolutionary forces and the national bourgeoisie as an immediate objective.

A recurrent theme in the PCM's pronouncements concerning the need for heavy industry was an almost messianic belief in the liberating impact of massive developments in the country's productive forces. In the 1940s,

28. Socialist students meeting in June 1934 called for the creation of a Polytechnic Institute aimed at "la preparación y capacitación técnica de los obreros para que puedan encargarse de la dirección de la producción económica." Martínez Assad (1979:92). See also Pérez Rocha (1978:97–128).

and especially during the left's brief flirtation with Browderism, these propositions were further inflated (Fernández Anaya 1944:6).[29] A leading PCM figure expressed the point with great clarity:

> Under socialism and capitalism productivity develops in ways hitherto undreamed of. This presents us with two roads—either fascist terror, which paralyzes development and signifies a return to barbarism, or the establishment of new relations on a world scale, which will allow these gigantic increases in production to be absorbed peacefully and permit further development of the forces of production (Fernández Anaya 1945).

Lombardo and his followers shared this economic obsession with productive forces. But what is distinctive about the culture of Lombardismo is its glorification of the state and its progressive nationalizing and anti-imperialist pretensions. Lombardo lent the authority and the considerable prestige of the left to the state's claim to the role of privileged interpreter of nation and nationality. Here Lombardo was not only drawing on the conventional Comintern belief that in a semicolonial setting only a strong state (*estado fuerte*) could coordinate the progressive alliance against imperialism. He was also making a conscious effort to draw on indigenous nationalist cults (almost always articulated by the intelligentsia) like that of the Aztec ruler Cuauhtémoc. Thus it is highly significant that Lombardo began his 1952 presidential campaign at the site where Cuauhtémoc's remains were supposedly buried, with a speech invoking the memory of the last of the Aztec emperors:

> Padre Cuauhtémoc: tú nos legaste, con tu conducta y tu sacrificio, el mandato eterno de defender a México contra la opresión venida de afuera. Yo te prometo, en nombre del Partido Popular y el mío propio, creyendo ser fiel interprete. . . . (R. Bartra 1982:190–91)[30]

Lombardismo represented the more authoritarian strains in the culture of Marxism—a Mexican blend of Legal Marxism and British Fabia-

---

29. Browderism refers to the orientation of the Mexican Communist party (and many other Latin American parties) in 1944–45 when, under the influence of Earl Browder, the PCM made moves to dissolve itself and its party structures in line with the "liquidationist" theme of the CPUSA strategy.

30. Lombardo was not alone in this political reading of Cuauhtémoc. David Siqueiros (still a member of the PCM) wrote in 1951, "I see in Cuauhtémoc a prototype of Mao Tse-Tung, . . . the leaders of the Viet Minh, and the fighters for the nationalization of Iran's oil." Cited in Folgarait (1987:36). The mix of Stalinism and cultural nationalism in Lombardo's utterances also recalls the poem of the Cuban poet

nism. It owed its strength in part to the ideological and political alliance established between its practitioners and the state bureaucracy, in whose ranks an extraordinarily large number of Lombardistas and ex-Lombardistas worked. Here, interesting parallels can be traced between Lombardismo and the Fabian tradition within British socialism. Stuart Hall and Bill Schwartz's description of the Fabian project can, without too much violence to history, be applied to Lombardismo.

> Their dream was of a fully regulated, fully administered collectivist society in which state surveillance would be an essential condition of civic conduct. Regulated collectivism should replace the regime of unregulated individualism. . . . They elevated the bureaucrat, the expert and the administrator to the position of the leading cadre of their struggle for a new society (Hall and Schwartz 1985:23).

Lombardismo, like Fabianism, was an often illiberal and statist tendency. Like some of the Fabians, Lombardismo was never anti-Soviet. In fact, as Pablo Gómez has put it:

> hizo del estatismo obrero de la U.R.S.S. y los demás países socialistas su aspiración y objetivo, y de esa manera asimiló los dogmas más sobresalientes del estalinismo. Por esta razón, la lucha contra este socialismo fue particularmente difícil (P. Gómez 1981:22–23).

A prime example of Lombardismo in action is provided by the career of Víctor Manuel Villaseñor, even though he broke with Lombardo in the late 1940s. Villaseñor began his career as a lawyer and diplomat, positions he maintained until 1934. During the mid-1930s he became a collaborator of Lombardo and of the newly formed CTM, and part of the team designing the PRM's second Six-Year Plan (*Plan Sexenal*). He was also president of the Sociedad de Amigos de la U.R.S.S. (Villaseñor 1940:36–37; 1976).

Of all the currents within Mexican Marxism, it was Lombardismo that was most intimately bound up with the image and practice of the caudillo, the authoritarian populist. Lombardo himself unquestionably emulated this figure for most of his life. An intellectual by training, Lombardo devoted a good portion of his life to the labor movement: first the CROM (Regional Confederation of Mexican Workers) of the 1920s; then the CTM, which he helped found and led from 1936 until the early

---

Nicolás Guillén: "Stalín, capitán a quien Changó proteja/y a quien resguarde Ochún." See Monsiváis (1982:8).

1940s. But Lombardo, almost invariably referred to as "El Maestro" by his supporters, viewed politics and parties as educators of the ignorant masses. The paternalist and authoritarian overtones of this form of politics are overwhelmingly present here: "Trató a los proletarios como un grupo de alumnos congregados en la aula," one writer has neatly put it (R. Bartra 1982:183–84).

The legacy of Lombardismo has been extremely ambiguous. The tradition of revolutionary nationalism rendered large sections of the left impotent for many decades, encouraging the swallowing of gigantic myths about the progressive potential of the Mexican revolution. More seriously, Lombardismo's ostensible sensitivity toward the national culture did not seem to encourage a critical analysis of the achievements of revolutionary nationalism to see how far they could be used in emancipatory politics (Corrigan and Sayer 1985:206). On the other hand, no political movement or organization can survive for long (certainly not for the sixty years the PRI and its predecessors have managed to stay in power) if it has not been able to engage to some degree the deeply felt socioeconomic, cultural, and political needs of the population.[31] The enduring appeal of Lombardismo and the associated tradition of revolutionary nationalism can be looked at in the same light. Recent political events have underlined this point with great clarity. The emergence of the neo-Cardenista opposition during the election campaigns of 1987–88 revealed that revolutionary nationalism still has enormous convocatory power in Mexico. One has only to read Adolfo Gilly's impressions of peasant responses to Cuauhtémoc Cárdenas's presence in the Laguna region to see how powerful and galvanizing an effect these intense mobilizations had on people formed within a Marxist culture (Gilly 1988:47–68).[32]

31. Carlos Pereyra made this point quite well when he wrote, "Las organizaciones políticas no pueden echar raíces profundas en una sociedad si no encuentran en el propio proceso histórico de esa sociedad las fuentes de su actualidad ideológica y política. . . . Considerar a la revolución mexicana como un movimiento susceptible de animar sólo un proyecto favorable a las relaciones sociales de tipo capitalista significa una visión muy pobre de esa revolución y, sobre todo, equivale a renunciar al mejor trasfondo histórico de la lucha popular" (1981:26).

32. "Los ví en la Laguna, ejido tras ejido, pueblo tras pueblo. Ví en sus ojos algo que nunca, en un cuarto de siglo, había visto en los rostros mexicanos. No ya la ira, la indignación, el coraje, la fatiga, la indiferencia, la exasperación: ví en sus ojos la esperanza." Gilly (1988:48).

And yet the Lombardista and revolutionary nationalist tradition is once again revealing some of its historic weaknesses.[33] It is now more than five years since the fraudulent July 1988 elections, and the center-left opposition (Party of the Democratic Revolution, or PRD) is not in a healthy state. It is difficult to avoid the conclusion that the neo-Cardenista upsurge has been stymied, not only by continuing electoral fraud and government repression, but also by the movement's failure to encourage new forms of democratic participation that might offset the caudillismo that has, sadly, been so visible in the practice of the PRD.

The PCM and Agrarian Reform in the Laguna

The tradition of statism, scientism, and productivism from which Mexican Communism drew did not render the party incapable of comprehending and responding to the long and varied history of peasant and worker resistance and collective action in the areas in which its members operated. The history of the PCM's involvement in the Laguna area of Coahuila and Durango, particularly in the struggles that preceded the great land expropriation of 1936, shows this. Traditionally, analysts have explained the mobilizations of 1930–36 by reference to the organizing skills of labor and agricultural worker organizations in the Laguna region, as well as local PCM cadres. Or the mobilizations have been seen as a response to the immiseration and dislocation caused by ("external") crises such as the Great Depression. Another explanatory focus has tied the nature and scale of agrarian rebellion to certain structural characteristics of the Laguna work force, particularly its high degree of proletarianization.

These are all important ways of explicating the agrarian insurgency of the first half of the 1930s. But an exclusive focus on structural issues can be misleading. While references to the capitalist character of Laguna agriculture, for example, are in general not misplaced, they tend to oversimplify the character of the region's social structure, assuming a correspondence between structural features (ownership of means of production and labor forms) and the development of particular forms of class identification and consciousness.

33. I readily acknowledge that the neo-Cardenista "push" is much more than simply a revival of "left PRIism," Lombardismo, and other earlier traditions. Cuauhtémoc Cárdenas drew much of the strength for his campaign from hundreds of local and regional mobilizations of varied hue and origin.

An excessive concern with structural causation can also conceal the important connections in the Laguna between "peak" conjunctures of protest and prior traditions of struggle, some of which the PCM was able to tap.[34] Here the PCM was able to build on prior histories of peasant action, and on local collective memory of those actions—specifically the Juarista tradition of the Matamoros region. For example, while small peasant landholdings were uncommon, there was an important *tradition* of peasant and medium-sized smallholdings in certain areas of the Laguna. The best-known case is that of the army veterans of Matamoros and San Pedro, who received land grants from the Juárez government in the 1860s in exchange for services rendered in the campaigns against the French occupation. The usurpation of these lands by agricultural companies and their tenants with large holdings during the latifundist explosion of the late nineteenth century left deep scars in the memory of the Juarista veterans and their descendants. These people established a long record of continuous armed resistance to landowning authority during the Porfiriato (Vargas-Lobsinger 1984:18–120; Meyers 1984:251–54). The Matamoros and San Pedro areas would produce more than their share of leaders in the early years of the revolution, and several key figures in the peasant mobilization of 1935–36 (José Zárate, Domingo Sifuentes, Manuel Soria, and Santos Reyes—all of them with PCM affiliations) sprang from this reservoir of smallholder resentment (Martínez Saldaña 1980:87).

CONCLUSIONS

In the history of the Mexican radical left, the relationship between Marxism and Communism and the development of the Mexican state involved a process of exchange. Certain elements in the practice of Marxism and Communism in Mexico—viewed through the prism of the PCM and Lombardismo—strengthened the hegemonizing and regulating capacity of the state that emanated from the Mexican revolution; in particular the "scientistic," productivist, and statist orientation that so heavily shaped the Marxist tradition between the 1890s and 1960s. At the same time, the left assimilated certain characteristics of the dominant political culture. This two-way exchange was made possible by the

34. Steve Stern reminds us of the importance of situating analyses of agrarian rebellion within the long-term history of peasant resistance and engagement with the political world. Stern (1987:10–11).

similarities—some of them quite profound, others rather more shallow—between the culture of Marxism and Communism as it was received in Mexico and the political and ideological project developed by the architects of the Mexican state.

Most of the developments touched on in this essay represented attempts by intellectuals, professional cadres, and others in the vanguardist parties to develop representations of the past and present and visions of the future that could serve to mobilize their "target" constituencies. It is also important to study the ways prior traditions of struggle shaped the development of the left's practice "on the ground." Clearly, the Mexican Communist party meant different things to people in different regions, depending on the local mix of historical and cultural experience, the specificities of economic structure, and other variables. In some areas the PCM represented an opportunity to defend municipal autonomy and democracy; in others it provided chances to combat the corruption of worker syndicates and peasant unions and to fight under effective and disciplined leadership for better material conditions in factories, fields, and mines. In still other cases, support for the PCM may have been driven partly by the opportunities it provided for personal advancement in organizations and state bureaucracies in which party cadres exercised influence.[35] It is only on the basis of studies of particular conjunctures, however, that we will be able to examine what James Scott calls the "parochialization" and "syncretization" of the global, universalist messages delivered by revolutionary Marxists, and the "slippages" of meaning as these messages are absorbed and selectively reinterpreted (Scott 1977:219, 221).

35. This was particularly the case during the Cárdenas presidency, when party members occupied important positions in the federal state bureaucracy.

III

A Theoretical Reprise

WILLIAM ROSEBERRY

Hegemony and the Language of Contention

In soliciting papers for this volume, the editors pointed to two paradig-
matic bodies of scholarship that should inform our understandings of
"everyday forms of state formation": James Scott's work on a wide variety
of forms, acts, and "arts" of popular resistance to dominant orders (see
especially 1976; 1985; 1990), and Philip Corrigan and Derek Sayer's
study (1985) of a specific dominant order—the formation of the English
state, seen as a centuries-long process of economic transformation, political extension and construction, and cultural revolution that formed both
"the state" and particular kinds of social and political subjects. The
authors' task was to consider the relevance of these projects, developed
and applied to other world areas (Southeast Asia and England), for an
understanding of Mexican state formation and popular culture.

While the editors of this volume clearly intended for us to consider
Scott's and Corrigan and Sayer's works in relation to each other, to think
about how we might simultaneously examine the formation of orders of
domination and forms of resistance, it is also apparent that many of the
contributors have followed Alan Knight's lead in placing the works and
perspectives in partial opposition to each other—the "moral economy" of
the peasantry and other subordinate groups as opposed to "the great arch"
of the triumphal state.

Although it might be helpful to examine the various ways in which
each of these bodies of work speak to each other, I simply wish to point
out that each of their founding metaphors is taken from the work of E. P.
Thompson. Scott took Thompson's references to the "moral economy" of
the poor in eighteenth- and nineteenth-century England (1963; 1971) as
central image and starting point for his own theoretical model of peasant
consciousness in the face of capitalist expansion and the formation of

colonial states (Scott 1976). Corrigan and Sayer, in turn, take Thompson's critique of orthodox Marxist understandings of "the bourgeois revolution" as a challenge for their study of the formation of the English state (Thompson [1965] 1978a). Rather than locating "the" revolution at a single upheaval in the mid-seventeenth century, Thompson wrote of a long and particular history of statemaking and capitalist transformation, challenging Marxists to abandon readymade historical and political scripts and explore the historical formation of particular capitalist civilizations. For Thompson, the image of a "great arch" is both architectural (a towering and solid structure of bricks) and temporal (an arch of time during which the structure is built and through which it takes its dimensions and form). Both senses matter to Corrigan and Sayer: to write the history of the bourgeois revolution in England one had to write of a great arch spanning nine centuries.

Continuing the attempt to relate the works of Scott and Corrigan and Sayer in our understanding of Mexican state formation and popular culture, let us consider a third Thompsonian metaphor: the "field of force." Thompson proposes the image in his essay "Eighteenth-Century English Society: Class Struggle Without Class?" (1978b), in which he specifically addresses the problem of popular culture within relations of domination, arguing, "What must concern us is the polarization of antagonistic interests and the corresponding dialectic of culture" (ibid.: 150). In describing a field of force, he provides a suggestive image,

> . . . in which an electrical current magnetized a plate covered with iron filings. The filings, which were evenly distributed, arranged themselves at one pole or the other, while in between those filings which remained in place aligned themselves sketchily as if directed towards opposing attractive poles. This is very much how I see eighteenth-century society, with, for many purposes, the crowd at one pole, the aristocracy and gentry at the other, and until late in the century, the professional and merchant groups bound by lines of magnetic dependency to the rulers, or on occasion hiding their faces in common action with the crowd (ibid.: 151).

As he turns his understanding of such a field toward the analysis of popular or plebeian culture, Thompson suggests that its "coherence . . . arises less from any inherent cognitive structure than from the particular field of force and sociological oppositions peculiar to eighteenth-century society; to be blunt, the discrete and fragmented elements of older patterns of thought become integrated by *class*" (ibid.: 156).

This metaphor carries certain obvious but important problems. First, the magnetic field is bipolar, and most of the social situations with which we are familiar are infinitely more complex, with multiple sites of domination or forms and elements of popular experience. Because the field is bipolar, the patterns of the iron filings are symmetrical, again in ways that "the dominant" and "the popular" can never be. Finally, the image is static, for new filings fit quickly and easily within a preexisting pattern and field of force, without necessarily altering the pattern and with no effect on the field itself. Each of these problems is related to one or another of the metaphor's strengths: the image draws our attention to a wider field of tension and force, to the importance of placing elements of "the dominant" or "the popular" within that field, but its very clarity becomes a problem when we move from a two-dimensional template to the multidimensional world of the social, political, and cultural.

Let us, then, move to that multidimensional world, and attempt to understand social fields of force in more complex and processual terms. Are there additional and related concepts that can serve as suggestive guides? One concept that appears in several papers in this volume is the Gramscian understanding of hegemony. It is interesting that, given the editors' attempt to confront the works of Scott and Corrigan and Sayer, none of these authors is especially sympathetic to the concept. Scott, in particular, has registered the most vigorous criticisms, especially in *Weapons of the Weak* (1985) and *Domination and the Arts of Resistance* (1990). Challenging those theorists who understand hegemony as "ideological consensus," Scott stresses the lack of consensus in social situations of domination. The dominated *know* they are dominated, they know by whom and how; far from consenting to that domination, they initiate all sorts of subtle ways of living with, talking about, resisting, undermining, and confronting the unequal and power-laden worlds in which they live. Corrigan and Sayer are also impatient with notions of "ideological consensus," but they approach their criticism from the other pole of the field of force. The power of the state, in their view, rests not so much on the consent of its subjects but with the state's regulative and coercive forms and agencies, which define and create certain kinds of subjects and identities while denying, ruling out, other kinds of subjects and identities. Moreover, the state accomplishes this not simply through its police and armies but through its offices and routines, its taxing, licensing, and registering procedures and papers.

These are two powerful criticisms, from which ideas of "ideological consent" cannot easily recover. There is more to Gramsci and his use of the idea of hegemony, however, than the concept of consent appropriated by political scientists and criticized (forcefully and correctly) by

Scott, Corrigan, and Sayer. For one thing, Gramsci understood and emphasized, more clearly than did his interpreters, the complex unity of coercion and consent in situations of domination. Hegemony was a more *material* and *political* concept in Gramsci's usage than it has since become. For another thing, Gramsci well understood the *fragility* of hegemony. Indeed, one of the most interesting sections in the *Selections from the Prison Notebooks* ([1929–35] 1971) is his "Notes on Italian History," an analysis and interpretation of the failure of the Piedmont bourgeoisie to form a nation-state, their failure to form a bloc that could rule, through force and consent.

Let us return to the field of force and inquire whether a more material, political, and problematic concept of hegemony aids in understanding the complex and dynamic relations between the dominant and popular, or between state formation and everyday forms of action. Let us explore hegemony not as a finished and monolithic ideological formation but as a problematic, contested, political process of domination and struggle.

Gramsci begins his notes on Italian history with some observations concerning the history (and the study of the history) of "ruling" and "subaltern" classes. "The historical unity of the ruling classes," he writes,

> is realised in the State, and their history is essentially the history of States and of groups of States. But it would be wrong to think that this unity is simply juridical and political (though such forms of unity do have their importance too, and not in a purely formal sense); the fundamental historical unity, concretely, results from the organic relations between State or political society and "civil society" ([1929–35] 1971:52).

The "subaltern classes," on the other hand,

> by definition, are not unified and cannot unite until they are able to become a "State": their history, therefore, is intertwined with that of civil society, and thereby with the history of States and groups of States. Hence it is necessary to study: (1) the objective formation of the subaltern groups, by the developments and transformations occurring in the sphere of economic production; their quantitative diffusion and their origins in pre-existing social groups, whose mentality, ideology and aims they conserve for a time; (2) their active or passive affiliation to the dominant political formations, their attempts to influence the programmes of these formations in order to press claims of their own, and the consequences of these attempts in determining processes of decomposition, renovation, or neo-formation; (3) the birth of new parties of the dominant groups, intended to conserve the assent of the subaltern groups and to maintain control over them; (4) the formations which the subaltern groups themselves produce, in order to press claims of a

limited and partial character; (5) those new formations which assert the autonomy of the subaltern groups, but within the old framework; (6) those formations which assert the integral autonomy, . . . etc. (ibid.)

Let us consider several features of Gramsci's introductory comments that bear emphasis as we consider hegemonic processes. First, for both the ruling and the subaltern classes Gramsci implies plurality or diversity; unity is for them a political and cultural problem. Throughout his discussion, his emphasis is on the plural, on classes and groups.

Second, though the passage seems to imply that the unity of the ruling classes is unproblematic through their control of the state, Gramsci then proceeds in his "Notes" to examine the failure of the Piedmont bourgeoisie to unite with other regionally based dominant groups or to forge a unified ruling bloc that could control (or create) a state. He is, then, pointing to a problematic relationship. Unity *requires* control of the state (the subaltern classes, "by definition," are not unified because they are not the state), but control of the state by the ruling classes is not assumed. Such control is at once juridical and political (as we might ordinarily understand "the history of States and of groups of States"), and moral and cultural (as we consider the complex tensions among ruling groups and between ruling and subaltern groups in the relations between state and civil society). Any study of state formation should, in this formulation, also be a study of cultural revolution (see Corrigan and Sayer 1985).

Third, if we render the history of ruling groups and of states and groups of states as problematic, then an array of questions similar to those posed by Gramsci of subaltern classes needs to be considered. That is, we need to consider their "objective" formation in the economic sphere—the movements, developments, and transformations in production and distribution, and their social and demographic distribution in space and time. We *also* (not *then*) need to study their social and cultural relations with other groups—other "ruling" groups within and beyond their region or sphere of influence; subaltern groups within and beyond their region. What associations or organizations of kinship, ethnicity, religion, region, or nation bind or divide them? We also (not then) need to investigate their political associations and organizations, and the political institutions, laws, routines, and orders they confront, create, and attempt to control. As we consider such questions, the complexity of the field of force becomes clear. In addition to *sectoral* differentiation among distinct class fractions, based on different positions and roles within accumulation processes, Gramsci draws our attention to *spatial* differentiation, to the uneven and unequal development of social powers in regional spaces. His consideration of the failures of state formation and hegemony in the Italian peninsula begins with the difficulties imposed by regionally distinct fields of force.

Fourth, we need to ask the same questions of the subaltern classes, in their relationships to the dominant groups and political institutions.

Fifth, it is worth noting that Gramsci does not assume that subaltern groups are captured or immobilized by some sort of ideological consensus. At one point he raises the question of their group origins "in preexisting social groups, whose mentality, ideology and aims they conserve for a time," and he also considers the possibility of "their active or passive affiliation to the dominant political formations"; but in neither case is Gramsci's observation static or definitive. Rather, active or passive affiliation and the preservation of mentalities are placed within a dynamic range of actions, positions, and possibilities, a range that includes the formation of new organizations and institutions, the pressing of claims, the assertion of autonomy. This range is understandable solely in terms of (1) a field of force that connects the ruling and subaltern in "the organic relations between State or political society and 'civil society,'" and (2) a hegemonic *process* (see Mallon, this volume; Roseberry and O'Brien 1991). Gramsci's criteria and questions clearly imply a temporal dimension without necessarily leading to a teleology.

Sixth, the relations between ruling and subaltern groups are characterized by contention, struggle, and argument. Far from assuming that the subaltern passively accept their fate, Gramsci clearly envisions a much more active and confrontational subaltern population than many of his interpreters have assumed. Nevertheless, he places action and confrontation within the formations, institutions, and organizations of the state and civil society in which subordinate populations live. Subaltern groups and classes carry the "mentality, ideology, and aims" of preexisting social groups; they "affiliate" with preexisting political organizations as they attempt to press their own claims; they create new organizations within a preexisting social and political "framework," and so on. Thus while Gramsci does not see subordinate populations as the deluded and passive captives of the state, neither does he see their activities and organizations as autonomous expressions of a subaltern politics and culture. Like plebeian culture in eighteenth-century England, they exist within and are shaped by the field of force.

This is the way hegemony works. I propose that we use the concept *not* to understand consent but to understand struggle; the ways in which the words, images, symbols, forms, organizations, institutions, and movements used by subordinate populations to talk about, understand, confront, accommodate themselves to, or resist their domination are shaped by the process of domination itself. What hegemony constructs, then, is not a shared ideology but a common material and meaningful framework for living through, talking about, and acting upon social orders characterized by domination.

That common material and meaningful framework is, in part, discursive: a common language or way of talking about social relationships that sets out the central terms around which and in terms of which contestation and struggle can occur. Consider, for example, Daniel Nugent and Ana Alonso's examination, in their chapter in this volume, of Namiquipans' refusal of an *ejido* grant because the institution of the *ejido* carried with it a certain set of subordinate relations to the central state and denied a prior set of relations between Namiquipans and the central state, and between Namiquipans and the land. Consider as well the conflict Terri Koreck discusses in a recent essay concerning the naming of the community where she did her work (1991). Each name—Cuchillo Parado, Veintecinco de Marzo, and Nuestra Señora de las Begonias—expresses different interests and histories, different visions of community and nation. The state claims the power to name; to create and print maps with state-sanctioned labels. Community residents can recognize the right but refuse the name, *among themselves*. In both cases, villagers resist words; but the words signal and express material social, economic, and political relationships and powers. Struggle and resistance concern these powers (Namiquipans reject a certain kind of relationship with the state in their access to land). The state is able to impose certain words—to state, to name, to label. The state is not (necessarily) able to force villagers to accept or use those names. Namiquipans refuse the *ejido* label and thereby call up an earlier history of fierce autonomy. Koreck's villagers continue to refer to Cuchillo Parado and thereby attempt to refuse a certain kind of relationship with the state. In James Scott's terms, both use a "hidden transcript" with which to talk about their domination. But both public and hidden transcripts are intimately intertwined. They exist within a common discursive framework that grants both Cuchillo Parado and Veintecinco de Marzo meaning.

Clearly, some imposed words and institutions carry more power, and contention over them carries more of a threat to a dominant order, than others. We might assume, for example, that a community's rejection of the central institution of the state's new agrarian order presents more of a challenge than a village's continued use of a name like Cuchillo Parado. We might imagine that neither the central nor the local state has much reason to worry over what the villagers call themselves as long as "Veinte-cinco de Marzo" is uniformly named in state records and registries, and as long as maps "accurately" place the *pueblo* in relation to others in a homogeneously configured space. To the extent that the different names call up different histories (as they do here), however, points of conflict and challenge may emerge.

In neither Namiquipa nor Cuchillo Parado, however, have the villagers autonomously chosen the particular issue over which they will struggle; the issue, and the argument over names and institutional forms, was presented by the projects of a homogenizing state. Nor, for that matter, did "the state" choose this particular terrain for contention. Nugent and Alonso capture nicely the surprise of the representatives of the Comisión Nacional Agraria at Namiquipans' refusal to accept the state's generous offer of land and protection. The points of contention, the "words"—and the whole material history of powers, forces, and contradictions that the words inadequately express—over which a centralizing state and a local village might struggle are determined by the hegemonic process itself. Once they appear, regardless of the conscious intent of the state functionaries or villagers who first use them, they may seem to call up and call into question the whole structure of domination. Nugent and Alonso, for example, usefully discuss the apparent intentions of the agrarianists in Mexico City in the 1920s.

> A key point about the agrarian reform process . . . is that it was profoundly *distant* from the communities and people whose lives it was designed to reorder. The distance was physical, social, and rhetorical. CNA meetings took place in Mexico City, far from the affected communities. They were attended not by peasants but by members of the CNA—lawyers, bureaucrats, schoolteachers, and politicians, few of whom had risen through the ranks of the popular movements. They articulated the norms of the agrarian reform in edicts, proclamations, fact-finding rulings issued in state-controlled publications, and a host of internal memoranda circulated within the CNA and the CLAs. The language of the agrarian reform was laden with legal niceties and technicalities, and invocations of a national *patria* few peasants could relate to (Katz 1988d; Anderson 1983). The language was stripped of local references recognizable to the beneficiaries of the land redistributions; their respective communities, their *patrias chicas*—landscapes impregnated with generations of work, struggle, and meaning—were reduced to or recast as so-and-so many hectares of such-and-such a category of land for this-and-that type of use (this volume, p. 228–29).

Attention to such political and discursive processes and projects can illuminate many aspects of a complexly structured field of force. Within the central state, these aspects would include the intentions and struggles of agrarianists as they attempted to reform "the" agrarian structure, and their attempts to build and incorporate a following in the countryside; in local fields (Yucatán, Morelos, and Chihuahua, say), relevant aspects might be the differential and (for the agrarianists) surprising reception of their central reforms and structures. Beginning with the 1926 rejection of an *ejido* in Namiquipa, then, the analysis can move in various directions— "inward" toward the examination of differential social relations in Namiquipa, "outward" toward the exploration of regional and central political spaces—as it maps overlapping structures and processes of domination. It may, in short, take a particular object of contention or a point of failure in the establishment of a common discursive framework to examine each of the levels Florencia Mallon points to in her model of hegemonic processes.

Conceptualizing such process in terms of the necessity of constructing a common discursive framework allows us to examine both the power and the fragility of a particular order of domination. Let us consider, first, the power. "States," Corrigan and Sayer argue,

> state; the arcane rituals of a court of law, the formulae of royal assent to an Act of Parliament, visits of school inspectors, are all statements. They define, in great detail, acceptable forms and images of social activity and individual and collective identity; they regulate . . . much . . . of social life. In this sense "the State" never stops talking.
>
> Out of the vast range of human social capacities—possible ways in which social life could be lived—state activities more or less forcibly "encourage" some whilst suppressing, marginalizing, eroding, undermining others. Schooling for instance comes to stand for education, policing for order, voting for political participation. Fundamental social classifications, like age and gender, are enshrined in law, embedded in institutions, routinized in administrative procedures and symbolized in rituals of state. Certain forms of activity are given the official seal of approval, others are situated beyond the pale. This has cumulative, and enormous, cultural consequences; consequences for how people identify . . . themselves and their "place" in the world (1985:3, 4).

We see this in our examples from Chihuahua, in which the central state claims the power, through its administrative registers, institutes, and bureaus, to make maps and to impose uniform, centralized institutions on a heterogeneous countryside. We can also see how forms and languages of protest or resistance *must* adopt the forms and languages of domination in order to be registered or heard. "Y venimos a contradecir" is a powerful statement of community solidarity and opposition, but to be effective it is addressed to the proper colonial authorities, it follows (ritualistically) the proper forms of address and order of presentation, and it is registered in the proper colonial offices. It recognizes and addresses power even as it protests it; or it decries the abuse or misuse of power, implicitly recognizing a legitimate use of the same power. To the extent that a dominant order establishes such legitimate forms of procedure, to the extent that it establishes not consent but prescribed forms for expressing both acceptance and discontent, it has established a common discursive framework.

The problematic and fragile character of such frameworks must be stressed, however. Beginning with the linguistic level, common discursive frameworks, "a common language or way of talking about social relationships," are historically quite rare and have never been achieved in Mexico. Indeed, sociolinguists are increasingly drawn to the analysis of bilingual situations in which subordinate and dominant groups interact. They examine the various contexts in which "languages of solidarity" might be used by subordinate groups (see, e.g., Gal 1987; J. Hill 1985; Woolard 1985). At this level alone, then, hegemonic processes may break down. (This, too, provides an important entry point for the analysis of hegemonic processes; an examination of a state's language policies—its attempts to promote or enforce cultural and linguistic assimilation through a common, "national" language, or, alternatively, its promotion or protection of bi- or multilingual institutes, practices, and literatures. In each case, the examination of state and stated rationales for the policies, and of the tensions and struggles the policies address, can illuminate much wider political and cultural tensions.)

We can, however, explore the fragility of discursive frameworks at other levels as well. Let us return, for example, to Corrigan and Sayer's discussion of the ways in which "states . . . state." The forms of regulation and routine to which Corrigan and Sayer allude depend on an extremely dense, centralized, and effective state. This, too, has been rare in Mexico, despite the intentions, projects, and claims of the state and its officials in various periods. Witness, for example, Romana Falcón's assessment of local rule through the Porfirian *jefes políticos*. Brief reference to two other essays in this volume reinforces the point: Rockwell's analysis of rural schooling in Tlaxcala, with its complex tensions between central aims and directives and the efforts of local elites and teachers to serve and satisfy village needs and demands; and Mallon's examination of the conflicts between the central state and local politicos in the *sierra de Puebla* and elsewhere, stressing how the language, aims, and projects of liberalism receive particular inflections as they are inserted in regional and local class relations and political alliances.

Each case reveals ways in which the state, which never stops talking, has no audience; or rather, has a number of audiences who hear different things; and who, in repeating what the state says to still other audiences, change the words, tones, inflections, and meanings. Hardly, it would seem, a common discursive framework.

Of what use, then, are analyses of hegemony, or, as I would prefer, a "hegemonic process"? Remember that the primary architect of the concept used it partly to understand the failure of the Piedmont bourgeoisie to lead and form a unified nation-state. The concept's value for Gramsci in this particular event lay in its illumination of lines of weakness and cleavage, of alliances unformed and class fractions unable to make their particular interests appear to be the interests of a wider collectivity. In using the concept of hegemony in Mexico, I do not claim that we will suddenly discover a similar failure. If we conceive a hegemonic process and common discursive framework as (unarticulated but necessary) state *projects* rather than state *achievements*, however, we can advance our understanding of "popular culture" and "state formation" in relation to each other.

We may understand that relationship first and most obviously at those points at which the common discursive framework breaks down: where, for example, national holidays are disregarded and locally significant days or places (the birthday of a local hero, the site of a burial or battle, the boundary markers of an old land grant) are marked or revered; where, in other words, the language and precepts of liberalism are given regional inflections.

It would be wrong, however, to place these points of rupture—or the problematic relationship between the talking state and the distracted audience—into a simple power model that proposes an opposition between "the dominant" and "the subordinate" or "the state" and "the popular." The field of force is much more complex, as the laws, dictates, programs, and procedures of the central state are applied in particular regions, each of which is characterized by distinct patterns of inequality and domination, which in turn are the uniquely configured social products of historical processes that include prior relations and tensions of center and locality.

The particular merit of this understanding of hegemonic process, then, is that it aids in drawing a more complex map of a field of force. By focusing attention on points of rupture, areas where a common discursive framework cannot be achieved, it serves as a point of entry into the analysis of a process of domination that shapes both "the state" and "popular culture." This is also, it should be said, the particular merit of the essays in this volume. In their attempt to place popular culture in relation to state formation, these chapters challenge received understandings of each. Popular culture, in these essays, is no timeless repository of authentic and egalitarian traditional values; the state is no machine, manufacturing consent. Linking the two, and shaping each, is a multidimensional and dynamic field of force.

DEREK SAYER

Everyday Forms of State Formation: Some Dissident Remarks on "Hegemony"

I

It is exceedingly difficult to add anything to a collection of papers, such as these, which are extremely rich, empirically and historically, when their topic, the Mexican revolution, is one with which I am not especially familiar. It is the more difficult if, like me, you have a deep and inbuilt horror of abstraction—a horror that comes from an increasing appreciation of its integrity to characteristically modern forms of power. For there is a certain affinity between forms of power and forms of knowledge, to which I will return.

The single thing I think has most powerfully come out of these chapters is the sheer complexity of the issues they deal with. I thought it might be helpful to go through the contributions and look at how many different definitions of hegemony I could find, but at some point I gave up. This problem arises with just about every concept—including the concepts of state, popular culture, and revolution—around which this volume is organized. Many of these papers have an empirical density, an insistent specificity of particular times and places that constantly escapes the analytical categories we try to bring to bear on them. They have lots of loose ends, and often what I find most interesting *are* the loose ends. So

Thanks to Helen Robbins for transcribing some of my remarks to the conference, which served as the basis for this essay.

I am not going to attempt to provide anything that will in any sense unify what the previous chapters present. Instead, I want to offer some thoughts of my own, inspired by this collection of essays.

The exchange of written work and discussions leading to this volume invented categories like postrevisionism and neopopulism (a tiny example of everyday forms of state formation?) through which Philip Corrigan's and my book became elevated to something called a theoretical framework. Now, we ourselves never saw *The Great Arch*[1] as offering a theory of the state. It does have certain ideas in it about how one might study that object, whatever that object may be, but insofar as it offers any theories they are deeply embedded in the particular process of state formation that we are studying, which is that of England. It is instructive, I think, that neither Corrigan nor I have ever succeeded in being able to "abstract" the argument of the book for transplantation elsewhere. England is very peculiar in all sorts of ways, but *The Great Arch* is not a *case study* of something more *general*. English state formation is sui generis like any other—including that of Mexico. And this establishes severe limitations on the degree to which concepts and metaphors that we found helpful may be applied elsewhere. I do not think it useful to go around the world searching for monumental arches, complete or incomplete, or even stately viaducts, which can be put like a hat on the Mexican diversities these papers so graphically portray. Other images, such as Adolfo Gilly's of the Mexican state formation being more like a tree than an arch, may be very much more pertinent to understanding it.

II

Since Alan Knight uses rather strong terms to counterpose *Weapons of the Weak* and *The Great Arch* in his chapter, let me begin by recalling some of the questions James Scott poses in his own work. There are undoubtedly differences of emphasis between the way we approach the issues and the way Scott does. But they do not lie where they might obviously be looked for. In particular, in *The Great Arch* we are critical, and explicitly so, of standard uses of the concept of hegemony; and we are equally insistent on

---

1. Corrigan and Sayer (1985). A new edition of this was published in the Blackwell Ideas series, 1991, with a new postscript and bibliographic supplement. The postscript bears on some of the issues raised here. See also Corrigan (this volume: xvii–xix; 1990b); Sayer (1992).

the fragility of power and the permanent presence of alternatives. I would endorse all the points Knight brings out in his commentary on Scott's work: the apparent suddenness of the shift when things appear to change overnight; the reasonable inference that a subversive subscript was there all along; the Jekyll-Hyde quality of revolutions, indicative of the divided character of their subjects; the stew seething underneath the apparent compliance and deference from which we all too glibly infer "hegemony." And Jim Scott, I think, has put the problem I want to address very sharply in the foreword to this volume, where he asks four crucial questions. First, how cohesive historically *are* hegemonic projects? Second, even if they are cohesive at some level—of intellectuality—how cohesive are they when actually translated into *practice?* Third, even if these projects are successful at both levels, how *confining* are they, anyway? And fourth, who is the *audience* for this performance? Or are we just dealing with stories that elites tell themselves? The chapters in this volume underline again and again the pertinence of these four questions.

How cohesive historically are supposed hegemonic projects? These papers not only bring out conflicts within and between elites, breaking down any notion of the coherent state project; they also bring out a constant slippage where, behind the masks of the state, what we in fact repeatedly find is the petty, the personal, the corrupt, the backstabbing, the wheeling and dealing. This is nowhere better illustrated than in Romana Falcón's chapter on the Porfirian *jefes políticos* or Florencia Mallon's study of nineteenth-century Mexican politics. The former starts off by arguing in general, even "great archian" terms that those *jefes* were defining identities, imposing definitions of community by monopolizing such things as the permission to serenade. I think such apparent minutiae are very important as indices of *attempted* state formation in the everyday *Lebenswelt.* But Falcón goes on to demonstrate that in reality, of course, those *jefes* were ineffective, inept, and corrupt. They were constantly seeping away right out of the state, in ways that problematized the very existence of anything we might want to call by that name.

Regarding how effectively such projects are translated into practice, we have Elsie Rockwell's illuminating study of teachers and schools. What comes out most forcefully here is the polysemic, ambiguous, contradictory quality of these putative state forms: even as they oppress, they also empower. It is not a question of either/or, but both/and. This bears on Jim Scott's third question of how confining such projects are anyway. Even if we can assume the existence in Mexico of a hegemonic project at all, a number of recent studies suggest that if this project does confine, it does so in very complicated ways. Perhaps the best example of this, along with Rockwell's chapter, is Daniel Nugent and Ana Alonso's work on Namiquipa, Chihuahua. They find that villagers are challenging one hegemonic project with the documents of the other; and in the name, moreover, of the Spanish crown.[2] So did *The Great Arch:* think, for example, of the multiple connotations of the notion of "English liberties."

Regarding Jim Scott's last question—who is the audience for this performance—the chapter by Armando Bartra is particularly instructive. One thing it forcefully reminds us is that even if the state, as *The Great Arch* put it, never stops talking, we cannot be sure that anybody is listening. They may be snatching their "half-hour of pleasure" in whatever form. In fact, Bartra traces what in our terms is undoubtedly a process of cultural revolution that involves identity formation and deformation. We see new forms of individuality and intimacy in relationships to culture; the novelty of "laughing by yourself." We see homogenization overcoming regionalizations and the entry of "North American" culture into Mexican identities. We have new forms of differentiation, as we move into the 1940s, with specifically targeted comics for women, for children, and so on. But this apparently has little to do with the state, and it is disputable whether it is anybody's "project" at all, in any reasonable sense of that word. The politicians and intellectuals, meanwhile, *are* elaborating supposed hegemonic projects around the idea of the Mexican state and constructions of national culture and identity. But if Jan Rus's and Marjorie Becker's respective examinations of state-promoted indigenismo and agrarismo provide any indication, the fate of such projects remains shaky at best.

Roger Bartra is more blunt: in a recent essay, he employs Mexico's monumental exposition of national art and antiquities in the United States in 1990 as both a metaphor for the PRI's postrevolutionary cultural project and a vehicle for its critical dissection. Mexicans have grown tired of the state's long-running exercise in cultural manipulation; the project's destiny, he observes sardonically, is to end up in New York's Metropolitan Museum of Art, an exotic spectacle for gringo consumption (R. Bartra 1991).

2. Apart from their paper in this volume, see Alonso (1988d); Nugent (1989a). Also see the essays in this volume by Rus and Becker for further illustration of the complex, often contradictory manner in which so-called "hegemonic projects" confine the state's subjects. The recent work of María Teresa Koreck abounds with similar examples.

All this is to say that a priori, I am deeply suspicious of any grand claims to the existence of hegemonic projects, let alone their success. This was something we brought out, in fact, in *The Great Arch*; for instance, when talking about the 1830s in Britain. Yes, there were projects around, like those diversely inspired by Jeremy Bentham. But they certainly did not wholly define what happened. For me the value of many of these chapters is to bring this out sharply, clearly, and in very considerable detail; and it is their location in Armando Bartra's "modest beginnings," their concern with the trivial, the mundane, the everyday that I think gives them that power. This offers a salutary counterpoint to the grand abstractions and "dead Frenchmen" that normally dominate much of this area of discourse.

III

With this in mind, let me turn to the twin themes of resistance and rule— a term I feel much more comfortable with than the altogether more intellectual notion of hegemony. In their introduction to this volume, the editors draw on an under-appreciated article by Philip Abrams that we also cite in *The Great Arch*: "Some Notes on the Difficulty of Studying the State" ([1977] 1988). What Abrams argues is that "the state" does not exist. And if the state does not exist, we cannot and should not take it as an object of study. What Abrams suggests instead is that the state is a *claim* that in its very name attempts to give unity, coherence, structure, and intentionality to what are in practice frequently disunited, fragmented attempts at domination. In this sense "the state" *is* an ideological project (rather than an agency that *has* such projects). Again, Falcón's chapter on the *jefes políticos* brings this out very well, as does Jan Rus's discussion of *las políticas indígenas y indigenistas*. Abrams distinguishes between the *practice* of politics—politically organized subjection, he calls it—and the *idea* of the state, and says that the idea of the state is a "collective misrepresentation." The state is not the reality behind the mask of political practice; the state *is* the mask. If so, Corrigan and I would argue, we need to give the closest attention to how this idea of the state is constructed and sustained. But we should not, through our own categories, replicate this misrepresentation.

Most of the essays here do not. They are far more particular in what they actually look at; they deconstruct the grand narratives of statehood and their authority claims to purposiveness, unity, coherence, rationality. But when I think of the terms in which the contributors to this volume conducted a four-day discussion of everyday forms of Mexican state formation in early 1991, I recall how often we unthinkingly said "the state does this," "the state does that," "the state wants the other." Quite a lot of the time. It is a dangerous shorthand. But "it" slips very easily off the tongue when we are talking about "the state." This, I suggest, is an essential part of "its" power. It is also a "category error" that is especially seductive for intellectuals—and dangerous for those on whose bodies the "projects" of intellectuals are too often visited.

Everything I have said so far is an argument against reifying "the state" and "the project" of the state, but I think it equally dangerous and misleading to reify, to attribute undue coherence, concreteness, and solidity to resistance and "popular culture." This is brought out in the recent work of Terri Koreck, who argues that "counterhegemonic projects" do not need to have these attributes of coherence and solidity because they are not about the organization of domination (Koreck 1991). More simply, I would say, they are frequently not *projects*, and to describe them as such may be dangerously to misconstrue them.

I would also insist on a further rider, which is not irrelevant to twentieth-century history and some of its more characteristic tragedies. The presumed progression from unarticulated, latent revolutionary sentiment—the subversive subscripts—into a political project makes me deeply suspicious. What is going on here is a translation and a totalization. I want to ask, by and for whom? Usually it is intellectuals in positions of power, who articulate what they *claim* is already there as *vox populi*. Nevertheless, to translate is to traduce, to betray. There are ways of constituting popular culture—of constituting resistance—from the diversities we are trying to make sense of, which disturbingly mirror the way "the state" is itself ideologically constituted. And the implications of this totalization are not merely epistemological.

Nowhere is this made clearer than in Barry Carr's chapter on self-proclaimed "vanguards," in which he brings out the affinities between the attempted modernizing projects of various phases of Mexican state formation and Marxist "oppositional" discourses. I would suggest that in both cases we are in the same world of the logic of domination, and we need to beware especially that we do not conspire in this by our own uncritical use of its procedures and categories. I do not want to get into the issue of modernity, postmodernity, and so on here.[3] But I would suggest—and people have been saying this for a long time before the

3. For my views on these issues see Sayer (1987:126–49; and especially 1991).

postmodernists, going back to Max Weber[4] and beyond—that there is a certain parallel between the exigencies of scientific discourse (coherence, predictability, control, one thing following from another and being logically related to the other) and the technologies of domination themselves. All of them are logics of *control* which marshall things—and people—in particular ways; and all of them rest on an essential *abstraction*.

To repeat what I indicated at the start of this essay, the value for me of many of these papers is their refusal of that abstraction. So not only do I agree with what I think Jim Scott is saying on many things, but I would want to take the argument further and say that his critique needs to be extended to claims and historiographies that presume to speak for the oppressed. After 1989, and the global collapse of the most ambitiously totalizing "liberation" project of this century—I mean what used to call itself "scientific socialism"—claims to be "organic intellectuals" deserve to be treated with the healthy skepticism we bring to "the state" itself. Indeed, remembering some of Weber's remarks on the "devil of intellectualization," we might want to consider the possibility that the status of "organic intellectual" of anything other than a ruling class might just be a contradiction in terms.

IV

All this said, rule *is* accomplished, domination is secured much of the time, even in Mexico, whether or not this takes the form of imposing great arches. If what I have argued so far is headed in the right direction, explaining how this is accomplished becomes singularly problematic. It is at this point that our old friend hegemony usually waltzes its way onto the stage. I am not going to offer a theory of hegemony, but I do want to make three very brief observations on power—all of them skeptical of normal uses of the notion of hegemony—and with that bring this essay to a conclusion.

My first observation is that to my mind, rule is not centrally about either inculcating beliefs or securing consent, as many conceptions of hegemony tacitly presume. It is deeper and it is more pervasive and it is more insidious than that. Consider the example taken from Václav Havel,

---

4. For Max Weber I have in mind his famous essays "Politics as a Vocation" and (especially) "Science as a Vocation," both in Gerth and Mills (1970). See also Sayer (1991, last chapter).

of a greengrocer in Prague who hangs a sign in his window saying "Workers of the World Unite" (Havel [1977] 1987).[5] Following Havel, I would suggest that the form of power to which this act testifies relies centrally on the *knowledge* of everybody involved that they are "living a lie."

Havel's greengrocer had no interest in the fate of the international proletariat; he was merely participating in a ritual. But that "merely" is deceptive. And it is here, I think, that my emphases do differ from Jim Scott's. We cannot infer from the greengrocer's likely nonbelief in what the sign says that his action is *meaningless*. For his displaying the sign—or more dramatically, failing to do so—sent out signals, clear to all. There is a subscript here too, and it is the subscript of power rather than resistance. What displaying the sign signified was his willingness to conform, to participate in the established order as if its representations were reality. It also said, in a language all could read, that the greengrocer shared a real sociality with others, that of living the lie itself. Had he not displayed the sign, he would be challenging the everyday moral accommodations, grounded in an equally everyday fear, which everyone engages in and which make everyday life livable—even if at the cost of a corrosive derangement of "private" and "public" selves.

This analysis rests less on the greengrocer's being fooled than on his, and everybody else's, knowing complicity. It is cynicism, not ideological incorporation, that makes this system work. But this is consequential, for such ritual accommodations diminish and disempower their participants, and the participants know this, too. It is in effect a systematic mobilization of bad faith in which, like collaborators with an invading army, people are tainted as individuals by the ways in which they have to behave (and nobody, it follows, can be trusted). The critical point for theories of hegemony is that this is the exact opposite of "mystification" or "false consciousness." This power works through the way it forcibly organizes, and divides, subjectivities, and thereby produces and reproduces quite *material* forms of sociality.

Individuals live in the lie that is "the state," and it lives through their performances. Their beliefs are neither here nor there. What is demanded of them is only—but precisely—performances. Like actors (to invoke another metaphor sociologists are prone to employ, without always considering what it conveys) they merely have to behave as if they were the

5. This brilliant essay is to my mind one of the most important contributions to the sociology of power in recent years.

characters they are impersonating. Rituals, we argue in *The Great Arch*, are a crucial dimension of that power that represents itself as "the state" and us as members of a "body politic." Believers or not, participants are by their very actions affirming the power of what is sanctified. Hobbes had good reason for baptizing the state Mortal God. In ritual observances like the greengrocer's, "His" omnipotence is daily celebrated, even if his existence is, for many members of the congregation personally, a matter of doubt.

The second thing I would like to emphasize, following from that example, is the importance of coercion, very broadly conceived. If you ask why Havel's greengrocer is apparently content to live the lie, part of the reason is likely to be that he may lose his job or apartment or see his children denied a university education if he does not. The point may be generalized. Here I would underline some of the things that Alonso (1986) and Koreck (1991) say about the authoritative organization of spaces, of times, of identities. I do not think people wholly are what they are identified as; Havel's greengrocer doubtless had another life in his weekend cottage. In that discrepancy lies the space for resistance. But authority does routinely and insistently define the quotidian world in which we are constrained to live—in a multitude of ways. It does so, as Rockwell shows, for instance, through the ways a school organizes space and time, inescapably sinewing the rhythms of locality to those of the nation, even if there is room for contestation in the classroom.

Max Weber once classically distinguished power from authority. He defined authority as legitimate power, and much discourse on hegemony echoes him in this. I want to make a deliberately provocative emphasis to the contrary. To a very considerable degree, in my view, it is the exercise of power pure and simple that itself authorizes and legitimates; and it does this less by the manipulation of beliefs than by defining the boundaries of the possible. Power enforces the terms on which things *must* be done at the most everyday of levels: the license I have to get if I want to marry, if I want to drive; the number I have to carry on the little card in my pocket if I want to claim expenses for a conference in the United States and I am a Canadian citizen. This is an organization of the times and spaces within which individual life is lived. And it is profoundly coercive, whether or not it is experienced as such. Frequently it is, but people have no material choice but to "accommodate" to what is, for the time being, their social reality.

The third and final point I want to make vis-à-vis rule and hegemony is superficially contrary to this, but also makes sense of Havel's thoroughly knowing but apparently compliant greengrocer. Such state forms or enactments do not merely constrain. They may also empower and enable, often in differential ways (men against women, for example). Individuals and groups may creatively adapt and use the forms through which, on another level, they are confined and constrained. When I got my driver's license for the first time four years ago (I am not a North American, and I escaped that particular rite of passage in my youth), I found it enormously liberating. Not only could I get to work in ten minutes rather than fifty, without having to change buses in minus thirty degrees; I also had the freedom of the continent, a freedom I immediately took advantage of by driving from Montana to Maine. The chapters in this book offer many examples of how state forms enable people to do things they want to do, both individually and collectively, whatever the "project" of their "framers." Elsie Rockwell's paper I have already instanced. Florencia Mallon emphasizes the importance to the state of incorporating elements of counterhegemonic cultures as a "legitimating device" (these were her terms, not mine); in doing so, spaces were opened. Gilbert Joseph's essay demonstrates how, inconveniently for their betters, once peasants have been mobilized for political purposes they acquire a habit of refusing to disappear from the stage.

  Campesino may be in origin a homogenizing and, in many ways, repressive category that effaces differences, but it is also a category people can sometimes use to express their difference. Its invocation has meaning and power. This paradox stands out very sharply, if in some ways tragically, in Marjorie Becker's chapter. In postrevolutionary Michoacán, some of what we might regard as the most repressive elements in femininity as constructed by Catholic theology became sources of strength and power for some women under particular circumstances. When we are dealing with issues of power and resistance, then, we are in the presence of something that is deeply and eternally contradictory. It is very rarely a question of "the state" *here* and "resistance" *there.* That contradiction lies *within* the subjectivities and socialities rulers always seek to regulate, but never succeed in wholly constituting.

V

I will end with another paradox, again taken from Jim Scott. He says (somewhere) that prisons are run by the prisoners. I agree. I would also argue that most of the time that is exactly why they work as well as they do. This was the point of *The Great Arch*'s insistence that "the state" lives in and through its subjects: we were not arguing an "incorporation" thesis at the level of ideology or belief, but pointing to precisely the materiality of everyday forms of state formation.

To put it another way: to abstract out, reify, and monolithically counterpose "hegemony" and "resistance" is to misunderstand both. Another conclusion follows from this, in which again I would agree with Jim Scott. If the suggestions I have made in these remarks—or the multiple testimonies of these essays—hold water, the hegemony of the state is also exactly what is most fragile about the state, precisely because it does depend on people living what they much of the time know to be a lie. Once in a blue moon the Prague greengrocer, knowing full well what his action signifies, takes down the sign in his window, and all that is solid melts into air. At that point, "hegemony" is revealed for what it is: the intellectual equivalent of the emperor's new clothes.

It is not entirely beside the point, however, to record that what appears to have turned compliance into defiance in the case of the greengrocer, and catapulted Václav Havel into Prague Castle, was Mikhail Gorbachev's repudiation of the Brezhnev doctrine. As Max Weber also said (and *The Great Arch*, unoriginally, repeated), every state is founded, in the final analysis, on force.[6]

6. See Weber, "Politics as a Vocation," in Gerth and Mills (1970).

Bibliography

ARCHIVES

Mexico City

ACDN	Archivo de Cancelados de la Defensa Nacional
AGN	Archivo General de la Nación
	FG Fondo Gobernación
	CNA.Actas Comisión Nacional Agraria, Actas
	CNA.RP Comisión Nacional Agraria, Resoluciones Presidenciales
AGRA	Archivo General de la Reforma Agraria
AHDN	Archivo Histórico de la Defensa Nacional
AHSEP	Archivo Histórico de la Secretaría de Educación Pública
ATN	Archivo de Terrenos Nacionales
BN.AFM	Biblioteca Nacional, Archivo Francisco Madero
CEHMC	Centro de Estudios de Historia de México, CONDUMEX
	FDLI Fondo Bernardo Reyes
CGPD or CPD	Colección General Porfirio Díaz, Universidad Ibero-americana

Chiapas

SRA.Tuxtla	Archivo de la Secretaría de la Reforma Agraria, Delegación Chiapas, Tuxtla Gutiérrez

INAREMAC.BD   Instituto de Asesoría Antropológica para la Región Maya, A.C., Banco de Datos, San Cristóbal, Chiapas

Chihuahua

AEN   Archivo Ejidal de Namiquipa, Namiquipa
AGNCh   Archivo General de Notarías, Estado de Chihuahua, Ciudad Chihuahua
AJMN   Archivo del Juzgado, Municipio de Namiquipa, Namiquipa
AMCG   Archivo Municipal de Ciudad Guerrero
AMN   Archivo Municipal de Namiquipa
ASC   Archivo Seccional de Cruces, Municipio de Namiquipa
CIDECH   Centro de Investigación y Documentación del Estado de Chihuahua, Ciudad Chihuahua

Coahuila

AGHECZ   Archivo General Histórico del Estado de Coahuila de Zaragoza
AMS   Archivo Municipal de Saltillo
    JP   Fondo Jefes Políticos
    PM   Fondo Presidentes Municipales

Durango

AGCCA   Archivo General del Cuerpo Consultativo Agrario, Gómez Palacio

Michoacán

AMZ   Archivo Municipal de Zamora, Zamora
APC   Archivo de la Purísima Corazón, Zamora

Puebla

ACEP   Archivo del Congreso del Estado de Puebla
AGNEP   Archivo General de Notarías del Estado de Puebla

AHMTO	Archivo Histórico Municipal de Tetela de Ocampo
AHMZ	Archivo Histórico Municipal de Zacapoaxtla

Tlaxcala

AGET	Archivo General del Estado de Tlaxcala, Tlaxcala
	EP Fondo Educación Pública
	FRRO Fondo de la Revolución y del Régimen Obregonista

Yucatán

AGEY	Archivo General del Estado de Yucatán, Mérida
	RJ Ramo de Justicia

Peru

BNP	Biblioteca Nacional del Perú

United States

BL	Bancroft Library, Berkeley, California
NA	National Archives, Washington, DC
	RG Record Groups (59, 84)
	SD-CPR Department of State Consular Post Records: Progreso

NEWSPAPERS

DH	*Diario del Hogar* (Mexico City)
	Diario Oficial (Various capital cities)
DY	*Diario Yucateco* (Mérida, Yucatán)
	New York Times
PO	*Periódico Oficial* (Saltillo, Coahuila)
RdM	*Revista de Mérida* (Mérida, Yucatán)
RdY	*Revista de Yucatán* (Mérida, Yucatán)
	El Siglo XIX (Mexico City)
	El Tiempo (Mexico City)

BOOKS AND ARTICLES

Abercrombie, Nicholas, Stephen Hill, and Bryan S. Turner. 1980. *The Dominant Ideology Thesis*. London: George Allen and Unwin.

Abrams, Philip. [1977] 1988. "Notes on the Difficulty of Studying the State." *Journal of Historical Sociology* 1(1):58–89.

Abu-Lughod, Lila. 1990. "The Romance of Resistance: Tracing Transformations of Power Through Bedouin Women." *American Ethnologist* 17(1):41–55.

Adas, Michael. 1982. "Bandits, Monks, and Pretender Kings: Patterns of Peasant Resistance and Protest in Colonial Burma, 1826–1941." In *Power and Protest in the Countryside*, ed. Robert Weller and Scott Guggenheim. Durham: Duke University Press.

Aguilar, Citlali. 1991. "El trabajo de los maestros: una construcción cotidiana." Licenciatura thesis, Centro de Investigación y de Estudios Avanzados del Instituto Politécnico Nacional (México).

Aguilar Camín, Héctor. 1980. "The Relevant Tradition: Sonoran Leaders in the Revolution." In *Caudillo and Peasant in the Mexican Revolution*. See Brading 1980.

Aguirre Beltrán, Gonzalo. 1988. "Formación de una teoría y una práctica indigenistas." In *Instituto Nacional Indigenista: 40 Años*. México: Instituto Nacional Indigenista.

———, et al., eds. 1976. *El indigenismo en acción: XXV aniversario del Centro Coordinador Indigenista Tzeltal-Tzotzil*. México: Instituto Nacional Indigenista.

Agulhon, Maurice. 1970. *La République au village: les populations du Var de la révolution a la Seconde République*. Paris: Plon.

Albó, Xavier. 1987. "From MNRistas to Kataristas to Katari." In *Resistance, Rebellion, and Consciousness in the Andean Peasant World*. See Stern 1987.

Almada, Francisco R. 1964. *La revolución en el estado de Chihuahua*, 2 vols. Chihuahua: Biblioteca del Instituto Nacional de Estudios Históricos de la Revolución Mexicana.

Alonso, Ana María. 1986. "The Hermeneutics of History." Paper delivered to History Department seminar, University of Chicago.

———. 1988a. "Gender, Ethnicity, and the Constitution of Subjects: Accommodation, Resistance, and Revolution on the Chihuahuan Frontier." Ph.D. diss., University of Chicago.

———. 1988b. "'Progress' as Disorder and Dishonor." *Critique of Anthropology* 8(1):13–33.

———. 1988c. "U.S. Military Intervention, Revolutionary Mobilization, and Popular Ideology in the Chihuahuan Sierra, 1916–1917." In *Rural Revolt in Mexico and U.S. Intervention*. See Nugent 1988a.

———. 1988d. "The Effects of Truth: Re-presentations of the Past and the Imagining of Community." *Journal of Historical Sociology* 1(1):33–57.

———. 1992a. "Work and *Gusto*: Gender and Re-Creation in a North Mexican

Pueblo." In *Workers' Expressions: Beyond Accommodation and Resistance*, ed. John Calagione, Doris Francis, and Daniel Nugent. Albany: SUNY Press.

——. 1992b. "Gender, Power, and Historical Memory: Discourses of Serrano Resistance." In *Feminists Theorize the Political*, ed. Judith Butler and Joan Scott. New York: Routledge.

Aman, Kenneth, and Cristián Parker, eds. 1991. *Popular Culture in Chile: Resistance and Survival*. Boulder: Westview Press.

Amerlinck de Bontempo, Marijosé. 1982. "La reforma agraria en la hacienda de San Diego de Rioverde." In *Después de los latifundios*, ed. Heriberto Moreno García. Zamora: El Colegio de Michoacán.

Anderson, Benedict. 1983. *Imagined Communities: Reflections on the Origin and Spread of Nationalism*. London: Verso/New Left Books.

Anguiano, Arturo. 1975. *El estado y la política obrera del cardenismo*. México: Editorial Era.

Angulo, Andrés, ed. 1956. *Herencia política del Coronel Miguel Lira y Ortega*. México: Secretaría de Educación Pública.

Ankerson, Dudley. 1984. *Agrarian Warlord: Saturnino Cedillo and the Mexican Revolution in San Luis Potosí*. DeKalb: Northern Illinois Press.

Anonymous. 1946. "Los ideales de Hidalgo sólo se realizarán plenamente con un partido del proletariado." *Unidad Socialista* 2(3).

Arias, Jacinto. 1984. *Historia de la colonia de "Los Chorros."* Tuxtla Gutiérrez: Gobierno del Estado.

——. 1985. *San Pedro Chenalhó: algo de su historia, cuentos, y costumbres*. Tuxtla Gutiérrez: Gobierno del Estado.

Arizpe, Lourdes. 1973. *Parentesco y economía en una sociedad Nahua: Nican Pehua Zacatipán*. México: Instituto Nacional Indigenista/Secretaría de Educación Pública.

Arnold, David. 1984. "Gramsci and Peasant Subalternity in India." *Journal of Peasant Studies* 11(4):155–77.

Aubry, Andrés. 1991. *San Cristóbal de Las Casas. Su historia urbana, demográfica y monumental, 1528–1990*. San Cristóbal, Chiapas: INAREMAC.

Azuela, Alicia. 1986. "Rivera and the Concept of Proletarian Art." In *Diego Rivera: A Retrospective*, ed. Cynthia Newman Helms. New York: W. W. Norton.

Bailey, David C. 1978. "Revisionism and the Recent Historiography of the Mexican Revolution." *Hispanic American Historical Review* 58(1):62–79.

Bartra, Armando. 1985. *Los herederos de Zapata*. México: Ediciones Era.

Bartra, Armando, and Manuel Aurrecochea. 1988 and forthcoming. *Puros cuentos: la historia de la historieta en México*. 2 vols. México: Grijalbo.

Bartra, Roger. 1982. "Lombardo o revueltas." In *El reto de la izquierda*, ed. R. Bartra. México: Grijalbo.

——. 1987. *La jaula de la melancolía: identidad y metamórfosis del mexicano*. México: Grijalbo.

————. 1991. "Mexican *Oficio:* The Miseries and Splendors of Culture." *Third Text* 14:7–16.

Basadre, Jorge. 1970. *Historia de la República del Perú, 1822–1933.* Vol. 10. Lima: Editorial Universitaria.

Bastian, Jean-Pierre. 1986. "Metodismo y rebelión política en Tlaxala, 1874–1920." In *Memorias del Primer Simposio Internacional de Investigaciones Socio-históricas sobre Tlaxcala.* Tlaxcala: Gobierno del Estado/Universidad Ibero-Americana.

Baumann, Friedericke. 1983. "Landowners, Peasants, and the Expansion of Capitalist Agriculture in Chiapas, 1896–1916." *Mesoamérica* 4(5):8–63.

Bayly, C. A. 1988. "Rallying Around the Subaltern." *Journal of Peasant Studies* 16(1):110–20.

Beals, Carleton. 1931. *Mexican Maze.* Philadelphia: Book League of America.

Becker, Marjorie. 1987. "Black and White and Color: Cardenismo and the Search for a *Campesino* Ideology." *Comparative Studies in Society and History* 29:453–65.

————. 1988a. "Lázaro Cárdenas and the Mexican Counter-Revolution: The Struggle over Culture in Michoacán, 1934–1940." Ph.D. diss., Yale University.

————. 1988b. "Lázaro Cárdenas, Cultural Cartographers, and the Limits of Everyday Resistance in Michoacán, 1934–40." Paper given at the 46th International Congress of Americanists, Amsterdam.

————. 1989. "Cardenistas, Campesinos, and the Weapons of the Weak: The Limits of Everyday Resistance in Michoacán, 1934–1940." *Peasant Studies* 16:233–50.

————. Forthcoming. *Setting the Virgin on Fire: Lázaro Cárdenas, Michoacán Campesinos, and the Redemption of the Mexican Revolution.* Berkeley: University of California Press.

Beekman, John, and James C. Hefley. 1968. *Peril by Choice: The Story of John and Elaine Beekman, Wycliffe Bible Translators in Mexico.* Grand Rapids: Zondervan Press.

Beezley, William H., and Judith Ewell, eds. 1987. *The Human Tradition in Latin America: The Twentieth Century.* Wilmington: Scholarly Resources.

Beezley, William H., Cheryl E. Martin, and William E. French, eds. 1994. *Rituals of Rule, Rituals of Resistance: Public Celebrations and Popular Culture in Mexico.* Wilmington: Scholarly Resources.

Behar, Ruth. 1990. "Rage and Redemption: Reading the Life Story of a Mexican Market Woman." *Feminist Studies* 16:223–58.

Benjamin, Thomas. 1989. *A Rich Land, A Poor People: Politics and Society in Modern Chiapas.* Albuquerque: University of New Mexico Press.

————. 1994. "'La Revolución es un bloque': The Origins of Official History of the Mexican Revolution." *Mexican Studies/Estudios Mexicanos* 10.

Benjamin, Thomas, and Mark Wasserman, eds. 1990. *Provinces of the Revolution: Essays on Regional Mexican History, 1910–1929.* Albuquerque: University of New Mexico Press.

Benjamin, Walter. 1968. *Illuminations*. Trans. Harry Zohn. New York: Harcourt, Brace and World.

Berman, Marshall. 1992. "Why Modernism Still Matters." In *Modernity and Identity*, ed. Scott Lash and Jonathan Friedman. Oxford: Basil Blackwell.

Betancourt Pérez, Antonio. 1983. *La problemática social: ¿primera chispa de la Revolución Mexicana?* Mérida: Gobierno del Estado/Academia Yucatanense.

Bois, Paul. 1971. *Paysans de l'ouest*. Paris: Flammarion.

Bojórquez Urzáiz, Carlos. 1977. "El Yucatán de 1847 hasta 1851: breves apuntes sobre el trabajo y la subsistencia." *Boletín de la Escuela de Ciencias Antropológicas de la Universidad de Yucatán* 5:18–25.

————. 1979. "Regionalización de la política agraria de Yucatán en la segunda mitad del siglo XIX." *Revista de la Universidad de Yucatán* 21:32–45.

Bolio Ontiveros, Edmundo. 1967. *Yucatán en la dictadura y en la Revolución*. México: Instituto Nacional de Estudios de la Revolución Mexicana.

Brading, David A., ed. 1980. *Caudillo and Peasant in the Mexican Revolution*. Cambridge: Cambridge University Press. Spanish ed. 1985. México: Fondo de Cultura Económica.

————. 1988. *Mito y profecía en la historia de México*. México: Vuelta.

Bricker, Victoria Reifler. 1981. *The Indian Christ, The Indian King: The Historical Substrate of Maya Myth and Ritual*. Austin: University of Texas Press.

Bright, Charles, and Susan Harding, eds. 1984. *Statemaking and Social Movements*. Ann Arbor: University of Michigan Press.

Brinton, Crane. 1965. *The Anatomy of Revolution*. New York: Vintage Books.

Britton, John A. 1979. "Teacher Unionization and the Corporate State in Mexico, 1931–1945." *Hispanic American Historical Review* 59(4):674–90.

Brown, Peter. 1982. *Society and the Holy in Late Antiquity*. Berkeley: University of California Press.

Burch, Noel. 1969. *Praxis du cinéma*. Paris: Gallimard.

Bustamante Alvarez, Tomás. 1987. "Período 1934–1940." In *Historia de la cuestión agraria mexicana: Estado de Guerrero, 1867–1940*. México: Gobierno del Estado de Guerrero/Universidad Autónoma de Guerrero y Centro de Estudios Históricos del Agrarismo en México.

Buve, Raymond Th. J. 1975. "Peasant Movements, Caudillos, and Land Reform During the Revolution (1910–1917) in Tlaxcala, Mexico." *Boletín de Estudios Latinoamericanos y del Caribe* 18:112–52.

————. 1982. "Compadrazgo, Local Politics, and the Revolution in Tlaxcala (1910–1917): Some Questions, Hypotheses, and Comments." In *The Indians of Mexico in Pre-Columbian and Modern Times*, ed. Maarten E. Jansen and Ted J. Leyenaar. Leiden: Rutgers B.V.

————. 1985. "Jefes menores de la Revolución Mexicana y los primeros avances en la consolidación nacional: el caso de Tlaxcala (1910–1920)." Unpublished manuscript.

————. 1988. "'Neither Carranza nor Zapata!': The Rise and Fall of a Peasant

Movement that Tried to Challenge Both, Tlaxcala, 1910–19." In *Riot, Rebellion, and Revolution*, ed. Katz. See Katz 1988a.

——. 1989. "Agricultores, dominación política, y estructura agraria en la Revolución Mexicana: el caso de Tlaxcala (1910–1918)." *Revista Mexicana de Sociología* 51(2):181–236.

——. 1990. "Tlaxcala: Consolidating a Cacicazgo." In *Provinces of the Revolution*. See Benjamin and Wasserman 1990.

Buve, Raymond Th. J., and Romana Falcón. 1989. "Tlaxcala and San Luis Potosí Under the Sonorenses (1920–1934): Regional Revolutionary Power Groups and the National State." In *Region, State, and Capitalism in Mexico*. See Pansters and Ouweneel 1989.

Calagione, John P., and Daniel Nugent. 1992. "Introduction: Beyond Accommodation and Resistance on the Margins of Capitalism." In *Workers' Expressions: Beyond Accommodation and Resistance*, ed. Calagione et al. Albany: State University of New York Press.

Calvo, Angelino, et al. 1989. *Voces de la historia: Nuevo San Juan Chamula, Nuevo Huixtán, Nuevo Matzam*. San Cristóbal, Chiapas: DESMI/Universidad Autónoma de Chiapas.

Calzadíaz Barrera, Alberto. 1979. *Hechos reales de la Revolución*. Vol. 1. México: Editorial Patria.

Camacho, Salvador. 1992. *Educación socialista en Aguascalientes, 1934–1940*. México: Consejo Nacional para la Cultura y las Artes.

Cancian, Frank. 1965. *Economics and Prestige in a Maya Community: The Religious Cargo System in Zinacantán*. Stanford: Stanford University Press.

——. 1972. *Change and Uncertainty in a Peasant Economy: The Maya Corn Farmers of Zinacantán*. Stanford: Stanford University Press.

Cardoso, Ciro, ed. 1980. *México en el siglo XIX: historia económica y de la estructura social*. México: Nueva Imagen.

Carmagnani, Marcello. 1982. "Local Governments and Ethnic Governments in Oaxaca." In *Essays in the Political, Economic, and Social History of Colonial Latin America*, ed. Karen Spalding. Newark, DE: University of Delaware Latin American Studies Program.

Carnoy, Martin. 1984. *The State and Political Theory*. Princeton: Princeton University Press.

Carr, Barry. 1980. "Recent Regional Studies of the Mexican Revolution." *Latin American Research Review* 15(1):3–14.

——. 1992. *Marxism and Communism in Twentieth-Century Mexico*. Lincoln: University of Nebraska Press.

Casillas Moreno, Angelina. 1985. *La mujer en dos comunidades de emigrantes (Chihuahua)*. México: SEP.

Castillo Burguete, María T. 1988. "Producción y comercialización de granos básicos: el movimiento de la unión estatal de productores de maiz de Chiapas." Master's thesis, Universidad Autónoma Metropolitana, Xochimilco.

Cerutti, Mario. 1989. Untitled Ph.D. thesis (history), University of Leiden.

Chacón, Ramón. 1981. "Yucatán and the Mexican Revolution: The Pre-Constitutional Years, 1910–1918." Ph.D. diss., Stanford University.

Chakrabarty, Dipesh. 1985. "Invitation to a Dialogue." In *Subaltern Studies IV.* See Guha 1985.

————. 1991. "Subaltern Studies and Critique of History." *Arena* (Melbourne) 96:105–20.

Chartier, Roger. 1987. *The Cultural Uses of Print in Early Modern France.* Princeton: Princeton University Press.

Chassen-López, Francie. 1977. *Lombardo Toledano y el movimiento obrero mexicano, 1917–1940.* México: Extemporáneos.

Chaterjee, Partha. 1982. "Agrarian Relations and Communalism in Bengal, 1926–1935." In *Subaltern Studies I.* See Guha 1982a.

————. 1983. "Gandhi and the Critique of Civil Society." In *Subaltern Studies II.* See Guha 1983a.

————. 1986. *Nationalist Thought and the Colonial World: A Derivative Discourse?* Tokyo: Zed Books for United Nations University.

————. 1987. "Caste and Subaltern Consciousness." In *Subaltern Studies VI,* ed. Ranajit Guha. Delhi: Oxford University Press.

————. 1990. "The Nationalist Resolution of the Women's Question." In *Recasting Women: Essays in Indian Colonial History,* ed. Kumkum Sangari and Sudesh Vaid. New Brunswick: Rutgers University Press.

Chevalier, François. 1989. "La libertad municipal, antigua y permanente reinvindicación mexicana." *Revista Mexicana de Sociología* 51(2):433–49.

Cirese, Alberto. 1979. *Ensayo sobre las culturas subalternas.* México: Cuadernos de la Casa Chata.

Civeira Taboada, Miguel. 1974. "Francisco I. Madero contra Carlos R. Menéndez." Unpublished manuscript.

Civera, Alicia. 1988. "Política educativa del gobierno del Estado de México, 1934–1940." *Secuencia* (México) 5:39–50.

Coatsworth, John. 1976. "Anotaciones sobre la producción de alimentos durante el Porfiriato." *Historia Mexicana* 26(2):167–87.

————. 1988a. "Patterns of Rural Rebellion in Latin America: Mexico in Comparative Perspective." In *Riot, Rebellion, and Revolution.* See Katz 1988a.

————. 1988b. "Comment on 'The United States and the Mexican Peasantry.'" In *Rural Revolt in Mexico.* See Nugent 1988a.

Cobb, Richard. 1972. *The Police and the People.* Oxford: Oxford University Press.

Cockroft, James D. 1967. "El maestro de primaria en la Revolución Mexicana." *Historia Mexicana* 16(4):565–87.

————. 1983. *Mexico: Class Formation, Capital Accumulation, and the State.* New York: Monthly Review Press.

Cohn, Bernard. 1980. "History and Anthropology: The State of Play." *Comparative Studies in Society and History* 22(2):198–221.

Collier, George. 1989. "Changing Inequality in Zinacantán: The Generations of 1918 and 1942." In *Ethnographic Encounters in Southern Mesoamerica*, ed. Victoria Reifler Bricker and Gary H. Gossen. Austin: University of Texas Press.

Comaroff, John L. 1982. "Dialectical Systems, History, and Anthropology: Units of Study and Questions of Theory." *Journal of Southern African History* 8(2):143–72.

———. 1987. "Of Totemism and Ethnicity: Consciousness, Practice, and the Signs of Inequality." *Ethnos* 52:3–4:301–23.

Connell, R. W. 1987. *Gender and Power*. Stanford: Stanford University Press.

Córdova, Arnaldo. 1973. *La ideología de la Revolución Mexicana: la formación del nuevo régimen*. México: Ediciones Era.

———. 1974. *La política de masas del cardenismo*. México: Editorial Era.

———. 1984. "Nación y nacionalismo en México." *Nexos* 83.

———. 1989. *La revolución y el estado en México*. México: Ediciones Era.

Corrigan, Philip. 1975. "On the Politics of Production: A Comment on 'Peasants and Politics' by Eric Hobsbawm." *Journal of Peasant Studies* 2(3):341–49.

———. 1990a. *Social Forms/Human Capacities*. London: Routledge.

———. 1990b. "State Formation (Entry for a Dictionary) (1986)." In *Social Forms/Human Capacities*.

Corrigan, Philip, Bruce Curtis, and Robert Lansing. n.d. "The Political Space of Schooling." Mimeo.

Corrigan, Philip, Harvie Ramsay, and Derek Sayer. 1978. *Socialist Construction and Marxist Theory: Bolshevism and Its Critique*. New York: Monthly Review Press.

———. 1979. *For Mao*. London: Macmillan.

———. 1980. "The State as a Relation of Production." In *Capitalism, State Formation, and Marxist Theory*, ed. Corrigan. London: Quartet Books.

Corrigan, Philip, and Derek Sayer. [1982] 1985. "Marxist Theory and Socialist Construction in Historical Perspective." *Utafiti* 6(2):127–58.

———. 1983. "Late Marx: Continuity, Contradiction and Learning." In *Late Marx and the Russian Road*. See Shanin 1983.

———. 1985. *The Great Arch: English State Formation as Cultural Revolution*. Oxford: Basil Blackwell.

Cosío Villegas, Daniel. 1956. *Historia moderna de México: el Porfiriato*. México: Editorial Hermes.

Craig, Ann L. 1983. *The First Agraristas*. Berkeley: University of California Press.

Das, Veena. 1987. "Subaltern as Perspective." *Subaltern Studies VI*. Delhi: Oxford University Press.

Davidson, Alastair. 1984. "Gramsci, the Peasantry, and Popular Culture." *Journal of Peasant Studies* 11(4):139–53.

De Certeau, Michel. 1984. *The Practice of Everyday Life*. Trans. Steven Rendall. Berkeley: University of California Press.

Deere, Carmen Diana. 1990. *Household and Class Relations*. Berkeley: University of California Press.

De la Peña, Guillermo. 1981. *A Legacy of Promises.* Austin: University of Texas Press.

————. 1989. "Local and Regional Power in Mexico." *Texas Papers on Mexico* no. 88-01. Austin: The Mexican Center of the Institute of Latin American Studies.

Del Castillo, Porfirio. 1953. *Puebla y Tlaxcala en los días de la Revolución.* México: Zavala.

Díaz Soto y Gama, Antonio. 1953. "La ley agraria del villismo." In *El Universal* (México), April 22 and 29.

Domínguez, José Luis. 1981. "Situación política en el partido de Sotuta (1911–1916)." In *Yucatán: peonaje y liberación.* See González Rodríguez et al. 1981.

Douglas, Mary. 1966. *Purity and Danger: An Analysis of the Concepts of Pollution and Taboo.* London: Ark Paperbacks.

Dow, James W. 1974. *Santos y supervivencias: funciones de la religión en una comunidad otomí.* México: Instituto Nacional Indigenista/Secretaría de Educación Pública.

Doyle, William. 1989. *The Oxford History of the French Revolution.* Oxford: Clarendon Press.

Duarte Morales, Teodosio. 1968. *El rugir del cañón.* Ciudad Juárez: Editorial B. Herrera.

Durkheim, Emile. 1957. *Professional Ethics and Civic Morals.* London: Routledge and Kegan Paul.

Edel, Mathew. 1966. "El ejido en Zinacantán." In *Los zinacantecos,* ed. Evon Z. Vogt. México: Instituto Nacional Indigenista.

Eklof, Ben. 1990. "Peasants and Schools." In *The World of the Russian Peasant: Post-Emancipation Culture and Society,* ed. Eklof and S. P. Frank. Boston: Unwin Hyman.

Embriz Osorio, Arnulfo, and Ricardo León García. 1982. *Documentos para la historia del agrarismo en Michoacán.* México: Centro de Estudios Históricos del Agrarismo en México.

Engels, Friedrich. [1884] 1942. *The Origin of the Family, Private Property, and the State.* Trans. of 4th German ed. New York: International Publishers.

Escobar, Arturo. 1992. "Imagining a Post-Development Era? Critical Thought, Development, and Social Movements." *Social Text* 10(2–3):20–56.

Esponda, Hugo. 1986. *Historia de la iglesia presbiteriana en Chiapas.* México: Publicaciones "El Faro."

Evans, Peter B., Dietrich Rueschemeyer, and Theda Skocpol. 1985. *Bringing the State Back In.* Cambridge: Cambridge University Press.

Ezpeleta, Justa, and Elsie Rockwell. 1983. "Escuela y clases subalternas." *Cuadernos Políticos* 37:70–80.

Fabela, Isidro, ed. 1963. *Documentos históricos de la Revolución Mexicana: revolución y régimen constitucionalista.* Vol. 4. *El plan de Guadalupe.* México: Fondo de Cultura Económica.

Fabian, Johannes. 1983. *Time and the Other.* New York: Columbia University Press.

Falcón, Romana. 1977. *El agrarismo en Veracruz: la etapa radical (1928–1935)*. México: El Colegio de México.

————. 1984. *Revolución y caciquismo: San Luis Potosí, 1910–1938*. México: El Colegio de México.

————. 1988. "La desaparición de jefes políticos en Coahuila: una paradoja porfirista." *Historia Mexicana* 37(3):423–68.

————. 1989. "Logros y límites de la centralización porfirista: Coahuila vista desde arriba." In *El dominio de las minorías*. See Staples et al. 1989.

————. 1991. "Poderes y razones de las jefaturas políticas. Coahuila en el primer siglo de vida independiente." In *Cincuenta años de historia en México*. Vol. 2, ed. Alicia Hernández Chávez and Manuel Miño Grijalva. México: El Colegio de México.

————. Forthcoming. "El estado incapaz. Lucha entre naciones. Poder, territorio, 'salvajes,' y 'gefes de departmento.'" In *El mundo rural mexicano a través de los siglos: homenaje a François Chevalier*, ed. Ricardo Avila and Carlos Martínez Assad. Guadalajara: Universidad de Guadalajara.

Falcón, Romana, and Soledad García. 1986. *La semilla en el surco: Adalberto Tejeda y el radicalismo en Veracruz, 1883–1960*. México: El Colegio de México.

Farriss, Nancy M. 1984. *Maya Society Under Colonial Rule: The Collective Enterprise of Survival*. Princeton: Princeton University Press.

Feder, Ernest. 1971. *The Rape of the Peasantry*. New York: Doubleday.

Fernández Anaya, Jorge. 1944. "La industrialización del país—una necesidad histórica de México." *La Voz de México*, March 25.

————. 1945. "El marxismo de nuestros tiempos." *La Voz de México*, March 18.

Fernández Christlieb, Fátima. 1982. *Los medios de difusión masiva en México*. México: Juan Pablos Editor.

Figes, Orlando. 1989. *Peasant Russia, Civil War: The Volga Countryside in Revolution, 1917–1921*. Oxford: Clarendon Press.

Foglio Miramontes, Fernando. 1936. *Geografía económica agrícola del estado de Michoacán*. México: Editorial Cultural.

Folgarait, Leonard. 1987. *So Far from Heaven: David Alfaro Siqueiros's* The March of Humanity *and Mexican Revolutionary Politics*. Cambridge: Cambridge University Press.

Foner, Eric. 1983. *Nothing but Freedom: Emancipation and Its Legacy*. Baton Rouge: Louisiana State University Press.

Foster-Carter, Aidan. 1978. "Can We Articulate 'Articulation?'" In *The New Economic Anthropology*, ed. John Clammer. London: Macmillan.

Foucault, Michel. 1979. *Discipline and Punish*. Harmondsworth: Penguin.

————. 1980. *Power/Knowledge: Selected Interviews and Other Writings, 1972–1977*. Ed. Colin Gordon. New York: Pantheon Books.

Foweraker, Joe. 1989. *Making Democracy in Spain: Grass-Roots Struggle in the South, 1955–1975*. Cambridge: Cambridge University Press.

Foweraker, Joe, and Ann L. Craig, eds. 1990. *Popular Movements and Political Change in Mexico.* Boulder: Lynne Rienner.

Fowler-Salamini, Heather. 1978. *Agrarian Radicalism in Veracruz, 1920–1938.* Lincoln: University of Nebraska Press.

———. 1990. "Tamaulipas: Land Reform and the State." In *Provinces of the Revolution.* See Benjamin and Wasserman 1990.

———. 1993. "The Boom in Regional Studies of the Mexican Revolution: Where Is It Leading?" *Latin American Research Review* 28(2):175–90.

Frankenhalter, Marilyn. 1979. *José Revueltas: el solitario solidario.* Miami: Ediciones Universal.

Franz, David A. 1973. "Bullets and Bolshevists: A History of the Mexican Revolution in Yucatán." Ph.D. diss., University of New Mexico.

Freitag, Sandra B. 1989. "Popular Culture in the Rewriting of History: An Essay in Comparative History and Historiography." *Peasant Studies* 16(3):169–98.

French, William E. 1990. "Peaceful and Working People: The Inculcation of the Capitalist Work Ethic in a Mexican Mining District." Ph.D. diss., University of Texas, Austin.

Friedlander, Judith. 1981. "The Secularization of the Cargo System: An Example from Postrevolutionary Central Mexico." *Latin American Research Review* 16(2):132–43.

Friedrich, Paul. [1970] 1977. *Agrarian Revolt in a Mexican Village.* Chicago: University of Chicago Press.

———. 1986. *The Princes of Naranja.* Austin: University of Texas Press.

Frost, Frederick J. T., and Channing Arnold. 1909. *The American Egypt.* London: Hutchinson.

Gadow, Hans. 1908. *Through Southern Mexico.* London: Witherby and Co.

Gal, Susan. 1987. "Codeswitching and Consciousness in the European Periphery." *American Ethnologist* 14:637–53.

Gamboa Ricalde, Alvaro. 1943–1955. *Yucatán desde 1910.* 3 vols. Veracruz and Mexico City: Imprenta "Standard."

García, Velma. 1992. "Agrarian Reform and the State in Postrevolutionary Veracruz." Unpublished manuscript.

García Canclini, Néstor. 1982. *Las culturas populares en el capitalismo.* Havana: Casa de las Américas.

———, ed. 1987. *Políticas culturales en América Latina,* México: Grijalbo.

———. 1988. "Culture and Power: The State of Research." *Media, Culture, and Society* 10:467–97.

———. 1990. *Culturas híbridas: estrategias para entrar y salir de la modernidad.* México: Grijalbo.

García de León, Antonio. 1979. "Lucha de clases y poder político en Chiapas." *Historia y Sociedad* 22:57–87.

———. 1985. *Resistencia y utopía,* 2 vols., México: Ediciones Era.

Garrido, Luis Javier. 1986. *El partido de la revolución institucionalizada*. México: SEP.

Geertz, Clifford. 1973. *The Interpretation of Cultures*. New York: Basic Books.

Genovese, Eugene. 1974. *Roll, Jordan, Roll: The World the Slaves Made*. New York: Pantheon Books.

———. 1979. *From Rebellion to Revolution: Afro-American Slave Revolts in the Making of the New World*. Baton Rouge: Louisiana State University Press.

Gerth, Hans, and C. Wright Mills, eds. 1970. *From Max Weber*. London: Routledge.

Giddens, Anthony. 1981. *A Contemporary Critique of Historical Materialism*. Vol. 1. *Power, Property, and the State*. Berkeley: University of California Press.

———. 1987. *A Contemporary Critique of Historical Materialism*. Vol. 2. *The Nation-State and Violence*. Berkeley: University of California Press.

Gill, Christopher. 1991. "Campesino Patriarchy in the Times of Slavery: The Henequen Plantation Society of Yucatán, 1860–1915." Master's thesis, University of Texas, Austin.

Gill, Mario. 1955. "Mochis: fruto de un sueño imperialista." *Historia Mexicana* 5(2):303–20.

Gilly, Adolfo. 1971. *La revolución interrumpida: México, 1910–1920*. México: El Caballito. English trans. 1983. *The Mexican Revolution*. London: New Left Books.

———. 1988. "Crónicas de campaña." *Brecha* 5–6:47–68.

———. 1989. *Cartas a Cuauhtémoc Cárdenas*. México: Ediciones Era.

Gledhill, John. 1991. *Casi nada: A Study of Agrarian Reform in the Homeland of Cardenismo*. Austin: University of Texas Press.

Goldfrank, Walter L. 1979. "Theories of Revolution and Revolution Without Theory: The Case of Mexico." *Theory and Society* 7:135–65.

Gómez, Pablo. 1981. "De Lombardo a los pluralistas." *Machete* (México) 10:22–23.

Gómez, Nich Juan. 1976. "Algo de mi vida." In *El indigenismo en acción*. See Aguirre Beltrán 1976.

Gonzalbo Aizpuru, Pilar. 1991. "Algunas consideraciones para la periodización de la historia de la educación en México." *Revista Mexicana de Pedagogía* 2(8):29–34.

González, Luis. [1968] 1972. *Pueblo en vilo*. México: El Colegio de México. English trans. 1974. *San José de Gracia*. Austin: University of Texas Press.

———. 1978. *Zamora*. Gobierno del Estado de Michoacán.

González Herrera, Carlos. 1988. "El villismo frente al problema agrario." *Cuadernos del Norte* 1(3):18–25.

González Rodríguez, Blanca, et al., eds. 1981. *Yucatán: peonaje y liberación*. Mérida: Fonapas-Yucatán/INAH.

Gramsci, Antonio. [1929–1935] 1971. *Selections from the Prison Notebooks*. Ed. and trans. Quintin Hoare and Geoffrey Nowell-Smith. New York: International Publishers.

Gruening, Ernest. 1928. *Mexico and Its Heritage.* New York: The Century Company.

Guerra, François-Xavier. 1985. *Le Mexique: de l'ancien régime à la révolution.* 2 vols. Paris: L'Harmattan. Spanish trans. 1988. *México: del antiguo régimen a la Revolución.* 2 vols. México: Fondo de Cultura Económica.

Guerrero Tapia, José. 1979. *Chiapas: tragedia y paisaje.* México: published by author.

Guha, Ranajit, ed. 1982a. *Subaltern Studies I: Writings on South Asian History and Society.* Delhi: Oxford University Press.

————. 1982b. "On Some Aspects of the Historiography of Colonial India." In *Subaltern Studies I.* See Guha 1982a.

————. 1983a. "The Prose of Counterinsurgency." In *Subaltern Studies II,* ed. Guha. Delhi: Oxford University Press.

————. 1983b. *Elementary Aspects of Peasant Insurgency in Colonial India.* Delhi: Oxford University Press.

————, ed. 1984. *Subaltern Studies III.* Delhi: Oxford University Press.

————, ed. 1985. *Subaltern Studies IV.* Delhi: Oxford University Press.

————. 1986. "Chandra's Death." In *Subaltern Studies V,* ed. Guha. Delhi: Oxford University Press.

————. 1989. "Dominance Without Hegemony and Its Historiography." In *Subaltern Studies VI,* ed. Guha. Delhi: Oxford University Press.

Guha, Ranajit, and Gayatri Chakravorty Spivak. 1985. *Selected Subaltern Studies.* New York: Oxford University Press.

Guillén, Francisco Javier. 1934. "En defensa de Chiapas." Folder. Tuxtla Gutiérrez: Published privately, April 23.

Guiteras Holmes, Calixta. 1992. *Cancuc: etnografía de un pueblo tzeltal de los altos de Chiapas, 1944.* Tuxtla Gutiérrez: Gobierno del Estado.

Gutiérrez, Roberto J. 1981. "Juchitán, municipio comunista." *A: Análisis Histórico y Sociedad Mexicana* 2(4).

Hall, Linda B. 1990. "Banks, Oil, and the Reinstitutionalization of the Mexican State, 1920–1924." In *The Revolutionary Process in Mexico.* See Rodríguez O. 1990.

Hall, Stuart. 1981. "Notes on Deconstructing 'The Popular.'" In *People's History and Socialist Theory,* ed. Raphael Samuel. London: Routledge and Kegan Paul.

Hall, Stuart, and Bill Schwartz. 1985. "State and Society." In *Crises in the British State, 1880–1930,* ed. Mary Logan and Bill Schwartz. London: Hutchinson/ Centre for Contemporary Cultural Studies.

Hamilton, Nora. 1982. *The Limits of State Autonomy: Post-Revolutionary Mexico.* Princeton: Princeton University Press.

Hansen, Asael T. 1980. "Change in the Class System in Mérida, Yucatán, 1875–1935." In *Yucatán: A World Apart,* ed. Edward H. Moseley and Edward D. Terry. Tuscaloosa: University of Alabama Press.

Hansen, Roger D. 1971. *The Politics of Mexican Development.* Baltimore: Johns Hopkins University Press.

Harris, Marvin. 1979. *Cultural Materialism*. New York: Random House.

Hart, John Mason. 1987. *Revolutionary Mexico: The Coming and Process of the Mexican Revolution*. Berkeley: University of California Press.

Hartmann, Heidi. 1981. "The Unhappy Marriage of Marxism and Feminism: Toward a More Progressive Union." In *Women and Revolution: A Discussion of the Unhappy Marriage of Marxism and Feminism*, ed. Lydia Sargent. Boston: South End Press.

Havel, Václav. [1977] 1987. "The Power of the Powerless." In Havel, *Living in Truth*. Boston and London: Faber and Faber.

Helguera R., Laura. 1974. *Los campesinos de la tierra de Zapata*. Vol. 3. *Adaptación, cambio, y rebelión*. México: SEP/INAH.

Hernández Chávez, Alicia. 1991. *Anenecuilco: memoria y vida de un pueblo*. México: El Colégio de México.

Hernández Hernández, Claudio. 1987. "El trabajo escolar de un maestro rural." In *Los maestros y la cultura nacional, 1920–1950*. Vol. 3. México: Secretaría de Educación Pública. 51–90.

Hewitt de Alcántara, Cynthia. 1984. *Anthropological Perspectives on Rural Mexico*. London: Routledge and Kegan Paul.

———. 1985. *La modernización de la agricultura mexicana, 1940–1970*. México: Siglo XXI.

Hill, Christopher. 1975. *The World Turned Upside Down*. Harmondsworth: Penguin Books.

———. 1981. "Parliament and People in Seventeenth-Century England." *Past and Present* 92:100–24.

Hill, Jane. 1985. "The Grammar of Consciousness and the Consciousness of Grammar." *American Ethnologist* 12:725–37.

Hobsbawm, Eric. 1959. *Primitive Rebels: Studies in Archaic Forms of Social Movement in the Nineteenth and Twentieth Centuries*. Manchester: Manchester University Press.

———. 1973. "Peasants and Politics." *Journal of Peasant Studies* 1(1):3–22.

———. 1986. "Revolution." In *Revolution in History*, ed. Roy Porter and Mikulás Teich. Cambridge: Cambridge University Press.

———. 1990. *Nations and Nationalism Since 1780: Programme, Myth, Reality*. Cambridge: Cambridge University Press.

Hobsbawm, Eric, and George Rudé. 1968. *Captain Swing*. New York: Pantheon Books.

Holloway, John. 1980. "El estado y la lucha cotidiana." *Cuadernos Políticos* 24:8–28.

Huerta, Efraín. 1974. "Desconcierto." In *Los eróticos y otros poemas*. México: Joaquín Mortiz.

Huerta Jaramillo, Ana María Dolores. 1985. *Insurrecciones rurales en el estado de Puebla, 1868–1870*. Puebla: Universidad Autónoma de Puebla.

Hunt, Lynn. 1984. *Politics, Culture, and Class in the French Revolution*. Berkeley: University of California Press.

Huntington, S. P. 1971. *Political Order in Changing Societies.* New Haven: Yale University Press.

Inda, Angélica, ed. 1986. "Dos siglos en Chamula, 1778–1985." *Boletín del Archivo Histórico Diocesano (San Cristóbal)* 3(1–2).

Jacobs, Ian. 1983. *Ranchero Revolt: The Mexican Revolution in Guerrero.* Austin: University of Texas Press.

Jordán, Fernando. 1956. *Crónica de un país bárbaro.* Chihuahua: Centro Librero La Prensa.

Joseph, Gilbert M. 1980. "Caciquismo and the Revolution: Carrillo Puerto in Yucatán." In *Caudillo and Peasant in the Mexican Revolution.* See Brading 1980.

———. 1986. *Rediscovering the Past at Mexico's Periphery.* Tuscaloosa: University of Alabama Press.

———. 1988a. "Forging the Regional Pastime: Baseball and Class in Yucatán." In *Sport and Society in Latin America: Diffusion, Dependency, and the Rise of Mass Culture,* ed. Joseph L. Arbena. New York: Greenwood Press.

———. [1982] 1988b. *Revolution from Without: Yucatán, Mexico, and the United States, 1880–1924.* Rev. ed. Durham: Duke University Press.

———. 1990. "On the Trail of Latin American Bandits: A Reexamination of Peasant Resistance." *Latin American Research Review* 25(3):7–53.

———. 1991a. "'Resocializing' Latin American Banditry: A Reply." *Latin American Research Review* 26(1):161–74.

———. 1991b. "The New Regional Historiography at Mexico's Periphery." In *Land, Labor, and Capital in Modern Yucatán: Essays in Regional History and Political Economy,* ed. Joseph and Jeffery T. Brannon. Tuscaloosa: University of Alabama Press.

Joseph, Gilbert M., and Allen Wells. 1986. "Summer of Discontent: Economic Rivalry Among Elite Factions During the Late Porfiriato in Yucatán." *Journal of Latin American Studies* 18(2):255–82. Spanish version in *Región y Sociedad* (Mérida) 8(41):43–68.

———. 1987. "The Rough-and-Tumble Career of Pedro Crespo." In *The Human Tradition in Latin America: The Twentieth Century.* See Beezley and Ewell 1987.

———. 1988. "El monocultivo henequenero y sus contradicciones: estructura de dominación y formas de resistencia en haciendas yucatecas durante el Porfiriato tardío." *Siglo XIX* 3(6):215–77.

———. 1990a. "Seasons of Upheaval: The Crisis of Oligarchical Rule in Yucatán, 1909–1915." In *The Revolutionary Process in Mexico.* See Rodríguez 1990.

———. 1990b. "Yucatán: Elite Politics and Rural Insurgency." In *Provinces of the Revolution.* See Benjamin and Wasserman 1990.

———. Forthcoming. *Summer of Discontent, Seasons of Upheaval: Elite Politics and Rural Insurgency in Yucatán, 1876–1915.*

Jrade, Ramón. 1985. "Inquiries into the Cristero Insurrection Against the Mexican Revolution." *Latin American Research Review* 20(2).

————. 1989. "Religion, Politics, and the State: The Rural-Urban Alliance in Mexico's Cristero Insurrection." Paper presented at the Fifteenth Congress of the Latin American Studies Association, Miami, December 1989.

Judt, Tony. 1979. "'A Clown in Regal Purple': Social History and the Historians." *History Workshop* 7:66–94.

Kahn, Joel. 1985. "Peasant Ideologies in the Third World." *Annual Review of Anthropology* 14:49–75.

Kaplan, Steven L. 1984. *Understanding Popular Culture*. Berlin: Mouton Publishers.

Kaplan, Temma. 1982. "Female Consciousness and Collective Action: The Case of Barcelona, 1910–1918." *Signs* 7(3):545–66.

————. 1987. "Women and Communal Strikes in the Crisis of 1917–1922." In *Becoming Visible: Women in European History*, 2d ed., ed. Renate Bridenthal, Claudia Koonz, and Susan Stuard. Boston: Houghton Mifflin.

————. 1992. "Making Spectacles of Themselves: Women's Rituals and Patterns of Resistance in Africa, Argentina, and the Contemporary United States." Paper presented at the National Humanities Center, Research Triangle, NC, November 1992.

Katz, Friedrich. 1974. "Labor Conditions on Porfirian Haciendas: Some Trends and Tendencies." *Hispanic American Historical Review* 54(1):1–47.

————. 1976. "Peasants and the Mexican Revolution of 1910." In *Forging Nations: A Comparative View of Rural Ferment and Revolt*, ed. J. Spielberg and S. Whiteford. East Lansing: Michigan State University Press.

————. 1980. "Pancho Villa, Peasant Movements, and Agrarian Rebellion in Northern Mexico." In *Caudillo and Peasant in the Mexican Revolution*. See Brading 1980.

————. 1981a. *The Secret War in Mexico: Europe, the United States, and the Mexican Revolution*. Chicago: University of Chicago Press.

————. 1981b. "Rural Uprisings in Mexico." Paper presented at the Social Science Research Council Conference on Rural Uprisings in Mexico, New York.

————, ed. 1986a. *Porfirio Díaz frente al descontento popular regional (1891–1893)*. México: Universidad Iberoamericana.

————. 1986b. "The Porfiriato." In *The Cambridge History of Latin America*, ed. Leslie Bethell. Vol. 5. Cambridge: Cambridge University Press.

————, ed. 1988a. *Riot, Rebellion, and Revolution: Rural Social Conflict in Mexico*. Princeton: Princeton University Press.

————. 1988b. "Introduction: Rural Revolts in Mexico." In *Riot, Rebellion and Revolution*. See Katz 1988a.

————. 1988c. "Rural Rebellions After 1810." In *Riot, Rebellion and Revolution*. See Katz 1988a.

————. 1988d. "From Alliance to Dependency: The Formation and Deformation of an Alliance Between Francisco Villa and the United States." In *Rural Revolt in Mexico and U.S. Intervention*. See Nugent 1988a.

Katz, Michael B. 1987. *Reconstructing American Education*. Cambridge: Harvard University Press.

Kelley, Joan. 1979. "The Doubled Vision of Feminist Theory: A Postscript to the 'Women and Power' Conference." *Feminist Studies* 5:216–27.

Klehr, Harvey. 1984. *The Heyday of American Communism: The Depression Decade*. New York: Basic Books.

Knight, Alan. 1981. "Intellectuals in the Mexican Revolution." Paper presented at the Sixth Conference of Mexican and U.S. Historians, Chicago.

———. 1984a. "The Working Class and the Mexican Revolution, c. 1900–1920." *Journal of Latin American Studies* 16(1):51–79.

———. 1984b. Book review essay. *Journal of Latin American Studies* 16(2):525–26.

———. 1985a. "El liberalismo mexicano desde la Reforma hasta la Revolución (una interpretación)." *Historia Mexicana* 35(1):59–92.

———. 1985b. "The Mexican Revolution: Bourgeois? Nationalist? or Just a 'Great Rebellion?'" *Bulletin of Latin American Research* 4(2):1–37.

———. 1986a. *The Mexican Revolution*. 2 vols. Cambridge: Cambridge University Press.

———. 1986b. "Mexican Peonage: What Was It and Why Was It?" *Journal of Latin American Studies* 18(1):41–74.

———. 1987. *U.S.-Mexican Relations, 1910–1940: An Interpretation*. San Diego: Center for U.S.-Mexican Studies.

———. 1989. "Los intelectuales en la Revolución Mexicana." *Revista Mexicana de Sociología* 51(2):25–65.

———. 1990a. "Historical Continuities in Social Movements." In *Popular Movements and Political Change in Mexico*. See Foweraker and Craig 1990.

———. 1990b. "Cardenismo: Juggernaut or Jalopy?" *Texas Papers on Mexico* no. 90-09. Austin: The Mexican Center of the Institute of Latin American Studies.

———. 1990c. "Revolutionary Project, Recalcitrant People: Mexico, 1910–1940." In *The Revolutionary Process in Mexico*. See Rodríguez 1990.

———. 1990d. "Social Revolution: A Latin American Perspective." *Bulletin of Latin American Research* 9(2).

———. 1991. "Land and Society in Revolutionary Mexico: The Destruction of the Great Haciendas." *Mexican Studies/Estudios Mexicanos* 7(1).

———. 1992. "Mexico's Elite Settlement: Conjuncture and Consequences." In *Elites and Democratic Consolidation in Latin America and Southern Europe*, ed. John Higley and Richard Gunther. New York: Cambridge University Press.

Kohl, J. V. 1982. "The Cliza and Ucureña War: Syndical Violence and National Revolution in Bolivia." *Hispanic American Historical Review* 62(4):607–28.

Köhler, Ulrich. 1975. *Cambio cultural dirigido en los altos de Chiapas*. Mexico: Instituto Nacional Indigenista.

Koreck, María Teresa. 1991. "Popular Sub-versions in Postrevolutionary Mexico: 'Taking Up Reason' in the 'Longitude of War.'" Paper presented to conference

"Popular Culture, State Formation, and Revolutionary Mexico," Center for U.S.-Mexican Studies, San Diego, California.

Krauze, Enrique. 1976. *Caudillos culturales en la revolución mexicana*. México: Siglo XXI.

Laborde, Hernán. 1946. "La virgen de Guadalupe ha sido la campeona de nuestras luchas." *La Voz de México* 14:3.

Laclau, Ernesto. 1975. "The Specificity of the Political: Around the Poulantzas-Miliband Debate." *Economy and Society* 4(1):87–110.

———. [1977] 1979. *Politics and Ideology in Marxist Theory*. London: Verso Books.

Laclau, Ernesto, and Chantal Mouffe. [1985] 1989. *Hegemony and Socialist Strategy: Toward a Radical Democratic Politics*. New York: Verso.

LaFrance, David. 1984. "Puebla: Breakdown of the Old Order." In *Other Mexicos: Essays on Regional Mexican History, 1876–1911*, ed. Thomas Benjamin and William McNellie. Albuquerque: University of New Mexico Press.

———. 1989. *The Mexican Revolution in Puebla, 1908–1913: The Maderista Movement and the Failure of Liberal Reform*. Wilmington: Scholarly Resources.

———. 1990. "Many Causes, Movements, Failures, 1910–1913: The Regional Nature of Maderismo." In *Provinces of the Revolution*. See Benjamin and Wasserman 1990.

LaFrance, David, and G. P. C. Thomson. 1987. "Juan Francisco Lucas: Patriarch of the Sierra Norte de Puebla." In *The Human Tradition in Latin America: The Twentieth Century*. See Beezley and Ewell 1987.

Lagarde, Marcela, and Daniel Cazés. 1980. "Construcción del partido de masas. El caso de la Montaña, Guerrero: Parte 1." *Oposición* (February 24): 3.

Larín, Nicolás. 1968. *La rebelión de los cristeros (1926–29)*. México: Ediciones Era.

Leal, Juan Felipe. 1975a. "The Mexican State, 1915–1973: A Historical Interpretation." *Latin American Perspectives* 2(2):48–63.

———. 1975b. *México: estado, burocracia, y sindicatos*. México: Ediciones "El Caballito."

Le Bon, Gustave. [1909] 1952. *The Crowd: A Study of the Popular Mind*. London: E. Benn.

Lefebvre, Henri. 1988. "Toward a Leftist Cultural Politics: Remarks Occasioned by the Centenary of Marx's Death." In *Marxism and the Interpretation of Culture*, ed. Cary Nelson and Lawrence Grossberg. London: Macmillan Education.

Lerner, Victoria. 1979. *Historia de la Revolución Mexicana*. Vol. 17. *1934–1940: la educación socialista*. México: El Colegio de México.

Levinson, Bradley A. 1993. "*Todos somos iguales*: Cultural Production and Social Difference at a Mexican Secondary School." Ph.D. diss. University of North Carolina, Chapel Hill.

Leyes y Códigos de México. [1971] 1982. *Ley Federal de Reforma Agraria*. México: Editorial Porrua.

Lira, Andrés. 1983. *Comunidades indígenas frente a la Ciudad de México. Tenochtitlán y Tlatelolco, sus pueblos y barrios, 1812–1919*. México: El Colegio de Michoacán.

Lister, Florence, and Robert Lister. 1966. *Chihuahua, Storehouse of Storms.* Norman: University of Oklahoma Press.

Lloyd, Jane-Dale. 1988. "Rancheros and Rebellion: The Case of Northwestern Chihuahua, 1905–1909." In *Rural Revolt in Mexico and U.S. Intervention.* See Nugent 1988a.

Loera, Margarita. 1987. *Mi pueblo: su historia y tradiciones.* México: INAH.

Logan, Kathleen. 1990. "Women's Participation in Urban Protest." In *Popular Movements and Political Change in Mexico.* See Foweraker and Craig 1990.

Lombardi Satriani, L. M. 1975. *Antropología cultural: análisis de la cultura subalterna.* Buenos Aires: Galeana.

———. 1978. *Apropiación y destrucción de las clases subalternas.* México: Nueva Imagen.

Lomnitz-Adler, Claudio. 1992. "Concepts for the Study of Regional Culture." In *Mexico's Regions.* See Van Young 1992b.

Long, Norman. 1984. "Creating a Space for Change: A Perspective on the Sociology of Development." Inaugural lecture, Professorship of Empirical Sociology of Non-Western Countries, Agricultural University, Wageningen, the Netherlands, November 15.

Loyo, Engracia. 1994. "Popular Reactions to the Educational Reforms of Cardenismo." In *Rituals of Rule, Rituals of Resistance.* See Beezley, Martin, and French 1993.

Macías, Anna. 1982. *Against All Odds: The Feminist Movement in Mexico to 1940.* Westport: Greenwood Press.

Macintyre, Stuart. 1980. *Little Moscows: Communism and Working-Class Militancy in Inter-War Britain.* London: Croon-Helm.

Mahan, Elizabeth. 1990. "Communications, Culture, and the State in Latin America." *Journal of Interamerican Studies and World Affairs* 32(1):146–54.

Mallon, Florencia E. 1983. *The Defense of Community in Peru's Central Highlands: Peasant Struggle and Capitalist Transition, 1860–1940.* Princeton: Princeton University Press.

———. 1987a. "Nationalist and Anti-State Coalitions in the War of the Pacific: Junín and Cajamarca, 1879–1902." In *Resistance, Rebellion, and Consciousness in the Andean Peasant World.* See Stern 1987.

———. 1987b. "Patriarchy in the Transition to Capitalism: Central Peru, 1830–1950." *Feminist Studies* 13:379–407.

———. 1988. "Peasants and State Formation in Nineteenth-Century Mexico: Morelos, 1848–1858." *Political Power and Social Theory* 7:1–54.

———. Forthcoming. *Peasant and Nation: The Making of Postcolonial Mexico and Peru.* Berkeley: University of California Press.

Manrique, Nelson. 1981. *Campesinado y nación: Las guerrillas indígenas en la guerra con Chile.* Lima: Ital Peru-CIC.

———. 1988. *Yawar mayu: sociedades terratenientes serranas, 1879–1910.* Lima: DESCO.

Mao Zedong [Tse-Tung]. 1966. *Four Essays on Philosophy.* Peking: Foreign Languages Press.

Marcuse, Herbert. 1966. *One-dimensional Man.* Boston: Beacon Press.

Margolies, Barbara Luise. 1975. *Princes of the Earth.* Washington, DC: American Anthropological Association.

Marsden, Richard. 1992. "'The State': A Comment on Abrams, Denis, and Sayer." *Journal of Historical Sociology* 5(2):358–77.

Martín-Barbero, Jesús. 1987. *De los medios a las mediaciones: comunicación, cultura, y hegemonía.* México: Ediciones G. Gilli.

———. n.d. *Procesos de comunicación y matrices de cultura.* Barcelona: n.p.

Martínez Assad, Carlos. 1979. *El laboratorio de la revolución.* México: Siglo XXI.

———, ed. 1990. *Balance y perspectivas de los estudios regionales en México.* México: Universidad Nacional Autónoma de México.

———. 1991. "Dos versiones de la Revolución Mexicana." *Nexos* 167:78–80.

Martínez Saldaña, Tomás. 1980. *El costo social de un éxito político: la política expansionista del estado mexicano en el agro lagunero.* Chapingo.

Marx, Karl. [1867] 1906. *Capital: A Critique of Political Economy.* Vol. 1. Trans. Samuel Moore and Edward Aveling. Chicago: Charles Kerr and Co.

———. [1857–58] 1973. *Grundrisse.* Trans. Martin Nicolaus. New York: Vintage.

Marx, Karl, and Friedrich Engels. [1955] 1975. *Selected Correspondence.* Trans. I. Lasker. 3d ed. Moscow: Progress Publishers.

Mattelart, Armand, and Seth Siegelaub, eds. 1979–83. *Communication and Class Struggle.* 2 vols. New York and Bagnolet, France: IG/IMMRC.

Mauss, Marcel. [1925] 1967. *The Gift.* Trans. Ian Cunnison. New York: Norton.

Medin, Tzvi. 1982. *El minimato presidencial: historia política del maximato, 1928–1935.* México: Ediciones Era.

Medina H., Andrés. 1991. *Tenejapa: familia y tradición en un pueblo tzeltal.* Tuxtla Gutiérrez: Gobierno del Estado de Chiapas.

Mejía Pineros, María Consuelo, and Sergio Sarmiento Siva. 1987. *La lucha indígena: un reto a la ortodoxia.* México: Siglo XXI/Instituto de Investigaciones Sociales.

Mendieta y Núñez, Lucio. 1981. *El problema agrario en México.* México: Porrúa.

Menéndez, Carlos R. 1919. *La primera chispa de la Revolución Mexicana: el movimiento de Valladolid en 1910.* Mérida: Imprenta de "La Revista de Yucatán."

Meneses Morales, Ernesto. 1986. *Tendencias educativas oficiales en México, 1911–1934.* México: Centro de Estudios Educativos.

Mercado, Ruth. 1986. *La escuela primaria gratuita, una lucha popular cotidiana.* México: Centro de Investigación y de Estudios Avanzados del Instituto Politécnico Nacional.

———. 1992. "La escuela en la memoria histórica local. Una construcción colectiva." *Nueva Antropología* 42:73–87.

Meyer, Jean. 1971. *Problemas campesinos y revueltas agrarias, 1821–1910.* México: SepSetentas.

————. 1974a. *La Cristiada.* Vol. 1. *La guerra de los Cristeros.* Trans. Aurelio Garzón del Camino. México: Siglo XXI.

————. 1974b. *La Cristiada.* Vol. 2. *El conflicto entre la iglesia y el estado.* México: Siglo XXI.

————. 1974c. *La Cristiada.* Vol. 3. *Los Cristeros.* México:Siglo XXI.

————. 1976. *The Cristero Rebellion: The Mexican People Between Church and State, 1926–1929.* Trans. Richard Southern. Cambridge: Cambridge University Press.

————. 1984. *Esperando a Lozada.* Zamora: El Colegio de Michoacán.

————. 1986. "Haciendas y ranchos, peones y campesinos en el Porfiriato: algunas, falacias estadísticas." *Historia Mexicana* 35(3):477–509.

Meyer, Jean, Enrique Krauze, and Cayetano Reyes. 1977. *Historia de la Revolución Mexicana.* Vol. 11. *Estado y sociedad con Calles.* México: El Colegio de México.

Meyer, Lorenzo. 1978. *Historia de la Revolución Mexicana.* Vol. 12. *1928–1934: El conflicto social y los gobiernos del maximato.* México: El Colegio de México.

Meyer, Lorenzo, Rafael Segovia, and Lejandra Lajous. 1978. *Historia de la Revolución Mexicana.* Vol. 13. *1928–1934: Los inicios de la institucionalización. La política del maximato.* México: El Colegio de México.

Meyers, William. 1984. "La Comarca Lagunera: Work, Protest, and Popular Mobilization in North Central Mexico." In *Other Mexicos: Essays on Regional Mexican History, 1876–1911,* ed. Thomas Benjamin and William McNellie, Norman: University of Oklahoma Press.

Miliband, Ralph. 1970. "The Capitalist State: Reply to Nicos Poulantzas." *New Left Review* 59:53–60.

————. 1973. "Poulantzas and the Capitalist State." *New Left Review* 82:83–92.

Miller, Beth. 1984. "Concha Michel, revolucionaria mexicana." *La Palabra y el Hombre* 50 (Apr.–June): 23–27.

Miller, Simon. 1988. "Revisionism in Recent Mexican Historiography." *Bulletin of Latin American Research* 4(1):77–88.

Millon, Robert Paul. 1960. *Mexican Marxist Vicente Lombardo Toledano.* Chapel Hill: University of North Carolina Press.

Mohanty, Chandra Talpade. 1992. "Introduction: Cartographies of Struggle." In *Third World Women and the Politics of Feminism,* ed. Mohanty, Ann Russo, and Lourdes Torres. Bloomington: Indiana University Press.

Monsiváis, Carlos. 1981. "Notas sobre el Estado, la cultura nacional y las culturas populares en México." *Cuadernos Políticos* 30:33–44.

————. 1982. "Del muralismo al ballet folklórico." *Deslinde* 1:3 (December).

————. 1985. "La aparición del subsuelo. Sobre la cultura de la Revolución Mexicana." *Historias* 8–9:159–77.

————. 1987. *Entrada libre: crónicas de una sociedad que se organiza.* México: Era.

Montoya, Rodrigo, María José Silveira, and Felipe José Lindoso, eds. 1979. *Producción parcelaria y universo ideológico.* Lima: Mosca Azul Editores.

Moore, Barrington. 1969. *The Social Origins of Dictatorship and Democracy.* Harmondsworth: Penguin.

———. 1978. *Injustice: The Social Bases of Obedience and Revolt.* White Plains, NY: M. E. Sharpe.

Morales Sánchez, Alonso. 1976. "Fundación de la escuela de Tzopiljá." In *El indigenismo en acción.* See Aguirre Beltrán et al. 1976.

Mukerji, Chandra, and Michael Schudson, eds. 1991. *Rethinking Popular Culture: Contemporary Perspectives in Cultural Studies.* Berkeley: University of California Press.

Myers, Sharon. 1981. "Alcozauca, un presente de cara hacia el futuro." *Dí* (México) 20 (March 12).

Nash, June. 1970. *In the Eyes of the Ancestors: Belief and Behavior in a Maya Community.* New Haven: Yale University Press.

Nash, June, and Helen Icken Safa, eds. 1976. *Sex and Class in Latin America.* New York: Praeger.

———. 1986. *Women and Change in Latin America,* South Hadley: Bergen and Garvey.

Nava Rodríguez, Luis. 1978. *Tlaxcala contemporánea. De 1822 a 1977.* México: Progreso.

Nickel, Herbert J. 1988. "Agricultural Laborers in the Mexican Revolution (1910–40): Some Hypotheses and Facts About Participation and Restraint in the Highlands of Puebla-Tlaxcala." In *Riot, Rebellion, and Revolution.* See Katz 1988a.

Nugent, Daniel, ed. 1988a. *Rural Revolt in Mexico and U.S. Intervention.* San Diego: Center for U.S.-Mexican Studies.

———. 1988b. "Rural Revolt in Mexico, Mexican Nationalism and the State, and Forms of U.S. Intervention." In *Rural Revolt in Mexico and U.S. Intervention.* See Nugent 1988a.

———. 1989a. "'Are We Not [Civilized] Men?': The Formation and Devolution of Community in Northern Mexico." *Journal of Historical Sociology* 2(3):206–39.

———. 1989b. "Conflicting Ideological Views of the Ejido in Northern Mexico." *Texas Papers on Mexico* no. 88-03. Austin: The Mexican Center.

———. 1990. "Paradojas en el desarrollo de 'la cuestión agraria en Chihuahua, 1885–1935." In *Actas del Primer Congreso de Historia Regional Comparada, 1989,* ed. Rubén Lau Rojo and Carlos González Herrera. Ciudad Juárez: Universidad Autónoma de Ciudad Juárez.

———. 1991. "Revolutionary Posturing, Bourgeois Land 'Reform': Reflections on the Agrarian Question in Northern Mexico." *LABOUR, Capital and Society* 24(1):90–108.

———. 1992. "Popular Musical Culture in Rural Chihuahua: Accommodation or Resistance." In *Worker's Expressions.* See Calagione and Nugent 1992.

———. 1993. *Spent Cartridges of Revolution: An Anthropological History of Namiquipa, Chihuahua.* Chicago: University of Chicago Press.

Nutini, Hugo C., and Barry L. Isaac. 1974. *Los pueblos de habla náhuatl de la región de Tlaxcala y Puebla*. México: Instituto Nacional Indigenista/Secretaría de Educación Pública.

Nutini, Hugo C., Barry L. Isaac, and Betty Bell. 1980. *The Structure and Historical Development of the Compadrazgo System in Rural Tlaxcala*. Princeton: Princeton University Press.

O'Brien, Jay, and William Roseberry, eds. 1991. *Golden Ages, Dark Ages: Imagining the Past in Anthropology and History*. Berkeley: University of California Press.

Ochoa Campos, Moisés. 1967. *La Révolución Mexicana: sus causas sociales*. México: BINEHRM.

⸺. 1968. *La Revolución Mexicana: sus causas políticas*. 2 vols. México: BINEHRM.

O'Hanlon, Rosalind. 1988. "Recovering the Subject: Subaltern Studies and Histories of Resistance in Colonial South Asia." *Modern Asian Studies* 22(1):189–224.

O'Hanlon, Rosalind, and David Washbrook. 1992. "After Orientalism: Culture, Criticism, and Politics in the Third World." *Comparative Studies in Society and History* 34(1):141–67.

Olea Arias, Heliodoro. 1961. *Apuntes históricos de la revolución de 1910–1911*. Chihuahua: Impresora AIFFER.

O'Malley, Ilene. 1986. *The Myth of Revolution: Hero Cults and the Institutionalization of the Mexican State, 1920–1940*. Westport: Greenwood Press.

Osorio, Rubén. 1990. *Pancho Villa, ese desconocido: entrevistas en Chihuahua a favor y en su contra*. Chihuahua: Ediciones del Gobierno del Estado de Chihuahua.

Oyarzún, Kemy. 1989. "Introduction: Cultural Production and the Struggle for Hegemony." *Latin American Perspectives* 16(2):3–11.

Pansters, Wil, and Arij Ouweneel, eds. 1989. *Region, State, and Capitalism in Mexico: Nineteenth and Twentieth Centuries*. Amsterdam: Center for Latin American Research and Documentation.

Paoli, Francisco, and Enrique Montalvo. 1977. *El socialismo olvidado de Yucatán*. México: Siglo XXI.

Paradise, Ruth. 1991. "El conocimiento cultural en el salón de clases: niños indígenas y su orientación hacia la observación." *Infancia y Aprendizaje* 55:83–85.

Partido Comunista Mexicano (PCM). [1938] 1980. *Hacia una educación al servicio del pueblo: resoluciones y principales estudios presentados en la Conferencia Pedagógica del PC*. México: Imprenta Mundial.

Patch, Robert. 1976. *La formación de estancias y haciendas durante la colonia*. Mérida: Gobierno del Estado de Yucatán.

Pereyra, Carlos. 1981. "Socialismo, nación, y partido." *Machete* 101 (February).

⸺. 1984. *El sujeto de la historia*. Madrid: Alianza.

Pérez Rocha, Manuel. 1978. "Socialismo y enseñanza técnica en México, 1930–1940." *Problemas de Desarrollo* 19(36):97–128.

Porter, Roy. 1990. *English Society in the Eighteenth Century.* Harmondsworth: Penguin.

Post, Ken. 1978. *Arise, Ye Starvelings!* The Hague: Martinus Nijhoff.

Poulantzas, Nicos. 1969. "The Problem of the Capitalist State." *New Left Review* 58:67–78.

——. 1973. *Political Power and Social Classes.* Trans. Timothy O'Hagan. London: New Left Books.

——. 1976. "The Capitalist State: A Reply to Miliband and Laclau." *New Left Review* 95:63–83.

——. 1978. *State, Power, Socialism.* London: New Left Books.

Pozas Arciniega, Ricardo. 1944. *Chamula, 1943–1944.* Thesis. Instituto Nacional de Antropología e Historia. México.

——. 1952. "El trabajo en las plantaciones de café y el cambio socio-cultural del indio." *Revista Mexicana de Estudios Antropológicos* 12:31–48.

——. 1976. *La antropología y la burocracia indigenista.* México: Editorial de Cuadernos para Trabajadores.

——. 1977. *Chamula: un pueblo indio de los altos de Chiapas.* 2 vols. México: Instituto Nacional Indigenista.

Prakash, Gyan. 1990. "Writing Post-Orientalist Histories of the Third World: Perspectives from Indian Historiography." *Comparative Studies in Society and History* 32(2):383–408.

——. 1992a. "Can the 'Subaltern' Ride? A Reply to O'Hanlon and Washbrook." *Comparative Studies in Society and History* 34(1):168–84.

——. 1992b. "Postcolonial Criticism and Indian Historiography." *Social Text* 10(2–3):8–19.

Raby, David L. 1974. *Educación y revolución social en México.* México: SepSetentas.

——. 1981. "La educación socialista en México." *Cuadernos Políticos* 29 (July–September): 75–82.

——. 1989. "Ideología y construcción del estado: la función política de la educación rural en México, 1921–1935." *Revista Mexicana de Sociología* 51(2): 305–20.

Ramírez Rancaño, Mario. 1991. *Tlaxcala: una historia compartida.* México: Consejo Nacional para la Cultura y las Artes/Gobierno del Estado de Tlaxcala.

Rebel, Herman. 1988. "Why Not 'Old Marie' . . . or Someone Very Much Like Her?: A Reassessment of the Question About Grimm's Contributors from a Social Historical Perspective." *Social History* 13(1):1–24.

——. 1989. "Cultural Hegemony and Class Experience: A Critical Reading of Recent Ethnological-Historical Approaches." *American Ethnologist* 16(1):117–36, 16(2):350–65.

Reed, John. 1969. *Insurgent Mexico.* New York: International Publishers.

Reed, Nelson. 1964. *The Caste War of Yucatán.* Stanford: Stanford University Press.

Reed-Danahay, Deborah. 1987. "Farm Children at School: Educational Strategies in Rural France." *Anthropological Quarterly* 60(2):83–89.

Reina, Leticia. 1983. *Las luchas populares en México en el siglo XIX*, México: CIESAS.

Revueltas, José. 1974. "Cincuenta pesos por cada bracero guatemalteco." *Excélsior* (México), April 14.

———. 1979. *Los días terrenales*. México: Ediciones Era.

———. 1980. *Ensayo sobre un proletariado sin cabeza*. México: Era.

Reyes, Sergio, et al. 1970. *Estructura agraria y desarrollo agrícola en México*. 3 vols. México: Centro de Investigaciones Agrarias.

Rocha Islas, Marta. 1979. "Del villismo y las defensas sociales en Chihuahua." Licenciatura thesis, Universidad Nacional Autónoma de México.

Rockwell, Elsie. 1986. "Cómo observar la reproducción." *Revista Colombiana de Educación* 17:109–25.

———. 1992. "Tales from Xaltipan: Documenting Orality and Literacy in Rural Mexico." *Cultural Dynamics* 5(2):156–75.

Rockwell, Elsie, and Ruth Mercado. 1986. *La escuela, lugar de trabajo docente: descripciones y debates*. México: Centro de Investigación y de Estudios Avanzados del Instituto Politécnico Nacional.

Rodríguez O., Jaime E., ed. 1990. *The Revolutionary Process in Mexico: Essays on Political and Social Change, 1880–1940*. Los Angeles: Latin American Center, UCLA.

———, ed. 1992. *Patterns of Contention in Mexican History*. Wilmington: Scholarly Resources.

Rosaldo, Renato. 1987. "Politics, Patriarchs, and Laughter." *Cultural Critique* 6:65–86.

———. 1989. *Culture and Truth: The Remaking of Social Anthropology*. Boston: Beacon Press.

Roseberry, William. 1989. *Anthropologies and Histories*. New Brunswick: Rutgers University Press.

———. 1991. "Potatoes, Sacks, and Enclosures." In *Golden Ages, Dark Ages*. See O'Brien and Roseberry 1991.

Roseberry, William, and Jay O'Brien. 1991. Introduction to *Golden Ages, Dark Ages*. See O'Brien and Roseberry 1991.

Ross, Stanley, ed. 1966. *Is the Mexican Revolution Dead?* New York: Alfred A. Knopf.

Rowe, William, and Vivian Schelling. 1991. *Memory and Modernity: Popular Culture in Latin America*. London: Verso.

Rubin, Jeffrey. 1987. "State Policies, Leftist Oppositions, and Municipal Elections: The Case of the COCEI in Juchitán." In *Electoral Patterns and Perspectives in Mexico*, ed. Arturo Alvarado. San Diego: Center for U.S.-Mexican Studies.

Rudé, George. 1964. *The Crowd in History: A Study of Popular Disturbances in France and England, 1730–1848*. New York: Wiley.

Ruiz, Ramón Eduardo. 1980. *The Great Rebellion: Mexico, 1905–1924*. New York: Norton.

———. 1988. *The People of Sonora and Yankee Capitalists*. Tucson: University of Arizona Press.

Rus, Jan. Forthcoming. "Contained Revolutions: The Struggle for Control of Highland Chiapas, 1910–1925." *Mexican Studies/Estudios Mexcianos.*

Rus, Jan, et. al. 1986. *Abtel ya pinka/Trabajo en las fincas.* San Cristóbal, Chiapas: INAREMAC.

Rus, Jan, and Salvador Guzmán Bakbolom, eds. 1990. *Kipaltik: la historia de cómo compramos nuestra finca.* San Cristóbal, Chiapas: INAREMAC.

Rus, Jan, and Robert Wasserstrom. 1980. "Civil-Religious Hierarchies in Central Chiapas: A Critical Perspective." *American Ethnologist* 7(3):466–78.

———. 1981. "Evangelization and Political Control." In *Is God an American?* ed. S. Hvalkof and P. Aaby. Copenhagen: International Work Group on Indigenous Affairs.

Salas, Elizabeth. 1990. *Soldaderas in the Mexican Military: Myth and History.* Austin: University of Texas Press.

Samuel, Raphael. 1980. "British Marxist Historians, 1880–1980 (Part One)." *New Left Review* 120:21–95.

———. 1985. "The Lost World of British Communism." *New Left Review* 154:3–54.

Sanderson, Susan R. Walsh. 1984. *Land Reform in Mexico, 1916–1980.* New York: Academic Press.

Santis Gómez, Juan. 1976. "Breves notas sobre el horario flexible." In *El indigenismo en acción.* See Aguirre Beltrán 1976.

Sargent, Lydia, ed. 1981. *Women and Revolution: A Discussion of the Unhappy Marriage of Marxism and Feminism.* Boston: South End Press.

Sarmiento, Domingo. 1952. *Civilización y barbarie.* Buenos Aires: Librería El Ateneo.

Sassoon, Anne Showstack. 1980. *Gramsci's Politics.* London: Croom Helm.

Sayer, Derek. 1987. *The Violence of Abstraction.* Cambridge: Basil Blackwell.

———. 1991. *Capitalism and Modernity: An Excursus on Marx and Weber.* New York: Routledge.

———. 1992. "A Notable Administration: English State Formation and the Rise of Capitalism." *American Journal of Sociology* 97(5):1382–1415.

Schmitt, Karl. 1965. *Communism in Mexico: A Study in Political Frustration.* Austin: University of Texas Press.

Schryer, Frans J. 1980. *The Rancheros of Pisaflores: The History of a Peasant Bourgeoisie in Mexico.* Toronto: University of Toronto Press.

Schwartz, Bill. 1982. "The Communist Party Historians' Group, 1945–1956." In *Making Histories: Studies in History-Writing and Politics,* ed. Richard Johnson et al. London: Hutchinson/Centre for Contemporary Cultural Studies.

Scott, James C. 1976. *The Moral Economy of the Peasant: Rebellion and Subsistence in Southeast Asia.* New Haven: Yale University Press.

———. 1977. "Protest and Profanation: Agrarian Revolt and the Little Tradition." *Theory and Society* 4(1):1–38, 4(2):211–46.

————. 1985. *Weapons of the Weak: Everyday Forms of Peasant Resistance*. New Haven: Yale University Press.

————. 1987. "Resistance Without Protest and Without Organization: Peasant Opposition to the Islamic *Zakat* and the Christian Tithe." *Comparative Studies in Society and History* 29(3):417–52.

————. 1990. *Domination and the Arts of Resistance: Hidden Transcripts*. New Haven: Yale University Press.

Scott, James C., and Benedict Kerkvliet, eds. 1986. "Everyday Forms of Peasant Resistance in Southeast Asia." Special issue. *Journal of Peasant Studies* 13(2).

Screen Reader. 1977. *Screen Reader 1. Cinema/Ideology/Politics*. London: Society for Education in Film and Television.

Secretaría de Educación Pública (SEP). 1935. Federal Inspectors' Reports, México.

————. 1987. *Los maestros y la cultura nacional, 1920–50*. 5 vols. México: Secretaría de Educación Pública.

Seed, Patricia. 1991. "Colonial and Postcolonial Discourse." *Latin American Research Review* 26(3):181–200.

Seidman, Michael. 1991. *Workers Against Work: Labor in Paris and Barcelona During the Popular Fronts*. Berkeley: University of California Press.

Semo, Enrique. 1978. *Historia mexicana: economía y lucha de clases*. México: Ediciones Era.

Shanin, Teodor. 1983. "Marxism and the Vernacular Revolutionary Traditions." In *Late Marx and the Russian Road: Marx and the Peripheries of Capitalism*, ed. Shanin. London: Routledge and Kegan Paul.

————. 1990. "The Question of Socialism: A Development Failure or an Ethical Defeat?" *History Workshop* 30:68–74.

Sierra Camacho, María Teresa. 1987. *El ejercicio discursivo de la autoridad en asambleas comunales (metodología y análisis del discurso oral)*. México: Cuadernos de la Casa Chata.

Silva Herzog, Jesús. 1963. *Trayectoria ideológica de la Revolución Mexicana, 1910–1917*. México: Cuadernos Americanos.

————. 1969. *Breve historia de la Revolución Mexicana*. 2 vols. México: SEP.

Simpson, Eyler. 1937. *The Ejido: Mexico's Way Out*. Chapel Hill: University of North Carolina Press.

Siqueiros, David. 1971. "El Presidium del Comité Central del PCM sobre las declaraciones de Siqueiros." *Oposición* 1:21 (February 15): 2.

Siverts, Henning. 1965. "The Cacique of K'ankujk: A Study of Leadership and Social Change in Highland Chiapas." *Estudios de Cultura Maya* 5:339–60.

————. 1969. *Oxchuc, una tribu maya de México*. México: Instituto Indigenista Interamericano.

Skocpol, Theda. 1979. *States and Social Revolutions*. Cambridge: Cambridge University Press.

Smith, Gavin. 1991. "The Production of Culture in Local Rebellion." In *Golden Ages, Dark Ages*. See O'Brien and Roseberry 1991.

Spivak, Gayatri Chakravorty. 1985. "Subaltern Studies: Deconstructing Historiography." In *Subaltern Studies IV*. See Guha 1985.

————. 1988. "Can the Subaltern Speak?" In *Marxism and the Interpretation of Culture*, ed. Cary H. Nelson and Lawrence G. Grossberg. London: Macmillan Education.

Stacey, Judith. 1983. *Patriarchy and Socialist Revolution in China*. Berkeley: University of California Press.

Staples, Anne, et al., eds. 1989. *El dominio de las minorías: República Restaurada y Porfiriato*. México: El Colegio de México.

Starr, Frederick. 1908. *In Indian Mexico*. Chicago: Forbes and Co.

Stavenhagen, Rodolfo. 1970. "Social Aspects of Agrarian Structure in Mexico." In *Agrarian Problems and Peasant Movements in Latin America*, ed. Stavenhagen. New York: Doubleday.

Stearns, Peter. 1983. "Social and Political History." *Journal of Social History* 16(3):366–82.

Stern, Steve J. 1987. "New Approaches to the Study of Peasant Rebellion and Consciousness." In *Resistance, Rebellion, and Consciousness in the Andean World: 18th to 20th Centuries*, ed. Stern. Madison: University of Wisconsin Press.

————. 1988. "Feudalism, Capitalism, and the World-System in the Perspective of Latin America and the Caribbean." *American Historical Review* 93(4):829–72.

Sullivan-González, Douglas. 1989. "The Struggle for Hegemony: An Analysis of the Mexican Catholic Church, 1876–1911." Graduate research paper, University of Texas at Austin.

Swingewood, Alan. 1979. *The Myth of Mass Culture*. Atlantic Highlands: Humanities Press.

Taboada, Eva. 1985. "Educación y lucha ideológica en el México posrevolucionario (1920–1940)." In *Educación y clases populares en América Latina*, ed. María de Ibarrola y Elsie Rockwell. México: Centro de Investigación y de Estudios Avanzados del Instituto Politécnico Nacional.

Taggart, James M. 1975. *Estructura de los grupos domésticos de una comunidad Nahuat de Puebla*. México: Instituto Nacional Indigenista/Secretaría de Educación Pública.

Tannenbaum, Frank. 1929. *The Mexican Agrarian Revolution*. Washington: The Brookings Institution.

————. 1950. *Mexico: The Struggle for Peace and Bread*. New York: Alfred A. Knopf.

————. [1933] 1966. *Peace By Revolution: Mexico After 1910*. New York: Columbia University Press.

Tapia, Jesús. 1985. "El culto de la Purísima: un mito de fundación." Paper presented at the Seventh Meeting of Mexican and North American Historians, Oaxaca, October 1985.

————. 1986. *Campo religioso y evolución política en el Bajío zamorano.* Zamora: El Colegio de Michoacán.

Taylor, Peter, and Herman Rebel. 1981. "Hessian Peasant Women, Their Families, and the Draft: A Socio-Historical Interpretation of Four Tales from the Grimm Collection." *Journal of Family History* 6:347–78.

Taylor, William. 1979. *Drinking, Homicide, and Rebellion in Colonial Mexican Villages.* Stanford: Stanford University Press.

Terrazas, Joaquín. 1905. *Memorias del Señor Coronel Don Joaquín Terrazas.* Ciudad Juárez: Imprenta de "El Agricultor Mexicano."

Terrazas, Silvestre. 1985. *El verdadero Pancho Villa.* México: Era.

Thompson, E. P. 1963. *The Making of the English Working Class.* New York: Vintage. Reprint 1972, Penguin.

————. 1967. "Time, Work-Discipline, and Industrial Capitalism." *Past and Present* 38:56–97.

————. 1971. "The Moral Economy of the English Crowd in the Eighteenth Century." *Past and Present* 50:76–136.

————. 1974. "Patrician Society, Plebeian Culture." *Journal of Social History* 7(4):382–405.

————. 1976. *William Morris: Romantic to Revolutionary.* New York: Pantheon.

————. [1965] 1978a. "The Peculiarities of the English." In *The Poverty of Theory and Other Essays.* New York: Monthly Review Press.

————. 1978b. "Eighteenth-Century English Society: Class Struggle Without Class?" *Social History* 3(2):133–65.

Thompson, Richard. 1974. *The Winds of Tomorrow: Social Change in a Maya Town.* Chicago: University of Chicago Press.

Thomson, Guy P. C. 1990. "Bulwarks of Patriotic Liberalism: The National Guard, Philharmonic Corps, and Patriotic Juntas in Mexico, 1847–88." *Journal of Latin American Studies* 22:31–68.

————. 1991. "Agrarian Conflict in the Municipality of Cuetzalán (Sierra de Puebla): The Rise and Fall of 'Pala' Agustín Dieguillo, 1861–1894." *Hispanic American Historical Review* 71(2):205–58.

Tibol, Raquel, ed. 1972. *Diego Rivera, arte y política.* México: Grijalbo.

Trouillot, Michel-Rolph. 1990. *Haiti: State Against Nation.* New York: Monthly Review Press.

Tutino, John. 1986. *From Insurrection to Revolution in Mexico: Social Bases of Agrarian Violence, 1750–1940.* Princeton: Princeton University Press.

————. 1990. "Revolutionary Confrontation, 1913–17: Regions, Classes, and the New National State." In *Provinces of the Revolution.* See Benjamin and Wasserman 1990.

Urbina, Erasto. 1944. "El despertar de un pueblo: memorias relativas a la evolución indígena en el estado de Chiapas." Unpublished manuscript. Library of the Centro de Investigaciones Ecológicas del Sureste, San Cristóbal, Chiapas.

Valadés, José C. 1963–1967. *Historia general de la Revolución Mexicana*. 10 vols. México: M. Quesada Brandi.

Valdés Silva, Candelaria. 1990. "Los maestros rurales y el reparto agrario en la Laguna." Licenciatura thesis, Centro de Investigación y de Estudios de Avanzados.

Vanderwood, Paul. 1987. "Building Blocks But Yet No Building: Regional History and the Mexican Revolution." *Mexican Studies/Estudios Mexicanos* 3(2):421–32.

———. 1989. "Comparing Mexican Independence and the Revolution: Causes, Concepts, and Pitfalls." In *The Independence of Mexico and the Creation of the New Nation*, ed. Jaime E. Rodríguez O. Los Angeles: University of California Press.

Van Young, Eric. 1990. "To See Someone Not Seeing: Historical Studies of Peasants and Politics in Mexico." *Mexican Studies/Estudios Mexicanos* 6(1):133–59.

———. 1992a. "Mentalities and Collectivities: A Comment." In *Patterns of Contention in Mexican History*. See Rodríguez 1992.

———. 1992b. "Are Regions Good to Think?" In *Mexico's Regions: Comparative History and Development*, ed. Van Young. San Diego: Center for U.S.-Mexican Studies.

Vargas-Lobsinger, María. 1984. *La hacienda de "La Concha": una empresa algodonera de la Laguna, 1883–1917*. México: Universidad Nacional Autónoma de México.

Vaughan, Mary Kay. 1982. *Estado, clases sociales, y educación en México*. México: Fondo de Cultura Económica. English ed. 1982. *The State, Education, and Social Class in Mexico, 1889–1928*. DeKalb: Northern Illinois University Press.

———. 1987. "El papel político del magisterio socialista de México, 1934–40: un estudio comparativo de los casos de Puebla y Sonora." Unpublished manuscript.

———. 1990a. "Primary Education and Literacy in Mexico in the Nineteenth Century: Research Trends, 1968–1988." *Latin American Research Review* 24(3):31–66.

———. 1990b. "Women Schoolteachers in the Mexican Revolution: The Story of Reyna's Braids." *Journal of Women's History* 2(1):143–68.

———. 1991. "Socialist Education in the State of Puebla in the Cárdenas Period." In *El campo, la ciudad, y la frontera en la historia de México*, ed. Ricardo Sánchez Flores, Eric Van Young, and Gisela von Wobeser. México: Universidad Nacional Autónoma de México.

———. 1992. "Rural Women's Literacy and Education in the Mexican Revolution: Subverting a Patriarchal Event?" Paper presented at the Conference "Crossing Borders, Creating Spaces: Mexican and Chicana Women, 1848–1992," University of Illinois, Chicago.

———. 1994. "The Construction of Patriotic Festival in Central Mexico: Puebla (1900–1946)." In *Rituals of Rule, Rituals of Resistance*. See Beezley et al. 1994.

Vázquez, Josefina Z. 1970. *Nacionalismo y educación en México*. México: El Colegio de México.

Villaseñor, Víctor Manuel. 1976. *Memorias de un hombre de izquierda*. Vol. 2. México: Grijalbo.

Vivó, Jorge A. 1959. *Estudio de geografía, económica, y demográfica de Chiapas*. México: Sociedad Mexicana de Geografía y Estadistica.

Vogt, Evon Z. 1969. *Zinacantán: A Maya Community in the Highlands of Chiapas*. Cambridge: Harvard University Press.

Volosinov, V. N. [1929] 1986. *Marxism and the Philosophy of Language*. Cambridge: Harvard University Press.

Voss, Stuart F. 1990. "Nationalizing the Revolution: Culmination and Circumstance." In *Provinces of the Revolution*. See Benjamin and Wasserman 1990.

Wallerstein, Immanuel. 1988. "Comments on Stern's Critical Tests." *American Historical Review* 93(4):873–85.

Warman, Arturo. 1976. *Y venimos a contradecir*. México: Ediciones de la Casa Chata.

———. 1978. "The Revolutionary Potential of the Mexican Peasant." In *Toward a Marxist Anthropology*, ed. Stanley Diamond. The Hague: Mouton.

———. 1988. "Zapata/zapatismo." In *Riot, Rebellion, and Revolution*. See Katz 1988a.

Warner, Marina. 1976. *Alone of All Her Sex: The Myth and Cult of the Virgin Mary*. New York: Alfred A. Knopf.

Wasserman, Mark. 1980. "The Social Origins of the 1910 Revolution in Chihuahua." *Latin American Research Review* 15(1):15–38.

Wasserstrom, Robert. 1976. *Ambíguo progreso*. San Cristóbal, Chiapas: INAREMAC.

———. 1980. *Ingreso y trabajo rural en los altos de Chiapas. El caso de San Juan Chamula*. San Cristóbal, Chiapas: Centro de Investigaciones Ecológicas del Sureste.

———. 1983. *Class and Society in Central Chiapas*. Berkeley: University of California Press.

Weber, Max. [1918] 1958. "Politics as a Vocation." In *From Max Weber*, ed. Hans Gerth and C. Wright Mills. New York: Oxford University Press.

Wells, Allen. 1984. "Yucatán: Social Violence and Control." In *Other Mexicos: Essays on Regional Mexican History, 1876–1911*, ed. Thomas Benjamin and William McNellie. Albuquerque: University of New Mexico Press.

———. 1985. *Yucatán's Gilded Age: Haciendas, Henequen, and International Harvester, 1860–1915*. Albuquerque: University of New Mexico Press.

Wexler, Philip, Tony Whitson, and Emily J. Moskowitz. 1981. "Deschooling by Default: The Changing Social Functions of Public Schooling." *Interchange* 12(2–3):133–50.

Weyl, Sylvia and Nathaniel Weyl. 1939. *The Reconquest of Mexico: The Years of Lázaro Cárdenas*. New York: Oxford University Press.

Whetten, Nathan. 1948. *Rural Mexico*. Chicago: University of Chicago Press.

Williams, Raymond. 1961. *Culture and Society, 1780–1950*. Harmondsworth: Penguin.

———. 1977. *Marxism and Literature*. London: Oxford University Press.

———. 1980. *Problems in Materialism and Culture*. London: Verso.

Willis, Paul. 1977. *Learning to Labour: How Working-Class Kids Get Working-Class Jobs.* London: Gowet.

Winn, Peter. 1986. *Weavers of Revolution: The Yarur Workers and Chile's Road to Socialism.* New York: Oxford University Press.

Wolf, Eric. 1969. *Peasant Wars of the Twentieth Century.* New York: Harper and Row. (Reprint 1973. London: Faber and Faber.)

———. 1971. Introduction to *National Liberation: Revolution in the Third World,* ed. Norman Miller and Roderick Aya. New York: Free Press.

Womack, John. 1968. *Zapata and the Mexican Revolution.* New York: Vintage Books.

———. 1986. "The Mexican Revolution, 1910–1920." In *The Cambridge History of Latin America,* ed. Leslie Bethell. Vol. 5. Cambridge: Cambridge University Press.

Woolard, K. 1985. "Language Variation and Cultural Hegemony: Toward an Integration of Sociolinguistic and Social Theory." *American Ethnologist* 12:738–48.

Yúdice, George, Jean Franco, and Juan Flores, eds. 1992. *On Edge: The Crisis of Contemporary Latin American Culture.* Minneapolis: University of Minnesota Press.

Index

Abercrombie, Nicholas, 56, 63
Abrams, Philip, xvii, 19, 371
Abu-Lughod, Lila, 21n
Agrarian dispossession, 142n, 216,
    237, 240, 281–82, 350; resistance
    to, 218. *See also* Agrarian reform
Agrarian Law, the: fear of, 237–39;
    Namiquipans' rejection of, 230–36;
    violations of, 244
Agrarian reform, 56, 60–61, 100, 175,
    190, 209–46, 326n, 363; accom-
    plishments of, 73, 212; in Chiapas,
    265–70, 276–80, 284; and the
    communist party, 332, 350–51;
    and institutional state power, 72,
    101, 211, 292, 342; official dis-
    course of, 227–29, 232, 362; op-
    position to, 45–47, 49, 230–36; of
    Zapatistas, 38. *See also* Agrarian dis-
    possession; Cárdenas, Lázaro:
    agrarian reforms of; *Ejido*
Agrarismo, 47, 61–62, 175, 232, 370;
    state co-optation of, 213
Agraristas, 46, 51–52, 62, 213; rela-
    tions with Catholic church, 48–49,
    53
Aguascalientes (state), 41, 46
Aguillón de los Ríos, Justiniano, 179,
    184–85, 203n

Aguirre Beltrán, Gonzalo, 288n
Agulhon, Maurice, viii, x
Alamán, 61
Alarcón, Manuel, 103
Alcohol: sale of, 280, 282; monopoly
    on aguardiente, 288n
Alcoholism, 258; campaigns against,
    336–37; as resistance, 145. *See also*
    Sobriety
Alcozauca (town), 330, 331n, 335; as
    "red" ayuntamiento, 336
Alemán, Miguel, 332
Algerian revolution, 30
Alonso, Ana María, ix–x, 16n, 18, 22,
    139, 169n, 241n, 361–62, 370,
    375; on historical memory, 236n;
    on masculinity, 234n; on warfare
    between colonists and indigenes,
    206n, 245n
Althusser, Louis, 173n
Alvarado, Salvador, 139, 147, 164,
    167; liberal reforms of, 58, 163;
    and revolution in Yucatán, 42
Anáhuac, 341
Anarchism, 63, 326, 335, 339; repres-
    sion of, 160
Anarchosyndicalism, 340n
Andes, 13, 23, 165
Anguiano, Arturo, 249

Contributors

GILBERT M. JOSEPH is Professor of History and Chair of the Council on Latin American Studies at Yale University. He is the author of *Revolution from Without: Yucatán, Mexico, and the United States, 1880–1924, Rediscovering the Past at Mexico's Periphery,* and numerous articles on the Mexican revolution and the history of rural crime and protest. He is also the coeditor, with Allen Wells, of *Yucatán y la International Harvester* and, with Jeffery Brannon, of *Land, Labor, and Capital in Modern Yucatán: Essays in Regional History and Political Economy.* Currently he is completing a book with Allen Wells on elite politics and rural insurgency in Yucatán during the Porfiriato and early revolutionary era, as well as writing a social and political history of Mexico.

DANIEL NUGENT teaches anthropology and Latin American studies at the University of Arizona and is a managing editor of the *Journal of Historical Sociology.* Since the early 1980s he has carried out research in rural Chihuahua and has published articles on historical anthropology, agrarian struggles in northern Mexico, and the anthropology of work. He is the author of *Spent Cartridges of Revolution: An Anthropological History of Namiquipa, Chihuahua,* the editor of *Rural Revolt in Mexico and U.S. Intervention,* and the coeditor, with John Calagione and others, of *Worker's Expressions: Beyond Accommodation and Resistance.*

ANA MARÍA ALONSO teaches anthropology at the University of Arizona. She has conducted ethnographic and archival investigation in Mexico and the United States, and has held postdoctoral fellowships at the Pembroke Center for Teaching and Research on Women (Brown University) and the Southwest Institute for Research on Women (Tucson, Arizona). She is the author of a forthcoming volume, *Blood, Sex, and Gold: Honor, Gender, and Resistance on Mexico's Northern Frontier* and numerous articles on popular resistance, social memory, historical anthropology, gender, and ethnicity.

ARMANDO BARTRA is a political activist and scholar who is currently Director of the Circo Maya in Mexico City. He has carried out wide-ranging studies of the history and present condition of peasant and popular movements in Mexico. He is the author of *Los herederos de Zapata* and the editor of a selection of articles from the Mexican Liberal party's newspaper, *Regeneración*. Recently, with Manuel Aurrecochea, he completed a study of comics and the popular press in Mexico, which resulted in the publication of a two-volume work, *Puros cuentos: la historia de la historieta en México*.

MARJORIE BECKER is Associate Professor of History at the University of Southern California. Her extensive research has focused on rural Michoacán, and she has been a Visiting Fellow at the Center for U.S.-Mexican Studies in La Jolla, California. Author of *Setting the Virgin on Fire: Lázaro Cárdenas, Michoacán Campesinos, and the Redemption of the Mexican Revolution*, she has also published a variety of essays examining state and popular discourses, forms of resistance, and the dynamics of gender and class in the Mexican countryside during the 1930s.

BARRY CARR teaches Latin American history at LaTrobe University in Melbourne, Australia. He has written numerous books and articles on the Mexican and Latin American labor movement and left, including *El movimiento obrero y la política en México, 1910–1929* and *Marxism and Communism in Twentieth-Century Mexico*. He is the coeditor with Steve Ellner, of *The Latin American Left Since Allende*. Currently he is completing a volume on work and workers in the Cuban sugar industry during the 1920s and 1930s, part of a larger project assessing the impact of the Great Depression on patterns of labor and peasant mobilization in Cuba and Central America.

PHILIP CORRIGAN, a former librarian, is a prolific historical sociologist and teacher who has written numerous books and articles on the topics of state formation, the sociology of education, cultural studies, and social theory. With Derek Sayer, he is the coauthor of *The Great Arch: English State Formation as Cultural Revolution*, and some of his other writings are collected in *Social Forms and Human Capacities: Essays in Authority and Difference*. Formerly Professor of Sociology at the University of Exeter and head of the Sociology Department at the Ontario Institute for Studies in Education, he is a founding editor of the *Journal of Historical Sociology*.

ROMANA FALCÓN is Research Professor at the Centro de Estudios Históricos of El Colegio de México. In addition to numerous articles on the political and social history of Porfirian and revolutionary Mexico, she is the author of *El agrarismo en Veracruz, la etapa radical (1928–1935)* and *Revolución y caciquismo: San Luis Potosí, 1910–1938* and, with Soledad García, the coauthor of *La semilla en el surco: Adalberto Tejeda y el radicalismo en Veracruz, 1883–1960*. She is currently completing a book on Mexico's *jefes políticos* (local political bosses) during the late nineteenth and early twentieth centuries.

ALAN KNIGHT is Professor of Latin American History and Director of the Latin American Centre at St. Antony's College, Oxford University. He is the author of the award-winning two-volume history *The Mexican Revolution*, of *U.S.-Mexican Relations, 1910–1940: An Interpretation*, and of numerous articles on the modern Mexican past and the comparative history of revolution and social movements. He is currently working on a history of Lázaro Cárdenas's regime and Mexico during the 1930s.

FLORENCIA E. MALLON is Professor of History at the University of Wisconsin–Madison. She is the author of *The Defense of Community in Peru's Central Highlands: Peasant Struggle and Capitalist Transition, 1860–1940*, of *Peasant and Nation: The Making of Postcolonial Mexico and Peru*, and numerous articles on peasant politics, nationalism, the state, gender, and social theory. She is currently editing a volume on popular nationalism and state formation in Asia, Europe, and the Americas.

ELSIE ROCKWELL is Professor and past head of the Departamento de Investigaciones Educativas at the Instituto Politécnico Nacional in Mexico City. Trained in history and social anthropology, she is one of Latin America's leading educational theorists. With Ruth Mercado, she is coauthor of *La escuela, lugar del trabajo docente*; and with María de Ibarrola, coeditor of *Educación y clases populares en América Latina*. Her recent articles include "Tales from Xaltipan: Documenting Orality and Literacy in Rural Mexico" and "De la reforma constitucional a las controversias locales: la educación socialista en Tlaxcala."

WILLIAM ROSEBERRY teaches anthropology at the New School for Social Research. His first book, *Coffee and Capitalism in the Venezuelan Andes*, established new standards for the writing of historical ethnography. He has gone on to do comparative research on the peasantry in Colombia, the southern Andes, Mexico, and England. Several of his influential theoretical essays have been collected in *Anthropologies and Histories*. Recently he coedited, with Jay O'Brien, *Golden Ages, Dark Ages: Imagining the Past in Anthropology and History*.

JAN RUS is a social anthropologist who first worked in the village of Chamula as an undergraduate member of the Harvard Chiapas Project in 1968. For the last six years he has worked for the Instituto de Asesoría Antropológica para la Región Maya (INAREMAC) in San Cristóbal, Chiapas, helping native writers prepare and publish community studies, life histories, and short stories in Tzotzil and Spanish. He is currently completing a historical ethnography of the Tzotzils from the late colonial period through the 1980s.

DEREK SAYER is Professor of Sociology at the University of Alberta. He has published many books and essays on sociological method and social theory, including *Marx's Method*, *The Violence of Abstraction*, and *Capitalism and Modernity*. He is the coauthor of a number of texts with Philip Corrigan and others, most notably *The Great Arch*. A founding editor of the *Journal of Historical Sociology*, he recently worked for 18 months at the Institute of Sociology in the Czech Academy of Science.

JAMES C. SCOTT is Eugene Meyer Professor of Political Science, Director of the Program in Agrarian Studies, and Chair of the Council on Southeast Asia Studies at Yale University. Among his many books and articles on rural society and politics are *The Moral Economy of the Peasant: Subsistence and Rebellion in Southeast Asia, Weapons of the Weak: Everyday Forms of Peasant Resistance,* and *Domination and the Arts of Resistance: Hidden Transcripts.*

Library of Congress Cataloging-in-Publication Data

Everyday forms of state formation : revolution and the negotiation
of rule in modern Mexico / edited by Gilbert M. Joseph and Daniel
Nugent.

p.   cm.

Includes bibliographical references and index.

ISBN 0-8223-1452-5 (cl). — ISBN 0-8223-1467-3 (pa)

1. Mexico—Politics and government—20th century. 2. Mexico—
Politics and government—1867–1910. 3. Mexico—History—
20th century. 4. Mexico—History—1867–1910. 5. Political
culture—Mexico—History—20th century. 6. Political culture—
Mexico—History—19th century. I. Joseph, G. M. (Gilbert Michael), 1947– . II. Nugent, Daniel.

JL1281.E93   1994

320.972'09'04—dc20   93-40294   CIP